1 MONTH OF
FREE
READING

at

www.ForgottenBooks.com

By purchasing this book you are eligible for one month membership to ForgottenBooks.com, giving you unlimited access to our entire collection of over 1,000,000 titles via our web site and mobile apps.

To claim your free month visit:

www.forgottenbooks.com/free127260

ISBN 978-1-5281-6902-8
PIBN 10127260

HISTORY

OF

NORTHAMPTON

MASSACHUSETTS

FROM ITS SETTLEMENT IN 1654

BY

JAMES RUSSELL TRUMBULL

VOL. I

———

Of Patriotism is Liberty Born

———

NORTHAMPTON:
1898.

NORTHAMPTON, MASS. :
PRESS OF GAZETTE PRINTING CO.
1898

TO THE MEMORY OF

SYLVESTER JUDD,

JOURNALIST, HISTORIAN, ANTIQUARIAN,

WHOSE RESEARCHES MADE THESE VOLUMES POSSIBLE,

THIS WORK IS

RESPECTFULLY INSCRIBED.

PREFACE.

The written history of a community may be found in its Town, Church and Parish records; in the public and private correspondence and papers of its citizens; and in the County, State and National archives. Its unwritten history is shadowed in the lives, acts, opinions and traditions of the people. From these sources the historian gathers his materials, combining and weaving them into connected narrative. Tradition is but a side light, the flashing of whose uncertain rays dazzles and bewilders rather than illuminates the truth. Yet it has its uses, and may not be altogether overlooked.

Based upon the records of the town, treated in chronological order, and supplemented by such other documentary evidence as it has been possible to obtain, the volumes of this work are intended to present in some degree a connected history of this community during the first century and a half of its existence. This method of treatment, while it shows more consecutively, perhaps, the material, moral, social, religious, educational and political progress of the town, involves to some extent a repetition of topics, though not necessarily a reproduction of facts.

The History of Northampton contains much that is of interest to the beginnings of the towns in this section. In fact, all the plantations here had much in common. Many of the inhabitants of the later settled towns, joined by kinship of blood as well as contiguity of residence, were emigrants from the elder settlement. This community of interest unites the history of the older with that of the more recently established towns, and renders necessary frequent allusions to the neighboring plantations.

Most important in the construction of this work has been the MSS. collection of the late Sylvester Judd. He employed many years of his life in gathering material relating to the early history of Northampton and other towns in this valley. This MSS. now in the joint ownership of the Forbes Library and the undersigned, has been freely drawn upon. Its use in the compilation of these volumes has been invaluable. In fact, the possession of those documents was the main incentive to undertaking the task at all. In transcribing from ancient records, Mr. Judd modernized their spelling, and in many instances condensed their substance. Quotations from those papers are given as he copied them,

and in a majority of cases, reference is made to them in the text. In
other cases the orthography of the original documents has been strictly
followed.

The author is also under great obligations to Hon. George Sheldon of
Deerfield, not only for his kindness in response to personal inquiries,
but also for the aid afforded by his admirable History of Deerfield, recently published.

To Miss C. Alice Baker of Cambridge, Mass., special thanks are due.
The thorough original research of Miss Baker, among the public archives and monasteries of Canada, as well as among legal records in this
country, has added much of value to the general history of this region.

Acknowledgements are also due to Mr. Wilberforce Eames, Librarian of the Lenox Library, N. Y.; to Mr. C. B. Tillinghast, Librarian
of the Mass. State Library, Boston, Mass.; to Mr. C. A. Cutter, Librarian of the Forbes Library, Northampton; to Miss C. S. Laidley, Librarian of the Clarke Library, Northampton; to Mr. E. I. Clapp, City
Clerk of Northampton, for special favors; and to Mr. Edward Morris
and Mr. H. M. Burt of Springfield, Mass.

A distinct feature of the work is exhibited in the maps presented in
the first volume. One of them gives the location of the original home
lots of the first settlers, and is printed in red ink on transparent paper.
The other, printed in black ink, gives the present topography of the
same territory. By placing one above the other a glance will show the
changes in the ownership of real estate since the town was settled.

The frontispiece to this volume, a portrait of Rev. Jonathan Edwards, engraved by Miss Emily Sartain of Philadelphia, is from a picture now the property of Mrs. Eli Whitney, of New Haven, Ct.,
through whose kindness the copy was obtained. The original portrait
of Mr. Edwards was painted about the year 1740, at Boston, as is supposed by John Smybert, an artist of reputation, who came to this country in 1728, with Bishop Berkley. He painted portraits both of Mr.
and Mrs. Edwards, by order of a Mr. Hogg, to whom they were forwarded in Scotland. After his death, they were presented by his sister
to Rev. Dr. Erskine of Edinburgh, who on learning that they were the
only portraits of Mr. Edwards and his wife extant, sent them to Rev.
Jonathan Edwards, second son of the president, and they are now in
the possession of Mr. Eugene Edwards, of Stonington, Ct. In 1828,
Rembrant Peale of Philadelphia, copied this portrait, and from a pho-
tograph of that picture this engraving has been made.

It is not claimed that this history is exhaustive of the period of
which it treats, neither is it to be understood as original in all its researches. It is rather a compilation of facts, many of which have
already been published, emphasized and illustrated from such new and
original papers as it has been possible to procure. As a grouping of
the earlier incidents connected with the founding and progress of this
ancient town, it is hoped that the labor bestowed upon it, covering
nearly a quarter of a century, may not have been expended in vain.

J. R. T.

Northampton, December, 1898.

CONTENTS.

CHAPTER I.

ESTABLISHING THE PLANTATION.

CHAPTER II.

COMMENCING THE SETTLEMENT.

CHAPTER III.

ORGANIZING THE TOWN.

CHAPTER IV.

THE WITCHCRAFT SLANDER TRIAL.

CHAPTER V.

PERFECTING THE ORGANIZATION.

CHAPTER IX.

FOUNDING THE CHURCH.

CHAPTER X.

NEW MEETING HOUSE—HAMPSHIRE COUNTY.

CHAPTER XI.

RAPID GROWTH OF CHURCH AND TOWN.

CHAPTER XII.

POPULATION—TAXATION—REPRESENTATION.

CHAPTER XIII.

SPECIAL MUNICIPAL REGULATIONS.

CHAPTER XIV.

THE INDIANS—THEIR TREATMENT.

CHAPTER XV.

PROGRESS IN EVERY DIRECTION.

CHAPTER XVI.

REV. ELEAZAR MATHER.

CHAPTER XVII.

MATTERS ECCLESIASTICAL AND EDUCATIONAL.

CHAPTER XVIII.

WITCHCRAFT—TRIAL OF MARY PARSONS.

CHAPTER XIX.

KING PHILIP'S WAR—OPENING EVENTS.

CHAPTER XX.

CHAPTER XXI.

CHAPTER XXII.

WAY OF LIVING— ENFORCING SUMPTUARY LAWS.

CHAPTER XXIII.

KING PHILIP'S WAR—MRS. ROWLANDSON'S STORY.

CHAPTER XXIV.

KING PHILIP'S WAR—ATTACK ON NORTHAMPTON.

CHAPTER XXV.

KING PHILIP'S WAR—CONSOLIDATION FAILS.

CHAPTER XXVI.

KING PHILIP'S WAR—FIGHT AT TURNER'S FALLS.

CHAPTER XXVII.

KING PHILIP'S WAR—CLOSE OF HOSTILITIES.

CHAPTER XXVIII.

THE LAST INDIAN RAID.

CHAPTER XXIX.

LEAD DISCOVERED—MINING OPERATIONS.

CHAPTER XXX.

TITHINGMEN—INCENDIARISM—TOWN BELL.

CHAPTER XXXI.

DIVIDING THE COMMONS—GRAMMAR SCHOOL.

CHAPTER XXXII.

CHARTER VACATED—GOVERNMENT OF ANDROS.

CHAPTER XXXIII.

INDIAN MURDERS—MILITIA—FORTIFICATIONS.

CHAPTER XXXIV.

CAPT. COOK—TAXES—NEW CHARTER—SCHOOLS.

CHAPTER XXXV.

KING WILLIAM'S FRENCH AND INDIAN WAR.

CHAPTER XXXVI.

HATFIELD BOUNDARY—OVERSEERS OF THE POOR.

CHAPTER XXXVII.

MODERATOR—MILL RIVER—ORDINARIES—JAIL.

CHAPTER XXXVIII.

QUEEN ANNE'S FRENCH AND INDIAN WAR.

CHAPTER XXXIX.

QUEEN ANNE'S FRENCH AND INDIAN WAR.

CHAPTER XL.

QUEEN ANNE'S FRENCH AND INDIAN WAR.

CHAPTER XLI.

TURNING MILL RIVER—JOSEPH HAWLEY.

CHAPTER XLII.

COL. STODDARD'S MISSION TO CANADA.

CHAPTER XLIII.

SAW MILL—MINISTER'S SALARY—COMMON LANDS.

CHAPTER XLIV.

MEDAD POMEROY—FINANCES—PUBLIC BANK.

APPENDIX.

ILLUSTRATIONS.

AUTOGRAPHS.

MAPS.

Map of the home lots of the first settlers of Northampton.

Map representing the present topography of that part of Northampton occupied by its first planters.

Map of the Town of Northampton, published in 1831, showing the Divisions of the Commons and the Meadows, as well as the former course of Mill River. To face page 17.

HISTORY OF NORTHAMPTON.

CHAPTER I.

ESTABLISHING THE PLANTATION.

Hardships and Difficulties of the same general nature Menaced the Beginnings of every Town.

ONE-THIRD of a century elapsed after Plymouth Rock became immortal, before permanent settlers found their way into this immediate section of the valley. Gradually the fame of its fertile meadows and rich uplands, made known by the natives and heralded by explorers, spread among the settlements at the Bay, but years passed ere the hardy pioneer tested for himself the truth of these alluring reports. Civilization, delayed in its coming, burst suddenly upon the banks of the tranquil Connecticut. Four towns, the chronicles of whose progress have been presented in many an entertaining volume, followed each other almost within a twelvemonth. To trace the history of the beginnings of any town is to reproduce, to a certain extent, the commencement of many another. Yet each has its own peculiar characteristics, and each differs in many essentials from all the rest. The hardships incident to the establishment of a township in the wilderness, remote from neighbors, and dependent wholly upon its own scanty resources, beset the settlers here, even as they harrassed and disturbed the first years of every other inland plantation. Aware of the trials and dangers attending their undertaking, the early inhabitants came prepared to meet, and determined to conquer them all. With skill and resolution they set about their arduous task, and in a strong and confident spirit laid broad and deep the material, intellectual, social and religious foundations upon which rests to-day the noble superstructure of our beautiful city.

A Spice of World-liness Responsible for much of the Emigration.

No record exists pointing out with certainty the first appearance of white men within the limits of this town. It was not alone the great fertility of its bottom lands that attracted adventurers, but also the abundance of game that filled its forests and streams. The possibilities of the fur trade were speedily recognized by the new comers, and they quickly availed themselves of its benefits. Though the first emigrants were driven by religious persecution to cross the ocean, others soon followed them for commercial purposes, and many of the towns in Massachusetts were established the better to carry on trade with the natives. As settlements extended inland, these sentiments more and more prevailed, and though in some instances higher motives may have governed the migration, yet a spirit of thrift undoubtedly permeated the best intentioned of them. Townships were begun at Windsor, Wethersfield, Hartford and Agawam (Springfield), in 1635 and 1636. From these settlements came the planters of Nonotuck (Northampton), the details of whose history it is proposed to narrate.

Exploration Facilitates Trade with the Natives.

It is probable that the adventurers who first established themselves in Springfield, did not long remain unacquainted with the contiguous territory, and exploring parties ascended the river, before that town had been many years in existence. Among the inducements for occupying these lands the first was unquestionably a commercial one. All facilities for trade, of which exploration was one of the most feasible, were pushed forward at the earliest possible moment. But no attempt at a settlement here was made till Springfield had been eighteen years a town. The first substantiated record of the passage of Europeans through this territory, was that of 1638. That, however, was not an expedition for discovery, neither was it an attempt to open traffic for profit with the aborigines. It was a journey, forced by circumstances, and made for the purpose of sustaining life. On its results depended the existence of the settlers, the survival of the plantations. Impoverished by the war with the Pequods, the lower towns on the river were in great danger from starvation, and appealed to the Indians to sell them provisions.

Capt. Mason sent Northward for Supplies.

As a last resource, Capt. John Mason with two companions was dispatched up the river in search of food, in the spring of the year 1638. They journeyed as far as Pocumtuck (Deerfield), where they succeeded in purchasing an ample supply of corn, which was delivered by the Indians with a fleet of fifty canoes at Hartford and Windsor.[1] Forever to the credit of the red man be it recorded that he responded liberally and generously to the appeal of the strangers who came to supplant and drive him not only from the home of his fathers, but eventually from the face of the earth. The conqueror of the Pequods, fresh from that sanguinary conflict, which resulted in the annihilation of one Indian nation[2] came humbly suing another of the same race to preserve the victors from a lingering death. "Never was the like," says Mason, "known to this day."

Mts. Holyoke and Tom.

The two mountains that stood then as now at the southern entrance to Nonotuck meadows, undoubtedly received their names from Elizur Holyoke and Rowland Thomas, pioneer settlers of Springfield. Not many years after the successful mission of Mason, two parties went northward from Springfield to explore the country. Holyoke commanded the division that ascended the eastern bank of the river and Thomas that on the west. Tradition affirms that these parties standing where the river is narrowest, at the place once known as Rock Ferry, shouting across to each other, applied the names of their leaders to the respective mountains.[3]

1 "The year ensuing the colony being in extream want of Provisions, many giving twelve shillings for one bushel of Indian corn ; the Court of Connecticut imploying Capt. Mason, Mr. William Wadsworth, & Deacon Stebbin to try what Providence would afford for their relief, in this great straight ; who notwithstanding some discouragements they met from some English went to a place called Pocumtuck, where they procured so much corn at reasonable rates, that the Indians brought down to Hartford & Windsor Fifty canoes laden with corn at one time."—Mason's History of the Pequod war, Mass. Hist. Col. vol. 8, p. 153.

2 "There remained not a sannup nor a squaw, not a warrior or child of the Pequod name. A nation had disappeared from the family of man."—Bancroft's History of the U. S., vol. 1, page 402, Ed. 1852.

3 Holland's History of Western Mass., vol. 1, p. 54.

A New Settlement under Discussion.   The reports made by this expedition, and doubtless by other explorers, attracted attention to this desirable place, yet many years elapsed before decided action was taken. Fully occupied with their own affairs, the inhabitants of the newly planted towns had little time to bestow upon the foundations of others. Still reports of the desirability of these rich alluvial lands, became rapidly disseminated, and the project of forming a new town was under discussion for a number of years before any movement towards it actually took place. Certain citizens of the towns already in existence became especially interested in this matter during the year 1652. The fact that the first concerted measures looking towards a new settlement were taken early in May, of the following year, is an indication that the question had been previously under advisement. The capabilities of the broad meadows, annually enriched by the overflowing waters of the lingering Connecticut, as well as the suitability of the situation for trading purposes, aroused the enterprise and cupidity of the settlers in existing plantations, and the proposition to form a new town soon found many supporters.

Causes which Governed the Founding of the new Plantation.   The plan for the settlement of Northampton originated at Hartford. It was not fostered by nor did it grow out of any religious controversy whatever. The breach between Rev. Messrs. Russell and Stone, which resulted in the removal of the former with the most of his congregation, to the wilds of Massachusetts, and the founding of the town of Hadley, had not then culminated. This transaction appears to have been purely of a business nature[1]. The same influences prevailed which governed the settlers in the towns already alluded to : tillable land in abundance, facil-

1. Maverick's description of New England, written in 1660, and discovered within a few years, contains the following, which doubtless has reference to Northampton, though his ideas of distance seem somewhat vague. "Above Springfield, 8 Miles is another Towne at first Intended but for a tradeing house with the Indians, but the gallant Land about it hath invited men to make it a Towne. This Connecticott River is a great River before yᵉ Towne, bigger than the Thames above bridge."—N. E. Hist. and Gen. Reg., vol. 39.

"John Pynchon only survivor, asserts upon his certain knowledge that the great meadow in Northampton, which the town improves was the chief land aimed at." Affidavit of John Pynchon, relative to a correction of the boundary line of the town.

ity of trade with the Indians, and a laudable desire to better their condition in life by promptly seizing these advantages.   Imbued with that restless spirit which incited so many to brave the perils of the stormy ocean, as well as those of the savage wilderness, they but yielded to the impulses of the times in removing to new and untried districts.   Notwithstanding the worldly considerations which determined their movement up the river, the founders of Northampton were Puritans in the choicest meaning of that term.   Sincere believers, they endeavored to promote purity of religion in whatever circumstances they were placed. Satisfied that the true faith had found a permanent lodgment in the new world, they sought to extend and protect it wherever called upon to dwell.   With a form of worship, simple as the creed they professed, they wove their religion into the warp and woof of their daily lives, and asked God's blessing upon all their undertakings.   Consequently a reverent dependence upon Deity manifested itself in their public documents and pervaded their humblest occupations.

Petition to the General Court.   In May, 1653, twenty-four persons petitioned the General Court of Massachusetts for liberty to "plant, possess and inhabit Nonotuck."   These petitioners, with a single exception, residing within the jurisdiction of Connecticut, sought the aid of influential citizens living in the colony to which they desired to remove.   Consequently their petition was supplemented by that of three prominent inhabitants of Springfield.   The original document bears no date but that of its presentation in May, while the other was dated May 3, 1653 (O. S.).   Both petitions were presented to the General Court at the same time.   The former, signed by many Hartford men, and undoubtedly prepared some time in April, was as follows : —

"To the Right worshipfull Gouer^r And the worshipfull Magestrats Assistants & debutys of this much Hon^d Court your humble petition^r wish in crease of All filicity, your humble petisioners being fully p^rswaded of your former prompnes and pious indeauors To begin And settle Plantations in such places As Apeared conuenient within the liberty of your Jurisdiction and pattent for the further inlarging of the teritories of the Gospell of our Lord Jesus Christ And the common vtility of the publick weale Are therefore Imboldened to present these few Leins to your Judicious Consideration And there request therein that you would be pleased to giue and grant Liberty to your petisioners whose names Are subscribed and such as shall Joine with them According to your wonted Clemency Power Right And Authority from by And vnder you to plant posess and Inhabit the place being on Conetequat Riuer Aboue Springfeild Called nonotack As their owne Inheritance. According to their deuisions by estate And to Carry on the Affairs of the place by erecting A towne there to be gouerned According to the Laws directions & instructions they shall receiue from you: your humble petisioners hauing some Knowledge of the place by reason of the propinquity of our habitation to be a place desirable to erect a towne in for the furtherance of the publick weale by prouiding Corne and raising cattell not only for their owne but Likewise for the good of others the probogating of the gospell the place promising in an ordinary way of gods prouidence a Comfortable Subsistance whereby people may Liue And Attend vpon god in his holy ordinances without distraction. So committing you to the Guidance of the mighty Counselor we rest your humble petitioners:

Edward Elmor [Hartford].	Jonathan Smith [Farmington].
Richard Smith [Wethersfield].	William oughton [Holton]
John Gilberd [Hartford].	[Hartford].
William miller	Roberd Bartlet [Hartford].
John Allyn [Windsor].	John Cole [Hartford].
Richard wekly [Haddam].	Nicolas Acley [Hartford].
Thomas Burnum [Windsor].	John web [Stamford].
Mathias Trot [Treat]	thomas Stedman [New London].
[Wethersfield].	Thomas Bird [Hartford].
Thomas Rote [Hartford].	william Jans [New Haven].
wiliam Clark [Dorchester].	John North [Wethersfield].
Joseph Smith [Hartford].	Joseph bird [Farmington].
John Stedman [Hartford].	James Bird [Farmington].

Petition of the Springfield Men. Only three men signed the petition from Springfield. But they were the foremost citizens of the place, and were already well known to the authorities. From this document it appears that these men had no private ends to gratify. It was not for their own benefit that they petitioned the court, nor was the new town to be founded by or established in the interests of Springfield people. Neither of the petitioners ever resided here, and with the exception of Mr. Pynchon, none of them ever owned any land in the new settlement. The petition is appended:—

"To our highly honoured the Generall Court of Massachusts.

"The humble petition of John Pynchon, Eliezur Holliock and Samuel Chapin, Inhabitants of Springfeild, sheweth

"We hartily desire the continuance of your peace And increase of your subjects in these parts: In order where unto we humbly tender oᵣ desires that Liberty may be granted to erect a plantation about Fiue-teene miles aboue vs on this River of conetiquat if it be the will of the Lord the place being we think very commodius consideratis conside-randis or the containing Large quantitys of excelent Land and Meadow and tillable ground sufficient for two larg planttations a work wch if it should go on might as we conceiue proue greatly Advantagas to your Commonwealth to wch purpose there are diuers in our Neighboring plantations that have a desire to remoue thither with your Aprobation thereof to the number of twenty-five families at least that Already Appeer whereof many of them are of considerable quality for Estates and fit matter for A church when it shal pleas God to giue opertunity that way: it is oᵣ humble desires that by this Honˡ Court some power may be established her or som course appointed for the regulating of their first proceedings as concerning whome to Admit and other occor-oncess that so the Glory of God may be furethered and your peace and hapiness not retarded and the Inducement to vs in these desires is not any sinester respect of our owne but that we being so alone may by this means may haue som more neighbourhood of your Jurisdiction, thus not Doubting your acceptance of oᵣ desires we shal intreat the Lord to sit among you in all your counsils and remaine yours mos humble servants

<table>
<tr><td>Springfeild the</td><td>JOHN PYNCHON</td></tr>
<tr><td>6 of yᵉ (3) ᵐᵗʰ 1653.</td><td>ELIZUR HOLLIOK</td></tr>
<tr><td></td><td>SAMˡˡ CHAPIN."</td></tr>
</table>

Action of the Court. These two petitions which were presented to the General Court at the same time, were acted upon by that body, on the 18th of May, when the following vote, appointing commissioners to lay out the land, was passed:—

"In ansʳ to the peticon of seuerall inhabitants of Springfeild &c, craving liberty & authoritje to erect a new plantacon and touneship at Nonotucke, &c, itt is ordered, that Mʳ Jnᵒ Pinchon, Mʳ Elitzur Holioke, and Samuell Chapin shallbe, and heereby are, appointed a comittee to diuide the land peticoned for into two plantacons, and that the peticon-ers make choice of one of them, where they shall haue libertje to plant themselves, provided they shall not apropriate to any planter above one hundred acres of all sorts of land, whereof not above twenty acres of meadow, till twenty inhabitants haue planted & setled them-selves vppon the place, who shall have power to distribute the land, and give out proporcons of land to the seuerall inhabitants, according to theire estates or eminent qualifficacions, as in other tounes of this jurisdiccon."[1]

1 Records of Massachusetts, vol. 4, part 1, p. 136.

Report of the
Committee.

The above-named commissioners made their report to the Legislature, in November, 1654, having, however, in the previous May, given the following document to the proprietors, which was copied in full upon the town records. There is an important difference between them. In the former the town boundary is said to be "from the litle meadowe above theire plantacon, which meadow is called Capawonke or Mattaomett," while in the latter it is made to include that meadow. In their return to the Court, the commissioners omit to name the distance westward that the township was to extend, though it was correctly given in the document prepared for the settlers. In 1657, in a petition to the Legislature, the town prayed that the ambiguity in the grant might be cleared up, but no action was taken till thirty years afterwards, when the boundary line was rectified, but in the meantime the town had purchased Capawonke :—

"A Trew Coppy of the boundes of the plantation which the Committee appointed by the Hono'd Generall Court laid out to the Planters of Nonotuck.

"Whereas wee whose names are vnder written where appointed by the Generall Court of the Massachusets to lay out the land at Nonotuck for two Plantations, for the present wee haue only appointed the boundes of one of them to which we allow the greate Meddowe on the west side of Conecticut River as allsoe a little Meddowe Caled by the Endians Cappawonke which lyeth about two miles aboue the greate Meddowe the boundes of which Plantation is to extend from the vpper end of the little meddow called Capawonke to the great fales to Springfeild ward, and westward is to extend nine miles into the woodes from the river Conecticote lying vppon [the] east the foresaid Meddowes and vplands to belong to the Petitioners and such as shall come to plant with them, who according to the Liberty granted from the Courte haue made choyc thereof for them selues and their successors not molesting the Indians or depriueing them of ther Just right and propriety without Allowance to ther satisfaction.

By vs

JOHN PYNCHON
ELIZUR HOLYOKE

Springfeild, 9ᵗʰ of May, 1654.   SAMUEL CHAPIN."

The Red Men fairly Treated.

To extinguish the Indian title in the proposed plantation became the first duty of the commissioners. The aborigines in this portion of the valley were well aware of the power of the English. Though more than a decade had passed since the war with the Pequods, they had not yet forgotten the vigor and prowess displayed by the pale face soldiers in that campaign. Memory yet recalled to them the terrible punishment meted out to that nation for its cruelty and treachery. Yet all their own relations with the white men thus far had been amicable and peaceful. They found a speedy market for such articles as they had to sell, were readily admitted to the English settlements and were everywhere treated justly and fairly. Their land, of which they made scant use, and which was really of little value to them, was honorably purchased. In fact the establishment of the new settlement at Northampton did not dispossess the Indian owners of any thing held sacred by them. None of their cherished landmarks were removed, nor were they deprived of anything which they especially valued. No Indian village then existed within the limits of the town. There were here no burial places, hallowed by the mournful sentiments with which all nations and tribes invest the last resting places of their dead. On the meadow, at suitable intervals they raised a little corn. The river was valued mainly for the quantity of fish its waters yielded, and the forests were important only in proportion to the amount of game they secreted.

The Indians of Western Massachuse'ts. In Western Massachusetts the Indians paid yearly tribute to the Mohawks, who resided beyond the Hudson river. They were the most easterly tribe of the great Iriquois family. Few permanent Indian settlements were found in Massachusetts west of Connecticut river. That section of country, as well as what is now comprised within the limits of the state of Vermont, formed the Beaver hunting grounds of the Iriquois. The valley, north of the Connecticut line was occupied by several tribes or remnants of tribes, none powerful in themselves, and acting little in unison. The Nipmucks or Nipnets of central Massachusetts, seem to have held some sort of sway over these river tribes, while they in turn owed fealty to the more powerful Pequods, Wampanoags and Narragansetts.

Springfield was purchased of the Agawams, Westfield of the Waranoaks, Northampton and Hadley of the Nonotucks, Deerfield of the Pocumtucks, and Northfield of the Squakeags.

The Nonotucks.   The Nonotucks owned the lands on both sides of the river, from the falls at South Hadley to Sugar Loaf Mountain. The name Nonotuck signifies "The Midst of the River," and local historians have conjectured that its significance is derived from the numerous peninsulas and projecting points formed by the tortuous course of the river. The name was applied to that part of the valley extending north from Mts. Holyoke and Tom to the confines of Deerfield. Its spelling varied at different times, though Nonotuck was always used to designate Northampton.[1]

Indian Deed of Northampton.   The commissioners met with no difficulty in arranging terms with the Indians, and in September, they purchased Nonotuck. The instrument conveying the land to John Pynchon of Springfield, is given in full :—

"Bee it Knowne by these presents that Chickwallopp, Alias Wawhillowa, Neessahalant, Nassicohee, Riants, Paquahalant, Assellaquompas and Awonusk the wife of Wulluther all of Nanotuck, who are the cheife and prop[er] owners of all the land on the west side of Quonetticot River at Nanotuck on the one [part] Doe giue, Grant, bargaine, and sell vnto John Pynchon of Springfeild on the other pty to him his heires and Assigns, All the Groundes and Meddowes, Woodes and Pondes and W[aters] lying on the west side of Quonetticutt River, beginning [at] the small River (beelow Munhan) called Sankrohonk And so vpp by Quonetticutt River (to the leetle meddow called Capawonk namely to the leetle brooke or Gutter on this side Capawonk, which leetle brooke is caled Masquampe : And the Grounds lying Westward from Conecticut River (within the Compass aforenamed) for Nine Miles out into the woods, viz, as farr as Manshconish is from Springfeild, (for soe it was expressed to the Indians) All that tract of Grounds from Sankronk Riverett and Quonackquck Called Munhan, Pochnack, Petonwag, Aspowounk, Luckcommuck, Assattayyagg, Nayyagg, Nayyvumkegg, Masqump, and by Whatsoever other names the said groundes are caled And All out into the woodes from the great River for 9 miles within this Compass. The Aforesaid Indians and in pticuler Wawhollowa, Nenessahalant, and Nassachohe beeing the Sachems of Nanotuck doe for themselues and with the Consent of the other Indians and owners of the sd Groundes, sell, giue, and Grant vnto John Pynchon of Springfeild and to his Assignes for and in the Consideration of one hundred fathum

1   Nawattocke, 1637; Nowottok and Nawottock, 1646; Nauwotak, 1648; Noatucke, 1654; Nanotuck, 1653; Nonotucke, 1653, 1655, 1658; Norwotake, 1657; Norwootuck and Norwuttuck, 1657; Northwottock, 1656, 1661; Norwottock, 1659, 1660; Norwoottucke, 1659; Norwotuck, 1661. John Pynchon has in his accounts Nalwotogg, Nolwotogg, and Norwotog, and in his deeds, Nolwotogg.—Judd's Hist. of Hadley, p. 122.

of Wampam by Tale and for Tenn Coates (besides some small gifts) in hand to the said Sachems and owners, All the land Aforesaid as [by] these presents haue bargained granted and sould to the [said] Pynchon all and singuler the said landes free from all Cumbrances of Indians provided the said Pynchon shall plow vpp or cawse to bee plowed vpp for the said Indians Sixteene Acres of land on the East'ly side of Quoneticutt River which is to bee donn sometime next summer 1654 And in the meane time viz the next spring 1654, the Indians haue liberty to plant ther present Corne feildes, but after that time they are wholly to leaue that West side of the river. And not to plant or molest ye English ther.

" All the said Premises the said Pynchon and his assignes shall haue and enjoy Absolutely and Clearly forever [from] all in Cumbrances from any Indians or ther corne feilds. In witnesse of these p^{r}sents the said Indians haue subscribed their markes this Twenty-fowrth day of September 1653."

" These vnderwritten are witnesses y^t these are the markes of the Sachems within mentioned, And that they doe fully passe over the land within mentioned in the beehalfe of themselues and other owners to John Pychon of Springfeild and to his Assignes forever."

Eight years after the coming of the first settlers, Mr. Pynchon made over the property described in the above deed to the inhabitants of Northampton, by means of the following document, which was recorded by Elizur Holyoke " in the Publicke Records in page 15 " :—

Mr. Pynchon assigns the Property to its rightful Owners.

" Wher as the within mentioned grant or purchase of Landes of the Indians of Nanotuck is in the name of John Pynchon his heires or Assignes without mentioning of any other p^{r}sons, when as it was purchased in the beehalfe of severall p^{r}sons who had obtained a grant from the Generall Court for A plantation ther, Intending to plant and settle themselues in the said landes within mentioned. Now Know all men that I the said John Pynchon doe acknowledg myselfe to haue acted in the premises only as beeing Intrusted by the said p^r^sons now Inhabitantes of Northampton. And therefore doe hereby for my selfe, my heires Executors or Administrators Assigne and make over the within named p^r^mises and all the land, or whatever is therin Contayned, vnto the present Inhabitants of Northampton to them and to ther successors and heires for ever as witnesse my hand this 16th of January, 1662. JOHN PYNCHON."

"This assignement was acknowledged on the said sixteenth day of January, 1662.

Before vs

ELIZUR HOLYOKE }
SAMUEL CHAPIN } Commissioners."

Within the bounds named in the above deed was included all the territory now comprising the towns of Northampton, Southampton, Easthampton, Westhampton and a part of Hatfield and Montgomery. Beginning at the head of the Falls opposite the present town of South Hadley, the line extended northward, following the river to the southern boundary of Hatfield, and westward nine miles into the woods.

CHAPTER II.

COMMENCING THE SETTLEMENT.

First Meeting of the Proprietors.

TEN days had not passed after the date of the purchase, when a meeting of the planters was held, whether at Hartford or Springfield, is uncertain. At this meeting twenty or twenty-one persons were present. The name of Thomas Root appears twice, but only one person of that name settled in Northampton, and this duplication must be an error.[1] As in the deed already given, there are omissions, so in this document there are others, which are indicated by brackets. These were undoubtedly occasioned by the imperfect state of the records when copied from the old book, by order of the town in 1660. It may be unnecessary to state that they have in no way improved since that time. A transcript of the proceedings of this meeting is given below:—

"October 3th, 1653.

"It is agreed by the plantrs of Nonotuck which Petition to the Court in the [Spring] or any that shall Joine with them that they shall bee resident there [and] dwell themselues and ther families by the next Spring come [   ] next ensueing the date here of, or els every such prson as shall be deficient in that Kinde shall loose his mony paid for the purchase with the Charges that they haue binn att vnlesse hee shall giue such [reason] to the Company designed for that worke that the said Company [Please to] giue them more time.

Giles Whiteing	William Holton	Thomas Roote
Edward Elmer	William ffelle	Thomas Bascom
Thomas [ ]	William Miller	Henry Curtis
William Clarke	George Alexander	John Broughton
Robert Bartlett	Thomas Roote	William Hanum
John Gilburd	John Bayly	Daniell [Evarts]
John Webb	John King	Thomas Gridley."

1 Thomas Root was from Hartford, and he had a son Thomas, but he was scarcely ten years of age at this time, and the second of the name in this list could not have been intended for him.

1 3

Second Meeting of the Planters. On the 15th of November, another meeting of the planters was held. The action taken at that time is recorded on three separate pages of the oldest book of town records now in existence. Each of the following paragraphs represents a page of the record : —

(Page 1.)   "November 15, '53.

"It is ordered and agreed that all such personnes as shall goe up to nalwottoge the next Spring insuing the date hereof, there to dwell the next winter for the furdering and promotting the planting of the said place, it is agreed that euery singell man shall receiue foure akers of meadoe besid the rest of his Deuision, and euery head of a phamily shall receiue six akers of meadoe beside the rest of there diuision."

(Page 2.)   "November 15, 1653.

"It is agreed, ordered & declared by the Company designed for the planting of nallwottoge who pettitioned to the Generall Corte in the bay for Liberty to plant the said place, which petition being granted, it is agreed by the said Company the said place granted by the corte and purchased of the Indians, shall be aloted to 80 phamilys according to there names, Estates and qualifications."

[Here follow two paragraphs which were crossed with a pen on the record, in which it is proposed to divide one-quarter of the plantation between the twenty men[1] who signed the first petition and to choose five men to make the division.[2]]

" Thomas Bird   who shall haue power to receuie in
  Thomas Burnnum   such inhabitants as the shall Judg
  Robbard Bartlett   fitt for the Caring one the designe
  John Gilbirt   and to accommodate the according
  Ed Elmer   to the former rull which is a quar-
ter to 20 phamelys being in Estimation eight hundered Akers."

(Page 3.)   "November 15, '53.

"For the planting of a towne at Nolwottoge it is agreed by the Company to whom the Courte granted Liberty to plant the said place. It is agreed and Declared that euery persone or persons as shall take up any land at Nealwottoge shall inhabite them selues and phamilys foure years after there the first sitting Downe or planting themsellues and phamilyes in the said place before any such person or persons shall

1 An apparent discrepancy appears at this point. Attached to the first petition are the names of twenty-four persons (see page 6), but the proceedings of the first meeting of the proprietors contain only twenty signatures (without the duplicate of Thomas Roote), and undoubtedly the allusion is to the signers of those proceedings and not to the men who signed the first petition.

2 The paragraphs alluded to above are appended : "Moreouer it is agreed that 20 men that petitioned to Corte shall haue one quarter of the said lands to deuid Amounst them according to there names, Estat & qualification."
"It is agreed by the Company designed for Nallwottoge to make choys of flue men for the deuiding of the lands, who shall Deuide one quarter of the meadoe to 20 phamilyes, according to there names, Estats and qualifications."

haue power to lett or sell any such land without the consent of the towne, and in case that any man shall depart away from the said place before he hath dwellt there foure complett years as afore specified, all such lands shall fall into the towne's hands, vnles the person remouing shall giue the towne such sattisfiing resons that the towne shall giue grant Liberty to the persone or persons remouing to dispose of there lands. It is also agreed that in case any man that hath a proprietty in the said place shall dye either before he shall goe to the said place or hath dwelt there foure yeares, then the heires of the Deceased peartty or persone shall haue Liberty to make the best of any such lands of the deceased person or persons paying the Charges and Desearts of the said land."

It is quite probable that the paragraphs of the above document which were erased or crossed, never went into effect. The proposed division of one-quarter of the lands to the twenty men[1] who were present at the first meeting apparently was not carried out, as only eight of the number ever came here, and only two of the five men appointed to admit inhabitants and divide the property, settled in Northampton.

Under these rules and regulations the planters took possession of the new territory. No movement was made towards a settlement, however, till the next year. Winter was too near at hand when they were adopted to admit of emigration, though some of the proprietors undoubtedly came to spy out the land in 1653. The main object of the emigrants was to make good their claim, and provide some means of shelter before the commencement of another winter.

Forty-five names, including those whose surnames are blank because of the dilapidation of the records, as well as both the Roots, were signed to the first petition and to the formal agreement concerning the plantation.[2] At the October meeting for consultation and organization, only eight of the signers to the petition seem to have been present, but thirteen new names, counting the blanks, were appended. Only fourteen of the whole number—eight of the petitioners and six of those who attended the October meeting—ever became residents here, and some of these men did not come till the place had been several years settled.

---

1 It should be understood that the division as stated above did not mean that the inhabitants should be restricted to four or five acres of meadow land, but that none should have less. Many of them had much more. The agreement seems also to have meant that to the twenty men who paid the Indians for the land, should be given one-fourth part of the meadow, but that part of it was not consummated.

2 See pages 6 and 13.

Promptly in the Spring of 1654, the first settlers arrived to take possession of the newly
purchased plantation.   No information concerning the route they pursued has been obtained.   In all
probability they followed the course which afterwards became the traveled way to the southern towns.   This roadway, designated in some old deeds as the "cartway," and
in others as the "common cartway as we go to Windsor,"
entered the town very nearly where West Street is now
located.   The crossing at Mill River was at or near the site
of the present bridge, and the line of travel very nearly
coincided with that of the old highway to Easthampton,
Southampton, and Westfield.[1]   Whether they brought their
household goods on horse back, in ox carts, or left them to
come by way of the river, is unknown.   How many composed
the first band of settlers, where they selected their home lots,
and the day of their arrival, have never been recorded.
That some of them came in 1654, is unquestionable.   Imagination pictures the little company on a mild day early in
the month of May, halting wearily upon Meeting House
Hill.   Calm and peaceful stretch the wide expanding meadows, already smiling under the kindly influence of the genial
season.   The two mountains, covered to their summits with
green, are dimly seen through the intervening forests, as the
setting sun illumes their wooded heights.   On every hand
spreads the boundless forest.   The eye sweeps around and
beyond the bare tree trunks, noting an occasional open space,
fit location for the log cabins that will soon shelter the adventurers who have left kindred and friends so far away.
Dimly through the forest rises the smoke of the Indian
wigwams, and possibly between the trees are seen glimpses
of their dusky owners, watching the new comers with eager
interest.   They have little time to dwell upon the beauties
of the landscape.   They know that the broad river winds
through the fertile meadows and they can see the little
stream that divides their plantation.   Satisfied that their
journey has come to an end, they unload their weary beasts,
partake of their evening meal, and provide temporary shelter.   That these pioneers should have brought their families with them, on their first coming, is problematical.

1 "Before Hadley was begun, the Northampton people had a way to Windsor and
Hartford through Waranoke (afterwards Westfield)."—Judd's Hist. of Hadley, p. 42.

Naturally an advanced guard of men, prepared to stake out their claims, and build their houses, would precede all the rest.

Selection of Home Lots.
It is undoubtedly true that the first comers selected their home lots wherever there was an open space of land adapted to the needs of the house builder, and requiring the least labor in preparation. The men of that day were not adepts at clearing away forests, though nearly all of Northampton's pioneers had already some experience in founding new settlements. The meadows were the principal attraction, and facility of access to them would of course govern in the location of a permanent residence.

The homesteads first occupied in this town were situated on both sides of what is now Pleasant Street. It was first named Bartlett Street[1] in honor of Robert Bartlett, one of the first men to locate there. Quite a number of settlers whose names are not found among those already mentioned, must have accompanied the first body of emigrants. If proximity to Meeting House Hill is any indication of priority of settlement, then but few of the earlier promoters of the enterprise were among the first to arrive.

There is nothing to show by what method the uplands were distributed or how the adjustment of home lots was determined. While it might be inferred that, what was afterwards known as Meeting House Hill, would become the central point in the location of these lots, it is evident that such was not the case. All of the first selected homesteads were situated east of a north and south line intersecting that elevation. The uplands were undoubtedly more densely wooded than the section nearest the meadows, hence the work of clearing them for occupancy was proportionately reduced. Then the land on the streets named had many of the characteristics of meadow soil, which were lacking in other portions of the town, and consequently was more desirable.

1 In Hadley and other towns the first highways were decided upon before the home 'o' of the settlers were laid out. It was not then the custom to establish highways ·er the land of individuals.—Judd's Hist. of Hadley, p. 42.

2

Homesteads of some of the Original Promoters.

The eight settlers whose names were appended to the original petition were Edward Elmer, William Miller, Thomas Roote, William Holton, William Janes, William Clarke, Robert Bartlett and John Webb. It is quite probable that four of these men were among the first to arrive :—Bartlett, Elmer, Holton and Webb. The first three named among them settled on the west side of Pleasant Street. Bartlett's lot was at the lower end of the street, next to the meadow, and was nearly identical with the homestead of the late Wm. R. Clapp. Elmer and Holton had the next two lots north of Bartlett. Root, Webb, Miller and Janes, resided elsewhere. John and Richard Lyman, Joseph Parsons and Alexander Edwards were also among the early arrivals, but their names do not appear upon either of the already quoted documents. The two Lymans were the most northerly occupants of land on Pleasant Street, though their lots did not quite come up to Meeting House Hill, as there was unappropriated land enough above John Lyman's, four years afterwards, for a home lot of four acres for the minister. Richard Lyman's lot joined that of Holton, and the five lots above enumerated, embraced all the land between Pleasant Street and Mill River, from the parsonage lot to the entrance into that river of what was afterwards known as Pomeroy Brook.

Lots on the East side of Pleasant Street and elsewhere.

On the east side of Pleasant Street were five home lots. Three of them belonged to persons who signed the original petition. John Webb had two acres, bounded north on Main Street and east on the (Pomeroy) brook ; next to Webb, bounded west on Pleasant Street, and north on Main, was Alexander Edwards, (these two lots afterwards comprised the homestead of Gov. Caleb Strong) ; south of Webb and Edwards was William Janes ; next came Thomas Root, and joining him on the south was Thomas Mason. All these lots were bounded west on Pleasant Street. Samuel Wright Sr., had a home lot of four acres, extending from King Street to the brook, bounded south on Main Street, which included the site of the First National Bank and contiguous property. Joining Wright on the north was that of William Miller, extending from King Street to the (Market Street) brook. This locates all the eight settlers who signed the original petition, with the exception of William Clarke. He did not appear till 1660, and he had one of the first home lots taken west of Meeting House Hill.

Other Lots Granted to the Earliest Settlers. The six new names signed to the agreement of October, 1653, were those of George Alexander, John King, Thomas Bascom, Henry Curtis, John Broughton and William Hannum. It is somewhat uncertain when these men arrived, but they were here within two years after the settlement commenced. Joseph Parsons came probably before either of the six above-named, and his homestead was situated at the corner of Bridge and Market Streets, being bounded on the south by the former street. George Alexander established himself on Market Street. His lot was the next but one above that of Joseph Parsons. John Bliss, brother-in-law to Joseph Parsons, had the lot between Parsons and Alexander, and in the course of a few years it fell into the possession of Parsons. North of Alexander was the lot of William Hannum, and still north of Hannum was that of Henry Curtis. The lots of Bliss and Alexander, were in subsequent years, when transferred to other parties, bounded on the east by the "sequestered Ministers' lot," afterwards converted into a cemetery, which is still in use. John Broughton and Thomas Bascom had lots on the east side of Hawley Street. The most northerly lot on that street, bordering on Bridge Street, and now occupied in part as the site of the Norwood Hotel, was taken by Joseph Fitch. He was undoubtedly an early resident, as he was a member of the first board of selectmen, and it is quite probable that his next neighbors, Broughton and Bascom, came about the same time; Bascom, at any rate, was here in 1657. John King had the fourth lot on King Street, between whom and William Miller on the south, was the lot of David Burt. This completes the list of home lots awarded to the promoters of the enterprise, who were conspicuous at the preliminary meetings which inaugurated the movement, with the single exception noted above.

Size of Home Lots.
"Forlorn" Lots.
Meadow Lots.
To nearly all the first settlers home lots of
at least four acres were granted, though to
some much more land was given.   In most
cases the grant was all in one lot.   On the east side of
King Street, from the former residence of Eliphalet Williams to the homestead of the late J. P. Williston, the
home lots contained but two acres each.   In order to supply these deficiencies, a section called "Forlorn" was either
set apart or used by common consent.   This "Forlorn"
land was on the west side of King Street brook, above
Park, and from it two acres each were given to such of the
grantees on that street as were short of the requisite number.[1]   Apparently it was of limited extent, and was all required to equalize the home lots on King Street.   There is
no record of "Forlorn" land being given to persons living
in other portions of the town.   In this vicinity was the
place called "Miller's Lion's Den,"[2] so named in deeds.   It
belonged to William Miller, who owned the lot bounded
south by Park Street.   The first lot on King Street, that of
Samuel Wright Sr., contained four acres, but it was first
granted in two lots :—one to Samuel Wright Sr. and the
other to his son Samuel, who relinquished it to his father,
and was provided with a lot on Bridge Street, on a portion
of which now stands the new house of John L. Draper.
To the owner of each home lot were granted other lands,
meadow, upland or plain land.   The meadows were generally divided into small lots, no individual having all his
meadow land in one place.   The number of acres awarded
to different persons varied.   Some had but eight or ten
acres, while others obtained from thirty to fifty.   Meadow
lots usually contained three, six, eight, ten or more acres,
and those having the largest quantity held a number of lots,
sometimes widely separated from each other.

1 The "Forlorn" lots lay between King Street and the base of Round Hill, and
extended from "Lyman's Lane" (Park Street) to "Hawley Lane" (Spring Street).
They consisted originally of seven lots of two acres each, and the land was all given
to the settlers on the east side of King Street, to make their home lots up to the
standard size. "Miller's Lion's Den" was situated north of Hawley Lane.

2 It was a question when New England was first settled whether there were not
lions among its wild beasts. Some of the early writers believed that they existed
here, and many incidents were related concerning them. The catamount or panther
was the lion of the Indians, and probably from a den once occupied by these animals
on Miller's land, the name originated. Very few of them were seen in this section
after the settlement commenced.

Circuitous Course
of Connecticut
River.

From the boundary line between Northampton and Easthampton, at the northerly end of Mt. Tom, to the Connecticut River at the upper end of Hadley front street, the distance in a straight line is four and one-half miles. To reach the same points, by following the course of the river, as it ran at that time, a little less than eleven miles must have been traversed. Within these curves of the stream lie the rich alluvial lands of Northampton and Hadley. The most abrupt of them is at the southern line of the Northampton meadows. It was formerly known as the "Ox Bow," but is now generally called the "Old Bed." Through this bend the river flowed for three and one-half miles, adding but ten or twelve rods to its course towards the sea. It encircled about 300 acres of land which was then a part of Hadley, called Hockanum meadow. In 1840 the waters cut out a new channel across the narrow neck of land on the Hadley side, greatly straightening the course of the river. Afterwards that portion of the meadow was set off to Northampton.

Names applied to
the Divisions of
the Meadows.

The first settlers divided the meadows into many sections, giving to each an appropriate name. Either the conformation of the land, the course of the river, some local tradition, or an Indian name, seem to have determined these appellations. As the names appear in the earliest deeds, they must have been adopted when the land was apportioned.

The names of twelve separate divisions of the meadows are to be found upon the oldest book of real estate records. In the bend above "Shepherd's Island," along the river bank is "Old Rainbow," and adjoining it on the west, "Young Rainbow," named without doubt from the original shape of the land caused by the curve in the river; "Walnut Trees" division was laid out along the southern half of "Young Rainbow;" "Venturer's Field" extended from "Walnut Trees" to Pomeroy Terrace; there is a tradition that one or more families ventured to spend the winter of 1653, in a cave in the bluff at this point, hence the name; above "Venturer's Field" up to the present bridge across the river, extended the "Last Division;" on the river bank, opposite Shepherd's Island, was "Bark Wigwam;" following the Connecticut to the present mouth of Mill River, was "Middle Meadow;" between "Middle Meadow" on the south, and "Walnut Trees" and "Venturer's Field," on the north, were "First," "Second" and "Third Squares," the latter forming the eastern boundary; "Manhan Meadow," named from Manhan River, embraced the land now bounded on the east by Mill River, south by Connecticut River, "Old Bed," and west by "Fort Hill;" "Hog's Bladder" lay at the most southerly point of the "Ox Bow;" another lot of meadow land, containing 120 acres, "more or less," lying north of Hulburt's Pond, granted to John Pynchon, has since been known as "Pynchon's Meadow," but was not so called at that date.

Rule for Dividing Meadow Land. These names were applied to the meadows during the first years after the settlement began, and are many of them still as familiar as of old. The rule adopted for dividing meadow land was fifteen acres to the head of a family, three acres to a son, and twenty acres to £100 of estate.[1] Most of the uplands at first granted (except home lots), are distinctly stated to have been given in "lieu" of lands in the meadow; they were substituted when meadow land did not hold out, or when it proved to be swampy or otherwise untillable. Others had grants of upland because their home lots were smaller than the regulation size.

Payments for Land, 1659, 1660. None of the first settlers paid anything for their land except for the original purchase made by Pynchon, and the necessary expenses attending that transaction. Not till some years after its settlement did the town sell any real estate. A few settlers paid 10s. for their home lots in 1659 and 1660. In later years the town made several extensive sales of land, when money was needed for some specific purpose. At this time, however, the proprietors were not speculating in land, though one or two of the inhabitants seemed to exhibit a propensity that way, if the records of real estate conveyances afford any evidence.

1 In January, 1663, this rule was unanimously confirmed.

Land Records.   No real estate grants or sales of land were recorded previous to 1657, though Richard Lyman was chosen "Recorder of Lands," two years before that date. The peculiar form of recording deeds at that time, especially of those who first acquired land titles here, represents the property as "taken." According to the rule adopted Nov. 15, 1653, no person could acquire an absolute title to a home lot till it had been occupied four years. Sixteen home lots are recorded as having been "taken" in 1657, all of them, with two exceptions, in the month of December. If these men had lived upon their lots four years, there must have been quite a settlement here in the fall of 1653, but the records of both the proprietors' meetings held in that year, name the "next spring" as the time for commencing the settlement. There is no other indication that any portion of this territory had any inhabitants prior to the year 1654, and it may be that the condition referred to was not insisted upon. But seven of the settlers recorded as having "taken" land in 1657, were signers of either of the documents heretofore mentioned. It is possible that these sixteen men came here early in the spring of 165¾, according to the Julian method of computing time, then in practice, which made the new year begin March 25. If so, the four years of required occupancy might have been credited to them, after the device of "legal fiction," in 1657.

CHAPTER III.

ORGANIZING THE TOWN.

Preliminaries of the Organization. THE settlement commenced, home lots selected, houses built upon them, and the community gathered, there remained the development of the municipal organization. Certain rules and regulations governing the adjustment of land titles, at that stage a most important consideration, had been adopted by men, the majority of whom never settled here. The people, though few in number—not more than twenty or twenty-five families arriving during the first two years— recognized the necessity of united action, and at once availed themselves of the proper and legal method. It is not probable that the inhabitants long remained without authorizing some among them to manage the "prudentials" of the town. There was no question concerning the best system of administration. The colony laws designated what powers were delegated to communities, and scarce any of the settlers were without experience in the formation of new towns. Familiar with the principles of executive government that everywhere prevailed, and recognizing the town meeting as the unit of power, they entered upon the work of establishing the township.

First Town Meeting. A gathering of citizens was undoubtedly held within a few months after the first arrivals. Unfortunately there exists no transcript of its proceedings, and the day on which it convened cannot now be named. Only by means of the dates of certain acts that must have originated therein, can any approximation towards the time of its assembling be reached. The first record of the transactions of any town meeting is of one that occurred in December, 1655. But a petition to the General Court, presented in May of the same year, must have been acted upon at some previous assembly; and an agreement with certain citizens, which was to be fulfilled in the previous April, had already been recorded. The first settlers undoubtedly came during the spring and summer of 1654, and it is very probable that the preliminary town meeting was held in December or January following.

First Meeting House Erected.   Among the first public acts of the new town was the erection of a Meeting House; "a house for the towne," it is called. It was to be used not exclusively for public worship, but for such gatherings as the town had need. During the next hundred years, the meeting house was not invested with the religious sanctity of the present time. It was used for all town purposes, secular as well as religious.[1] The contract for this building has no date, but may be found in full upon the town records, and was probably awarded in the latter part of the year 1654 :—

"William Hoton   They are to build a house for the Towne
Richard Lyman   of Northampton of Sawen Timber 26
Joseph Persons   foot long & 18 foot wide, 9 foot high
John Lyman   from the lower p^t of ye cell to the vpper
Edward Elmore   part of the raisens.

"And to frame the roofe of Sawen Timber 4 paire of Rafters with coller beams, 7 great laths 5 inches broad, 3 inches wide, the Sparrs 6 inches one way & 5 the other, with the punching for the gable ends 5 below the coller beams one above. Two chimney peeces 4 braces for the roofe nailed on. Only the Towne must find ye nails & help toe raise ye roofe. Two halfe Somers & one Somer & mortice the Somers for the joyce and to make a doore way. Two window places the pieces 8 inches thick below & 6 above. This to be done by the midle of Aprill next vnder the same forfeit which the Town agree for their part for which the said partyes are to have 14^l of the Towne & ye foresaid partyes must out of this pay their rates to the house & the rest of the 14^l the Towne is to pay in worke or corne as they shall agree vpon by the midle of April next '55·"

1 Early in the present century, town meetings as well as sessions of the law courts were occasionally held in the meeting house.

Importance of this Document.

The preceding is an important document, inasmuch as it establishes absolutely certain facts. It shows that the five persons named in it must have been here in 1654; and that the name of the town was decided upon during the first eight months after its settlement. From it may also be inferred that one town meeting at least had been held before the new township was many months old. This contract was placed upon the record by Richard Lyman, who preceded William Janes in the office of recorder.

Log Houses.

As this was the first public building erected in the new town, it must be in some sense better than the log houses that sheltered the people. "Sawen Timber" was the material specified. The dwellings of the pioneers were constructed, the best of them, of hewn, most of them of unhewn timber, squared at the ends. When it is considered that sawn timber could be obtained only by great manual labor[1] it becomes evident that the edifice was one of special importance.

Petition to the General Court to appoint Justices.

Other important action which must have quickly followed if it did not precede the Meeting House contract, was the adoption of the petition to the General Court already noted. The fact that the name Northampton was used in the former document and not in the petition, is an indication that the latter may have been first in point of time. "Desirous to have a course of ordinary judicature set up among them," the inhabitants solicited the authorities to establish a government here. All that remains concerning this matter is the annexed order of the court, passed at the May session, in 1655:

"In ansʳ to the peticon of the inhabitants of Nonotucke, humbly desiring the establishment of a goument amongst them, theire peticon is graunted, and itt is ordered, that Willjam Houlton, Thomas Bascome & Edward Elmer shall & hereby are impowred as the threemen to end all smale causes, according to lawe here, they repayring to Springfeild, to Mᴿ Pinchon, Mᴿ Holiock, &c, who are authorized to give them theire oathes, as also the connstables oath to Robert Bartlett."

1 Saw Mills were introduced into the colony in 1631, but many years elapsed before any were in use in Western Massachusetts. Timber was sawn by means of the long saw resembling the common cross cut saw of to-day ; one man standing on the top of the log and the other in the pit underneath.

This original form of Justice's Court had jurisdiction in all cases where the claim did not exceed 40s., and was established "for avoyding of the Countryes charge by bringing small causes to Court of Assistants." The law applied only in towns where no magistrate lived. A majority of the commissioners had power to act, and either party if dissatisfied with the decision had the liberty of appeal. These commissioners were also empowered to solemnize marriages, and two of them were to be present on every such occasion. That clause, however, was repealed in a few years, and that authority given to the magistrates.

Constable. First Incumbents of that office. In thus establishing the judiciary the court also recognized another important office, that of constable, and in delegating to each of the above-named officers the powers authorized by law, acknowledged and confirmed the legal existence of the town. In fact, the local court would be of no avail without the proper officers to execute its decrees. The absence of both the original petition to the court, and the record of the town meeting, sanctioning it, leaves a doubt concerning the election of Bartlett to the office of constable.[1] There is no record of any choice of constable till 1660, when Nathaniel Phelps was elected. James Bridgman was chosen "Deputy Constable to continue so long as Nathaniel Phelps is constable," in 1658. Phelps was probably first elected constable in 1656 or 1657, and Bridgman was confirmed in that office by the General Court, in May, 1659. Robert Bartlett, however, was the first person who served in that capacity in Northampton.

The Town Named. Though Northampton dates its existence as a town from the year 1654, it had no definite act of incorporation. The name of the town had very

1 "By the law of England, the criterion of the existence of a Parish or Township is the presence of a local constable. * * We do not suppose that this has always been a conscious standard for legislative action in the recognition of towns, or for the actual determination of Town or Parish writs, but we claim that without a constable, or some power representing the corporate responsibility of the community for the preservation of the local peace, a Town would be an impossibility. There have been towns in New England without Selectmen, without Ministers, without a Church or a Common School, but there never was a Town without a Constable. He is the *sine qua non* of an organized Parish or Township, and that by the authority of the Common Law, than which there is no greater authority in the history of English institutions."
—Johns Hopkins University Studies, vol. 1, p. 21.

probably been adopted at one of the first legal meetings of its citizens.   Northampton, as is generally believed, was so called from an English town of that name, from which some of its settlers came; the suggestion is also made that the name was applied because the town was then the most northerly settlement on the Connecticut river.   Both facts may have had an influence.   The colonial authorities recognized its existence and established its legal status, when in answer to its first petition, a board of "commissioners to end small causes" was appointed.   In the first petition the new name was not used, for the court appointed the commissioners for the town of "Nonotucke."   The next year both names were employed, "Nonotucke alias Northampton."

Second Town Meeting.   The next Town Meeting of which any account can be found was held December 11, 1655.   This was the second gathering of the kind in the history of the town, and its record contains the first list of town officers.   Its proceedings are given in the following order : —

"The townsmen chosen for the town, Northampton, Dec. 11, 1655.

William Miller   )   to joyne wth the Townsmen
Richard Lyman   }   for makeing rates.
Joseph Fitch   )   William Hoton
                                        Edward Elmore.

"It is ordered & agreed by the Towne of Northampton That the Townsmen haue power to agree for a cow keeper or calf keeper.

"That the Townsmen haue power to make rates & gather them for prudent occations of the Towne.

"It is ordered y^t noe man shall trade any Bever in the Towne's Liberty but such as have Liberty from the Towne.

"It is ordered y^t all rates shalbe raised for this yeare according to the lands & estates that they putt in for when they receaued their lands."

This action was brief and to the point.   The agreements and orders then adopted, providing for the assessment and collection of taxes, fully organized and established the town government.   By general consent the few settlers then resident here placed themselves upon the common basis provided by law for the control of all rural municipalities.   In this sense it was the most memorable town meeting ever convened in this place. It fully recognized the existence of the town as a corporate body, and put the machinery of government in working order.

Cow Keeper. The undivided commons and the woods were the pasture grounds of the township, and the cow keeper had the care of the stock pastured in them. He was appointed by the town, his wages being collected from the owners of the cows, during the early years of the settlement, but afterwards individuals joined together and paid their own herders. In some cases children and youth were employed for this purpose, and they were required by law to busy themselves in some useful occupation while so engaged.[1] No one was allowed to be idle in those industrious communities.

The custom of general herding was characteristic of all the early New England settlements. At first came the cowherd, then the dryherd, afterwards the swineherd and the goatherd, followed by the shepherd, all a part of the system of herding that prevailed for a century or more. Here the method did not vary essentially from that adopted in other towns, though it is not certain that either hogs or goats ever reached the dignity of a special herder. The herd of cows was usually gathered in the early morning hours, not long after sunrise, and brought back in time for the evening milking. During the night the animals, for shelter or safety, remained in the sheds or barns, or some enclosure on the home lot. From this system was developed another institution of considerable value, the town bull. Interspersed throughout the town records are many entries relative to this important animal, and he appears among the oft repeated items of expenditure as long as the practice of communal herding was continued. The num-

---

1 By a law passed in 1642, selectmen were ordered to see that "such" (meaning children) "as are sett to Keep cattle be set to some other imploym't w'th all, as spinning upon the rock, knitting, weaving tape," &c. It was the custom in the old world for those who were ordered to take charge of herds while pasturing upon the commons to employ themselves meanwhile in some other useful labor, either spinning, weaving or knitting. In Scotland, knitting was an accomplishment more common among the boys than the girls. "Spinning upon a rock" was simply using the distaff, sometimes called the "rock and distaff." It was probably so called from the fact that at the lower end of the spindle was fastened a whorl or circular bit of stone to act the same part as that of a fly wheel to an engine. Weaving tape was done by means of a wooden frame, held in the lap or placed upon a table; a specimen of this machine can be seen in the museum at Memorial Hall.

ber paid for from the public purse, increased during a hundred years, from the single unruly animal that wandered
off to Panchus and was impounded at Hatfield, to ten or
more dispersed throughout the town.

Fur Trade.   To some extent the fur trade was a government monopoly, restricted by general laws,
and the towns would naturally jealously guard all that related to that branch of business.   Beaver skins were a most
valued factor in the early trade with the natives, and soon
became a leading article of exchange with foreign coun-
tries.   The account books of the first settlers, both here
and elsewhere, show the extent and volume of the trade in
furs, and the fact that it was first among the subjects considered by the town, evinces the importance with which it
was invested.

First Birth and   The first recorded birth in Northampton,
Marriage in   was that of Ebenezer Parsons, who was
Town.   born May 1, 1655.   He was the son of Cornet Joseph Parsons, and was slain in the first Indian
attack upon the town of Northfield, Sept. 2, 1675.

On the 15th of November of the same year, the first
marriage between residents of Northampton took place.
David Burt and Mary Holton were the parties to this
solemn contract.   Mary Holton was the daughter of William Holton, one of the first settlers and for years the most
trusted and respected man in the little community.   The
home lot of David Burt was the third on the east side of
King Street, and next above that of William Miller.   Here
he built his log house, and here the newly wedded couple
commenced their married life, coeval with the beginning
of the scarcely established plantation in which they had
taken up their abode.

Special Orders.   An order was passed by the town in February, 165⅚, allowing William Branch of
Springfield, to sell his "house and housing and fences belonging to his house to Thomas Mason, and the said Thomas
Mason is to have the said William's home lot."   This is the
only mention made of William Branch.   He probably pre-

empted his home lot with the other settlers, and built his house on it, but not having obtained a title to the land, the town permitted him to sell his improvements and gave the lot to Mason.   The home lot of Mason was situated on the east side of Pleasant Street, in the vicinity of the Belding's Silk Mill.—It was also "agreed that Joseph Person paying 20s. shall be freed from any offis in the towne of North hampton for this yeare."

Recorder Ap-   Another town meeting was held February
pointed.   28, 165⅚, at which but a single item of busi-
                  ness was recorded.   It was, however, a mat-
ter of considerable importance, though there were undoubtedly other men better fitted for the position than Elmore.
The vote was as follows :—

"Feb. 28, 1655.   It was voted and conclouded by the inhabitants of North hampton that edword elmore shall be recorder for the towne of North hampton for this yeere insoweing proueyd that those which have land recorded shall pay him for his paynes according to the order of the Towne."

The chirography as well as the orthography are somewhat peculiar, and both are hard to decipher.   Only one or two entries by the same hand exist.   There is no other evidence that Edward Elmore ever acted in that capacity.   If the record of the appointment is in his hand writing, none need regret that no more of it appears.   In the following December, Richard Lyman was chosen to fill that office.

Petition to the   The petition of 1655, for the establishment
General Court to of a government here, was followed the
confirm Judicial next year by another, asking for the con-
Officers and to es-
tablish a Court. firmation of the same men to end small
                  causes, but naming a new man for the office
of constable.   On account of the difficulty and expense of trials before the Court of Assistants in Boston, the peti-tioners request that a court of higher grade than that of the commissioners, should be established.   They suggest that it should be composed of the six men chosen to end small causes in the towns of Northampton and Springfield, should have jurisdiction in all litigation of greater value than 40s., and in all jury trials other than for capital

crimes ; the jurors to be chosen equally from the two towns. That document is given in full : —

"To the right worshipfull the Gouvenor and the worshipfull Magistrate assistante and the deputys of this much hounered Courte your humble petioners wish increase of all filicity your humble petioners being thankfull to this honnorable courte for the grant of our petions the last yeare conserning the Establishing of Gouvrment amounst us, and being fully persuaded of your promptnes and cordiallnes to seeke the good and comforte of all your subjects, and therefore bouldeness to solisset this hounnerable courte that the three men confermd by the court the last yeare for to ishue small cases to witt William Houlton Ed Elmer & Thomas Bascum might be confermed again for the next yeare & Thomas Rotte for a cunstable and that they might have their oath at Springfield as likwise our humble request to this hounnerable court is that they would be pleased to consider our condission being so remotte, it will be difficult and chargable to com so farr in all cases surmounting the value of forty shilling therefore our humble request is that although we desier to appeall to the court of assistants in cappetall crimes and causes of great consernment, yet in other cases this hounnerable court would be pleased to grant that they may be tried by the three men att Springfeild and the three men chosen from amounst our sellves and in cases that conserne a jury that it might be equally chosen from Springfeild and from amounst our sellves so we rest your humbl petioners committing with our prayer to the mighty counsellor the prince of peace.

From Norwottuck   WILLIAM JEANES
  alius Northamton   WILLIAM HULBURT
  Aprill 10, 56.   THOMAS WOODFORD."

Answer to the above   Whence these three men obtained their
   Petition.   authority to petition the General Court
does not appear.   Neither of them had then been chosen to any town office, nor is there the slightest indication that the inhabitants had directed them to forward such a document.   The court, however, responded favorably to the suggestion for the reappointment of the former commissioners, but in the matter of constable, some caution was observed.   The request that Thomas Root should hold that office was ignored.   The order was "y^t such counstable as shall be legally chosen there by the inhabitants of the sjd toune shall repajre to Springfeild," to take the oath of office.   It became necessary therefore, that Root should be elected to fill the office of constable, rather than nominated for it by any citizens, whatever their standing in the community, before he could be legally

sworn into the position.   Nothing appears subsequently to
prove that Root was ever chosen constable, and it is probable that Nathaniel Phelps was the first constable elected
by the town of Northampton.   A special reason against the
re-appointment of Bartlett as constable existed, aside from
the fact that there had been no election.

In regard to the request concerning the court, no reply
was made at this time, but within two years a tribunal
founded upon this suggestion was provided.

Robert Bartlett's
Misdemeanor.
Robert Bartlett had in the meantime fallen
under the censure of the law.   At the May
session in 1656, the General Court ordered
Messrs. Pynchon and Holioke to hear and report upon the
case of Bartlett, who was charged with having "committed a misdemeanor."   The result of this investigation is
not stated, but it could not have seriously affected his position in the community.   The next year he was chosen one
of the townsmen, was again elected in 1664, and afterwards
had much to do with town affairs.

Provision for As-
sessing Treas-
urer's Warrants.
At the same session the General Court passed
the following order defining the method of
assessing the Warrants of the Treasurer of
the Colony, upon the towns of Northampton and Springfield : —

"Forasmuch as the tounes of Springfeild and North Hampton are so
remote that the tresurer can not send forth his warrants to them, as
is provided by the lawe, Charges Publick, page yᵉ 9ᵗʰ, it is therefore
ordered by this court and the authoritje thereof, that the connstables
of the sjd tounes, from tjme to tjme, shall call together theire inhabitants in each toune, who shall assesse theire inhabitants and pay in the
same according to lawe, vnlesse at such time or tjmes as the Tresurer
shall send them warrants, as the former lawe provides, then to make
theire assessment accordingly."

The duty of the constable is here stated to be to make
the assessment.   Such a meaning may at least be inferred
from the wording of the order, though the intention may
have been that the constable and the inhabitants should
together levy the tax.   Whatever the design of the law
may have been, a new duty seems to have devolved upon
the constable, though it was only for a special and temporary purpose.

3

Frequent Town Meetings.

From this time onward town meetings were frequently held.   There are records of such meetings in February, April, August and December in the year 1656.   The business transacted related principally to measures for preventing "hoges" from getting into the meadows, fixing the penalty if any were found there, and regulating the time when cattle should be allowed to pasture in them.   A provision was adopted requiring every man to "set a stake at the beginning of his meadow fence with the too first letters of his name turned towards his own fence by the 21st day of April upon the forfitture of 1s."   It was also agreed that "the gaps in the meadow fence gate and bares shall be made up against hoges," by the 17th of April, "upon a penalty of 12d. for every rode that is not made up by the said time."   In August the following important vote was passed.   It is recorded by the same hand that noted Elmore's appointment as clerk: "It is ordered that no inhabitant of this towne shall sel or chang or macke away any of his lands in North hampton withoute lefe from the town until he have posessed it fower years."   In 1657, only four meetings were recorded, but during the following year no less than nine were held.

Land Titles.

The former rule regarding land titles, agreed upon before the settlement began, was by this vote adopted by the town.   No man was to own his land in fee simple till he had occupied it four years.   All grants of home lots subsequently made, contain this condition.   The provision was a wise one.   It discouraged speculation, tended to make the settlement permanent, and encouraged good citizenship.   The early settlers came here to live, every energy must be put forth to exist, and only through persistent, continued effort could the community be established.

Town Officers again Chosen.

At the meeting held in December, a complete list of town officers was chosen, but the page is so much defaced and torn that it is impossible to name with certainty the selectmen, though the list subsequently found upon a later record, contains the names of Joseph Parsons, Sam. Wright Jr., and Isaac Sheldon. Richard Limon (Lyman) and David Burt were chosen measurers of land, "and for their labor they are to have twelve pence for a home lot so measured by them and penny an achor for other divisions." At the same time Richard Limon was chosen "recorder of lands."

Delegates to the General Court Elected. At a meeting held February 13, 165⁴⁄₇, and recorded after the December meeting already referred to, "It was then voted that for the yeare ensuing, Samuel Wright Senior, Joseph Fitch and William Jeanes should bee committees and to be presented to the Gennerall Courte or Courte of Election in May next." The meaning of this vote is not clear. If these men were chosen deputies they never acted in that capacity, and it is doubtful whether Northampton at that time was entitled to representation. There seems to have been no petition or other question that was referred to the Legislature, which would be likely to require their presence before that body. What their duty was and why they were elected is a mystery.

Other Records of the year 1656. Other fragmentary and meagre memoranda of meetings held during this year remain, but nothing of historical value can be gathered from them. In the first volume of town annals, transcribed in 1661, the earliest town meeting noticed is that of June, 1657, and the archives have been continued without interruption till the present day. It is probable that a regular book of records had not previously been opened, but that many of the minutes of town business noted by the clerk upon his blotter, were never transferred, and consequently much that is of importance to the history of the first years of the town, has been lost. Most of the transactions already referred to or quoted, were found upon an ancient book of proprietors' records, which contains also all the original deeds.

Arrival of New Settlers. While the first comers were perfecting the town organization and making preparations for establishing the worship of God, other settlers were arriving. Young men of sterling character, many of them skilful mechanics, middle-aged men of sub-

stance, and occasionally citizens of riper years, were taking
up home lots. It is impossible to name the date of each
accession. No deeds were recorded previous to 1657, and
that is undoubtedly the date of record and not of possession. The first occupied home lots were laid off on what
are now known as Pleasant, King, Hawley and Market
Streets. The names of the owners on Pleasant Street have
heretofore been given. Those of other streets, necessarily
involving more or less repetition, follow.

Home Lots on Hawley Street. Three of the first residents on Hawley
Street have been already named. All the
first grants were on the east side of the
street. Next beyond Thomas Bascom came Robert Lyman,
then James Bridgman, and last on the street was the lot of
George Langton, part of which he gave to his son-in-law,
Thomas Hanchet.

Other Lots on Market Street. North of Henry Curtis, whose lot on Market Street has been designated, was a high-
way, connecting Market and Bridge Streets,
joining the latter street at the northerly line of the cemetery. Above this highway, on Market Street, was the lot of
Christopher Smith, and in the following order came the
lots of Arthur Williams, Henry Cunliffe and Joshua
Carter.

Home Lots on King Street. On King Street the lots were divided into
parcels of two acres each, situated on both
sides of the street. Samuel Wright Sr.,
had the first lot at the corner of King and Main Streets,
containing four acres. William Miller, David Burt, John
King, Walter Lee, Thomas Woodford, Isaac Sheldon, Samuel Allen, and Joseph Root, had two acres each on the
east side of King Street, extending from the highway to the
brook on Market Street. Every settler being entitled to a
home lot of four acres, an additional two acres was granted
to each of these men. The additions were located on the
other side of the street, west of the brook, commencing at
Park Street. William Miller had the first lot, and the
others were laid off contiguously in the order named above,

Samuel Allen's being the farthest north. Joseph Root had no land except on the east side of the street, coming two years after the others, and John Allen was granted four acres, above Root, in 1671. The land between the King Street brook and the highway was held as "commons," and was not disposed of for several years.

Home Lots on Meeting House Hill.
The lots upon the highways just named having been occupied, settlers began to cluster around Meeting House Hill. William Hulbert is first mentioned as having a home lot in that vicinity. He had four acres with a boundary near the present line of Gothic Street. South of him were John Ingersoll and Thomas Salmon. Above William Hulbert, where the Parochial School now is, was the homestead granted to Nathaniel Phelps. His son, Nathaniel Phelps Jr., had a grant west of his father, and together they owned a strip of land bordering on Park Street, from King Street brook to Prospect Street. A highway very nearly coinciding with Gothic Street, gave access to the brickyard, located on the brook, and Hulbert an outlet.

John Pynchon's Home Lot.
All the land on the south side of Main Street, including that now occupied by "Shop Row," comprising in all five and one-half acres, was recorded as having been granted in 1657, to John Pynchon. The record in this case is more than usually minute, giving distances as well as the points of compass. Within two years this lot was given to the minister, and a house built upon it for him. Mr. Pynchon either did not accept the property or else he relinquished it when a lot was wanted for the pastor. There is nothing on the registry indicating that it ever passed out of his possession. These records, however, were copied into another book in a few years, and this one was not transcribed. The stated boundaries of this lot show that Thomas Salmon had another on the west, but Salmon settled on the opposite side of the street and probably never owned one there. Mr. Pynchon had also a grant of 120 acres in the meadow, at the same time. Possibly he exchanged the home lot for the meadow land. The latter grant, which is still known as Pynchon's Meadow, he sold in a few years.

William Clarke and Henry Woodward's Lots. Previous to 1659, no one had ventured west of Meeting House Hill. During that year Lieut. William Clarke and Henry Woodward joined the settlement. Although William Clarke was present at the second meeting of the planters, in 1653, as his signature attests, he did not remove to the new town till six years afterwards. The two grants to Clarke and Woodward were the largest home lots that had then been awarded. Each contained twelve acres, and extended from the highway on the east to Mill River on the west. These lots joined each other at or near the present location of the main building of Smith College. Lieut. Clarke had the most northerly of the two lots, and still north of him was Edward Baker.

Home Lots on Elm Street. On the opposite side of Elm Street, the most southerly lot· was that of Ralph Hutchinson, granted about this time. South of Hutchinson was an acre and a half—a portion of it the lot now occupied by the Catholic Church—that remained in possession of the town till 1667, when it was given to Medad Pomeroy. In the meantime Hutchinson had sold to Increase Turner and Turner had "alienated" it to Jedediah Strong. North of Hutchinson was a lot of two acres, granted to Nathaniel, son of Lieut. William Clarke, and still north of Clarke was a home lot granted to Jedediah Strong, containing four acres. Strong sold it in a few years, and it soon after came into the possession of William Clarke, who transferred it in 1698, to Jonathan Hunt. The last named lot bordered on what is now Prospect Street. Beyond, and bounded easterly on Prospect Street, was the original lot granted to Jonathan Hunt. Then came Joseph Baker, and he was joined on the west by John Taylor. These lots were all granted from 1659 to 1661, and carried the line of settlers on the east and north sides of Elm Street, as far west as the present Round Hill Road.

Home Lots on Main and West Streets. On the south side of Main Street, commencing at the head of South Street, was a home lot which was in the possession of John Webb in 1660, though there is no record of its grant to him, nor of purchase by Webb. He sold it in that year to

Elder John Strong.   Then came the "Mill Lot," on which
was built the first grist mill; adjoining this on the west
was the home lot of Lieut. David Wilton, and next beyond,
and identical with the Forbes Library lot, was that of
Capt. Aaron Cook.   At the corner of West and Green
Streets, Alexander Edwards had a home lot, part of which
was granted by the town "in lieu of land he was to have
had in the meadow," and part of which he purchased of
other persons.   He removed to this location from the corner of Main and Pleasant Streets in 1660.

Home Lots south   About the time that lots were occupied on
of Mill River.   Elm Street, settlers ventured across Mill
                   River.   A swamp then extended along the
bank of the river where now are Maple and Fruit Streets.
This swamp was granted to Joseph Parsons, William Miller and David Burt.   Parsons had eight acres, including
two acres of upland, his being the most westerly of the
three lots, and the others three acres each.   The first home
lot on the upland was given to George Sumner; he was
bounded on the north by Parsons, Miller and Burt.   On
the South was Enos Kingsley.   These two lots extending
eastward to Mill River (as it then ran), included the present homesteads of H. L. Williams and E. H. R. Lyman.
South of Kingsley was William Smead, and still south of
him was Ralph Hutchinson.   Each of these lots contained
eight acres.   On the west side of South Street, next to the
river, were two acres granted to Elder John Strong.   Enos
Kingsley owned the adjoining lot which he bought of John
Webb, in 1660.   This lot occupied the site of the property
recently owned by the heirs of the late George Kingsley,
which remained in the family more than 200 years.   It
originally included the site of Lamb's Wire Mills.   Next
south of this lot was the homestead of John Searl, and
south of him was that of Nathaniel Clark.   These lots
were granted in 1659 and 1660, and some of them were the
lots for which the town required the settlers to pay 10s.
apiece.

This completes the general list of grants to the original
settlers, as described in the first book of deeds, though in
none of them were any names of streets designated.   When

these names were first applied is unknown, though it will be shown in a subsequent chapter that several of them had different appellations from those which they now bear. No evidence appears that any of them were adopted by vote of the town for a hundred years after these lots were granted.

Method of Procedure in the New England Settlements.   It was not so much the survival of old English customs as it was the practical demands of daily life, that decided the method of procedure in the municipal system of New England. The practice of the first dwellers in Northampton may have been based upon precedent, but they worked out the executive problem for themselves in accordance with their surroundings. Theirs was a government by the majority, not the rulership of a few. The community acting in concert, decided what was for the general welfare of the plantation. While many of the measures adopted or propositions discussed now seem trivial or inquisitorial, they were nevertheless essential to the then existing state of affairs.

Great care observed in Admitting Settlers.   The company organized for the settlement of Nonotuck, before a pioneer appeared upon the ground, appointed a committee of five persons who were empowered to "receive in such inhabitants as they shall judg fitt." The same careful supervision over the right of entry into the community was adhered to while the town was in process of organization. In later years it assumed a somewhat different phase, and obnoxious persons were "warned out of town." No one was allowed to join the plantation until permission had been granted, and in 1657, at almost every town meeting, inhabitants were admitted by special vote. With this absolute control of the right to inhabit was closely connected that of land ownership. Allusion has already been made to the vote denying the right of sale without permission from the town till after four years of occupation. This rule was continued as long as land was granted to new comers without remuneration. Another requirement was that the grantee should build upon and thus improve the property. In a number of cases persons, who through neglect of this regulation, had forfeited their home lots, were allowed further time in order to meet the conditions, and in several instances the land reverted to the town.

Fencing the Com-   Of prime importance to the best interests of
mon Field.   the new community was the enclosure of
                   the common field.   When the uplands were
opened to general pasturage, some protection must be afforded to the growing crops in the meadows, and where the holdings were small it was impossible that every owner, especially in the meadows, should fence each separate lot and maintain it against the annual floods.   The laws of the colony established the practice in such cases, and not many months elapsed after the first settlers arrived before the meadows were substantially fenced.   Whether this was done by agreement among individuals or by order of the town does not appear.   No account of any such transaction has been found, though in after years minute details concerning the reconstruction of the meadow fence were always entered upon the records.   Everybody in town at that time owned meadow land, and the proprietors without doubt, then as in after years, assessed the length of fence in proportion to ownership.   The meadows, though divided into small parcels, were in many respects considered as common lands.   While each citizen had the right of proprietorship in certain tracts, the community held the right of general control for the good of the whole.   Lest the greed of the few should incommode the many, the town made rules for the regulation of all, and in 1656, as previously cited, prescribed the dates when the meadows should be cleared of cattle and hogs, and ordered that certain repairs should be made in the fences.   The first systematic action of the town in reference to fencing the meadows was taken six years afterwards, and will be noted in its proper sequence.

CHAPTER IV.

THE WITCHCRAFT SLANDER TRIAL.

A Witchcraft Sensation. AN excitement of more than ordinary intensity prevailed in 1656. It pervaded the entire community, everyone apparently taking sides; some in proportion to their superstitious beliefs, others because they were envious or jealous of their neighbors; and for many a year the town suffered from the bitter feelings fomented by that contention. The antagonisms engendered thereby, entered into the every day transactions of the time, and undoubtedly had a marked influence in shaping the controversies over town officers that found their way into the courts within a year. The first intimation that belief in witchcraft had any foothold in Northampton, came from a trial for slander, in which some of the first families in the place were engaged, before the town had been two years settled.

The Trouble probably Originated in Springfield. Undoubtedly the seeds of the dissension were sown before the parties removed to Northampton. Both the principals in the affair lived in Springfield during the excitement consequent upon the witchcraft craze in that town, five years previous. All the circumstances of that memorable time were still vivid in their minds, and but little stretch of the imagination was needed to find a counterpart of those uncanny proceedings in the life of any one, when jealousy or hatred pointed out the way. All the individuals concerned in this affair resided in the same neighborhood, within a quarter of a mile of each other, nearly all of them on Market and Hawley Streets.

Joseph Parsons vs. Sarah Bridgman. In 1656, Joseph Parsons charged Sarah, wife of James Bridgman, with slander. He accused her of calling his wife a witch. The preliminary examinations in the case were in part taken before the commissioners for ending small causes in Northampton, and in part before the commissioners or magistrates at Springfield. The evidence for the prosecution seems to have been heard mainly by the Northampton commissioners, and that in behalf of the defendants by those of Springfield. All the testimony is on file in the Boston court records.[1] William Holton, Thomas Bascom and Edward Elmer, were the Northampton commissioners, and John Pynchon and Elizur Holyoke were the judicial authorities at Springfield.

The Slander founded on Unsubstantiated Report. Neighborhood gossip was the foundation of the story. It all originated with Sarah Bridgman, who sent the rumors flying. "Goody" Branch (undoubtedly the wife of William Branch, who sold out to Thomas Mason), who lived in Springfield, came to Northampton, as may be conjectured, to visit "Goody" Bridgman, and there was probably a gathering of friends to do honor to the occasion. Very naturally the conversation turned upon the all-absorbing topic of witchcraft. It soon drifted to personalities. The insinuation that Mrs. Joseph Parsons was suspected "of being a which" was amplified and enlarged upon, and finally the majority decided that it was something more than mere surmise. Mrs. Robert Bartlett ventured to disagree with the rest of the gossips, whereupon "Goody" Bridgman became "distasted" (disgusted) and had "hard thoughts" of her, "because she was intimate with the said Mary Parsons." Mrs. Bridgman repeated her story with embellishments, to Hannah Langton, another neighbor, relating the incident about her little boy, who, "when his knee was sore cried out of the wife of Joseph Parsons and said that she did hurt him and she would pull off his knee," and she also declared that others were "jealous" that Mrs. Parsons was "not right." At first Hannah was inclined to believe

---

1 To Miss C. Alice Baker of Cambridge, is due the entire credit of discovering and transcribing the testimony upon which the above account is based.

these stories, but was afterwards "sorry she should have had hard thoughts of her upon noe better grounds."

Mrs. Bliss Investi-
gates the Ru-
mors.

Margaret Bliss, mother of Mary Parsons, hearing these stories, lost no time in interviewing the author of them. Goodwife Bridgman was equal to the occasion, and told her to her face "that she did heare" that her daughter "was suspected to be a which." Mrs. Bridgman also said to Mrs. Bliss that she had been told that "some discontent" had arisen between "the blind man at Springfield and her daughter and that she had done him hurtte and that there was some words between the blind man and her daughter, and then the child of the blind man had fitts."

Cornet Parsons
brings Suit for
Slander.

Exasperated by these and similar statements, Joseph Parsons invoked the aid of the law to remove the disreputable imputation upon the character of his wife. That upon such idle talk rested the foundation of the slander case, which resulted in the trial and conviction of Sarah Bridgman, before the Magistrates' Court at Cambridge, in the month of October, is abundantly proved by the statements already quoted from the evidence given before the Northampton commissioners.

Voluminous Testi-
mony for the De-
fence.

During the month of August, 1656, voluminous testimony was presented in the case before the commissioners at Springfield. The evidence sworn to by the witnesses for Mrs. Bridgman, shows how the most common events resulting from natural causes, may be misconstrued and made to serve the most malicious purpose, under the influence of superstition. Some of it was evidently the outcome of jealousy and spite, and the whole was founded on a belief in witchcraft and dealings with the devil. These statements are important, not only because they present the opinions concerning familiar spirits then prevailing, but also because of the relations they bear to the after trial of Mrs. Parsons for the practice of witchcraft.

Testimony of Mrs. William Hannum. The wife of William Hannum, who lived on Market Street, a short distance above Mrs. Parsons, testified that she had "been warned by some of Windsor and some of Norwottuck (Northampton) to beware how I had to doe with Mary, the wife of Joseph Parsons." Notwithstanding this warning, Mrs. Hannum had considerable "to do" with Mary Parsons. She spun yarn for her and afterwards Mrs. Parsons asked her to let one of her daughters "goe there to dwel." But Mrs. Hannum, considering "what rumors went about her," refused. "But she, having allured my daughter," as the evidence reads, inspired the girl with a great desire to live with her. The mother, however, was decided, and declared that her daughter "should not goe thither to dwel if she might have £10 a yeere." In other words, she wouldn't be hired to consent. Then Mrs. Parsons found fault about the yarn, and charged that it "wanted of the tale in the threads in the knotts." Upon examination Mrs. Hannum found that it "did want almost in every knot of the yarn. Some tymes there would be but 18 threads in a knot for 40 or 28 for 40 & whch notwithstandinge when I spun it I did my best indeavor to give true account, and it was not found fault with till this tyme and soe I spun some more for her to recompence this defect." Afterwards more yarn was spun and that was short, though Mrs. Hannum declared that she had spun for others, "and could have my yarn hold out." After this the witness spun some "Ockum yarn" for Mrs. Parsons. To make things sure this time she sent for the weights belonging to the latter lady, and weighed the "Ockum" before witnesses, but Mrs. Parsons "sent me word it wanted weight." Then her daughter, "though formerly healthy, yet this summer hath been sickly and unhelpfull to mee wch though I know it may be by God's own immediate hand, yet it causes some jealousyes in me agt the said Mary, because it fell out within three or four days after I had given her a full denyal of my daughter's service." Here is the covert insinuation of uncanny dealings by Mrs. Parsons. The daughter, charmed with the idea of living with one of the richest families in town, was disappointed at the refusal of her mother, and moped and sulked and wouldn't help about the house work.

William Hannum
not only Corrob-
orates his wife,
but has G r i e v -
ances of his own. This evidence was bravely supplemented by that of William Hannum, husband of the previous witness, and father of the naughty Hannum girl. He was apparently a firm believer in witchcraft, and made definite charges against the accused. When the falling out about the yarn occurred, he said that "some discontented words passed on both sides." At the time of this unpleasantness, which "was in an evening in March," all his cattle were well for aught he could see, but "the next morning, one cow lay in my yard ready to dy." The animal "languished away and dyed about a fortnight after," though he "took great care night and daye, to save her, giving her samp, pease, wholesome drinks, eggs, etc., and this cow beinge younge was a lusty cow before this very tyme." On one occasion he saw Joseph Parsons beat one of his little children "unmercifully," on account of "loosing its shoe." His wife, Mary Parsons, "cominge to save it because shee had beaten it before, as she said, he thrust her away." The next day he heard his neighbors "talking how Joseph Parsons had in a sort beaten his wife." Then he perpetrated an astounding jest, by answering them, "one of you being his next neighbors must ride!¹ which manner of jesting I do not approve of or allow of in myselfe." Mary Parsons heard of this peculiar jesting the same day, and Mr. Hannum says "she dealt with me about it, showing her offense." And now comes the punishment: "And soe it fell out that the same evening," his "sow that had four younge piggs," was "missinge and we could not find her that night." After much search he came upon the sow in a swamp "and there shee stood with her nose to yᵉ ground, looking steadily as if shee had seen somethinge in the ground; soe I drave her home & before noon that day shee dyed. She till now was a lusty swine and well fleshed." Goodman Hannum owned a yoke of oxen, and as was the custom then and since, he exchanged work with his neighbors. He loaned his cattle to John Bliss, and afterwards borrowed Bliss's and Goodman Langton's teams "to break

1 It is but fair to Mr. Hannum to say that the point of his jest is made somewhat obscure by the illegibility upon the record of the word "ride." In all probability, if that is the correct word, he meant to imply that they must ride in the fashion imputed to witches, upon a broom stick.

up some ground." The cattle belonging to Bliss he put between the other two yokes, "because they were younge and not very fitt to goe behinde, much less before." About this time "Mary Parsons came to mee and did chide with mee for abusinge her brother's oxen," by putting them in "ye middle where they are always under the whip." They had some words about it and Mary Parsons "went away in anger." "Within three days after I was goinge to Windsor with my oxen and cart, and about 4 miles from our town as I was goinge, whether my oxe hung out his Tongue or whether he went to eat, soe it fell out that a wrattle snake bitt him by the Tongue and there he dyed." "These things," he says "doe something run in my mind that I cannot have my mind from this woman y^t if shee be not right this way, shee may be a cause of these things, though I desire to look to ye overwhelming hand of God in all."

Goodwife Bridgman sees Signs and Scents Witchcraft.

Sarah Bridgman, the defendant, thought she had some reason to suspect evil doings, and related her story at length. Soon after the birth of her child,[1] about a year before this trial, "as I was sittinge upp, havinge my child in my lap, there was somethinge that gave a great blow on the doore and at that very instant, as I apprehended, my child changed and I thought wth myselfe and told my girle that my child would dy, and I sent out the girle to looke who it was at the doore, but shee could see noebody about the house. Presently after the girle came in I looking toward the doore thorow a hole by the doore I saw to my apprehension, two women pass by ye door with white cloaks on their heads; then I concluded my child would dy indeed; and I sent out ye girle to see who they were, but shee could see noebody; this made me think there is wickedness in the place." She related how her eleven years old boy, when he was looking for the cows in a swamp, felt something give him a great blow on the head, striking his hat and beating him most to the ground. "He thought it was a bird, but could see nothing that did it." Soon after he fell over some "loggs" and put his knee out of joint. Evidently the

1 James, son of James and Sarah Bridgman, was born May 30, 1655, and died on the 14th of the following June. This is the first recorded death in the town.

fracture was set in a very bungling manner. The boy was
"in grievous torture while the man [the chirurgeon] staid
wch was 2 days, to ye man's admiration [wonder?] for he
was rather worse than before and he was in grievous torture for about a month : and before he was well he cried
out one night about break of day & with his cryinge
awaked my husbande, he cryed many tymes that Goody
Parsons would pull off his knee, there she sitts on the
shelfe : then I and my husband labored to quiet him and
could hardly hold him in the bedd for he was very fierce
and we told him there was noe body, yea say'd hee there
shee sitts on the shelfe and after hee say'd there shee is gone
and a black mouse followed her : and both I and my husband told him in this extremity that there was noebody on
the shelfe : yea there shee is doe not you see her, there shee
runs away, and a black mouse followed her, and this he
say'd many times and with great violence, and about sun
risinge he was like to dy in our apprehension."

The Husband Con-
firms in all re-
spects the Testi-
mony of his Wife.

James Bridgman, husband of the above
witness, agreed with his wife in every particular, reiterating in almost identical words
the scene in the early morning, with the
sick boy, saying, "and these things the child spake with
much earnestness."

Insinuations that
Mary Parsons
had Dealings
with the Evil
One in Spring-
field.

Witnesses were brought forward to prove
that Mary Parsons was under the influence
of the powers of darkness while she lived
in Springfield, during the witchcraft troubles
in that place. She was represented as hav-
ing been in the habit of wandering about at night with her
familiar spirit. It was also asserted that her husband tried
to prevent these nocturnal rambles by locking the door of
the house, and hiding the key. William Branch, Thomas
Stebbins, and among others, her husband's brother Benjamin, testified that they had seen indications of mental un-
soundness. Branch remembered, when they all lived in
Longmeadow, that Joseph Parsons told him that "wherever
he laid the key his wife could find it and would goe out in
the night and that when shee went out a woman went out

with her and came in with her, but sayd Joseph Parsons,
God preserve her with his angels." At another time while
they lived in Longmeadow, George Colton "told him that
hee following Mary Parsons in her fitt he followed her
thorow the water where he was up to his knees and shee
was not wett. This thing I told to old Mr. [William]
Pynchon, w^n hee was here and he wondered at it but said
he could not tell w^{ht} to say about it." George Colton affirmed that on several occasions "about ye tyme ye witches
were apprehended," Mary Parsons would act very strangely,
in the same way as the children of Mr. Moxon, "whom I
verily believe were possessed with ye divell." He further
stated that when Mary Parsons was taken in a fit she
would "run away and when she had run a pretty while
she would fall downe like one dead & when she came to
herselfe shee would strike & beat herselfe & others, & act
like a distracted woman." He denied having told Mr.
Branch that he followed her through the water. Richard
Sikes had seen Mary Parsons in the meadow about four
years before, when she had fallen down in a fit, and had
helped to carry her into the house. She behaved as others
did "in their fits about y^t tyme." Benjamin Parsons testified that "my sister Parsons" had fits like the Moxon
children; "My sister," he stated, "would sometimes teare
her cloathes and beate herselfe on ye breasts and beate those
y^t held her so strongly y^t we could hardly hold her sometimes, and sometimes in her fits she would run away and
we col'd not hold her & sometimes shee would fall downe
like one dead."

John Matthews reported a conversation he
had overheard between Joseph Parsons and
his wife. "Aboutt foure yeares ago being
at Joseph Parsons house, making barrels
upon occasion of some difference betwixt Joseph Parsons &
his wife he s'd to his wife y^t shee was led by an evill spirit
whereuppon shee s'd y^t he was ye cause of it by locking her
into ye sellar & leaving her. Joseph Parsons s'd further y^t
shee went over ye water & Colton after her and shee was
not wet only Goodman Colton was wet. She s'd also y^t
when her husband lockt her into ye sellar ye sellar was full

*John Matthews
tells how she
was Locked in
the Cellar.*

of spirits and she threw the bed staffe at y^m & ye bed cloaths & her pillow & yet they would not be gone & from this tyme shee told me it was y^t shee fell into her fitts some few days after." She said to Matthews that "ye spirits appeared to her like poppets as shee was washing her cloaths at ye brooke & then shee fell into her fitts." She likewise told him "y^t in her fits shee hath gone from her house in ye long meddow thorough ye g^t swamp in her shift & when shee came to herselfe shee could not tell how shee came to be there."

Sleeping in the Cellar likely to give any one Fits. Beds and bed clothes are not usually found in a cellar, and their presence can only be accounted for on the presumption that her husband had made a bed for her there, in the hope of preventing the continuation of her somnambulistic excursions. No wonder Mary Parsons saw spirits and had fits, if she was compelled to sleep in such a cellar as was generally to be found in the houses of that day.

Referees Rejected. The accused twice proposed to leave the matter to referees, but Parsons and his wife refused, preferring to abide by the decision of the court. Mary Parsons answered "what ye cort would give her shee would hold to."

Evidence in Rebuttal A number of witnesses were introduced to show that the child of Sarah Bridgman had been sickly from its birth. It lived about two weeks. Testimony was also offered to prove that Mrs. Hannum's spinning for other people was as defective as that she did for Mrs. Parsons. Two persons swore that the yarn spun for them by Mrs. Hannum "wanted of the tale some 4, some 5, and some 6 threads in the knot." John Broughton skinned the cow of William Hannum, that died in March, and he found a great quantity, "4 or 5 gallons" "of matter in the belly of the cow," sufficient as he thought to cause the death of the animal. George Alexander and Samuel Allen were present when the ox "was stung with the rattle snake." They saw "nothing but what might com to passe in ye ordinary way and they killed the rattle snake."

Sarah Bridgman
Arrested and
held for Trial.

After this testimony had been taken, a warrant was issued Sept. 8th, by Henry Burt of Springfield, Magistrate, for the arrest of Mrs. Bridgman, and she gave a bond in £100, with sufficient surety for her personal appearance at the next county court to be held at Cambridge, on the 7th of October, to answer to the complaint of Joseph Parsons for slandering his wife.

Decision of the
Court.

The above evidence, on file in the court in all its legal verbosity, was laid before the Honored Bench of Magistrates, who after due deliberation, rendered the following decision :—

"The court having read the attachmts and prused the Evidences respectively p'sented on both sides wch are on file with the records of this court do find that the dfft hath without just grounds raised a great scandal and reproach upon the Plant: wife: and do therefore order that the dft shall make acknowledgement before the Inhabitants of the places where the said Partyes dwell: vizt: North Hampton and also at Spring-feild at some Publick meeting at each place by order of Mr Pyncheon or Mr Holliocke or eyther of ym and in such words and manner as shall be suitable sattisfaction for such an offence and the same to be testifyed under the Hands of the said Mr Pinchon and Mr Holliocke, within 60 days next ensuing and in case of default having notice of the time at each place the said deffendant, vizt: James Bridgman shall pay damages to the pl: ten pounds sterl: Also this court doth order that the Defft shall pay to the Pl his coste of court, vizt: seaven pounds one shilling and eight pence."

Which Alternative
of the Penalty
was Accepted ?

No return relative to the payment of this penalty seems to have been made, and it is not known whether Mrs. Bridgman offered the personal and public acknowledgments required. Possibly her husband may have preferred to pay the £10 sterling, rather than permit his wife to undergo the humiliation of a public retraction.

Character and
Temperament of
Mary Parsons.

Mary Parsons was apparently a proud and nervous woman, haughty in demeanor and inclined to carry things with a high hand. She belonged to the aristocracy, and evidently considered herself a dame of considerable importance. A woman of forcible speech and domineering ways, she was not unwilling that her neighbors should have the benefit of her opinions on any subject touching herself or her family. A case, so flimsy and frivolous, founded on jealousy, prejudice and superstition, conducted before honorable and sensible men, could not well have reached any other decision. To that community, however, in those days of belief in the supernatural, it was serious and significant. Such gossip was an affront that Esq. Parsons could not overlook in a town in which he ranked as one of the first in worldly possessions. His wife had been seriously affected during the difficulties in Springfield, but she had at this time apparently recovered her health, and was not to be trifled with. Appearances indicate that she was something of a somnambulist. When the witchcraft excitement in the neighboring town was at its height, she would often lose control of herself, in the frenzy of those attacks, and wander off in the night till she fell from sheer exhaustion, unable when she came to her senses, to remember what had occurred. From the reported conversations with her husband, it may also be surmised that she was in some sense a psychologist, or mind reader. Wherever the key was hidden, she was sure to discover its place of concealment. For this reason she was banished to the cellar. With his wife safely disposed of behind the cellar door, Parsons had little need longer to hide the key. The excited and nervous condition of the community in which they were then living had a marked effect upon so sensitive an organization as that of Mrs. Parsons, and the continued strain would bring into activity those latent tendencies of her mind. While in Springfield, during those exciting times, no attempt seems to have been made to connect her with the evil in any way. Nor does she seem to have been even suspected at that time. It was reserved for the malice, envy and credulity of her neighbors in another settlement to cast that stigma upon her.

CHAPTER V.

PERFECTING THE ORGANIZATION.

Prosperity of the Town. MEMORABLE in the history of the town, were the two succeeding years, 1657 and 1658. From the first named dates the continuous record of town affairs, and the latter was especially signalized by successful efforts to obtain a minister. Within that time the number of inhabitants was considerably increased, specific action was taken on matters destined to work great good to the welfare of the new plantation, and several valuable enterprises were undertaken. Men of character, ability and means were among the accessions, thus assuring beyond question the stability and permanence of the settlement.

The Initial Book of Town Records. The first existing book of consecutive town records was commenced in 1661. With the exception of a few items relating to the very earliest transactions, the proceedings quoted in the foregoing pages, were not transferred to this volume. On it the bounds of the plantation, the first meeting of the petitioners, copies of the original Indian deeds, and several documents not of general interest, precede the regular town meeting records. Probably the proprietors' registry of deeds, was the old book referred to below. The first entry of town business is found on page 6, and is as follows:—

"19th february 1660

"The day and yere aboue written It was voted affirmatiuely by the Towne of Northampton that a Committe should be chosen to Consider what was orderly and of vse in the old Towne booke and to appoint some to Transcribe the same into the new booke. those that were impowred for this worke were these 7 vizt: William Clarke, David Wilton, William Holton, Richard Lyman, Joseph Parsons, Robert Bartlet,

Samuel Wright Junio[r]. these 7 aforesaid appointed and agreed with William Jeanes the Towne Recorder to Transcribe all that was ord[r]ly and of vse in the old Towne booke into the new booke."

Mr. Janes began his records with the preceding vote, followed by another passed at the same time, noting the choice of Nathaniel Phelps as constable. He then goes back to June, 1657, ignoring all business that had been transacted in the previous years. From that time, however, it is presumed that all meetings, legally called, were duly entered, though they do not follow each other in regular chronological order. The dates of the years, and of the months of the same year, are frequently intermingled. This lack of uniformity is often confusing, and when the atrocious writing and worse spelling of some of the clerks is taken into the account, there is great liability to error, which is in no degree modified by the several methods of dating then in use. In later years this second book was copied in a fair and legible manner, but the quaint and venerable appearance of the original, as well as the amusing interest in its execrable orthography, are missing.

Division of Manhan Meadow. Much of the land in the meadows had already been assigned to settlers, but almost the entire section of Manhan was still undivided. This was disposed of in part by the annexed special vote, adopted June 25, 1657 : —

"It was voted and agreed the day and yeare aboue said that the land in Munhan shalbe devided among the inhabitants now resident that haue not had ther proportion elsewhere only Reserueing 60 Acres for sequestred land at the hither end of the meddow and the corner of land behinde M[r] Pynchons land. And these to runn from the greate River to the Mill River only ther must bee a highway of two rods brode from the hither end to the outside of Henry Curtis lot to ly betweene Henry Curtis and Lieutenant Clarks lot and soe running to the hoggs bladder. William Holton, Joseph ffitch and Robert Bartlet are chosen for the measuring the divission and to be pd by the day for ther measuring."

It should be remembered that the course of Mill River was then close under Fort Hill, and that it is supposed to have entered the Manhan River near the point at which that stream joined the Connecticut.

Lieut. William Clarke, named as an owner in Manhan, was not at that time a resident of Northampton. His home lot was not granted till 1659, and not till that date did he become a permanent settler. There is no further record of this distribution. It seems highly probable that this was only a partial division, just enough of territory being laid off in the northern half to even up meadow land owner-ship. At all events considerable land in Manhan, at its "upper" or southern end, was granted in 1659, as a bonus to desirable settlers.

A Grist Mill begun. Another important work was commenced this year. The settlers had no means of grinding their corn except that which existed in every household. Springfield was the nearest point at which a grist mill was to be found, and that was altogether too dis-tant to be made generally available. Consequently a mill "for the use of the inhabitants of Northampton," was be-gun. It was a private enterprise, and probably did not make great progress that year. The town passed no vote in reference to the matter, although a lot of two acres, called the "mill lot" had been already set off. No record was ever made of the location or grant of the mill lot, but it is recognized in the boundaries of adjoining property, and upon it the first grist mill in town was built. This mill stood on the north bank of Mill River, just west of the Gas Works. Several years elapsed before it was ready for use. The facts concerning its construction will be given in another chapter.

Purchase and Deed of Capawonke. Though the Commissioners included Capa-wonke in the original "lay out" of the plantation, it was not fully purchased by Mr. Pynchon when he bargained for the rest of the land. The Indians held possession of it till 1657, when John Webb seems to have been authorized to buy it though there is no vote on record conferring upon him any such authority. From the following deed it appears that a portion of the purchase money had already been paid, and that Webb merely completed the transaction : —

"The 20th of July 1657, that I Lampancho the Sachem haue sould to the Towne of Northampton vppon Conechtecutt River haue sould all the land and Trees with all the Appurtenances ther vnto belonging caled by the name of Pewongenuch and haue receuied full and compleate pay

and satisfaction for the same with all the Damages soe that I doe Resigne the full Right and Title for myselfe and my heires for ever to the
Towne of Northampton.   The satisfaction for the said land I receuied
of John Webb of the same Towne beeing Thirty shillings which is the
Remander of the pay and am now fully satisfied for said land with
all the Apurtenances wher vnto I haue set my hand the day & yere
aboue written.
                    The marke of Lampancho
                                          alias Umpanchela.
Witnesse to the same
        WILLIAM JEANES
        WILLIAM HOLTON."

The price agreed upon for this parcel of land, as will be
seen by future transactions with this chief, was 36s., and
Umpanchela had already received a portion of his pay,
probably 6s., "to bind the bargain."

New Board of
Townsmen and
their Instruc-
tions.

During the first few years after the organization of the town, its officers were not all
chosen at the same meeting.   Selectmen
were elected in December, and the others at
different times.   In 1658, a change was made, and townsmen were afterwards voted for early in the year, though
not always in the same month.   Consequently the selectmen chosen in December, 1656, held over till the new board
took office in 165⅞.   The election occurred in February of
that year, and the selectmen were ordered not to "dispose
of any of the Townes land without the Townes consent."
Nothing indicates the necessity for any such instruction,
but there was evidently reason to believe that something of
the kind had been done, or a suspicion existed that it was
in contemplation.   In addition to the above vote, a system
of yearly accounting between the different boards of selectmen was ordered, and that it might be perfectly understood, the method was explained at length upon the
records : —

"It was then voted and agreed that the old Townes men shall giue
vpp ther accoumpt within a moneth after ther yeare is expired to the
new Townes men, that all accoumpts may bee prfected and Righteousness maintained and this to bee donn from yeare to yeare, viz: Mr
ffitch, Richard Lyman, William Miller are to giue vpp ther accoumpts
to Joseph Parsons, Sam: Wright Junior and Isaac Shelden, and the
said Joseph Parsons, Sam: Wright Junior and Isaac Shelden are to
giue vpp ther accoumpts to William Holton, Robert Bartlett and
Thomas Woodford."

Here named in the order of their election, are the first three boards of townsmen, supplying the names of the second one, which the imperfect town record made impossible to decipher. The first named were chosen in December, 1655, the second in December, 1656, and the last were elected February, 8, 165$\frac{7}{8}$. On the 29th of March it was voted "y^t M^r ffitch is chosen Townes man for this yeare during the other two Townes mens time."

Why Mr. Fitch was chosen selectman at this time, or whom he displaced, is somewhat uncertain. Robert Bartlett, as has been seen, had been under a cloud, and the natural supposition would be that he was dropped. Yet in April, when the names of the three selectmen appear upon the records, signed to the ordinance about the boat, that of Joseph Fitch takes the place of William Holton. Possibly Holton, having been sent to Boston by the town, as its agent before the legislature, may have resigned the office of selectman.

In December, 1657, Samuel Wright and David Burt were "chosen measurers for the yere ensueing ther wages 12^d a home lot & other lots 1$^d\frac{1}{2}$ p^r acre in Munhan & other Devissions 2^d p^r acre." In May following "James Bridgman was chosen by the Towne deputy Constable to continue as long as Natha Phelps is Constable." But there is no record of the choice of Phelps. In December 1658, "Mr Jeanes is chosen Recorder of land for the yere ensueing."

Justices chosen by Ballot.

When the town petitioned the General Court to establish a government here, that body appointed the justices. This year the commissioners to end small causes were chosen by ballot[1] in town meeting, and were doubtless qualified in the usual way at Springfield. The record dated "Feb. 8th 1657," (58) reads :—

"It was voted and agreed concerne the order of the choyce of the 3 men to end small cawses they shall first chuse one and hee that hath most votes by pap^{rs} shall stand for one and for the rest in order for y^t ther was chosen for the yere ensueing William Holton, Thomas Bascum the 3 men to end small cawses."

1 Voting by ballot had not at that time become the universal practice. Questions in deliberative bodies were usually decided either viva voce or by a show of hands. This custom prevailed in town meetings and in the General Court, unless otherwise ordered. This is the first time the ballot is mentioned as having been used here.

One name was omitted, though three men were chosen. The mystery, however, was solved at the first session of the county court, as will be noted in its proper connection. The name unrecorded was that of Edward Elmer, who had already served two years in that capacity. According to the court record, Elmer was first chosen, and then some other person elected over him. Probably the recorder was uncertain which of the two was entitled tò the office, and so named neither of them. Elmer it seems hurried to Springfield and took the oath, and the court sustained him. These officers continued to be chosen in this manner, and were annually recorded with the list of town officers. In 1663, the commissioners appointed days on which sessions of their court would be held.[1]

Meadow Land located by lot. Casting lots, an ancient method of deciding doubtful questions, was resorted to in town affairs as well as those of lesser importance in every day life. In March, 165⅞, the town voted that

"Mr Williams John Stebbens Joseph Root Joseph Jeanes shall cast lotts for ther proportion of Grasse Ground the first lot to ly next to Robert Haywart and soè successively downward in the Middle Meddowe."

Robert Hayward's lot was bounded east by the great river. Joseph Root drew one and a quarter acres adjoining Hayward, then John Stebbins four acres, next Arthur Williams five acres, and last Joseph Janes one acre and one rod. The location only was decided by lot, other considerations determined the quantity of land.

First Movement towards obtaining a Minister. The most important work of the year towards perfecting the organization of the town, was inaugurated at a meeting held on the 18th of March, 165⅞. Then it was that the proposition for obtaining a minister was first acted upon. The vote passed at that time is given in full : —

"It was then voted and agreed yᵗ William Holton is desired to solicite the Generall Court, and to act and propound several Cases that Concerne the Towne, as first to cleare vpp the Exposition of the grant bee-

1 "The three men appointed to end small Cawses, appointe the 1 second day in every other mo: to heare any Complaints yᵗ shalbe brought according to lawe. The first day the 1 second day of the 4: mo: and 1 second day of the 6 mo: 1 second day of the 8 mo: the 1 second day of the 10 mo: & the 1 second day of the 12 mo:"

ing somewhat Ambiguous, y^t grant is supposed to bee an Answere to our petition (56)

2^{ly} to propound Concerneing further power or helpe in matters of Judicature, either for helpe from the bay or from Springfeild. 3. to treate with Mr Willard, and end [   ] ing aboute a Mynester, and to haue Advice aboute [   ] two meeteings, And to Des^r Advise what course to take aboute ye p^{r}venting of excesse of liquor in comeing to o^r Towne and of Sider. All those y^t were p^{r}sent at the makeing this vote did promise to Consent to it in case y^t the major p^t of the Inhabitantes of the Towne doe approoue of it and consent to it.

Wm Holton	William Hulburd	Sam: Allen
Robert Bartlet	Joh: King	Wil: Hanu[m]
Tho: Roote	Da: Burt	Tho: Mason
Jos: Root	Walt: Lee	Jos: Jeanes
Wil: Jeanes	George Allexand^r	Joh: Ing^{r}sol
Wil: Miller	Chris: Smith	Rob: Lyman
Natha: Phelpes	Tho: Salmon	John Stebens
Hen: Curtis	Joh: Broughton	James Bridgman."
	Geo: Langton	

The Inhabitants Religious and Temperate.

Those who voted at this meeting it seems were a little uncertain whether the "major part of the inhabitantes" were of the same opinion as themselves. The above list of twenty-five names must have comprised a large majority of the "inhabitantes," as not more than thirty-eight settlers had received grants of land previous to 1658. Very probably the clerk, in order to give legal sanction to the acts of their accredited agent, recorded the names as people made known their sentiments concerning the order, and not at the time of the meeting. At any rate, there could have been but little opposition to the vote. The questions proposed were the most significant that had yet presented themselves, involving both the moral and spiritual welfare of the township. Small as the community then was, it appreciated the necessity of a settled minister. A meeting house had been two years built, and it was time that the regular ministrations of a pastor should be secured. The evils of intoxicating drinks had also become apparent, and some authority was desired whereby their influx might be controlled. This same spirit of temperance, so prominent the fourth year after the settlement of the town, still prevails. How best to deal with intoxicants is yet an unsettled problem in the regulation of town affairs.

Mr. Willard, whose assistance was requested, was undoubtedly Maj. Simon Willard of Boston, a member of the board of assistant magistrates.

A Rate of £30 Ordered.

The opening of the year[1] (March 25th) found the new settlement still in a thriving condition. Increasing numbers gave it strength and confidence. An ample harvest had rewarded the planters, and the town felt abundantly able to meet all demands. On the 29th of March, it was "voted and Granted that a Rate of 30[1] is to be levied and gath'd to pay the Towne debts." Rates had been voted three years before, to meet current expenses, "prudent occations," as they were called, but no definite sum had been named. Whether any money or its equivalent had been collected under previous action it is now impossible to determine. It seems hardly probable, however, that any tax had been gathered. The only payment the town had obligated itself to make was £14 for building the meeting house, and the sum of £30 was probably sufficient to cover all expenses to that date.

1 Some confusion concerning dates is likely to arise unless the several reforms in the calendar are kept in mind. The first change was made by Julius Cæsar, 46 years before Christ. By his division the solar year consisted of 365 days and 6 hours, adding one day every four years. This was denominated the Julian method or "Old Style." The present "New Style" was established by Pope Gregory XIII. in 1582. He eliminated 10 days from the month of October, which corrected the calendar back to 325 years after Christ, and it was called the Gregorian system. In 1752, the English Parliament struck out eleven days, and the present method became the usage in England and her colonies. Still further complications arise from the fact that the year began at different times. The Julian method began the year January 1st. But in the course of a few centuries, for religious or other reasons, this was varied and other dates were adopted:—March 1st or 25th or December 25th, being in most common use. The English began the year Dec. 25th until the time of William the Conqueror, 1066. His coronation occurring January 1st, gave them occasion to make the year begin at that time. In the 12th century the English government made March 25th the legal beginning of the year in church and state. This law was observed till 1752, when Parliament enacted that the year should begin on the 1st of January. Great inconvenience was caused by this change, and many old records have two dates. Double dates between Jan. 1st and March 25th were in use in England and America, both dates being designated Jan. 10, 1662-3, March 5, 1664-5. The first figure denotes the year commencing on the 25th of the previous March, and the second one that beginning Jan. 1st. The first of March was accounted the beginning of the year for a time in New England and the months were numbered 1st, 2nd, 3rd, etc. Thus the 15th 11th mo. 1661, meant the 15th of January, 1662; or the 17th of the 12th mo. 1662, indicated February 17th, 1663. This latter form is sometimes used in the Northampton records, but more frequently double dates are employed. In this work the present style of the calendar is followed. The figures at the top of each page denote the year as commencing on the first of January.

Ferry Established across the Connecticut River.

As the population increased, better facilities were demanded for crossing the Connecticut River. Indian canoes, or perchance a skiff owned by individuals, were as yet the only means of transit. These were not always at hand when wanted, and at best illy accommodated the public. A boat was built at the expense of the town, in 1658, but there is nothing on record to show its size, shape, capacity, or cost. The following rules concerning the use of this ferry were adopted :—

"Aprill 27th (58). An ord¹ for makeing and ord'ing the boate made by the Townes men vizt : First y' wee make choyse of Goodman Bartlet for the keeping of the kay if any pson or psons haue occation to vse the said boate they shall demand the kay of Rob: Bartlet. Secondly y' all sd pson or psons after y' thay haue had the key delivered to [them] shall stand to the hazard of the boate till the kay [is] Delivered to the proper keeper appointed by the Towne or to his assignes. Thirdly that those that make vse of the boate shall not leaue it aboue 30 rodde be[low] the lower end of the Iland y' is belowe the middle med[ow] neither aboue the lower end of the Ileland without [the] side y' is next the River vnd⁰ the penalty of two shillings 6d. for every such defect. Further that they shall lock it to such a place y' in an ordynary way it shalbe secure from takeing away vnlesse it bee vnlocked vnder the penalty of 5ˢ for every such defect. ffourthly y' noe pson or psons y' carry over the boat over the River shall not retaine it ther aboue an howre and halfe. Further that if hee or they shall keepe the key after they haue brought over the boate and locked it aboue one howre shall forfite 2ˢ 6ᵈ for every such Defect. ffurther if any pson or psons shall breake or loose the oares belonging to the boate shal either pay for them or provide as good as they were againe.

ROB: BARTLET ⎫
JOSEPH FFITCH ⎬ Townesmen."
THOMAS WOODFORD ⎭

This crossing place, the first provided by the town, must have been below the present ferry at Hockanum. It was probably near the turn of the river at the upper end of the "ox bow." The Island mentioned has disappeared. Robert Bartlett lived at the lower end of Pleasant Street, and his was the house nearest to the ferry. No great use could have been made of this boat except for farming purposes, as there was then no settlement at Hadley, and its position was much too far to the south for the convenience of communication with that town, had it been in existence. There was a way to Springfield on the east side of the river

before Hadley was settled, but according to these rules
the ferry seems not to have been intended for the use of
travelers.   The town owned no land on the east side of the
river, and it may be that the ferry was established for the
purpose of transporting hay or other produce from Hockanum meadow, obtained by poaching upon the colony pre-
serves.

Holton presents   William Holton, commissioned by the town
the Petition.   in March, to act as their agent and present
Answer of the
Court.   certain matters to the General Court, attended promptly to his duty, and appeared
before that body in the following May.   On the 26th of the
month the court took action upon the petition and the fol- ·
lowing answer was returned : —

"In ans^r to the petition of North Hampton it is ordered, that theire
condition in relation to a minister be forthwith comended to the reuerend elders, & theire help desired therein ; secondly that there shall be
two courts kept yearely by the comissioners of Springfeild & North
Hampton joinctly, or by any fower of them, the one at Springfeild on
the last Twesday in the first moneth, and the other at North Hampton
vpon the last Twesday in September, which Courts shall haue power to
heare and determine, by jury or wthout, according to the liberty the
lawe allowes in County Courts, all civill actions not exceeding twenty
pounds damage, and all criminall cases not exceeding five pounds fine,
or corporall punishment not exceeding tenn stripes, reserving appeales
in all such cases to the County Court at Boston ; and the sajd Court
shall haue power to graunt ljcences for the keeping of ordinarjes, or
houses of comon entertajnment, selling wine, cidar or strong licquors
according to lawe, & not otherwise, giving the oath of freedom or fidel-
litje to persons qualified, according to lawe, to binde to the peace or
good behaviour, to comitt to prison fellons & malefactors, as the lawe
allowes, & this to be during the Courts pleasure."

The Petition but   It will be observed that in the above quoted
partially An-   response by the Legislature, several matters
swered.   referred to in the petition were passed over
in silence.   Wherein consisted the ambiguity of the grant
has been previously explained.   The defacement of the
record renders uncertain whether the "two meetings" were
town or religious gatherings, but that request, as well as
the temperance question, were neither of them considered
by the General Court.

First Court ever
Convened in
Northampton.

By virtue of the above commission, appointed in answer to the petition for "help in matters of judicature," and following out the suggestion of the petition in April, 1656, the first court ever held in Northampton, convened Sept. 28, 1658. It was composed of John Pynchon and Elizur Holyoke of Springfield, and two or more of the Northampton Commissioners, whose names are not given. In February, 165⅞, Holton, Bascom and Elmore[1] were chosen by the town, and two or more of them must have been present. Elmore, however, could not have served, as he brought an action before the court. The cases recorded were few in number, and of little consequence. They were but the ordinary quarrels and contentions that naturally arise in such communities; yet they show the spirit of the times and the jealousy with which religious observances were guarded. The following is a literal transcript of the court records as made by Mr. Pynchon: —

"Att a Court holden at Northampton Sept: 28 58 By order of the Generall Corte appoynting the Comissioners of Springfield to joyne wth the Comission^{rs} of Northampton for the issuing of all Civill Actions not exceeding Twenty pounds & as in ye said Comission hereunder written more at large—appeareth uppon wch day abovesaid Mt John Pynchon & Elizur Holyoke of Springfield Attended for that service according to ye comission following :

[For this commission and order of the court see page 62.]

Upon wch 28th Day of September Thomas Roote Complayned of Robert Bartlett in an action of the Case for strikinge his the said Thomas his wife wth a long stick to p^rjudice.

Robert Bartlett acknowledginge his offence in the Court Both Plantiffe & Defendt agreed about the matter between themselves;

Joseph Parsons Complaynes agt John Webb for not delivering a Cow & Calf accordinge to bargayne, and thereupon Joseph demand 4£ of the said John wch the said John Owed him;

Upon hearinge of the busyness Joseph Parsons was content to accept of the Cow though the Calf were lost, the said John allowing the said Joseph 5s. wch he promised to allow & pay to the said Joseph.

Edward Elmer Complaynes agt William Holton & Robert Bartlett in an action of defamation in two particulars: 1. for affirming that the said Edward Elmer went down in a disorderly way to take his oath And 2^{ly} for chringe him the said Edward to be one that made a breach or rent in the Town Concerning the Lords dayes Meetings.

1 This name is spelled in two different ways: Elmore and Elmer. In the record of his appointment as recorder, made evidently by his own hand, it is written Elmore, and this form is occasionally used elsewhere, but ordinarily it is shortened upon the records, as in speech, to Elmer.

To the first particular in this Action ye Court did thus judge :

Wee cannot wholly free Goodman Elmer from blame in the transaction of the busyness in relation to the place that he was chosen to vizt a Commissioner for the Towne & judge disorder in his proceedings, though in regard of the overhastyness of the Town in choosing another, wch might be some occasion of his for goeinge down to Springfield where he took his oath, we fynd not ground for Wm Holton & Robert Bartlett to charge him with disorderly taking his oath seeing Edward Elmer did not look for or move to have his oath given him till it was putt to him ; yet we judge it not a defamation ; the speaking of a mans Faylings & infirmityes may be disorderly & yet not a defamation ;

for the 2^d particular we see not ground for Wm Holton & Robert Bartlett to charge Edward Elmer for makinge a breach or rent in the Town ; for it appeareth that the ill management of matters on both sides had been the occasion of the breaches in the Town. But it doth not appear that Edward Elmer was ye cause of them, & therefore to charge him for makinge the breach, we fynd to be some degree of defaming Him, though in regard of some blame worthy carriage found in goodm Elmer about those matters we lay noe damage uppon the Defendants to pay to ye plaintiffe.

John Elmer son of Edward Elmer complayning agt Goodwife Holton for charging him the said John to have stollen an axe—this action was taken up amongst themselves before any sentence passed uppon it.

Att the same Courte Joseph Parsons was chosen Clarke of the Band, & took his oath accordingly for the due execution of his office.

And the Town fyndinge a necessity for some one to Keepe an ordinary for entertayning strangers, they made choyce of John Webb for that service who had a licence graunted him in that behalf as also for the sellinge of wine Cider or stronge liquors ; this licence to continue for one yeare from this Court. Provided the said John Webb doe not suffer any Evil rule or disorder in his house during the said Tearme & that he doe behave himselfe therein, in all things accordinge to the Laws of this Jurisdiction of ye Massachusetts."

Another item of business of considerable interest to the people of Northampton, came before this court, but was unnoticed by Pynchon. The purchase of Capawonke and the payment of thirty shillings for it by John Webb, have already been chronicled. Umpanchela, it seems, became dissatisfied with the price he received for it, and petitioned the court for more pay. He claimed that although he had signed the deed, "he understood that the thirty-six shillings should have been made upp fifty shillings." His demand was acceded to, he received fourteen shillings more, and gave a quit-claim deed to the inhabitants of Northampton for the entire meadow.

Explanation of El-
mer's Suit.
The above case in which Elmer brings an action against Holton and Bartlett, throws a little light upon the record of the first choice by the town of commissioners to end small causes. Three men were voted for, but the names of only two of them were recorded. The finding of the court indicates that Edward Elmer was one of the commissioners chosen, and that for some unexplained reason another ballot was taken and some one else elected. Elmer it seems, in order to secure the office, lost no time before taking the oath. Holton and Bartlett undoubtedly censured him for this unseemly haste, calling it disorderly. The records contain no solution of the matter, as the court was not called upon to decide the legality of the election, and no mention is made of the third man chosen on the board of commissioners for that year; but Elmer undoubtedly acted.

"Clarke of the
Band."
This office, to which Joseph Parsons was appointed, was a most important one in the then existing military organization, especially where the company was without commissioned officers. The Clerk of the Band was the keeper of the muster rolls, inspector of arms and ammunition, and collector of fines. Having the general oversight of all the internal affairs of the company, it was his duty to report all defects to his superior officer. This is the first intimation that a military company existed in Northampton, and because it had not yet arrived at the dignity of commissioned officers, there was all the more need of a clerk. Three years elapsed before Northampton had recruited a sufficient number of men to enable the company to choose officers, and then it had barely enough to be entitled to a lieutenant and ensign.

First Tavern.
John Webb, who was chosen to keep an "ordinary," probably lived at that time at the corner of Main and South Streets, near the residence of the late Enos Parsons. This was the first tavern ever kept in town. The citizens were of the opinion that the best way to "prevent excess of liquors and cider from coming to town," was to control the sale of them.

Another Session of the Local Court.

Whether the trouble about "two meetings," alluded to in the petition to the General Court, heretofore quoted, had reference to the "breach or rent in the town concerning the Lord's dayes meetings," occasioned by the controversy with Elmer, it is impossible to say. A pretty lively quarrel seems to have been going on in the town about this time, both in religious and secular matters. The next session of the local court was held at Springfield, and Northampton parties were at hand with their special grievances, which as developed by its proceedings, show to some extent the state of feeling existing here. Mr. Pynchon's record of this court is as follows :—

"Springfeild March 29th 1659.

"Walter Lee of Northampton Plantiff agt Edward Elmer of ye same town defendant in an action of review of the case whereby the said Edward by sute at Law in the Town of Northampton recovered of ye said Walter, a hogg wth damage to ye vallue of six pounds.

"Edward Elmer Samuell Wright senior Alexander Edwards & John Stebbin Plant agt the Town of North Hampton Defdt in an action of ye case concerninge their turninge out some of the freemen from beinge Selectmen to wch office they were chosen.

"Benjamin Cooley P & Contra John Webb of Northampton Defdt in an action of debt of 8£ & for damage 4£, issued—see forward.

"The 29 day of March 1659 above mentioned beinge appoynted by the Honored Genrll Corte held at Boston, May 20th 1658 for the Keepinge of a Corte at Springfeild by the Comissioners of Springfeild & Northampton joyntly or any foure of them as in the Comission (a Coppy whereof is before transcribed more at large) appeareth, the three men chosen for Northampton Comissionrs appeared here for the holdinge of ye said appoynted & intended Corte wch three men were William Holton Arthur Williams and Richard Lyman together with ye Jury men that were chosen & Warned to appeare at the Court for the tryall of Causes vizt Tho Cooper Geo Colton Rowl Thomas Jonathan Burt Tho Mirack Tho Stebbin & Robt Ashley of Springfield and Tho: Woodford Robt Bartlett Joseph Parsons & David Burt of Northamton. But the said William Holton Arthur Williams & Richard Lyman not being under oath presented themselves by Certificate under the hand of the Constable of Northampton to be sworne. But then some of the said Town of Northampton objecting agt their three men as being not legally appoynted to the work they came for, in yt they were not allowed by any Superior Power as the Law provides; & in that they were non freemen as to this Comonwealth, and for other Causes, Therefore after the busyness was Longe debated the result was that ye could be noe Corte Legally kept here without further order from Superior Powers ; & soe the Assembly brake up.

"The diffrence above menconed between Benjamin Cooley p^l & John Webb deft being by them referred to be decided by Springfield Comissioners, it was by them concluded thus that beside the debt of 8£ due by bill to Benjamin Cooley, John Web should allow for forbearance of ye debt to this tyme wth some charges & damage accruing the Summe of thirty shillings."

A General Unpleasantness.

Here is abundant evidence that a "breach or rent" of formidable dimensions existed.

Evidently the two parties were at sword's points, and opposed each other on any question that might be in agitation. The trouble, whatever its source, must have been of several years standing, and probably originated in the developments of the slander trial, described in Chapter IV. To this lack of unanimity may be attributed the precaution of obtaining the signatures appended to the vote of March, 165$\frac{4}{5}$. The opposition to Elmer relative to the commissionership, had without doubt, its beginning in the misunderstanding about the religious meetings, and the disagreement about selectmen was but the legitimate outgrowth of the same quarrel. On the 10th of January, 165$\frac{8}{9}$, Thomas Root, Richard Lyman and Joseph Parsons, were chosen selectmen, and on the 11th of March, William Holton, Arthur Williams and Richard Lyman, were elected commissioners. If any other persons were chosen selectmen, or even voted for, at the first named meeting, no intimation of it can be found upon the records. The plaintiffs claimed that they were voted into office and then turned out, but nothing to substantiate their claim has been discovered. Naturally they sought to test the legality of these proceedings, and applied to the county court for redress.

The Plaintiffs Checkmated.

When Elmer, Wright, Edwards and Stebbins brought their action against the town, they were checkmated by the rejection of the Northampton commissioners on purely technical grounds, so that no court could be held. Under these circumstances, an appeal to the "Superior Powers" was the only way out of the difficulty; but it does not appear that the plaintiffs made any attempt to carry their case to a higher court.

Possibly the then existing method of electing town officers may have precipitated this contest upon the court.
The ballot was not then, so far as can be ascertained, in
general use, and an election decided by ayes and nays, or a
show of hands, in promiscuous and ill-governed meetings
(such as the records show to have prevailed), unless very
emphatic, was always open to contest. And through the
disorders common in such meetings, especially when any
exciting topic was uppermost, these men may have deemed
themselves elected, when to the cooler heads of the presiding officers, the contrary may have been equally clear.

The Legislature
Settles the Con-
troversy.

Prompt action was taken by the defendants
and the whole matter was speedily brought
before the General Court. William Holton
appeared at the May session with a petition or petitions,
though no record of his appointment as messenger, or any
order authorizing the presentation of such documents, is
on file. He was not a deputy, for the town was not represented that year. Probably the papers were hurriedly prepared and signed, and the petitioners delegated Holton to
introduce them. This memorial has not been preserved,
but its purport can readily be surmised from the foregoing
records of the county court and from the action of the
Legislature. Not only were town officers confirmed, but
sensible advice was given relative to the cause of dissension
in the community. The decision of the court concerning
selectmen, commissioners and constable, is as follows;
what was suggested about another cause of disagreement,
will be quoted hereafter : —

"In ans^r to the peticon of the inhabitants of Northampton, this
Court doth order, that Willjam Holton, Arthur Willjams & Richard
Lyman to end small causes there for a yeare, and that Joseph Parsons
& Thomas Roote, joyned wth them, be theire select men, and that
James Bridgman be connstable."

Holton Sworn in
by the Court.

These were the men who were recorded as
having been chosen to fill those offices in
January and March, the commissioners be-
ing the same who were rejected by the court; and at the
same time James Bridgman had been elected constable. To
prevent further quarreling, and at the same time to give due
effect to its mandate, the General Court further ordered : —

"That William Holton, who is chosen & allowed off as a comissioner at North Hampton, shall haue his oath giuen him by some of the mgists before the Court breake vp, & also be impowred to giue oath to the other two comissioners & connstable, to prevent any further trouble about it. Yᵉ sᵈ Wᵐ Holton tooke his oath accordingly before yᵉ Court."

No Similar Case on Record. The Pltffs. may not have been the Aggrieved Parties

On no other occasion were selectmen for Northampton ever appointed by the General Court. This decision settled the contention concerning town officers for that year, and established the number that should constitute the board of selectmen. Heretofore but three townsmen had been chosen annually; from this time till 1875, with the exception of an interval of seven years, five were elected. The persons appointed by the Legislature, it will be noted, were not those who applied for redress at the Springfield court. Four names are given as bringing the suit, but the town records name only three men as having been elected in January. Whether they were the aggrieved parties, or only brought the suit in behalf of others, is not made clear. Estopped by the decision of the Legislature, the case had no further standing in court.

Sale of Capawonke to the Hartford people. A Profitable Transaction.

The assured success of the new plantation soon began to attract attention. A controversy had arisen in the church at Hartford, and the question of removal to the plantation on the other side of the Connecticut River, was under discussion. A proposition was made by the Hartford people, who were about to settle in "Hadleigh," to purchase Capawonke, which had been bought of the Indians by Northampton, the year previous for thirty-six shillings. It is probable that Umpanchela had obtained an inkling of the negotiations in progress for the disposition of this property, and accordingly deemed this a good opportunity to press his claim for increased compensation.

In answer to the above proposal the town voted, October 17, 1658,

"that the maior part of the Towne haue giuen away Capawonk ther whol right and Title vpon these conditions as followeth: 1: That they shall come and settle two plantations one of the East side of the

greate River and the other of the west. 2: that they shall maintaine
a sufficient fence against hoggs and cattle. 3: that they shall pay Tenn
pounds in wheate and pease at Hartford the next spring ensueing the
date heare of. 4: That they begin the next May to inhabitt vpon it,
and that they shall not desert it for 7 yeres themselues and there families."

This bargain did not prove satisfactory, and its conditions were not complied with. On the second of March
ensuing, the town voted to grant it to them for £10

"in Case the Meddow that is on the west side of the great River
which is Weekwacon's Squaws Meddowe can not bee purchased vpon
Reasonable Termes, or the Meddow which lyeth above Lampanchus
meddow on the west side of the Great River if that cannot bee purchased vpon Reasonable Tearmes then wee the inhabitants of Northampton doe giue to Hartford Company, the above said Lampanchus
Meddow provided that the said Hartford company doe fence it substantially against hoggs [   ] and paying 10 poundes to the Towne."
But if both meadows could be bought then two plantations, one on each
side of the river were to be commenced, but if one of the meadows
was bought and the two plantations not begun, then the contract was
to be void.

By the above extract it appears that another meadow besides that of Lampanchus or Umpanchela, was to be added
before the bargain was concluded, but no entry was made
of any such purchase. Nine days after this vote a special
committee, composed of "Joseph Parsons, Mr Fitch and
John Webb" was appointed to "treat and agree with the
Hartford men y^t are to sitt downe by vs about the meadow
that wee commonly call Lampanchus caled by the Indians
Capawonke." They sold the meadow to the Hartford men,
or Hadley settlers, for "£30 sterling in wheat and peas to
be delivered at Hartford at the current price before June 1,
1659."

If this meadow comprised only the land bought of Umpanchela, and no further evidence appears that more was
purchased, then the sale proved a pretty good speculation.
This property had been obtained of the Indians the year
previous, for a few shillings more than the town now received for it in pounds, though compelled afterwards to pay
a little more. Had either or both of the above named
meadows been bought at prices similar to that paid for
Capawonke, the trade was still a most excellent one for
Northampton. In 1660, it was voted that the new town men

should have all the land commonly called Panchus on this condition, appointing a committee "to deliver this message to Newtone:" "they were to free vs from all Damage that our cattle should at any time doe them in the aforesaid land, and Alsoe that the land should be all common charges equall with o^r other land." Some trouble occurred about the boundary of Capawonke and several allusions to the "controversy" appear upon the records.

Aside from its speculative aspect, this proved a very profitable transaction. The land was several miles from the settled portion of the plantation, and for many years could not have been used to advantage. Its sale brought money or its equivalent, into the town treasury, when it was sorely needed, and secured the establishment of a new settlement in close proximity to Northampton, as well as another on the opposite side of the river. Good use was made of whatever was paid for Capawonke, whether cash or produce, as will be seen in the succeeding chapters, and the whole town was greatly the gainer by the bargain.

Measurers of Land three times chosen   The office of measurer of land seems to have been quite unpopular and difficult to fill. Two men, chosen in 1659, resigned or refused to serve. During that year the choice of measurers is three times recorded, each time with a new name. In January, Samuel Wright Jr. and David Burt were elected; in February, David Burt and Thomas Mason were chosen; and in June, David Burt and John Stebbins. For the first time a sealer of weights and measures was elected, in the person of James Bridgman, who had been appointed constable by the Court, and at the same time William Miller was chosen deputy constable.

Discouraging Position of Affairs and Petition for Relief.   In the fall of 1659, between forty and fifty planters were resident here. Many of them had large families, and the demands for bare subsistence were great and increasing. A few among them were mechanics, yet all depended upon the produce of the land for their means of existence. Little help could be obtained from abroad. The nearest settlement was distant many miles, the way to it was long and difficult, and transportation laborious and uncertain. The mill was in process of construction, but not nearly completed. In addition to this catalogue of hardship, a disastrous storm had deprived them of the principal part of the previous year's crop. Yet amid all these discouragements the little community cheerfully added to its burdens by the settlement of a minister and provided liberally for his maintenance. Feeling sensibly the weak and impoverished condition of the people, the selectmen, in October, petitioned the General Court for relief. This document, setting forth the deplorable condition of affairs, still preserved in the archives of the state, is presented in full : —

"The humble Petition of the Inhabitants of Northampton.

Wheras It hath pleased God in his pᵣvidence to bring youᵣ humble Petitioners to a Plantation that is remote from other Plantations, wher unto wee are Constrained to fetch in supplies, and Finding the burden exceeding heavy did set vpon the makeing of a mill, wᶜʰ hath bin very long a doeing, and exceeding chargeable to effect, to answere our endes, but is not yet pᵣfected, the Charges of the mill being soe heavy, that wee are much weakened in our estates by it, furthermore It pleased God in his pᵣvidence vpon the edg of harvest was 12 month to afflict vs by a dreadfull storme soe that wee were bereaved of the greatest pᵗ of our Cropp wᶜʰ was a greate disappointement to vs, and further wee are necessitated to be at severall other publicke charges for the setling of the Ordinances amongst vs, yoᵣ humble petitioners considᵣing yoᵣ Clemency and Tendᵣnesse have pᵣsented oᵣ Condition to the serious Considᵣation of the honor'd Court humbly Disᵣeing you to forgiue for some yeares ouᵣ rates and wee shall acknowledg oᵣselves Deerly Ingaged to you praying God to pᵣpᵣ all yoᵣ Consultations and Admynistrations.

WILLIAM HOLTON
JOSEPH PARSONS
ARTHUR WILLYAMS
RICHARD LIMAN
THOMAS ROOT.

Northampton 17ᵗʰ
    of the 8. mo: (59) by vs inthe }
        behalfe of the Town }

"The deputyes thinke meete to Allow the petitioᵣˢ their Country rate for two yeares vizᵗ of 1659 & of 1660 Desireing the Consent of oᵣ Honorᵈ magists hereto   WILLIAM TORREY Cleric
    "The magists Consent not   EDW RAWSON Sect."

The Petition Disapproved by the Inhabitants.   It is noticeable that while the names of the five selectmen are appended to the above petition, no record can be found of any vote instructing them to present such a document. The presumption is that they did so on their own responsibility. That their action in this matter did not meet the approval of a majority of the voters may also be inferred. When the next election for town officers occurred, an entirely new board of townsmen was chosen, with the exception of Richard Lyman. It may be well also, to remember that these were the selectmen appointed by the General Court, and possibly the desire to be avenged upon them for the manner in which they obtained the office, may have had an influence in preventing their re-election. At the annual meeting in the year 1662, the selectmen were "prohibited the giueing out of landes and the presenting any matters to the Generall Courte." No other petitions from Northampton are noticed in the Massachusetts archives from the close of 1659 to 1662. From this recital of facts there is reason to believe that the people as a whole did not sanction the petition for relief from taxation.

CHAPTER VI.

SETTLING THE MINISTER.

Rev. Eleazar Mather Invited to Settle. The Legislature Approves of the choice.

THE people, though few in numbers and poor in worldly goods, entered upon the work of establishing and sustaining the gospel ministry with zeal and ardor. The General Court, when first appealed to, "ordered, that theire condition in relation to a minister be forthwith comended to the reuerend elders, and theire help desired therein." Action seems to have been taken at once. Whether by Mr. Willard, whose services were solicited by the town, by the agent, Holton, by the reverend elders, or by them all together, is not known. At all events an invitation was extended to Rev. Eleazar Mather to settle at Northampton. Apparently aware of this fact, and approving the choice, the court at the same session at which the vote previously quoted was passed, gave still more emphatic expression to its opinion :—

"This Court being solicjted by one of the inhabitants of Northhampton in the name of the rest, to comend theire condition, wanting an able minister of the gospell to administer the things of God vnto them, to the reuerend elders, wch this court take themselves bound to further what ljeth in theire power, and vnderstanding that some of the sjd inhabitants haue an eye vnto Mr Eliazer Mather as a fitt man to administer the things of God vnto them, this Court judgeth it meete to declare y^t, in case God so encljnes the harts of those who are concerned therein y^t Mr Mather goe vnto North Hampton to minister vnto the inhabitants there in the things of God, they both approove thereof, & shall be ready at all times to encourage him in that service as there shall be occasion, in whatsouer may rationally & meetly be expected."

Mr. Mather desired to Preach on Probation.

In response to this recommendation, the town, a month later, on the 7th of June, gave Mr. Mather a call. "It was agreed by a vnanimous consent to desire Mr. Mather to bee a mynister

to them in a way of Tryall in dispensing his gifts." If this
vote was intended simply as an invitation to preach as a
"candidate," the result was favorable, for at a meeting held
in October, the town voted to "pay Mr. Mather 25¹ for halfe
a yeare, to bee trewly paid in Good and Merchantable pay
in wheate in this place," and the selectmen were instructed,
in January, to receive the amount which was "to be levied
on every inhabitant according to his due proportion."

He Accepts the   The new minister, young and unmarried,
Call.   had not at that time been ordained, but he
                  accepted the invitation, and came to the
little settlement with every expectation of making it a permanent residence. No church had yet been formed, and
his "way of Tryall" was protracted three years before
such an organization was established. That everything
was mutually satisfactory, subsequent action by the town
abundantly proves.

A House for the   In the following December the town ordered
Minister ordered, "that a Rate of a hundred poundes shalbe
and Built.   levied for the building of a howse for the
mynistry the said howse to bee finished for one hundred
poundes." Nothing seems to have been done about it that
year, and in June, 1659, the "fiue Townesmen" were ordered
to "lett out the mynestrs howse to build to see it bee donn
and Allsoe to see the 100¹ rate levied for the paying of the
worke men wᶜʰ the build the said howse, according to the
former agreement."

The house for the minister was erected at once, and was
probably ready for him at the time of his marriage in September of that year. In January, 1660, Mr. Mather was
given 40 acres of meadow land, and a

"home lott of 4: Acres and the howse that is built vpon the home
lott nere John Lymans to bee his owne property both the howse and
land except hee shall remove himselfe and family from this Towne to
some other place beefore hee hath bin heare fowre yeres from the time
of his first aboade in the Towne but if hee dy before the time bee expired (he continueing in this place) the said howse and land to remaine
to him and to his heirs forever. Allsoe it is to bee vnderstoode that if
he remooue after hee hath bin at some Charge about the howse or land
beefore the fowre yeares bee expired hee is to bee paid for it by the
Towne."

Location and De-
scription of the
Property.

Mr. Mather's homestead was situated at the corner of Main and Pleasant Streets, and embraced all the land now occupied by "Shop Row" as far west as the store of Merritt Clark. The house was two stories in height, without the usual projecting upper story, and stood facing Pleasant Street. It contained two front rooms and a kitchen on the first floor, a porch in front and a "leanto" at the rear. The cellar was small, extending partly under one of the front rooms. In the second story there were chambers above the two lower rooms, and another over the front porch. The property was sold in 1689, by Mr. Mather's heirs to John and Moses Lyman. In 1785, Seth Lyman sold part of the estate to Judge Samuel Hinckley. He lived a long time in the old house, and about 1794, built the mansion on Pleasant Street owned and occupied many years by the late Maj. Harvey Kirkland.

Capawonke Pur-
chase Money
Disbursed.

The "Hartford Company," which bought Capáwonke, paid promptly for it and in April the town appropriated the £30 purchase money, paid or to be paid by them. Twenty-five pounds were to be used for Mr. Mather's first half year's salary, instead of being raised by rate as had been previously voted. The other five pounds were "to be paid 56ˢ to William Holton paying pᵗ of Mr. Mather's Dyet and the other 44ˢ to Brunson of farmeington for worke donn about the mill." Joseph Parsons was designated to receive and disburse the whole sum. The agents of the Hartford company were "William Westhood of Hartford and Samuel Smith of Wethersfeild."

Other Gifts to the
Minister.

One of the first votes in 1659, was that of January 4ᵗʰ, when eighty acres of meadow land were "laid out for the mynistry." The income of this land was to be given to the pastor, or he was to have the use of it in addition to all other grants. During the following year a lot of forty acres of meadow land was set apart for Mr. Mather: seventeen and one-half acres in Middle Meadow, and the rest in land already sequestered. A parcel of forty acres for a standing lot for the ministry was also ordered to be measured, when the first named eighty acres were set apart, and Mr. Mather was to have his choice of either lot. The records show that he probably accepted the first of the two propositions, as he had ten acres in Middle Meadow, twenty-one acres in Manhan, and ten acres near Middle Meadow Gate.

Meadow Land Placed at his Disposal by Voluntary Subscription.   When Mr. Mather accepted the call an agreement was made with him, by which a certain quantity of land was to be placed at his disposal, to be given by him to such persons as came here to settle through his influence. Instead of voting land to them from unappropriated territory, the inhabitants each agreed to contribute a proportionate number of acres for this purpose. Nothing remains to show why it was necessary to resort to such a method as an inducement to settlers. It was a new departure, and one that was never repeated. Was it because of the existing quarrel, that a voluntary contribution was considered at that time the most available plan, or when it was found necessary to offer land to certain men in order to induce them to emigrate, was that considered the only legal means by which it could be obtained for such a purpose? It could not have been because of a scarcity of meadow land, for grants of it were made to others in that and succeeding years. Whatever may have been the reason, the result was most satisfactory. The annexed document not only shows who gave the land, and how much each person contributed, but it also furnishes a nearly complete census of the settlers at the opening of the year 1659. Only two or three men refused or neglected to donate land, and some of them were afterwards called to account for their remissness : —

"A coppy of the writeing y^t is in Mr Mather's hand aboute the pticuler mens land y^t were giuen him to dispose of for the common good of the towne of Northampton, January 6, '58:

"This p^t witnessts y^t wee whose names are heare subscribed doe pmise and engage to part with such some of lands the which our names are annexed vpon consideration of Mr Mather now resident amongst vs shall haue the disposing of the said lands to such inhabitants as the said Mr Mather shall judg behouffull and needfull for the well beeing of the Towne of Northampton to bee ordered according to the same

rule by wch wee devided the land o^rselves haue or shall haue in possession that is to say 20 Akers to 100^l & 15 akers to a pson as all the lands
that wee abate or part with shall be laid together at the vpp end of the
meddow wee commonly call Munhan

	Acres.		Acres.		Acres.
William Holton	10		87		127
Joseph ffitch his		John Brought^n lot in		William Hanum	3
whole proportion	10	M u n h a n 3 acres		John Hanum	1
Joseph Parsons	8	more or less	3	Tho: Bascum	4
Richard Lyman	9	Sam: Wright Jun	3	Henry Curtis	5
John Lyman	5	David Burt of his		James Bridgman	4
Tho: Roote	5	Venturers lot	3	Robert Lyman	3
Thomas Mason }	10	Joh: Stebbens	2	John Bliss	2
Sam: Allen }		Salmon	2	George Alexander	
William Hulburd	5	Rob: Haward	3	his lot in Y o u n g	
William Jeanes	4	Tho: Woodford	6	Rainbow contain-	
Alexander Edwards	5	John Ingersoll	3	ing 3 acres and a	
Rob: Bartlett	5	Will: Miller his Ven-		half more or less	3½
Nath: Phelps	3	turers Feild lot	6	Christopher Smith	3
Arthur Williams	5	Isaac Sheldon	6	Georg Langton	4
John King	3	Walter Lee	3	Sam: Wright Sr	4
	87		127		163½"

Edward Elmore
called to Account
for Land and
Money. The names of all the inhabitants in the
town who had received home lots, except
Edward Elmore, John Webb and Joseph
Root, appear in the above list. Elmore
owned eighteen acres in Manhan meadow, at the place
where the town decided to lay out the contributed land, and
he agreed to exchange it for an equivalent elsewhere. It
appears, however, that he did not carry out this arrangement, but sold the land the next year. William Clarke
was appointed in June, 1660, by the town "as ther agent
to demand of Edward Elmore a certain quantity of land
wch hee promisd to giue when the Rest of the Inhabitantes
gaue for a Common and publique good and if hee refuse to
giue then to prosecute the said Edward Elmore in what
way the said William Clarke see most meete." The same
agent was also authorized to treat other delinquents in this
respect in a similar manner. At the same meeting William
Holton and John Webb were appointed to act with William
Clarke "to call Edward Elmore to Accoumpt for money
that hee receiued of the purchasers," and if he did not
"giue a satisfying accoumpt of the same" to prosecute him.
The money claimed by the town of Elmer was undoubtedly

the amount he received from the sale of the land he had agreed to exchange. In the latter part of the same year, Isaac Sheldon, who promised to give six acres to Mr. Mather, agreed to "Resigne and Deliver upp foure acres of his land in hoggs bladder" in place of "his former gift," and he was to be paid for fencing and plowing it as much as two "Indifferent men shall Judge meete."

Mr. Mather "Bequeathes" the Land. From this table it is apparent that the aggregate of all the land contributed was 163½ acres. Possibly more was afterwards added by some who did not sign the agreement. One hundred and forty acres of it were located at the upper end of Manhan meadow and placed at the disposal of Mr. Mather. Fortunately the records indicate to whom he distributed this land. It is there stated that Mr. Mather "bequeathed with the consent and approbation of the town," * * * "a third part of seven score acres" in Manhan to John Strong Sr., David Wilton, and Aaron Cook. Each of these persons received "forty-six and a half acres, twenty-six rods and eleven foot more or less." In addition, the town granted them each a home lot of four acres. These lots were situated on Main and West Streets, commencing at the Baptist Church and extending to the homestead of S. L. Parsons. Elder Strong was opposite the latter on the west side of the street. These men arrived apparently about the same time during the year 1659. The deeds of Wilton and Strong were recorded in the fall of 1660, and that of Cook in April of the year following. Mr. Mather was the son of the first minister of Dorchester, was born in that place, where he had lived till the time of accepting the call here, and was so well and favorably known there, that it was believed his influence would be of great service in inducing emigrants to remove to Northampton; and so it proved, for a number of others from that place were received within a year.

The "Dorchester Men" receive their Land. There can be no reasonable doubt that these three persons became residents of Northampton because of the influence of the new pastor, and it is highly probable that they were not the only men attracted hither by the same consideration, for about this time several substantial citizens from Dorchester followed their example. On the first of June, the selectmen were empowered "to giue forth to Dorchester men the land that they mee bee inhabytantes in this Towne, vizt : William Clarke Henry Woodward and Henry Cunleife." The name of William Clarke is appended to the original petition, indicating that at that time he intended to come with the rest, still it may have been through the personal solicitation of Mr. Mather that he reached a final decision. About one hundred acres in Manhan meadow were granted to these men in 1659, in addition to their home lots. Their meadow land was located very near that "bequeathed" by Mr. Mather.

Mr. Mather's Advent Beneficial.

If these six men emigrated to Northampton at the suggestion of Mr. Mather, then he accomplished more for the permanent good of the town by his first coming than by the eleven years of arduous ministerial labor, which followed. The new town, now in its sixth year, had been fairly prosperous. Inhabitants had arrived as rapidly as could have been anticipated, crops had been reasonably abundant, and the Indians everywhere evinced a friendly disposition. But the situation was not altogether satisfactory. While the petition to the Legislature shows that the community was poor and distressed, subsequent events prove that the people were hopeful and courageous. They mildly repudiated the action of the selectmen, in petitioning the General Court, and willingly laid themselves under more onerous burdens. It was undoubtedly this impoverished condition of affairs that led the people to offer a bounty, by means of a subscription in land, to induce emigration.

Such was the state of affairs when Mr. Mather and the new settlers arrived. William Clarke and John Strong, Aaron Cook, David Wilton, Henry Cunliffe and Henry Woodward, brought new life and energy to the enfeebled town. Their coming was like the infusion of new blood into the veins of an exhausted patient. From the day of their arrival, these men took a leading part in the management of town affairs. Their energy, independence and public spirit soon wrought a marked improvement. All of

them were at once put into the harness, and from this date
the advance of the settlement was steady and vigorous.
Other settlers arrived during the year, most of them from
Dorchester.

A Perpetual Stand-   Not fully satisfied with the grants of land
ing Lot for the   already made for the benefit of the minis-
Mir stry.   try, still another tract of meadow was set
apart for that purpose. The proposition came up at the
March meeting, 1660, when a committee was ordered to lay
out a "home lot for the mynistry," "in some convenient
place that they can finde except the meeting house hill."
This order was, however, in the succeeding month, embodied in the following comprehensive vote :—

"April 16th, 1660. It was voted and agreed at a Towne meeting that
Joseph Parsons, Robert Bartlet and William Jeanes were chosen by
the Towne and impowred to measure out Twente nine Acres of land in
the middle Meddowe and twelue Acres of land more at the end of the
second Square lying at the Rere of the Ventorers fieild and this 41
Acres aforesaid sequestred for a prpetuall standing lott for the mynistry
and never to bee Alterd but to Contynew successiuely to that function
for the encouragement of the mynistry in the Towne of Northampton.
Considering the Absolute necessity of the Promoteing God's honor and
the Good of Posteryty. It is further voted and agreed that William
Jeanes Robert Bartlet and Joseph Parsons are to take care to see that
the aforesaid 41 Acres of land bee Recorded according to the trew
entent of the grante above said."

This forty-one acres of meadow land was accordingly
measured at the places specified, and duly recorded. It
was in reality the property of the town while the town was
the Parish, but in 1825, when the Second Congregational
(Unitarian) Society was formed, it passed into possession
of the First Parish. The yearly income of this land, which
still remains as it was originally laid out, is now devoted
to the payment of Parish expenses.

Pastor's Salary.   Mr. Mather's salary was fixed at £80, and
                   the year was to commence in April. For
the half year, up to that date, he was to receive £25. Here
is another most encouraging indication of returning prosperity. A community that voluntarily increased the pastor's salary from fifty to eighty pounds, had little need to
petition for a remission of its state taxes.

6

Another C o n t r o-
versy Dealt with
b y t h e General
Court.

Scarcely had the minister been settled when the community was again agitated by a conflict of opinion. Two years before the church was organized, the town was divided by an antagonism of sentiment, not upon doctrinal points, but apparently upon a merely technical matter. This discussion pervaded the entire settlement, and was undoubtedly an outbreak of the previous unpleasantness. That was apparently a question about holding meetings. This seems to have had reference to the method of conducting them. Very little light can be thrown upon the cause of this disagreement. When the law point concerning the choice of selectmen was referred to the authorities, this element of discord seems to have been coupled with it, and when the General Court appointed town officers it also administered a little good advice to the quarrelsome citizens. The order of the court in answer to that petition is the only testimony bearing directly upon the origin of the trouble. The document itself has disappeared, the town never took any action upon it that was recorded, and nothing further has been ascertained concerning the difficulty. At its May session in 1659, the court voted : —

"And in relation to theire carrying on the duty of the Saboath in Mr Mather's absenc, wherein the doe so much disagree, that though in some cases private men may excercise theire guifts, where there are such as are knoune, able, approoved, & Orthodoxe, yet for present, as things as are circumstanced wth them, the Court judgeth it theire best, safest, & most peaceable way, in the absence of theire minister, to assemble all at one place, & to spend the Saboath together, besides praying & singing, in reading and repeating of knoune godly, Orthodoxe bookes & sermons."

The advice given by the court was excellent, and all disagreement upon that matter seems to have been speedily adjusted by the organization of the church.

Position and Descrip-
tion of the F i r s t
Meeting House.

Religious services were first conducted in the small building, eighteen by twenty-six feet in size, erected soon after the people began to arrive. It was placed at the intersection of what are now Main and King streets, and stood probably in the vicinity of the hydrant, at the southeast corner of the present Court House lawn, though probably some feet farther

into the highway.   Main Street had then no existence and
the ascent of Meeting House Hill was quite abrupt.   For
many years the roadway was where Court Street now ex-
tends.   This meeting house was built of "sawen timber,"
had one door-way, two windows, one or more chimneys,
and very probably was destitute of a pulpit, or any other
internal feature peculiar to ordinary houses of worship,
though it may be inferred that a raised platform extended
on the side opposite the door.   The building faced south-
wardly, had a pitched roof, which is believed to have been
covered with thatch.   In a room used for meetings of all
kinds, it is not probable that any pews were ever placed.
Benches without backs were deemed good enough, and
where no one expected anything better, more luxurious
seats would have been superfluous.   There was no assignment of sittings, the meeting house not having reached the
honor of being "dignified."

In this little building Mr. Mather dispensed his gifts during his three years of probation.   The congregation could not
have been large, but there is no reason to imagine that the
sermons were curtailed to correspond with the paucity of
hearers.   All this preceded the formation of the church,
but when that association was perfected, a new edifice was
found to be essential, and the old house was abandoned to
other uses.   This was the second meeting house built in
Massachusetts west of Lancaster, the first having been
erected in Springfield about nine years before.   It was at
best a low and insignificant structure, one story in height,
the assembly room being but nine feet in the clear.

CHAPTER VII.

NON-RESIDENTS—FREEMEN—HIGHWAYS.

Thomas Burnham's Claim Satisfied. On a committee chosen in 1653, to "receive" inhabitants, appears the name of Thomas Burnham. He never became a resident, but claimed lands, and appointed John Webb his attorney. Five years afterwards the town voted thirty acres to Burnham, on condition that Webb, his "atturny shall acquit and discharge the Towne of Northampton of all future claimes and demandes concerneing his right of any land of the said Towne." Included in this grant was a home lot of three acres. The selectmen and Edward Elmore were ordered to "pfect the businesse with John Webb concerneing Tho: Burnums Land," and the next month Webb pledged himself "to bring in noe inhabitant either to possesse the home lott or the meddowes without the consent of this Towne." The people intended to prevent either Webb or Burnham from speculating with this land, by selling it to irresponsible persons or non-residents.

The Town votes to "Quiet Possession." Some question seems to have arisen concerning the division of meadow land, no doubt brought into prominence by the action of Burnham. The matter came before the town, and a vote was passed January 5th, to "quiet possession," according to the marginal endorsement on the record, which provided that

"Each man shall enjoy his first proportion of land in the meddowes and Swamps Devidable without any futher molestation, as alsoe the 6 Acres apeece or 3 Acres apeece giuen to severall men it is agreed for the ending of Contention about that all those men shall peaceablely enjoy the one halfe of yᵗ land."

84

This action was followed by another vote in the succeeding month of November, in which it was ordered that all persons who had not received their full proportion of land were to apply to the townsmen, who were to make good all such deficiencies. In a few months another vote to the same effect was passed, and the right of each man to his real estate thereby established.

Non-resident Petitioners not entitled to Allotments. The transaction with Burnham gave rise to still further action by the town. Several of the parties who petitioned for the new plantation declined or for some reason failed to settle here. In order to protect itself from similar claims by non-residents, the town voted in February : —

"ffor as much as ther haue bin sundry psons who did Petition to the Generall Court at the bay for a grant of this Towne Caled the Towne of Northampton, and some others that haue paid part of the purchase towardes the obtaineing of the aforesaid place, yet never to this time though the place haue bin inhabited this fowre yeres and upward, haue bin resident as inhabitantes whereby they haue bin justly deprived themselves of any clayme or propriety of any land heare. It is firmely ordered inacted and agreed by the Towne of Northampton that any such pson or prsons whatsoever upon the accoumpt and consideration of beeing a Petitioner for this land, or of beeing at any Cost charge or Trouble more or lesse towardes the purchase thereof, are, and forever shalbe disowned as for ever haueing any Interest right or Title vnto any land or Alottmentes in this Towne of Northampton."

This declaration settled effectually the claims of non-residents, and no more trouble occurred from that quarter.

Freemen only Eligible to Official Honors. Town meetings were then the most potent element in municipal government. By them all business, however trivial, relating to town affairs, was transacted, and its edicts were final. In those days not every one could act in town meeting. Freemen only, those who had taken the oath of fidelity to the general government, were permitted to hold office or vote. At first, church membership was an essential requisite, and none but full communicants could become freemen. Afterwards, non-church members were allowed to take the oath, and still later a property qualification was required before any one could obtain the right of suffrage. Town offices were shunned, and many persons declined to qualify themselves as freemen in order to escape official burden. Subsequently a law was passed by which all who were chosen to office, should serve or pay a fine of 20s.

No allusion to this qualification is to be found on the town records. It is probable—apparent by the rejection of the three commissioners from Northampton, as officers of the court in Springfield, because they were not freemen— that little attention was paid by the voters to this matter during the first years of the town's existence. Some of the men prominent in its affairs, holding offices, both civil and judicial, did not take the freeman's oath till 1662. Especially was this the case in relation to the commissioners for ending small causes designated by the General Court, when selectmen were appointed. William Holton, Arthur Williams and John Lyman, were with others, admitted as freemen at a court held at Northampton, in March of that year. And yet the General Court appointed them to a judicial position, in spite of this fact, which was made known at the Springfield court.

Fines for Non-attendance at Town Meetings. The necessity of holding frequent town meetings made attendance upon them burdensome, and people began to absent themselves. Meetings were held nearly every month in the year, and frequently several times in the same month. At last this neglect became so general that it was deemed advisable to institute measures for its correction. Accordingly a system of fines was adopted. Thus

"Whosoever hee bee that absentes himselfe from any Towne meeteing beeing warned[1] by the Townesmen or any other being the warner with order from the Townesmen, shall pay 12^d to the Towne for every such neglect or whosoever doth depart before the meeting bee concluded without leaue from the moderator shall pay 12^d for every such neglect. But for those meeteings yerely when the Towne are to Chuse Select men or other Towne officers beeing legally warned yet to neglect comeing for every such defect to pay 2^s 6^d vnlesse the delinquent can giue some Just Cawse for the same and the Towne soe judg of it, and if ther bee 13 Inhabitants shall make a beginning and what they doe shalbee Au-

---

1 Town meetings were warned by the beating of a drum, or the blowing of a horn or trumpet on the evening before the meeting, or by special notification, as stated above. They were generally convened at 9 o'clock in the morning, occasionally after a weekly lecture, or "on a trayning day," and one is recorded as having been held "sun an hour high, at night."

thentick and others not ther shall loose ther votes. And allsoe be fined 1ᵈ if they bee not at the beginning of the meeteing when it is orderly begun."

This order remained unchanged for twenty years, when the number constituting a quorum was increased to thirty, and absentees were fined 12d. each.

First Sale of Home Lots.   Among the arrivals in 1659, were George Sumner, Enos Kingsley and Ralph Hutchinson. The first two named came from Dorchester, and the last from Boston. To each of these men was granted for a home lot eight acres of upland, lying on the " westerly side of yᵉ Mill River." But by a special vote they were each required to pay twenty shillings to the "Townesmen at demand thereof," and were also to build upon the lots and hold them four years, before obtaining a title. At a subsequent meeting the amount to be paid for them was reduced to ten shillings, and the condition of four year's possession repealed. This was the first instance in which the town demanded payment for land granted to settlers. These were among the first home lots taken up on South Street. They were double the size of ordinary home lots, situated at some distance from the settled portion of the town, and by reason of the intervening river much more difficult of access. With these drawbacks it is not easy to understand why parties would be willing to pay for land when everybody else had obtained it for nothing. It is possible that the size of the lots may have been the reason why a price was put upon them.

William Smead, who came from Dorchester, had a grant, the next year, of eight acres of land for a home lot, on condition that he should pay ten shillings for it, as had the three men the year previous. His lot was laid out on South Street, adjoining that of Ralph Hutchinson. Capt. Cook, Ensign Wilton and John Strong, were granted thirty acres apiece over Manhan River, in a parcel of land lately purchased of the Indians, or the same amount each up Mill River; they were also to have twenty acres apiece of upland upon the plain beyond the mill. Here were 150 acres of land given away almost in the same vote that ordered Smead to pay ten shillings for his home lot.

Population of the   With the opening of the year 1660, the for-
Town in 1660.   tunes of the settlement began to mend. A
twelvemonth of average prosperity, re-
newed hope and strengthened courage. The number of inhabitants had been considerably increased, and among them
were several who afterwards became pillars in the church
and leaders in town affairs. The names of fifty-seven men
are recorded as having received home lots up to this date,
which would indicate a population of between 300 and 400.
Not a bad showing for a town but six years settled, and in
a country with a widely scattered population of but 80,000.[1]

New Route to the   Soon after the purchase of Capawonke by
Bay Proposed.   the Hartford company, Hadley was settled,
and was then called "Newtown," the name
usually applied to all new settlements. Desiring a better
route to the "Bay," the upper towns on the Connecticut
River attempted this year to improve the road in that direction. The annual burnings by the Indians cleared the
forests to a great extent of undergrowth, and there was little to impede locomotion in any direction. Though covered with trees, the country was open at every point of the
compass, and hills, streams and swamps, were the greatest
hindrances to travel. Indian paths, scarcely more than a foot
in width, crossed the territory at intervals, and were made
use of by the English. A passage-way for men and horses
was all that existed. It was for the purpose of improving
one of these pathways that the town voted in July to
"contribute towardes the laying out of a way from New-
towne to Nashway to the vallew of 30^s or 40^s." No results,
however, followed this action, and no passage-way for
carts or sleds to the Bay was made till after the close of the
century. The next year a committee was appointed to
"Treat with the New-towne men about a highway to New-
towne over the River and if they can agree to lay it out if
not to leave it to the County Court."

1 In 1660 the only English colonies on the American continent, after the emigration of half a century, were in Virginia, New England and Maryland, which are supposed to have contained no more than 80,000 inhabitants.—Holmes' American Annals.

Highways.   First among the duties of the settlers must have been that of determining the position of the highways. It was necessary that they should be decided upon before any home lots were granted, but no record of their location, other than as boundaries of such lots, was made. From the manner in which the topographical features of the town seem to have been followed in the matter of highways, it is very probable that a portion of it may have been carefully mapped out, before a single log cabin was built. The first highways upon which the town took action were those in the meadows, some three years after the settlement commenced, and the first allusion to any was to that in Manhan meadow, when in 1657, that section was divided.

In 1655, John Lyman and George Alexander were chosen "way wardens or Surveyors of Ways," but no further reference to these officers appears for five years. In the meantime a committee on highways was appointed which confined its work to roads already in existence. Though these roads were three, six or more rods in width, they were mere passage-ways for carts or paths for horseback riders. Most of them were studded with stumps, and sprinkled with rocks, and the cart ruts, worn deep into the soil, crooked and uneven, were the only indication of a roadway. At first little attention seems to have been paid to them, and after they began to be "worked," they were left flat and without adequate drainage. In some instances parts of them had to be re-located in a few years, on account of the deep gullies washed in them.

"Supervisers for the hywayes" were chosen in 1661, but only the name of James Bridgman can be deciphered. These officers, however, had no authority to lay out or alter highways. How long the term of office of the highway committee continued, is not shown. Probably they were chosen but for one year. Afterwards special committees were sometimes appointed to lay out specified highways, and sometimes the selectmen were charged with that work.

First Highway Com- John Stebbins and Samuel Allen were
mittee. West and chosen to "Joyne with the Selectmen to
Green Streets la'd
out. lay out high waies" in June, and in December this vote was re-affirmed. Their first
work was that of establishing West Street, which is thus
described on the records : —

"The aforesaid men mett the 26th of february to lay out the high
waie goeing from the Town goeing towardes Allexander Edwardes Meddow nere the Mill river: Wee began at Ensigne Wiltons lott and becawse of the hill and wepp Swampish grounde ther was laide in the
high way wee laid a leetle nerer to his lott * * * and soe upp to
* * the west corner of Captaine Cooks lott * * and then ther is
two waies to passe over the mill river, the one to goe over at the upper
end of Allexander Edwardes meddowe this to be six rodds wide, and
this way to goe on the north side of the marked trees downe the hill,
and the other to goe in the Carte way, except at the brow of the hill ther
it is to bee 6 rodd of the north side of the marked tree on the brow
wher it is to bee made, and soe to goe below Allexander Edwardes meddow over the mill river."

Ensign Wilton lived near where the Baptist Church
stands, and the above-named route was very nearly the
same as that of West and Green Streets as they now exist.
The Green Street branch was laid for use during high
water, when the river where the other highway crossed it,
became in consequence impassable. No bridges then existed and all streams were crossed at fording places. This
is the first record of the laying out of any highway in
Northampton, and this was the first committee appointed
for such a purpose. Alexander Edwards owned all the land
on the west side of West Street, south of Green.

Picturesque Irreg- While one of the picturesque beauties of
ularity of the Northampton is the irregularity of its
Streets.
streets, the esthetic taste of our forefathers, who established them, has often been called in
question. The statement that they were laid in paths made
by the cows on their way to pasture, has been many times
reiterated, and may still find believers. To attempt seriously the disproval of a suggestion so absurd, may seem
but little less ridiculous than the proposition itself. Yet it
can readily be shown that Northampton is indebted to na-

ture alone for the irregular beauty of its streets.[1] When West and Green Streets were established, there were already in existence nine other highways, though the names of none of them had then been recorded. These corresponded very nearly to what are now called Main, King, Market, Bridge, Hawley, Pleasant, South, Elm and Prospect Streets. There were other shorter streets or lanes, some of which have been discontinued, while others have become handsome and attractive. On each of the above-named streets settlers had taken up home lots and erected houses. Instead of dropping down here and there a house because a path in that direction happened to exist, the lots were laid off systematically, and the highways conformed closely to the peculiarities of the surface.

A glance at the map will establish this fact. The course of the principal stream, Mill River, had not then been changed. Its two tributaries, Market and King Street brooks, above their junction, near the head of Hawley Street, flowed for some distance nearly parallel. The first lots on King Street were granted on its easterly side, extending from the highway on the west to the brook (Market Street) on the east. Most of them were twelve rods wide, containing two acres, "more or less." West of and in some cases reaching quite to the highway, were the swampy lands formed by the King Street brook, so that nearly all the available land between the two brooks was utilized, the highway, of course following the trend of the brook. Market Street was laid east of and parallel with the brook of that name, just far enough from it to escape the marshy land that showed at intervals along its eastern bank, though a line of home lots was afterwards granted on the west side of this highway. Bridge Street was a continuation of Main, or rather Main Street was an extension of Bridge, for the latter was first established. Its course

1 "Northampton is built on ten streets, proceeding from the center with no very distant resemblance to the claws of a crab ; only somewhat less winding and less regular. It has been said that they were laid out by the cows ; and that wherever these animals when going to feed in the forests made their paths, the inhabitants located their streets. The probability is that the first planters, being both inclined and obliged to build near each other, placed their houses wherever the ground was sufficiently dry to furnish convenient building spots. In spite of this irregularity, the town, with its scenery, is a very interesting object to the eye."— Dwight's Travels, vol. 1, p. 328, pub. 1821.

was a little north of east, till it reached the bluffs bordering the meadows, when it turned sharply northward, following the bluff line to the Great River. South from Bridge Street, still along the edge of the bluff, near the present line of Pomeroy Terrace, was another highway, turning westward till it merged itself in Pleasant Street. Hawley street left Bridge at the easterly border of a swamp formed along Pomeroy brook, as it was afterwards termed, below the junction of King and Market Street brooks, and extended southwards till it reached the way leading from the meadow bluffs to Pleasant street. Pleasant Street was laid between two tiers of lots, one bounded west on Mill River and the other east on Pomeroy brook. South Street passed south from Main Street, down the hill to Mill River, at a point that afforded a good fording place. Crossing the river and the swampy land beyond, it conformed to the irregularity of the table land between the curves of Mill River, allowing space for home lots at each side. Many of the home lots on the west side of the street were bounded west by that river, and those on the opposite side had an easterly boundary on the same stream. Evidently there was "method in the madness" of the men who laid out the highways, the picturesque irregularity of which adds so much to the attractiveness of the town.

Original Names of Some of the Streets. Many years elapsed after the first home lots were taken, before any streets were named. On the original deeds and records the word highway is always used, and when a name was applied it usually had some local significance. Often a street was named from a prominent citizen residing upon it; occasionally from a notable characteristic of some dweller; and again the use made of it governed its designation. Thus, Pleasant Street was first named "Bartlett Street" from Robert Bartlett, one of the first settlers upon it; after the jail was built, as it happened on Bartlett's original homestead, it became "Prison Lane;" and at another time it was called "Comfort Street," possibly after the second and more comfortable stone jail was erected. Hawley Street was first known as "Pudding Lane," on account, as tradition says, of the puddings made by one of its residents and served to the family, whether from quality or quantity is not stated.   Prospect Street once had the dignified title of "Cow Lane," and its sinuous lines, reminding one of the bovines seeking pastures fair, are still an enchanting characteristic.   Possibly from this cognomen came the suggestion that all the streets were cow paths.   Then "Gallows Plain," so named from having been the place where capital punishments were inflicted, was changed to "Pancake Plain," and is styled in modern days "Hospital Hill." King Street is supposed to have received its name from John King, who was one of the first, if not the very first settler upon that highway.   Park Street was formerly called "Lyman's Lane;" Spring Street was known as "Hawley Lane;" and people now living were once familiar with the appellation "New Boston," given to the upper portion of Elm Street.   What is now North Street and vicinity was formerly known as "Earl's Plain."   John Earl bought property there in 1667, and his name was attached to the whole section.

New Meeting House in Agitation.   A vote passed in July, proves that the design of building a new meeting house was already in agitation, though no formal action was taken till the next year.   To Ralph Hutchinson four acres of land were granted, "provided hee leaue the last two Acres granted to him beyound Samuel Allens and allsoe provide 400 Clabbard for the meeting house."   Covering of that kind would hardly be needed for the old meeting house, and it may be safely assumed that the people, foreseeing the need of a new house of worship, made this bargain in advance in order to give Hutchinson ample time to prepare them.   No saw mill existed in this region at that time.   All sawed lumber was made ready at the saw pits. Clapboards[1] were split out like staves and hewn or shaved into proper shape.

1 "Clap-boards were originally cloven and not sawed and were thence called clove boards, and in process of time cloboards, claboards, clapboards."—Coffin's History of Newberry.
" Bricks were laid against the inner partition or wooden wall, and covered with clay.   Boards were placed on the outside, first called clayboards, then corrupted into clapboards."—Weeden's Economic and Social New England, vol. 1, p. 284.

Town Officers.
Clerk of the
Writs.

Town officers, as far as recorded this year were Townsmen: Richard Lyman, John Lyman, Henry Woodward, Henry Cunliffe and William Clarke. Commissioners to end Small Causes: William Clarke, Henry Woodward and Henry Cunliffe. For a number of years after the General Court united the Selectmen and Commissioners, the town followed that practice, but after the year 1671, there is no record of the election of commissioners. At least two of the same men were on both boards. Measurers: John Stebbins, and David Burt. Clerk of the Writs, William Jeanes; this being the first time that such an office was recognized. His duty, set forth in the law of 1641, creating the office, was to grant "summons and attachments in civil actions." The fees as fixed by the court, were 2d. apiece for warrants, 3d. apiece for a replevy or attachment, and 4d. apiece for a bond. Clerks of the Writs were licensed by the county Courts.

Accidental Death
of David Burt.

David Burt, son of David, the marriage of whose parents was the first that occurred in Northampton, was accidentally killed on the 30th of August. His mutilated body was found near the dwelling house, soon after dark. He was about four years of age, had been playing about the cart, and was trodden to death by the cattle or crushed by the clumsy cart wheels.[1]

1 An inquest was held, and the court record of this event is as follows: "Sept. 25, 1660, a jury of twelve men made inquiry concerning the death of David Burt, about   years old, son of David Burt of Northampton. The jury thought the child being busy about the cart that carted his father's corn, he was trodden down by the cart or cattle ; no person knowing it ; it being in the dusk of the evening."

CHAPTER VIII.

GRIST MILL—COUNTY COURT—MILITIA.

First Corn Mill.
Its Location.
FOR some years the settlers, following the example of the Indians, pounded their corn in the primitive native mortars. Some undoubtedly carried their grists to Springfield, but the distance to that town was so great, that the necessity of a mill within their own borders became more and more apparent as the population increased. The first allusion to a mill is that of 1659, both in the petition to the General Court for relief from taxation, and in the recorded payment to Bronson "for worke donn about the mill." It was probably commenced during the previous year, and was some two years in process of construction. It was erected on the north side of Mill River, on the mill lot. Probably the first dam was built in the vicinity of the present one, and the mill stood near it, as it was not then customary to make use of a canal to convey water to the wheel. A new dam[1] was built some years after, higher up the river, but it is not known whether it was for the use of the old mill or for a new one on the other side of the river.

Its Builders and
Final Transfer.
This mill was built partly by the town and partly by individuals, the town providing the site and paying for some of the work. The original owners were William Clarke, Alexander Edwards, Samuel Wright Sr., and Joseph Parsons. Robert Hayward was the first miller, and for several years operated the mill for the builders. In 1661, Hayward bought

---

1 Elder John Strong was granted two acres of land on the south side of Mill River, which was bounded on the "east by the highway near the old dam," and "west by the highway near the new dam." Unfortunately this record is without date, but the grant seems to have been made within a few years of the building of the first mill.

the property.   Previous to this transaction Samuel Wright
Sr. sold his interest to Alexander Edwards, and in June,
Edwards disposed of the half in his possession to Robert
Hayward for the "Some of eight pounds to be paid in
good merchantable wheat at 3^s per bushel, or in cattle,
corn price to bee paid in May next ensuing the date hereof,
and in case the said Robt Hayward doth sell his p^t of the
mill within three years, then the said Alexander Edwards
is to have the first offer of it."   The next year Hayward
bought the other half of the mill property of William
Clarke and Joseph Parsons.   The bills of sale mention it
as the "Mill of Northampton," but the lot is not named in
the transfer to Hayward.   In November of the following
year, 1662, both mill and lot were sold by Hayward to
Praisever Turner of Dorchester, possession to be given in
April.   The price named in the deed to Turner was "four
score and fifteen poundes."   Turner, who was a miller, sold
the "mill lot," in 1666, to David Wilton, whose home lot
adjoined it on the west.   When it was sold to Wilton, no
mention was made of the mill.   It was not successful and
was not in use many years.   There was not fall enough, and
the water set back in time of freshets so as to prevent its
running.   Another mill was built in a different location
about the time that Wilton bought the lot.

The "Mill Trench."   The waste water from this mill was carried
back to the river by means of a long trench
or water way, which crossed no less than four home lots,
and was a source of considerable annoyance to the parties
whose premises it invaded.   It traversed the western end of
the lots of John Webb (afterwards Elder John Strong),
Eleazar Mather, and John and Richard Lyman nearly on
the present line of the railroad, entering Mill River in
the vicinity of the tenement block of Loomis & Dailey.
John Webb, and Richard Lyman's heirs sought reparation
from the town on account of the damage to their property
by the trench.   In 1659, Webb was granted two acres of
land for "Dammage hee suffers in his home lott by Reason
of the Mill and Trench diging Gravell and for the liberty
of the Towne to mend and make upp breaches about the
Mill and Trench to haue egresse and Regresse to doe the

same." The heirs of Richard Lyman received no compensation till 1671. Webb occupied the corner lot at the head of South Street, which extended in after years as far west as the Academy of Music, and the other parties named had the first three homesteads on Pleasant Street.

This was the only mill in town during the first twelve years after its settlement. Its importance to the community is shown by the fact that in 1661, the town voted that "the mill bee free," which meant undoubtedly that the mill should be free from taxation. Three years afterwards the question of building a new mill was under consideration, but half a dozen years elapsed before another one was in operation.

Developments of the Year 1661. Events of lasting benefit to the welfare of the town followed each other in quick succession in 1661. Military and religious organizations were formed, the courts commenced their regular sessions, the town took upon itself the burden of erecting a new meeting house, and altogether the settlement received an impetus that carried it a long way forward.

County Court Established. Previous to this time, but one court had been held in Northampton, and that was convened three years before. In 1659, the General Court appointed the three commissioners in Springfield to hold two courts each year in that town or in Northampton, as they should determine, with all the powers and duties of county courts. At the same time "the commission graunted last year respecting Northampton," was repealed. This was a provision that the commissioners of the two towns should jointly hold one court yearly in each town. Probably the repeal was owing to the quarrel over the election of town officers that effected to some extent the efficiency of the former court. The Springfield commissioners did not recognize the necessity of holding any courts in Northampton for two years. In 1660, John Webster of Hadley, was made a magistrate, and a member of the court, serving till his death in 1661.

Court held in North-
ampton, and its
Business.

The first Court held in Northampton of which any record exists here, convened March 24, 1661. It was probably held at the "ordinary" or tavern, as was the custom before Court Houses were built, or it may have assembled at the meeting house. John Webb had been licensed to keep an ordinary two years before, and as far as is known, was the only innkeeper in town at that time. The proceedings of this court were as follows:—

"March 26, 1661. For holding this Co'te were p'sent M' John Webster, Capt. John Pynchon, M' Samll Chapin. And Elizur Holyoke, Record'.

"And for y' Jury these: David Wilton, William Clark, William Holton, Henry Woodward, John Lyman, John Stebbins, Andrew Warner, William Lewis, John White, Samuell Smith, Thomas Stebbins, Samuell Marshfield." [1]

The business of this court was not voluminous, and may be condensed into a few paragraphs. Capt. Thomas Savadge of Boston, brought an "action of debt," "to the value of Three score & ffoure pounds," against John Webb, in which a verdict for the plaintiff was recorded. John Bliss was non-suited in an action against Webb, "in that he gave not legall warning to the defdt for his appearance at the co'te," and was ordered to "pay 10' for the entry of his action."

Henry Cunliffe, of Northampton, having been summoned to defend a suit for slander by Francis Hacklington, and the latter not appearing, asked for compensation for his own time and for that of his witnesses. Hacklington was ordered to pay Cunliffe two shillings for damages, "Eighteen pence a peece for five witnesses" and "two pence for the summons."   '

Samuel Porter of Hadley, assigned his right and interest in his servant, Robert Williams, to William Lewis, "to serve in husbandry for five years" and "the said assignm' was allowed by this Co'te."

Goodman William Hannum of Northampton, was relieved from "trayninge, watchinge and wardinge by reason of age and the weakness of his body."

Thomas Coleman of New Towne, took the oath of Constable, and Joseph Parsons was "lycensed to keep an ordinary or house of Comon entertaynment in the Towne of Northampton for the yeere ensueing and he hath liberty graunted him to sell wines or strong liquors as need shall require. Provided he keepe good rule & order in his house."

---

1 Mr. John Webster was an inhabitant of Hadley, which was called "the New Towne at Norwottuck," on the court records. He was a man of ability, had been Governor of Connecticut, was commissioned a magistrate by the General Court of Massachusetts in 1660, and was authorized to "joyne w'th the comissioners in keeping the courts at Springfeild." He died at Hadley, within a fortnight after the holding of this court. Of the above-named Jurors, the first six were from Northampton, the next four from Hadley, and the last two from Springfield.

Widow Margaret Bliss of Springfield, complained of the "annoyance shee received by the passage of the water of the mill at Springfeild." Lieut. William Clarke of Northampton, and John White Sr. of New Towne, were ordered to view the premises and report to Mr Holyoke.

"The soldiery of Northampton presented the names of certayne persons whom they had chosen for military officers, viz.: William Clarke for Lieutennate: David Wilton for Ensigne bearer: William Holton for a Sergant: & John Hannum for a Drummer." These men were all confirmed except the Drummer; no notice was taken of him. "William Holton not quallifyed according to law for the office," was allowed "to doe the work of a Serjeant for the band at any tyme of military exercise till the next Gen^{ll} Co^{r}te, to whom they are to looke for his confirmation in ye office."

"It beinge p^{r}sented to this Co^{r}te that this winter past John Holton killed a wolfe uppon the Riuer betweene Northampton and New Towne the Riuer beinge frozen: The Co^{r}te determined that the said Two Townes should pay 10^s a peece to Goodman Holton for his son y^t killed ye wolfe."

John Pynchon presented his account as treasurer of the county, by which it appeared that there was due the county 13^l 12^s, which the court ordered to be expended in building a house of correction at Springfield, under the direction of Mr. Pynchon.

"These 15 persons of the Towne of Northampton whose names follow, viz.: Richard ffellowes, John Webb, Joshua Carter, Jonath Hunt, James Wright, Zachary ffeild, Tho: Copley, Joseph Barker, Thomas Hanchet, Ralfe Hutchison, Thomas Bascom, Samll Bartlett, Nehemiah Allyn, Thomas Roote & Judah Wright, tooke the oath of fidellity to this Comon Wealth in ye psence of the Co^{r}te."

"The votes of the ffreemen of the Townes of Springfeild and Northampton for a County Treasurer for the yeere ensueing were p^{r}sented to this Co^{r}te wch being opened & perused it appeared y^t Capt John Pynchon was chosen County Treasurer for this year."

William Holton sued Richard Treat for £5, a bill or bond, said to be in the hands of John Barnard of Hartford. Capt. John Pynchon was ordered to take up the bill and recover the £5.

Application seems to have been made for a new bridge "in the way to Springfeild on ye east side of the great Riuer over that brook where there is an old cart bridge now out of repayre." Joseph Parsons of Northampton, and Goodman Dickinson Sr. of the New Towne, were ordered to make a survey "where they judge it is most meet to make the bridge," to take charge of the construction and return their account at the next court.

A session of the court was held at Hadley, the same day, and fourteen citizens of that place took the oath of allegiance.

The will and inventory of John Harman of Springfield, was recorded on the 13th of May.

Duties of the County Court.

From the foregoing abridged statement of the business transacted at the first session of the County Court, held in Northampton, may be seen as well the multiplicity of its duties as the character of the cases that arose in the community at that time. There were no lawyers and no need of any. While the court was established to render justice between man and man in the simplest and most direct method, the litigation it had authority over was neither important nor intricate. Little law was required and very little administered. Capital cases were referred to the Court of Assistants at Boston. This Court was the only one in existence in the western portion of the Bay Colony. It had the powers of a Justice's Court, as well as those of County Commissioners, and had also jurisdiction in matters of Probate. It heard jury trials, administered the oath of fidelity, as well as the oath of office, granted licenses, ordered bridges, and county buildings erected, and confirmed military titles.

Train Bands.

Under penalties for disobedience the colony laws required every able bodied person over sixteen years of age to perform military duty. Training day therefore soon became an institution from whose labors few were excused. The General Court early established rules and regulations for the military government of the colony. At first train bands were to meet every Saturday, then once a month. Subsequently the times of meeting were changed to eight, then six, and then four times a year. The number of men required for a full company of foot soldiers was sixty-four; while a troop of horsemen was not to exceed seventy. Two-thirds of each infantry company were to be musketeers, and the remainder pikemen. Each musketeer must be armed with a musket and all necessary equipments, viz : a priming wire, scourer, mold for bullets, sword, rest, bandoleers, one pound of powder, twenty bullets and two fathoms (twelve feet) of match cord. The pikemen were to have a pike, corslet, head piece, sword and snapsack.[1]

1 For description of arms, accoutrements and exercises of the militia, see Judd's History of Hadley, pp. 224, 225.

First Train Band in Northampton. Companies of less than sixty-four men had no captains. For this reason no officers above the grade of lieutenant were confirmed by the county court in 1661. Northampton had a train band in 1658. Its numbers were so small, however, the clerk of the Band being the only person acting under the authority of the court, that no commissioned officers were appointed. This military company was recruited to the required standard within three years, and the officers elected by it were accepted by the court as before mentioned. Towns were required to keep on hand an ample stock of powder. David Wilton, who was appointed Ensign-bearer, furnished a set of "cullers" for the company, for which the town granted him a parcel of land.

Though the petition asking the appointment of the officers elected by the Northampton Train Band was presented at the court held in this town in March, action upon it was not consummated till the next session of the court, held at Springfield, in the month of August. At that time a certificate of the appointment of Lieut. Clarke and Ensign Wilton was issued, which was carefully copied upon the town records. They were not fully authorized to act, however, till the following year, when the General Court, at its October session, ordered that their commissions should be issued according to law. The disability of William Holton was removed in 1662, and he was qualified to act as Sergeant.

Regulations for Conducting Town Meetings. Penalties having been established in order to prevail upon people to attend town meetings, the necessity of rules and regulations governing their conduct when present, soon became apparent. The text of the order indicates that they were in the habit of acting like a parcel of school boys when assembled. To check the prevailing disorder, the following rules were prepared by the selectmen, and entered upon the records :—

"Northampton : 19th of 12th mo : 1660. [February, 1661.]
"At a meeting of the Selectmen Consid⸱ing [   ] that might bee for the well ord⸱ing of Towne meetings and finding by experience that Tumults and many Speaking at one time in such a Tumultous manner that It hinders the worke in hand and is Dishonorable to God and

greiuous to many p^rsons, Doe therfore order while any Comon busines
is in hand or vnd^r Consid^ration & debate, every man shall apply himselfe to the Common worke and not to be more Speakers than one at a
time loueingly and moderately vpon the Penalty of 12^d for every such
offence to be levied by distresse. Wee Intend not to hinder any man
to giue his Advise in any matter one at a time." [1]

Inducements offered   Anxious to secure all possible additions of
to Thomas Barber   reliable men, the citizens were ever on the
to Settle.   alert when any desirable accessions were in
anticipation. Thomas Barber of Windsor, had evidently
been prospecting hereabouts, and was deemed worthy to
become an inhabitant. The town not only voted to receive
him and grant him a home lot, but also to give him "liberty to looke out a plott of ground to the quantity of 20
acres and if it doe incourage him to come they grant [it to
him] vpon this condition, that he come and inhabit [and
make] improouemente of it within a yere after the date
[hereof]." This vote was passed in June. Mr. Barber died
during the next year at Windsor. Here was a generous
bid to obtain a new settler, somewhat in contrast with the
vote to sell home lots, adopted a short time before.

Pomeroy and Hunt   Two important acquisitions were made to
join the Settle-   the community in 1659 and 1660. Medad
ment. Votes re-   Pomeroy, the blacksmith, and Jonathan
specting them.   Hunt, the cooper, arrived during those
years. Both were heartily welcomed and specially encouraged. Pomeroy, however, was not the first blacksmith.
John Webb preceded him. Webb was a man of roving
disposition, a speculator in real estate, dealer in furs, and a
generally unreliable person. He is called a "brazier" in
certain deeds, and was probably a "tinker," doing a little
at several trades. Blacksmithing seems not to have been a

1 The experience of some of the earlier settled towns in reference to the government of town meetings seems to have been repeated in Northampton. The people
behaved as badly here as in other places, and on precisely the same lines. Almost
identical provisions for their orderly conduct at such times were adopted by the
town of Dorchester in 1645, and similar regulations may be found upon the records
of Dedham, Hingham, and other towns. Several of the most influential citizens of
Northampton were "Dorchester men," and when the same conditions confronted
them here, they applied the remedy with which they were already familiar. In Dorchester, people were fined for non-attendance, for leaving meetings without permission, while they were in progress, and special rules were adopted in order that
"confusion may be avoided and business more orderly dispatched."

congenial employment, and he sold his tools to the town. In 1660, these tools, consisting of "a paire of bellowes an anvill a hand hamm^r on hammer 3 p^r of Tongs a Bickorne a slice a naileing stake two cheesels one nayling hammer," were sold to Medad Pomeroy "on Termes." What the consideration was is not stated, but five years afterwards they were given to him unconditionally. Extra grants of land were made to those two skilled mechanics, both of which were coupled in one vote. They were based on the special trades of the grantees, and as the record contains nothing of a similar nature, the vote is given in full :—

"At a Legall Towne meeting 8 2: mo. 1661 (8th of April) It was then voted and Granted to Medad Pumry and Jonathan Hunt that they should either of them haue 16 Acres of land either of them 8 Acres within the fence feild and either of them 8 Acres by the mill River, And if the aforesaid land bee not soe good as ordynary land is in the fence feild y^t is to bee made good by quantity as it wantes in quality and that it is granted to them on this Condition that they shall inhabit in this towne and possess it in ther owne psons fowre yeares from the day of the date abouesaid, and doe the worke that belong to ther trades, that is to say to supply the Townes need of Smithery and Coopery ware. And it was further agreed that Robert Bartlet and Robert Hay-wert were those to determine ther land wether it were as good as ordy-nary land as abouesaid or not, if not to lay out soe much more in some Convenient place to make it equall according to the trew intent of this vote. Med: Pumry 6 Ac^{r}e in the mid: med: in lew of 5, 4 in lew of 3 in the swampe, 19 Ars upp mill river."

Their Home Lots. Medad Pomeroy's original home lot was on a street bounding the cemetery lot on the north, which has since been discontinued, but he after-wards bought another lot in the center of the town, and eventually his property embraced the land lying on Main Street, between Elm on the west and the present "Mansion House" on the east. Jonathan Hunt had a home lot on Elm Street, at the corner of Prospect. It embraced the property now owned by Drs. Seymour and Davenport, A. McCallum, and a portion of the Capen school lot.

These two men were honored and respected during the long years of their residence here. Both held many offices of trust and responsibility, and both were founders of fam-ilies whose descendants, prominent in many branches of human knowledge, are scattered throughout the land.

A New Boat.   In June, 1661, "It was voted affirmatively that the towne will build a new boat." Probably it was intended for the ferry at Hockanum, for Northampton apparently had no official connection with a ferry to Hadley till three years afterwards. Whether this boat was built or not is uncertain, for there seems to have been very little need of a ferry in the meadows at that time. Soon after its settlement, Hadley provided for a ferry, which was put in operation this year, and the further need of one at Hockanum is questionable.

William Clarke "empowred to joyne in marriage."   No person in Northampton, previous to this date, had been authorized to perform the marriage ceremony. Marriage was considered a civil and not a religious contract, and magistrates only were permitted to officiate. When William Clarke was confirmed as Lieutenant of the Northampton company, he was also "empowred to joyne in marriage such as shall desire the same, being published according to law." The law relating to publishments, enacted in 1639, provided that intentions of marriage should be "3 times published at some time of publike lecture or towne meeting in both the townes where the parties resided." In towns where no lectures were held the intentions were to "bee set vp in writing, vpon some poast standing in publike veiwe & vsed for such purpose only, & there to stand, so as it may easily bee reade by the space of 14 dayes." The publishment, when not posted, is by inference, supposed to have been made by announcement, "crying the banns," by the town clerk or some other official. Another conclusion, suggested by the wording of the law, is that the banns were not to be cried on the Sabbath, but at some week day meeting, preferably that of the weekly lecture.

Prison at Springfield.   The court ordered the surplus in the county treasury to be expended in building a House of Correction in Springfield, and the General Court, at its June session, directed that the county rate of Springfield and Northampton, for that year, might be used for the same purpose, if the house should cost more than sixty pounds.

CHAPTER IX.

FOUNDING THE CHURCH.

SEVEN years passed after the arrival of the
first emigrants before a church was formed,
though a meeting house had been built, and
a minister engaged. For three years the people attended
faithfully upon the ministrations of their chosen pastor,
readily granting from their slender resources, all that was
needed for his sustenance. Now the time had come for the
formation of the visible church, and on the 18th of June,
1661, that work was accomplished. The original entry on
the records of the church is as follows : —

"The Church was gathered at Northampton, 18. 4. 1661.

"The psons that begun that worke were in number 8, viz: Mr Eleazar Mather, David Wilton, William Clarke, John Strong, Henry Cunliffe, Henry Woodward, Thomas Roote, Thomas Hanchett. Messengers that were present were from 4. Churches: Mr Pelatjah Glover, Deacon Clap, Thomas Tilstone from the Church of Christ at Dorchester,
Mr John Eliot Sen., Goodman Williams, from the Church of Christ at
Roxbury, Capt. John Pynchon, Deacon Chapin from the Church at
Springfeild, Mr John Russel ye Pastor, Mr Goodwin, goodman White,
from the Church of Christ at Hadleigh, And at the same day after they
had entered into Covenant, they chose Mr Eleazar Mather to the office
of a Pastor which they had concluded to doe before, and desired Reverend Mr Eliot, and Reverend Mr Russel to ordaine him, which accordingly was done."

Four of the persons named as founders of the church,
viz. : Mr. Mather, William Clarke, Henry Cunliffe, and
Henry Woodward, were in April, "dismissed from the
church in Dorchester, to join with others for the gathering
of a church in Northampton." A few months afterwards,
the wives of the last three named were also recommended
to the new church here. During the next few years many
others from that place were enrolled as members. Only

two churches, at Springfield and Hadley, were then in existence in the county. The Hadley church had been formed about a year before, and Mr. Goodwin, named as delegate, was its ruling elder.

Covenant Adopted by the Church   The annexed covenant was adopted at the same meeting, and the names appended comprised all or nearly all who signed it during the pastorate of the first minister : —

"The forme of wordes expessing the Ch. Covenant entered into the 18 of the fourth 1661, by those that then begun that worke and afterward by such as were admitted into Ch. estate and subscribed ther names there vnto.

"Disclaiming all Confidence of, and any worthinesse in ourselves either to bee in Covenant with God, or to pertake in the least of his mercyes, and allsoe all strength of our owne to keepe Covenant with him, or to pforme the least spirituall duty any further than hee by his free spirit shall asist. But relying vpon the Tender mercy, and gracious assistance of the Lord through Jesus Christ, wee doe promise and Covenant in the presence of the Lord the searcher of all hearts ; and before the holy Angells, and this company, ffirst and cheifly, to cleave forever vnto God with our whol hearts as our chiefe, best, yea and only good, and vnto Jesus Christ as our only Saviour, Husband, and Lord, and only High Priest, Prophet and King. And for the furthering of this holy Communion with God the father and Christ Jesus, his sonne, wee promise and engage to obserue, and maintaine according to o' place and vtmost power all the holy institutions, and Ordinances which hee hath appointed for his Church, bewaileing the neglect ther of, and the sinfull defilements of the same with the Inventions and Corruptions of men.... And as for this perticuler Company and society of Saints, wee promise and engage in the prsence of the Lord that wee will Cleave one vnto another in brotherly loue, and seeke the best Spirituall good each of other, by frequent exhortation, seasonable Admonition, and Constant watchfullnesse according vnto the rules of the Gospell, and to performe each vnto other all duties that the Lord in his word doth require of vs, as brethren in Christ, and as fellow members of the same Individuall body of Christ, as long as the Lord shall continue our Church relation each to other....And allsoe wee promise and engage mutuall subjection one to another in all the Administrations and Dispensations according vnto God of all those dutyes which by our Covenant to God, and one to another, wee are bound to the pformance....These things wee all promise in the syncerity of our hearts as before the Lord the examiner, and tryer of all hearts beseeching him, soe to blesse vs, as wee shall truly indevour by his grace the faithfull observation of the same, and when wee through weaknesse shall fayle, then to wayt, and rely vpon the Lord Jesus Christ for pardon, acceptance, healing for his name sake. To this Covenant, and every part of it, wee willingly and syncerely ingage ourselues, and subscribe our names therevnto.

Northampton 18th 4. 1661.

Samuel Wright	Aaron Cooke	Eleazar Mather
John Marsh	William Holton	David Wilton
Thomas Woodford	Joane Cooke	William Clarke
Kathern Wilton	Mary Holton	John Strong
Abigaile Strong	Sarah Clarke	Henry Cunliffe
Margaret Wright	Susan Cunleife	Henry Woodward
Arthur Williams	Elizabeth Woodward	Thomas Roote
Mary Alford	Alice Hutchinson	Thomas Hanchet
Sarah Bridgman	Susan Allexand'	William Jeanes
George Allexander	Richard Lyman	Thomas Bascum
Isaac Sheldon	Hepzibah Lyman	William Hulburd
Mary Sheldon	John Lyman	Avis Bascom
Allexander Edwardes	John King	Ann Hulburd
William Hanum	John Ingersol	Elizabeth Curtis
Nathaniel Phelps	Mary Burt	These six last were
Kathern Williams	Sary King	added vnto the Ch.
Ann Bartlet	Abigail Strong Junio'	14th 5 m 61
Deliverance Hanchet	Josiah Duey	Joseph Eliot
George Langton	Mary Strong	Clemence Mason
Esther Mather	John Stibbins	Elizabeth Phelps
Dorcus Lyman	Sarah Allin	Robert Bartlet, excom-
Ruth Baker	Samuel Smith	municated and re-ad-
Hannah Langton	Mary Smith	mitted
Honor Hanum	Joseph Parsons	Richard Weller
these two were added	Sarah Hanum	Sarah Smith
to ye Ch. 18 of 6 (61)	ffreedom Strong	Joseph Leeds."

These Men Ancestors of the Present Inhabitants.

Such was the foundation on which was established the First Church of Christ in Northampton. Many of the persons whose names are signed to this document were ancestors of the present inhabitants of this and the neighboring towns, who still bear the same family name. The population of the town, when the church was organized, was probably not far from 300. The church records up to the death of Mr. Mather contain 228 names, which include those who were in full communion, and all who were admitted with their parents, as well as all who had been baptized.

Children Admitted to the Church with their Parents.

Of the seventy-one names appended to the covenant, only thirty-five were admitted as members during the year 1661. On the day of organization, eighteen children of six members (one had none and another no minor children), "were admitted with their parents," viz: seven of John Strong, five of William Clarke, one of Henry Woodward, two of Thomas Root, and three of Thomas Hanchet. During the next month eight others were admitted and up to the close of the year ending March 24, 1662, thirty others. In 1662, fourteen more children were added, making seventy in two years. All of these except five were born before their parents removed to Northampton. The parents were members of other churches, and their children were not baptized here. [1]

Payment of Church Expenses.   All the sacramental charges of the church were paid by contributions from the members. The first vote in reference to this matter that was ever entered upon the church records, is as follows : —

"The 13 of 1 mo. [March] 1666.

Voted and vnanimously agreed by this Ch. that each prson will Contribute towards defraying the Charge of the Sacrament three pecks and halfe of wheate for a yeare, this to bee paid in to the Deacon about the last of Septembr when hee shall call for it."

The Seven Pillars of the Church.   The eight men who laid the foundations of the Church were among the most eminent of the early settlers, and deserve such passing notice as the dim records of their time will allow. Whatever can be gleaned concerning Mr. Mather will be given in the future pages of this history. His associates in the work have been, not inappropriately, termed the "Seven Pillars of the Church." Comparatively little can be· learned respecting them. The simple statement that they were chosen year after year to fill certain town offices, and performed many other public duties, is nearly all that the records afford ; a slender background on which to outline even the most incomplete sketch of their lives, yet suffi-

1 Formerly it was the custom to baptize children the Sabbath after their birth, and if it occurred on that day, the ceremony was performed before the services closed. A child of Rev. Jonathan Edwards, born while he was conducting the afternoon Sabbath services, was presented for baptism when less than an hour old. The ordinance was administered by the minister without leaving the pulpit. The father usually, sometimes the nurse or some member of the family, carried the infant up the steps to the pulpit door. It is reported that on one occasion a woman and her husband, a man of intemperate habits, and loose character, presented their child for baptism. Mr. Edwards, knowing the reputation of the man, asked the mother to bring the child forward. The husband, much offended, refused afterwards to hear Mr. Edwards preach.—Judd MSS.

cient to show in some degree the character of the men. Their names, which stand first among the signatures to the covenant, were David Wilton, William Clarke, John Strong, Henry Cunliffe, Henry Woodward, Thomas Roote, Thomas Hanchet.

David Wilton, called more frequently on the records Ensign or Lieut. Wilton, was a man of more than ordinary ability. He was an Indian trader, and had in his possession much land in the meadows and elsewhere. His home lot covered the premises now occupied by the High School buildings, the Baptist Church, and Dr. Higbee's lot, extending from the highway to the river. At Dorchester in 1632, he became a resident of Windsor in 1635, where his trading operations began, and where he was much employed in public affairs, having been many times a Deputy to the General Court. Removing to Northampton in 1660, he became at once an active citizen and a leading man. He was chosen Ensign of the first military organization in Northampton, and was afterwards in 1663, appointed Lieutenant in the Hampshire Troop of Horsemen. Prominent in civil, military and religious affairs, he occupied many of the highest offices in the gift of the town. For a number of years he was annually chosen townsman, was often on the board of Commissioners to end small causes, one of the Judges of the County Court, a member of the first board of County Commissioners, and almost constantly employed in the public service. He was elected representative in 1665, was delegated by the General Court to lay out grants of land and treat with the Indians, and his reputation as an upright, public-spirited citizen was everywhere recognized.

Extensively Engaged in Trade. Lieut. Wilton was engaged in trade with both whites and Indians, at Windsor and Northampton. He purchased many goods of John Pynchon Jr. of Boston, for which he paid in furs, pork, grain, etc. Not only was he a manufacturer of liquors, probably cider brandy, or "apple jack," but in 1662, he had a special license granted him to vend them.

The court record states : "yet though he still liquors, but by a change in the law" could not sell without a license, permission was granted him to sell till the next court, "provided he sell not but to housekeepers of honest conversation." This was probably in the sense of a wholesale license and did not give him authority to retail by the glass. In his capacity as trader he sold many things to the town's people, soldiers and Indians.

Among the papers of the first Joseph Hawley, who married Lydia Marshall, granddaughter of David Wilton, is an account current between the latter and John Pynchon Jr. of Boston. It commenced in May, 1675, and continued till November of the following year. The charge against Wilton is £110; the credit, including the balance at the last settlement in April, 1675, of £34, is £204, showing a fair profit to Wilton. The following facts, condensed from these accounts, show the volume of business transacted by him in furs, within the compass of four months: April 13th, 1675, he sent to Pynchon a barrel of skins, included in which were 65lbs of Beaver, 43 Raccoons and 5 Pessows or Wildcats. Eleven days after, he forwarded by Preserved Clapp, 33 Wullunegs, 13 Opennockis (Martin), 10 Notomagus, 3 black Otter and 2 Fox. On the 4th of June, he sent by Alexander Edwards, 161 Openockis, 7 Notamagus (Mink), 3 Wallanoks (Woodshaws or Fishers). On the 16th he sent another barrel containing 102¼ lbs. of Beaver and 4 Wullanegs. Again on the 28th, he despatched still another barrel of furs, in which were packed 66lbs of Beaver, 33 Squashes (Muskrats), 13 Otters, 14 Racouns, 3 Wallanegs, 5 Notomagus, 1 Oppenockis. In addition there were 4 bushels of Indian corn, one Indian bag and 12lbs of Beeswax. In July, packed in a cider barrel, were 66lbs of Beaver, 4 Otters, 19 Squashes, 7 Racouns, one Fox, 2 Openockis. During this time he also forwarded 3 bbls. of Pork, and 2 bbls. of Flour. These goods were carted to Hartford, and there put on board vessels bound for Boston. The persons named, by whom the goods were sent, were responsible only for the cartage. He purchased of Pynchon, among other things, tobacco, taffety, salt, at 2s 6d per bushel, dowlas, hob nails, many yards of fine red cotton (probably for the Indian trade), "white ozenbergs," an hour glass, castor hat, silver buttons, quantities of duffels, stockings, cloves, mace, nutmegs, ribbon, "wood silk," gloves, etc., etc. He carried on business with Mr. Pynchon as early as 1668, and possibly before that date.

The private account book of Wilton shows that he entertained many officers and men during King Philip's war, in 1675 and 1676. He did not keep an "ordinary," but in common with other citizens "dieted" many of the troopers with whom the town was filled during those troublesome times. Capt. Mason, Maj. Treat, Capts. Appleton,

Watts, Poole and Lathrop were among his boarders. An extract from this account book will be found in the following pages.

Real Estate.   A personal friend of Mr. Mather, he received a portion of the land so generously donated by the citizens and placed at the disposal of the new pastor. He purchased the "mill lot," adjoining his home lot on the east, of Praisever Turner in 1676. In 1672, he petitioned the General Court to be relieved from further service as Lieutenant and for the confirmation of a mortgage of certain lands from Chickawallopp and Payquachalant. The court gave him his discharge, and "considering the petitioners long serving of the country, doe grant vnto him one hundred acres of land in that place desired." As he neglected to make good his title to this land, his heirs, in 1685, obtained a ratification of the grant. He died while on a visit to Windsor, in 1678. His only child, Mary, married the brave Capt. Marshall, who was killed in the Narragansett war. To her son, Samuel Marshall, he bequeathed most of his real estate in Northampton. At the time of his death, his home lot was bounded by the Forbes Library lot on the west, and included the lot on which the Academy of Music now stands. He owned in all 130 acres of land.

Penmanship. Often Employed as Recorder.   In penmanship, Lieut. Wilton surpassed most of his contemporaries. Many times chosen selectman, much of his bold and even chirography may be found upon the town record books. He was several times appointed recorder for the county court, when the illness of that officer, Mr. Holyoke of Springfield, prevented his serving, and his clear and regular writing is among the best on the court record.

Marriage.   Lieut. Wilton married Katherine (sometimes spelled Kathorn) Hoskins, daughter of Ann Hoskins, wife of John Hoskins Sr., by a former husband, by whom he had one child.

William Clarke   William Clarke, most frequently referred to on the
records as Lieut. William
Clarke, was among the most active and efficient of the
early settlers.   Not only is he remembered as one of the
seven pillars of the church, but as one of the most influential among the founders of the town.   He emigrated in
1630, at the age of twenty-one, coming over in the ship
William & Mary, with Rev. Mr. Warham, Roger Clap,
and other prominent men.   First he settled in Dorchester,
where he officiated as townsman from 1646 to 1653.   One
of the "Dorchester men," who arrived here soon after the
settlement of Mr. Mather, he remained to the end, the firm
and faithful friend of his pastor.   A man of quiet dignity,
self-contained, and ready of resource, he bore a more conspicuous part in the early history of the town, than any
others who lived here during the first twenty years of its
existence.   His reputation as a man of business preceded
him, and he was at once put forward in many affairs of
public importance, and so continued, a leader, till old age
compelled him to give place to younger but scarcely better
men.

Conspicuously En-   During the twenty-three years succeeding
gaged in Town   his first election as townsman, he was
Business.   twenty times a member of that body, and
for ten years he was regularly chosen one of the commissioners to end small causes.   He was the first citizen who
ever served as deputy to the General Court, and from 1663
to 1682, he was fourteen times elected to that office,
though not consecutively.   For twenty-six years he acted
as one of the associate justices of the county court.   In
1662, he was authorized by the General Court to solemnize
marriages, being the first person to hold that responsible
position in town.   He was frequently appointed by the
court to settle grievances with the Indians, was greatly interested in promoting the new settlement at Squakheag
(Northfield), and is named as having served as town clerk,
at the commencement of the second settlement of that
place, though there is no evidence that he ever lived there.
Several times he was chosen a commissioner with others, to

determine disputed boundaries between Northampton and neighboring towns. He supplied the commissary department to some extent during King Philip's Indian war, and the Legislature ordered the Treasurer to pay him in 1676, thirty-eight pounds, eighteen shillings for "porke and bisket" "delivered to the countrys vse." He built, or assisted in building the first grist mills, as well as the first saw mill ever put in operation here. So well was he appreciated as a man of business and pecuniary substance, that he was granted the largest home lot which up to that time had been given to any settler. But one other citizen was so liberally provided in that respect. This lot covered nearly all the north half of the Smith College property. Here he built his house and reared his large family of five sons and four daughters. Tradition states that he built a block house upon this lot which was used as a place of refuge during the Indian troubles. His dwelling house was burned in 1681, having been set on fire by a negro, as he averred in search of food.

His Military and other Duties. William Clarke was chosen Lieutenant of the first military company ever organized here, when that was the office of highest rank to which the company, on account of its small number of men, was entitled, was in active service during King Philip's war, and was at the same time a member of the military committee of the county. A man of great public spirit, resolute and capable, he was sure to be employed by the town in conducting any of its business requiring skill, knowledge, tact and determination. In 1671, he was licensed to sell "wine, cider or liquor for a year." He had large grants of land in the meadows and elsewhere and purchased many acres in different parts of the town. All his lands, embracing nearly two hundred acres, with the exception of 7¾ acres, he disposed of before his death to his sons, reserving to himself an annuity of £24.

Ardent, Patriotic, and Persevering. There are no records remaining by which to judge of his private life and character. Only through the public duties he was called upon to perform can any estimate of him as a man

8

and a citizen be reached. He was a hard worker, a pioneer in the best sense of the term. Enduring hardship with cheerfulness, meeting difficulty half way, conquering oftener than conquered, he stands one of the most prominent among the promoters of the plantation. Founder of a numerous family that has had worthy representatives during the entire history of the town, and whose descendants are scattered throughout the land, his name is honored and respected wherever it is found.

Marriage, Death, and Inventory. William Clarke was twice married. His first wife, Sarah, died in Northampton, in September, 1676, and the next year he married Sarah, widow of Lieut. Thomas Cooper, who was killed by the Indians when Springfield was burned, in 1675. He had ten children, all born before he came to Northampton. He died in 1690, aged 81 years. His personal property was inventoried at £131, and his will was mainly confirmatory of the division previously made of his real estate. Small sums of money were left to his children and £5 to the school.

Monument Erected to his Memory. In 1888, the descendants of William Clarke, from all sections of the country, united in erecting a memorial to his memory in the Bridge Street cemetery. The original slab of red sandstone still marks the location of the grave, and beside it has been placed a monument with an appropriate inscription.

John Strong Elder John Strong, first of the name who emigrated to New England, and progenitor of that most extensive family of Strongs, which is now represented in all sections of the country, came to Northampton in 1659. Born at Taunton, Eng., in 1605, he resided both in London and Plymouth. In company with 140 others, when twenty-five years of age, he sailed from Plymouth for the new world. They arrived at Nantasket, May 30, 1630, after a tedious voyage of seventy days. At Dorchester, where he first settled, he remained five years. In 1635, he removed to

Hingham, and in 1638, to Taunton, Mass., having taken the freeman's oath at Boston, two years before. Here he lived about seven years, when he went to Windsor, Ct., where he remained till he once more changed his residence to Northampton. While at Taunton, he was chosen Deputy to the General Court, consecutively from 1641 to 1644. He assisted in the planting of each of these towns, and was an active and honored citizen in them all.

By Trade a Tanner. John Strong and William Clarke came over in the same ship and settled in the same town. Both were especial friends of Mr. Mather, and Strong received a portion of the donated land. When John Strong reached Northampton he was fifty-four years of age. His experience in pioneer life enabled him to assume at once a position of prominence and responsibility, seldom accorded to new comers. During the forty years of his residence in Northampton, he was honored and trusted above most men, in secular and religious matters. Of his life here, however, little is known except what can be gleaned from the meager town and church records. A man of deep religious feeling, a Puritan emigrant to New England, braving the hardships of the wilderness that he might establish purity of religion and liberty of conscience, he would naturally be found among the foremost in establishing the ordinances of religious worship. By trade a tanner, he was the first and probably the only person who carried on that business—except as he brought up his son Ebenezer to the calling—during the entire period of his residence in town. John King was also a tanner, but there is no evidence that he ever carried on a tannery of his own. The original tan yard of Elder Strong, granted by the town in 1660, contained a quarter of an acre. It was situated on the King Street brook, a little north of the Hampshire Marble Works. The tannery was removed to Pomeroy brook, after his death, by some of his descendants, who owned the property since known as the Gov. Caleb Strong place, extending from Pleasant to Hawley Street. So great was the confidence in his honesty and integrity, that the town by vote directed all hides to be taken to him to be tanned at his own price.

Chosen Ruling Elder.

During his life in Northampton, he held perhaps a less number of public offices than many younger men, yet he was no less interested in everything pertaining to the best interests of the town. Prominent in the establishment of schools and a leader in church affairs, he was ever active in the temporal as well as the spiritual welfare of the community. The purity of his private life, the consistency of his christian character, his experience in worldly affairs, and his general intelligence, pointed to him as a proper person to fill the position of Ruling Elder. When Mr. Strong arrived no church had been formed, but when that organization was perfected, he was conspicuous among its promoters. With Mather, Strong, Eliot to foster and protect it, the feeble church, established upon the western borders of civilization, environed by savages, enveloped in the vast forests that everywhere covered the land, expanded with the growth of the town, and became the governing element for good in the new settlement. The position of ruling elder in the church was second in importance only to that of the pastor. Wise and capable, in the maturity of his powers, having assisted at the establishment of four other towns, Elder Strong's advice was sought, and his suggestions heeded, as well in matters relating to the community, as in the more private affairs of his fellow townsmen. The best efforts of his long life were everywhere devoted to the good of the people among whom he lived. To him more than to any other layman is the church indebted for its foundation and early growth. Among all the earnest, thoughtful men who planted the settlement at Northampton, not one was more influential, more painstaking, or more respected than Elder John Strong.

His Home Lot.

The home lot granted him by the town was situated on West Street, nearly opposite the present Parsons homestead. He soon sold it to John Webb, and purchased Webb's home lot at the corner of Main and South Streets, embracing within its limits the residence of the late Enos Parsons, and all the land westerly to the Academy of Music, extending from Main Street to the river. This property remained in the Strong family 103 years.

His Family and Descendants.   Elder Strong was twice married. His first wife, whom he married in England, died on the voyage over, and an infant child died about two months after his arrival. In 1630, he married Abigail, daughter of Thomas Ford. He had eighteen children, fifteen of whom lived to adult age. His death occurred in 1699, when he was 94 years of age. His descendants are numerous throughout the country, aggregating in 1871, but little less than 30,000.

Henry Cunliffe, one of the three designated as "Dorchester men," went to that place in 1644, remaining there fifteen years, when he removed to Northampton. His home lot was on North Street. While his life here was brief compared with that of others, yet he was a man of substance, highly respected and often employed by the town. For a number of years he was chosen selectman, several times one of the commissioners to end small causes, and was in every way an estimable citizen. A person of high moral character and strict integrity, he too is entitled to be ranked as one among the "seven pillars of the church." He died in 1673, leaving one daughter, who married John Webb. He willed his real estate to her two children, after the death of his wife, and "to Warham Mather, the son of Mr. Eleazar Mather, Pastor of the church in Northampton, in testimony of his profound respect for his progenitors and in particular his grandfather, Mr. Richard Mather, a legacy of £5."

Henry Woodward. Henry Woodward came with Clarke and Cunliffe from Dorchester. He is said by Clap to have been a physician, but no evidence has been found indicating that he ever practiced here. He received a large home lot, equal in dimensions to that of William Clarke, and adjoining it on the south. His ability as a man of business brought him constantly into public life. The three, Clarke, Cunliffe and Woodward, were often associated in office; several times as commissioners, and frequently as selectmen. He was many times placed upon committees of importance, and wielded considerable influence as a citizen of worth and respectability. When the "Hampshire Troope" of Horse was formed in 1663, Henry Woodward was chosen Quartermaster, and from that time he is often named on the records as "Quarter Mr Woodward." He was a member of the first board of Tithingmen in Northampton, having been appointed by the selectmen in 1678, and approved by the county court. In addition to his home lot of twelve acres, he owned about one hundred acres of meadow and upland, most of which descended to his son John. In 1665, the county authorities made an agreement with him to entertain the court, and he was granted a license to keep an ordinary and to sell liquors. This arrangement was continued till 1681. Most of the courts were undoubtedly held at his house during that time. His tavern was situated a short distance easterly of the present location of Smith College Hall of Music. He was accidentally killed at the upper corn mill in 1685. He had four children, three daughters and one son. One of his daughters married Medad Pomeroy, another was the wife of Jedediah Strong, and a third married Capt. John Taylor, all men of prominence in the history of the town. Notwithstanding the fact that he was a man of good business capacity and largely engaged in town affairs, an authentic signature by his own hand has not been found. On his will he made his mark, and several other documents in the Probate office are signed in the same way.

Thomas Roote was at Salem in 1637, at Hartford two years afterwards, and removed to Northampton in 1655. He was among the first settlers to arrive here, and was one of the signers of the original petition. A quiet, substantial farmer, though a weaver by trade, he never arrived at the position of leader. He was several times elected a selectman, and was one of the officers of the town when careful men were in demand. His home lot was on the easterly side of Pleasant Street, below what is now known as Pearl Street. He died in 1694, at the advanced age of 84 years. He had six sons and one daughter, all born before he removed to Northampton.

Deacon Thomas Hanchet came to Northampton from Wethersfield in 1660, though his name appears in the records of Saybrook and New London. He was by no means so prominent in town affairs as his colleagues. A modest, retiring man, of blameless life, he was well worthy the distinction of having been elected second deacon of the new church, to which position he was chosen in 1668. His home lot was the most southerly on Hawley Street, and was a portion of the lot granted to Thomas Langton, whose daughter he married. In a few years he removed to Westfield, and afterwards to Suffield, where he died in 1686.

CHAPTER X.

NEW MEETING HOUSE—HAMPSHIRE COUNTY.

A New Meeting House. Its Location and Description. WITHIN a month after the successful establishment of the church, the town voted to build a new Meeting House. There is reason to believe that the matter had already been under consideration, and a more appropriate time—the formal settlement of the pastor over the newly organized church—could not have been found. Possibly it was for this that the people had been waiting. The old log house, after seven years use for all public meetings, had become too small for the rapidly increasing township. Accordingly on the 12th of July, 1661, the town voted to "build a new meeting howse, of 42 foote square, and that they will lay out about it 150[1]." The committee "chosen and empowred to Cary on and finish this worke," were "William Holton, Ensigne Wilton, Robert Bartlet, Joseph Parsons, John Stibbens, William Clarke." Holton and Parsons had been members of the committee which erected the first "house for the Towne," the others, with the exception of Bartlett, were new comers. It is impossible to designate with accuracy the location of this house. It stood on Meeting House Hill, west of the first one, and is believed to have been placed in the highway nearly opposite the present entrance to Center Street. Grants of land on Meeting House Hill, between the new meeting house and the school house (the first meeting house was used for a school house in 1663) indicate that the two buildings stood some distance apart. The new house was square, with a roof rising in a pyramidal form towards a point in the center. On the apex was placed a "turret"—a small cupola—in which the bell was suspended. The rope hung down in the broad aisle, where the ringer stood. No bell, however, was in use in Northampton for many years after this edifice was built. In the meantime the inhabitants were called together for religious or other meetings by sounding the trumpet or beating the drum. Jedediah, son of Elder John Strong, was paid 18s. per year in 1677, 1678 and 1679, for blowing the trumpet. Whether this instrument was sounded from the meeting house turret or by the trumpeter through the streets, is unknown. No allusion is made to a turret in the vote authorizing the building, neither is there any intimation that dormer windows[1] were placed in the roof, but in all probability the fashion of the day in such edifices was followed.[2] Somewhat extensive repairs were made in 1694, but no vote can be found ordering them.[3] New sills and underpinning were then put in, and the turret repaired. The sum of £150 was appropriated for this meeting house when the town decided to build. In December, 1663, it was voted to "add three poundes more to the forty-six poundes for the building of the meeting house to Aro Cooke." There is no explanation of this vote, and no other allusion to this amount. In February, 166¾, "The selectmen made a Rate for the new meettinge houese and comited it to the constable," to the amount of £115.08.09. This is all that appears concerning the cost of the edifice, and very probably the rate included the £49.

Seats in the New House.   When the house was built, the question of seats (very few pews were then used) was not considered, but in June, 1664, it was voted that the "meeting house bee decently seated," and the building committee was "impowered to procure the

---

1 In some instances dormer windows were placed in the roof for lighting the galleries. Sometimes as in case of the towns of New Haven and Milford, Ct., a square platform, with a railing, surmounted the turret, on which the drum was beaten or the trumpet sounded. In time of war a sentinel was posted there.

2 Hatfield had a meeting house forty-five feet square. with "gable windows upon each square of the roof" New London, Ct., had one forty feet square "with turret answerable;" West Springfield had one forty-two feet square, with windows in the roof; and Wethersfield, Ct., one forty-two feet square, with gable windows.

3. In the account books of Joseph Parsons, Esq. and Jerijah Strong, are charges against the town, in the year 1694, for materials used in repairs about the meeting house. Parsons has items for "sawing two stocks for Preamady" (pyramid), for carting two great beams and for "work in underpinning yᵉ meeting house;" Strong charges for "fetching a sill," a post and stone, and for a "load of timber for the terit."

seateing of it, and what pay they shall engage for the doeing the worke the Towne doe engage by this vote to pay accordingly." The next year, when the first seating committee was appointed, two votes in reference to seats were passed, apparently inconsistent with each other. The first one provided that "every man shall pay for his own seat by an equal proportion," and the second one stipulated that the Town would "pay such pay as the Committee shall agree for seateing the meeting house." Probably the first vote had reference to the work of providing the seats and the second to the labor of assigning them to individuals.

Seating the Meeting House.   Apparently the new meeting house was several years in process of construction, and when completed it was not set apart for religious purposes by any dedication services. Like an ordinary public building, it was occupied by the people when ready for use. Town meetings may possibly have been held in it before any religious assembly met therein. One special preliminary, however, was always carried out before any Sabbath exercises took place, and that, next in importance after its construction, was the assignment of sittings. The town built the structure, the cost was taxed upon the people, and when it was ready for use, a committee was appointed for "seating" the meeting house. To every inhabitant was appointed a place, and each person was expected—and if he did not the law was at hand to compel him—to occupy it whenever divine service was held. The old world reverence for position or estate had not been entirely obliterated. Whatever of equality before the law of man or God, may have been elsewhere observed, equality in social or political life, or equality of honor in the meeting house, were nowhere recognized. In every other position in life one man might be as good as another, but in the house of God, the rank and dignity of every worshipper were distinctly marked by the seat assigned him on the Lord's day. In January, 1665, the following committee was chosen to seat the meeting house:—

"The two Elders, Capt. Aaron Cooke, Lt. David Wilton, Lt. William Clarke, Goodman Parsons, Goodman Bartlett." And "The rules yᵗ they are to Attend in this worke are these Age, Estate, Qualefications only Respecting ye commissioned officers, & Imptiality." Some delay occurred in the performance of this duty, or else the result was unsatisfactory. for in the month of August, 1665, the following entry is found upon the records:—"The Towne revookt theare former voate conserninge the seatinge of the inhabitance of North Hampton in the meettinge house: and haue Desired the Elders to doe it with all convenient speede."

The only person chosen elder at that time, of which there is any record, was John Strong. The other one must have been Mr. Joseph Eliot, who had been hired to help Mr. Mather about three years before, and was known as the "Teaching Elder."

Interior of this Meeting House. It is conjectured that this building, with a wide door facing the south, had four windows in each side, exclusive of the gables (if any existed), but no description of its external appearance has been found. An idea of its interior can be obtained only from the general statements regarding similar structures in other towns, built about this time. Opposite the door stood the pulpit, and at each side of it may have been a few pews for the minister's family, the deacons and other dignitaries. Two rows of benches, each bench capable of seating five or six persons, with a wide passage way between, forming the "broad aisle," covered most of the floor space. The men—men and women were not then allowed to sit together—occupied those at the right of the minister as he faced the congregation, and the women those at the left. Another row of benches was placed along the walls, separated by a narrow aisle from the central seats. In some of the meeting houses, pews, square or oblong, were arranged along the walls, and occasionally persons were permitted to build a pew for themselves. No galleries were put in when the building was erected, but they were afterwards added.

In December, 1670, "The selectmen ordered Medad Pumary toe cary on and manadge the buildinge of a gallarie and toe call in the mony dew for the planks of those that had them, and the mony thats dew from them that haue had seats and haue not payd: toe carry on the worke: and what is wanttinge we will cee it toe be provided toe finish the worke and this toe be done with as much speede as may be." In the following February, 1671 (19-11-1670), "The selectmen impowred Medad Pomery to build the other galrie also or to get it done."

Nine years afterwards a front gallery was built. The meeting house was not fully provided with pews for more than half a century after its erection. In 1720, the town voted "y^t all ye flank Seatts on each side The Meeting House should be made into pews: and that upon ye Towns Charge."

Second Fencing of the Meadows. While the small size of the lots into which the meadows were divided rendered the fencing of each lot inconvenient and expensive, the annual overflow of the great river made it impossible. Consequently the first settlers adopted per force, the English system of common fields. Up to this time the meadows had been considered as two fields, but the town voted in August, 1661, "that they shall ly both in a feild, and for the fenceing of the aforesaid feild that they will cast lotts wher every mans fence shall ly." A committee of seven men was appointed to lay out the fence. The quantity of fence each man was to build was determined by the amount of meadow land he owned, and its location was fixed by lot. This committee did not complete their work till the next year, and in April made an entry of their proceedings upon the town books, in which is recorded the length in rods, feet and inches of every man's section of fence. It is termed : —

"The Record of the order of the lotts of the fences cast for every mans Proportion of fence for his lands in the Common feild in Northampton as they ly sucessively beeing cast into Two Divissions of fence."

The first division began at the Great River, near the present bridge, and was built upon the bluff at the edge of the meadow, to the lower end of Pleasant Street, where it came upon Mill River. It was carried along the river bank to the vicinity of South Street bridge, where it crossed that stream, and was extended up on to the pine plain till it met the old fence. The second division began at "Hogg's Bladder" (the euphonious name given by the first settlers to a parcel of meadow lying near the junction of the Manhan with the Connecticut River, and which it still retains), "at the middle of the fence and running over the River uppon the upland till it comes to meate the first Divission." The fence, built on the high land above Mill River, in the rear of the South Street lots, encircled Hurlburt's Pond, crossed Manhan River and extended to the place of beginning named in the records. The proportion of fence to the acre in the first division was six feet, and in the second, four feet nine inches. In the first division there were sixty-five owners, and in the second sixty-six.

From this time onward the fence enclosing the common field was maintained at the expense of the proprietors of the meadow land. While the position of the fence remained substantially as given above, new regulations and adjustments to changed ownership became necessary from time to time. These are all detailed upon the records, and the more important features of them will be presented in the future pages of this work.

First Burial Place. Bridge Street Cemetery. The first death in Northampton occurred in 1655. James, infant son of James Bridgman, died on the 14th of June. During the next three years five deaths were registered. Where these dead were buried is not known. In February, 1659, the town voted "that the burying place shalbee upon the meeting howse hill," and it is probable that all interments to that time had been made there. The selection of this place so near the meeting house, was undoubtedly in accordance with the system of parish church yards that prevailed in their old English homes. Three years after, when the new meeting house was located upon another site, it was concluded to change the position of the burying ground.[1] But eleven deaths had been recorded up to the commencement of the year 1661. A committee, chosen in that year "to finde out a convenient place for yt vse," reported, April 23, 1662, in favor of a position on Bridge Street, "at the furthest corner of the Sequestered Mynisters Lott wher Mrs Jeanes was buried." Mary, wife of William Janes, died April 4, 1662, and was probably buried there in anticipation of the determination to use this lot for such a purpose. The portion of the minister's lot se-

1 " Their burying place is stated to have been on the meeting house hill until the end of October, 1661. I mention this as proof that burying in the centers of towns by the side of their churches, was originally the common custom of New England. This custom plainly had its origin in the superstitions of the Romish Church, which attributed a kind of sanctity to a cemetery consecrated by a clergyman.—Dwight's Travels in N E., 1821, vol. 1, p. 345.

lected was at the north-east corner of the present cemetery, and is still known as the "old part." The quantity of land set apart was not defined, but in after years, when it became necessary to fence the plot, its bounds were established. Since that time it has been several times enlarged.

Rectifying the Land Records. At almost every town meeting, grants of land, often covering many acres, were voted, and frequent errors occurred in recording them, which sometimes required town action for their correction. Measurements of land were never very accurate, all mistakes of that nature being effectually covered by the phrase "more or less." Instances appear in which the boundaries of the same lot, given when the property was sold, and no change had been made in the ownership of the adjoining lots, vary essentially. In part these may be attributed to faulty description and in part to careless registration. In 1661, a committee consisting of "Mr Jeanes and the Townesmen," was "chosen to Rectefy all errors about Recording lands."

Wheat the Circulating Medium. One of the most important crops raised in the valley at this time was wheat, and it became a common medium of exchange, though other kinds of produce were used to some extent. It was grown on all the interval lands throughout the valley, and was generally a sure and abundant crop. Every farmer raised more or less wheat and with it he settled, not only his taxes, but nearly all his other indebtedness. The town paid its taxes to the colony in wheat, the people satisfied their obligations with it, and with it the traders bought goods, which in turn were again exchanged for wheat. So far as the colony rates were concerned, the price was fixed by the Legislature, and that established its commercial value, though the towns frequently named the figure at which it should be received for taxes. The first intimation of any action of this kind having been taken was a vote passed on the last day of December, "that the Towne rates for this p^{r}sent yere wheat shall goe for 3^s 6^d per bushell."

Hampshire County Instituted. As the Connecticut river towns increased in numbers, population and importance, it became necessary in order "that publicke affairs may with more facility be transacted according to lawes heere established," to unite them under a county jurisdiction. A court with all the powers appertaining to a county court already existed, and a county treasurer had been several times chosen. Whether or not the towns took the initiative in this matter is uncertain. The first allusion to it upon the town records was in March, 166½ : —

"After lecture[1] the towne stayed did vote and Impower Lieutenant Clarke & Ensigne Wilton as a comittee to confer wt^h the committees of Springfeild and Hadley Concerneing the name of this County and the place y^t should be the shere Towne and all other matters of that nature and soe accordingly as the Case requires to p^rsent the same to the Generall Court."

The above action seems to indicate that town business was transacted at any meeting, whenever the people came together, and without the legal formality of a special warning. Possibly the drummer may have made his rounds the evening previous, though the record says that the "town stayed." One other item of business was transacted at this meeting. "It was further voted that the Townes men should hire a Cow Keeper and engage that the towne should helpe him in some worke at his neede towards his pay."

Order of the Court Establishing the County. The General Court, at its May meeting, established the County of Hampshire, including in it the three towns of Springfield, Northampton and Hadley. Its limits were prescribed in the following act passed on th 7th of that month : —

1 "After the churches had settled well down to their work, a weekly lecture—essentially a repetition of one Sabbath service—became a fixed institution." "Different days were selected for these observances, and people in the eastern section of the colony had opportunity to hear a sermon every day in the week by attending them in different towns."—Dexter's Congregationalism, p. 457.

As the number of towns increased in this section, they united in carrying on this service. After six towns had been formed in Hampshire County, the ministers in them united, and there was a lecture in each town once in six weeks. Hence they were called "six weeks lectures." It is stated that a daughter of Rev. Solomon Stoddard, in her youth, often walked to Hatfield, to attend lectures there and back again to Northampton the same day. The six towns were Springfield, Westfield, Northampton, Hatfield, Hadley, and Deerfield.

"The bounds or ljmitts on the south to be the south ljne of the pattent, the extent of other bounds to be full thirty miles distant from any or either of the foresajd tounes, & what tounes or villages soeuer shall hereafter be erected w^th^in the foresajd precincts to be & belong to sajd county; and further, that the sajd county shall be called Hampshire. * * * & that Springfeild shall be the shire toune there, & the Courts to be kept one time at Springfeild & another time at Northampton ; the like order to be observed for their shire meetings, that is to say, one yeere at one toune, & the next yeare at the other, from time to tjme. * * * All the inhabitants of that shire shall pay their publicke rates to the countrey in fatt catle, or young catle, such as are fitt to be putt off, that so no vnecessary damage be put on the country; & in case they make payment in corne, then to be made at such prises as the lawe doe comonly passe amongst themselves, any other former or annuall orders referring to the prises of corne notwithstanding."

The towns comprising the county seem to have had a voice in deciding its name and in designating the shire town, and the order of the court was undoubtedly in accordance with the result of the deliberations of the committees from all the towns.

County Commissioners. First Meeting in Northampton.

County Commissioners seem to have been chosen by the several towns, soon after the establishment of the county, but there is no record of any vote for them here. Their first meeting, as well as all the rest for the year 1662, was held in Springfield. On the 2^d^ of April of the following year, they met in Northampton :—

"At a meeting of persons chosen by the several towns, to order and settle the affairs of the county, viz: Capt. John Pynchon, Mr. Henry Clarke, Capt. Aaron Cooke, Lt. David Wilton, and Elizur Holyoke: They agreed that the beginning of the year for the shire meetings should be on the first day of March yearly; That the shire meetings shall be each other year at Springfield and each other year at Northampton in a constant course; All this year to be at Northampton, Springfield having had them last year. They agreed also that the commissioner chosen in March yearly by the shire commissioners to carry the votes for the nomination of Magistrates to Boston, shall be allowed 30^s^ from the County Treasury; the rest of his charges he is to bear himself. The person to carry the votes to be changed yearly, that no man be overburthened, except for necessity or convenience, they see cause to act otherwise."[1] This was the first meeting of County Commissioners ever held in Northampton.

1 Judd MSS. Deeds, p. 53

Wolves Their De-
structiveness and
the Methods Em-
ployed for their
Extermination.
Of all the wild animals that infested the forests in New England, wolves were undoubtedly the most destructive and annoying. They were accustomed to roam in packs, and hardly any domestic animal was safe from their depredations. Even after their hunger was satisfied, they frequently destroyed sheep, lambs, goats, calves, swine and poultry. Regarded as the greatest enemy of the farmer, every means was employed to exterminate them, and bounties were offered by the government for their destruction. In all the settlements men hunted them constantly, not alone to obtain the bounty, but to rid the community of the pests. One of the most effective methods of taking them was by means of pits. Long deep trenches were dug and lined with logs, from which the bark had been peeled, standing upright, and touching each other. These trenches were covered with a light frame work, upon which leaves and dirt were scattered to make the surface appear like the surrounding territory. Over it was placed a quantity of tempting bait. The wolves rushing forward in pursuit of the bait, would break through into the pit. Unable to ascend the slippery sides, they would be found alive by the hunters the next day. It was no easy matter to dispose of these ferocious animals, and the wolf pits were often the scenes of much excitement.[1] This method of capturing these animals was resorted to by hunters in Northampton, and the marshy ground at the foot of "Brick yard Hill," on the road to Florence, was called "Wolf Pit Swamp." Capt. Aaron Cook had a pit for the capture of wolves and doubtless there were others in other sections of the town.

A Price on their
ears. Famous
Wolf Hunters.
The bounty for killing wolves at this time was 40s. Of this sum, the county was required to pay one-half, 20s., the town 10s., and the colony 10s. Their heads were carried to the selectmen or constable, who cut off the ears and paid the bounty. The first wolf paid for by the town, of which there is any memorandum, was that brought by John Webb. Subsequent records prove that Webb killed many of these animals. Famous among wolf killers was

1 Upham's Salem Village, pp. 211, 212.

9

Capt. Aaron Cook.   In 1664, he received bounties for killing thirteen of them, twice the number destroyed by all
the other hunters in that year.   Two years after he killed
six more of them, and his daughter "brought a Woulfs
heade tooke out of his pite."   Among those killed by Capt.
Cook, was "a blacke Woulf's heade," which was considered something of a rarity.   During the year 1665, the
town fixed the price of wheat paid for wolves' ears at 4s.
per bushel.   The amount paid for these appendages varied
from year to year, and was increased as the animals, on account of their scarcity, became more difficult to kill.

Bridge across Mill   Having waded Mill River for about eight
River Voted, but   years, the settlers on South Street began to
not Built.   agitate the question of a bridge across that
stream, and succeeded in obtaining a conditional vote in
favor of building one : —

"At a towne meeting 14. 9. 1662, (14ᵗʰ of November) Voted affirmatively that they will build a bridg ouer the Mill River: that is when
the meeting house is finished so as is comfortable to meet in likewise
this vote satisfied the inhabitants on the other side for the present:
allso they haue liberty in the meane time to build a bridg if they see
cause: So they are freed from working in the common highways till
the town do build a bridg ther."

The bridge, however, was not built for a number of
years, and it may be supposed that the people living on the
other side of the stream remained satisfied to ford the river
while they were excused from working on the highways.

Prospect Street   An important highway, the southerly por-
Established.   tion of Prospect Street, was laid out this
                   year.   The reason given for it was the "ne-
cessity of a high way leading towards thomas luis his
house, and so to the Round hill."   Thomas Lewis occupied
a home lot which now forms part of the homestead of H.
R. Hinckley.   Commencing at the lot of William Clarke,
just above what is now "Warfield Place," the road followed probably the present line of Prospect Street, possibly
a little to the east of it, till it reached the lot of David
Burt, now the property of Prof. B. C. Blodgett.   Passing
north-east of that house, it must have turned abruptly to
the west in order to approach the lot of Thomas Lewis,

from which point it was laid very nearly where it now is to Elm Street.   At first it was proposed to run the road below Jedediah Strong's lot, which covered a portion of the homestead of Oscar Edwards, but, at his suggestion, it was changed so as to form the eastern boundary of Jonathan Hunt's home lot.   Hunt's lot extended sixteen rods on Elm Street and forty on Prospect Street.   In 1712, the road was altered at the request of Henry Burt (who had come into possession of the David Burt property), from the north-east side of his house to the north-west side, and then it was undoubtedly laid in a straight course across the front of Rev. Solomon Stoddard's homestead, formerly that of Lewis.

CHAPTER XI.

RAPID GROWTH OF CHURCH AND TOWN.

The Church Votes to Employ another Teaching Officer.

MR. MATHER officiated about a year after the formation of the church, without assistance,[1] when on account of failing health, it was found necessary to obtain help. In December, 1662, at a meeting held at the pastor's house, the church

"voted that two Teaching officers were appointed as ordinances of Xᵗ Jesus for his church, and that it was the duty of every Ch. to doe what lyeth in them that they may bee furnished with two Teaching officers, this voted nemine contradicente. It was then alsoe declared by vote of all vnanimously, that this Church had neede of another teaching officer, to bee joyned to their Pastor."

No recommendation was made at this meeting concerning the person to be employed. The church took the initiative, and made known its want. As church members only could be made freemen, and freemen alone could vote in town affairs, there could have been little doubt relative to town action.

Rev. Joseph Eliot Called.

There was no delay in the matter. This movement, having apparently been decided upon before presentation either in church or town meeting, was speedily pushed forward. Church action was taken Dec. 30, and in three weeks the question came before the town. At a meeting held in January, 1663 (23. 11. 1662) "it was voted vnanimously that they be willinge to settle Mʳ Eliote amongst theme. Alsoe at the same tyme as aboue Dated the Land that was Sequistred

[1] Mr. Mather's health began to decline before he had been many years settled here, and this was the occasion of the call to Mr. Eliot. — Dwight's Travels, vol. 1, p. 349.

for the menistrey is now granted & giuene by the Towne to Mr Josepth Eliote if he setle amonst vs." This last vote was far from unanimous. It was so unsatisfactory to many of the citizens that the following protest was afterwards entered upon the records : —

"Wee whose names are heare vnderwritten doe manifest our desent to the act of the Towne next aboue written viz in giueing away that pcell of land to Mr Joseph Eliot which the Towne formerly sequestred perpetually for the mynistery as witness our hands.

JOHN STEBING

JOSEPH PARSONS

WILLIAM JEANES

RALPH HUTCHENSON

The Marke of   ROBERT BARTLET

SAMUELL WRITE, Senoyer

The Marke of   ALEXANDER EDWARD

The Marke of   WILLIAM MILLER

SAMUELL WRIGH Jn^{or}."

Fifty Pounds Voted for his Salary. Although the proposition to give away the land already set apart for the ministry, met with considerable opposition, there was no open objection to employing Mr. Eliot and paying him a fair salary. The same meeting at which the preceding votes were passed, granted him "fifty pound for the next yeare," and the men who protested against giving away the sequestered land voted in favor of this measure. Yet there seems to have been a slight under-current of opposition, a bit of which came to the surface. The next year Praisever Turner was brought before the court for circulating a false report that certain of the leading men in town, had sent word to "Mrs. Eliot in the Bay, informing her that Northampton was not able to mayntagne Two Ministers." Those who were accused of sending the statement denied the rumor, and Turner was fined. In Turner's case the wish was undoubtedly father to the thought, yet he may have voiced the sentiment of a few who did not care personally to oppose the proposition.

Mr. Mather's Liberality. On the 26th of April, 1663, the town "vnanimously did desire Mr Elyot to stay to helpefull in the yere ensuing in the mynistry." It also voted to accept "of Mr Mathers 10^l towards Mr Elyots maintenance, and to free Mr Mather of his rate for the yere ensueing." It was furthermore "agreed that Mr Eliot is to haue 50^l for the yere ensueing." At the same time "Ensigne Wilton and brother Strong were chosen Committees to p^{r}sent the Townes minde to Mr Elyot." The call was accepted, and in May following it was voted "y^t brother Woodward bee hyred to fetch upp Mr Eliot."[1]

Mr. Eliot Remains but a short time.

Rev. Joseph Eliot was the second son of Rev. John Eliot of Roxbury, the celebrated "Apostle to the Indians." He remained in town but a short time, evidently not much more than a year or two. At the commencement of the year following his settlement, "1-(11)-1663" (January, 1664) the town voted

"toe giue Mr Eliote Eighty pound to build him a house. Also the Towne vouted to giue him Sexty pound for the yeare ensuinge for his maintinance and they desier him to acept of this motion and tender and contenew amonge theme—the meaninge is to build him a house in cace he setle amonge vs." * * "Deacon Holton and Thomas Bascom Senr." were chosen "toe present this there desier toe Mr Eliote."

He evidently declined the offer and this is the last vote concerning him upon the records. It is not known when he left town, but there were two elders here in 1665, and he must have been one of them. He subsequently removed to Guilford, Ct., where he was settled for many years. In the history of Guilford he is spoken of as the "renowned Mr. Joseph Elliot, a pastor after God's own heart. After this burning and shining light had ministered to this good people about thirty years, he deceased to the inexpressible grief of his beloved flock, May 24, 1694."

The Church makes Choice of a Deacon and Ruling Elder.

About the time that the church decided to employ another teaching officer, probably at the same meeting, it also voted to choose a Ruling Elder and a Deacon. "After Solemn and extraordinary seeking to God for his Direction

---

1 There is a discrepancy in the dates of town action concerning Mr. Eliot. The church first acted, "30-10-62" (Dec., 1662) ; the first recorded town vote is dated "23-(11)-1662," (January 63) ; then follow votes dated respectively "Aprill 26th, 1662" and "May 3^d (62)." The earlier town records were very loosely kept and meetings are not entered in their regular order according to dates. It must either be believed that the town passed all the votes calling Mr. Eliot and arranging for his removal here, and that Mr. Mather offered to give up part of his salary, before the church moved in the matter, or that there is an error in the year of the April and May votes. The above account is based on the supposition that such an error exists.

and blessing vpon vs in the choise of officers," the church elected John Strong, Ruling Elder, and William Holton, Deacon. On the 13th of May, 1663, these two persons were "ordained," the

"Elder by the Imposition of ye handes of Pastor and Mr Russel Pastor of Hadleigh; The Deacon afterwardes by the imposition of the handes of Pastor and Elder; The messengers p^{r}sent of the church of Hadleigh, Mr Russell Mr Goodwin. bro^r Goodman of the Church of Springfeild Deacon Chapin and Mr Holyoake who approovd of, and by these Deligates gaue the right hand of felowship."

Duties of these Officers. In accordance with the Cambridge Platform, the offices of Pastor and Teacher were distinct. The special work of the pastor was that of preaching and exhortation, while the duty of the teacher was to explain and enforce the doctrine. The Ruling Elder was to join with the pastor and teacher in acts of spiritual rule, in admitting members, ordaining officers and excommunicating offenders. This distinction of offices had then been generally adopted in the colony, but it gradually declined and at length entirely ceased. It was not considered the duty of the pastor to read or expound the scriptures in the pulpit, this was the work of the teacher; where there was no such officer, that part of the service was omitted, and the singing of a psalm only separated the opening prayer from the sermon.[1]

Town Meeting on a Training Day. Another indication that town business was transacted whenever the people were assembled, no matter for what purpose, occurred in 1662. On a previous occasion, "after Lecture" the people "stayed," and certain matters were acted upon, so again the record reads "Uppon a Trayneing day in June (62) It was then voted that James Wright had a dispensation of 12 month for his home lote." This undoubtedly means that James Wright had forfeited his right to a home lot in not having complied with the conditions on which it was granted, but on showing good and sufficient reasons for such neglect, he was allowed further time in which to secure a title.

1 Dexter's Congregationalism, p. 452.

Town meetings seem to have slowly developed into system and order. At first penalties were enacted to compel attendance; then by-laws became necessary to preserve order; now it had become equally important to provide for the proper presentation of business, and the selection of a presiding officer. The order adopted for this purpose, dated 15th 11th mo. 1661 (January 15, 1662) reads as follows:

"Inasmuch as nothing can bee don by any pson or Society without method and Order, and that not Attending it brings any people to Confusion. And for the better carying an end of our occations, with Comlinesse, Wee order that noe businesse shalbe proposed to the Towne, but what haue bin first Considered of by the Townese men, and by them presented to the Towne. Allsoe that the Towne meeteing shalbee begunn and Caried on by one of the Townes men and concluded by him whom they shall appointe this to be Attended for this present yere & till another bee made by vs who are chosen for this p'sent yere. in the name and by the Consent of the Townesmen.

DAVID WILTON."

From this vote it may be inferred that there had been great irregularity both in the holding of meetings and in the presentation of business. It is also apparent that no general method had been observed in conducting them. The present system of notifying voters of the business to be transacted, by warrants, had not then been developed, though the above rule was a move in that direction. In fact, a directly opposite course had been pursued. Any one presented to the meeting whatever happened to interest him. It appears also that there had been little uniformity in the choice of presiding officer, else there would have been no need to provide for the appointment of one of the selectmen "to begin, carry on and conclude the meeting." The only previous allusion to this officer was in 1659, when persons were forbidden to leave a meeting without permission from the moderator. It is very probable that this system of appointing a member of the board of selectmen to preside at town meetings, was continued for at least forty years. About that time the custom of electing a moderator to act through the year was adopted.

Division of the
Commons.
On the 17th day of February, 166⅔, it was "voted affirmetiuely that all the Common land within three miles compasse of the Towne is to bee Devided amongst the Inhabitants of this Towne according to each mans proportion." The same day on which the above vote was passed, on "the 17th of the 12 mo.," the following method of distribution was "voted affirmatiuely by the Towne vnanimously to be recorded" : —

"ffor as much as the Inhabitants of the Towne might haue swarued from the Orderes of the Gennerall Court in the Distributions of land becawse ther were but a fewe freemen amongst them And now ther beeing by the providence of God to the number of 22 freemen, and the Considering the differentes that might Arise aboute the thing before mentioned ; Therefore wee agree with the rest of the Inhabitantes of this Towne aboute the Divission of lands that ther Modell was good and Just wch was to the head of the famyly 15 Acres: to a Sonn 3 Acres: to a 100^l estate Twenty Acres, And therfore wee doe all Jointly togeather agree and order for the further establishing and Confirmeing of all the severall grants of land that every man shall enjoy his land as it is granted and Recorded."

This action not only confirmed all previous land grants, but it applied the same rule to the pending distribution. In the following December, an order was adopted concerning this division : —

"1. to lay it Convenient and as equall as it can bee not pine plaines. 2. Wood and Timber to be Common. 3. in three Divissions. 4. not to bee inclosed till it bee inclosed according to lawe and then to bee rated. The divission to bee According to p^rsons and estates."

Position and Names
of these Divisions.
It is not now possible to ascertain with accuracy the section of the town included within the "compasse of three miles," and divided under this vote, nor are the three divisions known with certainty. No record concerning them other than the votes already quoted, is believed to be in existence. In all probability they included what has since been known as the "Inner Commons" and "Little Division." They were probably situated west and south of the settled portion of the town. Beyond the "Inner Commons," joining them on the west, was "Long Division," divided many years afterwards, which extended from its northern to its southern boundary. The dividing line between these two divisions forming the western boundary of the "Inner Com-

mons," was about two and one-quarter miles from the meeting house. Starting from a point a trifle west of the present position of the Easthampton meeting house, the line extended northerly through "Seeger Swamp" to Mill River, touching it very near the dam of the Nonotuck Silk Mill, in Florence, thence it turned westerly and included "Broughton's Meadow." From the river above the meadow, the line continued in a north-easterly direction, running in a very irregular course till it joined the south boundary of the town of Hatfield, a short distance east of "Broad Brook." South of the Inner Commons, and extending to a point a little below Manhan River, were two divisions called "Lovefield" and "Hatefield." The south line of these sections extended from Easthampton meeting house, in a north-easterly direction to Mt. Tom, thence following the present south boundary of Northampton to the Connecticut River. The north line commenced at the upper end of Hurlburt's Pond, and extended westerly to the Rocky Hill road, which it followed till near Brush Hill, where it turned abruptly southwards, continuing in that course to the Easthampton meeting house. Whence the peculiar names of these two divisions were derived, and the reason of their application to this section, is not known. In a subsequent adjustment of common lands they were united under the name of "Little Division."

Three Irishmen and their Grants. Little sympathy was wasted by the pioneers of Northampton upon the Irish. Willing that natives of the Emerald Isle should become residents, lands were granted to them on conditions expressly prohibiting them from gaining citizenship thereby. Three grants of this character were made before the town had been ten years settled, each containing the prohibitory clause. The first was made to Cornelius Merry in the following language : —

"At a legall towne meting there was then granted to Cornellius the Irishman three akers of land vpon condition he build vpon it and make improuement of it within one yeer yet not so as to make him Capabele of acting in any town affairs no more than he had before it was granted to him."

Cornelius Merry was a servant of John Lyman, to whom he was indentured. He purchased a number of acres of land, and in 1663, married Rachel Ball. They had seven children, several of whom were prominent citizens of Northfield and Deerfield. When Northfield was first settled, he removed to that place, became one of its citizens and the owner of considerable land. "Merry's Meadow," in that town, was so named from him. He was actively engaged in King Philip's war, and participated in the "Fall's Fight."[1]

"Dauid Thro" was a countryman of Cornelius Merry, and he was granted three acres of land "vpon the same conditions that Cornelius the Irishman was." There is no record of Thro's land, but "David Frow" seems to have owned more or less property, and the two names probably refer to the same person. Frow's grant was on North Street, and he subsequently sold it to John Earl. He was an Irishman, an indentured servant in Northampton, and after his time was out, went to Springfield, where he married Priscilla, widow of William Hunter, in 1678.[2]

Matthew Clesson had three acres, which were "granted to him as the other Irishmen haue it granted theme not as a hom lote." Savage says that he was a servant in Northampton, and was probably indentured like the others. He was quite prosperous, and accumulated considerable property, owning at one time fifty-nine acres of land lying in twelve different parcels, all of which, with the exception of seven acres and sixty rôds, he purchased. His dwelling house was burned by the Indians in 1675, and the town made him other grants in compensation for his losses. He took the oath of allegiance in 1673. Rev. Solomon Stoddard, in 1684, bought the homestead which Clesson had of Thomas Lewis. Matthew Clesson seems to have been something of a man, though the town classed him with the "other Irishmen." He was twice married and had

---

1 In 1666, the court ordered "Cornelius Merry to be whipt 20 stripes for abusing the authority in this country and the English by seditious speeches." A portion of this penalty was remitted He had previously been fined 30s. by the court for a misdemeanor. He paid all but 10s. of the amount. His master, John Lyman, agreed to pay that sum, and 2s. costs, and the court ordered Merry to serve his master 12 days more after his term of apprenticeship had expired.

2 In 1665, David Frow (it was sometimes spelled Fro) was "presented at the court for contemning the constable's authority, commanding him into the meeting house in the time of God's ordinances last Sabbath." He was ordered to sit in the stocks during the court's pleasure.

a family of ten children, several of whom became prominent citizens of this and other towns in the valley.

These were not the only Irishmen in the place. Nearly all the first emigrants from Ireland, were children or young persons who came over for the express purpose of engaging as servants. Some made contracts for their services before embarking, accompanying their masters. Others of both sexes were "sold for their passage" money (these, however, did not all come from Ireland), that is, they agreed to serve some one who would pay their passage, long enough to settle the account. There were more Irishmen in town than those who have been named, but none of them received direct grants. In 1658, Joseph Parsons was given three acres of meadow land "for the estate hee had in his Irish man." His name has not been given, and no other reference to him has been found. Very slight allusion is made to Irishmen on the earlier town records, other than has been noticed, and it is very probable that their position in life had much to do with the estimation in which they were held. It is noticeable that the three acres granted to each of these men, was all the land that either of them, with the exception of Clesson, ever received from the town.

Compounding for the Price of Grain. Lieut. William Clarke was chosen to "treate with the Tresurer and compound with him about the price of the corne for our Countrey ratte this yeare." Whether by this vote was intended the County Treasurer or the Treasurer of the Colony is not stated. The "countery ratte" would cover both the county and the colony tax, though ordinarily used to designate the latter. The price fixed upon by the treasurer of the colony would establish the value of grain for all purposes. Once before the town had named the price of wheat, and that was for town rates in 1661, when "wheat was to go for 3ˢ 6ᵈ." Later, in 1663, the price of grain was decided upon:—"Wheate should be at thre shilings & sex pence pr bushell, and pease at thre shilings pr bushell and Indian Corne at toe shillings thre pʳ bushell tell they see cause to alter it."

Tavern Keeper Appointed Conditionally. On the 28th of June, 1663, Joseph Parsons was chosen to keep the Ordinary "tel the Towne can better feet them selfs with another that can doe it commendable and comfortable and then he haue promised to leaue it to the pleashuer of the Towne." All innholders' licenses were granted by the courts, and evidently in this instance the town merely designated the person it desired to have licensed. Mr. Parsons held a license for the two preceding years, and kept the tavern till 1665, when Henry Woodward was appointed.

Public Schools Established. During the first decade of its history, the children of the town of Northampton escaped the discipline of the town schoolmaster. It is not to be supposed that they were suffered to remain in ignorance of the alphabet, however much they may have suffered in making its acquaintance. Whatever knowledge they possessed was either obtained at home or at private schools, taught at the different houses. Public schools were first established in Northampton in 1664. The law of the Province provided

"yt ev'y towneship in this iurisdiction, aft' y⁰ Lord hath increased y^m to y⁰ number of 50 household^rs, shall then forthw^th appoint one wth in their towne to teach all such children as shall resort to him to write & reade, whose wages shall be paid eith' by y⁰ parents or mast'ʳˢ of such children, or by y⁰ inhabitants in gen'all, by way of supply, as y⁰ maior p^t of those y^t ord' y⁰ prudentials of y⁰ towne shall appoint; pvided, those y^t send their children be not oppresed by paying much more y^n they can have y^m taught for in oth' townes."[1]

In 1662, there were sixty-two male residents of Northampton to whom was apportioned the erection and maintenance of the common fence. All of them owned meadow land, and all were householders. In order, therefore, to comply with the provisions of the law, the town must now employ a school-master. Consequently on the "28-of the-(11) mo. 1663 (January 28, 1664), the Towne voted to giue Mr Cor-

[1] The law above quoted, while it allowed towns to make schools free, did not so direct. Free schools were many years under discussion before the towns generally adopted them. Opinions were divided, the poorer classes favored free schools, while the more wealthy, especially those without children to send, opposed them. Free schools did not become general till long after the commencement of the 18th century.—Judd's History of Hadley, p. 64.

nish sex pound towards the scoole & to tacke the benifet of the scollers proviuded that he teach Sex moneths in the yeare together." By this vote the town, in accordance with the custom prevailing elsewhere, decided to combine both methods, part of the tuition to be paid by the town and part by the parents.

James Cornish James Cornish, the first school-master in Northampton, lived at the corner of Main and Pleas-ant Streets, near the site of the present "Union Block," having purchased the lot of Alexander Edwards in 1660; coming to Northampton from Saybrook, Ct., about that time. When the town employed a school-master it also provided a school-house, the first meeting-house being used for that purpose, after the erection of the second one. The remuneration of the school-teacher was small, and the scanty six pounds, though supplemented by whatever the parents of the pupils paid, hardly sufficed for the support of the master and his family. Like most of the settlers, he was a farmer, and though he was required to teach school but six months in a year, it may be readily believed that he found it difficult to make "both ends meet." He was em-ployed in this capacity but a few years, for in 1667 another teacher was engaged. In a short time he removed to West-field, selling his home lot in 1699, to Ebenezer Strong. Mr. Cornish was without doubt a man of considerable ability and standing in the community, as the title of "Mr." which was then an honorable distinction, was prefixed to his name on the records. Whatever may have been his attainments, he had a habit of profanity, and sometimes indulged in what in those puritanical days, bordered on blasphemy, for which he was brought before the court and fined.[1] In 1687, he was appointed Clerk of the Courts under the administration of Sir Edmund Andros, and acted in that capacity for two years. Mr. Cornish peti-

1 Mr. Cornish was brought before the court in 1671 for taking God's name in vain in the summer of 1670. In town meeting at Westfield, in opposition to something Capt. Cooke had said, he answered "As God lives that which the Captain says is false." He owned the words before the court and labored to justify the expression. The court decided that such language was unfit to be used in ordinary matters, and fined him 10s. He was presented also for cursing, which was attested by George Sexton's two sons. The court ordered a fine of 20s., "highly resenting that such an aged man and of his quality and profession, should so dishonor God and give such evil example to youth and others."

tioned the county court, at its session in 1691, for remuneration for his services as clerk. He stated that "his clerkship under Sir Edmund Andros, subjected him to expenses in attending courts and other works of his office; for which he cannot as yet get due fees," and requested the court "to put him in some way to get his right." The court replied that the law was open for him, "he had liberty to sue." The towns, however, were ordered to pay what it was their duty to pay, the constables were to be inquired of as to the proper amount; and he was to be allowed what was right. Being represented as very needy, the court ordered that 20s. should be paid to him from the treasury, and "recommended to the towns to do something for him in charity." In 1695, he was living in Westfield, "being upwards of four score years old." He left two sons, James and Gabriel, and perhaps other children.

A Company of Cavalry Organized. The train band of Northampton was formed and officered in 1661. Three years afterwards a company of cavalry was organized. For the special "encouragement of raysing a troope of Horse in Hampshire," the General Court ordered, "that in regard they are but yett in their minority, for the present and vntill they can attajne to more, sixe and thirty horse shall be accounted a troope,"[1] and gave them liberty to choose all the necessary officers for such an organization. Accordingly the "Hampshire Troope" was formed in March, 166¾. At that time "Diverse persons of the soldiery from all the towns in Hampshire met at Northampton, and listed themselves into a Troope." The following officers were chosen and approved by the court:—John Pynchon, Springfield, Captain; Ensign David Wilton, Northampton, Lieutenant; Lieut. William Allis, Hadley, Cornet; Henry Woodward, Northampton, and George Colton, Springfield, Quartermasters. Lieut. David Wilton and Cornet William Allis died in 1678, and in October, Lieut. Philip Smith of Hadley, was appointed Lieutenant, and Joseph Parsons Sr. of Northampton, Cornet.

---

1 "A troop of horsemen was not to exceed 70 soldiers. Each trooper was to have a good horse, saddle, bridle, holsters, pistol or carbine, and a sword. A troop had a Captain, Lieutenant, Cornet, Quartermaster, Clerk, Trumpeter, and Corporals. Each trooper was obliged to keep a good horse at all times, and was allowed by the colony, 5s. a year."—Judd's History of Hadley, p. 225.

CHAPTER XII.

POPULATION—TAXATION—REPRESENTATION.

A Substantial and Satisfactory Increase in Wealth and Population. FROM its fifth to its tenth year, the growth of the town was rapid and substantial. During that length of time the population had more than doubled. With increase in numbers came added wealth, and both made possible all the benefits of an expanded social, religious and intellectual life, upon which were speedily to be grafted those political and economic burdens, common to every struggling plantation. The town was no longer a mere trading post. Its people had established themselves permanently, and the settlement was fast taking rank with the older and more populous communities. It had arrived at the dignity of representation, and could no longer ignore its political responsibilities. But few of the inhabitants, however, had yet become freemen. Among the seventy-eight heads of families composing the population in 1663, the names of but thirty are to be found on the church record, and but twenty-two, according to the vote in that year for dividing the commons, were freemen, who alone were entitled to exercise the right of franchise. Within a year, however, several others took the oath, and in 1664, the number had considerably increased.

Names of Settlers from 1654 to 1695, and other Statistics. The annexed list contains as far as can be ascertained, the names of all the settlers who came to Northampton previous to 1695. The date of their admission as freemen and the special trade or calling of each, when known, are also given, as well as the number of acres in meadow land and in home lots, awarded to each before 1660. Up to this date all persons sixteen years of age could be made freemen, but were not entitled to vote for magistrates. The law was changed in 1664, when the church membership qualification was repealed, and none under twenty-four years of age could take the oath of allegiance. This list contains the names of one hundred and twenty-two persons, and among them can be found but forty-eight who appear upon the record of the court as having taken the freeman's oath before 1666. Previous to 1690, most of them during the preceding eight years, more than fifty of the sons of those who arrived before 1663, became heads of families, to many of whom the town gave lands. Their names are not included in the following table. The location of the home lots of nearly all the settlers, whose grants of meadow land are named below, can be found upon the map accompanying this volume:—

SETTLERS FROM 1653 TO 1658.

	Occupation.	Freemen.	Home Lot.	Meadow Land.
Robert Bartlett		1663	4	57
Samuel Bartlett		1661		
son of Robert				
Edward Elmore[1]				72
William Holton[1]		1662		86
Richard Lyman		1662	3	81
Robert Lyman		1684	4	32
John Lyman	Shoemaker	1664	2	53
George Langton		1663	2	38
James Bridgman	Carpenter	1648	3¾	38
Thomas Bascom	Mason	1661	4	32
John Broughton			4	27
Joseph Fitch			4	60
Thomas Mason		1670	4	37
John Hannum		1680	4	15
Henry Curtis			4	34
William Hulburt			4	43
John Ingersol		1664	4	23
Thomas Salmon			4	22
Nathaniel Phelps		1663	4	29
Joseph Janes			2	8
John Stebbins			4	34
Edward Baker			4	22
Arthur Williams		1662	4	20

1 Number of acres in home lot not given.

1 0

	Occupation.	Freemen.	Home Lot.	Meadow Land.
Christopher Smith	. . .		4	17
Robert Hayward	Mill-wright	.	2	20
Alexander Alvord	. . .	1684		
Thomas Roote Sr.	. . . .	1661	2	51
Thomas Roote Jr.	. . .	1661		
William Jeanes	Teacher .	.	1662	2	34
Alexander Edwards	. . .	1664	2	72
John Webb	Brazier .	.	1661	2	37
Samuel Wright Sr.	. . .	1647	4	54
Samuel Wright Jr.	. . . .	1673	2	38
Judah Wright	. . . .	1661	4	
son Samuel Sr.				
William Miller	Tanner .	.		4	45
James Wright	. . . .	1661	4	
son Samuel Sr.				
David Burt	. . . .	1680	4	29
John King	Tanner	.	1664	4	26
Walter Lee	. . . .		4	19
Thomas Woodford	. . .		4	33
Isaac Sheldon .	. . . .	1663	4	31
Samuel Allen	. . . .	1683	4	26
Joseph Root .	. . . .	1684	2	10
Joseph Parsons	. . . .		4	81
John Bliss	. . . .		4	21
George Alexander	. . .	1663	4	.32½
William Hannum	. . . .		4	25
Rev. Eleazar Mather	. . .		4	41

FROM 1659 TO 1660.

	Occupation.	Freemen.	Home Lot.	Meadow Land.
William Clarke[1] .	. . .		12	86
Henry Woodward[1]	. . . .		12	46
Henry Cunliffe	. . . .	1644	8	20
Joshua Carter	. . . .	1661	3½	10
Thomas Hanchet .	. . .	1661	2	
Enos Kingsley	. . . .	1687	8	18
George Sumner	. . . .		8	8
Ralph Hutchinson	Carpenter	.	1661	8	8
John Sackett	. . . .		3	6
Aaron Cook	. . . .	1635	4	89
David Wilton	Indian Trader	1633	4	96
John Strong	Tanner .	.	1636	4	96
Medad Pomeroy	Blacksmith .	1663	4	32
Jonathan Hunt	Cooper .	.	1661	4	32
William Smead	. . . .	1680	8	6
Joseph Baker .	. . . .	1661	4	
Eldad Pomeroy				

1   Freemen when they came to Northampton.

FROM 1661 TO 1662.

Name	Occupation	Freemen	H'm Lot	Name	Occupation	Freemen	H'm Lot
Joseph Dickinson				Richard Weller		1663	4
Richard Fellows		1661		Praisever Turner	Miller	1664	
Zachariah Field		1661	4	Joseph Leeds		1663	4
John Taylor		1683	4	Josiah Dewey		1666	5
John Searl		1664	4	Increase Turner		1663	
John Earle				James Cornish	Teacher	1664	4
Thomas Lewis			4	John Allen		1663	4
Thomas Copley		1661					

FROM 1662 TO 1663.

Name	Occupation	Freemen	H'm Lot	Name	Occupation	Freemen	H'm Lot
Matthew Cole	Trader	1664		Thomas Dewey		1664	8

FROM 1663 TO 1664.

Name	Occupation	Freemen	H'm Lot	Name	Occupation	Freemen	H'm Lot
Nehem. Allen	Carpenter	1667	4	Geo. Fyler	Chirurgeon	1669	6
Samuel Marshall				Matthew Clesson		1673	13
Samuel Smith		1670	4	Cornelius Merry		1664	3
Rev. Joseph Eliot				John Marsh			3
David Frow		1664	3				

FROM 1666 TO 1669.

Name	Occupation	Freemen	H'm Lot	Name	Occupation	Freemen	H'm Lot
Israel Rust			4	Micah Mudge		1671	
Caleb Pomeroy		1663	6	Thomas Webster			
William Pixley		1674		John Hillior		1671	
Preserved Clapp		1671	4				

FROM 1670 TO 1674.

Name	Occupation	Freemen	H'm Lot	Name	Occupation	Freemen	H'm Lot
Rev. Solomon Stoddard		1673	4	Joshua Pomeroy			6
Timothy Baker		1671		Joseph Barnard			
Samuel Davis		1671		Robert Danks			
John Field				Joseph Hawley		1680	4

FROM 1677 TO 1680.

Name	Occupation	Freemen	H'm Lot	Name	Occupation	Freemen	H'm Lot
Samuel Judd		1684		James North			
Thomas Judd				Peter Bushrod			
Godfrey Nims	Cordwainer			William Wait			
Robert Price				William Wait Jr.			

FROM 1682 TO 1695.

Name	Occupation	Freemen	H'm Lot	Name	Occupation	Freemen	H'm Lot
Samuel Porter				Mark Warner			
Robert Porter				Nathaniel Dwight			
William Southwell				John Coombs			
John French				Benjamin Carpenter			

"The Oath of Aleagence wch By or^der from Our Honored Gen^11 Co^rte was to be taken respectively in Each Town of this Countie and was administered by ye Worshipful Majo^r Pynchon to ye severall Inhabitants & Persons within ye Townshipp of Northampton being convened together on ffeb^r 8 1678." The names of 124 persons are recorded as having taken the oath at that time. This was in accordance with an order by the King requiring the oath to be administered to all persons of suitable age within the colony. This oath did not confer the privilege of freemen, and was taken by every one.

Increase of Taxation, February, 1664. As the town increased in population and expanded its institutions, it naturally augmented its expenses. A new house of worship had been erected, an assistant in the ministry employed, the school had been established, and many other needed improvements adopted. To meet all these demands it became necessary largely to increase the taxes. On *the first of the last month in the old year (Feb. 166¾), the selectmen levied a rate for £288.12.8, for the following purposes :—

> "1 (12) 1663. The selectmen made a rate for the new meettinge houese and comted it to the constable—
> Some is 115.08.09
> A rate for Mr Mather 70.09.02
> A rate for Mr Eliote the Sume   .   .   .   50.00.00
> A Ratte for the Towne charges the Sume   .   19.15.11
> A Ratte for the countrie Sume is   .   .   .   32.18.10."

Very little Cash in Circulation. This was undoubtedly a large sum for so small a community to raise. It was not, however, paid in money. Had that been required the people would have been in straightened circumstances indeed. In those days very little money—gold and silver being the medium—was in circulation. While wheat was the prime factor, corn had also been made a legal tender for all debts, the price being fixed every year. Beef, pork, and furs, were also used in the system of exchange, and a community farming the rich lands of the Connecticut Valley meadows, had little trouble in meeting these demands. The salaries of the ministers were paid in produce, the price of which generally varied considerably from its money value. Debts and taxes were paid in the same manner, contracts in money were rare, and cash prices were seldom mentioned.[1]

Representation.
William Clarke
the first Dep'ty.

Northampton was not represented in the General Court till nine years after its organization. It contained the requisite number of freemen several years before that, but seems to have been in no haste to assert its claim in that respect. The town had been settled but three years when William Holton was sent as its agent to present certain matters to the Legislature, but he was not entitled to a seat in that body. William Clarke was the first Deputy ever chosen from Northampton, and he appeared as a member of the court at the May session in 1663. The law of 1653, provided that towns having "not more than thirty freemen shall henceforth be at libertje for sending or not sending deputjes to the Generall Court." All the expenses of the representatives were to be paid by the towns, and they were permitted to send one or two, as they might decide.

Position of Affairs
in the Colony.

The political situation in the colony at this time was somewhat critical. Under Cromwell, New England had been permitted to govern itself. He was too much occupied at home to give attention to the settlements across the sea. The most significant recognition of the colony on the part of Oliver Cromwell was an invitation to the Puritans to leave the home of their adoption and settle in Ireland, and after that proposition had been declined he urged them to re-

1 "Thus did this handfull of people, the tenth year after their establishment in this wilderness, pay one hundred and twenty pounds sterling for the ministry of the Gospel during one year, a greater salary than their descendants have probably ever paid, till within the last ten years, even nominally ; and worth in reality about three times as much as the greatest which they have ever paid. Yet three of the inhabitants could now pay the whole sum with less inconvenience, than the whole town at that time. Few specimens of liberality and attachment to religion can be found in the world of a more honorable nature. It is to be remembered that these people were under no extraneous influence Everything was spontaneously done by every man."—Dwight's Travels, ed. 1821, vol. 1, pp. 345, 346.

Commenting upon the above paragraph, in the History of Hadley, page 54, Mr. Judd observes :—" Northampton gave Rev. Eleazar Mather a Salary of £80 in 1658, and Prest. Dwight, who had not examined the old currency of New England, represented this as 80 pounds sterling. This is a mistake. It was paid in grain, and the value was not more than £60 in Massachusetts pine tree money. There never was a sterling currency in these towns."

move to the Island of Jamaica. Richard Cromwell was
never proclaimed Protector here, and never interfered in
the government. Charles II. had been upon the throne
more than a year before he was publicly recognized
in the colony. News of his accession was received in Boston, in July, 1660. It came on the same ship that brought
over the two regicides, who spent so many years of their
lives hidden in the neighboring town of Hadley. No public notice was taken of the event by the authorities; a
proposition to send an address to the King having been
voted down at the October session of the General Court.
It was deemed advisable, however, a few months later,
after having received a certified copy of the proceedings of
Parliament, to memorialize the new government, and in
December, addresses to the King and Parliament were prepared and forwarded. These were graciously received, and
a reply, accompanied by a mandate for the arrest of Goffe
and Whaley, was transmitted. Search was made for the
regicides, but they had escaped to Connecticut and did not
come to Hadley till the next year. A committee for the
settlement of the government of New England was appointed in 1661. Through the representations of this committee, founded upon surmise, Massachusetts was accused
of a design to cast off her allegiance, effect an alliance with
Spain or adopt some other equally desperate remedy, rather
than admit of appeals from her authority. Upon this
point a controversy arose, and the royal government, re-
solving to establish the principle which the Long Parliament had waived, insisted upon subjecting the colony to
the Navigation Act.[1]

Declaration of   Though the colonists rejoiced in the appar-
Rights Published. ent good will of the King, and observed a
June, 1661.   day of Thanksgiving in recognition thereof,
they were well aware of the uncertain condition of affairs.
A declaration of natural and chartered rights, prepared by
a special committee, and adopted at a special session, was

---

1 The importation of merchandise into any English Colony, except in English vessels, manned with English crews, was forbidden. All foreign commerce must be conducted with England alone   Certain specified articles only could be exported, and
to no other than English ports.—Palfrey's History of New England, vol. 2, p. 444.

published by the General Court in June, 1661. The position of the colony and the views of its leaders were set forth in this document with all the fearlessness of patriotic determination. In it they declare that their liberties under God and their patent are "to choose their own governor, deputy-governor, and representatives; to admit freemen on terms to be prescribed at their own pleasure; to set up all sorts of officers, superior and inferior, and point out their power and places; to exercise by their annually-elected magistrates and deputies, all power and authority, legislative, executive and judicial; to defend themselves by force of arms against every aggression; and reject as an infringement of their right any parliamentary or royal imposition, prejudicial to the country, and contrary to any just act of colonial legislation." The duties of allegiance were narrowed to a few points, which conferred neither profit nor substantial power on the mother country or its sovereign.[1]

The King Proclaimed. Commission sent to England. The King's Letter in Reply. February to October, 1662.

It was not till two months after the promulgation of this manifesto, that the restoration of King Charles was acknowledged by public proclamation. The formalities of the occasion were meager, and the whole affair heartless and devoid of enthusiasm. The enemies of the colony in England were active and influential, and orders were received from the crown in the autumn for the appointment of a commission to be sent over to meet their accusations. Rev. John Norton and Simon Bradstreet were appointed, and after much delay finally departed on their mission. Received with courtesy and treated with respect, the messengers were permitted to return in a few months, with a letter from the King. This missive was perhaps less unacceptable than had been feared, but still it was not altogether satisfactory. The charter was confirmed conditionally, and a general amnesty for all past political offences except treason, was granted. The King demanded the revision of the laws of the colony. The rights of citizenship were to be conceded to peaceable Episcopalians; all persons of honest life, Quakers excepted, were to be admitted to the Lord's Supper,

1 Bancroft's History of the United States, vol. 2, pp. 73, 74.

and their children to baptism; every one was to take the oath of allegiance; the administration of justice was to be in the King's name, and the elective franchise was to be extended to all who were possessed of sufficient estate.[1]

The King's Letter, so long under Di (i ss n that English Commissioners were sent to adjust matters, April, 1663.

"His Majesties gracious letter," came before the General Court at its session in October. It was immediately voted that all process of law should be made in the King's name, and all further action upon the document was postponed till the next session of the court, the letter in the meantime having been published. In the following May that document was referred to a special committee, who were to report when the Legislature next assembled, but no report was ever made. The requirements concerning the qualifications of freemen and voters, were considered at the midsummer session in 1664, and the Church Membership qualification was repealed, but voters must own property of a certain amount, be of orthodox religion, and twenty-four years of age. Upon the other propositions of the document, the deliberations were so long continued, with so little prospect of a decision favorable to the demands of the crown, that all sorts of rumors, true as well as false, were reported at the English Court. At length the patience of the King became exhausted, and four commissioners were sent over to adjust matters.

The Charter Protected. Orders Concerning the Commissioners. A Day of Fasting and Prayer Appointed, Sept 1664.

Aware of the dangers that threatened, the General Court took such measures to avert them as prudence demanded. The charter was placed in the hands of a trustworthy committee for preservation. Due courtesy was to be shown to the commissioners, but no armed force from the war ships which conveyed them was to be allowed to land.[2] Then followed proceedings characteristic of the age. A day of fasting, humiliation and prayer was appointed, to be held on the first of Sep-

1 Barry's History of Massachusetts, vol. 1, p. 383.

2 Four vessels of war, conveying 450 soldiers, destined, with additional forces from New England, to proceed against the Dutch at Manhattan, brought the Commissioners. Massachusetts voted to provide her contingent of soldiers, but they were not needed.

tember. Indeed so momentous were the concerns of the colony, that during the year three such days of religious self-abasement were considered necessary, viz. : in June, September and November. No more efficient method of reaching every inhabitant of the colony could have been devised. There was no release from attendance upon this ceremonial. The law enjoined the presence of every able bodied citizen upon every religious observance, and before the close of the services on the designated day, the state of affairs between the Commonwealth and the mother country was made familiar to every one within the jurisdiction of the colony of Massachusetts Bay.

Another Address to the King, October, 1664. Fearful lest their charter privileges might be abridged, and unwilling to concede all that the King demanded, the colonists were disposed to temporize, yielding, or seeming to yield in non-essentials, yet holding tenaciously all they deemed of importance. In this crisis clear heads and adroit statesmanship were needed. Determined to nullify as far as possible the action of the commissioners and yet avoid an open rupture with the King, an address was prepared. Though couched in respectful language and reciting the privileges already granted, the hardships endured, the poverty of the people, and their loyalty to the king, the real meaning of the document was the recall or the revocation of the commission. More in hope of wearying the English government by prolonging the correspondence, "which might be continued till a new revolution" occurred, than with any expectation of changing its course, the colonists not only forwarded their address, but sent letters to prominent and influential noblemen, known to be friendly to the colony. Neither were received with favor, and the position of affairs was still critical and uncertain.

The Commissioners Baffled at every point Abandon the Struggle, 1665. Having concluded affairs with the Dutch, three of the commissioners returned to Boston, early in the year 1665. Their demand that the entire male population of the colony should be assembled at Boston on the next election day, to hear the message of the King, was rejected, and for sev-

eral weeks a spirited correspondence was carried on between
the General Court and the commissioners. The latter,
wearied with the discussion in which they gained no advantage, at length determined to assert their authority.
They decided to hold a court, "in which the colony was
cited to appear as defendant." The General Court forbade any such proceeding. When the commissioners
opened their court, a herald appeared, and having sounded
a trumpet, made proclamation in the name of the King,
and by authority of the charter, formally forbidding any
to abet the commissioners. This proclamation was made
in several places. Satisfied of the futility of further contention, the commissioners abandoned the struggle, after
an ineffectual attempt to influence New Hampshire and
Maine.

Massachusetts De-   King Charles, having sent letters of reproof,
fies the King.   decided to transfer the scene of negotia-
Sept., 1666.   tions, and ordered the colony to send agents
to England. The General Court, in September, after due
deliberation, preceded by lengthened religious services, refused to accede to this demand. No damaging results followed this defiance. England, engrossed by the calamities
of the time, and burdened by the profligacy of its rulers,
made no further immediate attempts to interfere with the
affairs of the Puritans of Massachusetts.

William Clarke,   Such in brief was the condition of the col-
first Deputy,   ony politically, during the years in which
Chosen in 1663.   Northampton was first represented in the
legislative councils of the Commonwealth. Little has
been developed indicating the sentiment of this small
community concerning these grave questions, but at the
same time no lengthy dissertation is needed to show how
the patriots of Northampton viewed them. Well aware of
the vital importance of the controversy then just entered
upon with the restored monarchy of Great Britain, they
made choice of their most trusted and worthy citizen, William Clarke, to fill this prominent position. When he was
elected in 1663, affairs had not reached their crisis. At
that time the King's letter was under advisement, and the

determination had been reached to preserve the charter at all hazards. The town records are silent concerning this first election of deputy to the General Court, as well as of most of the others in its early history, and it is only through the archives of the colony that any data in reference to Northampton's representatives are to be obtained. Whatever may have been his previous opinions, it may be believed that Clarke returned from the session imbued with the prevailing spirit of resistance to the unacceptable demands of the King.

Two Deputies Chosen in 1664. Hadley Men Recorded as Serving for Northampton. At the next session of the General Court, Northampton is recorded as having two representatives. Three sessions of the court were held in 1664, one in May, one in August, and still another in October. At the first session in that year the names of Lieut. Samuel Smith and Mr. William Lewis are given in the colony records, as the representatives from Northampton, while none are named as being present from Hadley. Both of these men were residents of Hadley, and had represented that town the previous year. At the August session, William Holton and Lieut. William Clarke are named in the archives as the deputies from Northampton, while Samuel Smith and John White represented Hadley. It is not probable that Northampton made choice of Hadley men as representatives for one session, and afterwards elected two of its own citizens for another the same year, when the law provided that deputies were to serve one year. In the absence of all local records bearing upon the case, it may be surmised that this town was not represented at the May session of the Legislature in 1664, but through some error the deputies from Hadley were assigned to Northampton.

Deputies hear from their Constituencies. Others Chosen in 1665. Warned by Parson Mather on the Fast day in September, of the dangers threatening the colony, the people of Northampton were ready to sanction whatever measures the General Court should see fit to adopt. Their representatives thus fortified and strengthened, undoubtedly returned at the October session, prepared to approve the address to the King, and agree to any other course of action deemed essential to the preservation of the liberties of the Commonwealth. The next year, David Wilton and William Holton were chosen deputies, and from that time onward Northampton has been duly represented in the Legislature.

Northampton forwards an Address or Petition to the Legislature the next year. When Wilton and Holton appeared at the May session, in 1665, they carried with them a document[1] showing the spirit as well as the sentiments of their constituents, and their desire to uphold and maintain the "ancient rights, liberties and privileges" of the colony. It was carefully prepared, and contains the signatures of eighty-six of the inhabitants of Northampton, comprising nearly every male person in the place, above twenty-one years of age. In it was set forth the settled determination of the people to resist every encroachment upon their rights, accompanied by an earnest plea that the Court would resolutely maintain all the advantages that had been thus far gained. It is in the handwriting of James Cornish, and is appended in full : —

"Northampton, April 19, 1665.

"To the honorable and much honored Generall Court assembled at Boston, 3ᵈ May, 1665 :

"The humble petition of the Inhabitants of Northampton, most humbly sheweth, that being not insensible of the sad frowns of God upon us, and threatenings towards vs, manifested both by signs from heaven & earth of his displeasure, hauing forsaken our first love, & forgotten to do our first works which wee came into this land to do ; the Lord having made it of a wilderness a fruitful field to us ; wherein wee haue enjoyed much of the presence of God, affording vs his own ordinances both civil & ecclesiastical in his own way & according to his own institution & that for so long a time ; and now fearing the subversion thereof, wee, owning you the fathers of our countrey, under whose shadow wee look for protection under God. Our humble request is that you would vouchsafe seriously to weigh and consider the case & state of our countrey, churches, plantations, familyes & persons & also the end wherfore wee & our predecessors haue adventured our liues familyes & estates to purchase ; Is it not a quiet & peaceable enjoyment of God in his ordinances & the advancement of the King-

---

1 Petitions and addresses showing the prevailing sentiments of the people, were from time to time forwarded to the General Court from various towns in the colony. Hadley sent a lengthy address, dated April 25, 1665, and others were also presented from different sections of the Commonwealth.

dome of Jesus Christ without humane traditions or molestacon. Wherfore our most humble request and petition to this hono^{r}ed Court is that you would bee pleased to Stand for confirme & maintayne our former & ancient rights, libertyes & previleges, both in Church & Common wealth (wch God himselfe hath bestowed & Christ hath purchased for vs) without any variation or altering from his most holy, strict rule in his word. This most humbly crauing you to grant o^r humble request wee heartily desire the father of all mercyes & giuer of all counsell to guide & counsell you to doe what is according to his good will & pleasure and humbly take leaue to leaue to his guidance & to remayne praying for yor peace & prosperity.

yor most humble petitioners

ELEAZAR MATHER,
AARON COOKE,
WILLIAM CLARKE,"
and 83 others.

The effect of these petitions upon the General Court, presenting in forcible language the opinions of the people, could not be otherwise than .beneficial, upholding and strengthening the position already taken by that body. There was no question about the disposition of the colonists. They were ready to maintain with courage and firmness the principles so conscientiously set forth in these documents. While manifesting in many ways that their loyalty to the King was not mere lip service, they asked to be allowed to retain the already established form of government, without encroachment or material change.

CHAPTER XIII.

SPECIAL MUNICIPAL REGULATIONS.

Minute Regulations for the Government of the Township. ONE noticeable peculiarity of these early times was the minuteness of the ordinances for the general and individual management of the community. Emigrating to New England for the establishment of permanent homes, the settlers bent all their energies to solve the problem of existence in the most rational and economical manner. The plan upon which their form of town government was founded seems to have been a survival in part of the communal system of the old world. Indeed they had no other formula upon which to base their practice. It was not to strike out new paths in administration or politics, or social economics, that they crossed the ocean, but to enjoy freedom of conscience, and lead honest, sober, and christian lives. They had no quarrel with the old methods of subsistence or the old ways of managing neighborhood affairs. But they adapted the methods with which they were familiar, to the changed circumstances of their environment. The allotments of land to each settler, the territory held in common, the use of the meadow and its fencing, each had its prototype in the English village.[1]

1 "The wood land and pasture land of an English village were still undivided, and every free villager had the right of turning into it his cattle or swine. The meadow land lay in like manner open and undivided from hay-harvest to spring. It was only when grass began to grow afresh that the common meadow was fenced off into grass fields, one for each householder in the village; and when hay-harvest was over, fence and division were at an end again. The plow-land alone was permanently alloted in equal shares both of corn-land and fallow-land, to the families of the freemen, though even the plow-land was subject to fresh division as the number of claimants grew greater or less. * * * The life, the sovereignty of the settlement resided solely in the body of the freemen whose holdings lay round the moot-hill or the sacred tree where the community met from time to time to deal out its own justice and to make its own laws. Here new settlers were admitted to the freedom of the township and by-laws framed and headmen and tithingmen chosen for its government."—Green's History of the English People, vol. 1, chap. 1, pp. 10-13.

By-laws for Regu-
lating the Mead-
ows, the Com-
mons, and the
Highways.

Orders and by-laws enacted for the protection of the Commons, the Meadows, and
the Highways, everywhere abound in the
annals of the town. One of the earliest recorded municipal votes was for the regulation of the
meadow in relation to pasturage, or the trespassing of
stock thereon, but previous to this there must have been
an order for fencing them. In the commons each inhabitant held an undivided proprietary right. That each
should profit by that privilege without infringement upon
the liberties of others was the end and aim of all these
provisions. While the personal belongings of each settler
were strictly defined, and rigidly insisted upon, there was
also much in common that required special attention.

The Rights of all
Guarded and
Protected.

The regulations and by-laws which follow
were the most minute and particular of
any yet adopted by the town. They well
exhibit the prevailing spirit of the body politic, in
which every man's property was protected from the encroachments of every other person, and the good order and
prosperity of the community secured. The paternal hand
of the government in jealously guarding and curtailing the
selfish propensities of the individual in order that they
might conserve and benefit the interests of all, is everywhere visible in all the enactments of the first settlements
of New England.

Order Relating to
Timber cut upon
the Commons.

An order was adopted in 1661, but not recorded for a couple of years, concerning the
length of time timber should be permitted
to lie upon the commons after being cut. Three months
was the limit fixed, upon penalty of forfeiture. "But in
case hee twart cutt it it may [lie] three moneths longer, but
if it bee not taken away att the 3 monethes end then it
shalbee forfeit, vnless it bee hewen and cloven upp, then it
shall not be forfeite." People were also prohibited from
getting "any candlewood to burne it to Cole or for Tarr
within the Compass of six miles of the Towne on the penalty of Tenn shillings a load." Thirty-eight years after

no candlewood was allowed to "be got within seauen [miles] from yᵉ meting house."¹ The punishment in this case was the forfeiture of the product.

Ample Protection for the Meadows.   In 1662, the town adopted a series of orders relating to the meadows, but not till 1664, was the clerk, William Jeanes, ordered to transcribe them upon the "Towne booke." The first had reference to the driving of cattle or swine through the corn fields in Manhan, "wher ther is noe common drift way." They must either be "yoakt or led in a Coard from the time of the first of May till the Indian corne be gathered on the Penalty of twelue pence yᵉ head to bee to the informer." The second provided for repairing the fence and gates of the common field. Fences were to be "suffitiently made vpp and repayred on or before" the 30ᵗʰ of March, "upon the penalty of 2ˢ 6ᵈ per rod for every defect;" and the gates were to be repaired before the middle of March, upon a penalty of "five shillings a gate." A third order prohibited indiscriminate mowing in the highways in the "common Corne feelds and Meddowes," by those who had no land bordering on them. Those whose lands were separated by the roads had liberty to mow all the land in them. Where different parties owned on opposite sides, each was entitled to mow one-half of the highway. For disobeying this order the penalty was the forfeiture of the grass or hay or the value of it, to the person owning on the other side of the way. The fourth by-law forbade persons while at work in the meadow, or at any other time, permitting their "cattle to trespasse by eateing other men's grasse," without the consent of the owners of the land. Whoever trespassed in this manner should "forfeit to the pty Damnified two shillings for every time for every beast." Section fifth related to the driving of "Cattle with ther Cartes or suffering them to trespasse on other mens Corne and Meddowe," the trespasser to forfeit two shillings to the party injured for every such unlawful act. A sixth pro-

---

1 Resinous pine, split into convenient size, called "candle wood," and pine knots were used for candles and for kindling fires. This candle wood was so named from the fact of its use for lighting the way about the house at night. Farmers were accustomed to gather every fall a quantity of pine knots and hearts of pine trees. They would almost as willingly commence the winter without hay as without a good supply of candlewood.—Judd's History of Hadley, pp. 302, 303.

vision was that all swine taken in the "meddow or in the Corne feilds after the middle of february that are not well and substantially runge," should be liable to a fine of "twelue pence a hogg," viz. :—10d. to him that should impound them and "two pence for the pounding;" and all "hoggs" taken in the meadow after the middle of April, were "lyable" to the same fine whether "they be runge or yoaked." Any swine found in any enclosure other than their owner's, were subject to a similar fine. The seventh order had reference to clearing the meadows of stock of all kinds previous to the 10th of March, and "from that time soe long as corne be on the Ground," the penalty being the same as in the preceding order.

Bailiffs Chosen.   On the 28th of January, 1664, "John Stebben and Enos Kingslo were chosen Bayleus for the Towne to cleare the meadows of all Cattle & Swine that are trespasers and Impound them that we may preserf our corne & grass." The town voted to place the above regulations on the records, the month following the election of Bailiffs, in order undoubtedly, that they might know their duties. These officers were also called "Meadow Bailiffs," "Howards," and "Haywards," but never before were they named on the records, though the laws they were chosen especially to enforce, were enacted nearly two years before.

Illegal Voting for   At a town meeting held "the 6th of the 11th
Selectmen.   mo. 1663, (January 6, 1664), David Wilton, William Clarke, Decon Holton, Joseph Parsons, Robert Bartlet," were chosen selectmen. So much illegal voting was perpetrated at this election, that an appeal was made to the County Court "in a paper Subscribed by diverse persons & presented to this corte as a breach of the Law of the Common Wealth;" the jury presenting the matter as an "illegal choyce of Select Men." The court decided that there was not "sufficient reason for this presentment, and that the Select Men are not invested in their places contrary to law. And therefore doe advise & desire the said Select Men to act in their places to which

11

they were chosen." Some half-a-dozen men were indicted
for illegal voting at the same session of the court. They
confessed their error and were fined. Wherein consisted
the irregularity is not stated, though there is reason to believe that two of them were not of legal age to vote.

Strict Orders Con-   The selectmen were required by law to ex-
cerning Fences.   ercise rigid supervision over all fences, be-
                     ing subject to a fine of £5 for non-compli-
ance. In 1664 and 1665, the town passed stringent by-laws
in reference to making and maintaining fences :—

They were to "bee fowre foote and halfe high and soe thicke and
stronge as that they keepe out Orderly Cattle." The fence viewers
were instructed to examine the fences at least once a month from
March to September, "or as oft as the Townes men shall desire," upon
a penalty of 5s. for every neglect. They were to "bring in a list of
every mans defect to the Townes men: only they are first to aquant
the owners prsently and set them a time to repaire it and then to see if
it bee don at the time, if not to take witnesses with them prooue the
defect of ye fence or fences, and then presently repaire the fence or
fences, and bring the defects soe prooued to the select men, and they
shalbe paid dubble for all ther labor, care, cost and trouble, about it
according to law." If the fence viewers neglected their duties they
were liable to a fine of two shillings and six pence per man. A vote in
1683, provided that the "penalty for the least defect in the fence shall
be twelve pence," and the same amount per rod for every defective rod.
In March, 1665, the town voted "that the greate River is accounted
Judged and determined to bee a fence."

Streets to be Kept   Another by-law was provided in June for
Clear and no   keeping the streets clear of all incum-
Horse Racing
Permitted.   brances detrimental to their use. The high-
                     ways as originally laid out, were of sufficient
width to allow of considerable private occupation, and
still leave plenty of space for ordinary passage. This order
provided that

"the highway goeing into the Meddow from Mr Mathers howse till
wee bee come past Robert Bartletts howse (Pleasant street) bee cleared
of wood and timber and Cartes and all lumber that ther may bee a
Cleare passage for man and beast on the penalty of Ten shillings forfeite to the Towne by those psons that shall soe incumber the highway."

Soon afterwards the rule was applied to all the streets
in town. Another provision, especially in the line of good
morals, was adopted at the same meeting :—

"Likewise it was ordered and voted that if any shall runn rases with ther horses or mares in any streete in this Towne shall for every such offence pay 2ˢ 6ᵈ the one halfe to yᵉ Towne & the other halfe to the informer."

Sunday Feeding of Cattle in the Meadows Prohibited, March 6, 166⅝. In a community where the constable had power to compel attendance upon Sunday services, it would hardly seem necessary to enact a special law prohibiting the feeding of cattle in the meadows on the Sabbath. Yet it was found necessary to pass the following ordinance : —

"Wheareas theare hath bine found by experience that many take libertie toe keepe theare Cattle with in the corne-feilds in the meadow on the lords Day : and much Damadge is don thearby besids the profanation of the Sabath by yonge peple toe gether : for the prevention wherof we the Selectmen doe order that noe person shall keepe any sort of cattle within the aforesaid feild or meadow on the Lord's Day on the penaltie of toe Shillings sex pence pʳ head a tyme to him that shall fiend take or complaine of any transgression in this kinde. Nor shall any pʳson hopple any hors or mare within the sayd feild toe leaue them all night on the penaltie of fiue Shillings a pese" to the informer.

First County Roads in Hampshire. The Line on both sides of the river. The first order of the County Court concerning highways in this section of Hampshire County, was made in 1664. Complaints of defective roads coming before the court, a committee of five persons was ordered to lay out and survey a highway on both sides of the river between Hadley and Windsor. In May this committee made their report, which is entered in full upon the town records. The highway began at "Hadley Townes end on the east side of the great river," extending southwards "to the end of Mount Holyoke," and thence to "Seanunganunck" (Chicopee) and Springfield, thence to Longmeadow, and on through "Namrick," to the "divideing line betweene the collonyes." On the west side of the river beginning at the said dividing line, the other road was to extend northwards to "Waronoack ;" from Waronoack hill "wher the Tradeing howse stoode" to the passage of the river, thence "thorow the other meddowe to the greate hill," to Manhan river, and in Northampton it was to lie "along the common fence side vnto the great river." The ferry was to be appointed by the

next County Court, and each town was to make its own
landing place. The town of Hadley was to make and maintain the highway and bridges from that town to Seanunganunck; Springfield to do the same from the latter place
to the foot of the falls; and in case it "appeares to be our
Collonyes right over Namerick brook" that part of the way
was to be made and cared for by the County. The ways
and bridges from the landing place at the great river, to
the top of Waronoack hill, were to be made and kept in
repair by Northampton, and thence to Windsor to be made
and maintained by Hadley and Northampton mutually.[1]

Line of the High-
way in North-
ampton.
These highways were laid by the committee
most if not the whole of the way along the
then existing roads. It is believed that the
one on the west side of the river followed the present route
of Bridge Street, and so through Main to South Street, extending along what is now termed the "old road" to Easthampton, and was very nearly the same as the present way
from that town to Westfield. A road to Windsor through
Westfield (Waranoak), already existed, and the county
assumed control of it by this order.

Six men were appointed by the court to survey these
highways, two from each of the towns interested. Capt.
Aaron Cook and Henry Woodward were from Northamp-
ton, Andrew Warner and William Allis from Hadley, and
George Colton and Benjamin Cooley from Springfield.
The report was signed by all of them with the exception of
William Allis.

Highways of Gen-
erous Width.
Land was plenty, and of comparatively little value except in the meadows or within
the settled village, and there was no scrimp-
ing of the roadways. The committee was very careful to

1 It may be worthy of note that in the return of the committee concerning the
lay out of these highways, Mts. Holyoke and Tom are both mentioned. The first is
called by the name it now bears, but the other is termed the "greate hill." Apparently Holyoke had been christened, but Tom was then unnamed, and the poetic description by Dr. Holland, of their naming (see p. 3) was but a figment of the imagination. In 1667, Mt. Tom is referred to upon the town records as the "great mountaine," but was first mentioned by name, in 1736, when it was proposed to "fence
in Mt. Tom for sheep."

specify at every point, the width of these roads, which were to vary from two rods, in the meadows, to four, six, eight, twenty, and in some places forty rods.[1]

The Cart the Principal Vehicle of Transportation. At that period the best roads were rough and uneven, little else than ruts or tracks for carts, scarcely any other wheeled vehicles being then in use. Few streams were bridged, and many times fording was difficult, if not dangerous. The country rate, paid in wheat, had to be carted to Hartford, and thence shipped to Boston. No boats were in use above Hartford for many years. Everything brought into town, as well as everything taken out of it, had to be carried in these clumsy vehicles or on horseback. Both Northampton and Hadley carted their grain to Hartford or Windsor. In 1664, the town agreed

" y^t what the Cuntry pay shall fall short in paying for the Carteing downe the Cuntry Rate to Hartford for this yeere y^t the Towne will beare an equall charge according to each man proportion in Towne rate, that noe man may be burdened by Carteing or otherwise by reason of ye price of Corne."

Burning the Woods. In order to prevent the growth of underbrush, so that there might be no hindrance to the pursuit of game, the Indians were accustomed to burn the woods annually. It was done both in the spring and fall of the year. By this means the weaker trees were destroyed, and the more vigorous, occasionally remaining in groups, gave the country a park-like appearance. So free were the forests of undergrowth during the sixty years following the first settlement of the town, that they were penetrable in every direction for horsemen. On this burned over land, the grass grew rapidly in the spring, where the trees were few, affording excellent pasturage. The first planters adopted this Indian custom, systematized it, and brought it under the regulation of the law. Indis-

1 " These were the first county roads in Hampshire. They followed the ways previously used by the early settlers. These three towns maintained for some years two roads near forty miles each from Hadley and Northampton to Connecticut line, which was then supposed to be south of the present north line of Windsor. Northampton and Hadley sent men and perhaps teams. to repair roads where Suffield now is. They were complained of in September, 1668, for defective way between Waranoke and Windsor. They amended the defects and were discharged in March, 1669, on paying the recorder's fees. The large streams, Chickopee, Manhan, Waranoke, and others had no bridges."—Judd's History of Hadley, p. 44.

criminate burning of the woods was forbidden by the General Court, and the towns took charge of the matter, within their own limits. The English, varying from the practice of the aborigines,[1] established the time of the annual burning between the 10th of March and the 30th of April. These woodland pastures were of great value and were highly prized. In Northampton the burnings were mainly confined to the western section of the town, extending to the hills of Westhampton and Williamsburg. In 1664, Joseph Parsons was ordered to burn the woods on the easterly and northerly sides of Mill River, two or three miles above Broughton's Meadow, and Robert Bartlett had instructions to burn them on the westerly and southerly sides of the same river. This practice of burning the woods was continued for nearly one hundred years. The sections included in this vote, were in the westerly portion of the town, beyond the present village of Florence.

The First Chirurgeon.   The first chirurgeon (surgeon) mentioned among the early settlers was George Fyler. In 1664, the town voted to receive him as an inhabitant, and gave him a home lot of six acres, and thirty acres more on condition that he should settle here, build upon his home lot, and remain in town four years. The County Court, at its session in the following March, granted him this license to practice:—

"George ffiler of Northampton being prsented to this corte as one reasonably well fitted & quallifyed for a Chirurgion was allowed by this corte to such work service & employment."

His home lot, located at the upper end of Elm Street, he sold to Jedediah Strong, in 1677. He did not long remain in town, removing to Westfield in a year or two. In 1674, he lived at Shelter Island, having in the meantime become a Quaker. At the March term of the court in 1673:—

"George ffiler of Westfeild being prsented by the Jury for diverse disorders & being examined firstly, for entertayning Quakers last Sum-

1 "The salvages are accustomed to set fire to the country in all places where they come and to burn it twice a year, viz. at the spring and the fall of the leaf. The reason that moves them to do so is because it would otherwise be so overgrown with underweeds, that it would be all a coppice wood and the people not be able in any wise to pass through the country out of a beaten path. This custom of firing the country is the means to make it passable and by that means the trees grow here and there as in our parks and makes the country very beautiful and commodious."—Morton's New England Canaan, pub. in 1632.

mer he owns he did entertayne them being necessitated thereunto because none else would as he sayes. George ffiler sayth he shall before the World own that he is one of them whom yᵉ world calls Quakers: Also he is pʳsented for absenting himselfe from God's publike worshipp on yᵉ Sabbaths he ownes he has genʳally absented himself geneʳally last winter; his speeches have been contemptuous of the Ministers of the Word and their work, viz. that they turne over 20 or 30 Authors in a weeke to patch up an houres discourse or two on the Sabbath. And tho he would pʳtend that he meant not the ministry in that town or of N. England yet by the testimonyes it appears otherwise: He seems to be a very Seminary of corrupt heriticall opinions tending to poysoning & corrupting the minds of them with wᵐ he hath to doe. And in Speaking of the religion of the Quakers (he speaks of it as distinct from that pʳfessed by our Nation in this countrey) he calls it Our religion, that is his own & such as hee. The said George ffiler for his venting of his hetorodoxyes & adhering to the pnicious wayes of the Quakers was pʳtested agᵗ by the Coʳte & admonisht thereof. And for his absenting himself fro Gods Ordinances on the Sabbath haveing been formʳly admonisht thereof both by yᵉ Woʳppˡˡ Majoʳ Pynchon & also by Westfeild Comissionʳs was now also admonisht yʳ of by the Coʳte: And it declared to him that it was in order to further dealing with him except he reform his course therein. And for his contemptuous & scandalous speeches of the ministry of this countrey & of Christ's holy institutions as denying the Sacramts, &c. he is sentenced to pay a fyne to yᵉ County 5ˡ or eles to well whipt." Thomas Noble of Westfield, engaged to see the fine paid.

Precautions against Pauperism. John Brace Warned. John Sackett's Man, Patrick, provided for. Thos. Buckland Proceeded against.

Carefully the townsmen endeavored, not only to prevent their own people from becoming paupers, but to protect the town from being burdened with those from other places. They scrutinized closely the condition morally, religiously, politically and industrially of every individual who sought to become an inhabitant. If any, perchance, were liable to require assistance from the authorities, he was forthwith invited to emigrate, or give security for his support. On the 5ᵗʰ of December, action was taken in reference to several questionable characters. It was ordered "that John Brace yᵗ liues with Joseph Dickinson shall haue notice to depᵗ the Towne." Brace made application to be permitted to remain, and on the 9ᵗʰ it was voted "that if hee continue till the first of february next hee is to bring in security to the Townes men that hee shall not bee any way chargable to the Towne." "The man that came lately out of y⁰ bay as hee says," had been hired for one year by John Sackett, and he was not molested, but the town decided by this vote that he was to be looked after. "As for Patrick wee agree that those yᵗ brought into yᵉ Towne be caled in question about bringing in." Pat., it seems was sick, and "wee order that hee should haue some bedd clothes, and doe intreate Mrs. Williams to entertaine him" during his sickness, at the expense of the town. In some cases it was found somewhat difficult to get rid of unsatisfactory persons. In 1667, the selectmen brought a case of this kind before the County Court. Thomas Buckley, or Buckland, had recently removed to Northampton, "whom for diverse good considerations that Towne could not allow of to reside there." The selectmen "haveing warned him to depᵗ the Towne," the court ordered him to leave "upon penalty of being pᵣoceeded agᵗ for contempt," and "all pᵣsons as shall entertayne him are to turne him away within 6 days after the publication" of the order of the court, otherwise they became liable to prosecution at the next session of the court, "for their misdemeanor," unless they gave security to "yᵉ comissionᵣˢ of that Town to save the Towne and county harmless for his abiding among them." This order did not seem to produce the desired effect, or it is possible that some one became security for him, for Buckland was still in town in 1673. He was then bound over for his appearance at court on charge of misdemeanor, but he ran away, and his bond, for which he pledged his horse and flax, was declared forfeited.

A New Mill in Agitation.   At a town meeting in 1663, when the question came up "concerning a motion aboutt the making of a new mill, the Towne granted the same toll to the builders that Hadley giues." This matter seems to have been in agitation for several years. At the time this vote was passed a committee was chosen to "Issue the businesse" of selecting the "Twenty Acres of land to bee laid to the mill." No action seems to have been taken under either of the above votes, for in February, 1665, Praisever Turner, owner of the then existing mill, offered a motion that the town should provide another mill. Consequently it was voted that "they doe desire Lt. Clarke to goe on with building a new mill and they will Ratifie a grant of land formerly made to the builders of ye mill." The next year a vote was adopted ordering the selectmen to "lay out A way ouer the River conveniente to the plase whear the new mill is to be set," and "that thear shall bee A bridge butt for A horse pasadge." The work, if actually begun, was not pushed forward very rapidly, for in July, 1666, the following agreement was made with the mill builders:—

"27 (6) 1666. At a Legale Towne meettinge in our Towne in the Debate aboute the mill with Lieft Clarke and Thomas Meekins Senr the Towne proposinge toe them to get the mill forward after there apologie: they proposed to the Towne toe be released of the ingadgment: to which the Towne would not consent: on which goodman Meekens acknoleged himselfe ingaged with Leif Clarke to build a mill in North Hampton for the vse of the Towne and then proposed to the Towne thr^e propositions: ferst that the Towne would giue them a day worke a man with toe oxen of them that haue them to Cart gravell toe the dam. to that the Towne granted by a vote they would giue them a day a peece with there teams they fiending tumbrels & giue the seasonable warning.

"2 proposition was that when he was redy to sete downe the foundation of the mill the Towne should aford him soe many hands as he should need to helpe sete her downe and ram her they giuinge seasonable warninge and pay them when the mill did goe toe get corne to pay them.

"3 proposition that the Towne should helpe them with thre hands a day somtyms fower such men as they should desier to worke with them tell the mill did goe and that the Towne should satisfie them for there labor in cace they called for there pay before the mill did goe: to wit goodman Meekens part: and he would pay them againe: the men they desiered wheare Tho Lues, Ralph Huchenson, Enos Kingsley Sargeant Kinge, Samuell Wright John Stebben: Tho Duwe Thomas Stronge John Liman: to this proposition the Towne and the persons nominated consented: the tyme goodman Meekins set to begirle on the worke was the next 5 day com seuen night which will be the 6 of Agust and to contennew on the worke tell the mill did goe, lis god by any Extraordinary prouidence shold hender as by sickness lamenes breach of his mill or the Like that should befall himselfe or his men.

"Alsoe the Towne voted that the commettie chossen to set vp the bredge to goe over to build this mill should haue power to cale out hands and set it vp spedily."

Location of the New Mill. Thomas Meekins, above referred to as "Goodman Meekins," was an inhabitant of Hadley. He was a mill-wright and assisted in building mills in Hadley as well as Northampton. These votes indicate that the town had become somewhat impatient at the dilatory proceedings in reference to the new mill, and were ready to make any arrangement that would secure its speedy completion. It must have been built on the west side of the river, nearly opposite, but a little to the north, of Maynard's Hoe Shop. A highway was laid to it through the home lot of William Clarke, for which he received a grant of twenty acres of land, but a few years after, when the mill was removed, he gave up the land, the highway was returned to him, and the twenty acres reverted to the town. The upper highway to the river (now Green Street), laid out when West Street was established, was discontinued the year that this mill was built, consequently a new and direct road to it was made through what is now a part of Smith College property. In 1667, John King and Thomas Dewey engaged to "maintaine the Bridge over the Reaver Leadinge to the New Mill for the space of seaven years" for 20s. a year. If the bridge was carried away they were "toe repaire it againe in ten weeks tyme," and were "then to have fiue pound out of the towne stocke the next yeare which was to be part of seauen pound before expressed."

Another Mill Built.   This new mill did not prove very satisfactory, and was not in use many years. In March 16$\frac{70}{11}$, William Clarke proposed on certain conditions, "to remove the mill from the place where it now is, and to build it about the red rock, at this side the river." This location was in the rear of the residence of F. N. Kneeland, in the vicinity of the "old tannery," erected many years afterwards. The mill was built by Lieut. Clarke, and served the purposes of the town for a number of years. It was assaulted by the Indians in 1675, and was either burned by them or within a year or two, as another mill was in use lower down the stream in 1678 or 1679. Broken stones and partially burned timbers, remains of the old mill, were still to be seen in that vicinity in 1830. A petition to the General Court from the town of Hatfield, in April 1678, represents Northampton as destitute of a mill.

CHAPTER XIV.

THE INDIANS—THEIR TREATMENT.

Indians of the Connecticut Valley. THE Indians of the Connecticut Valley differed very little from those in other sections of the country. They led the same nomadic life, here to-day, there to-morrow, with few ties to bind them long to any place. Little is to be found upon the records locally descriptive of their manners or customs. They had no villages within the limits of Northampton, and few permanent settlements within the borders of what is now known as Hampshire County. While the squaws tilled a small portion of the meadows, the men occasionally did a little fishing, and at other times amused themselves in hunting, trapping and fighting. The Nonotucks, who owned this territory, though perhaps the most numerous of the four western tribes, were not conspicuous, and held no important position among them. Their sachems had little influence, either in their own tribe or among the neighboring Indians.

The Natives very Friendly. When Northampton was settled, the red men in this section of the valley were few and scattered. The chiefs, who claimed authority to sell land, readily parted with it, and their followers, who had no knowledge of the nature of a deed, occupied and used it nearly to the same extent as before. They mingled with the white men on the most friendly terms, erecting their wigwams, when permitted, upon the home lots of the inhabitants, and seeking their protection when danger threatened.

The Indians gained nothing by their Intercourse with the Whites.

In New England the first settlers regarded the Indians as pagans, and measuring them by the standard of their own superior intelligence, often treated them with cruelty and injustice. In this section, however, there is no indication of any intentional wrong done them. While the white men scrupulously purchased the land and honestly paid for it, their dusky friends were regarded as heathen, scarcely worthy of respect. Too lazy to work, improvident and wasteful, apt scholars in vice, but obtuse learners in civilization, the Indians gained nothing by contact with the whites. Though the pale faces treated them as inferiors and had little in common with them, an even handed justice was sought to be established between the races. Not only were the Indians held amenable to the laws of the new comers, but the latter also were punished for crimes or trespasses against the aborigines.

Neither were they Impoverished by the Settlers.

But a meagre remnant of the red race occupied this territory, and they were neither incommoded nor impoverished by the advent of the English. At first they were permitted to plant corn in the meadows, the whites plowing the land for them. Game was nearly as plentiful in the forest as ever, and there was no lack of other supplies needed for their daily consumption. Pecuniarily they were benefitted by the change. A market was opened wherein they found a ready sale for their furs, and such other articles of traffic as they were able to manufacture.

Their Food and Improvidence.

Before they came in contact with the civilization of the old world, the Indians lived in a simple and primitive manner. Their food, clothing and habitations were obtained from the woods, the streams, the meadows and the uplands. Clothed in the skins of the wild animals, whose flesh stocked their larders, sheltered by the wigwams which were formed in part of the twigs and branches of the forest that concealed their game, they lived children of nature, untutored and unknown. Their food consisted mainly of the flesh of wild animals, fish, fruits, ground nuts, chestnuts, acorns, corn, beans and pumpkins. They also made use of certain edible roots. Their cooking utensils were few, some hollowed out of soapstone, others made of clay. Parched corn, beaten fine and mixed with fat, formed a substance called "nocake," and corn, pounded and sifted through baskets, and made into samp, was much used. Fish were caught at certain seasons of the year and dried. There is scant evidence that they made use of dried meats to any great extent. Children of to-day, they made little or no preparation for the future. Evidence, however, exists that they had receptacles for storing corn and other articles, "Indian barns,"[1] the settlers called them, yet they had little forethought and lived always in the present; feasting and carousing while food was plenty, only to endure the pangs of hunger and starvation when the supply was exhausted.

The Indians Detested Labor.

All attempts to make industrious men of the dusky warriors failed. The squaws were the working partners, planting the fields, carrying the burdens, and performing all the drudgery. The men detested menial labor, but would endure hardship, privation and fatigue with fortitude and courage while on the war path, or engaged in hunting. In some cases the settlers endeavored to make servants of the Indians. Children captured during the war were bound out to the farmers, but their service was seldom satisfactory. The government of the colony was guilty of selling Indian prisoners into slavery, but there is no evidence that any from this section were thus inhumanly treated.

Indians at War among themselves.

The river Indians were frequently at war among themselves, and the settlers in the valley suffered at times considerable inconvenience therefrom. Most powerful and belligerent among them were the Pocumtucks at Deerfield, who were almost constantly on the war path. After the close of the Pequod war, there followed six years of uneasy peace between the Indian tribes, preserved in a great measure by the efforts of the English. But in 1643, the Narragansetts

1 These Indian barns or caches were excavations in the ground for storing provisions, and have been found in abundance in certain sections of the valley. For a description of them, see Sheldon's History of Deerfield, vol. 1, pp. 76-78.

engaged in an inroad upon the Mohegans, who were only saved from severe defeat by the assistance of the colonial troops. Four years afterwards the Narragansetts, the Mohawks, and the Pocumtucks entered into an alliance against the Mohegans under Uncas. An attack upon him was made by the Narragansetts, but repulsed. Through the mediation of the English, the expedition was finally abandoned. Uncas once more commenced the war in 1655, by an attack upon the Podunks in Connecticut. The Pocumtucks retaliated and fell upon Uncas, defeating him. Badly demoralized, the latter sued for peace through the intervention of the English. At first the Pocumtucks refused to listen to their overtures, but at length an arrangement was concluded. Uncas, however, paid but little attention to the treaty, and soon after marched against the Naunautucks. He was promptly called to account by the English, and open hostilities were for the time avoided. In 1657, another alliance against Uncas was fomented by the Pocumtucks; and the Mohegans, once more defeated, would have been annihilated, but for the aid of Connecticut troops. Previous to this last outbreak, the Pocumtucks asked consent of the Government of Massachusetts to make war upon Uncas. The General Court attempted to arbitrate between the belligerents, but without avail. This war continued several years, and in 1659, the English again endeavored to make peace between the tribes, in which they were eventually successful, although the Pocumtucks at first declined.[1]

The Mohawks Attack and Defeat the Pocumtucks.   Hostilities were resumed between these Indians in 1663, when the Pocumtucks and their eastern allies, attacked and defeated the Mohawks. The latter sued for peace, but their overtures were rejected and their ambassadors slain. In 1664, the English having taken possession of New York, the Mohawks made a treaty of peace with them. By this means they not only gained the friendship of the whites, but also neutralized the Hudson river tribes. Soon after they made a treaty with the French. Having thus secured themselves against

1 For a full and comprehensive account of these Indian wars, see Sheldon's History of Deerfield, vol. 1, pp. 50 to 70.

the interference of other foes, the Mohawks immediately assembled a powerful force, and attacked and defeated the Pocumtucks and their allies. The Pocumtucks never rallied after this disaster.

Northampton Men zealous for Peace.

These constantly recurring Indian wars did not promote the welfare of the people of the valley, and they joined heartily in all the efforts to secure and maintain peace. While no action concerning these troubles was taken by the town, its leading citizens were energetic in their endeavors to prevent or extinguish the warfare. John Winthrop Jr., in a letter to Thomas Willets, dated "Hartford, July 27, 1664," mentions the successful efforts of certain Northampton settlers, in pacifying the Pocumtucks : —

"I heare that the English of those vpper plantations vpon this river (wᶜʰ are belonging to the colony of the Massachusett, and live below the lowest of those Hylanders) some of them that had any knowledge of them, and had oportunity to speake wᵗʰ them, did psuade them much to peace wᵗʰ the Mohoaks : and in a letter lately from Mʳ Pinchon (since I acquainted him wᵗʰ that intelligece fro your selfe) I am informed that in pticular Lieftenat Wilson [Wilton] of Northamton, and Mʳ Clarke of Hadly [Northampton] (I thinke one of the magistrates there) did psuade the Pacotuck Indians, to accept of the wampam, and make peace with them, and it is reported heere that those two, and some others were sent purposely fro the English of those upper plantations to the Pacotuck fort to labour wᵗʰ them to make peace ; and in your letter there is a passage, that some English of the towne of Hadlye were witnesses of peace made wᵗʰ those Indians."[1]

War Parties annoy the Settlers, and harbor Rogues.

During these years the English had their hands full in protecting themselves and striving to conciliate and keep the peace among the warlike tribes. Though friendly to the whites and evidently too fearful of their vengeance to provoke them too far, nevertheless their war parties were a constant annoyance to the settlements.[2] Armed bands of Indians were forbidden to come near the English towns, or to "invade or affront any English person or house." White rogues took advantage of these disturbances and sometimes found refuge and security for their plunder with the Indians.

1 Mass. Hist. Coll. 5th series, vol. 8, p. 89.

2 "They presse so neare and sometimes into the houses of the English as to theire great disturbance and which tends directly to the breach of peace betwixt vs and them if not speedily preuented."—Letter to the Pocumtucks, Sept. 3, 1659.

An instance of this kind occurred in 1659. John Webb and other inhabitants of Northampton, complained that "two Dutchmen, one Irishman, and one ffrenchman," had stolen "seuen mares and other cattle," and driven them to Pocumtuck. They suggested that the Sachem, Wonopequen, should pursue and apprehend the thieves, and bring back the stolen property, for which service they promised him 50s. for every mare. The chief agreed to the proposition and sent word to the Northampton men to come and receive their stock. Webb and the rest went to Pocumtuck, saw the mares in possession of the Indians, and the thieves in their company. The chief refused to deliver them according to the agreement, but demanded "great sums of wampum, coates, shirts, liquors, &c," saying that he had bought them of the Indians, and that each mare was worth £20. After spirited negotiations, conducted by the authorities, this as well as other stolen property, carried within the Indian lines for safe keeping, was returned to its owners.

The Indians Apply for Land on which to build a Fort. In 1664, the Indians made application to the town for a gift of land on which to build a fort. Their request was granted on the following conditions, and David Wilton, John Lyman and Joseph Parsons were appointed by the town "to deliver ther minde to the Indians" : —

"1.   ffirst they shall not break the Saboath by workeing or gameing or caring burdens or ye like.

"2.   They shall not pawway on that place or any wher els amogst vs.

"3.   They shall not gett liquoer or Sider and drinke themselues drunk and soe kill one an other as they haue donn.

"4.   They shall not take in other Indians of other places to seat amogst them, wee alow only Nowutague Indians yt were the Inhabytants of the place.

"5.   They shall not breake downe or fences and let in Cattle and Swine but shall goe over a stile at one place.

"6.   The Murdrers Callawane and Wurtowhan and Pacquallunt shall not seate Amongst them.

"7.   They shall not hunt nor kill or Cattle or Sheepe or Swine wth ther doggs if they doe they shall pay for them."

Position of the Fort Uncertain. Its Probable Location. These rules and regulations were accepted by the Indians, and their fort was built. Its exact location is uncertain,[1] and historians differ as to its position. Indian forts are said to have existed at three different places in Northampton. One was built on Fort Hill, South Street, another on Fort Plain, Easthampton, and a third on the bank of the Connecticut River, half way to Hatfield. If this one was situated on "Fort Hill," South Street, the land it occupied had already been granted for home lots, and settlers were living upon them. It does not seem probable that the owners of that property would have submitted to such an imposition without vigorous protest. Yet subsequent action by the town[2] seems to point to the fact that this fort was not far from the inhabited portion of the plantation. If it was at either of the other points—at opposite ends of the town—its proximity would not have been an inconvenience to the people or rendered necessary the expulsion of its occupants, within a few years. As neither record or tradition point to any other spot, within the settled portion of the town, Fort Hill, South Street, must be assumed to be the correct one. The small number of Indians in this vicinity would scarcely need, nor would the settlers willingly give them, land for another fort, when they made such bad use of the one they occupied. That three or even two Indian forts were in existence within the limits of Northampton at the same time is highly improbable. Undoubtedly that on Fort Plain, Easthampton, had then been abandoned. They also had a fort between Northampton and Hatfield, "on the top of the high bank of the Connecticut, opposite the north-west corner of Hadley

1 "This fort is said to have been built on the northerly end of Fort Plain, which is now Easthampton."—Rev. Solomon Williams' Fast Day Sermon, 1815, p. 10.

"This fort was built in the heart of the town ; at a distance perhaps of thirty rods from the most populous street."—Dwight's Travels, vol. 1, p. 349, Ed. 1821.

2 In June, 1670, "the Selectmen consideringe the greate abuse by the Indians in horible drunkennes profaning the Saboth breakeinge downe our fences and in steelinge our Corne and in keepinge Swine about the fort that distroy our Corne : we therfore order that noe person shall giue the Indians libertie to toe build a fort within the meadow fence although it be on his owne land and alsoe we order that they shall not keepe any Swine about the fort lis they be shut up in sties : and alsoe that the Indians shall contennew noe longer in ther old fort then til a moneth after migheltide [Michaelmas] next."

Great Meadow,"[1] in 1675, and were driven from it in the first year of King Philip's war. They probably took possession of this elevation when ejected from their place near the center of the town in 1670. That was the last point of land ever held by the Indians in Northampton.

Unsatisfactory Neighbors. Knowing the propensity of the red men for carousing, their love of liquor, and the temptation, seldom resisted by unscrupulous whites, to sell intoxicants to them, it appears strange that a gathering place should have been allowed them in the very center of the village. Though the conditions on which this permit was accorded were vigorous and minute, it is evident that the people soon regretted their generosity. There was constant friction. When in their cups the Indians were turbulent and quarrelsome; when sober, lawless and thievish. Frequent cases in court, to which they were parties, furnish abundant evidence that they were exceedingly troublesome neighbors.

The Grist Mill Burglarized. Much annoyance undoubtedly occurred from the lawlessness of the Indians, and many of them were brought before the courts and punished for their crimes. On the other hand, white men also suffered for cheating or maltreating the Indians. The mill of Praisever Turner (the first grist mill ever built in Northampton), was broken into by an Indian named Wenawen, in 1665, and "divers tools and meal to the value of 30s.," stolen. In a short time the Indian was arrested, arraigned and put under bonds for trial. Failing to appear, he and his sureties, Chickwallop and Sopos, were ordered to pay Turner twenty fathoms of wampum, valued at forty shillings, for his loss from the mill and charges about the suit.

An Indian Lad Murdered, and Cattle and Swine Killed. Depredations by the Mohawks were frequent during the year 1667. Most flagrant among them was the murder of an Indian lad, a servant of Nathaniel Clark, who was killed in the meadows during the summer. He was shot while riding

1 Judd's History of Hadley, p. 126.

his horse, "the skin and hair of his head being taken away." About the same time many cattle and swine were destroyed in the meadows by the same party of Indians. Some of them were killed and portions of their flesh carried off, while others were wounded. Complaint was made to the General Court, and such forcible arguments brought to bear upon the chiefs of the Mohawks, that within a couple of years the savages made restitution for these unlawful acts. Twenty pounds worth of leather was placed in the custody of the County Court for this purpose. The amount was apportioned to those who suffered, in proportion to their loss. To Northampton £7 was awarded, viz. : "to the heirs of Nathaniel Clarke, for his Indian Servant, killed by said Magnaws, £3.10; to Joseph Parsons £1.10; and the rest, 40ˢ. to Joseph Parsons, Joseph Leeds, Thomas Mason & Enos Kingsley, to be distributed by Lt. Clarke." Hadley received £8, and Springfield £5. The leather was placed in the hands of Simon Lobdell of Springfield, and he was to pay the award in shoes in "merchantable ware and reasonable prices."

Hampshire Appeals to the General Co't in 1668. These outrages became so frequent, that the Deputies from Hampshire County complained to the General Court, and an attempt was made to bring the Indians to a sense of their responsibility. The court ordered that the Indians should choose a Sachem, who could be held responsible for all such injuries. Lieut. William Clarke, Lieut. David Wilton of Northampton, and Lieut. Samuel Smith of Hadley, were appointed agents to attend to that duty, and Chickwallop was chosen chief by the Nonotucks. He was not a man of much influence, and acted only as a figure head, for the English to aim at when they sought redress. These newly appointed chieftains, others having been selected elsewhere, took advantage of their position and sold land right and left, putting the proceeds into their own pockets. This state of affairs came to an end with the close of King Philip's War, in 1676. After that date the troubles were with non-resident Indians and their French allies.

Indian Misde-
meanors.

Several Indians at Springfield and Northampton, complained of for traveling and
working on the Sabbath, were fined a certain number of bushels of corn. Afterwards they were
charged with drunkenness at the fort in this town, and
with resisting the constable and his assistants. Arrested
and taken before the court, they pledged a quantity of
wampum for their appearance for trial. As they did not
present themselves at the proper time, their pledge was declared forfeited. A part of it was paid to the constable,
Thomas Bascom, and his assistants, and the rest went to
the county.

Case of Petomanch.

An Indian, named Petomanch, committed
divers thefts and robberies at Northamp-
ton and Hadley, and escaped to Quabaug (Brookfield). Being pursued, he came to the Indian fort in this town. An
attempt was made to arrest him there, but a companion,
named Wuttawan, helped him to escape. Several Indians
testified to this fact, and Wuttawan was arrested and held
as a hostage. After consultation among themselves, the
Indians promised to use all their endeavors to catch the
real thief. If he could not be "found and got alive they
agreed to deliver up Wuttawan again (who upon this engagement was set at liberty), or otherwise make satisfaction as the court shall order."

Quequelatt Ar-
rested for En-
ticing three Lads
to run away.

Quequelatt was arrested in 1668, for aiding
Godfrey Nims, Benoni Stebbins and James
Bennett in their attempt to run away to
the French. He was charged with taking
their money to help them away and for telling "lyes about
yᵉ design." He was sentenced to be "well whipped with
20 lashes," and ordered to "restore the money and goods
he took of yᵉ lads to carry yᵐ away," and the record continues "whipt he was accordingly."

Story of the three
Northampton
Lads.

The case of these three young lads is best
told as it is set down in the records of the
court before which they were arraigned,
which was held at Springfield, September 24, 1667 :—

"James Bennet, Godfrey Nims, & Benoni Stebbins, young lads of Northampton being by Northampton Comission's bound ouer to this Co'te to answer for diverse crimes & misdemean's comitted by them, were brought to this Co'te by ye Constable of y^t Towne wch 3 lads are accused by Robert Bartlett for that they gott into his house two Sabbath dayes when all the family were at the Publike Meeting : On ye first of wch tymes, they vizt. Nims & Stebbins did ransack about the house & tooke away out of diverse places of the house vizt. 24 shillings in silver & 7^s in Wampam wth the intention to run away to the ffrench : All which is by them confessed, wch wickednesse of theires hath also been accompanyed with frequent lying to excuse & justify themselves, especially on Nims his p^t, who it seemes hath been a ringleader in their villainyes : ffor all wch their crimes and misdemeano's this Co'te doth Judge y^t the said 3 lads shalbe well whipt on their naked bodyes vizt. Nims & Bennet wth 15 lashes apeece & Benoni Stebbins with 11 lashes. And the said Nims & Stebbins are to pay Robert Bartlett the summe of 4^l being accounted treble according to law, for what goods he hath lost by their meanes. Also those psons that recd any money of any of the said lads, are to restore it to the s'd Robert Bartlett. But there being made to the Co'te an earnest petition & request by Ralfe Hutchinson father-in-law to ye said James Bennet & diverse other considerable psons y^t the said Bennets corporall punishment might be released by reason of his mothers weakness, who it is feared may suffer much inconveniency thereby, that punishment was remitted upon his father-in-law his engaging to this Co'te to pay ffive pounds to ye County as a fyne for the said Bennets offence, wch 5^l is to be paid to ye County Treasurer for ye use of ye County. Also John Stebbins, Junio^r being much suspected to have some hand in their plotting to run away. This Co'te doth ord^r ye Comission's of Northampton to call him before y^m & to examine him about that or any other thing whereon he is suspected to be guilty wth ye said lads, & so act therein according to their discretion, attending law. Also they are to call the Indian called Quequelatt who had a hand in their plott & to deale with him according as they fynd."

John Stebbins Jr., a brother of Benoni, acknowledged, at a court held in March of the next year, that he had been privy to the plot of Bennett and Stebbins to run away, and the court, because he had concealed his knowledge of it, sentenced him to be "whipt on the naked body with ten stripes or eles to pay 40^s to the County Treasurer." His father paid the fine.

What became of the Boys.   Godfrey Nims afterwards settled in Deerfield, and was probably the ancestor of all of that name in the country. He became the owner of considerable property, was in the "Falls Fight," and was an honored and respected citizen. James Bennett, who was fifteen years old at this time, was the son

of Francis Bennett of Boston, and came here with his
mother, who married Ralph Hutchinson. He married
Mary Broughton, daughter of John Broughton, in 1675,
and was slain while returning from the "Falls Fight," the
next year. Benoni Stebbins was the son of John Stebbins,
and but twelve years old. He removed to Deerfield, married Mary, widow of James Bennett, became a prominent
and useful citizen, and was killed by the Indians in the
attack on Deerfield, in 1704.

The Law for White
and Red Men alike.

While the courts of law were open as well
to the Indians as to the white men, the
former very seldom availed themselves of
the privilege.[1] But few cases can be found upon the records in which the Indians sought redress at law. They seemingly had little faith in the justice of the race which not
only enacted but administered the laws, by which they
claimed their rights. The annexed statements show, however, that justice, at their demand, was not denied them.
The Springfield Indians complained of Samuel Marshfield,
for unfair dealings concerning certain lands of which he
had obtained possession by mortgage. At the suggestion
of the court, arbitrators were appointed, and Marshfield
allowed the Indians a certain portion of the land, which
satisfied them. An Indian of Westfield, complained that
his corn was damaged by the cattle of the English. The
matter was adjusted to the satisfaction of the complainant.
Other cases of a similar nature appear, where restitution
for damage to fences or crops, was obtained. When the
Indians discovered a barefaced attempt to cheat them they
were always righted by the courts.

Selling L i q u o r to
the Indians. Un-
availing attempts
to prevent it.

Fond of strong drink, the Indians, when
under its influence, were quarrelsome and
unruly. The most severe laws which had
been enacted against selling liquor to them,
were constantly evaded. Many of the English in the several towns in the county were prosecuted for violations of

1 "In seven years, from 1661-68, at Plymouth, there are 15 prosecutions against Indians for trespass or stealing while there are only three prosecutions against whites
for trespass on Indians."—Weeden's Economic and Social History of New England,
vol. 1, p. 29.

these laws, but the evil was not abated. In the court record of 1670, appears the following paragraph : "The woefull drunkenness among the Indians cries aloud to use the utmost laudable means to prevent what may be of that sin among them." Many cases of the unlawful sale of liquor to the Indians appear upon the records of the court, women[1] being accused as well as men. The cupidity of the whites defied all restrictions, and the sale continued despite all efforts to curtail it by the officers of the law.

[1] John Harmon was fined 20s. in 1672, " for his wife's selling cider to the Indians, which they also say was only water cider." John Clark of Springfield, was fined for selling cider to them, which he also claimed was only water cider. " But because it was such as in all probability an Indian was drunk by it, and in that condition shot and killed another Indian, he was fined 40ˢ." Goodwife Miller of Northampton, was fined 45s. in 1673, for the same offence. She acknowledged that she sold them some sour cider mixed with beer, and afterwards petitioned for an abatement of the fine, but it was not granted. Her husband paid the fine and 2ˢ 6ᵈ for recorder's fees.

CHAPTER XV.

PROGRESS IN EVERY DIRECTION.

The Records Contain the History. DURING the next few years the history of the town is to be found mainly upon the record book of its meetings, and much that had a beneficial effect upon the subsequent prosperity of the place was inscribed thereon. The development of its industries was fostered and protected by wholesome enactments, and many primary and formative laws and regulations, that have given strength to the community and permanence to its institutions, were then adopted. A brief statement of the most important business transacted in them indicates progress in every direction.

Weights and Measures. Town Brand. Soldiers to buy Powder. James Bridgman was the first person in town chosen "Clerk of the Markets," or Sealer of Weights and Measures. This occurred in 1659, before the municipality had provided proper implements for such a purpose. Five years later the town was indicted for not having obtained standard weights and measures from the proper authorities. About this time, and probably in consequence of this action by the court, all weights and measures were directed to be delivered to the Clerk of the Markets. At the same time a town brand was also decided upon. The device was to be "NH," and the town ordered "y^t Lt. Wilton speake to Medad Pumry to make one." Towns were obliged by law to keep a stock of powder on hand, and it was voted "that the barrel of powder shalbe opened and supply all the souldiers that want powder in the Towne, provided they bring 3 pecks of wheat for a pound of powder." This was in accordance with a law of 1641, which provided that every one should buy powder, paying in grain.

184

The Need of Home Manufactures Recognized. The Government Imports Sheep.

Among the first enactments by the General Court, looking towards the establishment of home manufactures, were those for the encouragement of wool growing. Exports of cloth and clothing material from the mother country had been much lessened on account of the war in England, consequently laws on that subject were made as early as 1645. At first it was proposed to increase flocks of sheep, by ascertaining who would buy them at 40s. a head, so that there might be some course taken for the sending for them into other parts abroad. Any one was to be allowed to keep sheep in any common belonging to the town, and when the commons were "stinted," "ffive sheep were to be accounted to one great beast." Dogs caught killing or worrying sheep were to be hanged forthwith.

Spinning made Compulsory.

In 1656, because of the very great scarcity of clothing, compulsory spinning was ordered by the General Court. "Women, girles & boyes" not necessarily employed in other duties, were "enjoined to spinne according to their skills and abilyte." Every family was to be assessed one or more spinners, and those who were employed a greater part of the time in other business, were to be assessed one-half or one-quarter spinner. "A whole spinner was to spinn for 30 weeks every year, 3 pounds per week of lining, cotten or woolling and proportionally for a half or quarter spinner, under penalty of 12^d for every pound short." The selectmen were to enforce this law, dividing the town into sections of ten, six or five families, and appointing some person as overseer in the several sections. The amount received for fines was to be "improved for the encouragem^t of those that are diligent in their labor." Not only were the people required to spin wool, cotton, flax, etc., but their representatives were ordered to impress upon them the necessity for "the soweing of the seeds, both of hemp and flax." Whether the selectmen of Northampton ever respected this statute has not been ascertained. Certainly the town never took any action relative thereto, and it may be surmised that the law was not enforced.

A Shepherd Em-
ployed.

Sheep raising in Northampton began a few years after its settlement, and had increased to such an extent in 1664, that a Shepherd was employed by the town, and no sheep were allowed on the commons without a "constant keeper," under "penaltye of fower pence pr Sheepe evarie tyme soe Taken with out a keeper." Near the close of the century large tracts of land in different sections of the town were set apart for sheep pastures. John Webb was among the first in this town, who purchased these animals. He bought, in 1662, a flock of "30 sheep, ewes and lambs," of John Pynchon, for £20. David Wilton was engaged with Mr. Pynchon in a "sheep venture," in Rhode Island, a few years before Wilton removed to Northampton. The outcome of this enterprise is not known, though the fact that Pynchon had them for sale indicates that the business had been successful on his part.

Excused from High-
way and Ferry
Rates.

In February, 1665, the town voted to relieve certain of its citizens from ferry and highway rates, seemingly without any adequate reason. Judging from the record, the men had only to ask to have their taxes abated, and the request was readily granted. While they did not desire any roads or ferries for themselves, these men seem to have been perfectly willing to use those made for the public. The account of this transaction cannot be better stated than in the language of the record itself :—

"13th of the 12 mo. 1664 [February, 1665]. At a legall Towne meeting John Webb Senior desired to bee freed from the Towne charge about the ferry hous & ferrie rate and highwaies, becawse hee desired noe highwaies to bee made for him nor ferridg, but when hee goes over hee will pay his owne ferridg. John Earele is to haue ye same privelidge."

Lands Forfeited
and the Forfeit
Abated.

Early in the year it was declared that "all home lotts and other landes that haue not Attended the condition of the grante is iudged and determined to bee forfitt." In April, George Sumner's home lot was taken away from him on these grounds, while "John Allin, Zachary ffeild, Nathanael

Dickinson, James Wright which were forfeit had ther grants renewed provided that they attend the conditions of ther former grante." Sumner undoubtedly made application to be dealt with as liberally as the others had been, for in August the selectmen were ordered, inasmuch as his "hom lott was forfete" and the "Town tooke the forfete," to "giue him what can be spared from the publicke vse." George Sumner was among the first settlers who paid for their home lots, and it may be that he claimed exemption from the penalty incurred on that account.

The Constable's Account for one year.

The settlement with the Constable, William Miller, for the year 1665, fixes the town rate for that year at £74.8.4. His account, extended in full upon the record, is of interest as showing the prevailing method of transacting town business, as well as the volume of it for that year :—

"26. 10. [December] 1665. Counted with William Miller Constable: he was then depter—by a rate for the vse of the Towne beareing date 10-12-1664 (February 10, 1665)

the Som is		74.8.4
William Miller creditt		
By a list of depts the townsmen ordered him to pay	56 .9 .9	
Payed for careing downe the country Rate upon the town charges	2 .2 .0	
Payd to the townsmen 7^b 1^q wheat . .	1 .2 .6	
Payd to henery Woodward	4 .8 .1	
More to David Burt	0 .7 .6	
More to Enos Kingslye	0 .6 .6	
More to Medad Pumery	0 .3 .6	
More to Samuell Write	0 .1 .3	
William Miller payd to David Wilton by order	4.17.07	
Payd to Goodman Roote Senr for his bull 5^s 2^d Selling the Towne Mesher 6^d a day worke 6^d, all is	00.07.07	
Paid by William Hulburd paid Dauid Wilton	02.02.00	
by pay behind for his bull toe yeare . .	00.07.00	
by payment to you for Robert Butterworth	01.13.01–	74.8.4

"This fower pound seauentin shillings & 7^d David Wilton haue repayd to the Towne as will apeare on a paper booke on which is recorded how he tooke it from the Towne and haue the Townsmen account of it in the yeare 1666.

"29.11.65. Wheras Henry Woodward leptor above 4.8.1
he hath ballanced the account w^t the s tmen 4.8.1"

Highway Discon-   As already narrated, a highway had been
tinued.   established in two branches identical with
what are now known as West and Green
Streets, crossing Mill River at two points. In 1666, the
town gave up the northern branch, Green Street, to Alexander Edwards, from whose home lot it had been taken.
The good and sufficient reason offered for discontinuing
this portion of the highway, was because it was of "noe
vse for the end intended." It had been originally laid out for
"a passadge over the reavr in floode tyms when they could
not pas beloe but now the reuer haue wrought such a
deepe Chanell in that place that maks it vnpasable."

An Equal Valua-   Another vote passed this year established
tion of Home   the town rate on home lots. They were all
Lots.   to be valued alike for purposes of taxation.
The order reads that "all home lotts granted or that shall
be granted by the Towne to any p'son shall be vallued and
rated to all Publiq Charges at fiue pound estate."

Bridge over Mill   There was great delay in building a bridge
River again be-   over Mill River. The matter came before
fore the Town.   the town at intervals, votes were passed ordering its construction, and ommittees for building it were
appointed, but the work for ome reason did not progress.
In 1662, the first vote on this subject provided that the
bridge should be built when the meeting house was finished, the people on Sou Street in the meantime being
excused from highway ra s. Three years after the question was again in agitatic. The meeting house had been
"comfortable to meet in" for more than a year; but no
movement seems to have been made towards erecting the
bridge, and the settlers n the south side of the river became impatient. In 16 3 (20-12-1665), on "motion of Enos
Kingsley and the rest the neyghbores on the southerly
side of the mill river ' a committee of five persons was
chosen to do the wo; but they were instructed not to
"exeed the charge of horse bridg on the townes account."
Probably this vote unsatisfactory, the people interested insisting upon something better. though they did not
care to accept the tow s implied invitation to add from

their own pockets whatever might have been needed for a more substantial structure. At any rate nothing seems to have been done about the matter at that time. Four years afterwards, in August, 1670, the town once more voted "to build a bridge over the mill rever acordinge toe our Ingadgment toe that side," and again appointed a committee of five persons "toe get it don with all possible speed." In this connection there is a vote under date of "January: 2:1670" (1671), adding two more to this committee, and giving them "power to detirmin wher this bredg shall be made and how and whether ther must be a bred our the riuer & trench."

Bridge Completed after Ten Years of Agitation.

In this particular case, bridge building seems to have been slow and tedious work, and two years more were consumed in the construction of this one. In 1673 (6th January, 1672), another committee of three persons was appointed "toe carry on the worke till it was finished." It is difficult to understand why there should have been so much delay. The cost may have had something to do with it, at first, as the South Street settlers were apparently not disposed to pay anything more towards it than their legal assessment, and the town had just completed new meeting house. It is possible also that the relief m a highway tax might hav been deemed by a majoi of the town a sufficient offse to the inconvenience of f ling the river, on horseback or crossing it by means of   ping stones. Whatever may have been the reason, certa it is that an agitation of more than ten years was required efore the first bridge was built across Mill River. It was completed in 1673, and was located very nearly on the site of the present old bridge, probably a little farther up the str m.

Thomas Mason's Account as Constable.

In 1666, Thom s Mason, the constable, seems to have had little difficulty in the settlement of his a ount with the town. The trouble grew out of the freigh the wheat in which the country tax was paid, and w is the treasurer refused to allow. The record of this affa r as follows :—

"Whereas the treasurer hath not as yet giuen a discharge to Thomas Mason, Constable for the Country rate in the year 1666, it was agreed on by the Sellect men to record the amount that was deliuered to the tresurer by William Clark because there was no obiction against it but only for the caring of the wheat from Windsor to Hartford which he refused to pay for all though he had sayd that if the aboue sayd Clark hauing again spoke with the constable and found it honest he would accept but afterwards forgott as he sayd that he had sayd so. the acount is as followeth.

The constable is debpter as apears by warrant   £40.15.10
Cont[r] Credit[r]

To 18 troopers	04.10.0
To Capt. Coke for killing 8 wolues . .	04.00.0
To Cornellius Merye for killing a wolf .	00.10.0
To Jo Web to wolues	01.00.0
To nayls & work to make a bin .	00.10.0
To Carting 101 bus. Wheat . . .	05.01.0
To 101 bu. of wheat shipt . .	25..5.0 — 40.16.00 "

The payment of the country rate in wheat must have been cumbersome and expensive. It was first carted to Windsor, thence to Hartford, where it was shipped to Charlestown. Appended to the above account is the certificate of the ship-master : —

"June the 6, 1666.   Receiued aboard the bark Speedwell from Thomas Mason, Constable of Northampton, to say one hundered and on bushill of wheat wherof 3[b] & half a peck was taken out to pay the boats hier. Receued by me to be delliuered to M[r] Richard Russell of Charlstown, the danger of the s[e] s excepted.

WILLIAM JANSON."

Delinquent Constables called to Order. Some of the constables seem to have been delinquent about collecting the rates, and it was found necessary to call them to an account, accordingly the townsmen ordered

"that Robert Bartlett and John Liman shall gather and pay all that is behind of all the rates that were comited to them to gather and pay in according as they had order before the tenth of aprill next insuing and if either of them do faile they shall forfitt to the towne twenty shillings for each of them beside all the damage."

Second School Teacher Employed. James Cornish served as school-master at most but three years.   After his engagement in 1664, there is no further allusion to schools upon the records till the "7th of January, 1666," (1667).   He either received his subsequent appointment from the selectmen, or else no school was carried on during those years. His successor was William Jeanes, with whom the following arrangement was made : —

"It was Agreed and voted that William Jeanes was hired by the Towne to teach Schoole one yeare, and for his encouragement and satisfaction for his Attendance vpon that worke the Towne and himselfe came to this conclusion and Agreement.

"1ᵗˡʸ Impʳ for the yeare hee is to haue out of the Towne stock Tenn poundes wᶜʰ the Townsmen pʳmise to pay.

"2ˡʸ ffowre pence pr weeke for such as are in the primer & other English books.

"3. Six pence pr weeke to learne the Accidence wrighting Casting Accounts.

"4. In case ther be a neglect yᵗ they doe not come constant 3 days shalbe accounted as a weeke."

Parents the first Teachers. Early schooling in New England was of a very primitive sort, the text books as well as the methods of the old country being employed. The only educated men were the clergy, and those persons who were engaged as teachers were generally prepared to impart only the rudiments of knowledge. Before schools were established, laws were enacted by which parents were enjoined to teach "their children and apprentices perfectly to read the English tongue." Instances are not rare where persons were brought before the courts and admonished for neglecting this requirement.

Text Books and Course of Study. Text books were few and the course of study limited. The entire curriculum was embraced in the above vote, and consisted in reading, writing, the accidence, (or rudiments of English or Latin Grammar) and casting accounts. Primers for the younger scholars, psalters, testaments and Bibles for the older ones who had learned to read, were the books most in use. The "horn book," which contained the alphabet, the nine digits, and the Lord's prayer, all on one page, so called because its cover was made of "translucent horn," was employed to some extent in New England, but not much in Northampton. Spelling did not come in till later, as the town and other records abundantly prove. "Dillworth's" Spelling Book, which became so popular in the next century, had not then been introduced. The "Accidence" (whether English or Latin is not stated), was somewhat used in the Northampton schools, but the accounts of the early traders in Northampton do not record the sale of any such books. Arithmetic, "casting accounts," as it was called, could not have been taught from books, as few treatises on that subject had yet found their way into these Connecticut valley towns. The schools seem to have been divided into what might·be considered two grades, and the compensation was graduated to suit each department.

William Jeanes o r J a n e s, came from England in 1637, settled in New Haven, June 4, 1639, and was admitted a freeman in 1648. He was by profession a school-master, and taught in New Haven for a number of years. In 1651, he proposed that the town should pay a portion of the salary of the teacher, instead of the whole being paid by the parents of the children. He went to Wethersfield soon after, and New Haven offered him " £10 from the town and the rest from the parents to teach boys and girls to read and write." He did not accept this offer, but came to Northampton in 1656. His home lot of two acres was the second one on the easterly side of Pleasant Street. One of the earliest settlers of Northfield, he carried on religious exercises there, in the capacity of Teaching Elder, till the town was destroyed by the Indians, in 1675. There is a tradition that divine services were held in the open air before a meeting house was built, and that during the first summer, Elder Jeanes preached under an oak tree. He did not return to Northfield after it was first abandoned, and died in Northampton, in 1690. He was twice married, his second wife being Hannah, daughter of Thomas Bascom, and widow of John Broughton.

His Character and Qualifications. Mr. Jeanes appears to have been a man of more than ordinary ability, and was sufficiently educated for the grade of schools he was called upon to teach. An excellent penman, he was chosen recorder of lands in 1657, which office he continued to hold for many years. He it was who made the first entry on the church book of records, and the first thirteen pages of that volume, written in a clear, plain and even hand, are still as legible as when they were inscribed nearly 250 years ago. No record of his appointment or election as Teaching Elder has been found, and it is not known when he attained to that position. He is first named as Elder after his removal to Northfield.

Schools during the next few years, 1669 to 1676. The immediate future of the school after the year 1667, is somewhat uncertain, and could not have been very satisfactory. Nothing of importance can be gleaned from the records for the next three years, and in fact very little has been learned respecting them during the seven years following the engagement of Mr. Jeanes. He was hired for but one year, and no mention is made of further service. He went to Northfield in 1670. The next allusion to schools was in March, 1669, when the town voted "that they are willing to haue a scole master for the yeare insueing." Within a couple of years the school appears to have been closed, for early in 1671, the following vote was passed, the wording of which seems to imply that no school was then in existence in Northampton : —

"The Town considering of the great want of a scolemaster for the instructing of Children and youth haue for that end apointed Mr Soloman Stoderd and Elder Strong to treat with Mr Watson[1] to see whether he may be ataind to come and settle among vs for to cary on a Scole and if there be like ly hood of attaining him then to make report to the Towne on what terms he may be procured." Evidently the committee did not succeed in obtaining his services, for in May of the same year, it was voted "to giue a scolemaster 30^l a yere prouided that one can bee procured fit for such an imploiment that is to say that shal be able and fit to teach an instruct children and youth to Read english and to write and cast acounts at least."

In this case the selectmen were instructed to act, but it is not probable that Mr. Watson was engaged. According to the records, no further attention was paid to schools for five years, but from other sources it is clear that in 1674 and 1675, a school teacher had been employed. Action

1 Probably Caleb Watson of Hartford, who graduated at Harvard College in 1661, taught school in that town in 1674, and for a number of years after. He certainly did not settle in this town, and there is no evidence that he ever taught school here. He was the first school-master in Hadley, where he was employed in 1667.

13

was again taken by the town in 1676, when it was voted to
"giue M^r [Joseph] Hawly An Invitation to teach schole
in this Towne on the same conditions or termes as formerly."
The selectmen, under the former vote, had hired Mr. Hawley a couple of years before. From his own accounts there
is proof that he taught here first in 1674, as will be seen in
the proper chronological order.

Orders Concerning   Much trouble and loss were occasioned in
Swine and Horses   the meadows by swine rooting up and de-
in the Meadows.   stroying "our corn and peece." In August,
1667, the matter was brought before the town and stringent
orders passed for the protection of these crops. In the
regulations adopted it is stated that previous orders for
preventing such damages were "inefectual for the end because of Swomps and high bushy places into which the
hogs run away and cannot be got to pound." Any person
finding swine within the fence "of the corne feild" insufficiently "yooked or ringed," might demand "toe shillings
for every Swine be they beger or less excepting sucking
pegs of sex weeks old." Proof of ownership was to be
deemed sufficient without impounding them. This order
did not remedy the evil, and three years afterwards another
proviso was added. All swine so taken were to be impounded at once, and if one man could not drive them he
was authorized to call in such assistance as was required.
The pigs were to be appraised and as many of them sold as
would pay the "charges for poundinge damage and driv-
inge;" the owner was allowed twenty-four hours in which
to redeem them. A similar order was passed regarding
horses found in the corn fields. If in case either of swine
or horses, the owner failed to pay the charges "the Townsmen were toe make distres upon his goods and take the
pay and pay it by the constable."

Duties Imposed   The General Court "being sencible of the
upon Importa-   great necessity to regulate the way of rays-
tions.   ing moneys for the defraying of the publick chardges of the comonwealth," in November, 1668,
enacted that there should "be a custome imposed on all
goods & merchandizes * * imported into this jurisdic-

con * * from after the first of March next coming."
Upon "all goods, provissions & merchandizes, two per
cent;" upon "horses, mares & neate catle, of what age
soeuer, five shillings a peece;" and upon "wheate & all
other graine, three pence for euery bushell." This law,
generally unpopular throughout the colony, was especially
obnoxious to the river towns, and Northampton, Hadley
and Springfield, took prompt measures to express their dissatisfaction. Committees were appointed by each of them
to take the matter into consideration, and after deliberation
they decided to appeal to the Legislature for relief. Accordingly these three towns at once sent in their protests
against the law. The action of Northampton in the premises follows : —

"At a Legall Towne meeting the 14th of the 10 mo : 1668 (December)
"It was then voted and agreed that the committee impowered by
the Towne to treate with and Transact the businesse with the neighboring Townes and if neede bee with Hartford, the whole matter is left
to ther wisdome and discression to Consider of the late order made by
the Honord Generall Court with Respect to Hartford in the excise of
two pence pr bushel.   the persons impowred are

LT. WILLIAM CLARKE
DECON WILLIAM HOLTON   } Committee."
JOSEPH PARSONS

Northampton Pe-   From this vote resulted the annexed peti-
titions against   tion, which recites forcibly the reasons of
the Law.   their disapproval. The river towns were
particularly aggrieved because of the opportunity afforded
the neighboring colony of Connecticut to retaliate by imposing a duty on all articles while in transit; the petition
representing that such action was already in contemplation. The only route for the transportation of freight was
by way of the river, and the people of this section of Massachusetts were unwilling to run the risk of any addition
to this already heavy burden. Not only were they compelled to pay freight, but also the expense of making and
keeping in repair the cartway to the head of navigation.
William Clarke, chairman of the above committee, was
chosen deputy for 1669, and upon him devolved the duty of
presenting the petition. Much opposition to this law was
manifested in all parts of the Commonwealth, as the Legislature promptly discovered at its next session : —

"To the Right Wor[ll] Wor[ll] and much Honord the Governour Deputy
Governo[r] and the Rest of our Honor[d] Magistrates & Deputyes Assembled in Generall Court at Boston.

Right Wor[ll] Wor[ll] and much Honord

"Amonge the high and Peculier favoures wherewith the Lord hath
dignified his poore people in this wilderness and o[r]selues in p[t]iculer,
this may not bee accounted the least, that wee haue such Godly, Prudent, and Faithfull Rulers set over vs, vnto whom wee may vpon our
necessities suppleacte for our releife in our Distressing difficulties, and
that with well grounded assurance, not to bee disown'd in the time of
o[r] neede : The Consideration whereof hath encouraged your Petitioners the Inhabitants of Northampton to Address o[r]selues vnto you in
this our Petition humbly shewing.

"May it please you that wheras ther was a lawe made as wee are informed the last Sessions of o[r] Honord Gene[ll] Court Respecting laying
of Custome or Trybute vpon Corne or other provisions that are brought
into the several Portes within this Collony, and this Order, as wee are
allsoe informed doth not exempt, but reach and bring in our neighbour-
ing Plantations belowe vs vpon Conecticut Riuer.

"Wherupon wee are informed that they are like to doe soe by vs allsoe, and some of them doe tell vs that they will make vs pay for all,
and allsoe tell vs that if 2[d] p[r] bush: will not, 4[d] or 6[d] shall, and if 2[s] 6d
p bar, will not 5[s] shall.

"Wee know your worships vnderstand that wee haue noe way to
Transporte our Corne and Provisions but thoroe them, and wee find it
very Difficult and Chargable, for it will Cost 1[s] p bush. to Winsor, and
2[d] p. bush. from thence to Hartford, and 6[d] p. bush. from Hartford to
Boston. And many times wee are exposed to warehouse roome. Bee-
sides all this wee haue binn at very great Charge in laying out, in makeing and maintayning highwayes, and Bridges, to make them fitt for
Traveling and Carting. And if wee should pay Trybute and Custome
at Hartford or elswher in Conecticut Jurisdiction, wee Conceiue the
burthen will bee soe heavy that wee feare will Cawse some Amongst vs
to bee thinke themselves about speedy remooueing. And Allsoe bee a
meanes to retard and hinder the proceeding and goeing on of any Plantation aboue vs.

"Much honord in the Lord wee feare allsoe that the putting this
lawe in Execution vpon o[r] neighbours and loeuing Confederates (who
through the Good hand of Gods Providence vpon vs, have soe liued in
loue, and Peace to geather without such Taxes) hath in it a Tendency
to breake the bond of Peace and loue: Therefore whether it were not
better to let the Children goe free, and lay taxes and Custome on
strang[rs].

"Therefore wee humbly begg and craue of you, that you would bee
pleasd to stopp and p[r]vent the execution of that order vpon our neigh-
bouring Collony, If it may bee: Or else to make some pvission for your
Petitioners that they may not bee pvoked to doe to vs as is aboue
exprest, that wee may still haue free Passage thoro them. And allsoe
that loue and Peace may bee still Continued as formerly.

" Which wee leaue to your Godly wisdome to act and doe that which you thinke meete for you^r Petitioners, thus Craueing p^rdon for our boldnesse, Intreateing allsoe that your worshipps would be pleased to take candidly what wee haue said, as we intend the same, not in any measure to reflect, but only to mention, and make known our grevances to you, soe you^r Petitioners shall pray.

Northampton

4th 11^{th mo} 1668.

JOHN STRONG
WILLIAM CLARKE
WILLIAM HOLTON
JOSEPH PARSONS"
and 104 others.

Everybody's Name on the Petition. This memorial was written by William Jeanes, which accounts in some measure for the peculiar orthography of the document. (Spelling was not among the studies in the schools when Mr. Jeanes taught them.) About half the signatures were also written by him, and the intention evidently was to include those of all the males in town twenty-one years of age and over. The petition contains the genuine autographs of the most prominent citizens, and the other names were undoubtedly added in order to increase its effectiveness as representing the unanimous sentiment of the community.

Many Towns Petition against the Duties. Similar protests against this enactment were presented from towns in all parts of the Bay colony, and the unfavorable judgment of the people was soon made manifest. While these appeals did not at once compass the entire repeal of the duties imposed, they had the effect of causing a reduction of the rates in 1669, and a suspension of them in reference to Connecticut and Plymouth, the following year. The cost of transporting wheat from Northampton to Boston, was according to the above document, 1s. 8d. per bushel. There was at that time very little boating on the river above Hartford. The river towns of both colonies had many interests in common, and a war of imposts would have been most unfortunate.

Highway to the foot of the Falls. When the town was first settled the nearest point at which uninterrupted water communication could be obtained was Hartford, and every thing but a few light articles was carted to

that place, and shipped to the Bay. Some years afterwards light draft boats were put upon the river between
Springfield and Hartford, and the up river towns provided
landing places, Hadley on the east, and Northampton and
Hatfield on the west side of the river, just below Willi-
mansett Falls, which were then within the bounds of
Springfield. In 1668, Northampton voted to build "a
cart bridg over munhan River for the cariage of o^r Corne
and Trade to the foote of the falls." A committee was appointed to take charge of the matter, and "to confere and
agree with Panchus [Hatfield] men and to carry on this
designe both respecting the bridg & the highway to the
foote of the falls."

Boating on the river above Hartford, was probably commenced about this time; the boats with Northampton
freight continuing up the stream till the falls obstructed
further progress. Northampton men are found engaged as
boatmen, in 1679 and 1680, and that is the first record of
water transportation above Springfield, though from the
preceding vote it may be inferred that such had been the
practice for twelve or more years. Many of the lighter
articles of merchandise were undoubtedly carried in canoes
even after the larger boats came in use. There was for
many years much carting of freight to Windsor and Hartford, notwithstanding the cheaper carriage by water.
When the boundary between Springfield and Northampton
was finally adjusted in 1685, special privileges were granted
to Northampton in order to reach the "boating place below
the falls." In 1674, the town voted to join with Hatfield
in constructing "a pasable Cartway over the mountaine for
vs toe transport our goods down by water."

CHAPTER XVI.

REV. ELEAZAR MATHER.

Death of Rev. Mr. Mather.

EIGHT years after his ordination here the community was called upon to mourn the death of its beloved pastor. But a decade had passed, and during that brief interval he had endeared himself to the hearts of his people, and established a reputation as a preacher of no small capacity. The facts attending his settlement have been fully sketched, but few and meagre are the details to be gleaned from the imperfect records of his brief ministry. He passed away in the prime of life, respected, beloved and honored.

Early Life. A Graduate of Harvard College.

Rev. Eleazar Mather, first minister of Northampton, was the son of Rev. Richard Mather of Dorchester, and was an elder brother of the celebrated Dr. Increase Mather. He was born at Dorchester, May 13, 1637, and at the age of nineteen was graduated at Harvard College. Quite early in life he became seriously impressed, and devoted himself to the Christian ministry. Within two years of his graduation he became so favorably known to the public, that when a minister was wanted at this new settlement in the wilderness, he was selected for that position. Nothing is known respecting his early life, and but little concerning the few years of it spent in Northampton.

He found the People in Disagreement.

Reared among the hardships and privations common to all the pioneer plantations of Massachusetts Bay, he was well fitted for the duties that awaited him upon the banks of the Connecticut. Thoroughly grounded in the religious tenets taught by his father, the first minister of Dorchester, he became a strenuous supporter of the "Congregational way," as understood and administered by the clergy of that day. He

came here in response to a vote desiring him "to bee a Mynister to them in a way of Tryall in dispensing his gifts,"
and served three years before the people were ready to establish the church and place him at its head.   On his arrival
he found an antagonism already existing in the community, which gathered such force before his formal settlement was consummated, that the authority of the Legislature was invoked in order to its adjustment.   Something of
the difficulty may have been due to the bitterness engendered by the witchcraft slander controversy, which occurred two years before he was called, and something to
the unfortunate quarrel over town officers, a little later,
but the question that came before the General Court arose
directly from friction caused through his own absence.
These dissensions have been touched upon in the preceding
pages, but their real cause is hidden by the mists of years.
The dim records of the past afford no adequate solution of
them and present no suggestion of their satisfactory arrangement.   The colonial records contain the only intimation relating to the last named controversy, which proved to
have been a difference of opinion concerning who should
officiate in the absence of the pastor during his novitiate.
A very trivial affair it would seem at the present day,
when all such matters are settled beyond question, but it
was one among others which at that time set the whole
town by the ears.   The cause of these absences may be
conjectured when a certain event which occurred in the
fall of the year 1659, is recalled.   Of course the formal settlement of the minister ended all serious dispute on any such
point, and his influence seems to have healed, for the time
being at least, the dissatisfaction then prevailing.   No exciting events occurred during his residence here.   No Indian wars ravaged the country, and few disturbing elements
of political significance invaded the tranquility of the people.   The never varying routine of life in the settlements
was not marred by any serious disaster or any imminent
danger sufficient to call forth the heroism of either pastor
or people.   But in the quiet of those favorable years, he
helped to organize and establish the church and community which have survived, strengthening with years, for
nearly two centuries and a half.

A Member of the   Barely twenty-one years of age when he
Synod of 1662.   entered upon his duties, he soon developed
                    a genuine love for his work that brought
all his energies into play. He lived in a time of religious
controversy, when principles were adopted which unsettled
the religious opinions of New England for nearly a century. The position which he assumed, though it drove
Jonathan Edwards from his pulpit, is now the unquestioned belief and practice of Congregationalism. Mr.
Mather was a member of the Synod, called by the General Court in 1662,[1] at which was adopted the celebrated
"half-way covenant." This covenant was strongly antagonized by a minority of the Synod, and a spirited discussion arose. Mr. Chauncey, president of Harvard College,
and Mr. Davenport of New Haven, boldly opposed it in
print. Mr. Allen replied to Mr. Chauncey, and Mr. Richard Mather answered Mr. Davenport. The two sons of Mr.
Mather, Eleazar and Increase, dissented from the decision
of the Synod,[2] and its conclusions were not immediately
adopted by the church at Northampton.

Mr. Mather's Let-   Though it is not known that the Northamp-
ter to Mr. Dav-   ton pastor took any active part in the dis-
enport.   cussions of the Synod, he has left on record
some interesting statements concerning the internal work-
ings of that body. In a letter to Mr. John Davenport of
New Haven, dated "4th of 5th Mo. 1662" (July 4, 1662), Mr.
Mather writes :—

"The reason why there were soe few, not above 10 or 12 that appeared to act contrary to what the Assembley voted, was because they
would allow every one his interpretation in the debate, & thence sundry inconsiderately voted for that which when it was too late they

1 A Synod of above 70 met in Boston, Tuesday, 11-21 March, 1662, and after two
adjournments reached its results in the September following. The result was a
qualified and subordinate membership, allowing baptized persons of moral life and
othodox belief to belong to the churches so far as to receive baptism for their children and all privileges but that of the Lord's supper for themselves. This was carried in the Synod by a large vote, 60 or more to less than 10.—Dexter's Congregationalism, pp. 470, 471.
    The subjects propounded by the court for the consideration of the Synod, were :
"Quæst 1. Who are the subjects of baptisme. Quæst 2. Whither, according to the
word of God, there ought to be a consociation of churches, & what should be ye
manner of it."—Records of Massachusetts, vol. 4, part 2, p. 38.

2 Hutchinson's History of Massachusetts Bay, vol. 1, p. 224.

wished they had not done.   There was scarse any of the Congregationall principles, but they we[re] layen at by some or other of the
Assembly, as relations of the worke of grace.   The power [of] voting
of the fraternity in Admission, &c.: profession of vissible faith, & re-
pentance (to vse their owne words) as it was intended by the Synod in
46, not to be looked at in such as were Baptized in the church in reference to the Baptisme of there Children.   Mr Parker of Newbery was
one of the gr^t Antagonïsts of the Congregationall way & order, tho. it
not being the work of the p^rsent Synod to determine those matters, his
many motions to consider whether wee were in the right ecleseasticall
order, were not attended.   All dissenting is esteemed intollerable &
dissenters are accoumpted & charged to be the Breakers of the peace
of the churches, Adhærents to Brownisticall notions, & what not."

He Dissents from
the Synod's De-
cision.

All who dared to oppose the decision of the
Synod were bitterly denounced, but Mr.
Mather could not conscientiously agree to
its propositions.   He preferred to suffer the obloquy he declares to have fallen upon dissenters rather than assent to
what he considered an innovation upon the heretofore established custom and procedure of the church.   No action was
taken by the church here till about six months before the
death of Mr. Mather.   This delay of seven years, apparently
without any serious consideration of this important question, was no doubt due to the high respect entertained for
the opinions of the pastor.   The principles involved had
been freely and continuously under discussion throughout
the country, and must have challenged comment here as
well as elsewhere.   The apparent unanimity of the church,
when the propositions came up for action, indicates that
the people, familiar with the subject, had already decided
upon their course.

Mr. Mather's Let-
ter Concerning
Non-conformists.

The intolerance of old England caused
many non-conformists to look with longing
eyes to New England as a place of refuge.
Many ministers came over and many others would have
followed but for the uncertain state of affairs between the
colonists and the mother country.   While the Massachusetts Bay Colony was threatened with the loss of those privileges which alone rendered it a desirable asylum, the harrassed and bewildered religionists of that day hesitated to
add to their sectarian discomforts the material hardships
of a new and untried existence in the wilds of America.

Upon this point Mr. Mather writes as follows in another paragraph of the letter to Mr. Davenport, already quoted : [1]

"As touching newes from England. * * * Many thinke of removing out of England tho. they know not whether. There is a minister, one Mr Allen, come over lately (well acquainted with Mr Hooker) a Congregationall man, & one intimate with M^r Th: Goodwin, who reports that it is thought by the sober Godly people, it had beene better for the Countrey if they had not sent soe many addresses & Agents, which is reported to be a discovery of there pusalanimity & want of courage to stand for the cause they came hither for. Many are expelled heere this sumer. Mr Bartlit of Bidiford & his son were shipt for N: E:, but an Oath was imposed vpon them both afore they could get out of the harbo^r & that stopt them, for they chused rather to dye in prisson than take it." [2]

His Characteristics, and the Results of his Labors.
Earnest and untiring in the performance of every duty, a fair degree of success rewarded his labors, and the church flourished under his ministrations. Not only was he a very zealous preacher and a staunch upholder of the "Congregational way," but he was a most exemplary man. Possessing in a marked degree the governing characteristics of the Mathers, he was a person of decided opinions, and his sermons were eloquent and persuasive. The church was organized in 1661, and during that year thirty-five persons were admitted ; the next year there were twelve more admissions ; the year following saw nine new names added ; in 1664, five ; in 1665 and 1666, there were three in each year ; and in 1667, four more, making in all, seventy-one members in full communion at the time of his death. Feebleness of body greatly restricted his most effective work, and so keenly did he realize the loss occasioned thereby, that he voluntarily relinquished a portion of his salary towards the support of an assistant, well knowing that the community could ill afford to pay two pastors. His death took place on the 24th of July, 1669, at the age of 32.

1 Hutchinson alludes to this letter of Mr. Mather (see History, vol. 1, p. 225, note). His quotation, however, embodies part of a letter written by Rev. Mr. Rutherford to Mr. Davenport, which he credits to Mr. Mather. The first four lines are from the letter of Mr. Rutherford, and the rest comprises the last two sentences of Mr. Mather's letter quoted above. (Compare Hutchinson, vol. 1, p. 225, with Mass. Hist. Col. Series 4, vol. 8, pp. 190 and 194.) Hutchinson quotes Mr. Mather as saying "Many are *expected* here this summer," but in the "Mather papers," published in Mass. Hist. Collections, Series 4, vol. 8, pp. 192, 194, the word is *expelled*.

2 Massachusetts Historical Collections, 4th Series, vol. 8, pp. 192-194.

Sermons Published after his Death. Rev. Richard Mather, who died a short time before Eleazar, counseled his younger son, Increase, to pay particular attention to the spiritual interests of the rising generation. Eleazar also treasured the dying words of his father, and preached several sermons, shortly before his own death, in which he carried out this last injunction. The substance of these sermons was published in 1671, under the title "Serious exhortations to the present and succeeding generations in New England, earnestly calling upon them all to endeavor that the Lord's gracious presence may be continued with posterity; being the substance of four sermons preached at Northampton by Rev. Eleazar Mather." Upon one of these pamphlets, Dr. Increase Mather penned the following:—"The first sermon was preached June 13, 1669; the second, June 27, following; the third, July 4th; the fourth and last, July 11th. After which day my brother Eleazar lived not in health able to preach; for July 13 he took to his bed and July 24th he went to rest in the Lord, to keep everlasting Sabbath in heaven."

Tributes to his Memory. Few indeed are the tributes to his worth and talents left by those who had personal acquaintance with him, and it is only from others who judged him by the results of his labors, that any estimate of his character can be obtained. Rev. Cotton Mather, his nephew, writes of him as follows:—

"Here (Northampton) he labored 11 years in the vineyard of the Lord, and then the 12 years of his day's labor did expire, not without the deepest lamentations of all the churches as well as his own, then sitting along the river of Connecticut. As he was a very zealous preacher and accordingly saw many seals of his ministry, so he was a very pious walker, and as he drew towards the end of his days, he grew so remarkably ripe for heaven in a holy, watchful, fruitful disposition, that many observing persons did prognosticate his being not far from his end."

Rev. Jonathan Edwards, in his "Narrative of Surprising Conversions," speaks of him as "one whose heart was much in his work, abundant in labors for the good of precious souls, he had the high esteem and great love of his people, and was blessed with no small success."

Eleazar Mather   Rev. Mr. Mather married Esther, daughter of Rev. John Warham, first minister of Windsor, Sept. 29, 1659. They had three children, Eunice, who married Rev. John Williams of Deerfield, was captured by the Indians, and slain on the march to Canada, when that town was destroyed in 1704; Warham, who lived at New Haven, and Eliakim, who died when quite a young man.

Mr. Mather's Estate, Inventory and Probate.   He left no will, and at the September session of the Probate Court, in 1669, the estate was presented for Probate. The inventory as taken August 23^d, by Mr. John Strong and Dea. William Holton, was as follows:—

"*Imprimis* Pewter, brass fire irons, earthen ware, table wth other small things in ye kitchen	£14.05.06
It. feather bed & bedding belonging to it wth bedsted & trundle bed in ye parlour	07.10.00
It. Cupboard, table, chaires, stooles, fire irons, wth other small things there	05.10.06
It. barrells, tubs, trayes with their contents in ye cellar	02.10.06
It. apparell, money, watch	29.07.06
It. feather bed, bedding, lynnen, chests, trunk, wth other small things in ye kitchen chamber	25.08.06
It. rugg, blankett, Coverlett, bedsted, &c. in ye little chamber	03.17.00
It. nayles, fruit, Sugar, flax, Saddles, bridles, wth small things in ye porch chamber	07.06.06
It. wheat, Indian corn, small bed & bedstead, salt, flax wheeles, pillion, bags, &c.	09.00.00
It. tubbs, ax, spade, beetle, wedges, collar, bees	03.12.00
It. crop of Hay & corn in ye barn	13.00.00
It. ye prentice youth	06.00.00
It. house, barne, outhousing, orchard, Homelot	140.00.00
It. accomodation of meddow with ye appurtenances	160.00.00
It. liveing Stock, horses, Kine, Swine, Sheep, &c.	47.00.00
It. bookes with some other small things	60.08.00
	534.16.00
Out of which ye estate is in debt about	10.00.00
Remaynes	524.16.00"

Mrs. Mather was appointed administratrix and the "corte ordered one hundred and forty pounds to ye eldest son, & one Hundred pounds to ye daughter for y^t shee is the eldest child, & one Hundred pounds to ye youngest son by reason of its youngness & infirmityes accompanying it whereby it is accounted that there must be more than ordinary charges in its education." The rest of the property, amounting to £184.16.00, was given to Mrs. Mather, and she was to "have the improvement of ye whole estate till the children shall attayne such age as their portions are to be paid to them, viz: to the sons at one & twenty years of age & to the daughter at eighteen years of age."

Mr. Mather desired that Capt. Pynchon would act the part of overseer to his wife and children and the court appointed him, associating with him in the trust, Elder John Strong. The estate was to be expended, or as much as should be required, in bringing up and educating the children. Housing, land and books were to stand as security for the children's portions, but the overseers were allowed to sell the books or parts of them, if necessary, giving security for the money received.

In 1675, Mrs. Stoddard (Mrs. Mather had in the meantime married Rev. Solomon Stoddard) reported £25 not returned in the inventory, and the court added that amount to her share.

Salary of Mr. Mather.   Mr. Mather left a comfortable estate valued, according to the above inventory, at more than £500. His salary, while it was undoubtedly equal to that paid in other towns, was small. The town first voted to give him £25 in merchantable wheat for a half year's salary, then it was increased to £80 per year, and he afterwards relinquished £10 towards the salary of his assistant. For two years he received £70, and the rent of the sequestered land, but after that time there is no further allusion to his salary upon the records. His compensation was never paid in pounds sterling, and seldom was any of it paid in money. Gold and silver were quite scarce in the inland towns, especially in those upon the frontier. Provisions, country pay as it was called, consisting of wheat, peas, and corn, at prices established by the town, which were generally considerably higher than their money value, were the medium. The £80 salary of Mr. Mather, if paid in money at 6s. to the dollar, would have been only about $266.66, but when paid in wheat at 3s. 6d., peas at 2s. 6d., and Indian corn at 2s. per bushel, was considerably less. On the small compensation paid them, the clergy managed to live comfortably, bring up their families, and leave a fair estate.

Every Minister a Farmer.
It should be remembered that every man in the community was a farmer. The minister was no exception to this rule. Mr. Mather had a homestead of four acres, with a dwelling house and other buildings upon it, and forty acres of meadow land given him in fee simple. Besides this, he had the use of the land sequestered for the ministry, consisting of forty acres more. The inventory of his estate proves that he practiced farming to a considerable extent. He had live stock valued at £47, and produce in the barn, worth about £20 more. An "apprentice youth," whose services were appraised at £6, was probably his main assistant in farm work. Neighbors and friends were always ready to help, and many a day's work upon the farm was given by the parishioners to aid the minister.

Fire Wood always Supplied.
In addition to the salary, it was the practice to supply the minister with fire wood. This custom was probably adopted later, as no mention of it is made during the life of the first two pastors. But in after years large quantities of wood were furnished, especially during the pastorate of Jonathan Edwards. Other and valuable gifts were constantly being made, and many a substantial donation found its way to the larder of the pastor. It is possible that the grants of land to the first two ministers contained trees enough to keep them in fire wood (though no upland appears to have been given to Mr. Mather), but afterwards when the wood lands had all been divided, it became necessary for the town to furnish them with fuel.

Duties of the old time Ministers.
Notwithstanding the exacting duties of the clergy, and they were severe and onerous, the minister found time to accomplish considerable manual labor. In fact, the demands of existence compelled him to till the ground. Two sermons, and they were by no means the thirty minute discourses of modern

days, had to be prepared every week. The weekly lecture was imperative, though in this section it was finally changed, by the union of several towns, to a "six weeks lecture." There were fasts and thanksgivings in abundance, when the besetting sins of the times or the political complications of the day, had to be set forth in strong colors. Catechising the children once a week, and the frequent pastoral visits from house to house, the minister having special oversight of the daily lives of his parishioners, could not be omitted. There were no marriage fees to eke out the scanty salary. Marriage was considered only a civil contract, and was solemnized by magistrates. Funerals were conducted with much ceremony, and in many instances at great expense. The sermon, if any was considered necessary, was delivered in the meeting house, from which the people marched to the cemetery in couples, females first in case of a woman, and males in case of a man, to the sound of the slowly tolling bell. In early times religious services were seldom held at the grave, though the minister was usually present. Ordinarily he was the only college educated person in the settlement, though sometimes, young college graduates, aspirants for the pulpit, taught school, and some of them sought the opportunity of studying theology under the tuition of the village pastor. Before the establishment of schools of a sufficiently high grade to fit pupils for college, the minister was able to add a trifle to his income by initiating a few boys into the mysteries of Greek and Latin. The clergyman seldom mingled in local politics, yet his advice was continually sought, and to his decision controversies and difficulties were constantly referred. Official correspondence with the government, in a majority of cases, fell to the lot of the clergy. During King Philip's war much of the correspondence from this section with the authorities at the Bay, was carried on by the ministers at Northampton and Hadley. Though exempted by law from military service, many of them volunteered as chaplains, when important expeditions were undertaken. The brief letters of the Hampshire clergymen, describing local events, especially during the Indian wars, became the foundation for the history of the times in which they lived, and are now in many instances the only data extant. Busy men, leaders in civil as well as ecclesiastical affairs, they exerted an influence commensurate with their spiritual calling.

Influence of the Church in Promoting the Settlement.
During the formative period of the settlement, the Church, as in all New England villages, became one of the most important factors in its development. It was the foundation of the political as well as the spiritual life of the community. Not to be a Church member argued ill for the standing and position of any person. Intent that "the glory of God might be furethered," the pioneers of this region, fostered, protected, cherished and obeyed those divine precepts which formed the ground work of their faith and the bulwark of their religion. Jealous of the appearance of evil, zeal sometimes overstepped prudence, and sharp contentions about religious matters were the result. However bitter might have been their personal feelings, there was always unanimity towards the preacher. The ministers in the original plantations of Massachusetts Bay were all men of superior education and great piety, very many of them possessing business talents of no inferior order. Then ministers were settled for life. The pastoral relation was considered too sacred to be readily severed, and when the clergyman became infirm from age, and unable to perform his manifold labors, the town always provided a colleague.

CHAPTER XVII.

MATTERS ECCLESIASTICAL AND EDUCATIONAL.

An Invitation Extended to Rev. Solomon Stoddard.

EFFORTS to obtain a new minister must have followed closely upon the death of Mr. Mather. The town was deprived of its pastor in the latter part of July, and in less than three months a movement to fill the vacancy began. William Clarke and Aaron Cook were deputies to the General Court, one or both of whom were undoubtedly present at its October session. Armed with authority, and probably accompanied by a special committee, they at once instituted inquiries to ascertain if any one could be obtained. A prominent clergyman of Boston recommended Rev. Mr. Solomon Stoddard as better "qualified than any other person with whom he was acquainted." This advice was promptly acted upon and the proposition brought before Mr. Stoddard. He had just returned from two years' service in Barbadoes, whither he went in search of health, and was about to embark for England, having already placed his baggage on board a vessel which was to sail the next day. Yielding to the earnest solicitations of his friend and the committee from this town, the proposed voyage was relinquished, and he decided to come to Northampton. By whom this committee was appointed, or of whom it was composed, cannot now be ascertained.

Terms of Settlement.

Nothing was entered upon either church or town records relative to any preliminary action that may have been taken concerning the call to Mr. Stoddard. The church book contains no reference whatever to the matter, and the first recorded vote of the town was the following, subsequent events indicating that Mr. Stoddard was already preaching here when it was passed :—

"At a legall Towne Metting 4 March 16$\frac{6}{7}\frac{9}{0}$ the townes propositions to Mr Solomon Stoder on conditione of hª settlement among vs and cary on theᴧwork of the ministry.

"1 voted vnanumusly that thay hope by the blesing of god on them to giue Mr Solomon Stodder one hundreed pound yearly as long as he continueth among vs and carieth on the worke of the Minestry alone this the ingage to pay in curent pay as formerly they paid to Mr Eliezer Mather.

"2 to giue him one hundreed pound in consideration of building a house to be paid within two or three years.

"3 that the Towne will within fiue or six years procure for Mr Stoder twenty acors of land within our fenced feild fit for Plowing and Mowing but the towne doth ingag that in case thay can procure it soner that they will."

The Town Reiterates its Offer to Mr. Stoddard. Though the exact date of Mr. Stoddard's removal to Northampton is uncertain, the fact that he married the widow of his predecessor, Mrs. Esther Mather, on the 18th of March, 16$\frac{6}{7}\frac{9}{0}$, is strong presumptive evidence that he delayed not in coming, after his interview with the Northampton committee. Undoubtedly he immediately commenced preaching, "by way of tryall," as was the custom. On the 29th of August, 1670, a committee of nine persons, viz :—

"Elder John Stronge, Lieft William Clarke, Decon William Holton, Dauid Wilton, Ensigne John Limon, Joseph Parsons, Thomaε Roote Senr, Robort Bartlete, Sergeant John King" were "chosen by the Towne and Empowred toe ackt in all matters in reference toe the settlement of Mr Solomon Stodord, viz : to giue Mr Stodord a hundred pound insteede of twenty acors of Land which was formerly voted by the towne to giue him, and alsoe to giue it him souner if they see goode. This committee was alsoe empowred by the towne toe by Land if they cee goode that is now toe be sold. * * and whatsoeuer this commitie doth in reference toe the premises the Towne doth theretoe agree, ratiefie and confirme." They were given full power "toe ackt accordinge toe there best discresion for the setlement of Mr Sollomon Stodord ether toe giue the sequestered Land or part of it or agree with him otherwise as they see goode not exseeding the toe hundred pound which is besid his yearely mayntenance." In September, after "serious consideration" the committee "determined toe by or procuer a hundred pounds worth of Land in the meadow plowinge and moueinge Land

and giue toe Mr Stodord : this toe be don betwene this and March next
ensuinge : 2^{ly} we will giue Mr Stodord on hundred pound a yeare for
his mayntinance acordinge toe the Towne vote March 4th 70 whearof
the income of the Sequestred land shall be part of it or elce he shall
haue the Sequestred land in his owne hand toe emproue himself if he
see goode as part of it and the remainder we will make goode: Conserninge the third proposition that we would giue Mr Stodord a hundred pound in consideration of buildinge him a house and toe pay it in
toe or thre yeare we will deliver him a hundred pounds worth of the
Sequestred Land for he toe Emproue or take the benifite of til we pay
him that hundred pound, which we will doe in two or thre years tyme.
* * Alsoe we will give Mr Stodord a home lot of fower acors if he
pleace. all these terms spesified we will doe and performe by the bliss-
inge and help of god in cace Mr Stodord doth sitle and abide amongst vs."

After Two Years
he Accepts the
Call.

Mr. Stoddard took ample time to consider
the matter, and did not formally accept the
call till 1672. In that year grants of land
were voted in accordance with the previous agreement, and
the town also purchased twenty-four and three-quarter
acres of meadow land from the widow of David Ensign;
six acres were in Great Rainbow, five in Little Rainbow,
six in Venturer's Field, and seven and three-quarters in
Walnut Trees divisions. He also received four acres within
the common fence, near the pound (at the lower end of
Pleasant Street), and this twenty-eight and three-quarter
acres undoubtedly comprised the £100 worth of meadow
land promised. An account, carried out upon the records,
shows that the town paid for the land bought of the Estate
of David Ensign, the sum of £92.2.6. This statement fixes
the price of meadow land at £3.14.5, or at six shillings to
the dollar, at about $12.40 per acre. Mr. Stoddard did not
immediately avail himself of the gift of a home lot, and
none was granted him till 1684. In 1673, however, "the
towne voted Mr Stoddard should be pay^d fiftie pound of
that hundred pound we ingaged toe giue him toe build a
house." For seventeen years or more after his marriage
to Mrs. Mather, he lived on the Mather homestead, at the
corner of Main and Pleasant Streets, in the house built by
the town and given to the first minister. In 1689, when
the youngest son of Rev. Eleazar Mather became of age,
that homestead was sold to John and Moses Lyman.

The New Pastor Ordained. On the 7th of February, 167½, Mr. Stoddard definitely accepted the call to the pastorate, in a letter addressed to the "Rev. John Strong, Ruling elder of the Church of Christ at North-ampton."[1] The installation, however did not take place for several months. The only account of the ceremonies of that occasion is found in the book of church records, inscribed in the handwriting of Mr. Stoddard himself:—

"Sept. 11th, 1672. Solomon Stoddard was ordained Pastour to the Church at North-Hampton by M[r] John Strong Ruling Elder of that Church & M[r] John Whiting Pastour to the Second Church in Hart-ford, & M[r] John Russell Pastour of the Church at Hadley gave the Right hand of ffellowship in the name of the Second Church at Hart-ford, the Churches of Gilford, ffarmington, Winsor, Hadley, Spring-feild & Hatfeild, whose messengers were present."

The Church Ac-cepts the "Half-way Covenant." When Mr. Stoddard commenced his labors in Northampton, he found that the "half-way covenant" had been fully accepted by the church. Two meetings were held, one in December, 1668, and the other in February, 1669. At the first one the subject of baptism was considered; at the other that of the consociation of churches, and both were consented to and approved by the church. This action was in accordance with the result of the Synod of 1662, as "commended to their consideration by Order of the Honno[r]ed Gn[ll] Court." Apparently nothing further was accomplished under these votes from the death of Mr. Mather till the installation of Mr. Stoddard. In November following that event, a spe-cial vote was passed which provided

" That from year to year such as grow up to adult age in the church shall present themselves to the Elders, & if they be found to under-

1 In this letter, after referring to the invitation of the church and people that he would undertake to be their pastor, he says :—" without eyeing that power and grace which God has treasured up in Jesus Christ, it were altogether vain for me to at-tempt such an undertaking. The best is, that when we have the command of God for our warrant,we have his promise both for assistance and pardon. I do therefore ven-ture to declare, that it is my intention, some time this next summer, to answer your desire in accepting of your invitation, giving up myself the residue of my days to the service of the house of God in this place; beseeching you, who are not altogether unacquainted with the difficulties, temptations and burdens of such a work, nor wholly strangers to my unfitness, to bow your knees to the Father of our Lord Jesus Christ, earnestly begging that he would fit me by his Spirit for so solemn a charge, and make me a blessing unto you and your posterity; that I may be enabled to be a faithful steward, and that my labor may not be in vain; that light, and peace, and the power of religion may be continued in this plantation."—Rev. Solomon Williams' Historical Sermon, April 13, 1815, pp. 19, 20.

stand & assent unto the doctrine of faith, not to be scandalous in life, & willing to subject themselves to the gouernment of Christ in this Church, shall publickly own the covenant & be acknowledged members of this church."

One "form of words expressing the Summe of the covenant to be used in Admission of members into a state of education," and another "to be used in the admission of members unto full communion," as well as the form of acknowledgment by the church in each case, were also entered upon the records. This continued to be the governing principle of the church for many years. In the course of time this system of "large congregationalism" drifted into the more lax method of admitting all to the full privileges of the church. It was argued that faith sufficient to justify the baptism of children was ample to admit the parents to the church as full communicants. This practice was not confined to Northampton, but became almost universal in Congregational churches. About the beginning of the eighteenth century, Mr. Stoddard propounded his theory that "the Lord's Supper is instituted to be a means of regeneration." This was the distinctive "Stoddardean doctrine." His proposition was strongly opposed by the Mathers—Increase and Cotton—and as strenuously defended by its author. The controversy became quite general and nearly every clergyman in New England ranged himself upon one side or the other. Church practice of course differed, but whatever bitterness of feeling was engendered thereby soon died out, and the antagonism upon this point "did not interfere with fellowship or disturb the peace." When the church formally assented to the half-way covenant, it also decided upon certain propositions, "Respecting Dutyes and Privilidges of the Children of the Covenant and the due and Orderly managment ther of," adopted a profession of faith, consisting of forty-six articles, and amended and enlarged the church covenant.

Admissions to the Church. During the first four months after Mr. Stoddard's settlement, 104 persons "Personally took the covenant" or were admitted to "a state of education." Many of them had children, who were baptized, and to some of the adults the same ordinance was administered.

Controversy over the Establishment of the "Old South Church," Boston, 1669 to 1771.

During the interval between the death of Mr. Mather and the settlement of Mr. Stoddard, came the disruption of the First Church in Boston, though the controversy which led to it had been going on for some years. People in this section became somewhat interested in the matter, and Northampton and Hadley exerted incidentally an influence in shaping the result. It is not needful to enter extensively upon the details of this transaction, though a brief synopsis may be necessary. After the death of Rev. Mr. Norton and Rev. Mr. Wilson, Pastor and Teacher in this church, a call was extended to Rev. Mr. Davenport of New Haven, who accepted. The deceased pastor and teacher, as well as a majority of the members of the church, strongly favored the new covenant. Consequently the call to Mr. Davenport, who vehemently opposed the decision of the Synod, though sanctioned by a majority vote of the church, provoked a heated debate, and a number of the influential members of that body, refused to acquiesce in his settlement. They finally withdrew, and proceeded to organize what has since been known as the "Old South Church." The First Church declined to dismiss the seceders, but an ecclesiastical council recognized them as a new church. This revived the discussion of the "Half-way covenant" throughout the country. Gov. Bellingham, who sympathized with Mr. Davenport, called an extra session of the Magistrates, but they declined to act. Throughout New England the churches ranged themselves on the two sides of this contention. Favor to the First Church meant opposition to the Synod, while support of the new Church signified concurrence in its decisions.

A Memorial from two Hampshire Towns.

The next suggestion, bearing upon this question came from Hadley and Northampton. An address or memorial from those towns brought the matter before the General Court. This document bears date May 3, 1670. It referred to the depressed condition of the churches, which indicated that the Lord instead of his wonted blessing

"hath shewed us both many signes of his displeasure against and departure from us: which if he proceed to doe then is that fearful woe

Hos: 9: 12 accomplished toward us. This Consideration and fear whereof occasioneth us to present this our humble Enquiry to this Honoured
Court viz Whether the rods of God upon our churches and land have
not this speaking voice to us that there should be some publike and
solemn enquiry what it is that hath provoked the Lord (who doth not
afflict willingly but if neede be) against us."

This memorial was signed by Henry Clarke, John Russell, Samuell Smith, in the name of the freemen of Hadley,
and by William Holton and William Clarke of Northampton, "in the name of Sundrey of the freemen there who
have had Consideration of the above mentioned premises."
These last two named gentlemen were the deputies from
Northampton for that year.

The Legislature   In the House of Deputies the petition was
takes Action   referred to a committee of five persons, to
upon the Ad-
dress.   which the magistrates added another member. This committee, after a "large time
of consultation," were unable to agree, and majority and
minority reports were presented. These coincided mainly
concerning the cause of God's displeasure and the means
by which it was to be removed. The majority denounced
in particular the "innovation in doctrine and opinion, worship and practice then prevailing," but did not refer explic-
itly to the existing controversy concerning the new church,
though that was evidently the animus of their strictures.
To this the minority demurred. The report of the majority was approved by the deputies, but their action was not
concurred in by the magistrates, who desired "a clearer
exposition" of certain parts of the report. A second paper
was sent to the magistrates disapproving of the proceedings relative to the "Old South," and censuring certain
parties concerned in them. This not proving satisfactory,
still further correspondence ensued between the two
branches of the government, and at length finding that
they could agree upon nothing else, they adopted the usual
course in such cases, ordered a day of fasting, humiliation
and prayer, and dropped the subject. By this time the
question had become wholly political, and at the ensuing
election parties were divided between the old and the new
church in Boston. A majority of the former members of
the House of Deputies were succeeded by new ones and the

complexion of that body was changed. The matter was revived in the next House, by a memorial from fifteen of the most distinguished clergymen in the colony, and the establishment of the new church was sanctioned by the legislature.

Vote of the North-ampton Deputies, 1671. There seems to have been no special reason why the people of the Connecticut valley should have concerned themselves particularly about the formation of a new church in Boston. The supreme importance of the principle underlying the whole controversy was in a sense sufficient to account for it, yet the matter, certainly in a local point of view, had much less significance for this, than for the eastern section of the Commonwealth. Peter Tilton of Hadley, was undoubtedly a prime mover in the affair. He was a member of the committee that considered the memorial from Hadley and Northampton, and the majority report was in his hand-writing. It has been insinuated that the petition origina-ted at the suggestion of Gov. Bellingham, between whom and the Rev. Mr. Russell, a very friendly feeling existed. Messrs. Clarke and Holton were re-elected deputies from Northampton, and although they signed the memorial of the Hadley men, they finally voted with the majority in sustaining the new church. At this time Northampton had no settled minister, though Mr. Stoddard had been called, and was then preaching here. The church, how-ever, of which William Holton was a deacon, and William Clarke a member in full communion, had already approved and adopted the decision of the Synod.[1]

Fine for not clos-ing the Meadow Gates. Tax Commissioner Appointed. In March, 1670, "it was voted affirmatiuely that if any shall let in any Cattell into the Meadow and not folow them or get them out or if any person shall Leaue oppen any of the Meadow Gats he shall be fined fiue shillings." In accordance with a law passed in 1647, "for a more equall & ready way of raysing monyes for defray^g publicke charges in time to come," in the month of August, "En-

---

1 Sprague's Annals, vol. 1, p. 96; Judd's History of Hadley, p. 85; Palfrey's His-tory of New England, vol. 8, pp. 83-86; History of Old South Church, vol. 1, pp. 90-107.

signe John Limane was chosene Commishener toe Joyne with the selectmen toe take the state of the Towne and cary the list toe Springfeild and meete with the Comishen-ers acordinge toe Law." The valuation lists of the several towns in the county were to be considered and perfected by Commissioners who were to meet at the shire town, and transmit the same to the Treasurer of the Commonwealth. This is the first record of any action by the town under this law. It is not probable, however, that the law had been ignored up to this time. There must have been a fail-ure on the part of the town clerk to record, rather than a neglect on the part of the town to appoint.

Land set apart for Schools. Permanent provision was made for schools this year, a quantity of land being seques-tered for that purpose. This was the foun-dation of the fund for the use of schools which was many years in existence. The town voted in January, 16$\frac{70}{71}$, to set apart

"A parcell of Land containing 80: or a hundreed Acors, if it can be found: for som publick vse as for in corragment of a scole or for what vse the Towne shall se good—and that this may be speedly done there was then a comitte chosen to Lay out this Land and to see that it bee Laid out where it may bee most for the Townes profit."

Location and Rent of the School Land. Two parcels of land were "found" fit for this purpose, the next year; both were on Manhan River, near Bartlett's Mill, now Easthampton. One tract of land containing eighty acres, was situated "a little aboue the cart way as you goe ouer the river and so vp the river on both sides, running from the brook a little above the cart way to Thomas Dewey's meadow, westerly;" and the other of twenty acres was "be-low the falls in munhan that are below the cart way." This land was leased apparently for a long term of years. That part of it above the mill was rented in two parts, one at 16s. and the other at 64s., bringing in an income of £4 yearly. The portion below the mill, called the upper and lower meadow, was also leased in two sections, at 15s. each per year. This land was held by the town for more than seventy years, when it was sold and the proceeds funded for the use of the schools.

A Poll Tax to pay the Minister. Other Rates and a Penalty for False Returns. In January 16$\frac{70}{71}$, it was voted that "all householders and Ratable persons shall pay 2^s 6^d per head to the ministers Rate for the year insuing." Stock was to be rated the same as it was "estemd in making the contry rate," and mowing and plowing land was to be rated at "twenty shillings" per acre. It was also voted that "if any in bringing in a list of Estate shall keep back any part of his estate he shall be Liable to be Rated double for that Estate which he keeps back if it can be found." This vote was repeated in 1674.

Land Grants to be acted on at two Meetings, and Town Business to be Recorded with greater care. Apparently there had been much irregularity in the granting of land. Many errors had crept in, and frequent votes were required to correct them. In order to prevent such inaccuracy in future, as well as to check inconsiderate and unsatisfactory grants, a vote was passed at the above meeting providing "that in granting of Land it shall be first be motioned at one Towne meeting and not granted but left to the Consideration of the Towne till the next meeting." At the same time provision was made for a more careful record of the proceedings of the several town meetings. An order was adopted "that all matters coming to the Towns considderation shal be writen downe in som lose paper before that it be voted by the Towne and then recorded verpatum in the Towne Book." If a vote of this kind had been previously passed and enforced, the early records would now be of much greater value.

Commissioners to end Small Causes no longer Elected. This year there disappears from the town proceedings the familiar record of the annual election of Commissioners to end Small Causes. After this date they appear to have been appointed by the County Court. When William Clarke was chosen a Justice of that court, special provision was made for the continuance of these officials in Northampton and Hadley, though the office had been abolished in Springfield, when Mr. Pynchon became a member of the County Court. Commissioners were appointed by the court till 1684, when all local record concerning them ceases. When Sir Edmund Andros reorganized the judicial system of the colony, this special form of Justice Court was continued, but appointments to it were not recorded by the clerks of the court. Under the new charter, Commissioners to end Small Causes were superceded by Justices of the Peace. It will be noted that these officers for Northampton were first appointed by the General Court, afterwards elected by the people, and then appointed by the County Court. In every case they were sworn into office by the court.

Precautions against Harboring Strangers. Colony laws were passed in the year 1637, imposing fines upon towns and persons entertaining strangers, or allowing them to remain more than three weeks without a license; friends and relatives came under the same restrictions. The reasons for these strict regulations are not far to seek. Even with the comparatively scanty emigration of those days, it was important that the towns should be protected against whatever there was of it that might become detrimental to them, and the inland plantations in particular would naturally avail themselves of a law securing them from its evils. Everywhere social and religious harmony was recognized as the principal foundation of the government, and everything tending to its demoralization must be under strict control. That danger in this direction was imminent, and that cases requiring treatment had already arisen, may be inferred from the following vote, passed in March, 167⅔ :—

"Whereas a greate deale of troble dettrament and Charge haue been brought vpon this Towne by reason of reseauinge into the same forreners and Strangers: wee doe therfore by this order and by this it is orderred: that who soe ever in this Towne shall bringe intoe it or reseaue intoe his famaly a forrener or stranger or any man from abroode and enterteyne him in his house aboue ten days without libertie frome the selectmen shall forfite toe the Towne ten shillings for evary weeke soe enterteyninge him."

Rotation in Office. Frequent change in official incumbents, but for other than political reasons, seems to have been one of the cardinal virtues, and in order to re-

lieve citizens of onerous public duty, as well as to distribute the honors of citizenship more evenly, the town voted
in 1674 : —

"Wheare as the inhabitants of this Towne haue for sunderrie years
made choice of Townsmen the same that wheare in the yeare before
and it beinge toe greate a burden for the same men toe be soe often im-
ployd in that worke and others eased the select men takinge the matter
intoe consideration doe order that for tym to come noe man shall be
chosen toe be a Towns man aboue toe yearse toegether and but on or
toe of them toe be chosen a second tyme nether."

Grants of Saw Mill Privileges. For sixteen years Northampton had been
without a saw mill, and when the matter
was first agitated, in 1667, the town made
very generous propositions towards the promotion of such
an enterprise, by offering the builders twenty acres of land,
if the mill should be completed within three years. The
grantees, John King and Medad Pomeroy, however, failed
to carry out their obligation, and in 1670, the same grant
was made to Joseph Parsons Sr., with the additional con-
cession that "the mill was to goe rate free, in all the comon
Towne rates due from him and his heirs soe long as he
keepe the mill goeing for the Townes vse." Rev. Mr. Stoddard, who had just begun to preach here, seems to have
joined in this venture. They built the mill, on Mill River,
just below "Baker's Meadow," probably in or near the
present "Bay State" village, and received the land offered
for it from the town. Joseph Parsons had "the land for
his father's mill" over Munhan river, and Mr. Stoddard
had what has since been known as "Stoddard's Meadow,"
on Mill River, in the present village of Florence. Mr.
Stoddard sold his right in the "mill place" in 1689, to John
Parsons, but no mill was there at the time. This was the
first saw mill constructed in Northampton.

In 1674, David Wilton, Medad Pomeroy, and John Taylor, had liberty to "set vp" a saw mill "on the brooke on
the right hand of the Cart waye goinge over Munhan river
on this sid that runs intoe the river and whilese the mill
is in vse theye haue granted them ten or twilf acors of
Land for a pasture." They were also granted "the Libertie of the Commons toe fall timber." This mill was probably built by the grantees, and was the first one erected
within the present limits of the town of Easthampton.

Joseph Hawley, Notwithstanding the provisions for schools
School-master, made two years before, there is little evi-
1674-1682.   dence that the school-master had yet become
a permanent fixture. Town action in reference to the employment of teachers, previous to 1671, has already been
given, and though the records contain no notice of a school-
master till five years after that date, yet the account books
of Mr. Joseph Hawley show that he carried on a school
here in 1674, for which he was paid in part by the town.
Mr. Hawley, just graduated from Harvard College, came to
Northampton in that year for the purpose of teaching
school, and from that time it is believed that continuous
schools have been maintained in this town. For at least
eight years he was thus employed, though there seems to
have been a partial intermission during the Indian war of
1675 and 1676, his school being open only about two months
in each of those years. He had between forty and fifty
scholars, but probably never so large a number at any one
time. Very few attended all the year, and some only for a
few months. His was the first school in town, taught by
a man, at which it is known that girls were present. They
were private pupils, no part of their tuition being paid
from the public funds, and presumably they were not present at the same session as the boys. Of these girls, eleven
in number, two were taught writing at 10s. each, and
among them were Mary and Hester Stoddard, daughters of
Rev. Solomon Stoddard.[1] For boys he charged four pence
a week for reading and writing, and Latin scholars six
pence per week; girls generally paid four pence per week,
though some were charged six pence. What the scholars
paid, which may have averaged forty scholars at 10s. each,
amounted to £20, and the town was taxed for the rest, perhaps £10 or £15 more. These school rates seem to have
been put into Mr. Hawley's hands for collection, and he received directly from the parents, not only what was due
on their private account, but their school tax also.

1 The girls taught by Mr. Hawley were Mary and Hester, daughters of Rev. Solomon Stoddard; Hannah, daughter of Isaac Sheldon; Sarah, daughter of Joseph Root;
Mary, daughter of John Taylor; Sarah and Waite, daughters of Preserved Clapp;
Sarah, daughter of Israel Rust; and Mary, daughter of Samuel Marshall; Thankful
and Johanna, daughters of John Taylor, were taught writing at 10s. each.

Subscriptions and Rates for Rebuilding the "Castle."

The fortification in Boston harbor,[1] called the "Castle," was burned March 21, 167$\frac{2}{3}$. A "free contribution" to rebuild it was commended by the Governor, Magistrates and Deputies. The committees of militia in the several towns were to take charge of the work of raising these contributions. This was done, and Northampton gave 41s. These subscriptions proving insufficient, taxes were levied to make up the deficiency. Those who had subscribed were to be considered in the rate. The amount assessed upon and paid by Northampton, in addition to the contributions, was £26.9.2. Hadley subscribed 93s. 7; Hatfield 92s. 6; Westfield 43s. Part of these subscriptions was allowed for freight. The rates for these three towns were, Hadley, £23.17.4; Hatfield, £11.5; Westfield, £12.3.3

Settlement of Northfield.

It was in 1671, that thirty citizens from Northampton, and three from Hadley, petitioned the General Court for the grant of a plantation at Squakheag. Their application was denied, but was renewed the following year, was then favorably acted upon, and the next spring the settlement was commenced. Twenty-two residents of Northampton and one of Wethersfield, "ingaged to do their indeavour to attend the conditions of the grant," and among them are to be found the names of Elder John Strong, Joseph Parsons Sr., Samuel Wright Sr., and William Jeanes. The name of William Clarke does not appear upon either petition, but he was employed to lay out the township, and was prominent in establishing the town. Nearly all of the twenty home lots at first set off were taken up by Northampton men, but were not all occupied by them. Those who did not become squatters themselves sent representatives to make their title good.

It is evident that this movement had in it some speculative elements. The first petition contains the gist of the matter. Finding themselves in a "great measure straightened," they ask for a new township. The real truth

---

1 This fortification was situated on Castle Island in Boston harbor, about three miles from that city. It was erected in 1634, and having fallen into decay, was rebuilt in 1643, at a cost of not less than £4,000. Burned in 167$\frac{2}{3}$, it had been immediately reconstructed of stone. It was to defray this expense that the subscriptions were ordered and the tax levied.

was that they were in pursuit of more meadow land. Having absorbed all that was available at home, they sought new fields, some undoubtedly with a view to the establishment of their sons, but most of them for their own pecuniary advantage. Northfield was but an out-settlement of Northampton. Important town officers were non-residents, and for many years its record books were kept here.

Contributions for Harvard College, 1672-1680. Harvard College, fostered, protected and sustained by the government, had not only received repeated grants of land and money, but voluntary subscriptions throughout the colony, for its benefit, were continued for years.[1] In 1669, when apparently its further usefulness depended upon the erection of a new college building, the system of town donations was resumed, and from 1672, pushed with renewed vigor. These "voluntary contributions" were enforced by statute. The Commonwealth held the contribution box and ordered the people to cast in their gifts. As might have been expected, considerable difficulty was experienced in obtaining returns under this system of compulsory generosity. For eight years or more the matter lingered, and those who did subscribe were dilatory in making payments. It should be considered, however, that during this period occurred King Philip's war, and that the devastated towns had little to pay with, however good their disposition might have been. Several statutory hints were required before the purses of the people could be opened to any great extent, or their donations made available. An order was issued in 1678, to levy by distress upon all persons who refuse to "make payment of what they have subscribed."

Northampton on the Black List. Two years afterwards the selectmen of the several towns were ordered to inquire into the matter, and make return "of what is don or to be donn," under penalty of £20. A list of the names

1 In 1652, the General Court ordered that a "voluntary collection be comended to the inhabitants of this jurisdiccon for the raising of such a some as may be jmploied for the majntenance of the præsident, certajne ffellowes and poore schollers in Harvard Colledge." Every town was to choose some one to "take the voluntary subscriptions." Evidently the people did not respond in a satisfactory manner, for in 1654, the towns that had not complied with the recommendation, were again ordered to appoint collectors for the college.

of twenty-two delinquent towns follows, and among them appears that of Northampton. This subscription did not commend itself to the inhabitants, as but few of the towns in the colony made any response during the many years it had been in progress. Of the thirty-two towns represented in the General Court in 1680, twelve had paid, and twenty were on the black list, which also included two others not represented that year. Northampton subscribed £29.17.10, in flax, summer wheat, and flour, but the expense of transportation and other drawbacks, which were deducted from these enforced donations, reduced the amount applied on the subscription to £20.9.4. This contribution is nowhere recognized by the town; it was obtained, without doubt, through the authority of the selectmen, who were empowered by the statute to appoint canvassers. The original paper,[1] containing the names of eighty-five subscribers, is still in existence; it shows that the work was commenced in 1672, and there are other entries in each of the next three years. Five years more, however, passed before the gifts were collected and forwarded.

1 This subscription paper, partly copied by Rev. Solomon Stoddard, is still extant in the Judd MSS. Collection. See Appendix A.

CHAPTER XVIII.

WITCHCRAFT—TRIAL OF MARY PARSONS.

Prevalence of Superstition.

IN New England, the early settlers were in no sense superior to the superstitions and delusions of the times in which they lived. Belief in the supernatural was universal. Having implicit faith in signs and omens, they read in the sky warnings of coming events, and gave prophetic interpretation to any unfamiliar phenomenon. Many occurrences, the results of natural laws, were often ascribed to unseen or occult influences, and any extraordinary incident was sure to be attributed to the direct interference of some higher power. The local history of Massachusetts abounds in corroborative facts.[1] This belief was by no means confined to the ignorant. It permeated all classes, the learned as well as the unlearned. Scholars, professional men, clergymen, acknowledged the existence of witches, and the common people imputed many of the events of every day life, seriously affecting themselves, or neighbors, to this evil influence. None doubted its reality, and in every civilized country the practice of witchcraft was made a capital offence. Nor is the superstition banished by the light and

1 These omens were generally noticed just before some important event took place. Immediately preceding the outbreak of King Philip's war, strange appearances in the heavens were reported by Increase Mather and others: such as the "d.scharge of artillery and small arms, accompanied by the beating of drums as in battle. In several places invisible troops of horse are said to have been heard riding through the air." As the first squadron of soldiers was marching to attack King Philip, in 1675, an eclipse of the sun took place, and upon it was distinctly visible to the superstitious militia men, the outlines of an Indian scalp. Previous to the attack on Deerfield, in 1704, Rev. Mr. Stoddard reports, according to Penhallow, that "a few nights before the assault was they were strangely amused [amazed] by a trampling noise round the fort as if it were beset by Indians." Again, quoting from the same authority, just before the attack on Pascommuck, "the people of Springfield heard a great shooting; unto some it seemed to be at Westfield, to others at a village, and to some again in the woods; so that many hastened to their assistance; but when they came all was still and quiet, the reason whereof is hard to assign, & yet we have repeated instances in history of the like nature."

civilization of the nineteenth century. In all parts of the world, civilized or barbarous, the same belief prevails. Four-fifths of the human race at the present day are said to believe in witchcraft.[1]

Witchcraft Excitements in Massachusetts. The records of the past show with what an intolerant spirit the crime was punished. Catholics and Protestants persecuted alleged witches with equally intemperate zeal. The cruelty of the punishment was commensurate with the adjudged enormity of the evil. Burning alive at the stake[2] was the horrible death meted out to those who had been convicted of witchcraft, though large numbers were hanged. None, however, were burned for this practice in Massachusetts. Throughout the settlements in America the signal atrocity of this great wrong was recognized, and stringent laws were passed for its suppression. The first execution in Massachusetts colony for this crime was that of Margaret Jones, who was hanged at Boston, June 15th, 1648. Eight years after Widow Anne Hibbins was executed in the same city. An unusual excitement existed in this direction in Massachusetts from 1681 to 1683. Many were tried, and several persons suffered the death penalty. During the succeeding decade, comparative quiet prevailed, with an occasional outbreak, but in 1692, the witchcraft craze burst into fierce flame in Salem and vicinity. Within a year nearly two hundred persons were accused and arrested. Some escaped from prison, others died there, nineteen were put to death, and one hundred and fifty were released when the excitement subsided. Plymouth colony leaves but two cases on record, one in 1661, and the other in 1677.

1 Century Magazine, January, 1892, p. 408.

2 "The belief in witchcraft was world wide. It had been stimulated by Pope Innocent VIII, one of whose agents boasted of having burned 900 witches. In our colonial era, some of the German states were burning 600 a year, while in Italy, Switzerland, and Sweden the slaughter was also terrible. In the sixteenth century, as is estimated, Continental Europe sacrificed 100,000 lives on this ground. * * * The Pope stimulated the Roman Catholic nations to activity, as Luther and Calvin did the Continental Protestants; and the Churches of Scotland and England were both zealous in destroying witches. Under the Long Parliament were 3,000 of these victims, and in ten years of its session there were 4,000 in Scotland. Most of these suffered the horrible death of burning alive, though many were murdered by ordeals. Mackay estimates that in a period of time which is more than covered by the life of John Alden of the "Mayflower," 40,000 of these executions took place in England. This was an extravagant estimate; but the fact that he thought it reasonable indicates that the actual result must have been horrible."—Pilgrim Republic, pp. 491, 492.

Witchcraft Trials in Hampshire County, 1651-52.

Several trials for witchcraft occurred in Hampshire County, but no executions. The first case was that of Mary Parsons, wife of Hugh Parsons of Springfield. She was tried for witchcraft and for the murder of her child, in 1651. On the former charge she was acquitted, but pleaded guilty to that of murder, and was sentenced to death. At the time of her trial she was quite sick, and the feeling prevailed that she would die before it was completed. There is no record of her execution, and it is believed that on account of sickness she was reprieved and probably died in prison. She was deranged. Her husband, Hugh Parsons, was accused of "having familiar and wicked converse with the devil and of using divers devilish practices and witchcraft," and tried the following year. The jury found him guilty, but the magistrates did not consent to the verdict. The case came before the General Court, May 26th, 1652, when he was judged not to be guilty of witchcraft, and was discharged.[1]

The First Case in Northampton.

The first case of witchcraft in Northampton came to trial in 1674. Mary Parsons, wife of Cornet Joseph Parsons, one of the first settlers in town, and one of its most prominent citizens, was the accused. She was the daughter of Thomas Bliss of Hartford, a woman of more than ordinary intelligence, and of unquestioned respectability. Her accusers were also persons of high standing and good reputation. How much revenge, jealousy, or spite may have influenced the prosecutors is not known, but there is reason to believe that the imputation grew out of an old quarrel of some eighteen years standing, the facts concerning which have been narrated in a previous chapter.

Samuel Bartlett, and his father-in-law, James Bridgman, whose wife was the defendant in the suit for slander, were the complainants. Both were men of substance,[2] and were greatly respected in the community.

Mary Parsons charged with Witchcraft.

Freed from all suspicions of evil doings by the result of the slander trial, the position of Mary Parsons in the community would seem to have been firmly established. The punishment in-

1 Judd's History of Hadley, p. 234.
2 Bartlett left an estate inventoried at £1,477, and Bridgman one of £100.

flicted upon the defendants, would be expected at least to deter any from offering further inuendoes or insinuations derogatory to her character. But such was not the case. Eighteen years afterwards, the same family revived the slanderous gossip in the form of distinct charges of witchcraft. It was not the loss of cows, or oxen, or swine, that was attributed to her this time, but the fearful and terrible accusation of causing the death of a human being. The Bridgman family still cherished the old grudge, though the mother had been six years dead.

Mary Bartlett's sudden Death Suggests Witchcraft.

Samuel Bartlett, son of Robert, in 1672, married Mary, daughter of James Bridgman. She died suddenly within two years. The husband and the father imagined that her death was caused by some "unnatural means," and superstition at once suggested witchcraft. Now was the time to revenge the slander case, and the parties who suffered from it were not slow to take advantage of the opportunity. Samuel Bartlett's wife died in August, and the case against Mary Parsons for witchcraft was entered at the September term of the court, held in Springfield.

The Rumor Spreads through the Town.

Suspicions of evil, started by Bartlett and Bridgman, at once took wind, and soon the surmise that Mary Parsons, the witch, had caused the death of Mrs. Bartlett, filled the town. The gossips stirred up the community on the subject, and Mrs. Parsons soon caught the rumors. She was a resolute and determined woman, met her accusers voluntarily, and in person, when they came before the court. She denied the imputation, and no doubt, cited in proof of her innocence, the abortive attempt to slander her in previous years.

Proceedings of the Preliminary Trial.

The testimony in this trial has not been discovered, but it may be presumed that much that was used in the previous case was reproduced.[1] So far, as recorded, the proceedings of the preliminary trial in this case, are as follows :—

1 A portion of the testimony in the slander trial was found in duplicate, upon the files of the court, and it may be inferred that copies of it were made for use on this occasion.

"County Co^rte holden at Springfeild, Sept. 29th, 1674.

"There Being exhibited to this Co^rte diverse testemonyes on Oath from Northampton of Mary Persons declaring Causes of jealousies & Suspition of Witchcrafft in y^t Town & Diverse of the testemonys reflecting on ye wife of Joseph Persons Senr, she haveing intemation y^t such things were bruited abroade & y^t she should Probably be called in Question for Reason aforesayd, she volentaryly made her appearence in Co^rte, desireing to Cleare her self of such an execrable crime & ye testemonyes being Reade before her & she examined thereupon, the Co^rte thought meete for speciall Reason to referr ye matter to fjurther Disquesition when she should be called fforth to make ffurther Answer & it being soe declared to her she was for Present dismist.

"Sam^ll Bartlet of Northampton haveing lately lost his wife to his greate greife as he expresseth and ye rather for y^t he Strongly suspects y^t she dyed by some unuseall means, viz, by meanes of some evell Instruem^t he presented to the Cor^rte diverse Evedences to shew the grounds of his fears & suspition. Alsoe Goodman Bridgeman sending to ye Co^rte & Intreating that Diligent inquisition may be made, Concerning ye Death of ye sayd Woeman his Daughter for y^t he also Strongly suspects, she come to her end by some unlawfull & unatureall means & for ye Diverse of ye testemoneyes doe reflect on Goodwife Persones Sen of Northampton ye Co^rte haveing Read ye testemonyes doe thinke it meete y^t ye case should be ffurther Look^t into & therefore doe refferr ye sayd case & all other things Concerning ye sayd Goodwife Persons y^t have beene now Presented to ye ajournm^t of this Co^rte which is to be kept at Northampton ye 18th Day of Novemb^r next, for further Disquisition & doe order y^t she be warned there to attend to answer w^t shall be objected agst her & ye witnesses are to be warned to appear to testify before her viva voce w^t they have already given in upon oath concerning her."

"The 18th of November being come, for speciall Reasons, Major Pynchon ajourned the court to the 5th day of January, 1674.

"Jan. 5, 1674, the Co^rte meet at Northampton at the time Appointed

"ffor the Holding of this Co^rte were present Majo^r John Pynchon & Assistant Mr Henry Clerke Left. Wm Clerke Lef^t David Wilton. The Recorder Capt Holyoke was absent not being well. Left Wilton was ordered and appointed to officiate as Clerk to this Co^rte.

"Mary Parsones the wife of Joseph Parsones Senr Appeared. Alsoe Sam^ll Bartlett whome this Co^rte ordered to produce ye witnesses in ye matter reffering to Goodwife Parsones suspition of witchcrafft. And ye sayd Goodwife Parsones being Called to speak for her self, She did assert her own inocency often mentioning it how Cleare she was of such a Crime, and y^t the Righteous God knew her Inocency with whome she had left her Cause.

"There havinge beene many Suspitiones of Witchcrafft at Northampton & severall testemonyes concerning the same, of Persones suspected, Exhibited to the Last County Co^rte in Septr Last at Springfeild by Persones then & there comeing Voluntarlie some to give in Evidence & others there appeareing also without Sumondes to Cleare themselves of soe execrable a Crime. Alsoe James Bridgeman sending to y⁰ Co'te y' Diligent inquesition might be made Concerning the Death of his Daughter Sam¹¹ Bartlets wife, whome both Goodman Bridgeman & Sam¹¹ Bartlet suspect she Came to her end by some unatureall meanes & for y' Diverse testemoneys reflect upon Mary Parsons y⁰ wife of Joseph Parsons Sen', it being alsoe affirmed y' there were many more Witnesses y' would come in in y' case. The Co'te then thought meete to order Mary Parsones to appeare at y⁰ Co'te now hither ajourned, who accordingly appeareing as abovesayd. Alsoe Sam¹¹ Bartlett appeared, whome y⁰ Co'te ordered to Produce y⁰ testemonyes in y⁰ case, which being Brought in & y⁰ Co'te ffinding them many & various, some of y^m being demonstrations of witch craft & others sorely reflecting upon Mary Parsons as being Guilty that way though y⁰ tryall of y⁰ Case belongs not to this co'te, but to y⁰ Co'te of Assistants, Yet Considering y⁰ Remoteness, and y⁰ Season of y⁰ yeare & many Difficultyes if not incapeabilityes of Persones there to appeare some being soe weake, This Co'te tooke y⁰ more paines in inquireing into y⁰ case. Appointed a jury of Soberdized Chast woeman to make Diligent search upon y⁰ Body of Mary Parsones, wheather any markes of witchcraft might appeare, who gave in there account to y⁰ Co'te on oath of w' they ffound (which) with all y⁰ testemoneys in y⁰ case y⁰ Co'te orders to be sent to Boston to our Hono'ed Govern' by y⁰ ffirst oppertunitie, Leaveing it to his Wisedome & Prudence in Communicating y⁰ matter to y⁰ Hono'ed Magestrates for y⁰ ffurther Proceeding therein as they shall see cause. And y⁰ Recorder of this Co'te is accordingly to take care y' all y⁰ writeings & Evedences in y⁰ case be Ready & Delivered to y⁰ Worshipfull Majo' Pynchon who is desired to write to y⁰ Govern' concerning this matter.

"Itt is ffurther ordered y' Mary Parsones shall make her appeareance Before y⁰ Govern' or magestrates or Co'te of Assistantes to answer to w' she is suspected of in case she be called or required theretoo by Authority & her Husband Joseph Parsones to become Bound in a Bond of 50' for his wives appeareance accordingly if required before y⁰ 13ᵗʰ May next. And accordingly Joseph Parsons Sen' being sent for & comeing before this Co'te acknowledged himself Bound to y⁰ County Tresurer for Hampshire in y⁰ sum of fifty Poundes Sterling that his wife Mary Parsones if required thereto shall appeare at Boston, Before y⁰ Govern' Magestrates, or Co'te of Assistantes or any Co'te between this & y⁰ 13ᵗʰ May next, to Answer unto w' she is suspected off viz: witchcraft, and in case of her non appeareance accordingly upon lawfull Sumons theretoe, Being Sent to or left at y⁰ House of y⁰ sayd Joseph Parsons then the sayd Joseph Parsones is to forfeite y⁰ Sum of fifty Poundes aforesayd to y⁰ County Treasurer for y⁰ use of y⁰ County, this y⁰ sayd Joseph Parsones Acknowledged in Courte whereupon his wife was Discharged ffurther attendance at Present."

Proceedings before the Court of Assistants.

The case came before the court at Boston in the following March, and Mrs. Parsons, having been indicted by the Grand Jury, was committed to prison, while awaiting trial, where she remained till the middle of May. Below may be found the action of the court :—

"At a Court of Assistants held at Boston 2ᵈ of March 1674, Mary Parsons presented and indicted for witchcraft.

"The Grand jury was called againe and they perusing severall evidences sent doune from the County Court at North Hampton, relating to Mary Parsons, the wife of Joseph Parson, they presenting an Indictment against hir on suspition of witchcraft leaving hir to further triall. The Court Ordered hir comittment to the prison in Boston there to remaine & be kept in order to hir further tryall.

"This Court is Ajourned to the 13ᵗʰ of May next at 10 of the clock in the morning.

"It is Ordered that the Secretary Issue out his warrants for such & so many of the wittnesses as oune within a moneth. Mr. Danforth, Mr. Ting & Major Clark shall with the Secret. on their perusall determine to be necessary and that a letter be writt to Major Pynchon to Accomdate yᵗ Affaire relating to Mary Parsons.

"Att A Court of Assistants on Adjournment held at Boston, 13ᵗʰ of May 1675.

"Att this Court Mary Parsons the wife of Joseph Parsons of Northampton in the County of Hampshire in the Colony of the Massachusets being presented & Indicted by the Grand Jury was also Indicted by the name of Mary Parsons the wife of Joseph Parsons for not having the feare of God before hir eyes and being Instigated by the divill hath at one or other of the times mentioned in the evidences now before yᵉ Court entred into familliarity with the divill and comitted severall acts of witchcraft on the person or persons of one or more as in the sayd evidences relating thereto, refference being thereto had Amply doeth and may appear and all this Contrary to the peace of our Soveraigne Lord the King his Crowne and dignity, the lawes of God and of this Jurisdiction. After the Indictment and Evidences in the Case were Read the prisoner at the barr holding up hir hand & pleading not Guilty putting hirself on hir triall, the Jury brought in their Verdict they found hir not Guilty, & so she was discharged."

Value of the Missing Testimony.

Concerning this memorable trial, no further report can be obtained. While the testimony in the comparatively unimportant slander case has been preserved, that taken in the capital trial for witchcraft has disappeared. It would be of great local importance if the "testimonies" referred to in the record could be found. To note the difference, if any, between the evidence produced at the two trials would give a more comprehensive insight into the inner life of those early days, by showing to what extent the imaginations of the aggrieved parties could carry the most insignificant incidents of their daily surroundings. Possibly that used in the defence at the slander trial was again made to do duty when the situation was reversed. At any rate it was equally abortive in each case. Mary Parsons was not only compelled to stand trial on charge of practicing witchcraft, but she also suffered the added indignity of imprisonment in Boston, while waiting the action of the court. This must have been extremely humiliating to a person of her pride and dignity. But she came out of this trial as she did out of the other, with flying colors. The furor against witches which followed many years after, had not at this time begun, men were able to weigh testimony without prejudice, and to render a verdict creditable to their sense of humanity and justice.

Mrs. Parsons Speaks for herself. The fact that Mrs. Parsons voluntarily appeared before the court, "desiring to clear herself of such an execrable crime," and that subsequently she argued her own case before the court, must not be overlooked. On both of these occasions she met her accusers boldly, protesting her innocence, and showing "how clear she was of such a crime." Attorneys were then an almost unknown quantity, especially in the inland towns, and criminal lawyers had little occasion for existence. It seems to have been customary for the accused to argue their own cases, and other instances of women speaking in courts of justice are not unknown.[1] In this trial, Mrs. Parsons was "called to speak for herself," and from the meagre report upon record, undoubtedly did so most effectively.

1 "In 1667, a woman spoke in town meeting in Windsor, in a case which concerned her, and not without effect." In 1677, "widow Editha Holyoke of Springfield, went into court and 'spoke in the case' relating to her share of her husband's estate." —Judd's History of Hadley, p. 235, note.

Another Member of the Parsons family Arraigned for Witchcraft.

Not satisfied with attempting to fasten the crime of witchcraft upon Mary Parsons, some one, probably the same parties, endeavored to include her son, John Parsons, in that or a similar misdemeanor. At the same court before which she was tried,

"Some testemonyes being procured in Co'te Reflecting on John Parsons yᵉ Coʳte have Reade & consedered yᵐ doe not ffinde in yᵐ any such weight whereby he Should be Prosicuted on suspition of witchcraft and therefore doe discharge yᵉ sayd John Parsones of any ffurther attendance."

Undoubtedly John,[1] like a dutiful son, had endeavored to uphold the dignity of the family and the innocence of his mother. In so doing he incurred the enmity of the Bartletts and Bridgmans, hence the attempt to include him in the prosecution and trial for witchcraft. The testimony against him must have been worthless, for the court paid it little attention.

Joseph Parsons Disgusted, goes back to Springfield.

No wonder Joseph Parsons, after this endeavor to make witches of two members of his family, became disgusted with Northampton, and within a few years left the town. In 1679, he purchased the home lot and other real estate of Lieut. Cooper, in Springfield, who was killed in King Philip's war, and removed to that place soon after.

Witchcraft "Vehemently Suspected."

John Stebbins of Northampton, died suddenly in March, 167⅜. The manner of his death was considered quite unusual, and the common belief was that he had been killed by witches. He was part owner of a saw mill on Broad Brook or Manhan River, and the facts would seem to indicate that he came to his death by an accident at the mill. An inquest was held by a jury of twelve men, who returned a verdict, which while it did not directly charge witchcraft, showed that they more than half believed it had something to do

1 John Parsons was the third son of Joseph and Mary Parsons. He was born in Springfield, and at this time was 24 years of age. This accusation did not injure him in the estimation of his fellow townsmen, and he became a man of prominence and influence. He was called Captain, and was in service during the Indian Wars. Several times he was chosen a member of the board of selectmen. His home lot was on Bridge Street, where John W. Hubbard now lives, and there he resided till his death, in 1728.

with his death. Two examinations were made of the remains, and two reports were handed in to the court. In
the first one they declared that there was a "warmth and
heate in his Body y^t dead persons are not usual to have;"
they reported that there were "fower places upon his brest
y^t seemed to have been Pintched, though the doctor informed y^m that in his life time there was a swelling between the Pintches;" his neck was as flexible as that of a
living person; upon his body were found "several hundred of spots" that looked as if "they had been shott with
small shott," and when they were scraped there were holes
under them. On the second examination, which must have
been made soon after the first one, they found, as would
very naturally follow, "the body somewhat more cold y^n
before, his joynts more limber," and several bruises on different parts of his person, which they had not previously
discovered. The jury reported to the County Court in
April, and Samuel Bartlett, brother-in-law to Stebbins,[1]
and who seems to have been witch finder in general for the
town, brought in all the testimony he could obtain. This
evidence, which cannot now be found, was sent to the
Court of Assistants at Boston, but no further action was
taken. Undoubtedly the testimony pointed to some suspected person, but no one was named on the records. As
Samuel Bartlett had something to do with this case in the
way of hunting up evidence, it may reasonably be surmised that his vision was again directed to the Parsons
family. Possibly this last suspicion, if it took that direction, clinched the decision of Joseph Parsons and his wife
to return to Springfield.

The Case of Mary
Webster.

Other persons suspected of witchcraft in this
part of Hampshire County, were brought
before the courts, but no one was executed
for that crime within its precincts. Most prominent in the

1 John Stebbins was the son of Rowland Stebbins of Springfield. He came to
Northampton in 1656, and lived at the lower end of "Pudding Lane," now Hawley
Street. His saw mill was situated within the bounds of Easthampton. He was a
large farmer and owned real estate valued at between £400 and £500. There is a tradition that "while sawing at his mill, the logs would roll over him, set in motion by
witches, by which he was severely bruised. It was also stated that a large number
of women were summoned by Joseph Hawley, to examine and touch him, intending
in this way to discover the witch. Blood flowed when a certain woman touched him,
but only one could see it, so nothing was done."—Judd MSS.

annals of the time was the case of Mary, wife of William Webster of Hadley. A full account of this transaction may be found in Judd's History of Hadley. Charges were preferred and a trial before the court in Boston, in 1683, resulted in the acquittal of the accused. This verdict, however, did not restore the woman to the good opinion of the people of Hadley. Cotton Mather relates with much minuteness, how, about two years after, it was supposed that Mary Webster caused, by her machinations, the death of Philip Smith, an eminently reputable citizen of the town of Hadley. He was sick for some time, and during his illness various unaccountable manifestations were frequent. Public opinion ran so high against her that a "number of brisk lads" of the town "gave disturbance to the woman" on several occasions. At one time the "disturbance" consisted in dragging her from her house and hanging her up till she was almost dead. After taking her down, they rolled her in the snow for some time, buried her in it, and there left her. She survived this barbarous treatment eleven years, and died in 1696, aged about 70.[1]

Mary Randall Arraigned.   The last case of suspected witchcraft in this town, and section, was that of Mary Randall. She was "presented" in 1691, on the usual charge of "familiarity with the devil." George and John Alexander and others, were her accusers. The County Court judged that there was "vehement suspicion" of guilt, and ordered that the case should be continued one year. She was sentenced to be sent to prison or to give bonds in the sum of £10 for her good behavior, and appearance at court. Her father became her bondsman, but the case was never called for trial. William Randall[2] was discharged of his bond in 1692.

A Characteristic Tradition.   Tradition is responsible for the statement[3] that Noah Strong thought a pigeon hawk which frightened the pigeons from the nest was a witch, and he shot at it with lead without effect. He

1 Judd's History of Hadley, pp. 236-239.

2 William Randall did not live long in Northampton, if he ever resided here. His daughter is named in the record as " of Northampton," while the father is said to belong in Enfield.

3 Judd MSS.

then shot his silver sleeve buttons and broke the hawk's wing. The same day a woman whom he had displeased, returned from Bartlett's mill with her arm badly bruised or broken. He was sure she was the witch. She was the wife of Bernard Bartlett, and had the reputation of being a witch. This legend may be dated during the second quarter of the eighteenth century.

Northampton Soil bad for Witches. Comprised in the foregoing statements, as far as known, are all the facts or traditions relative to witchcraft in Northampton. It is noticeable that while there were many persons who believed that the powers of darkness were permitted to meddle in the affairs of life, the test cases, in all but one instance, were confined to the same parties. The first gossipy rumors that brought on the slander trial, as well as the first real charge of uncanny practices, and the second intimation of evil doings, originated among the same families. Bridgman, Bartlett and Stebbins were connected by marriage. No evidence appears hinting even at the name of the person upon whom the accusation fell, in the case of John Stebbins, and the most ·natural suggestion is that the finger of suspicion again pointed to the Parsons family. While Northampton was not wholly free from this universal belief, it escaped the horrors that a few years afterwards cast such a reproach upon the eastern section of the Commonwealth. Evidently witches did not flourish here to any great extent, or the people were less excitable than in other places.

CHAPTER XIX.

KING PHILIP'S WAR—OPENING EVENTS.

Northampton at Peace with the Indians During its Minority. FOR twenty-one years the people of Northampton and other towns in the county, lived peaceably with the Indians. In all their intercourse with the red men, the pioneer settlers of this town treated them honorably, and the utmost confidence prevailed on both sides. Their wigwams were scattered about the town in all directions, and the Indians "in all times of danger and war had been wont to seek shelter by getting and crowding into our home lots, as near our houses as possible, and begging house-room for their stuff and themselves."[1] This amicable state of affairs came abruptly to an end in 1675, for then commenced the first of those Indian wars that wrought such destruction to life and property, not only throughout this valley, but in all portions of New England. Almost before suspicions of uneasiness among the tribes began to be entertained, the Indians about Northampton showed signs of dissatisfaction. Mr. Stoddard says of them in a letter to the council of Connecticut:—"A little before the tidings of the war with Plymouth brake out, * * * they on a sudden, without any cause given, plucked up their wigwams, took away their goods which they had laid up in our houses, and this they did at once." With the first rumors of an outbreak, the Northampton Indians (the Nonotucks) became distant and suspicious, and were soon detected in acts of treachery towards the English. They finally joined the enemy and fought their former friends and neighbors with vigor and cruelty.

1 Letter of Rev. Solomon Stoddard.

Constant Friction Between the Races. Abundant cause for antagonism between the white men and the Indians existed on every hand. Distasteful as the habits of the natives were to the settlers, they became more disgusting and annoying, as the former learned the vices of the English, and the conflict between civilization and barbarism developed into greater intensity as time advanced. Five years before, the Indians had been turned out of the fort granted them near the center of the village, and no one was allowed to offer them ground upon which to build another. This was but one among many sources of dissatisfaction that embittered the feelings of the Indians towards the settlers.

Known in History as "King Philip's War." This first among the series of Indian hostilities that desolated the land, has received the name of "King Philip's war." It was commenced by his own immediate followers and virtually ended with his death. Philip, chief sachem of the Wampanoags, was generally believed to have instigated a conspiracy among the Indians of New England, having for its object the uprising of all the tribes for the purpose of exterminating the white settlers. His personality pervaded every movement of the war, and to him was attributed every atrocity of the savage foe.[1] Hence his name became permanently identified with the conflict.

Probable Origin of the name of King. How Philip obtained the appellation of King[2] is uncertain. He was the second son of Massasoit, and upon the death of his brother Alexander, succeeded to the government of his

1 "Philip became a theme of universal apprehension. The mystery in which he was enveloped exaggerated his real terrors. He was an evil that walked in darkness; whose coming none could forsee, and against which none knew when to be on the alert. The whole country abounded with rumors and alarms. Philip seemed almost possessed of ubiquity, for, in whatever part of the widely extended frontier an irruption from the forest took place, Philip was said to be its leader."—Irving's Sketch Book, pp. 367, 368.

2 "By name Philip, commonly for his haughty and ambitious spirit nicknamed King Philip."—Hubbard's Indian Wars, p. 70.

"But at all events the Indian King Philip is a mythical Character."—Palfrey's New England, vol. 3, p. 223.

S. G. Drake, in a note p. 18, in Church's History of the Indian War, says: "which names they received from Gov. Prince of Plymouth, probably from Philip and Alexander of Macedon." Doubtless that belief prevailed at the time, and the prefix of King was thoughtlessly bestowed upon him.

tribe. The brothers, Wamsutta and Metacome, soon after the death of their father, appeared at Plymouth, and requested the Governor to give them English names. Gov. Prince complied, naming Wamsutta, Alexander, and Metacome, Philip. Whatever of kingly authority attached to the government of Massasoit, descended by right to his successor, Philip, but no such title was recognized among the Indian tribes of New England. The chief sachem of the Wampanoags had dominion over several other petty sagamores, and was at one time at the head of a powerful nation. In the time of Philip, the tribe had become greatly reduced by war, and after the settlement of Plymouth, it had been decimated by the small pox, and probably at the time of the outbreak numbered less than 250 fighting men.

Philip Estimated by his Contemporaries. Historians differ materially in their estimate of Philip's character, ability, and influence. Contemporary writers, some of whom were actors in the scenes which they describe, and others writing within a few years of the close of the war, are bitter in their attacks upon him. To them he was but a barbarous savage, without redeeming qualities; a blood thirsty butcher, intent only upon pillage, massacre and torture. [1]

1 In a series of pamphlets, by a "Merchant of Boston," issued in 1676 and 1677, he is termed "Prime Incendiary and Pestilent Ring Leader."

Rev. Wm. Hubbard, of Ipswich, in his "Narrative of the Indian Wars in New England," published in 1677, calls Philip that "grand rebel" and "notorious traitor." * * "the devil who was a murderer from the beginning, had so filled the heart of this savage miscreant with envy and malice against the English." * * "Yet did this treacherous and perfidious catiff still harbor the same or more mischievous thoughts against the English."—pp. 71, 77.

Capt. Thomas Church, who commanded the expedition in which Philip was killed, published "A History of Philip's War," in 1716. He evinces the greatest contempt for his antagonist; awards him hardly ordinary ability; says he was always "foremost in the flight;" records on seeing his dead body: "and a doleful, great, naked dirty beast he looked like," and ordered, that "forasmuch as he had caused many an Englishman's body to be unburied, and to rot above ground, that not one of his bones should be buried. And calling his old Indian executioner, bid him behead and quarter him."—p. 125, Drake's Ed. 1829.

Cotton Mather, commenting upon the death of Philip, uses the following language: "And in the place where he first contrived and commenced his mischief, this Agag was now cut in quarters, which were then hanged up, while his head was carried in triumph to Plymouth, where it arrived on the very day that the church was keeping a solemn thanksgiving to God. God sent them the head of Leviathan for a thanksgiving feast."

Philip viewed in the first half of the present Century.

As time softened the asperities of the conflict, these prejudiced opinions gave way to more liberal sentiments, and vituperation was changed to hero worship. The verdict rendered during the first fifty years of the nineteenth century, was as extravagantly laudatory as that of his contemporaries had been bitterly defamatory. Every sentiment of patriotism, all the abilities of statesmanship and military skill were attributed to him, and he was given a high position in the annals of fame.[1]

A more Modern Estimate.

More recent writers are inclined to endorse the opinions of those who lived nearer his time. They regard him as little better than the most unimportant sachem of the period in which he lived. He is described as a person of little talent, scant judgment and less sense. Accorded none of the characteristics of a leader, he is represented as without influence, and never prominent in any engagement, conspicuous only in flight. The judgment of the earlier historians was evidently largely tinged with prejudice, and that of the second epoch, as strongly swayed by sentiment, but it may also be conceded that the opinions of more recent chroniclers are not altogether free from a dash of exaggeration.

1 A biography of Philip appeared in the Analectic Magazine, in 1814, which speaks of the "military skill and prowess of Philip," "his fertility in expedients," etc.—Vol. 3, p. 508.

"The death of Philip in retrospect, makes different impressions from what were made at the time of the event. It was then considered as the extinction of a virulent and implacable enemy; it is now viewed as the fall of a great warrior, a penetrating statesman, and a mighty prince. It then excited universal joy and congratulation, as a prelude to the close of a merciless war; it now awakens sober reflections on the instability of empire, the peculiar destiny of the aboriginal race, and the inscrutable decrees of heaven."—Holmes' Annals of America, vol. 1, p. 383, pub. in 1829.

"Philip was unquestionably a great warrior and a mighty chief, in whom rested the confidence and the hope of the confederated tribes. The noble deeds which he performed in 1676, in the defense of his unfortunate people, would not suffer in comparison with those of the renowned heroes in our own cause in 1776."—Thacher's History of Plymouth, p. 145, pub. in 1832.

"King Philip's talents were of the highest order. As a politician he was the greatest of savages. * * Never perhaps did the fall of a warrior or a prince afford more scope for solid reflection. Philip was certainly a man of great powers of mind. * * It [his death] is now viewed as the fall of a great warrior, a penetrating statesman, a mighty prince."—Fowler's Historical Sketch of Fall River, pp. 9-11.

"He [Philip] needed but a whiter skin and a better success to have made him a hero whose name should linger on men's lips, and whose praise should be celebrated in song."—Holland's History of Western Massachusetts, vol. 1, p. 132, pub. in 1855.

Philip, squalid Indian though he was, will always stand conspicuous in the history of his time, and cannot truthfully be dismissed to oblivion as a nonenity.[1]

The Truth lies be-tween these Judgments. Neither of these estimates is absolutely correct. The truth lies midway between them. While Philip was by no means the contemptible, cowardly, insignificant being he is represented to be by one class of historians, neither is he entitled to all the attributes of patriotism or military skill with which he has been invested by other writers. His designs may not have been as far reaching, nor his plans as comprehensive as some have supposed, but he undoubtedly originated the outbreak of 1675, had a certain influence among the Indian tribes, and gave both the government of Plymouth Colony and Massachusetts Bay considerable trouble.

Philip Insincere and constantly Plotting, may have Organized the Outbreak. That Philip organized an extensive plot, embracing all the Indian tribes of New England, and arranged all the details for a general and simultaneous onslaught upon the English settlements, is not proved by contemporaneous history or corroborated by subsequent events. Yet it is impossible not to believe that the subject had been brought

1 " Philip, in great qualities, did not surpass many other sachems in New England and other colonies. Indeed, some Nipmuck sagamores seem to have been as enterprising and efficient actors in this bloody and desolating war, as Philip himself. The great foresight, profound schemes, and unbounded influence attributed to him are to a great extent imaginary." * * " He was the terror of New England for fourteen months. Schemes were attributed to him which he did not contrive, and deeds which he did not perform; and he was charged with the atrocities and cruelties of others. He was not in the attacks upon the Hampshire villages in 1676."—Judd's History of Hadley, pp. 135, 182, pub. in 1863.

" He had been widely distinguished from other red men who were engaged in inflicting the misery of this terrible war, and who, so far as we may now judge from their recorded conduct, possessed capacity and character at least equal to his. * * And the title of King, which it has been customary to attach to his name, disguises and transfigures to the view the form of a squalid savage whose palace was a sty; whose royal robe was a bear skin or coarse blanket, alive with vermin; who hardly knew the luxury of an ablution; who was often glad to appease appetite with food such as men who are not starving loathe. * * If a war had been elaborately concerted by a man of sense, it is scarcely to be supposed that it would have been entered on without a competent supply of munitions."—Palfrey's History of New England, vol. 3, pp. 222, 223, 227, ed. 1864.

" Nothing in his character from first to last, indicates any forethought or shows the least trace of heroism. Most surprising is it to learn that Philip is not known to have taken part in any one of the fights of the war, nor even,to have been in the immediate vicinity of any one of them after the initial skirmish,at Pocasset Swamp."—Pilgrim Republic, p. 551, pub. 1888.

to the attention of the several tribes.   Philip undoubtedly wrought them up by active negotiation or subtle insinuation, to a heat that needed but a spark to kindle into active warfare.   The entire history of the time shows that he was either frequently engaged in plots against the whites or his enemies industriously lied about him.   Rumors of his machinations coming, from time to time, to the notice of the Plymouth authorities, he was frequently called upon to explain his conduct and persuaded to make new treaties.   Every rumor prejudicial to Philip was carefully investigated, but always in that spirit of contempt born of conscious superiority, which admits of no alternative but submission.   He yielded to every demand of the English, signed such treaties as were proposed, and finally gave up his guns conditionally.   These were to be security for his good behavior "so long as they [the English] shall see reason."   In a short time the guns were confiscated on the flimsy pretext that some of them had been kept back, and the colonists believed that "the cloud might blow over." Two treaties were forced from Philip four years before the war broke out, but he had slight respect for these solemn contracts.   With little idea of English methods, and because the white men had power to enforce the terms they offered, he submitted.

Without Support he must have been Annihilated.   Had the war been entered upon by Philip alone, without concert or understanding on the part of other tribes, it must have ended with the first encounter.   Philip, defeated and fleeing for his life, would have been treated by them as an outcast, who could not be too quickly sacrificed for the purchase of their own peace and security.   A vanquished chief without influence, would have met with scant commiseration from men who through his means found themselves involved in an unexpected and unwelcome war.   But Philip had friends everywhere.   The Narragansetts cared for his women and children, the Nipmucks not only received and sheltered him, but even while he was detailing to them the ill success of the Mt. Hope fight, vigorously attacked the English, who were seeking them on an armed errand of peace and friendship.

Sausamon Denounces Philip. Is murdered, and his murderers Executed.

In the early part of the year, came rumors that Philip was again uneasy, and was once more plotting against the English. Sausamon reported that Philip was not only intending mischief, but was endeavoring to enlist others in his designs, and those statements have never been denied. Indeed the strongest evidence of their truth lies in the fact that the informer paid the forfeit of his life for his intelligence.[1] The immediate trial and execution of the murderers of Sausamon, roused the Indians to thoughts of vengeance. Had his report been untrue, little reason would have existed for killing him. Had there been no general uneasiness among the red men, and no idea, however indefinite, of approaching hostilities, the bare fact of the execution of men proved to have been guilty of murder, would have had no greater effect upon the tribes than had other and previous executions of Indian criminals. There is certainly reason to believe that they had long harbored hostile designs against the English.[2]

Philip not ready when the War Commenced.

The war began prematurely.[3] Some of Philip's young men, eager for plunder, sacked several houses in one of the eastern towns. This act precipitated hostilities. Few preparations had been made, and it seems probable that Philip had done little more than sound the different tribes as to the feasibility of such a combination as he proposed. The matter was in contemplation when Sausamon's disclosures were made. It is in evidence that the Connecticut River In-

1 "Last winter the Gov. of Plymouth was informed by Sausamon, a faithful Indian, that the said Philip was undoubtedly Indeavoring to raise new troubles; and was endeavoring to engage all the Sachems round about in a war against us. Some of the English also that lived near the said Sachem communicated their fears and jealousies concurrent with what the Indian had informed."—Narrative of Commissioners of Plymouth, Sept. 9, 1675.

2 "But this calm was deceitful; for, while every thing was apparently quiet, Philip was maturing his plans, rallying his forces, and preparing for war. The reality of this plot we are aware has been doubted; but the proofs of its existence we do not feel at liberty wholly to reject."—Barry's History of Massachusetts, vol. 1, p. 408.

3 "Its execution was fixed for the spring of 1676; but, as some say, by the rashness of Philip's young men, and against his own judgment and that of his counsellors, it was precipitated a year earlier."—Ibid.

dians[1] had knowledge of the proposed uprising, for certain suspicious actions of those at Northampton have been recorded. Rev. Solomon Stoddard, in a letter detailing the grounds for disarming the "Norwottog" Indians, writes:—

"In the winter and in the beginning of the spring our Indians gave cause of suspicion, in that they who were wont in former years to prefer earnestly for ground to plant on, even the most part of the winter and spring, now this spring desired not ground to plant till the time of planting was come, and it was almost too late. When they planted and the corn was come up; many of them deserted it and went to Quabaug to our enemies. Wappaye, the Indian, told Dea. Goodman, a little before the war broke out in Plymouth Colony, that this summer there would be a war between the English and the Indians; this he spake positively besides other bad words. * * * They shot several bullets at our men, as in Northampton meadow, at Parsons' boy; one in the town at the watchman; one at or close by Ens Cooke and another at Hadley; one at John Clary, passing by the fort in the road between Hatfield and Northampton; one in Hatfield meadow. * * * An Indian woman who had carried it as respectfully to the English as any we know among them, came with great earnestness and seeming affection and trouble, and told the English that then two of Philip's men were come to the fort. The Frenchman, Normanville, travelling towards Quabaug, saw (as he testified) these Indians who told him they had been at Mendon, and were coming to Norwotuck to persuade these Indians to join in the war; these he described so that our men plainly knew them. Our Indians afterwards shewed one of them to our men, testifying that he was one of them. * * * Their carriage was surly and insolent; one threatened to knock a maid on the head; another said the Indians would give him such a house, another told a woman that shortly she would bake bread for him; they vapored that the English were now afraid of the Indians. A squaw counselled good wife Wright to get into the town with her children and said she durst not tell her news, for then the Indians would cut off her head. They also solicited our men to entertain the Quabaug Indians but five days before they rose against the English. Wappawy, the Indian, confessed that he and several of our Indians had been with Philip, and named several of them."

The War opened by an Attack on Swansea. Sausamon was murdered in January, 1675. His murderers were tried and executed early in June. On the 24th of that month occurred the attack on Swansea, which opened the war, although a few houses had been rifled four days before.

1 "That the Indians had a conspiracy amongst themselves to rise against the English is confirmed by some of the Indians about Hadley."—Hubbard, p. 78.
"The Indians about Hadley confessed such a plot."—Hutchinson, vol. 1, p. 234.

Now Mr. Stoddard says that the Indians about Northampton began to act suspiciously in the winter, which must have been soon after the charges were made against Philip. This is good evidence that the disturbing elements were at work which in all probability originated with the Sachem of Pokanoket. That the Indian tribes were slow to take up arms after the first blow had been delivered, simply indicates that the conspiracy had not ripened, and that the commencement of the war was in a measure accidental.

Philip Driven from Mt. Hope and Po- casset Neck.

Philip established his headquarters at Mt. Hope, but he soon found it a very inconvenient place of residence. Troops from Plymouth Colony and from Boston, ordered out when intelligence was received of the assault on Swansea, were soon on the ground, and in the latter part of June, Philip was driven from his position. He fled to Pocasset, but did not tarry long. Unable to hold that point, he evacuated the place about the last of July, and went to the camp of the Nipmucks, at Wennimisset. In the meantime, however, the settlements at Dartmouth, Taunton, and Middleborough were assaulted, many houses burned, and a number of the inhabitants slain. So close was the pursuit of Philip, after leaving Pocasset Neck, that some thirty of his followers were killed or captured, and he was compelled to abandon about one hundred of his women and children.

A Treaty with the Narragansetts.

While these events were transpiring, the Commissioners of Massachusetts Bay,[1] Plymouth Colony and Connecticut, determined if possible to forestall Philip in his combinations with other tribes by making treaties on their own behalf. An armed party escorted the envoys who were empowered to treat with the Indians. Negotiations were concluded with the Narragansetts, and a treaty made with them which was

---

1 In 1672, the three colonies of Massachusetts Bay, Plymouth and Connecticut, entered into a confederacy, or rather revived the old confederacy established in 1643. It was a league for mutual defence which the then threatening position of Indian affairs demanded should be renewed. Among its provisions was the establishment of a quota of troops to be raised by each colony in time of war, and on this basis, that from Connecticut, which was so often so opportune to this section, was furnished. The proportion of troops to be contributed by each was for every one hundred from Massachusetts, sixty should be furnished by Connecticut, and thirty by Plymouth.

signed by a few of the old men. The young men were for war, and were ready to join Philip, but the old men were in favor of peace. This treaty, signed July 15th, was as usual, dictated by the English. The Narragansetts agreed to every thing required of them, promising to sell to the English whatever subjects of Philip were within their dominion, and to resist any invasion of their own, or of English territory by him. They also gave hostages for the fulfilment of their compact.

An Attempt to Treat with the Nipmucks.   This paper peace with one tribe was followed by a similar attempt to form another with the Nipmucks. But it was altogether too late. On the 14th of July, the latter tribe attacked Mendon, and seven or eight persons were killed. The Nipmucks were encamped at Wennimisset, about eight miles from Quabaug (Brookfield). From Brookfield eastward to Lancaster, there were no English settlements. In the vicinity of this little town, which contained but sixteen families, this tribe had gathered in great numbers. "Capt. Edward Hutchinson of Massachusetts, was sent" to force a treaty from them, and a conference with the Indians was agreed upon. On the 2d of August, the ambassador, accompanied by three citizens of Brookfield, and escorted by Capt. Wheeler and twenty troopers, set out for the place of rendezvous, which was upon a plain at some distance from the Indian camping ground. No Indians were found there.

The Ambush and Attack on Brookfield.   Persuaded by the Brookfield men who had perfect confidence in the honesty of the red men, the party proceeded to hunt them up. After marching four or five miles towards the Nipmuck encampment, they were lured into an ambush and eight of their men killed. Five were wounded, among them Capts. Wheeler and Hutchinson. Of this number, three, including Capt. Hutchinson, soon died. The discomfitted English, conducted by their Indian guides, found their way into the town of Brookfield. In a fortified house, where they were joined by most of the inhabitants, they withstood the onset of the savage foe for three days. On the evening of August 4th, Major Simon Willard, with forty-seven men, arrived and drove off the enemy. The town was soon after abandoned by the settlers.

Philip not in this Fight.   It is not positively known that Philip was personally concerned in the fight at Brookfield, though it is affirmed that he arrived at the camp of the Nipmucks, the day before it occurred.[1] When he joined the Nipmucks, he brought with him, besides women and children, forty men, thirty of whom were armed with guns, and the rest with bows and arrows. After the engagement he gave three of the sagamores about a peck each of unstrung wampum, which they accepted.

1   Palfrey's History of New England, vol. 3, p. 159.

CHAPTER XX.

KING PHILIP'S WAR—THREE TOWNS ABANDONED.

The Seven Thriving Valley Towns. AT this time scattered within a distance of fifty miles, along the valley of the Connecticut River, under the jurisdiction of Massachusetts, were seven well established and thriving settlements. Between Springfield and Northfield were Westfield, Northampton, Hadley, Hatfield, and Deerfield. Springfield and Northampton were the older towns, and Deerfield and Northfield the most recently settled. The newer towns were composed mainly of emigrants from the others. Hence there was established a community of interests between them all.

The War Surges Westward. The war, now in full progress, soon enveloped the towns of Western Massachusetts. During the remainder of the year the enemy attacked Deerfield, Northfield, Hatfield, Hadley and Springfield. That Philip planned these assaults or commanded at either of them is uncertain. Nothing definite is heard from him till the following spring, when he was seen by Mrs. Rowlandson while in captivity. It is not probable that he was idle, but there is no proof that the valley tribes yielded the leadership into his hands. Contemporaneous writings, however, show that every attack was attributed to him. Reports of commanders and others in authority, assume that Philip was the instigator and ubiquitous leader in all these encounters.

Vigorous but Unavailing Pursuit of the Enemy. Major Pynchon of Springfield, at the head of affairs in this section, when he heard of the attack on Brookfield, sent to Connecticut for reinforcements. Seventy men, forty dragoons, and thirty Indians, under command of Capt. Watts, were at once dispatched to Springfield, where they were joined by

Lieut. Thomas Cooper, with twenty-seven dragoons and ten Indians, and the whole ordered to the seat of war. They reached Brookfield on the 7th of August, and found there two full companies from the seaboard, commanded by Capt. Richard Beers of Watertown, and Capt. Thomas Lothrop of Beverly. Major Willard, with this detachment, numbering about three hundred fifty men, marched for the encampment at Wennimisset, but the enemy had fled. The woods were scoured in all directions without avail; not an Indian could be found. On the 9th, Capt. Moseley, sent with reinforcements and supplies to the eastern troops in the field, but with orders to continue in pursuit of Philip, reported at Brookfield. Further search for the enemy revealing nothing, headquarters were established at Hadley, where the entire force was concentrated. A thorough and extended scout was made on both sides of the river, about the 16th of August. Not an Indian was seen, but about seventy deserted wigwams were destroyed.

Friendly Indians Assist in the Pursuit. Many friendly Indians joined the whites in these expeditions. In addition to the number sent up from Hartford, thirty others under Joseph, son of Uncas, ranged the woods in pursuit of the hostiles. Some of the Northampton or Nonotuck tribe were also employed about this time, but Major Pynchon suspected their fidelity. It was believed that they were treacherous, giving warning by shouts of the approach of the English.

The Nipmucks Retreat to Payquyag. After the destruction of Brookfield, the Nipmucks fled and for a long time no trace of them could be found. The entire country was thoroughly searched in this vicinity, up and down the river, and as far east as Brookfield, but their hiding place was not discovered. It was finally ascertained that the enemy had fled northerly and were at Payquyag, (Athol) and other places in that section of what is now Franklin County. Here they remained in security, living upon the supplies captured at Brookfield. When these were exhausted they began to plunder the flocks of the settlers, driving off large numbers of sheep from Northfield.

Capt. Watts Re-
turns to Hart-
ford.

On the 22^d of August, Capt. Watts, having returned from scouting, was at Hadley, and the Bay forces were at Brookfield. Major Pynchon desired Capt. Watts to remain longer and reconnoitre in the vicinity of Payquyag, in the hope of discovering the enemy, but he soon returned to Hartford with all his troops. Garrisons were sent to the more northerly towns; twenty men to Northfield, and ten men to Deerfield. On the 23^d of August, Capts. Lothrop and Beers were at Hadley.

The Authorities
Decide to Dis-
arm the Nono-
tucks.

Many of the Nonotuck Indians were still living in the river towns, though not on the former terms of friendship with the settlers. They had a fort on the high bank of the Connecticut River, between Northampton and Hatfield. It was "opposite the northeast corner of Hadley Great Meadow," and was occupied about this time by a large body of Indians, among whom were Nonotucks, Pocumtucks, and other strangers. Soon after the war broke out, having reason to suspect the fidelity of the Nonotucks, the committees of militia in the Hampshire towns, decided to demand their arms. They professed friendship, and gave up their guns willingly. But in a few days, owing to their continued protestations of good will, and in accordance with a proposition made by them to join the forces sent against the enemy, their arms were returned to them. Suspicions being again aroused, the council of commanders held at Hadley, on the 24th of August, after due deliberation, decided once more to disarm them. Accordingly a messenger was sent to the fort, but he was put off with an evasive answer, and desired to come again. On his return he was received with insults. The temper of the Indians being thus disclosed, Capts. Lothrop and Beers determined to take away their arms by force the next morning.

The Indians Steal
away, are Pur-
sued, and the
first Fight in the
Valley Occurs.

While the Northampton troops were ordered to march as near to the fort as possible, Lothrop and Beers were to cross the Connecticut from Hadley, and endeavor to cut off their retreat up the river. The enemy, however, suspected the manœuver, or had received intelligence of it, and when the two divisions met at the fort, near day-break, they found nothing but the body of an aged sachem, who, refusing to go with his comrades, had been killed by them. After sending back a portion of the Northampton soldiers to guard the town, the commanders pushed forward with about one hundred men, "at a great pace after them."[1] Capts. Lothrop and Beers, proposing as Mr. Stoddard states, "to parley with the Indians," apparently disregarded the most ordinary military precautions, and were intent only upon coming within speaking distance. Their men had orders "not to make any shot upon them first."[2] The Indians, less pacifically inclined, following the tactics employed at Quabaug, hid in ambush, and the first intimation of their presence, was the discharge of about forty guns upon their unsuspecting pursuers. Five soldiers were killed by the fire of the Indians, and three others died subsequently of their wounds. "One man was shot in the back by our own men." The English charged upon the Indians in the swamp, and then fought them in their own way from behind trees. For three hours the fight continued, when the Indians fled, leaving behind them "much of their luggage." The place where this action occurred is said to have been at "Wequamps on the Pocumtuck path."[3]

The Loss on both Sides.   Nine persons were killed in this first encounter with the Indians in the Connecticut Valley. Only one of the slain was from Northampton, Samuel Mason, only son of Thomas Mason. The others were Azariah Dickinson, son of Nathaniel Dickinson of Hadley; Richard Fellows of Hatfield, son of Richard Fellows, deceased; James Levens of Roxbury; John Plumer of Newberry; Mark Pitman of Marblehead; Joseph Person of Lynn; Matthew Scales of Rowley; and William Cluff of Charlestown. John Parke of Water-

---

1 Rev. Solomon Stoddard's Letter, Mather's History.

2 Rev. Mr. Stoddard's Letter to the Connecticut Council.

3 Sheldon's History of Deerfield, p. 91. Judd's History of Hadley, p. 144, states that "the place is now unknown." Hubbard says it was "about ten miles above Hatfield at a place called Sugar Loaf Hill." And according to Rev. Mr. Russell of Hadley, "at a swamp beyond Hatfield."

town was shot in the elbow. The loss of the Indians is not known. A squaw captured soon after, and some children, who came into the camp the next day, reported that they lost twenty-six men. Mr. Judd doubted this statement, and believed that they lost no more men than the English. An Indian, Menownet, who was in the fight, affirms that no Indians were killed.

The Nonotucks forever Abandon their Stamping Grounds. In the early morning hours of August 25th, 1675, the Nonotuck Indians, accompanied by their families, and bearing with them all their worldly goods, left their native haunts never to return. They joined the Pocumtucks near Deerfield, and both tribes made common cause against the English. The result of this union was soon made manifest, by a joint attack upon Deerfield.

Reinforcements sent from Hartford. News of the fight at Sugar Loaf was sent to Hartford by Major Pynchon, and on the 26th of August, George Graves, with twenty men, was dispatched to "assist the plantations at Norwottog." He came to Northampton. Major Talcott was again ordered to Springfield to consult with Major Pynchon, and on the 3d of September, Major Treat, who had been appointed commander of the Connecticut forces in the field, came up with about ninety dragoons, reaching Northampton the day following.

Connecticut Men, Officers and Soldiers Quartered in Northampton. When the reinforcements reached Northampton they were quartered on the inhabitants. Officers, privates, Indians and horses, were distributed throughout the town. Some were billeted only for a few meals, others were enforced guests for days, and some for weeks. David Wilton seems to have had his share of them. Major Treat, Capt. "Cely," Lieut. Standley and Ensign Marshall, were at his house early in September, and Major Treat and other officers and soldiers, as well as Indians, were there at different times. There must have been considerable bustle and activity about town, as well as much anxiety and alarm among the inhabitants.

Deerfield Attacked and Partially Destroyed.

On the first of September, occurred the first Indian attack upon any town in this section. About sixty redskins suddenly appeared near the town of Deerfield. They gave the alarm by shooting James Eggleston, who was searching for his horse, and the people sought safety in their fortified block houses. After losing two of their number, the enemy abandoned the attack on these places of refuge, and proceeded to the work of pillaging and burning the deserted dwellings and barns of the settlers.

The "Angel of Hadley," a Myth.

Familiar to every school boy is the legend of the "Angel of Hadley." How the regicide Goffe, doubly risked his life to save the people among whom he was in hiding, not only to the bullets of the Indians, but to the keen eyes of royalty searching everywhere for the murderers of the king, has become a part of the history of the times. Alas, this story of true heroism has been relegated to the regions of romance. In brief, the narrative reads :—On the first day of September, 1675, on a day of religious services, while the people of Hadley were assembled in the meeting house, the Indians suddenly appeared. Though the settlers believed in God, they clung to their guns, and kept their powder dry. But they were without a leader and in the utmost confusion. "Suddenly a grave and elderly person appeared in the midst of them. In his mein and dress he differed from the rest of the people. He not only encouraged them to defend themselves; but he put himself at their head, rallied and instructed them, and led them on to encounter the enemy, who by this means was repulsed. As suddenly the deliverer of Hadley disappeared. The people were left in consternation utterly unable to account for this strange phenomenon. It is not probable that they were ever able to explain it." [1]

William Goffe and Edward Whalley, two of the judges who passed sentence of death upon Charles. I., King of England, escaped to this country in 1660, and four years afterwards came to Hadley, where they were secreted in the house of the minister, Rev. Mr. Russell. Only the pastor's family and two others knew of their presence

[1] Hutchinson's History of Massachusetts, vol. 1, p. 269, note.

there. In after years, when the participators in these scenes were all dead, and knowledge of his residence there was no longer dangerous, Goffe became the "Angel of Hadley." The story was so interwoven into the annals of this region that for nearly two hundred years no one doubted its authenticity. Historians differed as to its date, some placing it on the first of September, and others carrying it forward to June of the following year, but none questioned its truth. In 1874, George Sheldon Esq., author of the History of Deerfield, and the leading antiquarian of the Connecticut Valley, demonstrated the improbability of the statement. He could find no authority for the reported attack on the first of September, and as Hadley was the headquarters of the troops in this part of the county during Philip's war, suggested that there could not at any time have been a lack of soldiers, with experienced commanders, sufficient for the protection of the town.[1] As this discussion has no direct connection with this history, it is not necessary to enter upon its details. The arguments against the appearance of Goffe at Hadley, are at least plausible if not convincing, but it is difficult to destroy at once a faith cemented by centuries of unquestioned belief. There is no reason to suppose that any further light will ever be thrown upon this transaction. To the student of history it must remain at best a questionable incident. But the great majority of readers, conversant only with the long prevailing version of the legend, possibly never informed of the doubts advanced against it, will still continue to believe in the "Angel of Hadley."

Northfield Assailed and laid in Ashes. On the 2d of September, while the fires at Deerfield were still smouldering, Northfield was assailed by the Nipmucks and Wampanoags. A party at work in the meadows was surprised and eight of their number killed. The men who survived, together with the women and children, took refuge in the block house, where they successfully defended themselves, but were unable to prevent the savages from destroying their property. Of the eight men killed, two, Ebenezer

1 New England Historical and Genealogical Register, Oct., 1874.

Parsons and Nathaniel Curtis, belonged in Northampton, and three, Samuel Wright, Ebenezer Janes, and Jonathan Janes, though settlers at Northfield, were emigrants from this town. Samuel Wright was the son of Samuel Wright Sr., one of Northampton's original settlers. He married Elizabeth Burt, at Springfield, in 1653, and within three years removed to Northampton. He was forty-six years of age, and left a family of eight children. Ebenezer and Jonathan Janes were sons of William Janes, from fourteen to sixteen years old. Ebenezer Parsons was the son of Joseph Parsons, his birth being the first one recorded at Northampton, and he was just twenty years old. Nathaniel Curtis was the second son of Henry Curtis, and was about twenty-four years of age. Samuel Wright Jr., son of Sergt. Samuel Wright, was severely wounded.[1] John Peck of Hadley, Thomas Scott, and Benjamin Dunwich, probably eastern soldiers, were among the slain. Northfield contained at this time about sixteen families.

Capt. Beers, sent to succor Northfield, is Ambushed and slain. After the fight at Wequamps and the attack on Deerfield, the condition of the outlying towns was considered critical. On the 3ᵈ of September, Capt. Beers was sent from Hadley, with a force of thirty-six mounted men and some carts, with orders to secure the garrison at Northfield. At this time nothing was known of the attack on that place, and when within three or four miles of his destination he encamped. The next morning, leaving his horses in camp, under guard, Beers set out for Northfield.

---

1 In a petition to the General Court, for aid, dated May 3, 1703, he says: "In the first Indian war, I was pressed up to Northfield, under Capt. Lothrop, and there left a garrison soldier; soon after which the Indians besieged that fort; they killed my father and shot a bullet into my hip bone. From thence I was brought to Hadley, under care of Dr. Westcarr, where I was till winter. The doctor dying, I shifted from one surgeon to another till the spring. In April following, I went to Hartford to Mrs. Allyn, where I was about seven months, all which time I paid for my diet and chirurgeon out of my own estate, and although I attained to so much strength as to walk about and carry on some business, it hath been with much pain and difficulty, for the bullet remaining still in my hip bone, the wound continually runs and hath done so these fifteen years; though at times it is almost dried up, yet it breaks out again and especially of late years it grows worse and worse so that I am almost disabled for labor, and what I do is with much pain and difficulty. Considering my family has grown so great, I now for the first time petition for relief." June 1ˢᵗ, 1703. the General Court granted him £10; also 40s. a year for life. He died in 1734, aged 80. He had a family of nine children.

Probably he had not even then learned of the attack, and had no suspicion that there were any Indians about, for he took no precautions against surprise. Scarcely had the march begun, when he "was set upon by a great number of Indians from the side of a swamp where there was a hot dispute for some time."[1] Unable to make head against the enemy, Capt. Beers retreated to a hill near by, and was soon after killed. His small party, deprived of their leader, "fought till their powder and shot where spent,"[2] and then the survivors made the best of their way to Hadley, having first buried the body of their captain. The scene of this action is now known as "Beers' Plain" and "Beers' Mountain." Twenty-one of the English were slain, and thirteen reached Hadley in safety. This detachment was composed mainly of troops from the Bay. It contained several men from Hadley, but none from Northampton. One soldier returned after wandering in the woods for six days, almost famished; and another taken prisoner, was with the Indians during Mrs. Rowlandson's captivity.

Reinforcements again sent from Connecticut. Major Treat, whose arrival at Northampton has already been noted, had orders to send home all the Connecticut troops, except the twenty-nine men garrisoning the different towns, but when intelligence of this disaster reached Hartford, on the 5th, one hundred Mohegans and Pequods were ordered to reinforce Major Treat, while twenty dragoons, under Sergt. Joseph Wadsworth, were sent to Westfield, and twenty, under John Grant, to Springfield.

Maj. Treat marches at once to the Relief of Northfield. Recognizing the pressing need of immediate relief to Northfield, Major Treat with a force of one hundred men, began his march to that place, on Sunday, Sept. 5th. Like Beers, he encamped a few miles from the town, and on the morning of the 6th, reached his place of destination. Though no Indians were seen on the march, there were fearful indications on all sides of the malignity of the savages. The heads of Beers' soldiers stuck on poles, and the bodies of

1 Rev. Mr. Stoddard's Letter.
2 Mather's History.
17

others, dangling from trees, by chains hooked into their
jaws, were among the horrid sights that met their eyes.
While a detail of Treat's men were busy burying the dead,
they were fired upon by "about fourteen Indians."[1] No
one was killed, though Major Treat was hit by a spent ball.
Disheartened by the repeated exhibitions of the barbarity
of their inhuman foes, and fearful of another attack, orders
were issued for an immediate retreat.   Leaving the cattle
behind, and the dead unburied, the retrograde march commenced the "same night."   The next day Capt. Appleton,
who had just arrived from the Bay, started from Hadley
with reinforcements, and soon met Treat and his command.
Appleton endeavored to prevail upon Treat to turn about
and resume the offensive, but his forces were too much demoralized by what they had seen, as well as wearied by
their long night march, and all returned to Hadley. Many
of the cattle followed the army, and were soon afterwards
brought into that town.

Capt. Appleton's
Opportune Ap-
pearance.
No record has been found of Capt. Appleton's orders to march to the Connecticut
Valley, nor of the force he brought with
him, neither is it known where he met Major Treat's retreating and panic stricken army.   This memorable march
was made on the night of the 6th of September.   Ham-
pered by the darkness, and impeded by the train of fleeing
inhabitants, its progress must have been slow and tedious.
Capt. Appleton probably started on the morning of the 7th,
and met the returning forces a short distance from Hadley.
It is hardly probable that this company of fugitives and
soldiers dared to encamp during that long and fearful night,
but pressed forward with all speed, anxious only to reach
a place of safety.

Destruction of
Northfield.
After Northfield had been abandoned, the
Indians destroyed the fort and the remaining houses, and the town was without inhabitants for seven years.   It contained nearly as many people
as Brookfield, and had been but two years settled.

1 Rev. Mr. Stoddard's Letter.

A Defensive Policy Adopted, but is not Sanctioned by the Commissioners. The commanders of the troops held a council of war on the 8th, at which it was decided to act on the defensive, leaving a garrison in each town. Capt. Appleton was accordingly sent to Deerfield on the 10th. After reporting this decision to the authorities at Hartford, Major Treat and the Connecticut troops were recalled, except small garrisons of sixteen men at Westfield, and fifteen at Springfield. Neither the Connecticut Council nor the Commissioners of the United Colonies, approved of the action of the officers in the field, and the Commissioners voted Sept. 16th, to raise one thousand men for service in the valley. The Massachusetts and Connecticut troops were to be under the authority of Major Pynchon, with Major Treat as second in command. Of these men, five hundred were to be "dragoons or troopers with long armes." Massachusetts was to furnish five hundred twenty-seven soldiers, Connecticut three hundred fifteen, and Plymouth one hundred fifty-eight.

Deerfield a second time Attacked and Plundered. The Indians were still lurking in the vicinity of Deerfield, watching every movement of the garrison. On Sunday, Sept. 12th, while a party of soldiers were returning from religious worship at Stockwell's fort to their station at the north stockade, they were fired upon by Indians in ambush, and one man wounded. They all succeeded, however, in escaping to the fort. The enemy rushed upon the abandoned stockade, capturing the sentinel, whom they afterwards killed, and destroyed the fortification. Capt. Appleton soon drove the Indians from the town, but deeming his force too weak to engage in offensive operations, without exposing his strong hold to capture, he sent to Northampton for reinforcements. In the meantime the enemy plundered the village, burned several houses that had escaped the previous conflagration, and gathered large quantities of provisions, which were taken to their rendezvous at Pine Hill. The next night a party of volunteers from Northampton and Hadley, marched to the relief of Appleton, and on the 14th he directed his entire force against the Indian encampment at Pine Hill; but ere he reached the place it had been abandoned.[1]

1 Sheldon's History of Deerfield, p. 99.

Capt. Samuel Moseley came to Hadley, with a company of sixty Bay soldiers, on the 14th, and was ordered to Deerfield. Major Treat arrived at Northampton on the 15th or 16th, and Capt. John Mason was ordered to lead a company of Mohegans and Pequods to the Nonotuck plantation. This little army established headquarters at Hadley, and it soon became necessary to replenish the commissary department. Large quantities of wheat were then raised throughout the valley. The fertile meadows of Deerfield yielded ample crops of this important product; and at this time there were about three thousand bushels standing in stacks at that place. Major Pynchon, who owned nearly all of it, sent orders to have it threshed and made ready for removal.

For this purpose, a sufficient number of teams and their drivers were impressed, and Capt. Lothrop and his company were ordered to guard the train. On the 18th of September, in the early morning hours, he set out on that fatal march, reaching Deerfield unmolested. With the grain in bags, and some furniture of the inhabitants, loaded upon the carts—eighteen in number—the cavalcade started on its return to Hadley. They proceeded in safety some miles, and had reached a small stream in the town of Deerfield (now South Deerfield), without discovering any signs of the foe, when the escort halted to await the arrival of the teams. Many of the soldiers had placed their guns upon the carts, and tempted by the luscious grapes hanging by the wayside, dispersed to gather them. At this moment, the Indians, lying in ambush, suddenly opened fire upon the soldiers. Many were killed by the first discharge, and others were speedily slaughtered by the foe, who rushed from their concealment ere the white men had time to obtain their arms. Capt. Lothrop fell early in the action, and only "seven or eight of the English escaped."

Capt. Moseley, with a force of sixty men, who had gone out in another direction to hunt for Indians, was four or five miles distant when he heard the firing, and came with all haste to the scene of the encounter. When he reached the ground, he found the Indians stripping the slain, plundering the carts, ripping open the grain bags and feather beds, and scattering their contents in the mud. Moseley promptly attacked the savages, though they outnumbered him ten to one. For five or six hours he continued the fight, but towards evening, when Moseley, exhausted by his efforts, was about to withdraw, Major Treat arrived, and together they drove the Indians westward, pursuing them till darkness put an end to the conflict. With one hundred white men and sixty Mohegans, Major Treat left Northampton, that morning, his destination being Northfield, at which place he had been ordered to establish a military outpost. When the sound of battle reached him he hastened to the field, where he arrived "just in the nick of time." That night the troops marched to Deerfield, taking their wounded with them. The next morning Treat and Moseley returned to the battle field, and there hastily buried their dead. A spot was selected a short distance from the scene of the ambuscade, and sixty-four bodies were interred in "one dreadful grave."

The number of the slain is not accurately known. It has been variously estimated, some accounts placing it as high as ninety, while others name but sixty. Sixty-four men killed would probably come nearest to the truth. A report was made to the government at Boston (probably by officers in the field) of the burial of "sixty-four men in all," which would seem to be sufficient evidence as to the number slain. No Northampton men were engaged in this conflict. The soldiers were nearly all from the eastern part of the state, "the very flower of the County of Essex." Of the seventeen teamsters belonging in Deerfield, not one returned. These were the only residents of the valley who were known to have lost their lives in this encounter.

The Indian loss was reported at ninety-six, but it cannot be relied upon. They carried off or concealed their dead, and no accurate estimate of their loss has ever been obtained. The number of Indians engaged is variously stated at from five hundred to twelve hundred. Mr. Judd thinks five hundred is too large a number. He says "If the Indians were four hundred, they were six times as numerous as the soldiers." [1]

1 Judd's History of Hadley, p. 150.

Monument Erected.   One hundred sixty years afterwards an appropriate monument was erected and dedi-
icated to the memory of the slain in the fight at "Muddy
Brook," which was afterwards, because of the massacre,
named "Bloody Brook."

Deerfield Aban-   A few days subsequent to the defeat of
doned.   Lothrop, the garrison was ordered away,
and the inhabitants of Deerfield abandoned
the place. It contained more than twenty families, most
of them from other towns in the valley. This was the
third village deserted within the limits of Hampshire
County, during the few months in which the war had been
in progress. Up to this time the success of the Indians
had been uninterrupted, and panic and uncertainty prevailed everywhere. The inhabitants of Northfield and
Deerfield fled to the remaining settlements in the county,
which by this addition, and the troops quartered in them,
must have been filled to overflowing.

Northfield no longer   This disaster so disconcerted the plans of
Tenable. Soldiers   the Hartford Council, that the design of
in the Hampshire
Towns.   occupying and fortifying Northfield was
no longer feasible, and orders to certain
other Connecticut forces to reinforce Treat at that place,
were countermanded. About the first of October, Capt.
Samuel Appleton had a company at Hadley, Capt. Joseph
Sill another at Northampton, and Capt. Samuel Moseley a
third at Hatfield. Within a few days Lieut. Phinehas
Upham with thirty men, and Capt. Jonathan Poole of Reading, with thirty-five more, arrived. The Indian allies from
Connecticut returned home on the 23d of September.

Major Pynchon Re-   Major Pynchon, whose farm-house and
signs is Com-   barns at West Springfield, had been burned
mand,hand pt.
Appleton is Ap-   by the Indians on the 26th of September,
pointed.   and who had previously sent in his request
to be relieved from the duties of commander-in-chief, resigned on the 30th. Among other reasons, he urged the distressed state of his affairs at home, "the sorrows and afflic-
tions my dear wife undergoes and her continual calls to me

for relief and succor, she being almost overwhelmed with grief and trouble and in many straits and perplexities which would be somewhat holpen and alleviated by my presence there." Accordingly on the 4th of October, the Council appointed Capt. Samuel Appleton of Ipswich, commander-in-chief of the united forces, and on the 12th, he took command.

Treachery of the Springfield Indians. They lure the troops to Hadley.

In carrying out the instructions of the Hartford Council, dated August 28th, Major Pynchon did not disarm the Springfield Indians, but took hostages of them, who were sent to Hartford. They kept faith with the English till after the disasters in the upper towns. Doubtless incited by the representations of Philip, and encouraged by the success of their friends, they determined to aid in the proposed extermination of the English; their hostages having, in the meantime, succeeded in escaping. In accordance with the newly approved policy of offensive warfare, Major Pynchon concentrated all his forces in Hadley, on the 4th of October, preparatory to an extensive movement against the enemy. The savages, cognizant of all that was passing among their foes, gathered in force in the vicinity of Springfield, for the purpose of making an attack as soon as the troops marched away. Indeed it may have been part of their tactics to entice the bulk of the garrison to Hadley, by means of a false demonstration, as Pynchon gives as a reason for hastening to that place, a rumor that large bodies of Indians had been seen thereabouts. Probably the inhabitants of Springfield would all have been slaughtered had not Toto, a friendly Indian of Windsor, informed the authorities of Hartford and Windsor, of the threatened raid. Information of the impending danger was instantly dispatched to Westfield and Springfield, and thence to Hadley. Major Pynchon, with Capts. Appleton and Sill, with one hundred ninety men, immediately countermarched to the relief of the beleaguered town. Major Treat was on the west side of the Connecticut River, and started from Westfield, while Pynchon marched on the east. Treat reached a point opposite Springfield, about eleven o'clock, but being without boats could not cross. Several hours afterwards, Pynchon arrived, the enemy fled, and Treat crossed; but their work had been completed and the town was in flames.

Burning of Spring-
field.

Warned by the messengers from Hartford, the inhabitants of Springfield, gathered in the block house, with whatever of worldly goods they were able to take with them. Early on the morning of the 5th of October, no signs of Indians being discovered, Lieut. Thomas Cooper and John Miller rode out to reconnoitre. They were fired upon soon after leaving the fort. Miller was killed, and Lieut. Cooper so severely wounded, that he fell from his horse dead, as the animal reached the fort. Then followed the usual scene in this sanguinary warfare. The Indians, beyond gunshot from the fort, completely destroyed the town. Thirty-three houses and twenty-five barns, with their contents, were burned, including the corn mill of Major Pynchon. Only fifteen houses remained standing in the town plot. On the west side of the river, and in the outskirts on the east side, about sixty houses were left, with much corn in and about them. One woman was killed and two men died of their wounds a few days after.

The Indians and
their Loss.

The number of Indians engaged in this attack is estimated as being from one hundred to five hundred. About forty Springfield Indians and several hundred from up the river composed the party of the assailants. When the troops arrived, the enemy disappeared, and several days elapsed before any trace of them could be obtained.

Appleton takes Com-
mand. Hampshire
Garrisons.

Major Appleton, on taking command of the valley forces, immediately commenced offensive operations. Scouting parties were sent out in all directions, and great efforts made to locate the foe. The several towns were garrisoned as follows: Capt. Seeley, with sixty Connecticut soldiers, was at Northampton, Capt. Moseley at Hatfield, and Capt. Poole, with Lieut. Upham and sixty men, were at Hadley. Major Treat and part of his force had been suddenly recalled on the 8th. He returned to Hampshire in about ten days.

He Starts for North-field, but goes to Fa field. On the 15th, Major Appleton ordered out his whole force, intending to march towards Northfield, where it was believed the main body of the Indians was encamped. All responded but Capt. Seeley, who declined as Appleton says, because he thought he had not a sufficient commission. On the march news reached him that the enemy had gathered and were forming a barricade of rails near Pocumtuck. Appleton at once changed his course and crossed the river to Hatfield. A night expedition was planned against Pocumtuck, but it soon became evident that the Indians were on the alert, and the army returned to its quarters.

Major Appleton "sorely beset." In his correspondence, under date of Oct. 16th, Major Appleton reports that he was "sorely beset." Indications of Indians in the immediate vicinity were abundant, and notwithstanding the fact that Northampton had a garrison of fifty or more men, Capt. Seeley was clamorous for reinforcements. Appleton writes from Hadley : —

"This evening very late, I am assaulted with a most vehement and affectionate request from Northampton (who have already with them about fifty of Capt. Seeley's men) that I would afford them a little more help, they fearing to be assaulted presently."

Plenty of Indian Signs. That this alarm was not altogether groundless, is proved by the report from Capt. Moseley, made while the Northampton messengers were preferring their request, that signs of the enemy had been discovered within a mile of Hatfield. During the next few days the troops were kept pretty busy endeavoring to ascertain the whereabouts of the Indians. Appleton needed reinforcements, and in the absence of Major Treat and the Connecticut troops, was unable to do effective work. Information had been obtained of the discovery of a plot for a general uprising of all the Connecticut Indians, and this was the cause of the recall of Major Treat. Only prompt action, it is believed, saved the threatened towns from annihilation. Hartford and all the principal towns were marked for destruction, and general consternation prevailed throughout the Colony.

An Indian R u s e,
followed b y a n
Attack on H a t -
field.

The anticipated assault which had kept all the river towns in a ferment, fell upon Hatfield, on the 19th of October, when seven or eight hundred Indians attacked that town. Hoping to draw the English, as usual, into an ambuscade, the enemy devised a stratagem, which was partially successful. They set fires in the woods several miles distant, hoping to entice the bulk of the English forces outside of their fortifications. These fires were set northerly of the town, and Moseley sent a scout of ten mounted men to reconnoitre, who of course readily fell into the trap set for them.[1] Only one of the ten scouts escaped, three others were captured, and six were killed. At this time the town was garrisoned by Capts. Moseley and Poole, and Lieut. Upham, with their companies. Major Appleton was at Hadley, and on hearing the alarm, marched to the assistance of his subordinates. The attack was made about four o'clock in the afternoon, but the garrison was well prepared. Capt. Poole was stationed at the north end of the town, Capt. Moseley at the center, and Major Appleton occupied the south. After a conflict of two hours the enemy retired. Major Treat, who had just arrived at Northampton from Westfield, reached the scene of the encounter in time to render substantial aid. Only one man was killed in the direct assault. Of the three scouts who were captured, one of them was barbarously tortured to death, and the other two were released and sent home in the following March, to report what they had seen. "At last after the burning of some few barns with some other buildings, the enemy hasted away as fast as they came on."[2]

This defeat discouraged the Indians, and the main body withdrew from this part of the country in a short time. Straggling parties of them remained, however, in the hope of obtaining a few scalps or picking up a little plunder.

1 " On Wednesday, the 19th of Oct., a party of Indians about seven miles off Hatfield, in the woods, made several great fires, to make the English think they were there, but as soon as ever they had set fire to the woods, they came directly towards Hatfield and about two miles from Hatfield, they lay in the bushes by the way side, undiscoverable. thinking to cut off the English in their way to the fires."—Present State of New England, from a merchant in Boston to a friend in London, p. 166, published in 1675.

2 Hubbard's Indian Wars, p. 134.

CHAPTER XXI.

KING PHILIP'S WAR—RAID ON NORTHAMPTON.

Northampton Suffers in common with other Towns. NORTHAMPTON had endured less inconvenience thus far in the war than most of the neighboring towns. No direct assault had yet been made by the foe, but in common with the rest, the town had freely contributed men and means for mutual defense. Scarce an engagement had occurred in which some of its citizens had not taken part. The towns up the river contained numerous settlers from Northampton, and among them were many who, while they were classed as residents of those towns, were closely connected with Northampton families. While the troops in active service were mainly from other sections, from the Bay and from Connecticut, there were among them volunteers from many towns in the valley.

Two of its Citizens Slain on their own Homestead. During the first months of the war no resident of Northampton was killed within its limits. The people were in constant apprehension of danger from marauding savages, and work, especially in the meadows, was carried on with fear and trembling. It was not till September that the dreaded blow fell, and the first who were killed in the town were slain in sight of their own household. On the 28th of that month Praisever Turner and Usacksby Shakspeare[1] were killed. Praisever Turner came to Northampton in 1657, when he was twenty-one years old. He had served an apprenticeship as a mill-wright, and bought the first mill ever built in the town. His home lot was on Elm Street, and proba-

1 The name is given in a printed "Register of deaths in Northampton from the first settlement of the town in 1653, to Aug. 1824," as "Isaac Abbee Shakspeare." It is also written in a Note as "Uzackabee Shacksbee."

bly embraced the lot east of what is now known as "Paradise road." The earliest account of this tragedy is contained in a letter to the Connecticut council, from Major Pynchon, dated Hadley, Sept. 30, 1675 :—

"Two days ago 2 Englishmen at Northampton, being gone out in yᵉ morning to cut wood, but a little from the house, were both shot down Dead, having 2 bullets apiece shot into each of their bodies. The Indians cut off their scalps, took their arms, and were gone in a trice: though the English run presently thither, at yᵉ report of yᵉ guns, but could see nothing but yᵉ footing of 2 Indians."

They were proba-
bly Killed in
"Paradise."
This statement embodies all that is known concerning the death of these two men. They were undoubtedly slain by rambling Indians, seeking scalps. At this time the town was full of soldiers, some of whom were soon in pursuit of the foe, but they escaped unmolested. It is probable that they were killed in or near what is now known as "Paradise," as Turner's home lot bordered upon and undoubtedly included a portion of that delectable section. They would hardly venture very far from home, indeed Pynchon says, "a little from the house." Of Usacksby or Isaac Abbee Shakspeare, nothing is known. Pynchon calls him an Englishman, but that was simply another name for white man. He was in the employ of Turner, and it may be imagined that they went out after breakfast to replenish the wood pile.

Several Men At-
tacked in Pynch-
on's Meadow.
A few days after the fight at Hatfield, on the 28ᵗʰ of October, a number of Indians, probably stragglers from the horde which had invested that town, suddenly appeared in Northampton. They attacked a party of seven or eight men, who had ventured to gather their harvest from Pynchon's Meadow. This meadow is situated at the most westerly turn of the "Ox Bow." It is bounded on the south by Hurlburt's pond, into and through which at that time Mill River flowed. Their weapons were deposited at some convenient point, but no sentinel was posted. The Indians, who doubtless had been watching them, seized their guns and endeavored to surround the party. But the English at once detached their horses from the carts, and mounting

them fled. One of the men, however, managed to obtain possession of his gun, shot an Indian, and escaped with the rest of his companions.

The Indians enter South Street and burn Houses and Barns.

Pursuing the fleeing settlers directly into the town, the assailants entered South Street and "burnt four or five houses and two or three barns that stood some distance from the principal settlement."[1] Major Treat with his company, was stationed here at that time, and sent a detachment in haste after the marauders, but as usual without effect. Four houses and as many barns were destroyed. The buildings that were burned belonged to Enos Kingsley, Ralph Hutchinson, Preserved Clapp, and William Smead. They were at that time the most southerly of the settlers on that street. Enos Kingsley lived on the homestead, part of which has since been known as the Starkweather estate; William Smead occupied the adjoining home lot on the south, and Ralph Hutchinson the next one. Preserved Clapp lived on the other side of the street, nearly opposite the house of Ralph Hutchinson. These men lost every thing, houses and contents, and barns with all their crops. They were thus thrown upon the charity of their neighbors and townsmen for shelter and food. The following winter the town was fortified, and applications were at once made by the sufferers for building lots within the palisades.

The Sufferers Ask, and the Town Grants them other Home Lots.

With a single exception, these persons were probably all who were then living south of Mill River, and when they made application for safer places of residence, within the line of fortifications, the town took the following action : —

"Janeary 1 : 1676 (77). Preserved Clap made A motion for A peice of Land to build A house and barne on : his own being burnt by the enemy. The towne considering thereof made A choice of A Comitte to veiw the Land he desired and to Lay out to him what they thinke may be conuenient and Also to veiw what other Land may be found to sute other persons in the like condition and to Acommidate them as farr as may be."

1 Rev. Solomon Williams' Historical Sermon, 1815, p. 11.

It may be supposed that this committee proceeded at once to their work, and selected the grants, but if they did so, no report of the result of their labors was made till December of the following year, when the persons to whom the awards were made, desired the town to confirm the acts of the committee. Application for these home lots was not made till 1677; in the meantime another serious disaster occurred, and a number of other buildings were burned. In their report, the committee include all these losses, and say that they "Laid out sundry small parcels of Land to seuerall person on condition they Build on it and liue on it three years." These lots were located in or near the center of the town, wherever unappropriated land could be found. In some instances they were taken from the highway, but most of them were set off in the vicinity of Meeting House Hill. Grants designated on the town records as "given in the time of the Indian war," were made to four parties who lived on South Street, and from that record it is possible to ascertain who were the sufferers from the Indians who attacked the settlers in Pynchon's meadow.

War Grants to the South Street Men. Preserved Clapp, who first petitioned for a safer place to live, was given a small piece of land, but its location has not been ascertained. Enos Kingsley's lot was at the lower end of Pleasant Street. Ralph Hutchinson's grant was on the west side of King Street, between the brook and the street. William Smead had half an acre at the corner of Main and South Streets, including what afterwards was the site of the Edwards Church. Most of these lots were barely large enough for a house and barn, some of them embracing in the aggregate but sixty rods of land. They were not regarded as temporary dwelling places, but as permanent residences. Several of the recipients continued to live upon them, apparently never returning to their first granted homesteads.

Three Persons killed in a Meadow. The Indians, embolden by their success in burning houses and barns, appeared again the next day, October 29th, when they killed three persons. These people, Thomas Salmon, Joseph Baker, and Joseph Baker Jr., were at work in the meadow, and that is all that is positively known concerning the place or manner of their deaths. After the attack on the men in Pynchon's Meadow, it is not probable that two men and a boy would have ventured very far into the meadows unprotected. In the same paragraph[1] which notes the killing of these persons, it is stated that the Indians attempted to burn the mill, but it was so well defended that they were unable to effect their purpose. This mill was probably the one built in 1671, at Red Rocks. If this was the mill attacked, it is quite probable that the meadow in which the men were killed was the small one at the upper or western end of "Paradise." They were probably not very far from the mill, which it seems was well guarded, and undoubtedly considered themselves within hailing distance of succor, should the enemy appear. From the fact that the Indians at once assaulted the mill, it may be inferred that the men were killed very near it, being discovered by the enemy while on their way to the attack.

The Persons Killed. Two of these last victims were men prominent in the settlement, and could not readily be spared. Joseph Baker was the son of Edward Baker, and lived on Elm Street. His home lot was on the opposite side of the street from the lot originally granted to his father, and comprised the property on both sides of what is now Henshaw Avenue. Joseph Baker Jr., his son, was a lad but ten years of age. Thomas Salmon was an original settler, and had a home lot on Meeting House Hill, which he sold in 1668.

Danger Everywhere.
The Savage Foe
on the Alert.
While the foe was thus constantly skulking about, the plantation was in a state of great excitement. Danger lurked on every side. Men had been shot and scalped almost within sight of their own doors, and the good-wife, when her husband went forth to his daily toil, knew not that she should ever again behold him living. Though the town swarmed with soldiers, they were powerless to protect. No part of the settlement was safe. Watching every opportunity, the en-

1 Rev. Mr. Williams' Historical Sermon.

emy were ready to pounce upon any who in the least exposed themselves, and a man and a boy laboring in the meadows, narrowly escaped capture. It is not known who they were, nor in what part of the meadows they were at work. During the months of October and November, there were rumors of Indians about Hatfield, many tracks were discovered, and the cattle came running violently into the town. Majors Treat and Appleton had the forests in the vicinity of Northampton and Hatfield, and as far as Deerfield, thoroughly searched, but not an Indian was seen. Yet while the soldiers were thus actively employed, eight or ten buildings were burned, three persons killed, and two others very nearly captured, in this town.

Martial Law Declared. Events such as have been described thoroughly dispirited the inhabitants of the surviving towns of Hampshire County, many of whom had deserted their homes, and others were considering the expediency of following the example. This disaffection became so extensive that Major Appleton deemed it his duty to take measures to counteract its influence. He accordingly, on the 12ᵗʰ of November, issued a proclamation to the inhabitants of Springfield, Westfield, Northampton, Hadley and Hatfield,

" ordering that no person shall remove from or desert any of these towns so long as forces are continued here for their defense, without liberty under the hand of the commander-in-chief, in each town, nor shall any go out of the towns without a pass under the hand of. the commander-in-chief. * * * And if any be attempting or preparing to depart otherwise, all officers civil and military are hereby impowerd & required to prohibit their departure & also to secure them & their estates & bring them to the chief officers."

Soldiers withdrawn, but the Towns Garrisoned. Satisfied that the Indians had retired to winter quarters, Major Treat and the Connecticut forces left for home on the 19ᵗʰ of November, and Major Appleton did not remain many days longer. Under orders from the Council, small garrisons were left in each of the towns in Hampshire County. At Springfield, thirty-nine men remained, under the command of Major Pynchon ; at Westfield, twenty-nine men, under Major Aaron Cook ; at Northampton, twenty-six men, commanded by Lieut. William Clarke ; at Hadley, thirty men, under Capt. Jonathan Poole; and at Hatfield, thirty-six men, under Lieut. William Allis. Acting under instructions from the authorities, Major Appleton appointed a council of war for the security of the towns of Northampton, Hadley and Hatfield, consisting of the commissioned officers in each town. In addition the following persons were named as members of the council: Lieut. David Wilton of Northampton; Dea. Peter Tilton of Hadley; and Sergt. Isaac Graves of Hatfield. Capt. Jonathan Poole was made president of the council.

Northampton Pe- When it became evident that the campaign
titions for a Gar- had ended, and that the troops were about
rison. to be withdrawn, the Northampton Committee on Military Affairs, consisting of William Clarke, John Lyman and John King, addressed the following letter to the council. In it, after representing in strong terms the poverty of the town, they offer to subsist a garrison of forty men:—

"By the blessing of the Lord upon that help which you have put unto us, we are not at present in such eminent danger as formerly, the body of the Indians being not discovered in these parts since their defeat at Hatfield, so that our expectation is that your Hon^s: will call off great part of the Army, yet we trust you will not leave us wholly destitute, partly because we are Assured that there are some parties of the enemy still remaining, watching their opportunitye to destroy our men, so that we cannot with safety follow our occasions, partly because we are so remote, that if the Indians should return, it would be too late for us to send for help. We are loth to burden the country, whose expenses have been great already, but if the Lord will lay burdens upon us we must with silence submit to his holy will: were it a thing within our compase, we should not be backward to maintaine a garrison at our own charge: but the loses & expenses by reason of the war have been such, as renders us uncapable of such a thing: our losses in our Hay, corn, Buildings & seed-time are very considerable: neither is it a small matter, that the necessities of poor people that belong to the higher plantations, will call for from our hands: yet being unwilling to be unnecessarily burdensome: we shall not we hope be over craving: we shall desire as small a garrison, as we can judge any ways competent, & upon as easy terms for the country, as our present poverty will allow us: if your Hon^s: shall see cause to leave with us forty men, we shall be content to diet them at our own charge: we leave our motion with you: we can doe no lesse in faithfullnesse to our selvs & the Country but represent our case before you, & Request for what we judge is needful in order to our safety, leaving it with your selvs to judge of

1 8

the reasonablenesse of our motion: Thus with many thanks for the great Care you have had of us, we desire the Lord to support your hearts under your great burdens, & Guide you in the right way: we take leave & rest your humble servants.[1]

WILLIAM CLARKE
JOHN LIMON
JOHN KING

Northampton, Nov:9:75.　　　　　　in the name of the Town."

Secretary Rawson wrote to Major Appleton: "We concur, but think less will do for Hatfield and Hadley, but leave it with you." The result was that both Hatfield and Hadley had larger garrisons than Northampton.

The Troops March against the Nipmucks, and the Campaign ends. With the disappearance of the Indians in the fall of 1675, the campaign virtually closed in this section, and nothing more was heard of them till the opening of the ensuing spring. Appleton and Moseley were ordered to march against the Nipmucks, who had been making trouble. With all the forces available outside of the garrisons, these two officers started about the 20th of November, to reinforce the troops already operating in that region. The Indians did not await the coming of the soldiers, and the latter, after destroying a large quantity of corn, continued their march towards Boston.

Number of the Indians engaged, and the English losses. Most of the devastation and destruction already suffered by the river towns had been caused by the local tribes of Indians. They were aided by the Nipmucks, who were able to furnish much the largest number of warriors.[2] During the few months in which the war raged in the year 1675, about one hundred forty-five persons were killed in Hampshire County; forty-three or forty-four were residents of the county, and more than one hundred were from the eastern part of the Commonwealth. Every town in the county, with the exception of Hadley and Westfield,

1 This Letter is in the handwriting of Mr. Stoddard. Mass. Archives, vol. 68, p. 48.

2 Mr. Judd says that the Deerfield, Hadley and Northampton and Springfield Indians may have had one hundred fifty fighting men, and the Nipmucks could furnish about three times as many more. "The Indian warriors in and about Hampshire County were not more than six hundred at any time, and most of them were Nipmucks."—History of Hadley, p. 158.

had been partially destroyed. Brookfield, Northfield and Deerfield, had been deserted, though Brookfield was still to some extent, used as a military post.

Hampshire Towns Fortified.

Thus far during the struggle the towns had but slight protection against the foe. In most of them, block houses, forts, and occasionally a "forted" house, had been provided as places of refuge. These generally proved a sufficient shelter for the inhabitants, who had been compelled, however, in too many cases, to witness from them the destruction of cherished homes, toil earned crops, and valued stock. The Indians, finding that they gained nothing by attacking these places, soon desisted, and turned their attention to the destruction of the surrounding property. It is not known that any provision had yet been made in this town for the safety of its inhabitants. Nothing had been voted by the town for any such purpose, and if anything in that direction had been accomplished, it was probably done under the general laws then existing. The need of more efficient safeguards, by means of which not only life, but property, might be made secure, led the towns of Northampton, Hatfield, and Hadley, to adopt a plan of general fortification, and during the fall and winter of 1675, palisades were erected about the more thickly settled portions of those settlements.

Method of Fortification by Palisades.

These palisades[1] or fortifications were constructed of cleft wood about eight feet long above the ground, set close together and joined at the top by a flat strip of wood pinioned to the posts. In some instances rails were used. The cleft timber was hewn off at the edges so that the pieces were nowhere less than two inches in thickness. This rude defence, inadequate against a civilized foe, was found to be ample against the savages. Accustomed to this method of fortification, the Indians did not hesitate to attack the towns so defended. But a single experience in breaking

1 Indian fortifications "consisted of wooden palisades, strongly secured, with an internal gallery, from which the besieged party, under cover, might repel the assailants with missile weapons." From these the English undoubtedly obtained their ideas of enclosing their towns with palisades.

through them taught the red men a lesson that was never repeated. Of the three towns, Northampton erected much the longer of these structures, but all the houses in town were not included within the line. When the town was afterwards attacked, a number of houses standing outside of the defences were burned. There is no record of any vote or order by the town for the erection of these defensive works, nor is there any account of payment for them from the town treasury.

School House used as a Guard House.   The only vote recorded during this year, having any reference to the war, was that of June 30, in which the town "apoynted the Scoole house toe be the house for there wach house toe keepe the Court of gard in this troblesom tyme." This school house was in the center of the town, at the junction of Main and King Streets.

Location of the First Line of Palisades.   Very little information relative to the location of this line of palisades can be obtained from the records of that date. It was wholly on the north side of Mill River, and enclosed the meeting house and the houses nearest to that point. During the first French and Indian war, ten years after this one closed, a new line of similar fortifications was erected at the expense of the town, and its position defined upon the records. As it followed the first one in part, there is a possibility of locating the latter with approximate accuracy. Commencing on Bridge Street, just above the cemetery, the north-eastern line of which was then very near its present position, it probably followed the easterly boundary of the home lots laid out on Hawley Street. There was a highway at that time, very near, probably a little west of the present location of "Pomeroy Terrace," and undoubtedly the palisades were built along that highway till they reached Mill River, at a point just below the residence of the late William R. Clapp. Thence turning up that stream they were continued along the river bank to the rear of and beyond the Forbes Library lot, and crossing West Street, enclosed the house of Alexander Edwards, very near, but a little south of "Plymouth Hall." Thus far very little doubt remains concerning the position of the palisades, but all further data are wanting. The fortification of 1690, began at the house of Alexander Edwards, and joined the older one at the cemetery by a route clearly defined, but the line of the first one between these two points can only be conjectured. Probably it took very nearly a straight course, crossing Elm, State and Park Streets, reaching King Street, possibly as far up as the French Catholic church, and so on above the cemetery to the starting point on Bridge Street. This fortification was continued and repaired at intervals by vote of the town, and fourteen years afterwards it was renewed and enlarged. This was at best but a meagre defense, and against any other foe would have been valueless. But it answered its purpose, and undoubtedly saved the town from destruction.

Special Laws under which Fortifications could be Erected. In the absence of any special vote of the town, ordering the erection of this fortification, it may be inferred that it was built under the provisions of the general law of 1667. This enactment empowered

"the comittee of militia in euery toune, together wth the selectmen thereof, or the major part of them, to erect or cause to be erected, w^thin their tounes, either inclosing the meeting houses or some other convenient place, a fortiffication, or fort, of stone, bricke, timber or earth, as the places may be most capable, of such dimensions as may best suite their ability & vse; in which fortiffication the weomen, children & aged persons may be secured, in case of any suddaine danger, whereby the souldjers may be more free to oppose an enemy; for the effecting whereof, itt is hereby ordered, that the trayned souldiers, both horse & ffoote, in every toune, vpon their trayning dayes, shall be imploied about building the sjd fort at the guidance of the chiefe military officers of the toune; and all others exempted from ordinary traynings, who haue estates or bodily abillity, that dwell in the toune, or belong to it, they shall also, according to proportion contribute their help & assistance in bodily labour or otherwise, accordinge as the comitee of militia & selectmen shall order & appoint."

All who neglected or refused "to promote the sjd worke" were to be fined "fiue shillings a day a man." Where "teemes & carts" were needed, there was to "be allowed for a man two oxen & cart, in proportion to two souldjers labour, & so in proportion for greater teemes." This gave the authorities ample power to act without a vote of the town. The court further ordered that these fortifications should be forthwith taken in hand and prosecuted till they were finished.

Selectmen and Committee of the Militia.
For the year 1675, the selectmen were Lieut. David Wilton, John Stebbins, John King, Jonathan Hunt, and Medad Pomeroy. The military committee of each town, according to the law of 1652, consisted of the "magistrate in said town and the three chiefe military officers inhabitants of the said town, who should hold a commission from the General Court." William Clarke, one of the Associate Justices of the County Court, Lieut. John Lyman and Capt. John King, composed the military committee of the town. These men, undoubtedly acting under the above vote, caused the palisades to be built, but there is no data by which to determine the time of their construction. The first intimation that anything of the kind existed, was when the Indians broke through them in March, 1676.

Population and Extent of the Town.
Northampton contained a permanent population[1] of about five hundred persons, which at this time must have been considerably increased by the exigencies of the times. The growth of the place had been slow, and the new towns settled to the northward, had drawn away some of the young men, though all the survivors had ere this returned. According to a paper in the MSS. Department of the British Museum, the number of houses in town was one hundred.[2] The palisades did not by any means enclose all the settled portion of the town. South Street was entirely outside of the line, though few if any inhabitants were living there at this time, and many houses on the north side of Mill River were unprotected. Dwellings were scattered for the distance of a mile or more north and south of the meeting

[1] Grants of land to one hundred two settlers, previous to the year 1676, had been recorded. All but four of these persons were married and had families. The genealogical record shows that four hundred seventy-three children had been born to these individuals at this time. This would give a total population of six hundred seventy-three. During the twenty-one years that had elapsed since the settlement of the town, one hundred ten deaths had been recorded, leaving a total of five hundred sixty-three. A few had removed to other towns, consequently an estimate of five hundred as the aggregate number of inhabitants in 1675, must be very nearly accurate.

[2] See Appendix B.

house, in both directions, and nearly as far to the west; but
the majority of the people were grouped within half the
distance from that point. Those farthest west were little,
if any, beyond the Round Hill road on Elm Street. A line
commencing at the Central Massachusetts railroad bridge,
over the Connecticut River, running west to and encircling
Round Hill, crossing Mill River near the center of "Paradise," thence turning south-easterly, intersecting South
Street about on the line of Fort Street, and so to the bluff
above the meadow, would probably enclose nearly all the
homesteads occupied in Northampton, in 1675.

Very Little Town Business transacted during War Time. Scant reference is made upon the records to
the transaction of town business, during the
first year of the war, two pages containing
all that was accomplished. Military affairs
were the most important, and they were managed by the
military committee and the selectmen, without town action.
A committee of seven persons was chosen "toe order the
settlement of all the high ways in the meadow and toe rectifie errors therein." The intention was to make them con-
form "as neare as posible toe the originale bounds." This
work was not very speedily accomplished, probably on account of the unsettled state of affairs, and six years afterwards another committee was empowered "to finish the
said work and to stake all such ways as are needfull."

David Wilton's Account Book. 'At this time the town was filled with soldiers and friendly Indians, who were quar-
tered upon the inhabitants. They were
constantly coming and going, and altogether the times were
quite lively throughout the settlement. Many of them,
officers as well as soldiers, found entertainment at the house
of David Wilton, near the site of the Baptist Church. His
account book is still in existence. It contains charges and
memoranda made at this time, and undoubtedly gives a
fair sample of the manner of billeting soldiers among the
inhabitants. This old volume, written nearly two and a
quarter centuries ago, while the events just narrated, were
in progress, with its quaint spelling, and black, unfaded
ink, is here in part transcribed, as a portion of the history
of the period, not elsewhere to be found :—

"Soldiars Acount : i prise

Lift Cooper on pound tobackoe . . .	00.00.10
Daniell Allexander on pound	00.00.10
Ebenezer Jeans on pound	00.00.10
delivared Sargeant Kinge 6^{lb}½ chece . . .	00.02.08
toe the Soldiars on pound tobackoe . .	00.00.10
toe Capt. Lathrope[1] a knife	00.01.02
toe the indians on duzen knifs . . .	00.05.00
more at ferst fight 8^{lb}½ Chece loafe bread . .	00.04.00
teame toe cary provision to hadley toe hands on went	
ouer the River	00.02.00
to constabl quiar paper for malisia Counsle hadley	00.00.10
more on Chece & loafe bread . . ,	00.01.10
a quart Lickquor to ye Soldiars fight . . .	00.01.06
Samuell Marshall[2] & his horse in the first fight a day	
& a night	00
Samuell Marshall & his horse prest toe Windsor or	
hartford toe days	00.10.00
by chece toe Medad Pumry , . . .	00.03.04

26th 6th

Connighticot men came toe my house toe board, 4 men	
& 4 horses	00.03.04

When Major Treet[3] came y^t night quartered at my
house ye Major Capt Cely Lieft Standley, Ensigne
Marshall on more   also y^t night thre indians next
morninge all fower & 3 indians breakfast y^t night
and tell went away : 7 horses, they went away last
day about on clocke & came toe my house againe
tuesday night & at my house quarterred fower men
and thre indians

y^t night 7 horses—next day 5 horses morninge at
breakfast 4 : men : 6 indians toe major & his men
a bushell of ots

8th of ye 7th

good man pumry at night tooke from me 3 horses

To the indians by order the comittie of the malishia	
at Hadley ferst and after by order from Major	
Generall Pynchon toe the first Indians on duzen	
knifs	00.05.00
To Major Treat fower yards dufal . . .	01.08.00

1 Capt. Thomas Lothrop, who was killed at Bloody Brook.

2 Samuel Marshall was son-in-law to David Wilton, and lost his life in the Narragansett fight, Dec. 19, 1675.

3 The above date, "26th 6th" month, seems to indicate that Major Treat came up on the 26th of August, but it evidently belongs to the preceding entry, and the "Connighticot men" were undoubtedly the dragoons under Geo. Graves, sent up on the 25th. The other officers under Treat, were in the service here during the fall, and Capt. Seely was killed in the Narragansett campaign.

toe the Surgeant peare drawers a spoune toe lb suger
    ½ Ell blew lininge al 00.05.05
toe yᵉ indians came with Capt. Mason a duzen & eight
    knifs all is 00.08.04
by toe Lether Skins to macke Shows   .   .   00.10.00
by ¾ of a mouse [moose] Skin & half another   .   00.16.00
by thre yards of dufull for Stockings   .   .   01.01.00
by toe peare yarne Stockings to Soldiars   .   .   00.07.00
———————
05.00.09

beside yᵗ aboue on night at my house and breakfast
    being toe meals 10 men & 9 horses is
when Capt. Mason[1] came vp night and morninge ½
    . bushell peace boild bread meat & bear [beer] to the
    Indians for there breakfast all is   .   .   00.05.00

When Capt. Munson[2] came vp with 46 men at my
    house dined 6 men & 6 horses had ots in the stra
23ᵗʰ of yᵉ 7ᵗʰ 75

Major Treate returned toe my house & 9 men these 9
    men dined with me : yᵗ night following super 17
    men & 13 horses in pastuer & brakfast in morn-
    inge & at diner 13 men all is
next day after the comesary ordered me 6 men & 4
    horses :
Major Treate and toe men went toe Hadley the last of
    the 7ᵗʰ and came againe the next day and hee &
    his men went to Hadley the second of the 8ᵗʰ at
    even 75)
the 4ᵗʰ day I quartered 4 men & thre horses. 5ᵗʰ day
    at morninge all went to Springefeild[3]

Major Treate had when he went toe Squakeek[4] halfe a
    bushell & halfe a picke white peece .   .   00.01.08
Constable Leeds prist my horse to Squakeeke was out
    toe days   00
the 7ᵗʰ of the 8th moneth at night came thre men toe
    quarter yᵗ night and morninge Super lodging and
    breakfast 00.03.00

1 On the 15ᵗʰ of Sept., Capt. John Mason was ordered "to take a guard of English, and take under his conduct the Mohegans and Pequods and other Indians that shall be listed and lead them up to Norwotuck and the plantations up the river, and to command them there."

2 On the 19ᵗʰ, Lieut. Thomas Munson, who commanded the soldiers from New Haven County, had orders to march to "Norwottog and then up the river to our army." Ensign Stephen Burrit, from Fairfield County, had similar orders, and together their commands made up the forty-six men mentioned.

3 This was the date of the burning of Springfield, when all the troops in this section were hurried off to that town.

4 He set out for Northfield on the 18ᵗʰ of Sept., the date of the massacre at Bloody Brook.

11 day of the 8th Leift Clarke brought toe my house
    toe of Capt: Ceelies men to quarter
13th day at even Capt. Ceelie & Leift. Burrit came toe
    my house toe quarter so all fower quartered with
    me toe the 25th day y^t was toe weeks fower men is 01.14.00
Major Treat his Leift & Ensigne & toto came the 23th
    & went away 25th almost a weke for on man
    horses 7, at night al 00.07.00

Constable Baker prest toe Chesies: 11   .   . 00.04.00
Comesary Pumary prest toe bushels and halfe of wen-
    ter wheate 00.08.06
by a snapsacke prised by Constable Burt for John
    Broughton & lost 00.03.00
toe the Soldiars Lift Cooper Ebenezer Jans & Daniell
    Allexander each on on pound tobackoe at 10^d p^r lb 00.02.06

delivared by Major Treate & his comisaries order toe
    John Cooke toe peare stockings   .   . 00.06.06
alsoe toe Tho. hieot peare stockings this was Capt.
    Ceelies man 00.03.00
alsoe toe totoe a Cannadee Indian, Wascoate & a peare
    of shows & a Tewell [towel] all   .   . 00.09.03

Major Treate came backe 25 day at night sam day they
    went away y^t night, y^t day I had 7 men & 7 horses 00.05.00
25th 8th 75
    came toe men toe my house to quarter of Capt. aple-
    tons[1] men & abode but thre meals   .   . 00.02.06

this 25th at nown Major Treat came in toe my house toe
    quarter he & his men y^t night & next day 8 horses
    wh wr eight and abode in all on moneth want a
    a day at 4^s per week is 06.08.00
the horses come toe 00.04.00
29th
Major Apleton dined at my house and 13 of his men,
    14 in all 00.04.00
toe Mjor Treat a Chece 4^{lb}   .   .   . 00.01.08

17th of the 9th
    Capt Apleton & his ofisers & Soldiers dined at my
    house 15 men a counsle beinge held there, all is 00.06.00
beinge ordered I kept thre horses at house & good part
    of the tyme 4 of them: tyme beinge thre weeks
    want a day, all is 01.00.00
& gaue them Corne [unintelligible]

---

1 Capt. Appleton was made commander-in-chief in the valley, in place of Major
Pynchon, retired in October.

besids this Capt. Wats[1] quartered at my house toe
   weeks 00.08.00

More toe men: on day—Westfeild gard

26th of 8th

Constable brought toe indian children toe my house
   and abode there

24th of 9th 75

Comesary Pumary sent me toe quarter toe Soldiars and
   tooke of on at weeks end the other abode—they
   were Such & bapson, Samuell Such went on 31
   Agust so he quartered with me 40 weeks and Bapson on weeke

more toe Captane poole[2] eight yards want halfe a quarter tradinge cloth at 7s .   .   .   02.15.00
more by his order toe a Soldier and given his note toe
   the comisary toe yards & half more of duffule at 7s 00.17.06
more toe Neccolas Mason pear Stockings   .   . 00.02.04
more to Samuell Souch peare Stockings the Stockings
   I gave him.
more to William Willis a yard and halfe trading cloth 00.10.06
Capt. Lathrope a knife 00.01.02
to Lift Cooper Daniell Allexander and Ebenezer Jeans
   and on mor 4 lbs tobacko 00.03.04
to William Jaquish a knife 00.00.05
to John Smith toe knifs 00.01.05
to Jacob Burtton a knife & pips   .   .   .   00.01.00
to Samuell Ransford a knife   .   .   .   00.01.00
to William Howard a knife   .   .   .   00.00.05
                                    ——————
   this bil sent ye Bay by 04.14.02

Reseaved of Major Treat on the Counterry acounte
   13lb Leade at 6   .   .   .   .   .   00.06.06
alsoe reseavid of Comisary Pumry a hatt   .   .   00.11.00

Wilton states that the country owed him for dieting
   soldiers and other expenses, May 1, 1676, £19.9.6."

1 Capt. Watts was from Connecticut, came up when Brookfield was destroyed, but
his name is not mentioned afterwards. It is possible that he may have been here
while preparations were in progress for the Narragansett campaign.

2 Capt. Jonathan Poole, from the eastern part of the Colony, in Major Appleton's
command.

CHAPTER XXII.

WAY OF LIVING—ENFORCING SUMPTUARY LAWS.

Agriculture the Business of the Community.

FARMING was the chief occupation of the people, and indeed everybody depended upon the product of the land for subsistence. Mechanics tilled the soil, and every householder was the owner and cultivator of meadow land. With uncouth and heavy tools, many of them of wood, they carried on the agriculture of their day, and raised the crops which became at once their means of support and medium of exchange. They were hardy, industrious, God-fearing men, contented with their lot, and enduring the hardships of pioneer life without a murmur.

Their Tools and Farming Implements Rough and Ungainly.

The tools and implements of agriculture in use by the first settlers were massive and ponderous. Most of them were constructed by village mechanics, who patterned after those with which they had been familiar in the old country. The art of working in iron was but feebly developed, and many of the farm tools were made of wood. The mould-board of the old-fashioned plow was a straight piece of wood, sometimes shod with iron ; the coulter and share were of iron, and the beam was long, curved and heavy. It was an awkward and ungainly tool, very difficult to manage. Mechanics, called "plough wrights," manufactured the majority of them, but many were made by carpenters and blacksmiths in every town. In Northampton, Thomas Dewey made the wood work of a plow for David Wilton, for 6s., in 1673. The iron work, share, coulter, etc. (probably furnished by Medad Pomeroy), cost 24s. 6d. Most of the harrows had teeth of wood, hardened by fire, but these were soon discarded for teeth of iron. Carts were large, solid and heavy. Their wheels were in many instances sawn from solid plank, and were used without tires or boxes. Many old shovels had a wooden frame and were shod with iron. Some of them, however, as well as spades, were of iron, except the handle. Hoes were large and heavy, especially the broad hoe. Medad Pomeroy, the blacksmith, made broad hoes, spades and axes, for each of which he charged five shillings. These cumbersome implements greatly taxed the strength of men and animals.

Habits of the People. Their houses, nearly all built of logs, were but scantily furnished, and contained little beyond the bare necessities of life. Their flocks and herds supplemented what the soil provided, and the nimble fingers of the housewife, and her daughters, manufactured the fabric, as well as the garments that clothed the family. They lived quiet and contented lives, attending two services at the meeting house on Sundays, and town meetings regularly on week days, at least most of them did, as often as the business of the community demanded attention. Their food was coarse, but nutritious. Corn and wheat and rye were the staple at every meal; meat was abundant, pork, beef, mutton, wild game and fish, were plenty; potatoes were unknown, but turnips, cabbages, beans and a few other vegetables, were used to a considerable extent.

Food, Table Furnishings, and Table Manners. Wheat bread was in more common use at that time than in after years. "Rye and Indian" bread, consisting of one part rye and two parts Indian meal, came into use when wheat became scarce, and its popularity continued well into the present century. The first settlers learned from the Indians the use of corn meal, which made its appearance on the table in some form at nearly every repast. It came in the shape of hasty pudding, as corn cake, as boiled Indian pudding, and sometimes as samp and hominy. Succotash, beans boiled with corn in the milk, was another dish derived from the Indians, which is still welcomed everywhere. Bread and milk were much used, especially among the

younger portion of the family, and bread and cider were
substituted when milk was wanting. Cider that was beginning to ferment, taken before it became sour, to which
water was added, was warmed over the coals. Molasses
was used to sweeten the cider, and toasted bread broken
into the mixture. Tea and coffee did not come into general
use till the middle of the eighteenth century. Three meals
every day was the common practice. For breakfast, meat
was seldom provided, but bread and milk or bread and
cider, hasty pudding with milk or molasses, and sometimes
porridge or broth, made of peas or beans flavored by being
cooked with salt pork or beef, was the usual fare. Dinner
was deemed the most important, and some kind of meat or
fish, with vegetables, was always served. Supper sometimes comprised cold victuals, left from dinner, with the
usual adjuncts of bread and milk or cider. Crockery was
almost unknown, but pewter dishes and wooden ware
jostled each other on the cupboard shelves. In some instances food was brought upon the table in large wooden
platters, cut into convenient size, from which each guest
helped himself in turn. In many houses plates were not
to be found at breakfast, and forks were not in general use
before 1700, though pewter and wooden spoons were common. People dipped their hands into the platter containing the food, and however unrefined it may appear, there is
abundant reason to believe that our forefathers were in the
habit of eating with their fingers.

From the large   The pioneers of Northampton were many of
Families of the   them blessed with large families. Some of
Settlers came
the Founders of   them had ten, twelve, fifteen, and seven-
other Towns.   teen children. Twenty-five among those
who came here within the first ten years after settlement,
had three hundred thirty children born to them. Many
of their sons became themselves heads of families, and
grants of land were made to them. When new towns were
projected at Northfield and Deerfield, many of these young
men were among the original settlers. The older citizens
of Northampton became the corporators or "engagers" in
them, their sons occupied the home lots and established political and religious institutions therein. Of the first peti-

tioners for the establishment of Northfield, all but three were citizens of Northampton; ten Northampton names are found upon the early records of the town of Deerfield, and one-third of the householders there in 1675, had been residents in this town. Very few of the older inhabitants of Northampton removed permanently to these new settlements.

Bad Condition of Affairs in the Fall and Winter. During the fall and winter of the year 1675, the condition of affairs in the valley must have been discouraging, and it is not strange that the commander-in-chief felt compelled to place the county partially at least, under martial law. The future was dark and unpropitious, and there seemed to be no immediate prospect of relief. Hadley, Hatfield and Northampton were all that remained of the more northern settlements. To describe the situation in one of them portrays the condition of all. Equally harrassed, none escaped the peculiar trials and perplexities of the times, and though some suffered in a less degree, all were grievously burdened. In addition to the hardships attendant upon the war, winter set in with more than ordinary severity. The cold was intense, snow fell in unusual quantities, rendering communication with other towns very difficult, and some of the time quite impossible.

The Prospect in Northampton Gloomy and Discouraging. Northampton was not a frontier town and had not, like the others, sustained any concerted attack by the Indians. Yet her citizens had enlisted in the various expeditions and numbers of them had been killed; others had been slain within sight of their own firesides; many houses and barns had been burned; the town was filled with soldiers billeted upon the inhabitants; fugitives from the abandoned towns sought protection here, and could not be denied; the meadows had been only partially planted; the slender harvest following an interrupted seed time, could not be wholly gathered; much of the hay and grain stored in the barns had been destroyed; and altogether the outlook was most discouraging. Many of the inhabitants had furnished provisions and other material to aid in carrying on the war, and were compelled to wait years for repay-

ment.[1]   The loss of so many buildings and barns and such
quantities of hay and grain, proved a serious obstacle to
the keeping of stock[2] which had greatly accumulated, and
it became quite a problem how to subsist the cattle and
horses.

The Pressure of Taxation caused by the War, adds to the Burdens of the Time. Supplementary to the drain of supporting an increased population, came the burden of war taxes.   During the year 1675, ten country rates[3] had been laid by the government.   Early in the year, three rates were laid, one to be paid in August, one in October, and another in December.   In October seven more country rates were levied, three to be paid before the last of November, and the other four before the last of March.   These rates were not pressed for collection upon the country towns that had

1   Rev. Solomon Stoddard petitioned the General Court, June 3, 1679, for relief.   He says that he had disbursed for the county in the war, to the value of £20, as per account. That he is in need of his due, "having sustained considerable loss in proportion to my estate in the war," "and it will not answer my occasions to have it paid little by little out of the rates of the town."   His claim was allowed, and was to be paid by the Treasurer, but to appear in the general account of the county.   Medad Pomeroy, in a petition to the Governor and Council, dated Northampton, April 3, 1678, states that at the beginning of the war he had much provision which was to pay a debt due to Capt. Brattle, but it was all taken for the war and he can get nothing out of our county rates that will pay it.   He says there is due him on his first account to May, 1676, £36, when his dues to the county are taken out, and he hopes they will order him to be paid "said £36 that he may pay his honest debts, which are a burden to his spirits."   There is no record of any action by the court on Medad Pomeroy's petition, and he had in all probability, to await the dilatory action of the town and county authorities.   Lieut. William Clarke, more fortunate than some others, received, in 1676, an order on the State Treasurer for £38.18, for stores furnished.

2   Major Appleton writes from Hadley, Nov. 10, 1675 : "There will be a necessity of sending home many of our horses or else the towns here will be undone, the war hath so hindered their getting of hay and so many cattle are come in from other places that are desolated, that many are likely to perish.   One cow is already offered for the wintering of another."—Appleton Memorial, p. 130.

3   A country rate was equal to one penny on every pound in value of estate in the lists, and one shilling and eight pence on each poll.   The prices of grain allowed in payment of taxes, as fixed by the Council, were Wheat 6s., Rye 4s. 6d., Barley and Peas 4s., Indian Corn 3s., 6d., Oats 2s.   The grain was to be delivered to the Treasurer at the expense of the towns.   Those that were paid in money were allowed an abatement of one-quarter.

   "Down to the year 1645, it was the practice to levy a tax of a specific sum and apportion it among the towns.   In 1646, a different method came into use, a regular poll tax was determined, at first of 1s. 8d., afterwards of 2s. 6d., payable by males, within the jurisdiction, sixteen years old and upwards ; and a tax on property and on the profits of mechanics and tradesmen, of a penny in the pound.   The revenue from these two sources constituted one rate. * * The sixteen rates levied in the Colony in 1676, included the enormous assessment on property of 1s. 4d. in the pound or nearly seven per centum on the valuation."—Palfrey's History of New England, vol. 3, p. 230.

suffered from the war, and in final settlement, accounts for subsisting soldiers and other war expenses were allowed, in offset. No payment was made on these assessments by Northampton, in 1675, and the next year sixteen rates were added, making twenty-six rates assessed in two years. A single rate for Northampton was £22.2.10, and the aggregate in 1675 and 1676, reached £575. To this must be added the cost of "dieting" the soldiers detailed as a garrison, which the town assumed. There was still another outlay on the tax account, and that was the cost of transportation to Boston of the grain in which it was paid. The direct pecuniary burdens of the people, exclusive of their own individual losses, were large, while their resources, by reason of the war, were greatly diminished. In October, 1676, Northampton was abated, out of the last ten country rates, £18.12.6, on account of losses by the enemy.

Mr. Stoddard enumerates the then Besetting Sins. The letter to Increase Mather, dated Sept. 15th, written by Rev. Solomon Stoddard, already quoted, and published in Mather's History, after detailing the events of the war, closes with the following paragraph:—

"I desire that you would speak to the Governour that there may be some thorough care for a reformation. I am sensible there are many difficulties therein, many sins are grown so in fashion, that it becomes a question whether they be sins or not. I desire you would especially mention oppression, that intolerable pride in clothes and hair; the toleration of so many taverns especially in Boston, and suffering home dwellers to lie tippling in them."

The General Court Recognizes these Evils. This letter of Mr. Stoddard was followed by special action on the part of the General Court, though how much that missive may have influenced that result is doubtful. At the November session of the Legislature in 1675, a law was passed in which the prevailing sins of the time were enumerated and penalties provided against whoever indulged in them. The several sins mentioned by the eminent Divine from Northampton, were embodied in it, and he must have regarded its passage with great satisfaction.

19

Sumptuary laws[1] were already upon the statute books, and their enforcement in this section had not been neglected, but they were deemed insufficient. Under previous laws, seven married women of Northampton were "presented" in 1673, for wearing silk contrary to law, and all but one acquitted. At the same court nine married women of Springfield, nine of Hadley, seven of Hatfield, and three of Westfield, were also presented for the same offence. Some were admonished, others fined, and a few acquitted.

Many Young Peo-
ple of North-
ampton Defy the
Law. "Pride in clothes and hair," seems to have been amply illustrated in Mr. Stoddard's parish, and many of the young in his own congregation took occasion to defy the law. The action of the General Court in this matter promptly awakened public sentiment, and the moral suasion of the pulpit, no doubt brought to bear by the Reverend pastor, was strongly supplemented by the stern commands of law. The authorities proceeded with the work in hand, and an effort was speedily made to enforce the new statute and suppress these "heinous sins." On the 27th of March, 1676, twenty-three persons were presented at the court, in Northampton, "for wearing silk in a flaunting manner and for long hair and other extravagances contrary to honest and sober order, and demeanor not becoming a wilderness state, at least the profession of christianity and religion." Six of them were married women, six were unmarried,

---

1 The law enacted in 1657, declares "or vtter detestation & dislike that men or weomen of meane condition, educations and callings, should take vpon them the garbe of gentlemen, by the wearinge of gold or silver lace, or buttons or poynte at theire knees, to walke in greate bootes ; or women of the same ranke to weare silke or tiffany hoodes or scarfes, which though allowable to persons of greater estates or more liberall education, yet we cannot but judge it intollerable in p'sons of such like condition." Any person with an estate of less than than £200, who offended against this law was made liable to a fine of 10s. The selectmen were empowered to assess all who "exceed theire rankes & abilitie in the costlynes or fashion of their apparraill in any respect, especially in the wearinge of ribons & great bootes," at £200. An amendment was made to this law in 1662, in which its provisions were applied to children and servants. Not only was the wearing of rich garments prohibited, but "taylors" were forbidden to make or fashion them. The penalty for a first offence was admonition, for a second, a fine of 20s., and as the number of offences multiplied, an increase of the fine to 40s. The law of 1675, provided a fine of 10s. for a second and each succeeding conviction, but did not repeal the former statutes.

probably young girls, and the rest were young men. Two of the young unmarried women were the daughters of Elder John Strong.[1]

Hannah Lyman boldly asserts her Independence. Offenders in other Towns. At a subsequent session of the court, "Hannah Lyman of Northampton, was presented for wearing silk in a flaunting manner, in an offensive way and garbe, not only before, but when she stood presented, not only in ordinary times, but in extraordinary times, when the people of God were falling before the Lord in public humiliation in respect of the heavy judgments and calamities that were threatening to come upon us." She was sentenced to pay a fine of 10s. Hannah seems to have been an offender of more than ordinary boldness, ready to show off her fine attire, not only in the meeting house on Sundays and fast days, but in the faces of the Justices while they were trying her case. She was the daughter of Richard Lyman, deceased, and about sixteen years of age. At the March court, forty-five persons from different towns in the county were fined for wearing silk in a "flaunting manner," and for wearing long hair. Of these offenders, eighteen were residents of Springfield, five of Westfield, nine of Hadley, and thirteen of Hatfield. Eleven were married women, fifteen unmarried, and nineteen young men.

All Efforts to Enforce the Law Prove Futile. Attempts to carry out this law were continued in 1677 and 1678, and other fines were imposed, but it soon became a dead letter. Four years later the law was again invoked, and the five Hampshire County towns, Northampton, Hadley, Hatfield, Westfield, and Springfield, were indicted for not assessing

1 These persons were: the wife of Samuel Davis; Mary, wife of Samuel Holton; wife of Nathaniel Phelps; Mary and Hester Strong, "daughters of Mr. Strong;" Elizabeth Lyman; Sarah Edwards; wife of John Alvord; William Holton; Nathaniel Alexander; Jonathan Root; Mary Munden; wife of John Searl; Elizabeth Edwards; Abel Janes; Thomas Lyman; John Root; Samuel Langton; Samuel Wright; Joseph Wright; wife of Joseph Edwards; Esa-iah (Hezekiah) Root; Benoni Stebbins. The prisoners were all admonished and ordered to pay clerk's fees, 2s. 6d. each, and "so acquitted." The wife of Samuel Holton, "who having formerly offended and not reforming, she is fined 10s." She was charged with "wearing silk hoods and scarf in a flaunting manner." Sylvester Judd suggested that "this pride in long hair may allude to wigs which were coming into fashion." The new statute mentions "perewiggs" and "borders of hair" worn by "some women."

such of their inhabitants "as were excessive in their apparel, wearing silks and other forbidden apparel beyond their ranks." But it was of no avail. The æsthetic taste of the women, endorsed by the more liberal minded among the men, thrust aside these sumptuary laws of straight-laced puritanism, and nothing more is heard of them.[1]

1 People in general must needs have worn very plain clothing. Every article of dress was home made in every sense of the word. The material was manufactured, and the garments cut and made by the inmates of the farm house. Skins of animals were used to some extent, more especially for servant's clothing, the buckskin garments of the natives being adopted in some degree by the settlers. They could at first afford nothing better, yet as prosperity increased, the taste for finery crept in, and became so general that laws were especially framed to curtail the extravagance. With the taste for gold and silver ornamentation, and silk and lace, came the fashion of wearing long hair by the men. The Governor, Deputy Governor and Magistrates of Massachusetts entered into an association to prevent the wearing of long hair in 1649. They denounced the custom "of wearing long hair after the manner of ruffians and barbarous Indians," as "contrary to God's word," "as a thing uncivil and unmanly," "whereby men do demean themselves * * and do corrupt good manners." They entreat the Elders to manifest their zeal against the practice.

CHAPTER XXIII.

KING PHILIP'S WAR—MRS. ROWLANDSON'S STORY.

General Results of the War thus far, and Dreary Prospects.

AT the beginning of the winter of 1675, the results of the war had been extremely disastrous to the people of Hampshire County. Everywhere the enemy had triumphed. Town after town had been abandoned and destroyed, and Hadley and Hatfield were now frontier settlements. Upon the approach of cold weather, the foe had disappeared, but the whites could by no means congratulate themselves that the enemy had been conquered. Only at great cost and suffering and by the most heroic exertions, had any of the Hampshire settlements escaped destruction. All had suffered severely, and business of all kinds had been greatly crippled. Nor was there reason to believe that the trouble was over. The avowed object of the enemy was to sweep the English from the country; and encouraged by their success, a fiercer onset and more vigorous prosecution of the war was to be expected with the opening of the spring. None knew where the blow might fall. Though fortifications had been erected, and every other precaution suggested by prudence had been observed, yet the haunting suspicion of unknown evils, born of uncertainty, embittered all the future.

Perfidy of the Narragansetts.

The first treaty with the Narragansetts, in July, not having been regarded by that tribe, another arrangement with their chiefs was made in October. They then promised to surrender all hostile Indians under their jurisdiction within ten days. Again they failed to meet their obligations, and fearful lest this powerful tribe should suddenly take the war path, the

Commissioners of the United Colonies determined to move upon them. Five days after the expiration of the time fixed in the treaty for the delivery of their prisoners, the commissioners decided to raise a force of one thousand men for service in the Narragansett campaign, and Gov. Winslow of Plymouth, was appointed commander-in-chief of the expedition.

Situation of the Indian Fort, and Officers of the Army.
The Narragansetts had chosen for their winter quarters a naturally strong position, and within its limits were concentrated most of the tribe. Five or six acres of upland, situated in the midst of a swamp, had been so strongly fortified by rows of palisades, as to present an obstruction nearly a rod in thickness. A rude bridge of felled trees, four or five feet from the ground, protected by a block house, formed the main entrance. The fort was situated in what is now the town of South Kingston. Major Appleton, Capt. Moseley, Lieut. Upham, Major Treat, Capts. Seely and Watts, who had done such excellent service in this section during the summer and fall, were with their commands engaged in this enterprise. Major Appleton commanded the Massachusetts quota, Major Bradford that of Plymouth, and Major Treat, who was second in command, that of Connecticut. The army marched in the dead of winter, in deep snow and intense cold, the frost to a great extent neutralizing the protection afforded the Indians by means of the swamp.

Assault and Capture of the Indian Fort.
On the 19th of December, after passing an exceedingly cold night without shelter, and having marched eighteen miles through the deep snow, the assault was delivered. The Massachusetts troops led the attack, followed by the Plymouth and Connecticut forces. The Indians fought with desperation, and their assailants lost many men and a number of officers in the first encounter. Undaunted by the loss of their commanders, the men rushed forward over the narrow bridge, and soon forced an entrance within the palisades. For several hours the conflict raged. Once the English were driven out of the enclosure, but they rallied, renewed the assault, and ultimately captured the fort. The English

lost eighty men, who were either killed outright or afterwards died of their wounds.   Lieut. Upham and Capt. Seely were severely wounded and soon after died.   In addition, one hundred thirty-eight men were wounded.   The number of Indians collected within the fort is said to have been three thousand five hundred.   Their loss is not accurately known, though a captive reported that one thousand were slain.   The fort was entirely destroyed, and all the wigwams and a large store of provisions gathered there, were burned.   Having no protection from the inclement weather, the English troops were compelled to retrace their steps by a night march, amidst thick falling snow, to a place where the wounded could be properly sheltered. Midnight had long passed ere the weary though victorious army found rest.

The Indians Flee in all Directions.   This blow completely dispersed the tribe. The Indians fled in all directions, but such was the condition of the weather that no immediate pursuit could be made, nor was attempted. Many of them went into camp near Ware River, north of Brookfield, and others on the west side of Connecticut River, opposite Northfield.   The fugitives from the captured fort probably betook themselves to these several camps.

The Whereabouts of Philip Unknown.   The movements of Philip during the winter are not positively known. He was supposed to have had with him a body of from four hundred to five hundred men, but it is not probable that he had one-half that number.   It is said that he spent a portion, if not the whole of the winter, at "Scattacook," (Schaghticoke) in Renssellaer County, about twenty miles north of Albany, four miles east of the Hudson, and upon the north side of the Hoosick River.[1]   Some of his followers probably retired to the Narragansett country.   Philip was reported to have been sick, but it is believed that he was absent part of the time on an expedition to Canada, endeavoring to obtain reinforcements from the Indians in that country.

1 Gov. Andros' letter to the Commissioners. Colonial Records of Connecticut.

The Tribes get up a Mass Meeting. The principal rendezvous of the tribes was in the valleys of Manchester and Sunderland, in Vermont, and probably in this vicinity, a grand gathering of the Indians was held about the latter end of March. One authority locates it "three days journey towards the north-east, from the place where King Philip lay (which was between thirty and fourty English miles from Albany[1])." Wherever it was, there was a mass meeting of what remained of Massachusetts Indians, as well as others from sections of the country to the westward. All the discontented tribes were represented, and many savages, eager to gather scalps and plunder, joined these headquarters. The chiefs of the several tribes, Wampanoags, Pocumtucks, Narragansetts, and Nipmucks, were present, and it was in many respects the most representative gathering of the red men that had taken place since the war commenced.

A Great Display and its Purpose. It is highly probable that at this time the plan of the next season's campaign was discussed and decided upon. One of the most obvious considerations was to impress upon the English the number and power of the army under their control. The means of accomplishing this result were at hand. English prisoners were in their custody, and it was only necessary to display their whole force in the presence of these men and send them home to report. This was accordingly done with all the pomp and circumstance of which they were capable. It will be remembered that in the fight at Hatfield, on the 19th of October, two of the ten scouts sent by Capt. Moseley to reconnoitre, were captured. Before them, all the fighting men it was possible to muster, were marched and counter-marched. Paraded in three ranks, the forces of the red chiefs were inspected and counted by the prisoners, and every effort was made to impress upon them the size and effectiveness of the army of braves ready to take the field in the spring. When the show was over the captives were released and sent to Albany. They reported that they had seen two thousand one hundred men, mostly well

1 Narrative of a Merchant of Boston, p. 226.

armed, ready to renew the warfare.[1]   They also stated that the Indians at the rendezvous "in a vapouring manner, declared that their intent was first, to destroy Connecticut in the spring, then Boston in the harvest, and afterwards the Dutch (meaning what the Dutch had here[2])."

Philip not seen by the Scouts.	Philip was not seen by the returned scouts. Undoubtedly he was present at the assembly and participated in its deliberations.

His reported visit to Canada seems to have been partially successful, as the captives saw about five hundred Canada Indians at the rendezvous.   From this time till within a few days of his death, Philip was with the Indians in the Connecticut valley.   There is no evidence that he actually took part in any of the encounters, or that he planned any of the raids.   He seems to have been an agitator rather than a fighter.

The Plan of Campaign. Supplies of all kinds very scarce.	The first essential in the approaching campaign, an attempt to intimidate their enemies by reports concerning their military resources, had been carried out.

Their intention was apparently to establish a camp at a point where their non-combatants could rest secure and obtain food for their future subsistence, while their fighting men vigorously attacked the settlements on the river.   Their present necessities were great, provisions were scarce and starvation imminent.   But there was another equally pressing need.   Their supply of ammunition was nearly exhausted, and before hostilities could be renewed, more must be obtained.   An attempt to exchange prisoners captured at Lancaster for powder in Canada, failed.   But negotiations

---

1 One of the returned scouts reported that "he came up to an Indian Rendezvous made by a mighty Sachem near Hoosick river, towards Canada, where one of them told one and twenty hundred men, compleat: and the Indians themselves drawing out into three ranks (that he might view them better) made him tell them over three times; who he said were generally well armed, with good fire arms—and most of them young men; few so old as forty. And that amongst them were about 500 of those with straws about their noses, commonly called French Indians. That neither King Philip, nor that party, consisting of about four hundred, were with them, and that the said Philip's own men were not above one hundred; himself being very sickly and having but little authority or esteem among them."—Present State of New England, Merchant of Boston, p. 226.

2 Ibid, p. 227.

with the Dutch at Albany brought better results. Several Dutchmen, some of whom formerly resided at Springfield, had, according to reports from Indian sources, brought them four bushels of powder, and promised more.[1] Thus equipped, a raid upon the town of Northampton for supplies was determined upon early in March, 1676. This attack and its general results will be described in a following chapter.

Canonchet Suggests Planting the abandoned settlements, goes for Corn, and is beheaded, April 3, 1676.

Canonchet, chief of the Narragansetts, proposed that the meadows in the abandoned English settlements, on the Connecticut River, should be planted with corn. They had no seed, and Canonchet himself, volunteered to lead an expedition to Seaconck, a town near Mt. Hope, to obtain a supply. He succeeded in his undertaking, but on his return was surprised and captured by the English. Life and freedom were promised him provided he would bring his tribe into submission to the whites. He refused the offer with scorn and was executed the day after his capture. A portion of his band escaped with the precious seed, and considerable areas of land were planted at Northfield and Deerfield.

The Massachusetts Council send out Indian Spies.

During the winter of $167\frac{5}{6}$, James Quannupaquait, a native Indian, and another by the name of Job, were sent into the Indian country as spies. The information which they obtained, afterwards proved to be correct, but the authorities were in no condition to act immediately upon it; consequently many of the eastern towns were attacked and much suffering ensued. These spies went to the encampment at Wennimisset, and about twenty miles from the old fort at Quabaug, they found three hundred fighting men, with their women and children. They learned of the proposed raid upon the eastern section of the colony, and named the day of the assault upon Lancaster. Quannupaquait made

1 The charge that powder had been furnished to the hostiles by residents at Albany, during Philip's war. was made the subject of official correspondence between the Governors of Massachusetts and New York. As nothing positive could be proved, however, the matter was dropped.

his statement[1] in Boston on the 24th of January. No troops were available,[2] and the pre-arranged attacks were carried out in accordance with the programme. The towns were unprotected and fell an easy prey to the invader.

The Campaign of 1676. Capture of Mrs. Rowlandson. The campaign of 1676 was opened by the combined forces of the Nipmucks and Narragansetts in the eastern section of the colony. Lancaster, Chelmsford, Medfield, Weymouth, Mendon, Eel River, Sudbury, and Groton, all suffered during the months of February and March. Large numbers of the inhabitants were killed and others captured, many buildings were burned and much property destroyed. In the attack on Lancaster, Mrs. Rowlandson, wife of the pastor, and her three children were taken prisoners. The parsonage had been fortified, but the inmates were finally driven out, twelve of the forty-two[3] occupants having been

1 Quaunupaquait started on his expedition on the 30th of December, 1675, and was at the headquarters of the enemy, about twenty miles north of Quabaug old fort, on the 4th of January. Here within a compass of three miles he found about nine hundred men, women and children, about one-third of the whole number being fighting men. They belonged to a number of different tribes. He was told that Philip's winter quarters were within half a day's journey of the fort at Albany. Some dissatisfaction with Philip was reported. Sancumachu, a Hadley Sachem, was ready to kill him, because he had brought all this trouble upon them. They had lived very well with the English before. Provisions were plenty, venison abundant, as on account of the deep snow, deer could be easily killed. Corn was getting to be scarce, but they intended to come down upon Lancaster, Marlboro, and Groton, in order to obtain a supply. Lancaster was to be first attacked, and it would take place in twenty days (which would bring the date about the 8th of February; it actually occurred on the 10th of that month). Guns were plenty, some of them had been taken from Capts. Beers' and Lothrop's men. Ammunition was scarce. The Dutch refused to sell them powder, but the Mohawks obtained it for them. He reported that Mons. Normanville had been in communication with Philip, and had told the Indians not to burn the English mills, nor meeting houses, nor the best houses of the English, as the French would send reinforcements, three hundred Indians with arms and ammunition in the spring, and that the French intended to possess the plantations on the Connecticut River.—Mass. Historical Collections.

2 After the fall of the Narragansett fort, the colonial forces retired to Wickford, where they remained some weeks, in an almost starving condition, the severe weather rendering the transportation of provisions by sea impracticable; the Connecticut forces had been withdrawn to Stonington. The soldiers of Massachusetts and Plymouth still remained in active service, several skirmishes took place, and some damage was inflicted upon the enemy, but provisions were scarce, the Indians hard to come at, and about the 5th of February, the Bay troops retired to Boston.—Palfrey's History of New England, vol. 3, pp. 181, 182.

3 Mrs. Rowlandson says: (page 8, edition of 1853,) "of thirty-seven persons who were in this house, none escaped either present death or a bitter captivity, save only one." Mr. Judd says there were five soldiers in the house, making the whole number of inmates forty-two. Palfrey also gives the number as forty-two. Mrs. Rowlandson makes no allusion to any soldiers in her house, but says that twenty-four persons were captured, twelve killed and one escaped.

killed.   Mrs. Rowlandson published a narrative of her
trials and sufferings while in captivity.   Her captors traveled mainly through this section of country, which im-
parts to her record a certain local interest, while her sad
recital of hardship, as well as her vivid description of the
manners and habits of the natives, warrants a somewhat
lengthened allusion to her account.   She seems to have
been treated with more than ordinary courtesy, and the
privations she endured were apparently no greater than
those of her captors.

Mrs. Rowlandson's   Mrs. Rowlandson was taken captive Feb-
Captivity.   ruary 10th, 167$\frac{5}{6}$.   As she left the garrison
house, carrying her six years old daughter,
both mother and child were wounded.   That day they went
about a mile and camped.   The next day an Indian took
compassion on her and carried the child upon a horse while
the mother went by its side on foot.   Finally she took the
child in her arms and carried it till she fell from exhaustion.   Late in the afternoon snow began to fall, and she
spent the night sitting in the snow before a little fire, holding her child, who was in a high fever and constantly calling for water.   Her own wound was stiff and sore so that
she could move with difficulty.   On the 12th, "sun an hour
high," the party reached an Indian town called Wennimisset (in New Braintree, about eight miles from West
Brookfield).   Here they remained many days, and here her
daughter, after suffering nine days without adequate nourishment,[1] died and was buried.

Her Children and   While here, her two captive children came
Robert Pepper   to visit her.   The son Joseph was with a
visit her.   smaller band about six miles distant, and
the daughter was in the village.   The Indians had threatened to kill her wounded child, but preserved her own life
in the expectation of ransom.   On the 13th she saw Robert
Pepper of Roxbury, who had been captured at the fight in
which Capt. Beers was killed.   He had been almost to
Albany to see Philip.

[1] "There being not the least crumb of refreshment that came within either of our
mouths from Wednesday night to Saturday night, except only a little cold water."—
Mrs. Rowlandson's Narrative, p. 10.

Length of her Captivity. She was with the Indians till May 1st, a period of eighty-two days. During this time they were almost constantly on the move. They did not remain long at any place, and during the period of her captivity the location of their camp was changed twenty times. Occasionally they went forward swiftly, as if hotly pursued, but generally their pace was moderate. Their wanderings were mostly within the limits of what was then the County of Hampshire, and to her they appeared aimless.

The Indians Rejoice over their Barbarity. Mrs. Rowlandson was captured by a Narragansett Indian, who sold her to Quinnapin, brother-in-law to Philip. While they were in camp at Wennimisset, the Indians sent out expeditions against Medfield, Sudbury, and other places. On their return there was much rejoicing over the number of English slain, and the spoils obtained. After the attack on Medfield, they signified by whooping that twenty-three of their enemies had been slain. Some scalps were brought in, and a Bible, which was part of the plunder, was given to Mrs. Rowlandson. They claimed to have killed one hundred English at Sudbury, and lost but five or six of their own number. The party was considerably increased about the 3d of March, and after a rapid march they soon arrived at Paquayag River. Here dry trees were cut, a raft built, and the whole party ferried over. There were many hundreds of them, old and young, some sick and some lame, but "the greatest number of them were squaws."

Glean the Fields at Northfield. On the 6th, they burned their wigwams and hurried on apparently fearful of pursuit. The next day they were at Northfield, where the Indians gathered what had been left of the last harvest, planted with the seed which Canonchet lost his life in obtaining. They threshed the sheaves of wheat, frozen together, gleaned ears of corn and wheat scattered about, and managed to obtain a few ground nuts. Whole fields of wheat and corn had been abandoned and were spoiled. By this time they had wasted the stores plundered from the English settlements, and were in an almost starving condition.

She Visits Philip, is
asked to Smoke,
requested to make
Clothes f o r his
Boy, and Invited
to Dinner.   .
About the 8ᵗʰ of March, she was ordered
to cross the Connecticut River to see
Philip, but while crossing it, the Indians
were apparently scared by the appearance
of English scouts, and Mrs. Rowlandson's
party suddenly started off before embarking, and traveled
some four or five miles up the river.   They must have been
many miles above Northfield, when she actually crossed
the river to "Philip's Crew."   Many warriors were there,
apparently rejoicing over their victories.   She made the
acquaintance of Philip, who asked her to smoke, "a usual
compliment now-a-days among saints and sinners."   Smoking seems to have been one of her accomplishments, but
she had not practiced it during her captivity, and refused
the proffered civility.   Formerly, when she had taken two
or three pipes, she was "presently ready for another, such
a bewitching thing it is."   Philip asked her to make a shirt
for his boy, for which he gave her a shilling.   This money
she offered to her mistress, but was told to keep it, and she
bought a piece of horse flesh.   Afterwards Philip requested
her to make a cap for his son and in payment invited her
to dinner.[1]   The whole company seemed to have been half
starved most of the time.   She gives a detailed account of
their filthy manner of living and the disgusting food they
were compelled to eat.   Yet she says they were very particular about the water they drank.[2]   Her master and sev-

1 For dinner Philip gave her a "pancake. about as big as two fingers; it was made
of parched wheat beaten and fried in bear's greese; but I thought I never tasted
pleasanter food in my life.   There was a squaw who spake to me to make a shirt for
her sannup, for which she gave me a piece of bear.   Another asked me to knit a pair
of stockings, for Which she gave me a quart of peas.   I boiled my peas and bear together, and invited my master and mistress to dinner; but the proud gossip, because
I served them both in one dish, would eat nothing, except one bit that he gave her
upon the point of his knife. * * * Then came one of them, and gave me two
spoonfules of meal, to comfort me; and another gave half a pint of peas, which was
more worth than many bushels at another time. * * * Here was a squaw who
gave me a spoonful of meal; I put it in my pocket to keep it safely, yet somebody
stole it, but put five Indian corns in the room of it; which corns were the greatest
provision I had in my travel for one day."—Mrs. Rowlandson's Narrative.

2 "Their chief and commonest food was ground nuts; they eat also nuts and
acorns, artichokes, lily roots, ground beans, and several other weeds and roots that
I know not.   They would pick up old bones and cut them in pieces at the joints and
if they were full of worms and maggots, they would scald them over the fire to make
the vermin come out and then boil them and drink up the liquor and then beat the
great ends of them in a mortar and so eat them.   They would eat horses guts and
ears, and all sorts of wild birds which they could catch.   Also, bear, venison, beavers, tortoise, frogs, squirrels, dogs, skunks, rattle snakes; yea the very bark of trees;
besides all sorts of creatures and provisions, which they plundered from the English."—Ibid.

eral others started to go to the French in Canada for powder. The party was met by the Mohawks and four of them were killed.

She hears from Home and Travel's farther.

Thomas Reed, who was captured at Hadley, and John Gilbert, taken at Springfield, were in the camp with her at different times. Reed had seen her husband and brought welcome intelligence from him. Gilbert was a mere youth; she found him scantily clothed, and almost frozen; gave him a place near a fire, and did what she could for his comfort. After leaving Northfield, the Indians went into Vermont, and crossing the Ashuelot River, came again to the Paquayag, through which they waded, and on the 19th were in sight of Wachuset. Philip was with them, and no doubt had been all the time. Negotiations for the ransom of Mrs. Rowlandson had been opened, and several letters had passed between the Indians and the council in reference thereto. Philip was strongly opposed to her release, but told her that she would probably be free in about three weeks.

At Home Again.

Mrs. Rowlandson reached home about the first of May, twenty pounds having been paid for her ransom. Her son and daughter, whom she saw at intervals during her captivity, were redeemed soon after her own release.

A new Levy of Troops Ordered to Concentrate at Brookfield.

On the 8th of February, three days after the soldiers were withdrawn from the field, a levy of six hundred men was ordered. The command of the Massachusetts forces was conferred on Major Thomas Savage of Boston, and Major Treat remained at the head of those from Connecticut. Confirmation of certain information obtained by the spies was brought by Mary Shepherd, a girl fifteen years of age; who, on the 12th of February, 1676, was captured at Concord. She escaped from Wennimisset, and on horseback fled through the forest to the settlements. An expedition against the encampment at Wennimisset was organized at once, and the newly levied troops were ordered to concentrate at Quabaug, in three weeks. The several detachments united on the 2^d and 3^d of March, and leaving a garrison at Brookfield, proceeded the next day against the Indian encampment. The savages, well informed of the movements of the English, abandoned it before the troops arrived. They fled northward, and Mrs. Rowlandson notes the hurried march to Paquayag (Miller's) River, as well as the manner of crossing it from the 3^d to the 5th of March. Major Savage pursued the Indians to the river, but fearing that an attack might be made upon some of the river towns, took up his line of march to Hadley, where he arrived on the 8th of the month.

CHAPTER XXIV.

KING PHILIP'S WAR—ATTACK ON NORTHAMPTON.

Command of Major Savage, and its Disposition. IN Hampshire County, at this time, under the command of Major Savage, were the four companies of Capts. Moseley, Whipple, Gilman and Turner, the latter coming from Marlboro, February 29th, with eighty-nine foot soldiers. A garrison of eleven men was left at Brookfield, and Capt. Turner, with the remainder of his company, was stationed at Northampton, where he was joined by Major Treat, March 13th. Capt. Moseley was ordered to Hatfield, with two companies, and the rest of the troops remained at Hadley, where Major Savage established head-quarters. These dispositions had scarcely been perfected, when the Indians who had been pursued from Wennimisset, turned suddenly, and in force attacked Northampton.

Preparations at Northampton. On the 14th of March, 1676, occurred the most serious, and apparently the only organized attack upon Northampton during the war. It opened the campaign of the second year, on the part of the Indians in the Connecticut valley. During the previous fall and winter, palisades had been erected about the most thickly settled portion of the town, north of Mill River. The inhabitants doubtless considered themselves reasonably secure within their fortifications, and the sequel proved that these precautionary measures were none too promptly adopted. They certainly were the means of saving the town from destruction.

The Tribes con-
cerned in the At-
tack, and a Rea-
son for the
Movement.
This attack was made by the river Indians, aided by the Nipmucks, and Narragansetts, as well as those who fled from Wennimisset, and had been pursued to Paquayag. About the 9th of March, the last named fugitives joined Philip's forces, crossing the Connecticut River at a point above Northfield.[1] Soon after this union, the plan of an assault on Northampton was concocted, and preparations for it commenced. The names of the Indian leaders in this expedition are not known. It may be that Philip himself planned and led the attack. He was present at the Indian camp about this time. But there is no positive evidence that he had anything to do with the raid. Reduced to the verge of starvation, the savages must replenish their larder at all events, and in the shortest space of time. Presumably the enemy had learned that the forces under Major Savage, which pursued them, had been distributed throughout the towns, and while the attempt was fool-hardy and hazardous, circumstances compelled them to take the risk. On the 6th of March, the pursuit by Major Savage was relinquished, and eight days were suffered to elapse before the plan was matured; time sufficient to place reinforcements in all the settlements.

Mrs. Rowlandson
tells how the
Enemy Prepared
for the Raid.
Mrs. Rowlandson thus describes the preparations made for the attack:—"Now the Indians gathered their forces to go against Northampton. Over night one went about yelling and hooting to give notice of the design. Whereupon they went to boiling ground nuts and parching corn, as many as had it, for their provision, and in the morning away they went."[2] The assault was made on the north and east sides of the town with great impetuosity, though the most serious demonstration was at the lower end of Pleasant Street. Here the defences were quickly broken through, and a desperate conflict ensued.

1 Mrs. Rowlandson's Narrative, p. 20.

2 Mrs. Rowlandson gives very few dates in her narrative and it is somewhat difficult to fix the day of the month upon which some of the occurrences named by her transpired. The late Sylvester Judd, in a series of notes upon her statements, arranges the chronology of the entire volume, and those figures have been followed thus far. He names March 13th as the date of the preparations for the attack on Northampton.

A slight Discrepancy in the Reports, but that of Major Savage undoubtedly Correct.

The number of the assailants must have been quite large, as the enemy appeared simultaneously at three points.[1] There seems to be a slight disagreement between the statement of Major Savage and that of Rev. Mr. Russell, both of whom were at Hadley, and whose letters constitute the only reliable record of the occurrence. Major Savage says that the attack was made "in three places at once," while Mr. Russell's letter states that "the enemy broke their works in three places." Hubbard follows the account of Russell, and other historians have adopted his statement. The report of Major Savage was probably correct, and it is corroborated by other facts. He undoubtedly had information from his subordinates in command, and was himself upon the ground soon after the affair terminated. Houses were burned outside the fortifications at three different points, and this fact confirms the account of the commander-in-chief. Then Mr. Russell says that only one house was burned within the fortification, while it is well known that four others were destroyed outside of the palisades. If three openings had been made in the defences, of sufficient size to admit the foe, it is but reasonable to suppose that other houses would have been burned within them.

Three Points of Attack Identified.

This assault seems to have been organized with considerable skill, and was certainly executed with vigor. The plan of three simultaneous onsets was well devised, and but for the size of the garrison, must have proved successful. In the absence

1 "The enemy fiercely assaulted Northampton in three places at once and forced within the lines or palisades."—Letter of Maj. Savage, dated "Hadley, March 16, 1676."

"On the 14th inst. the enemy * * * made a most sudden and violent irruption upon Northampton, broke their works in three places, * * * burned 5 houses, one within the fortification."—Letter of Rev. Mr. Russell, dated March 16.

"On the 14th of March, 1676, a large number of them broke through the pallisados at the lower end of Pleasant Street, in three places."—Mr. Williams' Historical Sermon, 1815, p. 15.

"March 14th, the enemy fell upon Northampton, and in three places broke through the fortifycation of pallizadoes set up round about the town a little before for their better security."—Hubbard, p. 205.

"On the 14th of March, at break of day, a large body of the enemy fell upon Northampton—broke through the surrounding palisades at three points."—Hoyt's Indian Wars, p. 215.

of any further contemporary testimony concerning the affair, convincing proof exists that the Indians appeared at three distinct and separate places. The position of the houses burned indicates with certainty the location of two of them, and no doubt exists concerning the third. Only at one point were the palisades penetrated, and it may be inferred that no serious attempt to break through them was made elsewhere. Viewed in any light, the raid on North-ampton seems to have been carefully designed and its sev-eral parts carried out in unison. It is comparatively easy to name the point of each assault. One was on the east-erly side of Round Hill, near the present residence of H. R. Hinckley; another on King Street, very near the homestead of the late Eliphalet Williams; and the third, and most desperate, at the lower end of Pleasant Street. The efforts of the savages were successful only at the latter point, and it is highly probable that the other demonstra-tions were but feints to distract and bewilder the English.

The Enemy En-trapped and Driven off. Having made an opening through the de-fences, the savage horde swarmed in upon the sleeping town. Though the Indians knew there were soldiers in every town, they undoubtedly believed that Northampton, on account of its situation, had the smallest garrison, and anticipated an easy victory with abundant spoil. Those who penetrated the palisades were caught in a trap, and in escaping through the aper-ture they had made, must have lost many men. The red men had slight respect for the defences adopted by the English, and with little difficulty in this instance, broke through them; but this single experience was sufficient. These apparently insignificant barricades, ever after proved effectual. In no other town so protected were the fortifica-tions molested.

The Repulse due to the Presence of both Turner and Treat. While the opportune arrival of Major Treat, on the evening of the 13th, contributed largely towards the safety of the town, Capt. Turner and his company were also in-strumental in its preservation. It is impossible to say what the result would have been had either of them been absent; both rendered admirable service, and to their combined efforts must be attributed the repulse of the enemy.

Size of the Assaulting Party. Different estimates have been made of the number of Indians engaged in this assault. Rumor always greatly exaggerated the attacking forces in these conflicts, and it is difficult to arrive at a reasonable conjecture concerning them. The startled dwellers at Northampton, when the town was encompassed on three sides by yelling savages, might easily have imagined that there were at least two thousand[1] of them. It should be remembered that reports had attributed to Philip an army of three thousand men, and he was believed to be the leader as well as the organizer of the expedition. Probably not more than five hundred Indians were engaged in this affair.

Strength of the Garrison. The garrison comprised seventy-eight men commanded by Capt. William Turner. It was reinforced on the evening previous to the assault by the command of Major Treat, which consisted of two companies of Connecticut troops, and may have numbered nearly two hundred men. To these may be added the militia company of the town, which must at this time have been in an efficient condition.

The Killed and Wounded. Considering the impetuosity of the attack, and the number of Indians engaged in it, the loss to the settlers was not great. Four men and one girl were killed and six men wounded. The persons killed were Robert Bartlett, Thomas Holton, and Mary Earle, residents of Northampton; James McRennal, one of Capt. Turner's men, and Increase Whelstone, another soldier.

Robert Bartlett was one of the original petitioners and a member of the first party of emigrants. His home lot was identical with that owned by the late William R. Clapp, on

1 " On the 14th inst. the enemy to the number of 2000 as judged."—Letter of Mr. Russell. " Two thousand Indian warriors! Strange delusion! There may have been 300 or 400."—Judd's History of Hadley, p. 164. " About 700 Indians encompassed Northampton, where they fought very resolutely for the space of an hour."—News from New England, p. 307.

Pleasant Street. Prominent in town affairs, his name appears frequently during the first years of the town. His
body was hastily buried in the highway in front of his residence, probably because it was deemed unsafe to attempt
burial in the cemetery, although it was within the fortifications.[1] In January, 1681, his son Samuel was granted "a
small parcell of Land, so much as is Conuenient and neede-
full to compasse his fathers graue be in the common highway." Thomas Holton was the youngest son of William
Holton, who lived on the home lot next but one above that
of Robert Bartlett. He was unmarried. Mary Earle was
the eldest daughter of John Earle, and was but twelve
years of age. Her father was not long a resident of Northampton, and did not at this time own any property in the
town. He married Mary, daughter of John Webb Sr.
Nothing is known of the two soldiers. One of them was
probably the sentinel, who in one account, was said to have
been slain.

Loss of the Indians. The number of Indians killed is not known,
and as usual in such cases, the estimates
vary. Caught as they were within the fortifications, it
seems probable that many of them must have been slain,
while struggling to escape. It may be supposed, however,
that before any large number succeeded in effecting an entrance, they found more soldiers than they bargained for.
Mr. Russell states: "There are said to be found slain
about a dozen of the enemy." Menownet, a friendly Indian, said that they had one killed and four wounded.[2]
Another but less trustworthy account places the Indian loss
at twenty.[3]

Loss of Property in   Fortunately the loss of property was much
Northampton.   less than could have been anticipated when
the number of buildings outside of the fortifications is taken into account. The letters of Major Sav-

1 Although it has been positively stated (page 276) that the cemetery was enclosed
by the palisades, the above circumstance seems to imply that such may not have
been the case. While there is reason to believe in the accuracy of the first statement, the line of defence in that section is not so clearly defined upon the records as
to render its identification absolutely certain.

2 History of Hadley, p. 164, note.

3 " State of New England," by a Merchant of Boston, p. 216.

age and Mr. Russell agree in the statement that five houses and five barns were burned, the latter adding that one was "within the fortification." From the records of land grants to the sufferers in the Indian war of 1675 and 1676, it is possible to name the persons whose buildings were burned, and consequently to designate their home lots. The only house destroyed within the palisades was that of William Holton, who lived on Pleasant Street, very near the dwelling of Robert Bartlett. It is conjectured that the defences were broken through in this immediate vicinity. John Holton, son of William and brother of Thomas who was slain, had a war grant of a small lot, containing sixty rods on Meeting House Hill, and to his brother Samuel was given a lot very near it of the same size. Neither of these young men had been granted home lots previously, though both had married. Why these grants, named as Indian war grants, were made to the sons while the father was still living, and their residence was within the fortifications, is not clear.

The other buildings burned at this time, all of which were without the line of palisades, were those of Alexander Alvord, who lived probably in the vicinity of what is now known as Pomeroy Terrace; John Alexander, who occupied what was known in later years as the Edwin Clark estate on Bridge Street; Samuel Allen, who lived on King Street, on the lot afterwards owned and occupied by Rev. Mr. Hooker, and later by the late Eliphalet Williams; and Matthew Clesson, who owned the lot on which H. R. Hinckley now resides.

Location of the War Grants to the above-named Persons.

Each of these persons received war grants at this time. Alexander Alvord's was on Hawley Street, near the site of the Chicago Beef Co.'s warehouse; John Alexander's was on King Street near the house now occupied by John Parnell; Samuel Allen was granted a small lot on Meeting House Hill, including the site of the present Court House. Matthew Clesson's lot of sixty rods, was west of King Street, on the brook above Park. There was some disagreement between Clesson and the town authorities in reference to this grant. In 1702, he was given a home lot of four acres "on condition that he quit the town of an engagement which he says they made to him concerning the burning of his house by the Indians in 1675." [1]

Other Special Grants made at this time. Other grants were made at this time to John Alvord and Joseph Hawley. [2] John was the son of Alexander Alvord and his grant was on King Street, in the vicinity of Allen Street. Nothing js known of the grant to Mr. Hawley, other than that it was "near the school house," in the vicinity of Meeting House Hill, probably where Court Street has since been located. On the records both are endorsed as "granted in time of Indian war," though it is not easy to understand how they could have been given on account of losses occasioned by that conflict.

The Facts Presented fix the Points of the Indian Attacks. It is apparent from these facts that the location of the original homesteads of the persons to whom were granted small lots on account of the burning of their houses, will determine the points of the Indian feints or assaults, on the 14th of March, 167⅚; consequently it is evident that these demonstrations were made on Prospect, upper King, Bridge and Pleasant Streets, the house on Pomeroy Terrace being burned by the party assaulting the latter point.

Grants were made to Twelve Persons. Twelve persons [3] received compensation in land because of losses in 1675 and 1676, but the number of houses burned, according to the most reliable statements was only ten. The owner of

1 Matthew Clesson bought the homestead of Thomas Lewis, with house and barn in 1667. He sold it to Solomon Stoddard in 1684, but no buildings are mentioned in the deed to Mr. Stoddard, who built a house upon it soon after it came into his possession. Clesson owned another home lot on upper King street, but there is no evidence that he had a house upon it at that time.

2 Joseph Hawley came to Northampton in 1674, and had a grant of a home lot on the east side of Round Hill in 1682. In 1685 he was permitted by a vote of the town to "haue and injoy the land formerly layd out for him by the Committee without building on it."

3 *Recapitulation.* Of the twelve persons to whom land was granted inside the fortifications, on account of the war of 1675-6, called war grants, Preserved Clapp, William Smead, Enos Kingsley and Ralph Hutchinson, lived on South Street, and were burned out in October, 1675; Samuel Allen lived on upper King Street; Alexander Alvord on what is now Pomeroy Terrace; John Alexander on Bridge Street; Matthew Clesson on Prospect Street; and William Holton on Pleasant Street. John and Samuel Holton, Joseph Hawley and John Alvord owned no homesteads, and the land given to the two last named, must have been for some other reason.

one of them received nothing, but his two sons had special grants, on this account, and two other persons who had no houses to burn, were rewarded in the same manner.

The Indians ob-
tained but little
Plunder and
took no Pris-
oners.

The plunder obtained by the enemy was inconsiderable. Mrs. Rowlandson says that they "returned with some horses, sheep and other things." No captives were taken by the Indians in this attack, and no one was killed outside the fortifications. The reason for this is obvious. Those families living without the palisades undoubtedly retired within them during the night, otherwise many more persons would have been killed and some would certainly have been captured. All of them without doubt had relatives within the fortifications, with whom they could find accommodations.

Driven from North-
ampton, the Ene-
my appear before
Hatfield.

Soon after their discomfiture at Northampton, the enemy suddenly appeared before Hatfield. Already aware of the attack upon the neighboring town, Capt. Moseley was prepared for them. But the Indians had no relish for any more fighting that day, and were not anxious to assail another fortified town. No demonstration was made and the savages speedily vanished.

Northampton again
Alarmed.

Two days afterwards Northampton had another alarm. The enemy were seen on two sides of the town in considerable numbers, about two o'clock on the morning of the 16th. [1] They undoubtedly designed another surprise and night attack, but found the inhabitants ready to meet them. Messengers were sent to Major Savage at Hadley, for assistance, but the Indians retreated without striking a blow, and never again threatened the place in force.

The Indians con-
tinue their Wan-
derings.

The enemy returned to their head-quarters at Squakeag, but they did not long remain quiet. Mrs. Rowlandson's narrative shows that they were almost constantly on the move up and down

1 "Being beaten off they marched towards Hatfield and were seen in several places about the town in considerable companies. I presently sent another company to strengthen that town. This morning, about two o'clock, we were alarmed again from Northampton, which was occasioned by some Indians being seen on two sides of the town."—Major Savage's Letter, dated Hadley, March 16, 167⅝.

the valley, seldom remaining more than a few days in any camp. Small parties still continued to infest the county, committing depradations in various quarters.

On the 26th of March, a party of sixteen or eighteen men, accompanied by women and children, while on their way from Long-meadow to attend church at Springfield, were waylaid by seven or eight Indians. One man and a woman were killed, and two men wounded. In the confusion, two women and their babes were taken prisoners. Major Pynchon immediately dispatched a squadron in pursuit. Sixteen men sent out by Major Savage, from Hadley, joined them the next morning, and the enemy were soon after discovered. While their pursuers were in sight, the savages dashed out the brains of the infants and knocked the women on the head. The Indians escaped in a swamp which the English horsemen were unable to penetrate. One man was killed in Springfield and two men killed and two houses burned in Westfield, during the winter.

Outrages Committed in Southern Hampshire.

About the first of April, some Hadley farmers, under an escort from the garrison, went to Hockanum to work. They were ambushed by the Indians, Dea. Goodman[1] and two of the soldiers killed, and Thomas Reed, another soldier, captured.[2]

A Tragedy at Hockanum.

1 Hoyt says that some of the party "went to the summit of Mt. Holyoke to view the surrounding country from the peak, and that Dea. Goodman proceeded some distance in a different direction to view the enclosures of his field." Hubbard says they ventured, contrary to express orders, "upon the top of a high hill near by, to take a needless and unseasonable view of the country."

2 "About this time they came yelping from Hadley, having there killed three Englishmen and brought one captive with them, viz: Thos. Reed. They all gathered about the poor man, asking him many questions. I desired also to go and see him, and when I came he was crying bitterly, supposing they would quickly kill him. Whereupon I asked one of them whether they intended to kill him? he answered me they would not—he being cheered a little with that, I asked him about the welfare of my husband and he told me he saw him such a time in the bay and he was well but very melancholy."—Mrs. Rowlandson's Narrative, p. 28.

CHAPTER XXV.

KING PHILIP'S WAR—CONSOLIDATION FAILS.

The Enemy Active in all Directions. THE war was not confined to any one portion of the colony. It covered all parts, and almost simultaneous blows fell in the two opposite extremes of the province. Groton was assaulted on the 13th of March, and Northampton on the 14th. On the same day that the people of Longmeadow were attacked, Marlboro was set upon and destroyed, Capt. Pierce and his company slain at Patucket River, Simsbury, Ct., burned, and Windsor attacked. The enemy were not at all points equally successful, yet they inflicted almost continuous destruction, in one section or the other, and kept the entire force of their opponents constantly on the move.

A Scheme to Concentrate the Connecticut River Settlements. With so large an extent of country to defend against a foe active, mysterious, merciless, appearing in exaggerated numbers on the same day at remote points, keeping the whole colony in terror and uncertainty, no wonder the authorities were at a loss what course to pursue. Under these circumstances, the Council, with limited means at its command, unable to provide adequate defence everywhere, or to garrison properly, so many towns, conceived the idea of concentrating the settlements in the Connecticut valley upon two points. The smaller towns were to remove to the larger. This scheme was broached in a letter from Secretary Rawson to Major Savage, under date of March 26th, 1676, from which the following is an extract:—

"That those our towns on Connecticut River do immediately consult and determine the putting themselves into such a position as may best accommodate their security and provision, which we judge must be by their gathering together in such places and numbers that they may be able to defend themselves, and some considerable part of each company be improved in planting * * * and in case this cannot be in each town, then the lesser towns must gather to the greater. To remain in such a scattered state, is to expose lives and estates to the merciless cruelty of the enemy, and is no less than tempting Divine Providence, and to quit our plantations one after another, refusing to comply to the present humbling and dreadful hand of the Lord against us, is to be our own executioners and we fear will be * * * to our ruin more than the sword of the enemy when too Late. Some that know those places best, do apprehend that Springfield and Hadley are the fittest places for their fortifying and planting."

Letter from Secretary Rawson to Major Pynchon.

Another letter from Secretary Rawson had been sent to Major Pynchon at Springfield, dated March 20th, 1676. In it the same method of concentration was proposed. Ordinarily such a suggestion would have been equivalent to a command, but the people were not ready to adopt this one. The Secretary says that he can see no other way

"But to come all together in some convenient place in the town and take in so large a fort that the proprietors may live in distinct houses or shelters * * * and Westfield must join with you and totally remove to you, for 'tis impossible to hold both towns, the enemy being so many in those parts and our army must remove from them, we are assaulted on every side * * * most of our frontiers are away off; our present work is to secure the principal towns upon the sea coast; we cannot see how your people can remove at present, but must ride it out as best you can; we speak not of particular persons but of the body of the people, for whither will you go, or how will you remove your corn and goods? The like advice we have given for the other towns upon the River, to come in all to Hadley[1] and fortify it well, and there by united strength it may be kept, but otherwise all will be lost according to reason. Suppose the enemy should plant upon your deserted towns; it is hoped when the corn is grown we may have ability to destroy it. We must strengthen the heart. Ammunition is scarce here. If your people be averse to our advice, we must be necessitated to draw off our forces from them, for we cannot spare them nor supply them with ammunition. We have ordered the Major to leave some of the garrison soldiers to strengthen you, if you are able to provide food for them."

1 Secretary Rawson seems not to have been aware of the relative size of the towns. Northampton was the larger, and Hadley, according to the proposal that the lesser should go to the greater towns, should have come to Northampton. But Hadley had thus far been the military head-quarters for this section, and was consequently considered the most important town.

The Advice of the Council Disapproved by the Towns Interested.

These two letters show that a state almost of panic prevailed among the leading men of the colony. Beset on all sides, the authorities knew not which way to turn. Needing all their resources for the defence of the eastern towns, they must devise some means by which the valley settlements could take care of themselves. The most feasible method seemed to be that of union for a common defence. Such a concentration and abandonment of towns must have resulted in the entire removal of the English from the valley. This advice was injudicious and disheartening. Fortunately the proposition found no supporters among those who were most immediately interested in the suggested movement. Strong, able and voluminous protests were showered upon the Council. The authorities had misjudged the spirit of the settlers. They were not yet ready to give up all that they had toiled so hard, and suffered so much to gain. They refused to yield their homes, their land, and their household effects to the fury of the savage foe. Such a course, while it would greatly encourage the enemy, and proclaim the panic existing among the English, would also add impetus to the reported designs of the French, as shadowed by the statements of the Indians, that they intended to drive out the English and recolonize the country.[1]

The towns met the case promptly and fearlessly. They were not disposed to follow the advice of the Council, and did not hesitate to give their reasons. Rev. Mr. Russell of Hadley, strongly antagonized the plan, though it did not contemplate the abandonment of that town.

Northampton Opposes the Proposition, and sends a strong Protest.

The leading citizens of Northampton were opposed to any such action. Satisfied that the people preferred to remain in their own town, and bravely meet whatever danger menaced, they forwarded a vigorous protest. Notwith-

---

1 One of the Longmeadow women, captured on the 26th, and rescued, reported a conversation with the Indians, which is thus alluded to by Major Savage in his letter to the Council, on the 28th of March: Among other things she said "That some of the French were lately with them, who persuade them not to burn and destroy the houses, but to make what slaughter they can of the people, because they intend to come and inhabit them, * * * and that they do intend to fall on these towns shortly." This statement confirms the report of the spies, made early in the year, and no doubt truly represents the designs entertained by the French.

standing the sufferings they had but just undergone, in a
savage attack by the enemy, which they had reason to fear
might be repeated at any time, they were unwilling even
to entertain a thought of leaving the place.   Saved only by
the most fortunate combination of circumstances, they preferred still to endure the suspense of sudden and unexpected assault, the labor and fatigue of constant watch
and ward, as well as the burden and expense of subsisting
and paying the wages of a garrison.   Their protest is
manly and courageous, and exhibits the patient endurance
and strong faith of the pioneers of the Connecticut Valley.
The following letter, in the handwriting of Mr. Stoddard,
was at once forwarded to Boston :—

                                    Northampton, March 28, 1676.
Hon^d :
    We are not unsensible that your ears are dayly filled with the cryes
of many people in this day of calamity, through all parts of the Country, & are loth to add unto your affliction, by bringing any unnecessary
trouble upon you : yet we dare doe no other in faithfullnesse unto ourselves & the Country, then present breifely our condition before you :
we dare not entertain any thoughts of deserting this plantation : the
Lord has wounderfully appeared of late for our preservation, & we
feare it would be displeasing unto him, if we should give up into the
hands of our enemies, by running away, that which the Lord has so
eminently delivered out of their hands, when they did so violently
assault us : if we should desert a town of such considerable strength,
it may so animate the enemy, & discourage other plantations, as may
prove no small prejudice unto the Country : besides there seems to us
a great necessity for holding this place for the releife of those forces
that may be improved in following the enemy : to bring provisions
either from Boston or Hartford for the supply of an Army in these
quarters is a worke of no small difficulty & danger : the want of
places of entertainment for an Army in these parts, may hazard the
losse of many opportunities : if we may be allowed to judge, there can
be no prosecuting of the warr in these parts to advantage unlesse this
& the two neighbour Towns be maintained : yet we must needs say we
feare it will be a worke too heavy for us to defend our selvs : late experience has taught us, that unlesse we had been furnished with considerable numbers of men besides our own, we had in likelyhood become
a prey to our enemies : the enemy has a great strength in these parts,
& probably does but watch for the drawing away of the army that
they may renew their attempt : our earnest request therefore to your
Hon^rs : is, that you would not suffer us to be left destitute : but allow
us what number of men you judge convenient for the holding of the
Town : & least the charge (the country being now at great expence)

should discourge from granting our desire, we will at our own cost, bear the charge of a sufficient garrison: if your Hon^rs. shall see cause to allow us fifty souldiers, beside those which have kept with us all winter, we will diet them freely & pay them their wages: whereas some have Informed the Councill that Springfeild is one of the most convenient Towns for others to repair to: your Hon^rs are much misled therin for the bulke of the Town is burnt allready: whereby they are uncapable to entertain others, & their land lies remote, most of it on the other side of the great river, so they are uncapable, we fear either to maintain themselvs or others: thus leaving our request unto your solemn consideration, & desiring the Lord to guide you & support your hearts under these sore exercises, we take leave & Rest

your humble servants

N-Hampton	SOL: STODDARD
mar: 28, 76	JOHN STRONG
	WILLIAM CLARKE
The generality of the Town doe	DAVID WILTON
consent to pay the garrison	JOHN LIMON
souldiers, rather than	JOHN KING
want them." [1]	

The Firm and Moderate Demand of the People of Northampton.
This document states the case fairly and offers strong reasons against the project of consolidation. Couched in firm and courteous language, the letter commanded a respectful hearing, and no doubt its arguments were accorded their due weight in the consideration of, and final disposition of the case. The citizens ask for a moderate garrison, only fifty men in addition to the number that had been on duty there during the winter. It will be remembered that Major Appleton left thirty-six men to do guard duty here the fall before. The people were ready to subsist and pay these men, notwithstanding their impoverished condition. This was but a scant garrison for so large a town while active hostilities were in progress, yet the inhabitants preferred to run their chances with it rather than abandon the plantation. To leave the settlement would give a death blow to their fondest hopes, and yield to the savage foe all they had struggled for and gained in twenty years. They "dare not" under the circumstances consider such a suggestion, and events proved that they were justified in their refusal.

1 Mass. Archives, v. 68, p. 182.

No Action taken
by the Town.
Apparently the town took no action on this proposition. If any meeting was called to consider the question, no record of it exists. While the letters to Major Savage and Col. Pynchon were declared to be advisory, they had all the authority of an order, and had the recommendations contained in them accorded with the sentiments of the people, their suggestions would have been promptly carried out. Issued in that form purposely, they were undoubtedly intended as feelers. Probably it was not deemed necessary that the town should act in an official capacity in reference to them at that stage of the affair. An informal meeting of the citizens may have been held, which authorized the protest, or it may have been decided upon by the military authorities. The document was signed by the clergyman, the ruling elder, the military committee, and two of the selectmen, one of the latter being a member of the committee on military affairs.

Westfield Protests.
Westfield also protested sharply, contending that if such a consolidation was to be made, Westfield was much the better place for it than Springfield. The committee argued that Springfield would be difficult to fortify, and not good to live in, as most of it had been burned, and the tillage land was remote, situated on both sides of the river. Westfield, they averred, could be more easily defended than Springfield, and the soil was better adapted to cultivation. The Council at Hartford advised them not to desert their plantation. They decided to contract and strengthen their fortifications, and asked for a garrison of thirty men.

The Council of Con-
necticut Disap-
prove, and the
matter is Dropped.
Correspondence passed between Rev. Mr. Russell of Hadley, and the Council of Connecticut, respecting the proposed concentration of towns. The Council strongly disapproved, and offered many convincing arguments against the project, sending an address to the Council of Massachusetts. They say that the enemy will destroy the deserted places, and possess the land to plant, and "one of the best granaries in your colony will be lost, which is so

much needed." Finding so great opposition to their suggestion among those most interested in it, the authorities
permitted the matter to subside.

The Town Accepts the Garrison. Whatever action may have been taken previously, it seems that the three towns of
Northampton, Hatfield, and Hadley, acted
in concert in reference to the garrisons. On the 8ᵗʰ of
April, "the towne voted to except of fifty souldiers to
keep garison in this towne acording to the proposition that
the commitee for Northampton Hadly and Hatfield sent in
the last leter to the counsil Baring date March 31, 1676."

The English ready for Peace. Harassed and stricken at all points, the English were ready to close the war in any hon-
orable and satisfactory manner. In the latter part of March, an attempt was made to negotiate a
treaty of peace with the Indians. Both colonies were
ready for a cessation of hostilities, but the overtures came
from Connecticut, which had suffered little in comparison
with Massachusetts. A flag of truce, borne by a party
of friendly Indians, conducted by Towcanchasson, was
sent to the tribes up the river, by order of the Connecticut
Council. The chief carried a document, dated March 28ᵗʰ,
1676, which contained a proposition for an exchange of
prisoners, and intimations that a treaty of peace would be
concluded with any of the sachems. The Indians received
these proposals with divided opinions. Burning to revenge
the disaster of December, the Narragansetts refused to
entertain thoughts of peace. The Nipmucks, the Pocumtucks, and other river tribes, inveigled into the war
through the diplomacy of Philip, and realizing that they
were left to carry it on with little or no help from him,
were weary of the strife, and would undoubtedly have welcomed the end of the war. The fishing and planting season was at hand, and in order to gain time, the Indians
were willing to parley. A vague and non-committal reply
was returned to the missive of the Council, by the chiefs
assembled at Northfield. Without delay the Council
answered the Indians. They repeated the offer to exchange
captives, or they would ransom the English prisoners, and

2 1

suggested that a meeting should be held at Hadley, within eight days, for the purpose of negotiating a peace. The Indian messengers or commissioners were to have safe conduct coming and returning, and a response was demanded within five days. No further notice of these propositions was taken by the Indians.

General Condition of Affairs. On the 26th of March, all the Connecticut soldiers had been withdrawn from the county, Major Treat was ordered on an expedition against the Narragansetts, but had been suddenly recalled to Hartford, to protect the settlements in Connecticut. In this immediate vicinity, since the attack on Northampton, no demonstration in force had been made. The Indians were busying themselves in preparations for defence, as well as in obtaining supplies of food. A large camp was established at some considerable distance up the river, and forts built for its protection. Their scouting parties were still hovering about the plantations, and cattle, horses and sheep were constantly stolen. The feeling of insecurity and disquiet which prevailed among the English, was greatly augmented when the troops were recalled early in April. In a few weeks it was reported that three hundred acres of corn had been planted by the savages at Pocumtuck, and that every fishing place on the river above Deerfield, had its camp of busy fishermen. Encouraged by the repeated success of their eastern confederates, aware of the panic existing among the English, and of the recall of the Connecticut, and a portion of the Bay forces, and believing themselves secure, the enemy spent much time in feasting and carousing.

Major Savage Recalled, but leaves Garrisons in the Towns. The disasters which befell the eastern towns, fourteen of which had suffered severely, caused the Massachusetts Council to recall most of the troops in the valley. Major Savage received peremptory orders, and marched on the 7th of April, to the assistance of the eastern army. He took with him four companies under Moseley, Whipple, Gilman, and Drinker, leaving Capt. Turner in command, with a force of one hundred fifty-one men. These were distributed in the following order: Forty-six men at Northampton, under Sergt. Fogg; forty-five men at Hatfield, under Sergt. Robert Bardwell; and fifty-one men at Hadley, under Sergt. Robert Prosser, while nine men had been sent to Springfield.

Capt. Turner asks to be Relieved of his Command. Quietness prevailed during the month of April. Considering themselves secure, the enemy continued the work of accumulating provisions. The withdrawal of so many soldiers, made it impossible for the commandant to pursue any other than a defensive policy. While this state of inactivity prevailed, the soldiers were suffering for want of clothing, and Capt. Turner in reporting their condition, asked to be relieved of the command on account of ill health.[1] No attention was paid to this hint, and he continued to serve till the famous battle at the Falls—since known by his name—in which he lost his life.

A further Reduction of the Garrisons. The military committees of the towns of Northampton and Hadley, considering the number of soldiers more than sufficient for guard duty alone, apparently desirous of relieving themselves of the inefficient and incapable among them, and seeking to lift the burden of supporting so many men, petitioned the General Court, on the first of May, for a reduction of the garrison by one-half. The country agreed to pay the wages of those remaining.[2] This reduction left but twenty-three men in Northampton, hardly enough it would seem for guard duty.

1 "The soldiers here are in great distress for want of clothing, both Linen and woolen. Some has been brought from Quabaug, but not one eighth of what we want. * * * I should be glad if some better person might be found for this employment, for my weakness of body and often infirmities will hardly suffer me to do my duty as I ought, and it would grieve me to neglect anything that might be for the good of the country in this day of their distress."—Letter of Capt. Turner, dated Hadley, April 26, 1676.

2 "In answer to the desire & motion of the comittees of Hadley and Northampton, the Court on consideration thereof, declare, that one halfe of the garrison souldjers in those tounes be, by the comanders there, dismist, as are most vncapable of staying there, as shall be directed or otheruise knoune ; after wᶜʰ being donn, the country shall pay the wages of the other remayning halfe of the sᵈ garrison souldjers from that time."—Records of Massachusetts, vol. 5, p. 91.

The Settlers ready to assume the Offensive.
Though one-half the troops had departed, the people were not disheartened. They did not propose to submit meekly to the insolence of their enemies, who, sitting down at their ease, almost within a stone's throw of the settlements, awaited the close of the fishing and planting season before they swept down upon the valley towns. Either because they were so completely absorbed in the immediate work of the season, or perchance awaiting the outcome of the pending peace negotiations, the Indians remained quiet during the latter part of April and the opening days of May. The inaction of their foes, however, did not lure the settlers into fancied security. Their courage rose with the imminence of the threatened danger, and they were ready to take the offensive. Well aware that an effective blow at this time would greatly cripple the enemy, and believing that under existing circumstances, a night attack upon the Indian encampment might be successful, they clamored to be led against the foe.

The Desire of the People to attack the Indians set forth in a Letter to the Council.
This feeling is well presented in a letter to the Council, signed by Capt. Turner and six others, doubtless members of the military committees in the several towns. In it the prevailing sentiment to "be out against the enemy" is made manifest, they consider that "the enemy is now come so near us, that we count we might goe forth in the evening, and come upon them in the darknesse of the same night." They say that "It is the generall voyce of the people here y^t now is the time to distresse the enemy, and that could we driue them from thair fishing, and keepe out though but lesser parties against them, famine would subdue them." These suggestions were destined to fulfilment in the course of a few weeks, the letter being dated the 29th of April.

Progress of the Peace Negotiations.
Negotiations for peace, entered upon by the Connecticut Council, were still in progress, and about this time Indian envoys on their way to Hartford, with an answer to the overtures of the English, arrived at Hadley. Mr. Russell sent a dispatch to Hartford advising the Council of the coming of the mes-

sengers, and giving a statement of affairs in the valley, similar to that of the above quoted letter, and of even date therewith. These savage emissaries returned with their reply about the first of May. Its purport was that a conference with the sachems should be held at Hadley, on the 8th of the month, and in preparation for that event, the Council ordered one hundred soldiers to march forthwith to that place. While these preliminaries were under discussion, and up to the time of the proposed meeting at Hadley, the inhabitants of the valley were advised to make no hostile movement lest the English captives in the hands of the Indians should be put to death.

They Fail and the War Spirit Increases.   Having accomplished their object—to gain time for fishing and planting—the Indians took no further notice of the last communication from the Connecticut Council. In vain the authorities waited for the delegation to arrive at Hadley. The proposed eight days lengthened to ten and twelve, but no Indians appeared. The bad faith of the Indians in this matter, intensified the feeling against them, and the aggressive war spirit gained added strength in all the Hampshire settlements. It was proposed to borrow the tactics of the enemy, and make a sudden and overwhelming night attack. If their encampment could be dispersed, their gathered stores destroyed, and their planted fields devastated, the enemy would be crippled indeed. This war feeling was greatly augmented by a raid of the Indians, who came down on the night of May 13th, to Hatfield upper meadows, and carried away from seventy to eighty head of cattle that had been turned out to pasture.

Thomas Reed Escapes and reports the Condition of Affairs among the Indians.   Thomas Reed, who was captured at Hockanum, April 1st, managed to escape, and arrived at Hatfield on the 15th of May. He reported that the Indians had been planting three or four days at Deerfield, that they were living "at the falls, on both sides of the river," that most of them were old men and women, and that there were not more than sixty or seventy fighting men.

CHAPTER XXVI.

KING PHILIP'S WAR—FIGHT AT TURNER'S FALLS.

An Immediate Demonstration Determined upon.

THE information furnished by the escaped captives, Gilbert and Reed,[1] focused the prevailing desire for an immediate demonstration. It was decided to make an attack upon the camp at the falls above Deerfield, since known as Turner's Falls.[2] Eager as they were to be led against the enemy, some necessary delay occurred in organizing the details of the expedition, and it was not ready to start till the evening of May 18th. This delay was in part due to the expectation of reinforcements from Connecticut, application for aid therefrom having been made. The force, including officers, chaplain and guides, numbered about one hundred forty-seven men,[3] nearly all mounted. There were thirty-five soldiers from the garrisons at Northampton, Hadley and

1 John Gilbert and Edward Stebbins, two Springfield lads, were captured early in the year. Gilbert came into Hadley, in the latter part of April, and Stebbins returned about the same time. Reed, as has already been stated, came into Hatfield about the middle of May.

2 "Several hundred Indians had taken station on elevated ground, on the right bank of the river at the head of the fall; a smaller party occupied the opposite bank, and another was stationed at what is now called Smead's Island, upwards of a mile below. As the English forces at Hadley and the adjacent towns, were not at this time very numerous, the Indians considered themselves little exposed to an attack, and had become remiss in guarding their station."—Hoyt's Indian Wars, p. 128.

3 Estimates differ relative to the number of men engaged under Capt. Turner. From one hundred fifty to one hundred sixty is the statement generally made by historians. The latest research in regard to this matter is that of Mr. George Sheldon, and the list given by him in his recently published History of Deerfield (vol. 1, pages 158, 159, 160) is undoubtedly the most correct of any in existence. Strange to say, however, in none of the lists given, either in print or manuscript, appears the name of Capt. Samuel Holyoke of Springfield, the real hero of the occasion, (though Mr. Sheldon gives it in an appendix at the close of his second volume). With his name added, the whole number of volunteers, who participated in that fight, was one hundred forty-seven, and this is probably as accurate as any roll that can be made at the present time. Capt. Holyoke died the same year, unmarried, and his name did not appear in the list of claimants for the land at Fall Town.

Hatfield; and twenty-five from those at Springfield and Westfield, under command of Lieut. Isaiah Tay of Boston. The rest was composed of volunteers from the five towns in the County of Hampshire. From Northampton twenty-two men,[1] under Ensign John Lyman; from Hadley twenty-six, and from Hatfield twelve, under Sergts. John Dickinson and Joseph Kellogg; from Springfield twenty-four, and from Westfield three, under command of Capt. Holyoke. This little army, composed wholly of volunteers, soldiers as well as citizens, assembled at Hatfield, on the 18th of May. It was commanded by Capt. William Turner, with Capt. Samuel Holyoke of Springfield, and Ensign John Lyman of Northampton, as subordinates. Rev. Hope Atherton, minister at Hatfield, accompanied the expedition as chaplain, and Benjamin Wait of Hatfield, and Experience Hinsdell of Hadley, were the guides.

The Expedition sets out on the evening of May 18. On the evening of the day already named, the little band of volunteers, after listening to a fervent prayer from Chaplain Atherton, started on its hazardous march of twenty miles. The ·night was exceedingly dark, and the way lay through dense forests encumbered with fallen trees and entangled underbrush, across swamps yet soft with the spring rains, against a numerous and wary foe. All night the dreary march continued, followed by the desperate morning fight. The route lay along the west side of Connecticut River, and midnight found them at the forsaken plantation at Deerfield. On they hurried over the Deerfield river, and here they narrowly escaped detection. In order to avoid the ford which was guarded by the enemy, they crossed the river near the mouth of Sheldon's brook. Notwithstanding this precaution, the Indian sentinels caught the sound of the splashing horses. They examined the fording place with torches, but thanks to the darkness of the night, nothing was discovered. Imagining the alarm to have been occasioned by a troop of moose, no

---

1 In 1736, the Legislature granted a township of six miles square to the survivors and heirs of all who were engaged in this fight. It was called Falltown (now Bernardston). Twenty-two names of persons who were certainly residents of Northampton in 1676, are given in the list prepared by the Legislative committee, as entitled to grants of land at Falltown.

further notice of it was deemed necessary. Turner continuing his march through "Greenfield meadow, passing Green River and a trackless forest of about four miles, halted on elevated land, a small distance west of fall river about half a mile from the Indian camp at the falls."[1] Here he dismounted his men and picketed his horses, leaving them in charge of a small guard. Little time was spent in preparation for the attack. After fording Fall River they climbed a steep incline, and found themselves close upon the Indian camp.

The Indians Careless in their Security, are Surprised and Slaughtered. Prosperous in their fishing operations, and successful in their cattle thieving raid, the Indians spent the day preceding the attack in feasting upon the beef and milk obtained from the recently stolen Hatfield stock. Completely surfeited by their debauch they slept soundly, posting no sentinels and keeping no watch. At break of day the assaulting party reached its position in the rear of and overlooking the hostile camp. Arranging his forces so that every shot would tell, Capt. Turner hurled them upon the sleeping foe. So thorough was the surprise that the English thrust their guns into the wigwams before the enemy were aware of their presence. Astounded by the attack, the Indians rushed out in the greatest consternation. On the one side the deadly foeman pouring in his murderous fire, on the other the swift waters of the cataract, left them no avenue of escape. In the confusion they darted wildly about, shouting "Mohawks, Mohawks!" Some took to their canoes and endeavored to get away by the river. Many threw themselves in without paddles, and were hurried by the rushing waters to speedy destruction. Some attempted to escape by swimming, but were soon drowned. Others were shot in the water, as their canoes, riddled with bullets, sank beneath them. Numbers were killed in their wigwams, and not a few sought shelter under the overhanging banks of the river, where they were mercilessly slaughtered. Capt. Holyoke is reported as having killed five "with his own sword," who were thus in hiding, and

1 Hoyt's Indian Wars, p. 129.

the soldiers plied the bloody work till the enemy were dispersed. The butchery was brief, but terrible. Slight resistance was made by the panic stricken foe, and but one of the assailing party was wounded. Another was killed by his friends, who supposing him to be an Indian, shot him as he came out of a wigwam. The camp was burned and every thing in it destroyed.[1]

The Tide of Battle Turns, and the English are Driven off.

The work of destruction was thorough and complete, and thus far the victory had been overwhelming. But now the tide of battle turned, and henceforth it was for the victors but a race for life. Too long the English lingered in the deserted camp. Reinforcements for the red men, from the adjacent camps, were at hand, and realizing the weakness of the attacking party, they set themselves in motion to retrieve the day. Capt. Turner immediately fell back towards the point where his horses had been picketed, with his men in some disorder. A party of Indians were seen crossing the river above the encampment, and about twenty of Turner's men volunteered to attack them. But the enemy proved too strong, and they were driven back upon the main body, having been nearly surrounded while mounting their horses. Another party of Indians coming up from below the Falls, had already attacked the detachment guarding the horses, but were dispersed by the arrival of Capt. Turner. By this time other Indians had crossed from the east side of the river, and gathering courage from added numbers, they attacked the English with great vigor.

1 "Captain Turner, by Trade a Taylor, but one that for his valour, has left behinde him an Honorable Memory * * * * marching all Night, came upon them before Day-break, they having no Centinels, or Scouts abroad, as thinking themselves secure by Reason of their remote Distance from any of our Plantations; Ours taking this Advantage of their Negligence, fell in amongst them, and killed several hundreds of them upon the Place; they being out of any Posture or order to make any formidable Resistance, though they were six Times superior to us in Number; But that which was almost as much, nay in some respect more considerable than their lives. We there destroied all their Ammunition and Provision, which we think they can hardly be so soon and easily recruited with, as possibly they may be with Men. We likewise here demolisht Two Forges they had to mend their Armes; took away all their Materialls and Tools, and drove many of them into the River, where they were drowned, and threw two great Piggs of Lead of theirs (intended for making bullets) into said River."—New and Farther Narrative of the State of New England, p. 240, Published in 1676.

The Retreat.   Capt. Turner, enfeebled by sickness, was hardly able to sustain the fatigue of such an expedition, and was not in a condition properly to meet the changed circumstances of the day. When he found that the savages were swarming about his little command in great numbers, he gave the order to retreat. Continuing with the main body himself, Capt. Turner placed Capt. Holyoke in command of the rear guard, and the homeward march began. At Smead's Island, about a mile below the Falls, was a large Indian camp. Reinforcements from that point soon joined the attacking party, and the entire Indian force fell upon the flank and rear of the retreating squadrons. Here a desperate fight occurred, and it was only through the most heroic exertions that the enemy was repulsed. Capt. Holyoke "received them with resolution and often drove them back." At last his horse was shot under him and several Indians rushed forward. He shot the foremost of his assailants, and by the help of his men escaped. As the day advanced the heat increased, adding materially to the indisposition of Capt. Turner. He soon found great difficulty in managing his horse, and lost all control of his men. When urged to turn back and assist the hard pressed rear guard, or halt till it could come up with him, he replied : "Better save some, than lose all." An English captive, rescued by the soldiers, reported that Philip was ready to fall upon them with a thousand men. This information, apparently confirmed by sharply renewed and more vigorous attacks, caused a panic among the troops. The guides differed as to the best line of retreat. Without an efficient leader, and left to their own resources, the men separated into several parties, arranging themselves under as many different commanders. The route of the English lay beside a thickly covered morass or swamp, which extended nearly to Green River. From this covert the Indians poured a destructive fire upon the weary and disordered army. While passing this thicket, one of the retreating squadrons was cut off by the enemy, and utterly destroyed. A soldier having lost the way was captured, and as was "afterwards ascertained put to death by burning."[1]

1 Hoyt's Indian Wars, p. 180.

Capt. Turner is Killed and Capt. Holyoke succeeds to the Command.

After running the gauntlet of the swamp, the main body reached Green River. Here Capt. Turner, while crossing, near "Nash's Mills," was shot and fell dead from his horse. The command then devolved upon Capt. Holyoke, who succeeded in making good his retreat, through Green River meadows, across Petty's Plain, Deerfield River and meadows, till he reached Hatfield. Throughout the remainder of the retrograde march, the English forces were hard pressed by a numerous and active foe, who followed them to the "Bars," on the road leading to Deerfield South Meadow.

It was a Brave and Courageous Undertaking.

This was by far the most severe fight that had occurred in the valley during the war. Less disastrous to the English than others, but longer continued and more destructive to the Indians. The bravery and hardihood manifested in undertaking an expedition of this kind in the face of such overwhelming numbers, were only equalled by the unflinching courage displayed during the disastrous retreat, when for more than ten miles, every inch of ground was sharply contested with a foe out numbering them more than three to one. The name of Capt. Turner was applied to the Falls, while the real hero of the conflict was Capt. Samuel Holyoke,[1] but his exertions on that occasion cost him his life. He never recovered from the fatigue and excitement of that day. Disease set in, and during the following Autumn he died, full of honor, and yet his name nowhere appears upon the lists of those who were present upon that bloody field.

Loss of the English.

The English lost according to all contemporary reports, thirty-eight men, all but one of whom was slain after leaving the Falls, on the homeward march. About one-third of the men killed belonged to the Hampshire towns. Mr. Sheldon gives a list of forty-one killed and three wounded. Among the former is the name of but one resident of Northampton, that of James Bennet. A printed record of deaths in this town,

1 "And if Capt. Hollioke had not played the man at a more than ordinary rate, sometimes in the Front, sometimes in the Flank, and Rear, and at all times encouraging the soldiers, it might have proved a fatal Business to the assailants."—Hubbard, p. 226.

published in 1824, gives, under the date of May 19th, 1676, the names of fourteen others as "all slain by Indians," all of whom, with the exception of Capt. Turner, were garrison soldiers here.[1] When the troops reached Hatfield, forty-five men were missing, and two mortally wounded. Two came in that night (Friday), two on Sunday, and two more on Monday. One of the latter was Rev. Mr. Atherton, Chaplain of the expedition.

No Approximate Estimate of the number of Indians Killed. It is impossible to estimate with any degree of certainty, the number of Indians engaged in this fight, and equally impossible to arrive at the number slain. The aggregate of Indian losses is variously given. Some of the Indian prisoners stated that four hundred were killed, others gave the number of slain and drowned as three hundred or upwards, still others avowed that only sixty warriors of the Pocumtucks, Nipmucks and Narragansetts, including three or four sachems, and some of their best fighting men, were lost. They also reported that many who were carried over the Falls, got on shore below them. Rev. Mr. Russell puts the number at two hundred, in a letter to the Council at Hartford. He says that they were counted by some of the soldiers. Sylvester Judd states: "It can hardly be credited that men could have found time during or after the fight to count the dead or drowning Indians. It is not unreasonable, however, to suppose that from one hundred and thirty to one hundred and eighty Indians, old and young, perished at the Falls that morning." Most of the slain were river Indians, who twelve months before resided in and near the Hampshire villages. From this disaster the Indians never recovered. It was a crushing blow. They lost more, if only sixty warriors were slain, than in any other engagement during the war, except in the Narragansett fight.

A Serious Blow to Philip. This encounter, notwithstanding its sad ending, was the most serious discomfiture that had befallen King Philip during the war. Not only was the encampment broken up and the

---

1 See Appendix C for list of Northampton soldiers under Capt. Turner.

fishing and planting stopped, but many of the leading sachems were killed. The Indians, however, remained in the vicinity, still menacing the settlements, and delivered one more blow before abandoning the valley forever.

Adventures of Jonathan Wells. It is not strange that the little army under Turner became quickly disorganized. All were volunteers—many of them mere boys —who had never before acted together. They lacked the unity imparted by discipline, and soon lost confidence in their leaders. When the guides differed as to the best line of retreat, they broke up into squads, each man apparently acting for himself. A number of soldiers, who became separated from the main body, wandered for days in the woods. Most remarkable among these adventures were the experiences of Jonathan Wells and Rev. Hope Atherton, both of Hatfield. Jonathan Wells, only seventeen years of age, was one of the party who first contended with the Indians for the recovery of the horses. Soon after mounting, himself and horse were wounded. His own wound was in the thigh, which had previously been fractured and never set, but had grown together. Maintaining his seat with difficulty, he managed to attach himself to such parties as he was able to keep up with. During his flight, he took upon his horse Stephen Belding, a sixteen years old companion. When he came up with Capt. Turner, he represented to him the difficult position of the rear guard, and urged him to turn back to its aid or wait till it could close up with the main body. But the Captain dared not run the risk of losing everything, and all pressed forward. Wells' wounded horse soon fell behind, and when about two miles from the Falls he found himself in company with a wounded man named John Jones. They soon lost sight of each other, and Wells while following Green River towards its source, in attempting to climb a mountain, fell from his horse in a swoon. The faithful animal remained beside him, and on recovering consciousness, he gave the beast its liberty, forgetting, however, to take provisions, of which he had a three day's supply, from the saddle bags. In the evening, to keep off mosquitoes, he built a fire, which spread so rapidly in all directions, that he escaped from it with difficulty. Having filled his wounds with tow and bound his handkerchief around them, he laid down to rest. During sleep he dreamed that his grandfather appeared and told him how to find the right course. Deerfield river was crossed with great difficulty by the help of his gun. Again he fell asleep, and on awakening saw an Indian approaching in a canoe. His gun, half filled with sand and water, was useless, but he presented it at the Indian, who jumped from the canoe and disappeared. Wells then went into a swamp, fearing that other Indians were about, and hid between two logs which rested partly on the water. He heard the enemy searching for him, stepping upon the very logs beneath which he was concealed, and pressing him under the water till he was nearly drowned. Some horse's bones that the crows had picked, and some rotten beans that he found in Deerfield meadow, formed his only nourishment till he reached Hatfield, on Sunday, "between meetings," having wandered forty-eight hours. He was received with great joy by his friends. Four years and more he suffered before his wounds were fully healed.[1]

Narrative of Rev. Hope Atherton.   Rev. Hope Atherton, first minister of Hatfield, volunteered to act as chaplain to the expedition. He became separated from the army in the hurry and confusion of the retreat, and was lost in the woods. In a sermon delivered to his people, May 24th, he described the events of that occasion:

"On the morning that followed the night, in which I went out against the enemy with others, I was in eminent danger through an Instrument of death; a gun was discharged against me at a small distance; the Lord diverted the bullet so that no harm was done me. When I was separated from the army, none pursued after me, as if God had given the heathen a.charge, saying let him alone, he shall have his life for a prey. The night following I wandered up and down among the dwelling places of our Enemies; but none of them espied me. Sleep fell upon their eyes, and slumbering upon their eyelids. Their dogs moved not their tongues. The next day I was encompassed with enemies, unto whom I tendered myself a Captive. The Providence of God seemed to require me so to do. No way appeared to escape, and I had been a long time without food. They accepted not the tender which l made, when I spake they answered not; when I moved toward

1 Sheldon's History of Deerfield, vol. 1, pp. 161 to 166.

them, they moved away from me. I expected they would have laid hands upon me, but they did not. * * * On the same day, which was the last day of the week, not long before the sun did set, I declared with submission that I would go to the Indian habitations. I spake such language as I thought they understood ; Accordingly I endeavored ; but God whose thoughts were higher than my thoughts prevented me by his good providence. I was carried beside the path I intended to walk in, & brought to the sides of the great river, which was a good guide unto me. The most observable passage of providence was on the Sabbath-day-morning. Having entered upon a plain I saw two or three spies, who I (at first) thought had a glance upon me. Wherefore I turned aside and lay down. They climb'd up into a tree to spie. Then my soul secretly begged of God, that he would put it into their hearts to go away. I waited patiently and it was not long ere they went away. Then I took that course which I thought best according to the wisdom that God had given me. Two things I must not pass over that are matter of thanksgiving unto God ; the first is, that when my strength was far spent, I passed through deep waters and they overflowed me not ; * * * the second is that I subsisted the space of three days & part of a fourth without ordinary food."

Mr. Atherton, after wandering from the 19th to the 22d, without tasting food, having managed by some means to cross the Connecticut River, came on Monday morning after the fight, into Hadley. It is claimed that he found his way to Hatfield and not to Hadley.

Rev. Stephen W. Williams, in a memoir of Rev. John Williams, published in the "Redeemed Captive," gives what purports to be an extract from the sermon referred to above. In this quotation he makes Mr. Atherton say : "and after several days of hunger, fatigue and danger I reached Hatfield." A copy of that sermon is extant, and in it Mr. Atherton does not name the town into which he came. Mr. George Sheldon suggests that the fight was on the west side of Connecticut river and Hadley on the east side, that he could scarcely have crossed that stream, and that "the 'deep waters' must have been Deerfield river." In the absence of any testimony on that point from Mr. Atherton himself, there is the evidence of Rev. John Russell of Hadley, who wrote a letter to the Connecticut authorities, on the 22d, the very day of his return, in which he states : "about noon Mr. Atherton came into Hadley." This statement ought to be conclusive.

In reference to the adventures of Mr. Atherton, and to the above sermon, Rev. Stephen Williams of Longmeadow, son of Rev. John Williams, author of the "Redeemed Captive," in a letter to President Stiles, dated June 8th, 1781, says : —

"In the fight upon their retreat, Mr. Atherton was unhorsed and separated from the company, wandered in the woods some days and then got into Hadley, which is on the east side of Connecticut River. But the fight was on the west side.

"Mr. Atherton gave account that he had offered to surrender himself to the enemy, but they would not receive him. Many people were not willing to give credit to his account, suggesting that he was beside himself. This occasioned him to publish to his congregation and leave in writing the account I enclose to you. I had the paper from which this is copied, from his only son, with whom it was left. The account is doubtless true, for Jonathan Wells Esq., who was in the fight and lived afterwards at Deerfield, and was intimately acquainted with the Indians after the war, did himself inform me that the Indians told him that after the fall fight, that a little man with a black coat and without any hat, came toward them, but they were afraid and ran from them [him] thinking it was the Englishman's God."

CHAPTER XXVII.

KING PHILIP'S WAR—CLOSE OF HOSTILITIES.

Reinforcements from Connecticut Arrive. INTELLIGENCE of the fight was immediately forwarded to Hartford, and on the 20th of May, Capt. Newberry, with about eighty men, was dispatched to Northampton. He arrived on the 22d, having left three men at Westfield. The Committees of Militia in the several towns kept their scouts traversing the county in all directions, and the position of the Indians was not unknown. The old encampment was partially reoccupied, and a force of the enemy was still in the vicinity of the Falls.

The People not Discouraged, but Clamorous to be again led against the Enemy. The courage of the people was not dampened by the disastrous ending of Capt. Turner's expedition. They were ready and anxious to go out against the foe at the earliest practicable moment. After the death of Capt. Turner, however, they were destitute of a proper leader and deficient in men. Consequently matters remained stationary during the rest of the month. Rumors of a large gathering of Indians at or near Squakeag, were prevalent, and it was believed that they were making preparations for a demonstration. Two days after his arrival, Capt. Newberry reports in a letter to the Connecticut Council, concerning the state of feeling existing among the people in the river towns. They were in favor of immediate action. The scouts reported that the Indians were apparently dwelling in security, and it was believed that they could again be surprised and effectively punished. Capt. Newberry hinted in his letter that dogs could be used to advantage, but it was not till the next century that Massachusetts enlisted blood hounds to help fight her battles with the aborigines. This suggestion to the Connecticut Council found no favor with the authorities, at least no notice seems to have been taken of it in any reply to Capt. Newberry. He writes from Northampton, May 24th, as follows :

* * * "I find their people very desirous for motion against the enemy, and according to best intelligence, cannot but judge it may be for great advantage to be doing as soon as may be. They seem to be secure by what return the Scouts make, and doubtless are not yet numerous. It is credibly affirmed that there is a considerable party at Quabaug, nigh 300 by the intelligence that is come from thence last night. So that we are apt to think if Maj. Talcott would please to come that way with his forces he might do good service both here & there. We only present the case & leave it to the prudent consideration of the Council, or if the Council see cause to send about 50 or 60 more soldiers and give their consent & advise to the matter we would willingly march up with what of their soldiers may be raised here, and do what spoil we can by Gód's assistance on one side of the river. Our soldiers are very willing to be doing something, rather than lie in garrison ; little is like to be got by garrisoning whatever may be saved. If the Council see not their way by all that is before them to send any More men this way, then we propound for your advice & counsel whether we may not go forth with what is here to be procured & make some trials. Surely I cannot but think it will be disadvantageous to the public interest to defer the matter any long time. We further propound whether it may not do well that Samuel Cross and those dogs he hath may not be advantageous to the present motion, to be sent up, if you see cause to have anything done." [1]

His suggestion that Major Talcott should march by way of Quabaug, was subsequently adopted.

Hatfield Attacked by the Indians. The enemy, however, were still active, and on the 30th of May, again assumed the offensive. About seven hundred[2] of them suddenly appeared before Hatfield. The men were in the fields attending to their usual labors, and at once retired within the fortifications. No attempt was made to penetrate the palisades, but the Indians confined themselves to the work of destruction and plunder. Houses and barns were pillaged and burned, and cattle and horses slaughtered. Unable to make head against the large number of assailants, the inhabitants did not venture to leave the

1 Judd MSS.

2 "The number of Indians may have been 250."—History of Hadley. p. 175.

stockades. Aware that help could come only from North-ampton or Hadley, the Indians posted one party in the meadow near the ferry, and another in ambuscade on the Northampton road. When the alarm was given in Hadley, twenty-five "active and resolute men" of that town went to their relief. Crossing the river in the face of the foe, they effected a landing without the loss of a man. This was a hazardous exploit, successful because of its audacity, contrasting strongly with the conduct of Capt. Newberry, later in the day. Gallantly charging the enemy, they fought their way towards the town, though "encompassed by a swarm of Indians," who lay in ambush behind every tree and shrub. In crossing the river one man had been wounded, but when within one hundred rods of the palisades, five of their number were slain. The Hatfield men, seeing the desperate state of affairs, sallied out to their rescue, or none of them had escaped. In this fight the Indians showed more than their usual courage and recklessness. They constantly exposed themselves, and disputed the ground with great tenacity. Capt. Newberry, at Northampton, was at once notified of the attack, and started to render aid. He somehow learned or surmised that the road to Hatfield was ambushed, and in order to avoid it, crossed the river to Hadley. Here, notwithstanding the example of the twenty-five brave men, he lingered, and could not get to Hatfield "by reason they lay so thick about the landing place."[1] The Indians continued their work of destruction, till satiated with slaughter and pillage, they departed, leisurely driving away all the Hatfield sheep.

The Losses on both Sides. Twelve houses and barns were burned by the enemy, and many horses and cattle wantonly butchered. The English lost five men, viz: Jobanna Smith of Farmington, Ct., Richard Hall of Middletown, John Smith[2] of Hadley, and two of Capt Swain's[3] garrison. Three men were wounded. Hat-

1 Letter of Capt. Newberry, dated Northampton, May 30, 1676.

2 He was the son of Lieut. Samuel Smith and ancestor of Oliver and other Hatfield Smiths—History of Hadley, p. 176.

3 Capt. Jeremiah Swain was in command of the garrison at Hadley, having succeeded to that position on the death of Capt. Turner.

field was not entirely destitute of soldiers at this time. When Capt. Savage was recalled, a garrison of forty-five men, under Sergt. Bardwell remained, and undoubtedly these men were still there, and rendered good service during the fight. The loss of the enemy was twenty-five men, killed during the skirmish with the Hadley reinforcements.

Capt. Newberry Reports Indians about Hadley.

Capt. Newberry it seems had already some experience in fighting Indians, and appears to have learned enough by it to go many miles out of his way to avoid an ambush, even at the risk of putting an impassable river between himself and the enemy. In a letter from Northampton, dated May 26th, he reports that a number of Indians appeared about Hadley at that time; that a man on his way to mill was shot at, and "pr'sently after foure men more being sent foreth as a scout to discover, were also shott at by seaven or eight indians and narrowly escaped. The Indians made sevoral shotts at yᵉ mill but throow God's goodness none was hurt." He went over to their assistance, "Saw many tracks and also where yᵉ indians Lay yᵉ Ambushments as we judged, but could not finde yᵉ Indians so as to make anything of it." He found "where they had newly kild nine horses young and old."[1]

Overtures for Redeeming Captives partially Succeed, but Negotiations for Peace Failing, the War was to be Vigorously Prosecuted.

Negotiations for the recovery of English prisoners in the hands of the Indians, opened in April by Gov. Leverett, were in a measure successful, and a number, among them Mrs. Rowlandson and her children, were redeemed. But the overtures for peace, already described, were without avail, and the Massachusetts government determined to prosecute the war with vigor. During the latter part of May this decision was made known to the Council of Connecticut. Accordingly the united colonies at once organized a formidable expedition to be sent into Hampshire County. It was to scour the country, beat up the headquarters of the enemy and drive them off. Massachusetts proposed to furnish a force of five hundred men, and de-

1 Sheldon's History of Deerfield, vol. 1, p. 171.

sired that Connecticut should send an equal number. The Massachusetts contingent, under the command of Capt. Samuel Henchman, started westward on the 5th of June. On the march he surprised a camp of Nipmucks, and killed and captured thirty-six of their number. He was at Marlboro' on the 9th, but did not reach Hadley till the 14th.

Major Talcott commands the Connecticut Forces. His Movements. The Connecticut forces consisted of two hundred fifty English horsemen, and two hundred Indians on foot, commanded by Major John Talcott. On June 2d they left Norwich, and in five days were at Quabaug, having killed and captured many Indians on the way. It was the intention of the Council that Major Talcott should attack the stronghold of the enemy at Wachuset, but this was afterwards deemed too formidable an undertaking, and the order was countermanded. Henchman also had orders to take Wachuset, but he failed to do so, and the place was left unmolested. Major Talcott learned from his prisoners that five hundred Indians, mostly fighting men, were encamped at Pocumtuck. Fearing an attack upon the river settlements before he could reach them, he pushed forward as rapidly as possible. On arriving at Quabaug, and not finding the Massachusetts men there as expected, he marched at once to Hadley. Head-quarters were established at Northampton, and here he waited impatiently for the appearance of Capt. Henchman. During this period of inactivity his provisions to some extent became unserviceable. He writes: "If you cause any bread to be made for this wilderness work it had need to be well dried; great part of our bread is full of blue mould and yet kept dry from wet." Major Talcott applied to Hartford for ammunition, ordering a barrel of powder and three hundred bullets, and cautioned the authorities to "remember flint stones." A detachment under Capt. Denison was sent to bring up the ammunition, and he arrived with it about midnight on the 10th. This loss of supplies by decay placed a heavy burden upon the community which was necessarily called upon to make good the deficiency. Again he writes: "Our delays in these parts do so exhaust their provision, that it is feared they cannot suit us with bread sufficient for the

field, intending to lay in for one week." Previous to the
11th, Lieut. Leffingwell with "40 or 45 horse," was ordered
to Windsor to bring up what bread could be obtained of
Dea. Moore, a baker at that place. Major Talcott awaited
the tardy movements of Capt. Henchman and the Massachusetts troops for about one week, sending messenger after messenger to hurry them forward. During this interval he reports no movements against the enemy, no attempt
to ascertain whether the statements of his prisoners were
true or false. He did not apparently employ his time in efforts to obtain intelligence of his foes, but remained in
camp, quiet and inactive.

The Plans of the English undoubt- edly known to the Indians, and they assume the Aggressive.   The Indians were undoubtedly aware of the movements of the troops. Both Talcott and Henchman had encountered parties of them, had slain and captured some, while others had escaped. From these they must
have learned enough to surmise that the two detachments
were intended for united action when they reached the valley. Knowing that the English forces had not yet effected
a junction, they devised an attack upon the town of Hadley, hoping no doubt to inflict serious damage before the
concentration of the troops.

The Attack upon Hadley.   On the morning of June 12th, the enemy appeared in force before Hadley, and made a vigorous attack upon the place. Capt.
Swain was in command. About seven hundred[1] Indians,
in two divisions, invested the town on opposite sides. They
were discovered about an hour after sunrise. Three un-
armed soldiers, who went outside the fortifications on the
south side of the town, contrary to orders, were slain. A
detachment was immediately sent out against the enemy,
who fled on the approach of the soldiers.

1 This seems to have been the stock number of Indians in all these attacks. Seven
hundred was reported as the number engaged in the attack on Hatfield, May 30, and
again seven hundred in this raid on Hadley. Mr. Judd says : "there may have been
250 Indians engaged in this enterprise. * * * There were not at this time 700 hostile Indian warriors in Massachusetts."—History of Hadley, pp. 178, 179, note.

The Enemy driven off.

This assault, as well as the one on Northampton, in March, seems to have been skilfully planned. Having drawn the attention of the English on the south side of the fortification and engaged a portion of their forces in pursuit of that division, the Indians fell with great fury upon the opposite side of the town, only to meet a vigorous resistance. A number of them, after setting a barn on fire, went into a house, either for shelter or plunder, but they were so terrified at the discharge of a small cannon, that about fifty of them came tumbling out of it in great haste. The Indians were pursued about two miles, and many of them were reported to have been killed. In truth, however, but three dead savages were found after the fight was over, though some of the captives confessed "that they had thirty men killed that day." This check effectually disposed of the Indians in the valley, and they made no further demonstration during the continuance of King Philip's war. [1]

Capt. Henchman arrives and the Army Marches up the River and down again.

When Capt. Henchman reached Hadley, he had under his command a force equal to that of Major Talcott, and united they formed altogether the most formidable body of troops yet sent into this section. On the 16th, the combined army started on an expedition up the river. Major Talcott moved up on the west side and Capt. Henchman on the east. Not an Indian was discovered. Pocumtuck was searched and the encampment at the Falls thoroughly overhauled, but no enemy was to be seen. A cold north-east rain storm set in, which continued through the 17th. Their arms, ammunition and provisions were much damaged thereby, and on Sunday, the 18th, the army returned to head-quarters. Scouting parties were sent out in all directions, but no Indians could be found. One party came across the body of Capt. Turner, and reported that they saw in several places indications of the burning and torturing of soldiers captured from his army.

[1] It is this fight at Hadley, on the 12th of June, that several historians name as the time when Goffe appeared.

Did the Mohawks Fight against Philip? After the encounter at Turner's Falls, it is believed that the Indians established another camp farther up the river, and from it sallied to the attack upon Hadley. In this connection occurs the statement that while the fight at Hadley was in progress, the Mohawks fell upon and sacked this Indian encampment, carrying away many women and children.[1] These reverses thoroughly discouraged the enemy and they gave up the struggle. Unable longer to make head against the English, they rapidly dispersed, and the troops were

---

[1] How much the Mohawks may have contributed towards the discomfiture of Philip's Indians, is uncertain. Authorities differ relative to their action during the war, and many stories were afloat concerning them. It was stated that Philip, desirous of inciting them to take up arms in his behalf against the whites, killed several members of the tribe, ascribing the deed to the English, but one of them recovering from his wounds, reported the truth, which so incensed the Mohawks that they slew fifty of Philip's men. The Mohawks, it was said, drove Philip from the vicinity of Hoosick River, in the spring of 1676; cut off the party he sent to Canada with prisoners to exchange for powder, and fell upon and despoiled the Indian camp while the fighting men were engaged in the attack on Hadley. Mr. Judd (History of Hadley, p. 182, note) says that the story of killing the scattered Móhawks for the purpose of involving them in a quarrel with the English "does not deserve the least credit," and (p. 183) "There is no evidence that the Mohawks came into New England and killed any hostile Indians." Dr. Palfrey takes the same ground (History of New England, vol. 3, p. 203, note). Referring to and quoting the account, he states: "This may be taken for one of the many wild stories born of the stimulated imagination of the time." On the other hand, Mr. Sheldon (History of Deerfield, vol. 1, p. 177) inclines to the belief that they inflicted serious injury upon Philip's Indians. He credits them with all the acts quoted above, appeals to a letter of Gov. Andros of New York, for proof of the attack on Philip's camp, and argues that these statements agreeing with well known facts, justify the allegations. In a letter of July 5, 1676, Gov. Andros writes that the "Maquas have done great execution on your Indian enemies," without specifying particulars. The Connecticut Council endeavored to find out from him what the Mohawks had done, but gained no information. The statement that they drove Philip's men out of the jurisdiction of New York, is contained in a letter from New York to the Connecticut Council, without date or signature. The report of the sack of the Indian encampment by the Mohawks, is thus detailed by Cotton Mather (Magnalia, vol. 2, p. 573): "And at the very time when the Indians were distressing Hadley, the Maquas fell upon their head quarters and slaughtered their women and children and carried away much plunder with them." Both Hubbard and Hoyt mention the assault by which, according to the former, "many," and according to the latter, "about 50 of Philip's men," were killed, but they place this occurrence previous to the fight at Turner's Falls, and neither of them notices the attack upon the Indian encampment, although Hubbard states, that it was reported by an Indian in June, 1676, that about fifty of Philip's men had been killed by the Mohawks. If Mather's account is true, no wonder the Indians disappeared, for the final victory of the war was won by Mohawks and not by the English. The departure of the Indians from this section, however, is attributed by Hubbard to other causes. He says (pp. 239, 240) that after the repulse at Hadley they "began to be at variance among themselves," and "from that time forward the several Indians that had for so long time been combined together resolved now to part, and every one shift for themselves, and return to their own homes." Attempts were made by the Connecticut Council to engage Gov. Andros to employ the Mohawks against Philip and his allies. This being known to the latter, led them to anticipate an attack, and very probably caused them to cry out "Mohawks! Mohawks!" when surprised at the Falls fight.

soon after withdrawn. Major Talcott returned to Connecticut on the 20th, and a few days after Henchman retraced his steps to the Bay. A campaign of less than a fortnight had virtually ended the war in this section. The Indians were scattered and fleeing in all directions. Capt. Henchman reports that they were in "continual motion, some towards Narragansett, others toward Wachuset, shifting gradually and taking up each others quarters and lay not above a night in a place." The same condition of affairs existed among the river tribes; in scattered parties they roamed northward and westward, and were never again able to make the most feeble demonstration against the whites.

Capt. Swain sends a Detachment to the Falls.

After the departure of Talcott and Henchman with their commands, the only troops here were the few under Capt. Swain at Hadley. On the 28th of June, he sent a force of thirty men up the river to Turner's Falls. They dismantled an Indian fort, spoiled quantities of provisions gathered and stored by the enemy, burned a hundred wigwams on Smead's Island, and destroyed about thirty canoes. Not an Indian was seen. Though parties of them afterwards crossed the valley from the eastward, the native dwellers here never returned to their former habitations.

A Request for Soldiers to guard the Harvesters Denied. Flying parties of Savages Pursued.

Though the Indians had disappeared, it was uncertain when they might return, and accordingly precautions were taken to guard against surprise from any straggling parties. It was feared that those who fled to the Hudson might come back with reinforcements at any time. Without guards it was not deemed safe for laborers to pursue their avocations in the more remote sections. Rev. Mr. Russell wrote to Connecticut, July 11th, asking for a detachment of thirty men to protect the harvesters, while at work in the out-fields, but none could be spared. The suggestion was made that men from different towns join in guarding neighboring settlements while the harvesting was in progress. Nothing of the kind seems to have been done, and fortunately the crops were gathered with-

out molestation. About the 12th of July, a party of Indians passed through Westfield, on their way to the Hudson
River. They were pursued by the garrison and citizens of
Westfield, but escaped. Another party crossed Connecticut River between Hadley and Springfield, on the 11th of
August, with Major Talcott in hot pursuit. He overtook
them at the Housatonic River, killed forty, and captured
fifteen of them.[1]

Capt. Swain Destroys the growing Corn at Northfield and Deerfield. On the 12th, the Massachusetts Council
ordered Capt. Swain to collect the garrison
soldiers from all the valley towns, destroy
the growing corn at Deerfield and North-
field, and then "march homeward." On the 22^d, while engaged in carrying out this order, at Deerfield, six Indians
were discovered. Capt. Swain tried to open communica-
tions with them. Failing in this, and fearing that others
might be near, he hastily destroyed the corn, and returned
to head-quarters. An Indian captive reported that many
guns had been secreted in the vicinity of Pocumtuck. The
next day, Lieut. Hollister and ten men, guided by the prisoner, were sent to the place of their concealment, but it is
not known that any guns were recovered.

Philip flies to his old home, hotly Pursued, and is Slain. This proved to be the last expedition of the
war. Philip was slain near Mt. Hope, on
the 12th day of August, by an Indian of his
own nation, and the war in this state was
virtually ended. Philip and about thirty Narragansetts
left Wachuset, probably about the 15th of June, on account
of a quarrel among his followers. Capt. Brattle, and afterwards Capt. Moseley and two companies of Capt. Henchman's troops, were sent after him. In the latter part of
June news came to Boston that Philip was at Swanzey and
Rehoboth, and on the 24th of July, Capt. Church, the renowned Indian fighter, with a body of English and Sacon-

1 Major Talcott was ordered with his command on an expedition to the eastward,
and marched from New London, July 20th, into the colony of Plymouth. On his return he came upon the trail of a party of fleeing Indians and pursued them. Not
finding provisions for his troops at Westfield, he continued the pursuit with such
food as could be obtained, but in a short time was compelled to send back the bulk
of his force. This was termed the "hungry march," and extended from near the
Taunton River to the Housatonnuc.—History of Hadley, p. 181.

net Indians, was ordered in pursuit. He pressed the fugitives hard and captured many of Philip's men, women and children, among them his wife and son. Capt. Church learning that Philip was at Mt. Hope neck, made a night march on the 11th of August, surrounded the swamp on the 12th, and during the attack Philip was slain, while endeavoring to escape.

Gov. Andros refuses to Sanction an Expedition against the Fugitives who fled to New York.

A vigorous protest was made by Major Pynchon against the recall of the troops. It was feared that the fugitives who had fled within the jurisdiction of the government of New York, would raid the Hampshire towns. The Council consented that Swain's command might join any force that should be sent from Connecticut against these parties. Permission to undertake an expedition into that section was asked of Gov. Andros, and he was also requested to give up six chiefs who had found refuge with the New York Indians. Both demands were refused. Andros replied that he would prevent any hostile demonstrations, and that "some of the Indians had fled to Canada, some to the Senecas, and most other nations have got some."

Capt. Swain Departs.

Capt. Swain and his men departed Sept. 1st, though a few of them remained several months longer. Some of the eastern soldiers became permanent residents in the towns composing the county.

First Capital Punishment in Northampton.

During the closing scenes of the war occurred an incident which has found slight recognition in the annals of the time. The first case of capital punishment in Northampton took place in July, 1676. Absolutely nothing is known concerning it but the bare statement of the fact. The name of the person executed, as well as the nature of his offence, are both unrecorded. That he was a soldier and suffered death for some breach of military law, is all that can be ascertained. His crime must have been of a more than usually reprehensible character, for the man, although condemned by court martial, was not executed in accordance with military usage, but suffered the more ignominious death by hanging. All that can be ascertained concerning this affair is the following extract from "Bradstreet's Journal"[1] :—

"July 1676. A Souldier in yᵉ Garrison at Northampton in yᵉ Collony, was hanged. * * * He was condemned by a councll of warre. He was about 25 or 26. He was but a stranger in this county, prest out against the Indians."

All the forces remaining in this section of the valley in July, were a few under Capt. Swain. The culprit was undoubtedly a member of his company from the eastern part of the colony, and was known to but few persons in Northampton.

1 Rev. Simon Bradstreet was the son of Gov. Simon Bradstreet. He was graduated at Harvard College in 1660, and was settled at New London, Ct. He left a journal of "remarkable providences and accidents general and particular," covering the interval from 1664 to 1683, from which the above is an extract.

CHAPTER XXVIII.

THE LAST INDIAN RAID.

Philip's Death ends the War.

THE death of Philip closed the war in Massachusetts. No treaty of peace was signed, and no stipulations to relinquish hostilities bound either party. Their acknowledged leader slain, many of their chieftains killed or captured, the Indians fled and the war died out. In Maine, the strife began in September, 1675, and continued till April, 1678, when a formal peace was concluded with the eastern tribes. The war in that section was no less virulent and sanguinary than in Massachusetts, but its details do not come within the limits of this narrative.

The constant Apprehension of Evil gives place to a Feeling of Confidence and Security.

For a long time after the disappearance of the enemy, the feeling of dread and uncertainty engendered by the conflict, still prevailed. An inroad from the Indians living in the vicinity of the Hudson River, incited by the fugitives from this section who had fled to them for protection, might come at any moment. Yet as time wore on and none of these forebodings were realized, the great tension of previous years relaxed, and the people went about their usual avocations in security. Relieved of the burden of war, everywhere in the settlements the old routine of affairs was resumed. No longer compelled to set a guard while they labored, or to carry a musket on every occasion, the constant apprehension of evil that so long embittered life in the plantations, had given place to a feeling of confidence and safety. A few of the hardy settlers had returned to Deerfield, and set about rebuilding their

blackened and desolated dwellings; and in all the towns
the work of repairing the ravages of the war was rapidly
progressing.

A Party of Indians **Suddenly on the 19th of September, 1677,**
suddenly fall about eleven o'clock in the forenoon, a party
upon Hatfield. of Indians from Canada, under Ashpelon,
attacked Hatfield. The inhabitants were employed about
their daily labors, some were in the meadows and others at
work upon the frame of a house, outside of the palisades.
Three of those employed on the house were killed at the
first fire; nine other persons were slain, four wounded, seventeen taken prisoners, and seven houses burned. All but
five of the whole number of persons killed, wounded and
captured, were women and children. Nothing more disastrous had befallen any Hampshire town, since the war
commenced. It occurred too when least anticipated. The
war, it was believed, had been permanently closed, and no
hostile Indians were supposed to be nearer than the Hudson River.

They Capture all Having committed this outrage, the enemy
the People at fled. About dusk they reached Deerfield.
Deerfield. Early in that year five men had returned to
their abandoned farms. They were busy erecting new
houses and otherwise preparing to re-settle the place, but
their families were not with them. On the day named,
having just finished their labors, and while preparing the
evening meal, the savage war whoop and the roar of the
Indian guns suddenly awoke the echoes of the evening sol-
itude. One of the men, Quintin Stockwell, ran into the
swamp, where he stumbled and fell. An Indian pursuing,
was kept at bay with an empty pistol. He told Stockwell
that all Hatfield had been destroyed, that great numbers
of Indians were about, and promised to spare his life if he
would surrender. All the men at Deerfield were captured,
and one of them soon after killed. These prisoners soon
joined the party having in custody those taken at Hatfield.
From their first stopping place a detachment was sent back
to Deerfield, which returned with ten horses loaded with
corn and other provisions.

The Raiders with their Captives move Northward.
The Indians at once started northward, Canada being their destination, and on the march the prisoners were staked down at night. At Northfield the party remained a short time, but when scouts reported pursuit by the English, they crossed Connecticut River, and resumed their journey. Halting near Putney, Vt., they went into camp, the direct march to Canada not beginning till about the 20th of October. Just previous to their departure a long wigwam was erected and preparations made for a dance, to be followed by torture of prisoners. Better council however prevailed, and the latter part of the entertainment was omitted.

Soldiers sent up from Connecticut.
A force of fifty men was sent up from Connecticut, under Capt. Watts, to aid in pursuit of the enemy. This company, joined by men from the settlements, followed the Indians some distance above Northfield, but did not overtake them.

Benoni Stebbins Escapes. Hadley Mill Burned. Indian Prisoners suggest Negotiations for the Redemption of the Captives.
On the march from Canada the band of Ashpelon separated, and a portion of it went to Wachuset. He ordered that section to join him at the Connecticut River. Benoni Stebbins, captured at Deerfield, accompanied the messengers. About eighty women and children obeyed the summons, and while on the return march, Stebbins[1] escaped, reaching Hadley, Oct. 4th. A small body of Indians appeared at Hadley about this time, and burned the mill, but some of the party were captured, or surrendered voluntarily. These prisoners pretended that they came to negotiate for the redemption of the captives taken at Hatfield and Deerfield. An arrangement was made for further consultation at Hadley. Sunday, the 14th, was named as the day, and the Indians released. Application was made to Connecticut for assistance and advice. Major Talcott and forty men came up on the 11th. No further attention was paid by the Indians to the proposed negotiations, and on the 20th of Octo-

1 Stebbins "reported that the Indians who attacked Hatfield, were about twenty-seven, including four women, and that they were of the old enemy, formerly neighbors who had fled to Canada."—History of Hadley, p. 184.

ber, they set out on their long journey to Canada. These
were the first of the many English prisoners who afterwards traversed that dreary wilderness. When about two
hundred miles above Deerfield, the Indians separated.
They crossed Lake Champlain on the ice, and after some
delay reached Sorrel. The prisoners suffered greatly on
the march, and were often threatened with death. Lack of
food aggravated the hardships of this wintry journey. For
some time they lived on horse flesh, eating all but four of
the horses stolen at Deerfield. Samuel Russell and Mary
Foote were killed on the way. The others reached their
journey's end in the month of January. Not willing to
be entirely deprived of their inhuman rites, the savages
soon after reaching Canada, in the vicinity of Chambly,
burned Sergt. Plympton at the stake. The surviving prisoners were dispersed among the Indian lodges or sold to
the French.

Reasons for the
Slight and Inef-
fectual Pursuit.
The men of the valley, aided by the troops
from Connecticut, could have easily annihilated the little band of hostiles that so
wantonly attacked the peaceful settlements. Ignorant of
the number of the raiders, fearful of falling into an ambuscade, and unwilling to expose their friends and relatives
to sudden massacre, they quickly abandoned the pursuit,
and the enemy encamped unmolested a little more than
thirty miles from the scene of their depredations, where
they remained a month. After the first few days, the Indians did not fear the English, but were apprehensive of
an attack from the Mohawks. The prisoners were greatly
interested in the overtures for their redemption, and urged
their captors to make some arrangement with the English,
but the counsel of Ashpelon, who was in favor of their return, and who undoubtedly had an eye on the ransom
money, was overruled.

Benjamin Waite and
Stephen Jennings
Redeem the Cap-
tives.
Among the captives taken at Hatfield,
were the wife and three children of Benjamin Waite, and the wife and two children of Stephen Jennings. When the ne-
gotiations with the Indians for the release of the prisoners
failed, Benjamin Waite determined to make an attempt to

redeem them. In this undertaking he was soon after joined
by Stephen Jennings. Procuring from the General Court,
authority to act in the matter, as well as an appropriation to
defray expenses, and armed with letters from Gov. Leverett
to the authorities at Albany, and in Canada, as well as to
the Indians who held the captives, they set out for Albany
on their way to Canada, Oct. 24th. Meeting with unexpected obstacles from the government of New York, they
were unable to commence their northward journey till the
10th of December. With a rough chart of the country
drawn upon a piece of bark, by their Indian guide (who
left them at the lower extremity of Lake George), in an
old patched, birch bark canoe, they passed through Lake
George, crossed Lake Champlain, and reached Chambly
on the 6th of the following January. Here Jennings found
his wife. Soon after at Sorel and vicinity, all the surviving prisoners were discovered. Unable to make any progress in their negotiations without the sanction of the
French government, they proceeded to Quebec. Well received by the Governor, they succeeded, by his aid, in redeeming the prisoners by the payment of two hundred
pounds to the Indians. Intelligence of the success of
Waite and Jennings, and of the probability of their return
with the ransomed prisoners in May, reached Albany,
March 2d, and was forwarded to Hatfield.[1] An escort of
eleven men under Capt. de Luisigney, was furnished by the
French government. On the 19th of April, 1678, they left
Quebec, and on the 2d of May, started from Sorel, on their
return. The government of Massachusetts paid the expenses of the expedition, but did not pay the ransom money.

The Homeward
Journey. Addi-
tions to the
Party.

The journey homeward, with so many
women and children to care for, was pro-
longed and wearisome, and they did not
reach Albany till the 22d of May. Of the
twenty-one persons captured at Hatfield and Deerfield, seventeen survived and returned to their homes. During their
detention in Canada, the party had been enlarged by the
birth of two children: one to Waite, born on the 22d of

1 Count Frontenac, Gov. of Canada, having occasion to communicate with the
government at Boston about this time, sent messengers to Albany, who brought this
information.

2 3

January, and another to Jennings, born in the latter part
of March. These children were named "Canada" Waite
and "Captivity" Jennings.[1] Waite and Jennings had been
absent seven months, and during that time no direct intelligence had been received from either of them. On their
arrival at Albany, Waite and Quintin Stockwell wrote letters to friends at home, which were dispatched by special
messenger. Waite urged his friends to hurry forward with
help, and he would endeavor to meet them at Kinderhook
or Housatonic. He says "We must come very softly because of our wives and children. I pray you hasten them,
stay not night nor day, for y[e] matter requireth great hast.
Bring provisions with you for us." These letters roused
the entire community to immediate action, and men, horses
and provisions were forwarded at once. On Monday, May
27th, having waited five days to hear from home, Waite and
his party started. They met the welcome cavalcade of
towns-people, at Kinderhook. The remainder of the journey
through the woods to Westfield, where they were met by
another retinue of friends and neighbors, and on to Hatfield, was soon accomplished. "The day of their arrival
was one of the most joyful days that Hatfield ever knew."[2]

A Contribution to   Waite's and Stockwell's letters were copied,
pay the Ransom.   carried to Medfield, on the 29th of May, and
                              forwarded to the Governor and Council.
The 6th of June had already been set apart as a day of fasting, humiliation and prayer. An additional proclamation
was immediately issued directing that the letters should be
read in all the pulpits, and recommending that a contribution should be taken up for the relief of the sufferers as
well as their rescuers, "And the ministers are desired to
stir up the people thereto." Contributions were made in
forty-six towns in Massachusetts Colony, and £345.1.6 were
collected. From this donation came the £200 paid to ransom the prisoners.

1 "Canada Waite married Joseph Smith, son of the John Smith who was slain in
Hatfield meadow, May 30, 1676; she was the grandmother of the late Oliver Smith
(founder of the 'Smith Charities'), and his five brothers. Stephen Jennings removed
to Brookfield, and his daughter Captivity, married Abijah Bartlett of that town."—
History of Hadley, p. 185.

2 Ibid, p. 186.

The Government takes Measures to Intercept the Marauders and orders the Towns to build more Compactly.

This sudden and unprovoked attack brought consternation and alarm, as well to the government as to the people in this section. Scouting parties were sent out from Northampton and other towns, and every precaution was taken to provide against further surprise. The Council of Massachusetts sent a communication to the sachems of the Maquas, reciting the outrage, urging them to intercept the party, and offering a reward for the recovery of any of the captives. A letter was also addressed to Capt. Salisbury at Albany, requesting him to send out Indians against the marauders. At the same session, October, 1677, the General Court passed the following order : —

"The tounes in Hampshire being in more hazard of the incursions of the heathen ennemy then some others, this Court doeth order, that each toune there doe endeavor the new moddelling the scittuation of their houses, so as to be more compact & liue neerer together, for theire better deffence against the Indians."

A commission was appointed, consisting of one person from each town in the county, to carry out the provisions of this order, Lieut. William Clarke being designated as the member from this town. Very little action was taken in this direction, and nothing of importance was accomplished except at Westfield.

The Meeting House Fortified.

No immediate action seems to have been taken by the town in regard to additional means of defense on account of this last alarm. But in March, 167⅞, about six months after the raid upon Hatfield, a vote was passed "to fortifie the meeting house and that each squadron are to take care to doe their proportion." Some organization had undoubtedly been adopted when the palisades were erected and the town divided into military squadrons, a part of whose duty was prescribed in this vote. The meeting house was surrounded by a line of palisades, similar to those which encircled the town. This was the second meeting house built in 1661 ; it was forty-two feet square, and stood in the middle of Main Street, a little east of the entrance to Center Street.

The Line of Palisades Renewed and Repaired.

In January, 167⅜, a vote was adopted with only eight dissenting voices, ordering the "making or maintaining of the fortification * * * till a more setled peace Apear." Every man was to "make and maintaine that particular part of the fortification wch is Already Laid out to him and that for what gaps shall Apear for which owners canot be found the same to be made up in A general way."

Peace made with the Mohawks.

While the death of Philip ended the war in Massachusetts, no treaty of peace had been made with any of the river tribes. In fact, none of them seem to have been left in this vicinity with whom to negotiate. The events of 1677 indicated that other and similar incursions might be expected. The Mohawks were an uncertain quantity, and now that Philip was dead and his followers dispersed, they might sweep down upon the settlements at any moment. They had been urged to take up arms against Philip, and under pretence of compliance, had harrassed the friendly or "Praying Indians," as they were termed. Occasional attacks had been made by them upon the friendly Indians, since the death of Philip, and considerable stock had been stolen from the English. In 1680, Major Pynchon had been empowered to go to Albany and conclude a treaty with them. This was happily accomplished and that tribe gave no further trouble.

Rectifying Highways in the Meadows, 167 to 1684.

As the years passed, and the town increased in population, trouble arose in reference to the highways in the meadows, and committee after committee was appointed to rectify their bounds. This was undoubtedly difficult and perhaps embarrassing work, which people in general shrank from undertaking. Without sufficient landmarks, owners of meadow lots, some knowingly and others heedlessly, had been all these years, encroaching upon the highways, and the town at last determined to re-establish them as originally laid out. A committee previously appointed for that purpose failed to attend to the duty, and on the 30th of June, 1675, a committee of ten persons was chosen to

carry out the vote then adopted concerning them.   It seems
to have made no greater progress than its predecessor, for
six years afterwards another vote was passed, appointing
still another committee to finish up the business.   In this
vote it was stated that "there hath bene by" this committee,

"some time spent in order therevnto and the worke not yet fully perfected the Towne considered thereof and were desirous the work should
be finished did therefore this 27 of Febb: 1681 make choise of Sar^t John
King, Isack Shelden Senr Dauid Burt and Samuel Allyn to finish the
said work and to stake out Al such ways as are needfull to be stakt out
And they are to doe it According to the originall as neare as may be
and According to what was done by the Aboue said committe."

Three years later this work seems to have been satisfactorily accomplished, and the town voted that

"for the preserution of the said Hiwaies it is ordered by the Towne
and Selectmen that each proprietor of Land shall set A bound marke
at the Corner of his lot ranging according as the Highwaies are now
laid out by the committe.   And if any man shall neglect to set a
bound marke as aboue shall forfit fiue shilings for euery years neglect
and it is ordered that euery mans bound marke be set up fairly to be
seen by the first of may next vnder the same penalty vnless it can be
made Appear to the selectmen that he be disinabled to doe it."

CHAPTER XXIX.

LEAD DISCOVERED—MINING OPERATIONS.

Western Hampshire Destitute of Mineral Deposits. IN the hills of Western Hampshire are few mineral deposits of great commercial value. The most promising are those containing lead. Veins of this mineral exist in nine different towns in the Connecticut Valley, but in none have the products been sufficient to pay the expense of mining. Most important among them are the mines in Northampton and vicinity. These were among the first known and worked in this country. Though they were said to have furnished material for bullets during the war of the Revolution, and have thus far proved of little other pecuniary value, yet they possess an historic interest that may not be entirely overlooked.

Robert Lyman Discovers the Mine and eastern Capitalists become Interested. The Northampton Lead Mine was discovered by Robert Lyman,[1] a man of roving habits and withal something of a hunter. He spent much time in wandering about the country, and in 1678 or 1679, found indications of lead in

1 Robert Lyman was the youngest son of Richard Lyman of Hartford. He came to Northampton with his two brothers, Richard and John, about the year 1655. His home lot was the fourth from Bridge Street, on the east side of Hawley Street. In the latter part of the century his mind became unbalanced, and he was "distracted," as the records state. In 1692, the court ordered the selectmen to take him in charge and "put out" the children. He married Hepzibah Bascom, his next door neighbor, in 1662, who died in 1690. She was the daughter of Thomas Bascom. They had ten children, six of whom were living when he became crazy. It is possible that disappointment concerning the mine, which did not "pan out" well, and of which he was one of the owners, may have unsettled his mind. In accordance with the order of the court, the selectmen indentured Wait Lyman, as an apprentice to Medad Pumry "to learn the art and mystery of a blacksmith." His master was to "instruct him in reading and writing and learn him some orthodox catechism." At the close of his apprenticeship he was to be provided with "two suits of apparel, £5 worth of tools, and a good bible."

358

the mountains in the western part of the town. So favorable were the representations made by him that capitalists in Boston were induced to investigate the matter. Hezekiah Usher[1] and Richard Wharton[2] became interested and urged the formation of a mining company.

Liberty granted to work the Mine. On the 27th of July, 1679, the subject was brought before the town, and a letter from the above named gentlemen, that occasioned "much discours and agitation," was read. The town being

"generally willing that ye thing that the gentlemen did so commend to the town mite proseed & go forward, did then pas the following vote, viz: that Robert lymon and any other of the Inhabitants of this town and haveing comon Rights in the town shall haue liberty to try and open any place within our bounds and to make vse of any sort of mines or mineralls: provided they atend law: and all thos that do not see cause to Joine in the work do resign and give vp their Rite & Enterest to those that go forward with the sayd mine this was a full & cleer afirmative vote."

This meagre record indicates that the prospect of mining wealth created considerable excitement in the quiet town. The letter of Usher and Wharton had considerable effect in arousing visions of affluence in the minds of the staid

1 Hezekiah Usher was a merchant of Boston, son of Hezekiah, the bookseller, but did not follow his father's calling. He was a successful business man, and left an estate valued at £1615, in which were inventoried 347 ounces of plate. His mining transactions here and at other places, show him to have been something of a speculator. In connection with Major John Pynchon and Mr. William Avery, he received a grant of 1,000 acres of land for mining purposes at Miller's River, above Deerfield, in 1685. He was a member of the company that endeavored, in 1688, to obtain from the crown a monopoly of mines in New England, but the government of Massachusetts opposed the movement, and it failed. At the time of his death in 1697, he practically owned the entire mining property in Northampton, as well as other mineral lands at Concord. In his will he bequeathed one-half his mineral lands, "if any thing considerable should be," to his brother Ting (Jonathan Tyng married Sarah Usher) and children, "and the rest for publique charges—only some what to be pay'd in to the hand of Mr. Dyer, for the reliefe of him selfe and some others that may have lay'd out more than is convenient in minerals, as myselfe at present think I have done." Mr. Benjamin Dyer received for fourteen shares of the Northampton mine, from the executor of Usher's estate, 20s. per share in April, 1697, and 40s. per share in June.

2 Richard Wharton was an active business man, largely concerned in the purchase of lands, and much engaged in work for the benefit of the public. He was called a lawyer by Felt, but Savage says that he was not a member of the profession. In 1671, in connection with John Saffer & Co., he was granted by the General Court, a monopoly in Massachusetts of making pitch, rosin, turpentine, etc., for a term of ten years. Under appointment as one of the Council of Sir Edmund Andros, he thwarted some of his oppressive designs, and went to England with others, in July, 1687, to complain against his measures. He died in London, in 1690. His estate was much embarrassed.

citizens of Northampton, and caused a lively debate in the meeting. Yet there were some who refused to be caught by the glittering prospect, so many that the clerk of the meeting deemed it advisable to add to his record that a "cleer" majority existed in its favor.

A Mining Company Formed.   The subject was in agitation during the summer, arrangements were made for the formation of a company to develop the mine, and a special town meeting was held Oct. 16, at which

"They then voted that al such persons as would Joine in the carrying out of y[t] Designe should meett on the 23: of this instant at Sun an hour high at night To giue in a List of their Names: And to them or to those person that shall then Apeare the Towne doe hereby giue vp all their right in that minne Lying About six miles off on the west side of the Towne."

At the meeting held on the 23[d] of October, a mining company was formed and the following list of names entered upon the records : —

WILLIAM CLARKE SR.	JOHN STRONG	SAMUEL DAVIS
ISRAELL RUST	JOSEPH PERSONS SR.	ROBERD LIMON
JOSEPH HAWLEY	JOHN KING	JOSEPH PERSONS JR.
PRESERUED CLAP	JOHN LIMON SR.	RICHARD LIMON
MEDAD PUMRY	MARTIN SMITH	SAMUEL BARTLET.

Arrangements made for Opening the Mine, 1680.   In the above list will be found the names of some of the leading men of the town; two of them, however, Joseph Parsons Sr., and Martin Smith, soon relinquished all their rights. In July of the following year, an agreement was made between the Northampton owners, and Usher and Wharton, by which the latter became proprietors of one-half of the mine. A contract was drawn up and signed by all the parties concerned, in which it was provided

"that there should be a present and speedy tryall made and prosecuted as farr as £30 will defray the charge and that every partner shall bare and defray his part thereof according to his interest; the one half to be defraied by the said Wharton and Usher."

An overseer or manager was to be chosen by the company, and no one was allowed to sell any share till he had offered the same to the company. This agreement was signed by Wharton and Usher, and by fifteen citizens of Northampton; the names of Ebenezer Strong and Alexander Edwards appearing in place of Joseph Parsons Sr. and Martin Smith. To what extent the labor of opening the mine was carried during the summer is not known, but the company soon discovered that considerable land was needed for its further development.

One Hundred Acres of Land granted to the Mine Own- ers.   It was decided that the mine could not be properly opened without a grant of at least one hundred acres of land, and a petition conveying that modest request was presented. The matter came before the town at a meeting held "Jannery : 2 : 1681," (1682) and the town voted to give

"them one hundred Acres of Land on these conditions, first prouided they make further prosecution of that designe and goe forward in it and make improuement of the Land then the Land to be theirs otherwise to returne to the Towne : 2 if they place inhabitants there it shall be such as the Towne doe Approue of : 3 they are to take the land together : 4 not to come nerer the Towne then the foot of the hills on which the minerals are."

This was not strictly mineral land, though it probably included the lead claim, but was a section of forest in the vicinity of the deposit. In all probability, the prospects of the mine were not at this juncture very flattering.

Location of the Mine.   The vein was situated about six miles from the center of the town, in a south-westerly direction, very near the point where the boundaries of the present towns of North, East, and Southampton join those of Westhampton. In after years the principal work upon it was carried on in the town of Southampton.

Several Northamp- ampton Men sell out to Hezekiah Usher.   Some of the Northampton owners soon became satisfied that the mine was not likely to prove very remunerative, and sold out. Mr. Usher had more faith in it, or else he was ready for a little speculation, and bought all that was offered. The grant of one hundred acres of land to the company was made in 1682, but during the previous summer, six of the fifteen Northampton men had left the company. In June of that year, John Lyman sold his share to Hezekiah Usher for 23s., and before the first of September, Samuel Davis, Ebenezer Strong, Israel Rust, and Joseph Parsons Jr., had parted with their holdings to Medad Pomeroy. During the same month, Pomeroy sold the same four shares to Mr. Usher for £4. Pomeroy undoubtedly acted as agent for Usher in this transaction, for in the deed to him these parties are named as the former owners. On the 8th of May, 1682, Hezekiah Usher gave to Joseph Hawley 45s. for his share or shares. The deed of sale recites that "one consideration moueing Mr. Hezekiah Usher to this agreement [was] that the aboue mentioned Hawley was one of the attorneys apointed by the other ptys and never carying anything to the company acct. for his trouble." In other words, Mr. Hawley was paid that amount for his holding, on account of legal services. This transaction made Mr. Usher the largest owner in the mine. May 12th, 1696, Ephraim Savage, administrator of the estate of Richard Wharton, sold one-quarter part of the mine to Hezekiah Usher for £10 "currant money." While this sale seems to fix the entire value of the mine at that time at £40, the transaction with Mr. Dyer, after the death of Mr. Usher, which occurred the following year, shows that it was then worth £3 per share. Only nine of the original owners retained their shares more than two years.

Col. Pynchon seeks Information about the Mine. Among the persons interested in the mineral deposits, not only in Massachusetts, but of Connecticut also, was Col. John Pynchon of Springfield. He had investments in lead and iron mines in both colonies; in fact, scarce an opportunity to turn an honest penny occurred within the circuit of his trading operations, which he allowed to pass without an investigation. It was not till after Mr. Usher had become owner of a majority of the shares, that Mr. Pynchon began to look into the matter. Possibly Usher offered to sell him part of his holdings, or it may have been that some of the Northampton owners sought to pay their debts to the Springfield trader with lead mining stock. However that may have been, there is no doubt that Pynchon looked the ground over, though no evidence appears that he ever held any pecuniary interest in the mine. The following extract from his account book proves that he thought the matter worthy an examination: "1682, May 2, I let Robert Lyman have a young cow of 3 or 4 years old to discover and show me and such as I shall take with me where his mineral matters are." Whatever else Robert Lyman may have lost or gained through his mineral discoveries, he seems at least to have received a dividend of one cow from his lead mine.

Northampton Men had no Funds to spare for Mining Purposes.

It is impossible to state to what extent the mine was developed by the original company. That they did not realize as largely from it as had been anticipated, needs no demonstration. The capital required for working purposes must have been largely furnished by the Boston owners. Those people who entered upon the undertaking, dazzled by the fascination always attendant upon mineral adventures, soon found that there was a constant necessity for increasing outlay, with little prospect of immediate return. Consequently the excitement soon died out, and could not be substantially revived even by the grant of one hundred acres of land.

The Mine is Abandoned.

Wharton and Usher carried on mining operations here for a few years, but apparently with no great success. No further allusion is made to the mine on the town records, and nothing more can be learned concerning it till the elapse of nearly seventy years. It was probably abandoned soon after the death of Mr. Usher.

New York Parties obtain Possession in 1764.

Sampson Simpson, a merchant of New York, associated with himself sundry individuals for the purpose of developing the mineral resources of the country. He obtained several grants from the crown, one of which covered the mineral lands in Hampshire County.[1]

1 Sampson Simpson, a Jew, was a wealthy merchant of New York. He was one of the company of twenty-four prominent merchants of that city, who in 1768, organized the New York Chamber of Commerce. He was also largely interested in lead mines in Middlebury and Roxbury, Ct.

"On the 5th of October, 1765, Charles Scott, Ethan Allen[1] of Vermont, Benjamin Stiles, Abram Bronson, Israel Bronson, John Frederick Stendall, Thomas Row, and three slaves, Tom, Cato and Cesar, left Roxbury, Ct., for Northampton, took possession of the mines and began to work them."

On the "29th of November, 1776" (probably 1766), Thomas Row, mining captain, writes to Mr. Sampson Simpson, as follows [2] : —

"I have been in Northampton as you desired me and find that part looks as though it would produce a great deal of lead ore ; the Messrs. Bronson think they have cleared £300 besides paying all the charges. I was at three places or mines, or rather veins, which are very large and are mixed very much with ore ; there is another about two miles from Bronson's. This vein is the largest I ever saw (Southampton lead mines), the first stone of ore taken out of the back of the vein, weighed above two hundred weight, almost solid. This vein is open 6 rods long and 4 feet wide, mixed very thick with ore ; there is one part of the vein that is above a foot pretty near solid."

The company purchased and leased land of the farmers in Northampton and Southampton. One of the mines was on the farm of Moses Bartlett, which he sold to the company. It was described in the deed as being situated in Northampton.

William Bowdoin and two others Purchase the Property in 1768, and proceed in its development. Within three years, the above company, after expending a few thousand dollars, sold its sixteen shares to William Bowdoin, brother of Gov. Bowdoin, and two other men from Worcester County, Mr. Bowdoin owning about half the shares. These men engaged in the enterprise with much ardor and resolution, expending large sums of money.

"It was the common opinion that the mine contained silver as well as lead. The excavation [commenced by the former company] was extended to the depth of about 50 feet ; and the water in it was raised by a pump which was worked by water-power. The water for this purpose was brought from the south-western part of Westhampton, two miles or more, and a ditch or canal was dug for more than half that distance. The northern branch of the Manhan river rises in a swamp

---

1 Gen. Ethan Allen, of Revolutionary fame, seems to have been engaged in these mining operations. He came to Northampton, and was afterwards at Southampton. When at the latter place "he exhibited some of those bold and dauntless traits of character for which he was afterwards so conspicuous. He was then also a profane scoffer, though less hardened than in after years. Rev. J. Judd [minister at Southampton], who occasionally visited the mine, once reproved him in a gentle manner for his profane jokes, and found him more circumspect afterwards."—Judd MSS.

2 Hunt's Merchants' Magazine, 1852, vol. 27, pp. 747, 748.

near the line between South and Westhampton, called Sodom swamp. The stream runs northerly almost to the center of Westhampton, then turns easterly, and finally southerly until it joins the main branch of the Manhan at Pomeroy's meadow. In its course north it is called Sodom brook, and in its course south, King's river. It forms about half of an ellipse or oval, and across nearly the widest part of this ellipse the water was conducted from Sodom brook to the mine. It was first directed into a swamp south of the house of Sylvester Judd then followed the course of a small stream that issues from the swamp some distance; it then left the channel of the brook and a trench was dug more than a mile to the mine; this trench may now be seen wherever the land has not been cleared.

"To pound the ore and separate it from the stone, a large building was erected, 30 or 40 rods from King's river, east or north east of the mine, and one-fourth of a mile or more below the saw mill called King's mill. The building with its machinery was called the Stamping Mill, but what kind of machinery was used, or what process the ore went through I have not been able to ascertain. The machinery was carried by water taken from King's mill pond, and carried in troughs over an uneven country, 80 or 100 rods. In some low places the troughs were 20 feet above the ground, and were supported by timbers built up in what is called cob-work. The ore was carted from the mine to the stamping mill.

"The proprietors persevered in their undertaking until the commencement of the revolution in 1775, when it was discontinued, and the stamping mill and the works at the mine gradually went to ruin. The two Worcester proprietors failed, but Mr. Bowdoin, being very wealthy was able to suffer the loss. They had purchased large tracts of land in the vicinity, which were afterwards sold to the farmers for about two dollars an acre. When they commenced, settlements had not been begun in Westhampton; the whole region about the mine was a forest." [1]

Six hammers or stamps were used for crushing the ore, and a smelting furnace was connected with the stamping mill. Many persons were employed, and while the mines were being worked the taverns of Timothy Pomeroy and Major Clapp were quite prosperous. Operations were at their height about 1770, and the mine became quite a place of resort for the whole country round about. [2]

1 Judd MSS., written probably about 1837.

2 In May, 1770, Solomon Pomeroy, Gershom Pomeroy, and Lemuel Boiden, of Southampton, were fined for working four hours on two Sabbath days at the Northampton lead mine in pumping water. Solomon was fined 10s. for each day and costs, amounting to 82s. 2d. He appealed to the Superior Court. The case against Gershom Pomeroy and Boiden was continued till the next court. That against Pomeroy was withdrawn, and Boiden failed to appear, forfeiting his bond. The men probably considered their Sunday labor a work of necessity, in order to prevent the mine from becoming flooded. Lemuel Boiden, or Bowdoin, was undoubtedly a relative of the principal owner.

Nothing further seems to have been done here till after the opening of the present century. In 1807, 1808, and 1809, Perkins Nichols bought of the owners of the land their mining rights, and the Southampton mine came finally into the possession of Perkins Nichols, Thomas H. Perkins, Isaac P. Davis, and David Hinkley of Boston. By consent of the parties, the property was conveyed to Dr. Solomon Bond in trust. Operations were commenced in the spring of 1809, with Luther Work as chief miner. He labored alone for about thirteen years, with no other company than his wife, but finally died of fever contracted by the foul air of the mine. In order to save the expense of pumping the water from the excavation, which had been a serious drawback to the former owners, an adit or tunnel, for drainage, was commenced. It was opened at the surface, some distance below the shaft, and the canal to it was about three-quarters of a mile long. The tunnel itself had to be driven into solid rock for a distance of eleven hundred forty-two feet, and a shaft was sunk for ventilation, to the depth of one hundred fifty-nine feet. It was owing to the perseverance of Mr. Hinkley that the works were continued several years after all the other parties had refused to advance more money to push forward the enterprise. Work ceased upon the mine in consequence of the death of Mr. Hinkley and his head miner.[1]

Prof. Benjamin Silliman, of Yale College, visited the mine about six years after its purchase by the above company.[2] He states that it was found extremely difficult to work the mine on account of the great quantity of water. For this reason the proprietors were induced to abandon temporarily the works at the vein, and commence running a level to it from the foot of the hill, about sixty rods distant. This undertaking had already consumed about four years' time, and would probably require about two years more of constant labor before it could be completed. Except for a few rods at the extremity of the excavation, where the

1 Hunt's Merchant's Magazine, 1852, vol. 27, pp. 747, 748.
2 North American Review, vol. 1, p. 335.

water was kept back by a dam, the bottom was covered with it to the depth of two feet. He gives a vivid description of his passage under-ground in a boat from the mouth of the tunnel to the point where the miners were at work. Except for about one hundred feet from the entrance, which is sand, supported by timber, the whole course of the cavern is through solid rock. He states that several shafts had been sunk to the depth of sixty or eighty feet. The level then extended seven hundred twenty-six feet, and at that point was one hundred ten feet from the surface. Five hundred feet from the mouth of the adit, a shaft had been cut from the bottom upwards, about ninety feet, for ventilation. Three hundred feet from the entrance a small vein of coal had been found.

A New Company Undertakes the Work.

The enterprise was again abandoned in 1828, after the company had expended about $75,000, and for twenty years no further attempt to develop these mineral lands was made. In 1849, the property was purchased by Charles Stearns of New York, who in 1851, again opened the Northampton mine. The following year he sold his right in it to Messrs. Sandford, Coit & Griswold. Mr. Stearns also sold a portion of the Southampton mine to J. R. Sturgis of New York, and the next year the company cleared out the excavation, timbered the old adit, and removed the water from the shaft. Soon after both mines were leased to a company of Cornish miners, who worked them for half the ore raised, and paid their own expenses. The Southampton mine was carried on under the superintendence of Capt. Samuel Pinch, and that of Northampton by John Patterson.

Description of the Mines in 1854, and an Opinion of their Metallic Value, by an Expert.

Prof. J. D. Whitney,[1] Geologist, inspected these mines in 1853 and 1854, and from his work on "The Metallic Wealth of the United States," published in the last named year, the following facts have been gleaned :

"In the spring of 1853, I found the adit level driven in 970 feet. * * * In March last, I found that the work had been stopped, although the end of the level was supposed to be within a few feet of the lode.

1 Prof. Whitney was the son of the late Josiah D. Whitney of Northampton. He was State Geologist of California, was employed by the United States Government in a geological survey of the Lake Superior region, and was afterwards Professor of Geology at Harvard College.

"The same vein, apparently, has also been recently opened a distance of about half a mile in a direction nearly north 20° east, in the town of Easthampton. Here the lode is large, * * but is destitute of ore.

"Farther on in Northampton, about two-thirds of a mile from the last mentioned opening, another attempt at mining was made in 1852 and 1853, but the work was abandoned when I was last there. Here two shafts have been sunk at 80 feet distance from each other, and to a depth of about 50 feet.

"The only place where any work is now doing (March 1854), is at the Northampton Silver Lead Mining Company's mine, next adjoining on the north to the one just described, and distant from it only 200 or 300 feet. Here a shaft has been sunk 65 feet, which is now discontinued, and an adit is driving towards the vein, and will intersect it near the bottom of the shaft.

"Although this lode is so well defined and wide, I cannot recommend its being farther worked. The cost of opening it would be very great, and there is no reason to suppose that it will increase in richness in depth. * * * I should recommend that the Southampton adit be continued to intersect the lode, provided the distance, when accurately determined, be not too great; and unless a considerable change shall be found to have taken place in the character of the vein, all farther attempts at working it should be abandoned."

The Mines again change Owner-ship.
These mining companies appear to have been as sanguine of success as any of their predecessors, but were like them doomed to disappointment. Though the indications seemed to suggest rich deposits, the cost of obtaining the mineral and putting it upon the market, left a very slight margin of profit. Messrs. Pinch and Patterson labored diligently a number of years, but finally, the work was stopped, probably from want of funds, and the mines again became idle. In the meantime the property passed into possession of Edward Anthony of New York; he made no attempt to expand its resources, but in April, 1863, sold the same to Stephen Hills Jr., of New York, who conveyed it to the "Manhan Silver Lead Mining Co." for $500,000. This transfer seems to have covered the mineral lands once owned by Sampson Simpson, then by Wm. Bowdoin and others, afterwards by Perkins Nichols, David Hinkley, and company, and subsequently by Messrs. Stearns & Sturgis. This company, the same year, sold the Southampton mine farm lands, consisting of eighty-three and one-half acres, to Thos. E. Hastings for $50,000. He immediately transferred that and other mining rights of which he be-

came possessed, to the "Hampton Mining and Smelting Co." of Boston, for $450,000. This company proceeded to open the mineral lands, having obtained control of both mines, commencing operations in 1863. Ninety feet of the adit still remained to be completed, and the work was carried on upon a much larger scale than ever before. About one hundred fifty men, mostly French Canadians, were employed. Two powerful steam engines were put into operation, machine and blacksmith shops were erected, and an efficient crushing machine brought into use. The business was managed by Thomas E. Hastings and C. W. Elton, and for two years or more, work at the lead mines was much more lively than at any time since their discovery. Mingled with the lead was a sprinkling of silver, and a few specimens of copper, as well as coal, were found. The output, however, was limited, and after an expenditure of considerable money, the corporation became bankrupt in 1865. The last transfer of these mines that has been discovered was that of December, 1865, when the Manhan Silver Lead Mining Co. deeded to the "Manhan Lead Co." this property, excepting that portion of it previously sold to Thomas E. Hastings, for the sum, as named in the deed, of $950,000. In 1868, this estate was advertised to be sold by the tax collector for delinquent taxes. It is evident that fictitious values were placed upon these mines, as the product did not at any time warrant the considerations named in the several deeds. This was the final attempt at mining in this vicinity. During the last thirty years the adit has become filled up, and the buildings have gone to decay. A few timbers, and the remnants of the iron work at the mouth of the shaft, are all that now remains of the many thousands of dollars expended in developing the lead mines discovered by Robert Lyman more than two hundred years ago.

CHAPTER XXX.

TITHING-MEN—INCENDIARISM—TOWN BELL.

Tithing-men the Meeting House Police.

In Northampton, tithing-men were first appointed in 1678. The true significance of this office was never very clearly understood, though in later years its duties related to but one day in the week—Sunday[1]—and were confined to the meeting house and vicinity. The tithing-man was the person who distracted the congregation by trying to prevent mischievous boys and girls from making a disturbance. He tapped the whispering urchin on the head, jogged the snoring deacon, tortured the ear of the somnolent female, or if the culprit was too distant, rapped sharply on the pew rail, pointing his black rod[2] at the offender. In Massachusetts, the office seems to have been created to search out and punish offenders on Sunday in the meeting house. Afterwards other duties were attached and the tithing-man became an officer of considerable importance, but when neighborhood espionage became unpopular, only his Sunday functions remained, and finally they too were dispensed with, or given to other officials.

Germ of the Law.

Long before the Puritans crossed the sea, the office of tithing-man was established in Old England, but it seems not to have been immediately recognized in the colonies. The first law of this character

1 " The oldest people in New England remember the Tithing-man as a kind of Sunday constable, whose special duty it was, in the old parish meeting house, to quiet the restlessness of youth, and to disturb the slumbers of age."—Johns Hopkins University Studies, vol. 1, chap. Tithing-men.

2 " The law required the tithing-man to have a ' black staffe ' two feet long, tipped at one end with brass about 3 inches as a badge of his office." In early times it is said that the " tithing-man's rod was tipped at one end, not with brass, but with a squirrel's tail. This end was used in awakening women."—Ibid.

adopted in this colony, and which may be considered the foundation of all similar enactments, was passed in October, 1654.[1] "Much disorder in tyme of publicke ordinances, in the meeting howses * * through vnreuerent carriage and behaviour of diuers young psons and others," was the reason assigned for its passage. Certain men were appointed conjointly by the "officers of the congregation and the selectmen," who were to see that these Sunday disturbers were properly punished. They had cognizance, not only of any disorder in the congregation, but "elsewhere near about the meeting house." First they were to use moral suasion and afterwards the magistrates were to take the culprits in hand. No name was applied to them at this time, but they were the first persons empowered "to p'vent pphanation of y[e] Sabboath in y[e] meeting howse." From this beginning was the full fledged tithing-man evolved.

Neighborhood Inspectors Appointed, who are called "Tything-men," and Cages ordered for Transgressors.

Among the enactments of the year 1675,[2] when long hair and silk apparel were prohibited, was one which required the appointment of inspectors of ten or twelve families, who should look after unlicensed liquor dealers, and hunt up and make lists of all idle persons within the limits of their respective districts. This was the second step in the institution of this office, and marks the establishment of a new group of officials, but they were not yet termed tithing-men. Two years afterwards, additional laws were enacted to preserve order on the Sabbath,[3] and the business of enforcing them was delegated to persons who were then for the first time called "Tything-men." They were given the powers of constables, but were to use them only in the absence of the latter officers. The law also provided that a cage should be set up in the market place in Boston, and in such other

1 Records of Massachusetts, vol. 4, pt. 1, p. 201.

2 Ibid., vol. 5, p. 62.

3 "And the select-men are hereby ordered to see to it that there bee one man appointed to inspect the ten families of his neighbours, which tything man or men shall & are hereby haue power, in the absence of the constable, to app'hend all Saboath breakers & disorderly tiplers, or such as keep licensed houses, or others that shall suffer any disorders in their houses on y[e] Saboath day, or evening after, or at any other time, & to carry them before a magistrate or other authority."—Ibid., p. 133.

towns, as the County Courts might designate, to which all criminals were to be consigned. This may be deemed in one sense a special pillory appointed for the punishment of Sabbath breakers. There is no record of any cage[1] having been set up in Northampton, though one was ordered by the court eighteen years afterwards. During the same year the scope of the tithing-man's duties[2] was enlarged, and he was ordered to inspect public as well as private houses of entertainment. In 1679, the law was once more changed and the powers and duties of these officers more fully defined and explained.[3] The selectmen were to take care that tithing-men be annually chosen, and sworn to a faithful discharge of their duties. They had been previously appointed by the selectmen, and confirmed by the court. Now they were "to be chosen in their several precincts," whether in general town meeting or in the separate districts is not stated. Nor is it clear whether or not they were to be nominated by the selectmen and voted by the meeting, or balloted for by the people. Eventually they were elected at the annual town meeting in the same way as other town officers.

1 These cages varied in size, sometimes they were ten by sixteen feet and partly covered, though always barred on one or more sides. One was built at Portsmouth, "twelve feet square, with stocks within it and a pillory on the top," at a convenient space from the meeting house. Persons confined in them were exposed to the congregation, passing and repassing on Lecture days. Cages were in use till 1718.

2 "It is ordered, that those tything men shall be and are hereby appointed and impowred to inspect publicke licensed houses, as well as private, and vnlicensed houses, houses of enterteinement, as also ex officio to enter any such houses, & discharge their duty according to law; and the sajd tithing men are impowred to asist one another in their seuerall precincts, and to act in one anothers precincts wth as full power as in their oune."—Records of Massachusetts, vol. 5, p. 155.

3 "And the sajd tything men are required diligently to inspect all houses, licensed or vnlicensed, where they shall haue notice or haue ground to suspect that any person or persons doe spend their tjme or estates, by night or by day, in tipling or gaming, or otheruise vnproffitably, or doe sell by retayle, w^{th}in doores or w^{th}out, strong drincke." They were also empowered to enter and search all such houses for liquor, seize the same and report the names of the owners to the magistrates for punishment. They were also ordered to inspect the manners of all disorderly persons, and if they will not listen to admonition, were to present their names to the magistrate, who will proceed against them. They were likewise directed to present the names of all "stubborne and disorderly children & servants, night walkers, typlers, Saboath breakers, by night or by day, & such as absent themselues from the publicke worship of God on the Lords dayes, or whateuer the course or practise of any person or persons whatsoeuer tending to debauchery, irreligion, prophaness, & atheisme among us."—Ibid., vol. 5, pp. 240, 241.

Importance of the Office.

Here is the tithing-man fully equipped, clothed with certain powers that give him a rank second only to that of constables. Having in charge the morals of the community, on week days as well as Sundays, authorized to deliver to the authorities for punishment certain transgressors, the tithing-man was in the original conception of the office, a person of no little consequence in the community.

Tithing-men first Appointed in Northampton.

Under these laws, the selectmen of Northampton, in March, 1678, appointed Henry Woodward, John Lyman, John Stebbins, Isaac Sheldon, Sergt. King and Jonathan Hunt, tithing-men, each "to take the charge of inspecting ten or twelve families of their neighbours." These names were presented to the County Court, at the March term, and confirmed. The selectmen were to define the districts within which the appointees were to act. Tithing-men from other towns were confirmed at the same time, and the court gave them the following special instructions:—

"All wch Persons as aforesd being Authorized ye Tithing men for ye Severall Townes as aforesd are hereby required faithfullie to act in inspecting of y^{ir} neighbo^{rs} Soe as y^t sin & disorder be prevented & Suppresd in there Severall Precincts, & as occâtion may be to assist one another & act in one another Precincts dischargeing ye office of tithing men, according to ye law made Novr 1675 may 1677 & Octob^r 1677 they haveing Refference thereunto. And ffurther this Co^{rte} doth now comend to these tithing men & require y^m dilegentlie to take Care y^t ye Sabbath be not Prophaned by Youth or Elder Persons sitting or standing abroad out of their Meeteing houses in ye time of God's Publique Worshipp wher by they are Exposed to many temptations & divertions. But y^t they doe check all such Persons & soe deale with y^m as thereby to Enforce them to goe in within there meeteing Houses where they may attend better and be in sight or otherwise to present there names in Case such doe not reforme, to ye Magistrats Comison^r or other authorities in ye Severall Towns to proceed against such as shall remayne refractory according as they shall see cause. As alsoe to have a vigelent eye upon such Persons y^t shall without just and necessary cause be unseasonablie abroade in ye Evenings from y^{ir} parents & masters ffamielies all Persons being to repaire to their Lodgeings or homes by nine of ye Clocke at night or rather Before. And what Persons Soe Ever they finde faultie herein in being abroade unseasonablie or otherwise faultie they are to admonish & hasten to y^{ir} own proper places of aboade wheather they are to repaire wⁿ it drawes towards Nine of clock at night. And in case of there neglect thereof or non attendance theretoo then to complaine of such to authoritie y^t soe they may be Brought to Better order or proceeded against according to there demerritt."

Here the duties of these officers are clearly set forth. From this time onwards till the commencement of the present century, it is presumed that tithing-men were regularly chosen. The next year they appear to have been voted into office when other town officers were elected. At that time "Capt. Cook, Henry Woodward, Nath. Phelps Sr., Isaac Shelding Sr., Neh. Allyn, Thomas Strong, John Bridgman," were chosen tithing-men and sworn into office "11 of february 1679" (1680). No others are mentioned till 1693, and from that date till 1736, there is no further record of them. After that their names appear each year in the annual list of town officers. The number varied in different years. In some only two names are recorded, and in others eleven seem to have been chosen.

Rev. Mr. Stoddard.   Rev. Mr. Stoddard had now been settled
First Revivals.   over the church seven years. He had already acquired a conspicuous position, not only as a pastor among the clergy of the colony, but in the town and valley, as a man of practical business talents, and excellent judgment. During the Indian troubles he had been recognized, to a great extent, as the mouthpiece of the local authorities, and such of his letters to the government of the colony and others, as are in existence, are recognized as among the most trustworthy records of the time. The attention he gave to business affairs did not, however, detract from or lessen his labors as a minister of Christ. His pastoral work bore rich fruit. An extensive revival, extending over several years, culminated in large additions to the church in 1679, and in 1683. These were the two most noted periods of religious interest during the first half century following the settlement of the town.

A Home Lot granted   Contrary to the usual practice of the town,
him in 1681.   Mr. Stoddard was not granted a home lot at the time of his settlement, though both meadow and upland had been given him. After marriage he resided in the house built for the first minister, eleven

years before he was provided with a home lot.   It consisted of four acres and was situated on the east side of Round Hill, in the vicinity of the present junction of Henshaw Avenue and Crescent Streets.   Mr. Stoddard never built upon this lot, but three years after he bought another, a little south of this grant, which he and his descendants occupied for more than a century.   When this lot was granted to Mr. Stoddard on Round Hill, the rest of the land on that eminence was "sequestered," ordered to "lie in common, and not be given to any particular person or persons."

New Regulations for Granting Home Lots. The necessity of a more compact settlement, so strongly emphasized during the war, as well as the changing condition of affairs consequent upon the steady growth of the town, rendered necessary new regulations concerning the granting of home lots.   This was accomplished in 1680, by the adoption of the following provisions, the last two conditions having been added eight years afterwards :—

"1st that they be taken vp as nere the towne as may bee so that may Joine to some other home lots or to some other Land that is laid out and Joines to other home Lots.   2dly that there be improuement made of them within one yeare after they are granted and cleared within four years of wood and brush.   3dly that they be no preiudice to Laying out of such high waies as the town may haue occation of.   4thly to pay Rates According to custom.   & fifthly that they shall not alienate them till they be cleared.   Sixthly that the home lot shall be kept clere seuen yeers."

A new Route to the Bay Proposed. From Northampton to Boston, the overland journey was long and tedious.   It could be made only on horseback or on foot.   The way was but a single track, marked on either hand by a line of blazed trees.   It was in no sense a road, could not be traversed by vehicles of any kind, and was very properly termed the "Bay Path."   From Northampton the earliest route was to Brookfield, where it joined the path from Springfield, thence there were three ways to Boston.[1] Nothing was transported over this route that could not be carried on horseback.   An attempt was made in 1681 to

1 History of Hadley, p. 45.

shorten this pathway. Cyprian Stevens of Lancaster,[1] reported that a "way might be laid out farr nerer so that A Man might Comfortablely ride from Lancaster in A day and the way far better than the old road by quabage." Stevens offered to lay it out and mark it "for four pounds in money for this Towns propportion." Accordingly a committee was chosen to treat with him. Hadley and Hatfield were also interested in the new way, and committees were chosen by those towns to confer with the Northampton committee. Evidently no arrangement was effected at this time. The suggestion contemplated merely a change in the direction of the "path," not the formation of a cartway. Many years elapsed before a roadway to the Bay for wheeled vehicles was made.

Burning of William Clarke's House. The house of Lieut. William Clarke, situated very nearly on the ground now occupied by the main Smith College building, was burned on the night of July 14, 1681. It was built of logs, and Clarke and his wife were living in it at the time. A negro, named Jack, set the house on fire. He confessed the deed and pretended that it was done, accidentally, while he was searching for food, swinging a burning brand to light his way. Jack did not belong in town; he was a servant to Samuel Wolcott of Wethersfield; was a vicious character, a forerunner of the great army of tramps now everywhere wearying the patience of the public, and had already been before the courts for other misdemeanors. His object undoubtedly, was robbery, and it is not probable that he went about the house searching for food even, with a lighted pine torch in his hands. Very likely after stealing whatever he could lay his hands upon, he set the house on fire to conceal the robbery, or from spite against William Clarke, who was at this time 72 years of age.

Capture and Punishment of the Incendiary. Jack was arrested in Brookfield or Springfield, and was brought before the court in Boston, where he plead not guilty. When his confession was read to him, however, he acknowledged

1 Cyprian Stevens was an early settler and prominent citizen of Lancaster. He probably had occasion to traverse this route frequently, and it was perfectly familiar to him. He may have been a courier, or was perhaps in some way connected with a system of transportation, and he seems to have been afterwards employed by the town in the conveyance of wheat to Boston.

it, and the jury brought in a verdict of guilty. The court believed his confession as to setting the house on fire, but did not credit his statement that it was done carelessly. He was sentenced to be "hanged by the neck till he be dead and then taken down and burnt to ashes in the fire with Maria, the negro." Maria was under sentence of death for burning the houses of Thomas Swan, and of her master, Joshua Lamb, in Roxbury. She was burned alive. Both of these negroes were slaves.[1] Why the body of Jack was burned is not known.[2]

Expenses of the Capture and the Trial.

Peter Hendricks was arrested as an accomplice and bound over for trial. Nothing appearing against him he was discharged. The expenses of this trial were allowed by the court in 1682, and are in part given below:—Joseph Hawley and Medad Pomeroy both went to Boston, on this case, as well as constable Woodward. Mr. Hawley's bill amounted to £3. He was employed fifteen days, for which he charged 30s.; horse 12s.; diet 14s.; shaving 4s. Dea. Pomeroy charged £3 9s. For time and expenses his account was the same as Mr. Hawley's, but he charged 4s. for making irons, and 5s. for time and expenses to Springfield. Constable Woodward had charge of the prisoner here, and took him with Hendricks to Springfield. He charged for two men to keep him (the negro), 2s. 6d.; two days diet 1s. 6d.; two men and three horses to Springfield (in charge of Jack), 13s.; two men and three horses to Springfield (in charge of Peter Hendricks), 13s.; a man to keep Peter, 6s.; and for his own time, 2s. The witnesses received £17 5s., and the total expense of the trial was about £25 3s. At that time £3 in money was equal to £4 in country pay, and the account was allowed on that basis.

1 Many slaves were burned alive in New York and New Jersey, and in the southern colonies, but few in Massachusetts.

2 Tradition has handed down the following items concerning the burning of Clarke's house: The negro fastened the door on the outside so that no óne could escape, and set the fire on the outside. William Clarke injured his hands considerably (pounded them it is said) in his endeavor to escape, and his wife was somewhat burned. John Clarke, grandson of William, a little more than a year old, was brought out of the house and laid beside the fence. There was powder in one of the chambers, and when it exploded the ridge pole was blown across the road, and one end forced into the ground. The negro had taken offence at something William Clarke had done in his official capacity, and set the fire in a spirit of revenge. He was discovered either at Brookfield, Springfield, or near New Haven, and identified by means of a jack-knife in his possession that belonged to the Clarkes.

Another Grant for a Saw Mill Site. The Saw Mill question was again in agitation in 1681, and a site for one was granted to Richard and Thomas Lyman, Samuel Wright and Samuel Parsons. They were to set up the mill within a year, not to damage the corn mill on the same stream, and if they abandoned the privilege it was to revert to the town. The place designated was above Broughton's Meadow.

A Bell Purchased for the Meeting House. Suit entered to Recover the Wheat sent to pay for it. A movement for the purchase of a bell for the meeting house was made in 1682. Previous to this time the only summons to public worship or to secular meetings had been by means of a drum or trumpet. For ordinary town meetings, the drum was sometimes beaten through the streets the night before, and doubtless the drummer "cried" the meeting at the same time. In September the town "votted to haue A good bell purchased that so they might haue it for their vse to call the Towne together on the Lords days and at other times. And Also ordered the Selectmen to Labour to purchase a good Bell that might be herd through the towne."[1] A bell was bargained for and doubtless obtained, yet a drum was used to notify a special town meeting in 1690. Some difficulty occurred in reference to the payment for this bell. In March, 1688, Enos Kingsley was empowered by a vote of the town "to Sue for the wheat sent down By Mr Stevens (to pay for the Bell) which he pretends was spoiled : & so gives no account for it." At the same time the selectmen were ordered "speedily to Raise a Rate for money : so much as will fully discharge what money is still due for the payment of the Bell." This bell was in use for about three-quarters of a century.

1 Throughout New England, in early times, meetings were warned by the drum or trumpet, beaten or sounded in some instances from the top of the meeting house, and in others through the street. Bells were substituted in the latter part of the seventeenth century. It was customary to sound the trumpet or beat the drum at nine o'clock at night. At Hartford in 1677, a hand bell was rung throughout Hartford Street, and at New Haven and in other places, the drum was beaten every morning an hour before day.

Every thing made at Home. First vote concerning a Fulling Mill. The first beginnings of New England were pre-eminently the days of home manufacture. Nearly every thing required for family use was made at the farm house. Carding, spinning, knitting, weaving, were carried on in nearly every household. Not only was the cloth required for domestic needs manufactured at home, but the garments were cut and made there also. Not every farm house, however, had its loom, and the business of weaving was a trade at which men of experience found ample employment. Fulling mills soon became a necessity, and were established in many towns. All the home manufactured cloth, before it was ready for use, had to be dressed and finished. No such mill existed in Northampton for more than a quarter of a century after its settlement. Previous to their erection, cloth was thickened by treading, beating or pressing, which was done at every homestead. The first action in relation to a fulling mill was taken in 1682, when Dea. Medad Pomeroy was granted a "plase to Sate a ffulling mill." It was to be located in "soum conueniant plase," but there is no evidence that he ever established such a mill.[1]

A Highway to the Grist Mill—Green Street. A grist mill was built on the east side of Mill River, near the present site of Maynard's Hoe Shop, in 1677 and 1678, and the town took action concerning a highway to it this year. This road was first laid out on the lot of Henry Woodward (now Smith College property). The committee, however, were dissatisfied with the terms offered by Woodward, and changed the road wholly to land of Alexander Edwards, which joined that of Woodward on the south. He gave it on the condition that a right of way should be granted him on Middle Meadow Hill, and he was allowed to erect two gates on the mill lane, one near his well and the other at the lower end of his orchard. Edwards relinquished his title "so long as there shall stand a mill for the town's use." This was the second lay out of what is now known as Green Street.

1 John Coombs, who came to Northampton, about 1695, was a fuller. He had a fulling mill adjoining Bartlett's mill on the Manhan River (Easthampton) in 1700.

Beer the Universal Drink. Made at Home. Beer was the common beverage among the early settlers of New England, and like everything else was home-made, but after the introduction of apple trees, cider took its place to a great extent. Barley was one of the principal ingredients, and the majority of settlers took care to plant a small patch of it, sufficient for their needs. Many times barley might have been seen growing on the home lot, near the dwelling house, as if it were a most cherished production. The grain was taken to the maltsters and made into malt. Usually the good wife brewed her beer once a week, generally on Saturday, and it was ready to drink on Monday. Very little barley sufficed for a brewing, malt being used only as the foundation. Many other constituents were added to give "body" to the beverage. Wheat, rye, and other grains were employed for this purpose, but barley yielded the largest per cent. of malt.

Land for Malt Houses granted from the Highways. The business of converting barley into malt was carried on by many individuals, but the first allusion to it on the records was in 1684. At that time Jonathan Hunt, who lived near the present residence of Dr. Seymour, was granted permission to "set up a moult house in the highway, by the South end of Samuel Smiths home Lot nere the Line betwne s'd Smiths Lot and William Clarks Lot." Smith's home lot comprised the property of Oscar Edwards and the Burnham estate, and the malt house was placed nearly in front of the latter. With the liberal allotments of land to the first settlers, there would seem to have been little need for further grants from the highways for the purpose of erecting buildings. Malt houses were probably as plenty in proportion to the number of inhabitants, as cider mills have since become.

CHAPTER XXXI.

DIVIDING THE COMMONS—GRAMMAR SCHOOL.

Division of the Commons.

ALL the township not granted to individual settlers belonged to the municipality and was known as "commons." It was used by the community in general, under such restrictions as were prescribed by the town. Sections of these commons had been at different times apportioned among the inhabitants. Very little information can be obtained concerning these allotments; almost the only record being the vote by which they were ordered to be divided. No survey of any portion of the town made during the first century of its existence is now on file. Yet the town exercised strict jurisdiction over these common lands, and at various times adopted by-laws and passed votes relative to their use or occupation. They were the property of the community held for the benefit of all. The meadow only was fenced, the undivided uplands remaining open and free to every one. A portion of these commons was divided in 1684, though the vote would seem to cover all the common land in town. In October of that year "The Towne taking in to consideration an act made by the Towne, Decem^r 12: 1663 concerning deuiding the commons they now did Agree to deuide All the Commons pine Land as well as others." In the previous distribution, pine lands had been reserved.

Rules Adopted Governing the Distribution.

The records do not specify which part of the commons was under consideration, though there is reason to believe that a comparatively small portion of them was divided at this time. All the common land within three miles "compasse of the Towne" had been given to individual settlers

twenty-one years before, as has already been stated, and it
may be surmised that this section lay to the south of the
already existing divisions; in fact, the measurers were ordered to begin in the vicinity of Manhan. An elaborate
method of partition was adopted, but there is no other clue
to the amount or position of the territory apportioned. It
was voted that the

"rule for deuision should be according to persons and ratable estate :
by persons was then Agreed only to be vnderstood as them or such as
were or are now householders. But it was then Agreed vnanimously
that notwithstanding the deuision or distribution made as is above exprest that all such Lands as are by this order to be deuided shall be
free for any vse of any of the inhabitants of the Towne to cut fire
wood or timber or to get stones or to feed cattell on vnless it be on such
Lands as shall be fenced Cleared and improued either for Pasturing or
for Corne." In this case it behooved all who were benefitted by this
division to proceed at once to the betterment of their possessions. A
committee of nine persons was appointed "to view and consider how
many devisions to make and in what manner." At the same time another committee, consisting of the selectmen and three other persons,
was "impowered fully and absolutely to act and do all things and matters referring to the laying out and dividing the commons and granting
home lots as amply and largely as if the towne themselves were mett
together."

At a meeting held in the following February, the committee of nine made

"their Report To the town of their thoughts And conclusions of the
order manner & Rule of Laying out of the Commons : which were as
followeth, viz :

"1. That Every head of A family shall be Accounted at one hundred pounds.

"2. Every Male aboue 21 years of age at 30 pounds : & all males
under y^t age at 15 pounds.

"3. That every person Bring in a true List of all his Land & Rateable estate by the first of march next Ensuing.

"4. That the measurers Go and Begin to Measure At that Division
which is to Be Layd out toward Munhan And Bring In an account of
what Land is there that so it May Be Distributed to every man his proportion.

"5. When that Division is Layd out to Every Man his share then
to Go and Lay out the next Division, And so to go on untill the s^d
work be finished.

"6. That Each man pay for ye Laying out of his own Divisions of
Land.

"7. That Land In the Meadow shall be valued at five pounds pr
Acre."

This report was adopted and measurers appointed, but there is no further record of the distribution.

Brick Making. A New Brick Yard Established. Bricks were not in great demand during the early years of the settlement. They were used mainly for chimneys, for hearths, and sometimes for paving rooms. Few brick houses were built in Northampton till after the commencement of the present century. Francis Hacklington was a brick maker, the first one here of whom there is any record. Previous to 1658, the town laid out land for a brick yard, on the west side of King Street, between Court and Park Streets, and it is probable that all of Hacklington's bricks[1] were made there. In 165⅜ he made a contract with John Pynchon of Springfield, to furnish a quantity of bricks for his new house. They were to be delivered in Northampton. The first brick yard was probably in use for about thirty years. Nothing indicates that bricks were made at any other locality till 1684, when the town "voted to Lay out A brick Lot ouer the mill riuer where Wm Holton & Thomas Limon burnt a Kill Lately." This was on South Street, probably in the vicinity of the brick yard owned for many years by the Day Brothers.

Joseph Hawley again hired to keep School. Mr. Hawley was the town school-master for a period of time extending over nearly eleven years. His first service commencing within a year of his graduation from Harvard College, he was employed almost continuously till 1682, and then occasionally for a number of years. An arrangement was made with him in January, 168⅘, "to keep school one year provided he keep ten moneth certain In twelve. And in case he be absent two moneths to Make up the time at The years end, & to Allow twenty pounds out of the town & as much for his schollers pr week as formerly In such pay as Mr Stoddard is Payd In." As he had already "kept a considerable part of his time," the other members of the board

---

1 In 1661, Francis Hacklington of Northampton, sued Alexander Edwards for "wrongfully attaching a kiln of bricks." Hacklington himself was brought before the court "for breach of the Sabbath in working by carrying bricks at his kiln." As it was his first offence he escaped with an admonition. He was not long a resident of the town.

of selectmen (Mr. Hawley being one) confirmed this agreement, "and desire him to keep out his year." The proviso relative to absence was probably intended to cover the time when he was serving as deputy at the General Court. He was a member of that body in 1685, and was present at the May session. In 1689, Mr. Hawley was again hired to keep school, on the same terms.

Boundary between Northampton and Springfield Established.

This year the boundary line between Northampton and Springfield was definitely settled. When the committee having the matter in charge, reported to the Legislature in 1654, the bounds of the new plantation at Norwottuck, the distance it was to extend westward from the river was omitted, and an attempt on the part of the town to correct the return in 1657, failed. In 1685, however, the General Court rectified the error by ordering the insertion in the records of the court the words, "from the great River nine miles into the woods." This of course rendered necessary the re-establishment of the boundary line between Northampton and Springfield, and committees were appointed to settle the matter. "Deacon Pumrey, Serj. King, Jonathan Hunt & Dauid Birt: were Chosen a committee to Joyn with Springfield Men to Lay out And settle the Bounds Between Springfield and oʳ town." This work was accomplished in the month of April, the committee from Springfield consisting of "John Pynchon, Esq., Samˡˡ Marshfield, Rolland Thomas, & Sergt. Samˡˡ Terry." They met on the 23ᵈ of April, but could not agree about the starting point on Connecticut River, and appointed another meeting on the 28ᵗʰ, when the matter was adjusted, "and soe we parted Lovingly." It appears from a detailed report entered upon the Springfield records,[1] that the commissioners from that town insisted upon establishing the line at "Stoney Brook," while the Northampton men claimed a more southerly point. Both parties finally agreed to the lower site; each having some ground for their contention. "Stoney Brook" was probably the small stream now known as "Roaring Brook," which enters the Connecticut about one hundred fifty rods above the present boundary line.

[1] Life and Times of Henry Burt of Springfield, pp. 172, 173.

Undoubtedly the Springfield men relied on the wording of the Indian deed, which is that the southern line began at "the small River (beelow Munhan) called Sankrohonk, and so up by Quonetticutt river." On the other hand, Northampton insisted on the wording of the report to the Legislature of the committee which laid out the plantation, of which Mr. Pynchon was a member. In that document the bounds are given as extending "doune to the head of the ffalls which are belowe them."[1] "After some debates" the Springfield commissioners "yielded to their Coming Lower" * * "neer about the upper great Falls." Had Springfield established its claim, Holyoke would long since have owned much of that part of Northampton, which it now so strongly covets.

The bounds as agreed upon were to begin at the "great Barr of the ffalls: That is above the first great Barr, next to Northampton," and extend westerly nine miles from the river. Northampton was to have the liberty of fishing at the Lower Falls in Springfield, without molestation, and the use of such highways as they may "stand in need of for transportation to the boating place below the ffalls."

Grants of Land in connection with the above Settlement. Three years after, Joseph Hawley was granted "fourty Acres of Land In the meadow on the south side of Manhan River In the meadow commonly called Lieut. Wilton's Meadow. This was on Consideration of his service In getting the town Bounds setled." Mr. Hawley was not a member of the committee, but was undoubtedly employed to aid in its work. It was the custom of the town to compensate its prominent men for extra services by gifts of land, when money was scarce and land abundant. Other grants similar in purpose may be found upon the records.

Another donation of somewhat doubtful value was made in this connection, as follows:—

"At the same time: the town Granted to Joseph Hawley and Samuell Bartlet All their Right And Interest In or unto that tract of Land Lying at the North Corner of Springfeild Bounds Being halfe a Mile

1 Records of Massachusetts, vol. 3, p. 360.
2 5

square: which Springfeild Claims And In Case they do maintain it And quietly Injoy it: it is to be In Lue of their share In the Commons in that Division: wch they did then Accept."

New Road to the head of Navigation n Connecticut River, 1683-1687.

A new and better highway to the Falls on Connecticut River, was first agitated in 1683. It was a cartway for the transportation of grain. A bridge was to be built over the Manhan River, near its mouth, and the road was to cross the mountain. A committee was appointed to examine and report. They probably reported unfavorably, for in 168$\frac{5}{6}$, liberty was granted to "Joseph Parsons & such others as should Joyn with him, to Make A Cartbridge over the mouth of Munhan river for y^r own proper use provided they Damnifie no mans propriety thereby." In January, 168$\frac{6}{7}$, these men came before the town with a proposition that they would "doe one halfe of it in case the Towne would doe the other halfe of it which motion the Towne excepted of." At the same time a committee was chosen to "view the way from sd bredge to the fall or below" with power "to call out hands to make the way fit for Carting of the provision in the Towne to the vsuall Landing place."

Warham Mather, School-master. A new Method of Payment Adopted.

In 1687, a change in the method of paying the school-master was made, and Warham Mather[1] was engaged as teacher. He had but recently graduated from Harvard College, and was the first native born citizen employed in that work. He was to be paid

"forty pounds for one year in case he keepe Schoole here in the time and to instruct And teach all such children as belong to the Towne as shall come to him. At the same time the Towne agreed to pay in general by way of Rate the Aboue said sum of forty pounds [that] is so much of it as the Schollers readers at three p[ence] pur week and writers at four pence pur weeke did [lack] of Amounting to the Aboue

1 Warham Mather was the second child of Rev. Eleazar Mather, first minister of Northampton. He was graduated at Harvard College, in 1685, and was the first native college graduate of Northampton. In 1688, he was sent to Northfield by order of Gov. Andros, "to be their minister for half a year." The people were to provide for his subsistence and the government was to pay him £15. In 1691, he petitioned the General Court for his pay, and the claim was allowed, but he did not get the money till nine years afterwards. Finally he settled in New Haven, where he held the office of Judge of Probate from 1716 to 1727. He died in 1745.—Judd MSS.

said sum the Schoole master being to keep An exact Account of what Schollers come to him And how long they were with him And the amount [there] of to deliver to the selectmen."

Heretofore the town had paid but £20, and the teacher had as much more as he could collect from the pupils, at prices named by the town. Now the amount was doubled and the town guaranteed its payment. The teachers found much difficulty in collecting their pay from the scholars, and this method was adopted to secure them. Joseph Hawley was employed three months of this year on the same terms, before Mr. Mather was ready. Mr. Hawley was again teacher of the school in 1688, after Mr. Mather went to Northfield.

Origin of Bartlett's Mills.
Samuel Bartlett proposed in 1687, to build a corn mill on Manhan River, below the cart-way to the falls. The town granted him the privilege of the stream for two miles, as long as the "mill stands and goes." The land was to lie next to Mr. Hawley's land. Two years after he was granted thirty acres of land on the south side of Manhan River, in "consideration of his building the Mill there, and in case he take up any Land Joyning to the Mill he is to Injoy it no longer than he keeps up a corn mill there." In this connection is the following entry: "Joseph Parsons enters his desent against the grant too Samuell bartlet above writen." Mr. Parsons was already interested in the mill business, being part owner of a grist and saw mill, on Mill River, hence his opposition to this grant. Bartlett built his mill in what is now the town of Easthampton. A grist mill has been in operation at that place ever since, known as "Bartlett's Mill," and for one hundred seventy-five years its ownership was continued in the same family.

Ferry between Northampton and Hadley.
The route of travel for persons on horseback between Northampton and Springfield was for many years through Hadley, there being no ferry for horses at Hockanum,[1] and no good road on the west side of the river, east of Mt. Tom. All the offi-

1 The first ferry across Connecticut River was established by the town at or near Hockanum.—See p. 61.

cers, as well as others, having business with the courts, from the southern part of the county, crossed the river at Hadley and not at Springfield.

Soon after the settlement of Hadley, a ferry was established across Connecticut River by that town. It was at the lower end of Hadley Street, and was reached on this side by a road through the meadow across "Old Rainbow." In 1664, a committee was appointed by the County Court to consider the matter. The court ordered that Northampton should "keepe ye said fferry in ye place where the above mentioned committee did determine y^t the highways between the two Towns should meet." Northampton was to manage the ferry "with sufficient vessels for attending on ye same for wch they shall have six pence a horse & two pence a person exceptinge for troopers when they shall pass too & fro for Military exercise, who shalbe carried at such tymes for three pence horse & man." Northampton was to provide the ferryman, and until some arrangement could be effected, Hadley was to run the ferry as usual. The committee attempted to change the location of the ferry, but Hadley objected, and the towns agreed the next year, that it should remain at the old place. The same ferryman, Joseph Kellogg, was retained, and for about twenty years no further record has been found. In 1686, a committee, consisting of Capt. Aaron Cook, Medad Pomeroy, and Jonathan Hunt of Northampton, was appointed by the County Court to consider the ferry between Northampton and Hadley. They reported at the June session the following year, that they had agreed with Lieut. Kellogg[1] to keep the ferry "at the usual place," for a year. This ferry was at the lower end of Hadley Street, where the first one was established soon after the settlement of Hadley. The road to it was through the Northampton meadows, the landing place being at the upper end of "Old Rainbow." No ferry-man seems to have been employed at the Hockanum ferry, established in 1658, and it was probably then

1 Lieut. Joseph Kellogg lived in Hadley, and had been appointed ferry-man when the ferry was first established by the town of Hadley, in 1661. He and his descendants continued to keep the ferry for nearly a century, and afterwards it was run by Stephen Goodman, who married a daughter of James Kellogg, grandson of the first Joseph. For many years it was known as "Goodman's Ferry." — History of Hadley, p. 46.

very little used, if not entirely abandoned.   Lieut. Kellogg
was to provide "sufficient boats and canoes for all sorts of
passengers, and good attendance in the day time, and in the
night when necessity required, but not after 9 o'clock for
men in their ordinary occasions." Ferriage was fixed for
man and horse in the day time at "8^d in wheat or 6^d in
money; for persons 3^d each, if one at a time and 2^d if more
than one; after daylight till 9 o'clock double these prices."
At other times at night and in extraordinary storms and
tempests and floods "on such terms as can be agreed upon
between the parties, or the ferry-man might refuse to carry
them." Troopers on service were to pay 3d. in money for
man and horse.   Magistrates and deputies were "freed from
paying, but as they have frequent occasion to pass on the
country's business the ferry-man is to bring his account of
ferrying for such persons" to the court "to be paid out of
the county rates if the court judge meete." This "dead
heading" of the officials was a new feature; previously all
had been obliged to pay.   No other crossing near the ferry
was permitted "except men to their day labor and then not
to encumber the ferry place." Kellogg was allowed one
assistant, freed from watchings and trainings; he was also
permitted to supply "lodging, horsemeat, or refreshing to
strangers in need" and to "take pay as ordinary keepers
do." No other person was allowed to carry passengers
within fifty feet of the ferry, unless the ferry-man neglected
his duty.

Grammar School
Established.

Every town containing one hundred families was required by law to support a grammar school, at which children could be fit-
ted for college.   Northampton must have had the requisite
number of families some time previous to 1688, but took
no action upon the matter till that year.   While the town
was liable to be "presented" at court for not maintaining
a grammar school, it saw fit in the vote establishing such a
school, to base its action upon the higher plane of educational needs, rather than upon the compulsory mandate of
the statute, as is shown in the accompanying vote:—

"At A Leagall Towne meetting January 2:1687 (1688) The Towne
Considering the need of A Schoole master that should be Able to in-

struct children and youth in Learning and so be able to instruct such children as their parents desire to bring vp to Learning to fit y^m for the colledge that so they may be fit ye Service of god in the church or otherwise in the publick voted to giue twenty pounds out of the Towne Stock this to Be beside what may be raised on the Scholers wch shall come to be Taught by him And ordered the Selectmen now to be chosen to procure one that may be suitable for the service Aboue expressed for the year insuing."

Undoubtedly the selectmen carried out the above vote, but unfortunately left no record by which the name of the first grammar school teacher of Northampton can be identified. In April, 1694, a vote was passed in reference to paying Mr. Stevens and Timothy Edwards for teaching school. It is probable that these persons were the grammar school teachers. Timothy Edwards[1] was the son of Richard Edwards of Windsor, Ct., and father of Rev. Jonathan Edwards.

Clark and Parsons'   Samuel Clarke and John and Joseph Par-
Mills.   sons were the owners of a grist and saw mill
                       on Mill River, situated nearly opposite the
present site of the Hoe Shop, in 1685. This grist mill was the one built in 1677, on the west side of the river, and to which a road was laid soon after. When the mill became somewhat dilapidated, and was in great need of repairs, in 1688, Joseph Parsons and William Clarke had liberty to build a new mill. A new dam was erected, and the "mill newly set up" in 1689. When the mill was first built, a bridge was put across the river, but probably high water had carried it away, or it had become unfit for use. Consequently a new highway was laid to the renovated mill in 1689. This highway was on the west side of the river and wholly on land belonging to the mill owners. The crossing was near the present West Street bridge, and the road followed the river bank to the mills. Both of them were on the same side of the river, the saw mill farthest down the stream. This grant seems to have been made to Lieut. William Clarke and Joseph Parsons, but Samuel, son of

1 Timothy Edwards "graduated at Harvard College in 1691, and received the same day the degree of A. B. in the morning and of A. M. in the afternoon, an uncommon mark of respect paid to his great proficiency in learning." He married Esther, daughter of Rev. Solomon Stoddard.—Clark's Antiquities and Historicals of Northampton, p. 216.

William Clarke, was part owner of the old mills, and was undoubtedly proprietor in connection with the Parsonses, of the new one also.   At all events it fell into his hands at the death of his father in 1690.   These mills were partially burned in 1697, but were immediately repaired.   The grist mill was but slightly injured, as it was in use again the same year.

The Lay-out of Park Street Recorded.   In 1688, the street known as "Stoddard's Lane," but since bearing the name of "Park Street," was officially established.   It had been in existence since the settlement of the town, but this was its first official record :—

"The town then (May 21, 1688) Appointed the Committee to order the Records: to Rectifie And Record that Highway that Goeth up to Mr Stoddards house: Between Deacon Phelps & goodman millers lots."

CHAPTER XXXII.

CHARTER VACATED—GOVERNMENT OF ANDROS.

Death of Gov. Leverett. Succeeded by Simon Bradstreet.

BEFORE the life struggle of the colony with its savage foe was fairly ended ; certainly before the wounds received in that sanguinary contest were healed, the controversy with the mother country, which brought about the revocation of the charter, and led up to the revolution of 1688, commenced. Gov. Leverett, who succeeded Gov. Bellingham, died in 1679, a short time before his term of office expired. During his administration occurred the conflict with King Philip, and the contentions with the English government, which brought such distress upon the colony, were entered upon before it ended. His death took place in March, and in May following, Simon Bradstreet, then seventy-six years of age, was chosen his successor, and remained in office while the charter government existed.

Very little Interest in Political Affairs manifested by Citizens of Northampton.

The controversy with England concerning the method of governing Massachusetts, based upon non-compliance with the Navigation Act, the purchase of the Gorges patent of Maine by the Massachusetts Bay Company, the opposition to Randolph, the English emissary, and other matters, resulting in the final abrogation of the charter, seem to have attracted little attention from the town, but are sufficiently pertinent to this narrative to demand a passing recognition. It is not to be supposed, however, that the patriotic citizens of Northampton took no interest in these proceedings. Though primarily absorbed in the welfare of their own little hamlet, still they were conversant with the affairs of the Commonwealth. Thoroughly

392

comprehending the political aspects of the time, they took part through their representatives, and bore their share of the responsibility in the acts of the general government. But the records are silent concerning any of these absorbing topics. Upon the question of sustaining the charter, there was an universal interest manifested throughout Massachusetts.[1]

The Charter Annulled, and the Government of King Charles Established. After a vigorous resistance on the part of the colonists, the charter was vacated by the English Court of Chancery, in 1684. Massachusetts then became the property of Charles II., King of England. As a body politic the Commonwealth ceased to exist. Having made the colony an appanage to the crown, the King proceeded to work his investment for the greatest profit. Col. Percy Kirk, afterwards famous for his cruelties in the Monmouth rebellion, was appointed governor. Though he had not then earned his infamous immortality, still his character for cruel discipline and brutal administration, had become well known, and the people were greatly disconcerted at the prospect. The title of the new governor was to be "His Majesty's Lieutenant and Governor General," and his authority was to be absolute. No longer were the people to have a voice in the government. The colonial assembly was abolished, and the governor was to choose his own council. Quit rents on all lands hereafter to be granted were made payable to the King, and he had power to increase them at will. The Church of England was to be established in Boston, and one of the meeting houses seized for its use. Plymouth Colony, which never had a charter, though every effort was made to obtain one, the provinces of New Hampshire, and Maine, and the Narragansett country, together with Massachusetts, were to constitute the "Royal Province of New England." Several months elapsed before the decree became known in Massachusetts. The first intelligence

1 " The farmers in the country talked of it at their hearthsides; the people of Boston pondered it in their warehouses, discussed it upon the Exchange, and in the halls of legislation. It went with them to the church, and was the burden of their prayers. The clergy were aroused, and their opinions and arguments, on the one side and the other, were given in writing, or uttered in public; and, as they had ever been loyal to the colony, so now for the last time they declared themselves irrevocably in favor of adhering to the Charter."—Barry's History of Massachusetts, vol. 1, p. 473.

concerning it reached Boston in January, 1685. Gov. Bradstreet and the Council immediately convened the General Court. A day of fasting and prayer was appointed and the usual address to the King was forwarded.

Charles II. James II. Prince of Orange.

Charles II. died in July, 1685. James II. succeeded him. Within three years William of Orange landed at Torbay, and before the end of two months, King James was an outcast, having fled to France, never again to return to his own country.

King James Proclaimed and the old order of things continued.

The brevity of the reign of James II. alone prevented the immediate consummation of the designs already formed concerning the government of the new province. So crowded with momentous events were the few years of his reign, that scant time remained for the consideration of that topic. Immediately after his accession to the throne, King James issued an edict, directing that all persons in authority in the Kingdom or the colonies should continue in office till further orders. The General Court was convened on the reception of this mandate, and the advent of the new King was proclaimed. A parade of the officials amid the acclamations of the people and salvos of artillery, sufficiently attested the loyalty of the province. This announcement of the King meant the confirmation of Col. Kirk, and it was believed both here and in England, that he would assume authority. But the rebellion of Monmouth found other and different employment for Kirk, and afforded another field for the display of his brutalities. In the absence of other instructions, the old order of things was resumed in Massachusetts, and the system of government in force under the charter was continued.

Indignation of the People at the Loss of the Charter.

Indignation at the loss of the charter, which they were powerless to prevent, prevailed among the people. Their resentment was shown in the elections of the year 1685, when those magistrates who had favored its surrender, were dropped and others elected in their places. Gov.

Bradstreet was re-elected, but by a much smaller vote than usual. This general indifference and despondency was sharply manifested by several towns which refused to elect deputies. So many of them declined that the court found it necessary to threaten some of them for their neglect. The existing form of government was considered only as provisional, liable to be entirely altered at the pleasure of the King, and while awaiting the change, it was not strange that the elections were without spirit or enthusiasm.

The Proposition of Randolph and the Establishment of the new Government.
Soon after the defeat of the Monmouth rebellion, Randolph bestirred himself in reference to the government of the province. He presented a scheme which, among other provisions, included a joint house of assembly, in which Massachusetts should have twenty deputies, Plymouth and New Hampshire nine each, and Maine eight. Windsor, Springfield, Hadley and Northampton, were to form one district. Opposed by the King, who declared against the house of assembly, the project fell through. Another annual election was held in Massachusetts, in 1686, and the Legislature once more assembled. Within two days Randolph arrived in Boston with the newly prepared programme. Sir Edmund Andros was appointed Governor; Joseph Dudley, President; and William Stoughton, Deputy-President, with sixteen Councillors. There was to be no assembly, and their government extended over the "Dominion of New England," as constituted by King Charles. On the presentation of the commissions of the newly appointed officials, the General Court adjourned to the second Wednesday of the following October. It never met again. Until the arrival of Sir Edmund Andros, the duties of his office fell upon President Dudley, who inaugurated and set in motion the new form of government. His rule was brief, continuing only about seven months. In December, Andros arrived.

Sir Edmund Andros. His Unpopularity and some of his Unsatisfactory Laws.
Emphatic and profuse were the professions of Gov. Andros, relative to the public welfare, and the hope thereby aroused that he would conduct affairs with prudence, awakened a gleam of satisfaction throughout the country. But

the rigor of performance soon thrust aside the mask of profession, and the true animus of the new administration became speedily apparent. Sir Edmund Andros was unpopular throughout New England. His administration was
arbitrary, his demeanor overbearing, his demands oppressive and burdensome.

A tax of twenty pence on each poll, and one penny in the
pound on estates, was among the first of his unsatisfactory
acts. The evident illegality of such an assessment caused
considerable excitement, and payment was refused by a
number of towns. Several town clerks, as well as other
prominent citizens, were arrested, fined and imprisoned for
resistance against this unjust tax. The fees of law officers
were largely increased, causing great hardship in the settlement of estates; land titles were declared defective, and
could be rectified only by the payment of an amount satisfactory to the government officials. Each town was ordered to elect a commissioner, who in connection with the
selectmen, should assess upon the town such sums as the
Governor and Council demanded. He established the
Episcopal Church, and caused a church edifice to be erected
in Boston for that sect. He even interfered with the prevailing system of town government, antagonizing the patriotic sentiment of the people, which above all things re-
sented any dictation in town affairs, by prohibiting all
town meetings but one in each year, "upon any pretence or
color whatsoever." The dislike occasioned by his course during King Philip's war, while Governor of New York, added
to his unpopularity, and it was strongly emphasized by the
suspicion that he secretly favored the Roman Catholic religion. Aware of the general discontent and anxious to
allay it, he made a tour of New England, ostensibly to take
"measures to prevent a second Indian war." He was absent from Boston eleven weeks, visited Hartford, New
York, and Albany, and extended his travels through the
Connecticut Valley. He was at Springfield and Northampton, and made a flying visit to Northfield.[1] About the
15th of October, 1688, he held a meeting of the leading

1 Randolph wrote that he intended to visit those places, but there is no evidence
that he crossed the Connecticut River. The committee for the re-settlement of
Northfield had a conference with him at Hadley by his own request. It would not
have been necessary to have called them to Hadley, if he came to Northampton, for
the majority of them were residents of the last named town.

men of the valley, both civil and military, at Hadley, at which the condition of affairs locally, and the method of protection against the foe, were considered. On the first of November, he issued orders for the raising of a force of six hundred men, consisting of ten companies of sixty men each. John Pynchon of Springfield, was made Colonel, commanding in the valley, and Aaron Cook of Northampton, Major. This was denominated "Standing forces for the defence of the country against the Indians."

Northampton obeys the Laws. These proceedings undoubtedly were of interest to the inhabitants of this town, but the records do not show that any of the questions in agitation came before any public meeting for discussion or action. Unlike some of the eastern towns, Northampton made no resistance to any of the arbitrary enactments of the Andros government. All the laws, except that one having reference to the holding of but one town meeting[1] in a year, seem to have been observed. Two town meetings were held in 1686, and in 1687, and four in 1688. In the latter year, the annual election of town officers, which had previously been held in January, was changed to the 21st of May, and six selectmen were chosen. The next year, the government of Andros having been in the meantime overthrown, five selectmen were chosen to serve "till the first second day in March, wch day the Towne did then order should be the day of election of town officers yearly or till further order be made," and "fully impowered sd Selectmen to order al the publick prudentials of the Towne and to make Rates according to Custom." At the May meeting in 1688, the law in reference to choosing a commissioner[2] to assist in making rates was complied with, and Joseph Hawley was elected to that post.

1 The new law named the third Wednesday in May as the time for holding the annual election for the choice of town officers, and also provided that "it shall not be lawful for the inhabitants of any town in this Dominion to meet or convene themselves together at a town meeting upon any pretence or color whatsoever, but at the times beforementioned and appointed for the choice of town officers."

2 All but three towns in Essex County refused to elect a tax commissioner, or allow the selectmen to levy any rate till it had been appointed by the General Assembly, concurring with the Governor and Council. Ipswich was made an example. Several of her leading citizens were brought before the Court, tried, condemned and sentenced to fine and imprisonment. Such vigorous measures soon stifled all resistance, and the towns submitted.—Palfrey's New England, vol. 3, pp., 526, 528.

Compliance with Law made Difficult and Expensive. The County Court.

For the purpose of controling and profiting by the fees accruing therefrom, certain legal business of the Province was concentrated in the hands of the Governor and his retainers. Probate on estates was to be granted only by the Governor or some person designated by him, and all deeds and mortgages were to be recorded by Randolph and his deputies, who were to be paid by fees. The latter were greatly increased, and the method of transacting the business was rendered exceedingly inconvenient by the necessity of referring all such matters to Boston for final action. In this section the courts were allowed to remain substantially as before. The principal change was the removal of the two clerks, viz. : Samuel Partridge, appointed for the northern part of the county, and John Holyoke for the southern section, and the substitution of James Cornish, the school-master, in their places. The following named persons constituted the "County Court or Court of Pleas and Sessions," held at Northampton, June 17, 1687 :—"Col. John Pynchon, Esq., one of his majesty's council and Judge," and Justices, five in number :—"Mr. William Clarke, Mr. Joseph Hawley, Mr. John Holyoke, Capt. Aaron Cook, Lt. John Allis.

Representatives from Northampton.

During the years before the abrogation of the charter, Northampton was represented at the General Court by her ablest men. Lieut. William Clarke, first chosen in 1663, was returned each year in succession from 1668 to 1677. From 1663 to 1668, the town was not represented, and in 1668, 1670, 1671 and 1677, Lieut. Clarke had a colleague. In 1683 and 1685, Joseph Hawley was deputy, and in 1684 and 1686, Medad Pomeroy represented the town. The latter was deputy when the charter was annulled. He was the last deputy from Northampton, elected by authority of the "Governor and Council of Massachusetts Bay." Under the new regime the house of deputies was abolished. These men, while there is nothing to show that they took any active part in the legislative discussions of the day, were undoubtedly deeply interested in the vital questions then agitating the public mind. It was no light task for the members from this remote section of the province, to attend the sessions of those momentous years, while the struggle to preserve the charter was in progress. The legislative year commenced in May. In 1684, sessions of the General Court were held in six of the twelve months, and the year following it was in session every month from May to and including November, adjourning on the 17th of that month to the next February. It is not probable that the member from this town was present at each of these meetings, as that would require continuous residence in Boston. The town would hardly deem it necessary to be at so great an expense (as each town paid its own representative), nor would the member be willing to remain so long absent from home duties. In some instances the fact is especially noted upon the records that the deputy was chosen for or to be present at one session only.

Andros Arrested and a new form of Government Inaugurated. In February, 1689, news reached Boston of the landing of the Prince of Orange in England, and the flight of James. On the 18th of April, Andros and his principal adherents were seized and imprisoned. This was a bold act. It was rebellion and the perpetrators placed themselves in a perilous position. But they had endured the oppressions of Andros and his subordinates till submission ceased to be a virtue. Those who were prominent in this movement met on the 20th, and established a provisional government, forming what they denominated a "Council for the safety of the People, and conservation of the Peace." Simon Bradstreet, now eighty-seven years of age, was chosen President, and Wait Winthrop appointed to command the militia. In order to strengthen their position with some semblance of authority from the people, summons were forwarded to each town to send two delegates to a convention, except Boston, which was to send four. This convention was called to meet on the second of May. But the time was too short, and only sixty-six delegates responded. All that could be done by that body was to call another convention, and on the 22d of May, representatives from fifty-four towns assembled. All but fourteen of the members had been instructed by their towns to insist upon the resumption of the previous form of government.

The Town Votes for the re-estab-lishment of the old form of Government. Northampton elected but one delegate—John King—probably at a meeting held May 16, 1689. At the same time a vote instructing the delegate, or rather indicating to him the opinion of his constituents, was passed, as follows : —

"Voted vnanimously that yᵉ Govenʳ Deputy Govenʳ and Asistants wᶜʰ were Chosen and Sworn in may in yᵉ yeare 1686, should be Continued in or Reasume their former power for the yeare insuing vnlesse orders come from England to the contrary."

There is no further record. Whatever discussion might have preceded the above action, either among the citizens individually, or at the meeting is unknown. There was practical unanimity of sentiment. The people were loyal and patriotic, ready to acknowledge fealty to the King, and equally ready to depose unjust and tyrannical rulers.

CHAPTER XXXIII.

INDIAN MURDERS—MILITIA—FORTIFICATIONS.

Indian War in
Maine.

Gov. ANDROS' hasty visit to the Hampshire towns was in part occasioned by the disturbed state of Indian affairs. During the summer and fall of 1688, the Indians of Maine, incited by the machinations of Baron St. Castine, and inspired by a spirit of revenge for wrongs inflicted upon them by the whites, fell upon the settlements of that section. They surprised Dover, killed and captured the inhabitants and committed depredations on other towns. Majors Church and Swain were sent against them, and the enemy were driven off. At the commencement of winter, the English troops returned to Massachusetts. While these hostilities were in progress, Indians came into Hampshire County, and several murders were committed.

Abandoned Hampshire Towns Reoccupied.

Soon after the close of King Philip's war, the people along the banks of Connecticut River began to resettle the towns that had been abandoned at that time. The first attempt was made at Suffield, in 1677; Deerfield was permanently re-occupied in 1682; and Northfield again inhabited three years later. A few settlers had returned to Brookfield shortly after, and a new town was incorporated at Enfield, in 1683. Ten years of peace had done much towards the re-establishment of these settlements. All the towns on the river had recovered from the disasters of the war, and were in a thriving and prosperous condition.

Suspicious Indians about. Several Persons Killed.
The native tribes who formerly occupied the country had departed, and only occasionally was an Indian seen in the villages. These were treated with friendliness and courtesy, and apparently the utmost good will prevailed. This state of things was rudely broken in upon during the summer of 1688. In the latter part of July, fifteen Indians, seemingly friendly, some of whom formerly lived in this vicinity, lodged at the house of Thomas Wells, in Deerfield. Their actions were suspicious, but they were not watched. Three days afterwards, July 27th, five friendly Indians were killed near Spectacle Pond, Springfield, and on the 16th of August, six persons—three men, two women and a girl—were killed at Northfield. These murders were believed to have been committed by this band, and the examination of certain Indian prisoners, captured about this time, seems to indicate that this party of savages was hired by the French government of Canada, to kill and capture friendly Indians and whites upon English territory.[1] Considerable alarm was occasioned throughout Hampshire County by these outrages. Major Pynchon immediately sent soldiers to Northfield, and thirteen men came up from Hartford. A garrison composed of men from nearly all the river towns, was maintained there from August to October. In November, a company of fifty-one men, commanded by Capt. Bull, was sent from Connecticut, by order of Gov. Andros, and the place was garrisoned during the winter. The few settlers remaining in the town, consisting of seventy persons, of whom only fifteen were men, petitioned the General Court for help the next year. A committee was appointed to take charge of affairs, and the little handful of people continued to reside there till 1690, when Northfield was abandoned for a second time, and no attempt was made to resettle the place for a quarter of a century.

The Militia of of Northampton Disorganized.
A spirited controversy arose in this town in 1689, relative to the officers of the militia company. Not a little bitterness of feeling was manifested, and the town was divided into parties over the affair. Considerable correspondence passed between

1 History of Northfield, p. 113.

citizens of the town and the authorities, and several letters dealing in sharp personalities were written to the government. After the abrogation of the charter, the local train bands became somewhat disorganized, and little if anything seems to have been done to preserve their efficiency. It appears that an organization had been continued here, but there is little to show that the company was in any condition for service. When Andros established his standing army, and appointed Pynchon and Cook regimental officers for Hampshire County, there was no efficient train band in Northampton.

Major Pynchon's Orders Defied. It is evident that the Northampton officers, Sergt. King in particular, questioned the authority of Pynchon, and a letter written by the latter in November, 1688, indicates that they refused to obey him.[1] The reason why the Northampton men declined to recognize the authority of Col. Pynchon is not clear. It could not have been because he received his commission from Andros. Their own, if they held any, came from the same source. If none had been issued to others, then the officers in command in 1686, were still in authority, and King was not one of them. Pynchon held supreme command in Hampshire County before Andros was made governor, and consequently a double reason existed why he should have been obeyed.

The Militia to be Reorganized. When it became evident that a war with the French and their Indian allies could not be avoided, the provisional government of Massachusetts provided for the reorganization of the militia. June 14th, 1689, an order was passed that all militia officers in commission May 12th, 1686, "not in any way disqualified, should be re-instated in their respective commands, and

1 He says that he "sent away 15 men from Springfield who readily attended; gave orders to yᵉ upper towns for more to make up 50. At Northampton, Sergt. King cavilled about my power, hindered yᵉ Committee of Militia, told them Springfield men would not obey me (though it proved otherwise), that I had no power and they mattered me not and would not give 3 skips of a louse for it, said yᵉ court could act nothing. He and Pomeroy [Capt. Medad] bid defiance to yᵉ old commissioned officers. Such a height of pride are matters come to there yᵗ nothing could or would be done by or from my orders and directions. But they said they would, if any came from Springfield, go as volunteers; and so there went about 10 men that way."—History of Northfield, p. 118.

that all vacancies should forthwith be filled up of meet persons to be nominated by the householders and soldiers of such company." John King, who that year served as representative, brought the order. The contention was whether the old officers—Capt. Aaron Cook, Lieut. Joseph Hawley, and Ensign Timothy Baker—commissioned in 1686, should continue in command, or a new list be chosen. Major Pynchon, as commander in the county, and in obedience to the order of the authorities, renewed their commissions, while the company and the town were in favor of another election.

Medad Pomeroy's Letter concerning the Difficulty. Medad Pomeroy took an active part in this contest and addressed several letters to the authorities in favor of an entirely new selection. In his first letter of July 18th, he represented that Capt. Cook was no longer a citizen of Northampton, that Lieut. Hawley was not satisfactory to the company, on account of the manner in which he obtained the office, and that Ensign Baker had never accepted the commission. The trouble with the last two named officers dated back to the spring of 1686. He represented that the captain at that time promised the company that they would be allowed to choose their own officers. But that he came with commissions for Lieut. Hawley and Ensign Baker, without having consulted the company or the persons whose places were to be filled. [The vacancy in the office of lieutenant was caused by the resignation of Lieut. William Clarke, and the ensign had some idea of removing to Northfield.] The commission to Mr. Hawley was delivered to him at that time, "though the company then manifested much dislike to the same." The ensign then in commission "utterly refused to deliver up the colors to the Captain's order, and men's spirits being at that time in such a heat it was evident it was no season to take the colors away by force." A petition was sent to the General Court soon after, concerning this trouble, but the change in government occurred before any action was taken. When the order came in 1689, he says that the selectmen applied to Mr. Hawley "to see when or whether he would call a meeting for nomination of Captain and other military officers, because then they would take that opportunity to choose selectmen and other town officers." He promised to let them know in a few days, but put the matter off from time to time, "made light of the order, and said it was only a rattle to please fools, as if the court sat in counsel to make rattles to please fools." The selectmen then called a meeting for the election of town officials, and "read the order about the choice of officers." "But Mr. Cook being come to town he and Mr. Hawley made much disturbance in the meeting and opposed the choice of officers as much as possible, requiring them to desist from that matter. But the town did generally vote, and among all the votes there were only 2 or 3 for Mr. Hawley. The men then chosen were, Preserved Clapp, Capt., John King, Sr. Lieut., Ebenezer Strong, Ens., by a very full vote." He closes as follows: "The Inhabitants of Northampton request the council and Representatives to confirm these officers, and did desire me to signify to you the reasons of their acts." Again on the 20th, Pomeroy writes, urging a speedy settlement of the question. He says "for we are in a very great confusion. The town appointed Lt. Hawley and others to look after the militia till further settlement was obtained from the court; but Maj. Cook, and Mr. Hawley, and Timothy Baker say they have sole power of the militia, and grant warrants to press men to go and keep garrison at Squakeag, Indians being seen there of late; which sending men there seems to be a matter which duty and humanity require; but we are in such a state that none regards them nor will any obey them. * * We have intelligence that 50 Indians set out from Albany 5 days ago with a design for mischief," and he again counsels prompt action, suggesting that if the old officers should be appointed he fears "it will be of ill consequence."

Major Cook Replies to Pomeroy's Letters. Major Cook writes a sharp letter of protest, under date of July 22d, in which he handles the private characters of Pomeroy and King with great severity. He asserts that he has not removed from Northampton, but having just married a wife in Hadley, he is residing there temporarily, keeping up his own house in Northampton, to which he intends to return as soon as he has settled certain family affairs. Sergt. King,

he says, maintains that "I am removed, and the orders gave
them liberty to choose a new captain; and with violence,
against the counsel of Mr. Stoddard and other gentlemen,
proceeded to the choice of a Captain and chose a cousin of
mine, sister Clapp's son, that I wish were fit for it, and I
would soon be quiet. He is no freeman and joins to no
church, but a companion with tiplers that would never
submit to our wholesome laws respecting the militia; he
was a sergeant of our company, but sundry times carried
so tumultuously we were fain to discharge him of his
office." Of Mr. Hawley he speaks in the highest terms,
representing that "King and others by secret plots and
acts weakened his hand to his ministerial work; and being
employed in town business, he joined in fining King for bad
fences, by which many poor men had great losses; on
which King railed on Mr. Hawley dreadfully for injustice,
and also since for punishing them for turning their cattle
into the common field before the time, and like unjust acts
as they call them (which I think meritorious and just). On
these accounts, this King stirs up the multitude against Mr.
Hawley to turn him out of his place and choose King in his
room." He also charges King with intoxication and states
that he "carried on so corruptly and wild that by complaint
of some to the Judge of the Assizes, he discharged him of all
office and ordered him to carry a musket in the rear of the
company." Cook accuses King and his party of having
acted since he came "from the court" [having been chosen
representative] "as if all the governor's and councillors'
powers were in their hands to judge and trample on Col.
Pynchon's power as a major." Major Cook also pays his
respects to "one Medad Pumry his brother in E— (I wish I
could say in good)," whom he represents as in no sense a
teetotaller. The new orders of the court concerning the
choice of militia officers, he thinks nullify former orders,
which gave the company power to nominate their own officers.

Major Pynchon's Letter on the Militia Question.

Major Pynchon wrote to the government,
concerning this difficulty, on the 30th of
July. He says that he has tried· to allay
"the disorders and irregularities of the soldiers in this county. * * But there is a party at North-

ampton who fall in with Sergeant King, or rather that are stirred up by him, who do so blow up discontents against their former officers as makes it difficult; and I understand it was carried on in design by himself, that he might be Captain, and it has so far prevailed that he is nominated for Lieut. having so many relations, as I am informed about 32 in that town by marriage and blood, who have holpen it on and are the faction in that business, Medad Pomeroy joining with them and being of them (which also helped him to the place of deputy) when as many of the most sober and considerate men are otherwise disposed." No one, he says, can "justly object against any of" the officers commissioned in 1686. Of Ensign Baker, who it is alleged did not carry the colors on the day on which his commission was received, Pynchon says, that it was on account "of his modesty" and out of courtesy to the old ensign, who " had his discharge because he was removing to Northfield." It was the last muster of the year, the former ensign was acting, and consequently the commission was not given to Baker at the head of the company, but he received it afterwards. Before another training day, came the change in government, and another ensign was appointed "(whom now that party would have to be their new Captain) and so Baker was prevented of officiating in the place till now, that the present authority hath restored him; and I apprehend they are as well with their former officers viz: Capt. Cook, Lt. Hawley and Ens. Baker, * * as they can be, if not better than by the new ones they intend to present." He argues that they were the officers of the company till new ones were chosen, as they were commissioned May 12th, 1686, and had not yet been displaced by the government from which they derived their authority.

The General Court settles the Quarrel by Confirming the former Officers. On the 29th of July, the General Court put an end to the quarrel by declaring that Cook, Hawley and Baker should be the officers of the company, on the ground of their former commission. In regard to Capt. Cook, the court decided that as he kept his residence in Northampton, and was doing military duty there, the objection urged against him on account of removal from that place, was of no value.

It was an Attempt to oust the old Commanders. This controversy, the counterpart of which in various phases of life, is by no means unknown at the present day, grew out of the unsettled state of affairs owing to the change of government. In reality it was an attempt to oust the former officers. Military honors were sought after in those days when titles meant something and gave the recipients position in the community. The decision of the court, however, seems to have been contrary to the desire of citizens, as was proved by their future action. The prospect for immediate active service was imminent, and the Northampton company was soon to have its share.

Sergt. King, the Prime Mover. He Threatens to Sue the Town. Sergt. King seems to have been quite active in this affair, and he undoubtedly aspired to the command of the company. When the "council for Safety," called for the election of delegates to establish a government, Sergt. King was chosen to represent Northampton, as Major Pynchon states, through the influence of Medad Pomeroy (whose daughter his son married). He figures soon after in a suit against the town, incited no doubt by his disappointment in not obtaining the coveted rank in the militia. The town refused "to pay him for going twice to the Bay as their Representative or deputy, And the Towne Looking on it that they sent him But once." King was chosen a delegate to the second convention, which met in May, re-established the old government, and ordered an election of deputies in accordance with former methods of procedure. Northampton held no election under this latter order. A General Court, consisting of the former magistrates and the newly elected deputies, convened in June, and King, evidently acting upon the supposition that he had been chosen deputy for the year, attended that session.[1] Hence the suit. Mr.

1 There is the evidence of Major Cook, that King was present at the June meeting of the Legislature, for he says that King brought the order for reorganizing the militia. That order was passed June 14th, 1689.

Hawley was chosen attorney to act for the town, March 5th, 16⅞⅚. King soon after withdrew the action. Mr. Hawley at once complained of him "for commencing a suit against the town of Northampton and making the town expense, and yet withdrawing his action & did not prosecute." At a session held March 25th, 1690, the court ordered King to pay the expenses of the town, amounting to 24s. 6d. King did not relish this rebuff, and the next year, having been in the meantime made lieutenant, sought redress by renewing his action. Mr. Hawley was again chosen attorney on the part of the town, and the case came to trial at the March term. The jury brought in a verdict against King, who had the costs to pay, amounting to 24s. 8d. He sued for £8.8.[1]

The Death of Capt. Cook again opens the Discussion.

The death of Capt. Cook occurred in September, 1690, and the question concerning officers for the military company, was again opened. Major Pynchon wrote to Mr. Hawley, requesting him to call the company together, for the purpose of nominating a captain, urging them to lay aside "all business prejudice, misguided affection, and act for the public good." He suggested that they might, if they saw fit, nominate an entire list of officers; yet he judged "it would be well to regard what is customary upon the removal of a captain," to advance the lieutenant to the place. His suggestion, however, was not followed. A town meeting was held, and new officers chosen.

Mr. Hawley Petitions the Court, and resigns his Commission.

Lieut. Hawley was requested to accept the position of lieutenant, or rather to continue in it and act with the others in military affairs, but he absolutely declined. In the following petition to the General Court, he describes the proceedings when the new officers were chosen, and resigns his command. The document is dated Dec. 8th, 1690:—

1 In 169⅘, Joseph Parsons presented an account against the town as follows:—" By going once to serve in the Gen'l Court in the year 93, not yet paid for, and twice in the year '94, money £12." If King sued for pay for service at both sessions, then it would seem from the above bill, that the average allowance for attendance upon a session of the Legislature, was £4. It must be presumed, however, that the town objected only to paying King for one session, having acknowledged the validity of that election, and that his charge of £8.8 for the last one was excessive, and may in some measure have determined the verdict against him.

"On Friday night the drum beat for calling the inhabitants together the next morning, but some did not come and others would not vote. Those present being desired to vote, 55 votes were for Sergeant Clap, which was far more than any other had; but whether that be a competent number for such a great town (one half of them possibly being relations) is with your honors to determine. However I would entreat he might be established for I perceive none in this town are like to hold an office of that nature except first being chose by the company; witness Ensign Baker who was commissioned before the change of government & since the Revolution confirmed, could never have the colors delivered to him notwithstanding all the Captain's commands, but were withheld by Serg' Clap, by consent of great part of the company, till his death: yet at this meeting, he laying down his commission & putting the Company to their choice, some said it was well done, and a cry was made let us choose him again, which immediately they did. Thus I have stated the case—am not against Serg' Clap's establishment as things are; but would request the court to dismiss me (though not backward to serve the country) for I am not so fond of a Lieutenant's place after I have lost so many weeks in that service, as to desire to hold it under one who is no freeman & but a 3ᵈ Sergeant."[1]

Militia Officers Confirmed.

Preserved Clapp was confirmed as Captain, and Timothy Baker as Ensign. Mr. Hawley persisted in his declination, which was accepted, and in the following February, John King was chosen lieutenant by the company and confirmed by the court. So Clapp and King obtained the places they sought, and afterwards did good service against the enemy.

A Vote of Amity and Forbearance.

Reports of the capture of Schenectady by the French and Indians, which occurred Feb. 18th, 16$\frac{89}{90}$, spread terror and dismay throughout the province, and immediate steps were taken in all the Hampshire towns to put them into the best possible condition for defense. Existing fortifications were repaired and strengthened, and such towns as were destitute at once set about constructing them. On the 26th of February, the following vote was passed. It shows that the people of Northampton, though but recently bitterly contending about military officers, were thoroughly aroused and ready to acquiesce in any measure considered necessary for the security of the town:—

1 Judd MSS.

"Whereas the concurance of And Agreement as one of Any Society in publick concerns is the strenth (And vnder god) y⁶ safety And p͏ʳservation of y⁶ same, and yᵗ y⁶ consideration that a condecending Spirit one to anther in matters of publick Affairs wherein both the honour of god and our owne Safty is Aduanced: we therefore do Agree and bind o͏ʳselves to this, viz: that the maior vote of y⁶ Towne shall detirmine in or as to making of fortification for o͏ʳ defence Against the enemy that tho we as to o͏ʳ owne Apprehentions or Judgment Are of Another p͏ʳsuasion: yet notwithstanding we will Aquiesse And rest satisfied with the detirmination of the maior vote of the Towne And readily to y⁶ vtmost of o͏ʳ power doe and p͏ʳforme each of vs o͏ʳ parts of y⁶ same: Voted vnanimously or very fully the day Above sd."

The old Fortifications Deemed Inadequate, and a new Line decided upon. Only an emergency of great moment could have called out an unanimous vote like the above. But it seems to have been needed, more especially in view of the spiteful controversy concerning military affairs that had been in progress for more than a year, and was then not fully ended. It paved the way for the order providing better and more permanent fortifications, which was adopted the following March. The old ones erected some fifteen years before, and repaired in 1677, had fallen into decay. It is true the meeting house had been fortified, but doubtless the palisades around that building had since been removed. During the era of peace and prosperity that followed King Philip's war, many new houses had been built, particularly west of the meeting house. Consequently the area to be enclosed within the fortifications had been much increased, which of course added greatly to the expenditure. The vote ordering these fortifications was passed in March, and describes the line upon which they were established sufficiently to trace them with considerable accuracy at the present time:—

"At A Towne Meetting, March y⁶ 5ᵗʰ 16⁸⁹⁄₉₀ The Towne Considering of y⁶ danger they were in of being Asalted by An Enemie did then Agree to fortifie the Towne in and as for the Compasse of it did Agree that begining At Allexander Edwards his house the fortification should run from thence to Ensigne bakers and so to Deacon Hunts and from thence to M͏ʳ Stoderds And so to John Kings and from thence to meete with the Line where the old fortification formerly stood in the most conuenient place And so to run round the towne y⁶ rest of y⁶ way About the place where it formerly was standing. And for the rule w͏ᶜʰ was to be Attended in making vp of sd fortification it was then Agreed that one

halfe of it was to be done by male p^rsons from 16 years old And vp-
ward.   And married p^rsons should doe three rods Apeice for their
heads And single p^rsons two rods Apeice for their heads And the other
halfe to be done by estats according to each mans due proportion ; only
those p^rsons wch Liue with out the Line or Compasse of the fortification
Aboue sd are wholy to be free from making Any part of sd fortification or paing toward ye same.   But in case Any of them shall see reason to Come in within the Aboue sd fortification that then eury p^rson
or p^rsons are to doe their part of it Abating one-third part Acording to
the rule Aboue sd."

Position of the New   A committee consisting of "John King
Fortification.   Sr., John Parson, and Medad Pumry,"
were chosen to "Lay out the fortification."
To trace the line of this palisade is comparatively easy.
Alexander Edwards lived on West Street, at its junction
with Green.   He owned nearly all the property lying between West Street and Mill River, south of Green Street.
His house stood on the north-easterly corner of the lot, in
the vicinity of "Plymouth Hall."   Ensign Baker lived on
Elm Street.   His lot included the land from the east line of
the Cooper estate to Mill River, and his house was in the
vicinity of the brick house, formerly owned by Gen. Lyman (now Miss Tucker's).   Dea. Hunt's house was very
near that now owned by A. McCallum.   Mr. Stoddard lived
on what is now the H. R. Hinckley homestead, and John
King lived on King Street, and owned what are now known
as the Dr. Fisk and French Catholic Church estates.
The line of fortification was erected along the rear of
Smith College administration building and the President's
house, to Miss Tucker's, thence a little to the east of Henshaw Avenue, to and beyond Mr. Hinckley's, and probably
followed a course just north of Park Street, to King's homestead.   Where it was located from the house of John King
to Mill River, is not definitely stated.   It was supposed to
have encircled the burying ground, but a certain fact, heretofore noted, seems to antagonize such a belief.   Possibly
it was continued along the rear of the Market and Hawley
Street lots, reaching the river near the lower end of Pleasant Street.   From that point it must have followed the
stream as far as the homestead of S. L. Parsons, and on to
the place of beginning.

Its Length.   This line of defense enclosed a much larger area than the previous one.   Its entire length, if it encircled the burying ground, was something more than two miles, and its construction must have involved much labor and expense.   While the old palisade, where it extended through the more thickly settled portion of the town may have been demolished, it is probable that the portion of it which was erected along the banks of the river was in a fair state of preservation.   This fortification was similar to the one which was built in 167⅝.   That had been thoroughly tested, and there was every reason to believe that this one would prove equally effective.

CHAPTER XXXIV.

CAPT. COOK—TAXES—NEW CHARTER—SCHOOLS.

Wide-spread and Virulent Malady. Fatal to many Prominent Men. MUCH sickness prevailed throughout the colony of Connecticut in the year 1689. Springfield was invaded by it, and so many persons disabled, that harvesting had to be partially abandoned. Northampton also suffered to some extent, the number of deaths from disease being greater than in any other year since the settlement began. In the two following years, however, the epidemic, as it might be called, found its way up the river, and among its victims were many prominent and influential men. During the summer of 1690, one hundred persons were at one time sick at Deerfield, and four-score at Northampton.[1] The disease was also fatal and wide-spread, the next year. During these two years, "agues and fevers" prevailed in all the river towns. The names of twenty-five persons are recorded upon the death roll of Northampton in 1690, and in 1691, twenty-three others were added. Among them were some of the older and most eminent citizens of the town. Included in the list are the names of William Miller, Lieut. William Clarke, Samuel Davis, Lieut. John Lyman, Alexander Edwards, Major Aaron Cook, David Burt, and William Janes, in 1690; William Holton, Dea. Jonathan Hunt, and Caleb Pomeroy, in 1691. These eleven men were among the original settlers of the town, and had been identified with its interests from the first. Several of them were eighty years of age and upwards, but most of them were in the prime of life, and all were still active in promoting the welfare of the place. Major Cook was captain of the military company; Dea. Hunt was one of the selectmen

1 Peter Tilton's Letter to Gov. Bradstreet, dated Hadley, August 23d, 1690.

and representative to the General Court; and William Clarke, whose monograph has been previously spread upon these pages, may be truthfully deemed the father of the town. The loss of so many of its leading citizens must have been a sad blow to the community, especially when questions of such grave importance were coming to the front, and dangers so threatening menaced state and town.

Aaron Cook Prominent among the first settlers of the town was Major Aaron Cook, whose death occurred on the 5th of September, 1690. A man of more than ordinary energy and ability, he took a leading part, not only in the settlement of Northampton, but in that of three other New England towns. Born in England, about 1610, he emigrated to this country when twenty years of age. He first settled in Dorchester, receiving the Freeman's oath in 1635. After a residence of about seven years in that place, he joined the community at Windsor, which emigrated thither under the guidance of Rev. Mr. Warham. Here he remained twenty-three years, a leader both in civil and military affairs. For many years in succession he served as juror and became well acquainted with the methods of legal business as conducted in the courts of that day. In 1656, he was employed by the town of Windsor to warn public meetings "by drum or trumpet on ye top of ye meeting house," for which he was paid "20s for ye yeare." His military service began in Windsor as a private in the train band of that town. In 1653, he was chosen lieutenant, and captain two years after. Lieut. Cook was appointed to the command of a company of sixty minute men, in 1653, to be ready at a day's warning to operate against the Dutch. The first troop of horsemen ever raised in Connecticut was placed under command of Major John Mason, the celebrated Indian fighter, and in 165⅞ Major Cook became one of its members.

He Removes to Northampton. Major Cook's name first appears on the town records in March, 16⅚⅜, in connection with the names of two others. To these three men is the town under greater obligations than to any like

number that assisted at its settlement. Those persons were
John Strong, David Wilton, Aaron Cook. They came here
about the same time, from the same town, influenced apparently by a common impulse, and undoubtedly at the solicitation of the same individual. The first home lots
granted to them were contiguous. Outlands were awarded
them in the same vote, and were taken up in adjoining
lots. Strong and Cook married sisters, daughters of
Thomas Ford. All were firm friends of Mr. Mather; they
came here at his invitation, and to them he "bequeathed"
the meadow land contributed by the citizens.

Is Immediately   Though land was granted him in 1660, it is
Elected to office.   not probable that he came here to reside
permanently till the following year. At
the election for town officers in 1662, and again in 1663, he
was chosen a member of the board of selectmen, and in
1662, was one of the commissioners to end small causes. He
was appointed on the first committee to seat the meeting
house, and his name leads all the rest on the first recorded
list of tithing-men ever chosen in town meeting. In 1668,
he represented the town in the General Court as colleague
with William Clarke, and he was appointed by the County
Court on the first committee ever named for laying out
highways in this part of the county. In 1663, he was
chosen captain of the Northampton military company, and
was afterwards chairman of the town committee on military affairs.

Changes his Resi-   His prowess as a hunter of wolves has al-
dence to West-   ready been narrated; during three years
field.   he received bounties on twenty-seven wolves'
heads. He became an expert at the business while residing
in Windsor. After living in Northampton between seven
and eight years, he removed to Warranoco (Westfield). He
was one of the original promoters of this settlement, and
in 1666, had a grant of fifty acres of land there on condition of immediate settlement, and a residence of five years.
Not complying with these requirements, the land was forfeited. The grant, however, was renewed in 1667, and the
next year he became an inhabitant. He did not remove to

Westfield till midsummer, as he was present at the April session of the General Court, as deputy from Northampton, in 1668. In September, he was chosen to go to the Bay to procure a minister for the new settlement, and was "to be in the Bay the first Sabbath in October."

Returns to Northampton. Further Public Duties here.
Major Cook remained in Westfield about ten years. He had a license to keep an ordinary from 1668 to 1672, and for two years was one of the selectmen. In 1678, he returned to this town, where he afterwards resided. Again he was pressed into the public service, was once more one of the selectmen, in 1685, was chosen captain of the military company, and was prominent, as has been heretofore noted, in the controversy relative to the militia, the year before his death. He was promoted to the rank of major by Gov. Andros, in 1688. In 1661, and in almost every year following till 1674, he was a member of the jury at the sessions of the County Court, both from Northampton and Westfield. He was appointed one of the Associate Justices of the Court of General Sessions of the Peace in 1680, and served in that capacity through life.

Real Estate, Will, Home Lot.
Major Cook was the owner of considerable property, possessing at the time of his death, real estate in four different towns in Massachusetts and Connecticut. The total inventory of his estate amounted to £526. His home lot and thirty-six acres of meadow land were scheduled at £330. A homestead in Windsor, had been previously given to his son Aaron, and another in Westfield, to Noah. Three hundred acres of land in "Hartford Colony," and a parcel of land at Windsor, are mentioned, but were valued at only £50. The personal estate was inventoried at £146. In his will was an item providing that a silver bowl "of six pounds price" should be purchased and presented to the "Church of Christ in Northampton, if continuing in the Congregational way." The bowl was obtained and was used for many years for baptismal purposes. His home lot of four acres was situated at the top of the hill above the Baptist Church, and included the site of the Forbes Library.

27

Married Life. He was four times married. His first wife was a daughter of Thomas Ford, and sister to the wife of Elder John Strong. His second wife was Joan, daughter of Nicholas Denslow. She died at Westfield, in 1676. In the latter part of that same year he married Eliza, daughter of John Nash of New Haven. His fourth wife was Rebecca, daughter of Nathaniel Foot, and widow of Philip Smith of Hadley. He had eight children, five by his first wife and three by his second. Only two of his five sons survived him, Aaron and Noah. Aaron settled in Hadley and became one of its leading citizens. From him are descended the families by the name of Cook residing in Hadley and other towns of eastern Hampshire. Noah lived some years in Hartford, but returned to Northampton, where he died in 1699. His descendants are still living here and in the neighboring towns.

A Man of High Character and Ability. Like all the early settlers of this new country, Major Cook was a farmer, and while in Westfield, for some years a tavern keeper. That he was a man of much executive ability is abundantly proved by the many public offices he held. Honest and practical, of sound judgment, and withal social and companionable, he soon gained popularity wherever he resided, and was rapidly advanced to positions of honor and responsibility. In all respects he was a worthy representative of the old time New England pioneer. He was a member of the church, admitted when it was organized in 1661. Of his military record very little is known.

Absentees from Town Meetings dealt with. Several times in its history had the town found occasion to take action in order to enforce attendance upon town meetings. Another instance was recorded in 1690. Possibly the law of Gov. Andros prohibiting them may have been the cause in some degree for this neglect. Whatever the reason, the fact that people absented themselves to such an extent made necessary the adoption of the roll-call system. At the November meeting in that year the following vote was passed : —

"At A Legall Towne Metting the Towne Considering that by too much experience it is found that many prsons Are from time to time

Absent from Towne meetting whereby those wch orderly come to Attend what worke or matters they are by the Selectmen called to Attend Are greatly discoraged the Towne therefore did order that ye Selectmen should take A list yeerly of Al such p^rsons as ought to Attend towne mettings And Att all Town meettings said Lists shall be called ouer And that All such persons (being duly warned) as shall not be p^rsent to Answer their names shall be fined twelve pence Apeice According to A former Towne order, votted by the towne Affirmatiuely Novem^r :20 :(1690). At a Legall Towne metting Decem^r 5 (92) the Towne did confirme the aboue sd order."

War Taxes Burden the People. Extra taxes occasioned by the war between France and England, which commenced in 1689, and continued nine years, placed additional burdens upon the people. To meet their own municipal expenses was in most instances a task sufficiently onerous, but when to them were joined the increased war rates, levied by a government that might be swept away by royal edict at any moment, the tax payers were not over zealous in cancelling the obligation. Northampton passed several votes which greatly delayed and well nigh repudiated their payment. In 1690, many rates were laid which the authorities found much difficulty in collecting. The failure of the attack upon Quebec, which occurred this year, crippled the government of Massachusetts financially to a great extent. Depending mainly upon the treasure which they expected to capture from the enemy to defray the expenses of the expedition, it was without funds to cancel current indebtedness. The soldiers were clamorous for their pay and were upon the point of mutiny, because it was not forthcoming. To meet this emergency the government emitted the first bills of credit ever issued in the colony. It was provided that these bills were to be received for all sums due the treasury. They soon decreased in value, and the soldiers were unable to realize more than twelve or fourteen shillings in the pound. The financial stringency was felt throughout the colony. In 1690, twenty single rates were ordered, one-third off for money. Gold and silver constituted the only money in circulation. Massachusetts began to coin money in 1652, but not in sufficient quantities to eliminate the English and Spanish coin then in circulation. Comparatively little, however, found its way into the more remote parts of the colony, and it is not strange that the settlers protested strongly against a money tax, and asked to be released from its payment. A petition to the General Court signed by Medad Pomeroy, Northampton, John Allis, Deerfield, and Samuel Partridge, Hatfield, dated October, 1690, in behalf of the several towns in the county, states that "not one in ten of the inhabitants of Hampshire County have any income of money in any manner of ways," whereby they are put upon almost impossibilities to answer the treasurer. "They beg that the country's condition may be considered and that it may be as of old when those that had silver paid silver, and those that had it not, goat's hair, ram skins, etc." They say "what we have we are willing to pay. We wish to bear our share of the burdens, but in such a way as is possible for us." Relief was afforded in many cases and abatements allowed to many towns.

One-third added to the Money Rate. In March, 16$\frac{89}{90}$, the town passed a vote in regard to the payment of the money rate. The government wanting money and not provisions to pay its soldiers, proposed to abate one-third of the rate if paid in money, but the town not having any money, could only add one-third and pay in produce. Not quite sure that this would meet the requirement, the constable was to be protected from any liability he might incur in carrying out the order. It was

"voted to pay what money Rates were now to be paid, in wheat and peas at the contry price. And to add one-third part more and by A 3ᵈ part they Declard and ordered that it should be so vnderstood and so paid that when any man was to pay 20ˢ in money he should pay 30ˢ in wheat and peas And so According to that rule for All other sums And at the same time they Also engaged to secure the constable from Any damage he might be Liable to suffer in his receiving it as above sd."

A Highway Rate Provided. Highway work had up to this date been under the control of the selectmen. They had power to call out men and teams to work upon the roads, at certain prices per day, fixed by the town at its annual meeting. The expenses for highways were included in and formed a part of the town rate. Citizens living in different sections of the town worked upon the roadways in their immediate vicinity, and the amount was allowed when the taxes were paid. This method proved unsatisfactory, and a change was made in 1690, when the town voted

"That all Towne highwaies should be carried on by way of Rate according to p^{r}sons And estats And if Any p^{r}son doth not worke out his share it shall be Added to their Towne Rate, Legall notice being given. And in case Any Apprehend themselues [burdened] they shall Apply themselvs to ye selectmen who Are hereby impowered to relieue them."

Road to the Falls to be repaired in connection with Hatfield. Hatfield and Northampton made use of the same highway for cartage to the landing place on Connecticut River, and together kept it in repair. The roadway, as well as the bridge over Manhan River, were in need of repairs, and in November, 1690, the town appointed a committee

"To treat with And Agree with Hatfeild men About the repairing and maintaining of the bridge ouer munhan River And likewise the highway Leading to it they also voted that on Reasonable Terms such as the comittee should Agree with y^m vpon, they should haue Liberty to cart through our Meadow And ouer that bridge."

Another Tax Levied. At the April session in 1691, the General Court ordered that a tax of £24,000 should be levied, to be paid in bills of credit, money or grain at money price (those paying in grain to be responsible for transportation). The tax was to be laid forthwith; the head money (poll tax) to be set as in the last twenty rates; one-half was to be paid by the first of September. Northampton had a special grievance against this levy. Fair treatment at least was demanded, and the town, by the following vote, refused to pay the tax till the prices for grain were made satisfactory. The vote was passed at the March meeting, 169$\frac{1}{2}$: —

" The Town Considering of their Inabillity to pay those great rates wch were made in order to paying their part with y^e contry of twenty and four thousand pound in money or provision at so Low A Rate as is specified in the treasorors warrant the Towne did then desire the selectmen not to deliuer said rate to the Constable and did also ingage to secure the selectmen from any damage for their not dellivering the same. The whole Aboue voted Affirmitively."

The Discrimination against Hampshire County. Not only did the government lay the tax, but it fixed the price of the commodities in which the greater part of it must be paid. In this case a discrimination was made against Hampshire by naming prices less than those in any other county.[1] The people of Northampton had little besides the products of the soil with which to meet this demand, and were unwilling to submit to what they deemed an injustice. The larger quantities of grain and other things required under the reduced rate would enhance the cost of transportation from this remote section of the country, and thus add to the burden. No wonder the people hesitated, at least long enough to apply for a readjustment of the terms of payment. At the next session of the Court, prices were equalized, but the tax was not well received, and its payment was greatly neglected.

The New Charter. In 1692, the new charter, granted by King William, went into effect. By it Massachusetts and Plymouth colonies, and the territories of Maine and Nova Scotia, were united under the name of the "Province of Massachusetts Bay." The King retained the controling power, and almost the only privilege conceded to the people was that of electing members of the house of Deputies. He appointed the Governor, Lieut.-Governor, and Secretary, while the General Court selected the members of the Council, subject to the approval of the Governor. This charter was accepted, Sir William Phips appointed Governor, and Massachusetts was once more placed under a permanent and reasonably satisfactory administration. A tax for £30,000 was laid payable in three installments, in 1692 and 1693. This tax was equally unpopular with the last, and payments were slow. Northampton had paid nothing in 1694, and was then in arrears to the amount of £329. Collectors (constables) did not pay

1 The prices for Hampshire County were wheat 4s., pease, barley and malt 3s., Indian corn 2s. 6d., pork 60s. per barrel, and beef 30s. per barrel. In other counties prices at the same time were, wheat 4s. 6d., Indian corn 3s., barley and malt 4s., pease 4s., oats 1s. 6d., pork £3 per barrel, and beef 36s. per barrel.

and sheriffs found great difficulty in enforcing claims.[1]   In 1693, the balance of rates due from Hampshire County was £1857.3.1.   This was ordered by the General Court to be paid in bills of credit or otherwise.

New Government, but Old Debts. Tax Payments Delayed.   Though the charter and the government were new, the old debts still remained, and provision had to be made for their liquidation.   In 1690 and 1691, a paper currency called "Bills of Credit," had been established, £40,000 in denominations from two shillings to ten shillings issued, and the new government made them current for all payments.   Taxes had been levied to meet these bills, but they were collected with so much difficulty, that every year more or less of this paper currency had to be reissued.   That the people were not disposed to pay these taxes can readily be imagined when towns like Northampton passed such votes as follow.   In May, 1693,

"The Towne voted the selectmen should keep the two last money Rates in their hands till micallmust[michlemas] next and not deliver y^m to the Constable And the Towne ingaged to saue the selectmen harmelesse."

Inter-Charter Representation.   From the arrest of Andros to the time when the new charter went into effect, Northampton was represented at one or more sessions of the Legislature each year.   In several cases hers was the only deputy from this county.   Sessions of the Court were numerous, and it was no small bill of expense for the towns to pay their representatives.   The General Court was in session sixteen times from May 9, 1689, to May 4, 1692.   At its second and third session, May and June, 1689, John King was present; at the seventh, May, 1690, Joseph

1 Samuel Porter, a Sheriff in the County of Hampshire, petitioned the General Court in 1695, about difficulties in the conduct of his office. Executions had been levied against several constables. He had seized their lands and estates, but could find nobody to buy them, partly because money was not to be had, and partly because people would not lay out money for lands or estates taken in such a way that they could not enjoy them with freedom. "It is expected," he states, that "I should bind myself and heirs by firm deed of sale, but I think I am not obliged to do this. Our constables, therefore, do not pay their corn rates."—Judd MSS.

Bridgham;[1] at the ninth in December, of the same year,
Medad Pomeroy; at the twelfth, May, 1691, Joseph Hawley and Jonathan Hunt; at the thirteenth, in October,
Joseph Hawley [Mr. Hunt died in September]; at the sixteenth, May, 1692, Joseph Hawley. Northampton came
within the provision which allowed towns the option of
sending one or two deputies. Advantage was taken of this
law in but a single instance. In 1692, a law was passed requiring towns to pay their representatives three shillings
per day in money, for attendance as deputies, and also for
their mileage in both directions. Payment was to be made
within a month after the court adjourned.

A Proposition for
Establishing the
"Bay Road."

In 1692, Rev. Mr. Stoddard proposed to the
town a scheme for a highway to the eastward for wheeled vehicles. Freight transportation to the Bay was circuitous, considerable time was
consumed in the passage, and there was great liability of
damage, especially to grain and provisions in the transit.
Every thing was carted to the head of navigation on Connecticut River, in Springfield, and was carried thence to
Boston by water. To remedy this, a passage way for carts,
across the country was suggested. A committee was
chosen and instructed to find

"out Away to the bay to goe with wagons and Carts for the more
safe transportation of our Commodities supposing that the Towns
Ajacent will goine with vs." John Parsons and Medad Pumry were
chosen "to treat with the other towns and fully to act in the matter."

This was apparently a revival of the design offered by
the Lancaster men in 1681, and was the second movement
towards the formation of the still famous "Bay Road,"
which was the main thoroughfare to Boston till railroads
were constructed. "The Towns Ajacent," Hatfield and
Hadley, did "goine with" Northampton in this undertaking. Each appointed a committee, who undoubtedly made

1 Joseph Bridgham of Boston, was the son of Henry Bridgham of Dorchester. He
was a representative for Boston, in 1697, and afterwards a Ruling Elder in the First
Church. Under the law which allowed towns to choose persons living in other
places to represent them, Northampton elected him. It is perhaps with a single exception, the only occasion on which the town was represented in the General Court
by a person not an inhabitant.

a preliminary examination, but did not report favorably. At that time it was not feasible, and many years elapsed before wagons or carts passed from the river to the bay.

Rates and their Payment. Mr. Stoddard's Back Pay Voted. Taxes were called rates, and were not levied as a whole, under the head of town appropriations, but each was laid for a distinct object. There was the country rate, or State tax; the county rate, or county tax; the town rate for municipal expenses; the minister's rate; the school rate; the highway rate; the shepherd's rate, etc. Each of these rates seems to have been collected separately by the constable. There was no town collector or treasurer. From the list of town debts in the hands of the selectmen, the amount due to each, individual was ascertained and deducted from his rate, and he paid the balance if any remained. Transactions between neighbors would often include the adjustment of rates. Instances occur in which one man would pay the taxes of several others in a settlement with the constable. The rates were paid in grain, produce or provisions. Very little money was in circulation, and of that but a small amount, if any, found its way into the pockets of the minister. In many cases the minister's rate was paid directly to him; he kept an account and adjusted it with the constable. People carried to him whatever they could most conveniently spare, and if it proved acceptable, the amount was passed to the tax payer's credit. The balance due from each person was certified to the constable, and it was his duty to collect and pay it to the clergyman. Prices of commodities were fixed by the towns and were generally based on those decided upon by the General Court in payment of the colony tax. This method of allowing each person to pay when and what he pleased to the minister, did not always prove satisfactory. Many persons were delinquent in making these payments, or the minister was unwilling to accept what was offered, either on account of an over stocked larder, or because of the inferior quality of the articles proffered. This trouble became so pronounced that the town had to straighten out the matter, as will be seen by the following entry on the records :—

"the selectmen considering That diuers p'sons were Behind in pai-
ment of M' Stoderds Rates or in diuers of y^m And that there ought to
be care taken that he might haue his due And Also that the Towne
might be secured from damage that might possibly fall on y^m hereafter
by such neglects; in consideration whereof the Select men then appointed Ensigne Timothy Baker And Medad Pumry to go to o' Reuerend pastor M' Stoder And demand a List of the p'sons who had not
paid their Rates or At Least of such as he would not Accept of So as
to discharge the Towne of their proportion that so the Select men might
Look After the same that M' Stoderd might haue his due And thereby
the Towne Also might not be in danger of any future damage thereby."

The above formed part of the record of a meeting held
in February, 169⅔. It was approved on the 6th of March
following, and the committee ordered "to manage the same
to effect so as to get A discharge of M' Stoderd from what
the Towne was obliged Annually to pay him for the time
past." This order was carried out, and in February, 169⅝,
Mr. Stoddard gave a written discharge upon the town
books, "of all dues" to him from the time of his "comming
to the Towne till the beginning of the yeere Sixteen hundreed & ninety-four."

A Change in the
Method of Carry-
ing on the Schools.
A new method of paying the school-master
was adopted the year previous. The town
assumed the entire responsibility and voted
"to giue forty pounds per yeer for A Schoole Master that
might be Attained fit for that worke and the aboue said
sum of forty pounds they Agree to pay for one yeare And
the Scholers to go free." Here was a radical change.
When the first school was established, the town paid the
teacher a few pounds, and he collected what he could from
the pupils. In a few years the salary was increased and the
sum to be paid by each scholar voted. Soon after the town
still further increased the salary and assumed the responsibility of its payment, but still required the same amount
from those who attended. Now individuals were to be entirely relieved, and the sum required was to be raised by
taxation. Considerable opposition was manifested to this
proposition, and more than one meeting was held before
the question was settled. At a special meeting called "to
Againe consider about a Schoole," the former vote was
confirmed, but some opposed it so earnestly, that they in-

sisted in putting themselves on record as voting in opposition. The following names appear as dissenting from the
vote:—

JOHN KING SR.	JONATHAN HUNT	ABELL JANES
ENOS KINGSLY	WILLIAM HOLTON	WILLIAM KING
JOHN LIMON	JOSEPH ROOT	HENRY BURT.

Need of some such Reform.
This reform, so strongly opposed by these
nine men, seems to have come none too soon.
Apparently as much delay or neglect oc-
curred in reference to paying the school-master's allowance
as had been experienced in gathering the minister's salary.
Several of the teachers, some of them at the head of the
grammar school, had not received the sums agreed upon.
It was to remedy this defect that the new system was
adopted. One instance of this deficiency is seen in the following vote:—

"April:30:1694. At a Legall Towne meeting the Towne considering
that there was mony due to Mr Steeuens[1] for keeping Schole As by the
returne of A committe who were chosen to inquire into that matter did
Apeare the Towne then voted that those companies of Selectmen in the
Seueral yeers that they were in office wch indented with sd Steeuens
should take effectual care in that matter to see that he had his pay According to what they Agreed for. And also to see what was behind in
Mr Timothy Edwards his dues those selectmen wch hired him to take
care truly to pay him his dues And so from time to time."

At the May meeting, in 1693, the town voted to continue
the above system of free schools for the next twenty years,
and ordered that the salary of the teacher should be forty
pounds per year.

Order to Build a New School House.
An order was adopted this year to build a
new school house, and a committee appointed with full power to carry out the
vote. Nothing is recorded concerning its location. Probably it was built in the vicinity of the old one, near the
junction of Main and King Streets. The structure in
which the school had been kept was the first public building erected in the town. It was built in 1655, used for public worship for about seven years, and had been occupied
for school purposes about thirty years.

1 Timothy Stevens was in all probability a son of the first John Stevens of Newberry. He was graduated at Harvard College in 1687, and married Sarah, daughter
of Tobias Davis.

Town Treasurer first Chosen, and the Cl'k made Register of Deeds.

During the first forty years after its settlement the town had no need of a Treasurer. The constable was the collector and the selectmen were the disbursing officers. To the constable the treasurer of the colony sent his warrants, and from the constable he received the consignments of whatever commodity was found most convenient in which to pay them. The transaction was simple and straightforward and the intervention of the treasurer was superfluous. As the volume of town business increased, the necessity of another officer to have charge of its bookkeeping became apparent, and in 1694, Medad Pomeroy was chosen Town Treasurer. This was the first time in its history that the town made choice of such an officer. Five years afterwards the General Court ordered that town treasurers should be chosen annually when other town officers were elected.

In 1690, the town clerk was made recorder of deeds. The town "chose Medad Pumry to be Towne Clerk who was to keep as well the Towne Book of grants and town acts as the book of Records who is hereby ordered not to enter anything therein but what shall be by order from y^e Select men."

A Cage ordered to be set up.

According to the law of 1677, "cages" could be set up in any town designated by the County Court. Action under this law was first taken at the March session of the Court of Common Pleas, in 169$. At that time the following order was adopted :—

"Whereas it is thought necessary that there be a sufficient cage erected or set up in Northampton for the speedy security of some turbulent persons. Therefore it is ordered by the court that Joseph Hawley Esq., cause the same to be speedily erected and sufficiently made and set up in such place in said town and of such bigness as he shall think suitable, at the charge of the county."

It is not known and there is no record to show, that there was more lawlessness in town at that time than had been the case previously, or that any special reason existed for a cage. What action Mr. Hawley took under this order is not stated. There is no further reference to the cage or its use.

CHAPTER XXXV.

KING WILLIAM'S FRENCH AND INDIAN WAR.

The First French and Indian War. Schenectady Destroyed. THE accession of William and Mary to the throne of England brought on hostilities between France and England, which soon extended to the colonies of America. This contest lasted nearly ten years and is known as "King William's War." It was the first of those French and Indian wars which extended over a period of seventy-four years, and between which, with a single exception, scarcely a decade intervened. No sooner had war been declared than a plan was concocted by the French government for a general attack upon the more northerly of the English colonies in this country. The command was given to Count Frontenac, who was made governor of New France (Canada). He entered upon the campaign with vigor. Two expeditions were sent out, one to New York, and the other to Maine. War was declared in May, 1689, and in February, 1690, the combined French and Indian forces fell upon Schenectady, N. Y., where they committed the most inhuman barbarities. Sixty persons were massacred, twenty-seven carried prisoners to Canada, and the rest fled, scantily clothed, to Albany.[1] Salmon Falls and Casco, Me., were also attacked, captured and the inhabitants murdered or carried captive

---

1 Fearing an attack upon Albany, Connecticut and Massachusetts sent ninety soldiers to that point in 1689, under Capt. Jonathan Bull. Of this force, twenty-four men were from Hampshire County, but only one is positively known to have been a resident of Northampton. A portion, if not all of Capt. Bull's command, was at Schenectady, when it was destroyed, and David Burt Jr., of Northampton, was captured and carried to Canada, whence he never returned. He was the son of David Burt, the first person married in Northampton, and was about twenty years of age. In the official list of prisoners carried to Canada, appears the name of John Webb, who may have been a resident of this town. Joseph Marks, of Brookfield, was among the captives, Samuel Beaman of Hatfield, was captured but escaped, and Robert Alexander and Jonathan Church of Deerfield, were slain.

to Canada. This raid so alarmed the country that the towns in Hampshire County constructed fortifications without delay. Those of Northampton have already been described.

Expeditions against Port R o y a l a n d Quebec.
So uncertain was the condition of affairs that at the suggestion of the General Court of Massachusetts, a meeting of the Commissioners for the several colonies was held at New York, in May. It was decided, among other things, to attempt the capture of Quebec. During the preceding month Massachusetts had fitted out an expedition, commanded by Sir William Phips, which had taken possession of Port Royal, in Acadia. Encouraged by this success and exasperated by the barbarities of the French and their allies, the colonies entered with alacrity upon this more hazardous undertaking. A fleet of thirty-two vessels, conveying two thousand men, with provisions for four months, sailed from Nantasket in August. The attack on Quebec failed, and in November, Phips returned humiliated and crestfallen.

Quota of t r o o p s from Hampshire County.
In the meantime provision must be made for the protection of the western frontier, and it was agreed that Massachusetts should furnish one hundred sixty men both for home defense and to secure Albany. Major Pynchon was ordered to enlist or impress sixty men from Hampshire County. To this he stoutly demurred, stating that Hampshire was not able to spare so many men. The towns were weak, scattered and exposed. A garrison of twelve men had to be kept at Deerfield, and there was constant warding, watching, and scouting from every town. "There never fails," writes Pynchon, "of 4 men every day with horses, that go about 12 miles off the town for discovery and sometimes upon intimation of danger 6 or 8 in a day and this course we shall hold to prevent surprise." In five towns in the county, there were four hundred fifty-four soldiers, of whom .Northampton could furnish the largest number. The fatal sickness then prevailing in this section, made it still more difficult to raise the men, and the order was so modified that only forty men were required from Hampshire County.

Of these, nine were from Northampton, eight from Springfield, four from Westfield, six from Hatfield, five from Hadley, five from Suffield, and three from Enfield. No troops from western Massachusetts joined the Quebec expedition. Reports of Indians near the upper Hampshire towns were so constant that the soldiers from this county were retained for home defense. The failure of the expedition against Quebec left the frontiers in greater peril than ever. The victorious French and their dusky allies, it was believed, would retaliate at once upon the outlying settlements of the colonies. Scouting parties were kept in the field throughout the year, a garrison was maintained at Deerfield, and the utmost diligence employed to guard against surprise.

Constant Vigilance the Price of Safety. Though no Indian atrocities were committed in this county during the year, alarms were frequent, and the military authorities were kept constantly on the alert. Reports of the enemy at the falls above Northfield, at Coasset, and at other places were plenty, and in June, Capt. Talcott came up from Connecticut, with a company of horsemen, but he did not remain long. Indians from New York were prowling about the country, insolent and unruly. Two of them were arrested, and one of them shot at Deerfield, while attempting to escape.

The Military Company of Northampton in good Condition. During the nine years in which King William's war continued, Northampton was not attacked, and none of her citizens were killed by the enemy. She furnished the required quota of soldiers, and was ready to meet any emergency. After the controversy concerning military officers had been adjusted, the company seems to have been thoroughly drilled, and when the opportunity came for active service, made an honorable record. The number of soldiers liable for duty in this town, was one hundred twenty-eight.

An Indian Camp near Deerfield. Pynchon Suspicious of them. About one hundred fifty Indians, men, women and children, from the vicinity of Albany, settled near the town of Deerfield. Their camp was on the side of the mountain, about a mile south of that town. The men busied themselves with hunting.　Game was scarce in the vicinity of Albany, but plenty in this section.　Major Pynchon was suspicious that they might make trouble, and wrote to the government concerning them.　He stated that they had a pass from the mayor of Albany, and he classes them as "oᵣ former **Enymy** Indians wᶜʰ Setled at Albany til now." Among them may have been and probably were some who had formerly lived in this region, and were familiar with those hunting grounds.　During the summer they had been quiet and peaceable, though some of them were insolent and thievish.　Major Pynchon in his letter to the authorities, already quoted, expresses fear that difficulties might arise with them, as some of the inhabitants sold them rum and cider.　"Were yᵉ Indians honest," he writes, "as they pretend, they may be advantagious in scouting & giving notice of an enemie if approaching; yet also being so Setled, they have opportunity of entertaining an Enemy & betraying yᵉ Townes, if they should pᵛᵉ false." [1]　He suggests the formation of a company of minute men in the upper towns, of from forty to sixty strong, who could be relied on in case of sudden attack, and by occasionally showing themselves in force, demonstrate that the towns were not altogether defenseless.　A proposition to write to the mayor of Albany concerning them, was also made by Pynchon, and he referred to the rumor of a projected invasion from Canada.

The Committees of Militia act in the Matter.　Samuel Partridge of Hatfield, and John King of Northampton, wrote to the government in behalf of the Committees of Militia of the several towns, January 1, 169½, relative to these Indians.　In this communication they report that some of the savages

"have been presumptuous and bold to take men's corn without leave and otherwise carry it proudly.　Their number as near as we can come at it, is between 40 and 50 fighting men, and about 100 women and children.　We propose that some order may be given concerning them, either to send them back to Albany, or for such a settlement among us that they may be under command of limits and bounds," so that it may be known with whom they have communication.　They request that a garrison may be allowed them such as had been provided the previous

---

[1]　See letter in full, Sheldon's History of Deerfield, pp. 222, 223.

winter, and propose that application be made to Connecticut for one hundred men for two months, while the rivers and lakes are frozen, and an enemy can pass on the ice. Major Pynchon endorsed this letter, saying that the Indians were then friendly, but were very unacceptable to the people.

Reply of the Governor and Council.

In their reply, the Governor and Council concur in the suggestion to communicate with the mayor of Albany, but are of the opinion that there will be difficulty in removing the Indians while they are peaceable and orderly; and suggest that their actions should be closely observed, but in a manner that will avoid giving offence. The authorities advise the use of great care in preventing the sale of strong drink to them; leave to Major Pynchon the responsibility of ordering out the emergency men as he proposed; and state that Connecticut has been notified to send forty or fifty men to Deerfield for garrison duty.

Pynchon lays down the Law to the Red Men.

Negotiations with the Indians were at once entered upon by Major Pynchon, who drew up a paper, in which he stated the case in plain and forcible language. He contended that they ought not to have settled among the English, without liberty from the towns, but as passes had been issued by the mayor of Albany for hunting, they might remain during the winter, if they behaved peaceably and soberly and orderly, but after that they must go back to Albany. He cautioned them to beware of strong drink. The white men, he said, were not allowed to sell it, but if they did the Indians would do well to report them. They were not to wander from their encampment without permits, nor to come into the towns after sunset, to disturb the watchers; nor to go armed into any of the settlements; and they would be expected to give notice of the approach of any enemies of the white men.

The Indians state their Case.

In answer to the above conditions, the Indians acknowledged that they should have asked liberty to settle; denied having any ill-will towards the English; desired that their squaws might be under the protection of the whites while the men

2 8

were hunting; confessed that their young men and squaws would buy liquor as long as the English would sell it, but were afraid to inform against those who sold the strong drink, lest mischief should be done them; and professed that they were ready to aid the white men by giving notice if any enemies should appear.

Soldiers arrive from Connecticut, and Pynchon organizes his Minute Men. Early in February, Capt. Whiting with fifty men came up from Hartford, and remained in garrison at Deerfield throughout the winter. Major Pynchon also organized two companies of minute men, and held them in readiness for immediate service. Scouts were kept constantly traversing the country towards Canada. In May, the Indians were called back to Albany.

Constant Excitement. No attack was made by the Indians in any part of Hampshire County from 1689 to and including the year 1692. Rumors of the enemy were frequent, and there was constant fear of an inroad. Intimations that an army of French and Indians was on the march from Canada, were current and the frontier towns were in a continued state of excitement. Some of the settlers in Deerfield were contemplating another removal, but the garrison from Connecticut and a further strengthening of the fortifications, allayed their fears.

Several Persons Killed at Deerfield. During the year 1693, the enemy appeared at different places in this county, and several persons were killed. In June, the three daughters of Widow Hepzibah Wells, living in Deerfield, were tomahawked and scalped. Two of the children died, but the other survived. At the same time Thomas Broughton,[1] wife, and three children were killed. Great alarm was caused throughout the county by these atrocities, and soldiers were hastily sent from the other towns to Deerfield. Two companies were ordered up from Connecticut, but their stay was short. Capt. Whiting, with another company, came soon after, and remained three

1 Thomas Broughton was the son of John Broughton, one of the first settlers of Northampton. He went to Deerfield from Northampton, at the time of its second settlement.

months. Canada Indians were supposed to be the perpetrators of these outrages. A hunting party of Scatacook,
N. Y., Indians were in camp about a mile north-west of
the town. Two of them, accused by some of the wounded
victims, were arrested. They were undoubtedly present
when the murders were committed, though not actually
guilty of any of them. Complaint was made by the rest of
the Indians to Gov. Fletcher of New York, and the matter
was brought to the attention of the Government of Massachusetts. The two Indian prisoners were ordered to be released by Gov. Phips, but they escaped before the order
reached the valley.

Indian Outrage at
Brookfield.

On the 27th of July, a party of Canada Indians, twenty-six in number, killed six persons at Brookfield, and carried away captive three others—a man, a woman, and an infant. The
child was killed the next night. Only a small garrison had
been assigned to Brookfield, and messengers were dispatched to Springfield for help. Major Pynchon called out
fifty-eight mounted men—twenty from Springfield, eight
from Westfield, and the rest from Northampton, Hadley
and Hatfield—and placed them under the command of
Capt. Thomas Colton, of Springfield.

Pursuit and Disper-
sion of the Enemy.

As a portion of the Northampton Company
served under Capt. Colton, the following
extracts from a letter of Major Pynchon to
Gov. Phips, dated Springfield, Aug. 1st, 1693, giving a minute and graphic account of this march and its results, are
of interest :—

"On Saturday, July 29, Capt. Colton began his march out of Quabaug about 10 o'clock in the morning (having been detained by the
rain) with 42 men, having left 16 at the garrison, because he knew not
certainly that the Indians had drawn off. He went to Wolcott's house
where the enemy kept their rendezvous, found their tracks to go
through Wolcott's lot, & followed the same—soon came to where the
enemy first lodged after the mischief at Quabaug, viz: Thursday night
last which was about 10 miles Northerly from Wolcott's house, where
they killed Mason's child which they had taken away, the mother, as
also young Lawrence about 18 years of age, being then captives with
them. After a small halt, our men came where, as they supposed, the
enemy dined the next day, their 2d day from Quabaug ; there they killed

a mare of H. Gilbert's, which they had taken to carry their load, & there also they had broken the drum taken from Lawrence's house. Our soldiers pursuing came to a great pond, 30 miles or more off Quabaug, where they found the enemy lodged the 2ᵈ night. Here they found a horse of Mason's killed, & fresh tokens of them, their fire not out, which encouraged the soldiers much though the way was hideous, swamps, stones, brush, &c., scarce passable for horses—went 6 or 7 miles further that Saturday with their horses; finding they could not get along with horses, they left all their horses & men that could not foot it; 19 men were dismissed & ordered to bring the horses after. Capt Colton with 23 men, the most likely, pursuing the enemy on foot, lightning themselves of their coats & without provisions; they hastened that if possible they might come upon the Indians before night. But night came on before any Indian could be seen, the Capt. having gone 7 or 8 miles very briskly, after he left his horse, and he was forced to take up lodgings. Way very bad. Horses came up within 2 miles of the foot that night (Saturday) which was 3ᵈ night the enemy had been gone.

"In the morning of Lords Day July 30, the men resolutely bent, thought they were near the enemy; & they set off early before the horses came up. When they had gone about 1½ mile, they came upon the enemy in a most hideous thick woody place, when within 3 or 4 rods of them they discerned them not, till they heard them laughing. Presently the Capt. made signs to his few men to come up & compass them about, who did accordingly, about 10 of his men only just at his heels, the place obscure, the enemy hardly to be seen, having also cut down bushes to shelter themselves, yet made a shot upon them, as many of our men as had advantage, the rest of our men also readily coming up gave their volley also, just as the Indians, rising up, being at breakfast about sun a quarter of an hour high. Our men could not all make shot at once, those that at first had not opportunity did it at the Indians beginning to budge away, none of our men failing; and the Indians not knowing or discerning them till the bullets were in some of their bodies, & others of them alarmed by the volleys, ran away; not having opportunity to fire on our men. The Capt. says the enemy fired but one gun, though some of the soldiers say another was fired & that the Indian quivered so he could not hold his gun steady. They all ran that had life to do it in an instant, & in such a hideous thicket that our men could not see nor find an Indian more. Our men killed 4 certain, outright, which the Capt. saw & is sure of; most of the soldiers say there were 6 killed outright, with one that being wounded, one of our men ran up to & dispatched with his hatchet. Many were sorely wounded & no doubt ran into holes to die, for our men say the brush was bloody in many places, which it was hardly possible to make discovery of, & Capt. Colton says he saw blood on the ground as well as on the bushes. The Indians ran away so suddenly that they left their powder & ball, though some snatched up their guns. Our men brought away 9 guns, 20 hatchets, 4 cutlasses, 16 or 18 horns of powder, besides 2 barks full neatly covered about, 1 or 2 lbs.

in a bark.   Also the scalps our men got from them & burnt them.   Our men here regained the two captives the enemy carried away, Mason's wife & young Lawrence, & brought them back in safety, leaving plunder which they could not bring off, rendering it unserviceable.   On their return they met their horses within 2 miles of them.

"The relation of Mason's wife (the young man was tired & amazed), a lively intelligent woman is, that these Indians that were at Quabaug were only 26, 4 more of their company went off from them.   They say they belong to Canada & were from Pemaquid.   Designed to fall upon Nashua, but their scouts sent thither found them in a watchful and careful posture.   They bent their way to Quabaug—saw a house by climbing a tree on a high hill (must be Lawrence's) lay about the place 6 days & at last did the mischief—would not go near the fortification— told Thos. Lawrence if he would tell them truly what men were in it, they would spare his life.   He told them 6.   Then presently they knocked him down & scalped him.   She says her husband having no weapon, beat them off a great while with his hand, till they cut his hand, and they were very cowardly afraid to meddle with her, that if she had a weapon, she thinks she might have escaped; many things she had of them, one of them speaking good English."   *   *   *

In a postcript Pynchon writes "What I much wonder at, one of the soldiers a Smith (blacksmith) of Northampton, says that one of their hatchets he knows well that he made it about a year ago."[1]

Some of these savages had undoubtedly lived in this section, and had come back to murder and plunder their former friends.   The soldiers returned to their homes on the 31st, leaving a garrison of six or eight men at Brookfield.

The Pursuit Rash and Venturesome.   The Soldiers Rewarded for the Service.   This pursuit of the savages through swamps and thickets, as well as the final attack upon their camp, was rash and venturesome.   The English escaped ambuscade and massacre only because the Indians did not dream of pursuit.   Colton pushed rapidly forward, upon an exceedingly fresh trail, apparently without the slightest precaution, and was almost as much surprised as the Indians themselves, when he discovered their camp.   He succeeded, however, and brought away substantial tokens of victory.   The General Court rewarded the men engaged in this expedition, and in December, granted them £40 and all the plunder obtained.   The latter was to be shared equally among the soldiers.   This equal division of the spoils dissatisfied the Northampton men and they quickly manifested their disapproval.

1 Judd MSS.

It seems highly probable that Capt. Preserved Clapp, Lieut. John King, and Ens. Baker, who were elected officers of the Northampton company, in 1690, served in this expedition. At least they were greatly interested in its results and were much displeased with the disposition of the spoils as ordered by the Legislature. In February, 169¾, they petitioned the Court, protesting against an equal division.

They urge first, that much plunder was left behind "which might have been brought away by men who came away empty." This they did "from choice, not necessity, and left much which became a supply to the enemy." Second, those who "brought away plunder have dearly earned it; they were 70 miles from home, wearied and spent loaded with their own arms and in danger of being pursued; what they have brought away is hardly a recompense for their labor; few men would have given 12ᵈ for a gun then. Third, Great part of the men that staid with the horses deserve blame rather than recompense; 10 men were sufficient to tarry, whereas 19 did tarry and would not be persuaded to adventure farther against the enemy. It seems hard that valor and cowardice should have the same reward; that the travel, hazard and labor of our men should be overlooked and others made equal to them, who deserted them and exposed them to danger."

This document was in the handwriting of Mr. Stoddard, but the remonstrance apparently was of no avail, and for once "valor and cowardice" were equally rewarded.

An attempt was made in 1694, to treat with the western Indians. Commissioners from Massachusetts, New York, New Jersey and Connecticut, with a guard of sixty horsemen from Connecticut, proceeded to Albany. Here a conference was held with a delegation from the Five Nations. Many presents were given to the Indians, but the result was not satisfactory. Little was gained beyond liberal assurances of friendliness and good will towards the English.

Deerfield was attacked by a body of French and Indians, under M. Castine, Sept. 15ᵗʰ, 1694. No intimation of the approach of the hostile army had been received, and the enemy were close upon the place before their presence was suspected. Daniel Severance, who discovered them, was shot, and the alarm thus given. Having failed in their intended surprise, the assailants were readily driven off. Two men were wounded, one of whom was Richard Lyman of Northampton, a member of the garrison. Mrs. Hannah Beaman kept school north of the fort, outside of the stockade. Hearing the alarm, teacher and pupils fled to the fort, which they reached in safety, though pursued and fired upon.

Friendly Indians Killed.

A small company of Albany Indians were engaged in hunting near the Ashuelot River and in August, eight or nine of them were killed by hostile savages. Major Pynchon sent Capt. Colton with a company of horsemen in pursuit of them, but without success.

A Party of Deerfield Men Ambushed.

In August, 1695, five Deerfield men started for the mill, three miles distant, with bags of grain on horses. Within a mile of the village they were fired upon by Indians, who were lying in wait for them. One of their number, Joseph Barnard, was wounded and fell from his horse. His companions remounted him and started to retrace their steps. In a few moments his horse was shot. He was placed upon another, but was again wounded before proceeding many steps. All managed, however, to reach the stockade without further mishap. Barnard lingered for some weeks, but eventually died of his wounds. Hot pursuit was made, but the enemy escaped. Pynchon in reporting this disaster states "Dearefeild men & a parcel of Nthampton men, y^t had bene vp ye River, being just come in, went out after y^m imediately, about thirty or forty men in al (beside more y^t followed from Hatfield & Nth)." After pursuing the enemy seven or eight miles, the trail was lost and they returned. About thirty men, under Lieut. Hollister, were sent up from Hartford, who ranged the woods for about three weeks and then returned, leaving a garrison of twelve men at Deerfield. Indians were reported as having been seen near Northampton, Hadley and Springfield, and constant scouting was carried on in all directions.

This attack upon the party going to the mill and the

death of Barnard, coupled with constant rumors of a force of six hundred French and Indians on their way to attack Albany and annihilate Deerfield, spread fear and distrust throughout the valley. It was harvest time, but people dared not venture into the fields to gather the crops without a guard.

The Exposed Position of Deerfield. Capt. Clapp ordered on duty there. Deerfield was the most northerly of the river towns. Its exposed position invited attack, and only the utmost vigilance could prevent surprise. Many straggling Indians infested the forests, and parties of so-called friendly Indians from the vicinity of Albany and elsewhere, were in hunting camps in different parts of the country, who sheltered, if they did not encourage, the marauders. Scarcely a day passed without reports of the appearance of hostile bands, followed by prompt but abortive pursuit. In addition to the garrison from Connecticut, soldiers from the river towns saw much service in Deerfield and vicinity. Upon a more than usually startling rumor of fresh Indian signs, Capt. Clapp of Northampton, with a detachment of twenty men from his company, "ye most apt for service," was ordered to "range ye woods and afford y^m all ye assistance they were able." They went to Deerfield on the 25th of September and "returned ye 27th at Night, making little or noe discovery of ye enymy." Yet Pynchon says that "one of ye garrison soldiers y^t was at Hatfield goeing vp to ye garrison, discovered two Indians about 2 miles on this side of Dearfield Fort & fired at y^m, as he says." Capt. Clapp, aware of the weakness of the garrison, was "very sensible of need of men to be sent vp to strengthen y^m & to guard & scout about while they issue their harvest." Thereupon Pynchon ordered sixteen men—eight from Northampton, and four each from Hatfield and Hadley—to report there for duty. They were to remain a week or ten days.

Surprise of the Belding Family. Notwithstanding the constant scouting and ready pursuit of the Indians, they continued to lurk about the settlements, falling upon some unsuspecting household in an unguarded moment. Daniel Belding lived a short distance outside the stockade at Deerfield. On the 16th of September, a party of Indians surprised a couple of lads, up Green River, who were lining bees, captured one of them and pushed on after the other, hoping to catch him before he gave the alarm. They came upon the Belding family, killed the mother and three children, and captured the father and three others. One of the children was tomahawked, but survived the blow many years. The Indians with their captives started at once for Canada. A portion of the garrison pursued, and had a harmless skirmish with them in Deerfield meadows. The prisoners were sold to the French in Canada, where they remained about two years. At this time there were in the garrison at Deerfield nineteen men from Northampton, some of whom were undoubtedly among the number that pursued the enemy. In Joseph Parsons' account book, they are named as soldiers who "went from Deerfield, Sept. 16, 1696."[1]

Friendly Indians Suspected. They Murder Richard Church. The "pretended friendly Indians," as they were called by Capt. Partridge, who were allowed to encamp in and about the Hampshire towns, for the purpose of hunting, were strongly suspected of being concerned in these outrages. Suggestions were made by the local authorities that they should be sent "over the sea or near the sea on some island." Did that mean that they were to be sold into slavery, as had been done in Philip's war? While these Indians were undoubtedly privy to the murders, it is not probable that they had up to this time perpetrated any of them. They showed their true sentiments towards the whites, however, in the fall of 1696. In October, a party of the New York Indians, encamped at Hatfield, murdered Richard Church of Hadley. This affair created considerable excitement throughout the county. Church had been hunting with a couple of Hadley men, and when the Indians found and killed him was in the vicinity of Mt. Warner, having parted with his companions some time before. The Indians had been ordered not to hunt on the east side of Connecticut River, and it was believed that they committed the deed in a spirit of revenge. The body of

1 For list of names see Appendix D.

Church was found towards morning of the next day. It had been partially stripped and scalped. Several Indians were tracked to the vicinity of Mt. Toby, and one was captured, but the rest escaped, and fled to the encampment at Hatfield. Here they were arrested, and the rest of the band disarmed and secured. Four Indians, supposed to be immediately concerned in the murder, were examined before three justices, the ministers of Northampton and Hadley also being present. They were questioned separately, and at first denied the accusation. One of them finally turned State's evidence and the rest acknowledged their guilt.[1] The prisoners were taken singly to the scene of the tragedy, where each described in detail, with little variation, the position of the several parties when the deed was committed. Two of the culprits charged the crime upon their companions. The four Indians were tried at a special session of the court of Oyer and Terminer, called for the purpose, on the 21st of October. John Pynchon of Springfield, Samuel Partrigg of Hatfield, Joseph Hawley, Aaron Cook and Joseph Parsons of Northampton, were the Justices. Two of the prisoners were indicted as principals and the others as accessories. They were each declared guilty by the jury, and the principals sentenced to be "shot to death," on the 23d of the month. They were accordingly executed at Northampton, under the direction of Samuel Porter, Sheriff of the county. It is not known where in Northampton the executions took place. There was no jail here at that time. This was an example of prompt justice worthy of more frequent imitation. The murder was committed on the 5th of October, the perpetrators were arrested, tried, convicted, and paid the penalty of their crime within eighteen days. But two days intervened between their arraignment before the court and their execution. The other two prisoners were kept in custody for a few months and then discharged.

Complaints of the Albany Indians. The Albany Indians were greatly incensed against New England by rumors and false reports concerning this trial, as they were made to believe that the culprits were innocent. Consid-

1 History of Hadley, pp. 263-265.

erable correspondence ensued between the governments of New York and Massachusetts, caused by the complaints of these Indians. A detailed copy of the trial and evidence was finally sent to the Governor of New York, and the matter was dropped in 1697. The band of Indians remained in their encampment between Hatfield and Deerfield, till April of that year, when they disappeared, and did not return, much to the satisfaction of the inhabitants.

Peace Signed at Ryswick.

War between England and France ended in 1697. A treaty of peace was signed at Ryswick on the 20th of September. It was proclaimed at Boston, December 10th, but was not officially made known at Quebec till September of the following year, consequently hostilities did not immediately cease.

Another Tragedy in Hatfield Meadows. Pursuit of the Party and Rescue of the Prisoners.

In July, 1697, Sergt. Samuel Field of Hatfield, was killed by the enemy. About a year afterwards, another tragedy occurred in Hatfield meadows. On the 15th of July, 1698, a short time before sunset, a party of four Indians attacked several men and boys, who were at work in the north meadow. John Billings and Nathaniel Dickinson Jr., were killed, and Samuel Dickinson and a lad named Charley ——— were captured. The father, Nathaniel Dickinson, had his horse shot under him, but escaped. The savages, with their captives, immediately started up the river in canoes. Intelligence of this affair was at once sent to Deerfield, thirteen miles distant. Suspecting that the assailants had escaped in canoes, a party of thirteen men, under command of Corp. Benj. Wright of Northampton, started the same evening in pursuit. In it were two men from this town, the rest were either Deerfield men or members of the garrison there. They proceeded up the river about twenty miles, to the present town of Vernon, Vt., reaching there about daylight. Having placed their horses in a safe position, they lay in wait upon the river bank. When the enemy appeared on the opposite side of the stream, the English fired and wounded one of them. The Indians and one of the boys jumped into the river and gained the shore. Seeing that the savages were about to kill the lad, fire was again opened, sending them instantly to cover. The boy managed to join his companion in the canoe, and both succeeded in crossing the river in safety. One of the Indians, attempting to intercept them, was shot. Five or six men then embarked in the canoe in order to get possession of the other one, which had lodged on an island, a little distance down the stream. The Indians concealed themselves on the opposite bank, and when the English approached, fired upon them, killing Nathaniel Pomeroy of Deerfield. He was the son of Joshua Pomeroy of Northampton, who removed to Deerfield in 1684, and was the last soldier who fell in this war. The Indians who made this raid were Pocumtucks, and were known to the captive boys.

The Pursuers Rewarded. Prisoners Redeemed.   In 1698, the men[1] engaged in this affair petitioned the General Court for compensation. This document was signed by Jonathan Wells, Joseph Hawley and Samuel Partridge. In it they say : —

"We are of opinion that the persons above mentioned ought to be well rewarded. The 3 first Newly come into Deerfield weary out of the woods, and upon hearing of the news from Hatfield, four of the town, with seven of the garrison joining with them, went away in the Night. Their Journey was difficult, their undertaking hazardous. The issue successful, & we hope of good consequence. The ready spirit of the Soldiers to go out tho under pay already, we beleive will be taken notice of for their incouragement. The time of their service may well be esteemed two dayes. They travelling all the Night Before and the first three the night after from deerfield to Northampton, where they did belong. They all found themselves horses and provisions."

In response to the above petition, the Legislature granted £22 to these men, to Benjamin Wright £3, to the "six inhabitants" £2 each, and to the garrison soldiers each £1. Col. Schuyler and others went to Canada, the same year, to rescue and bring back the English captives. Between twenty and thirty prisoners were redeemed; among them were the survivors of the Belding family, and others belonging in Deerfield.

1 The names of the persons who were engaged in this pursuit were the following : "Benj. Wright, Corporal of the troop, Leader; Benj. Stibbins, Jonathan Taylor, troopers, of Northampton; Thomas Wells, Benoni More, Ebenezer Stebbins, Nath. Pumrey, Dragoons; Corporal gillit, Benj. King, Jonath. Brooks, Sam'l Root, Jos. Petty, Jos. Clesson, Henery Dwit, Garrison Soldiers at Deerfield."

Joseph Hawley and Joseph Parsons were sent to Albany by the Council to report this outrage, as it was believed to have been perpetrated by a party of Scatacook Indians. They had a guard of five men, four of whom, Benjamin Wright, William King, Benjamin Stebbins and Jonathan Taylor, were from Northampton. The other was Corporal Gillett, so that all but one of them were participators in the pursuit. They were allowed by the General Court £33.12 for expenses, and £6.8 for services.

CHAPTER XXXVI.

HATFIELD BOUNDARY—OVERSEERS OF THE POOR.

THE boundary between Northampton and Hatfield was the cause of a lengthened disagreement between the towns, and the occasion of several suits at law between certain of their citizens. It commenced in 1694, and was not settled for a quarter of a century. This controversy seems to have been occasioned by a proposition from Northampton to perambulate the boundary line. From the Hatfield records it appears that the dissatisfaction was mutual, though subsequent entries upon those of Northampton, indicate that an examination of the old line was all that was then intended. Hatfield, in reply to this suggestion, stated that application had already been made to Northampton for an alteration in the line, at the same time demanding that they "must have more full satisfaction where the line shal go before we run the line," and specifying the desired changes. Northampton, however, insisted upon a survey of the existing line. Hatfield offered to run the line according to the grant of the General Court. Apparently no attention was paid to this overture by Northampton, and in February, 169⅚, a sharp letter was forwarded to the selectmen of this town, in which Northampton was accused of neglecting to settle the bounds. Hatfield was willing to run the line according to the records, from Capawonke meadow nine miles on a west line, arguing that

"as to your pretended settlement of bounds with Hadley, there was not then, has not been since any grant of court of such bounds to you or Hadley; and laying out such line can give you no title to the land. Hatfield had the first grant of said land, and we are wronged by your cutting wood and timber on said land. Your neglect may occasion much disturbance and law suits, and be of ill report. We desire to know whether you will run the line according to the Court's grant or no."

446

To this ultimatum probably no reply was made. Certainly there is no record of town action thereon.

Hatfield Petitions the General Court. On the 20th of May, Hatfield appealed to the Legislature about the matter. This petition stated that there had been several essays by Northampton and Hatfield "to state and settle their northerly bounds upon an east and west line, upon which bound rightly settled, Hatfield's southerly bounds depend," and requested directions concerning the same. In June, the Court appointed Capt. Wells of Deerfield, Lieut. Samuel Root of Westfield, and Mr. Luke Hitchcock of Springfield, "to hear what each town had to say, to view the lines, and make return."

Northampton Remonstrates. In August, the selectmen of Northampton forwarded the following document to the authorities. It is in the handwriting, of Medad Pomeroy, chairman of the board, and was evidently prepared by him:—

"Having heard by our representative that our neighbors at Hatfield have petitioned for a settlement of our north bounds; which thing seems very strange to us that they should be ignorant of now; a matter which they were formerly so well acquainted with, and themselves, with our town have run in perambulation without any question of our bound being settled, which bound hath been stated and settled for 35 years and no question about the same till within 4 or 5 years.

"1. We hope and trust the Honored Court will give us leave to speak for ourselves before anything be acted by them in the matter further.

"2. We thought it was a received principle that the General Court were to resolve such things as the Common Law cannot determine; And there our neighbors ought to have repaired for relief.

"3. We might plead the law in page 37 which says all town bounds shall continue as heretofore granted and settled, and shall be run once in 3 years and marks renewed, which thing has been attended to for 35 years by both towns peaceably and quietly till 3 or 4 years past.

"We hope you will leave the case as it was; the law being ordained to relieve towns and persons that are damaged where we judge they ought to have sought for relief.

MEDAD PUMRY
JOHN CLARKE
WM CLARKE
THOS SHELDEN
} Selectmen.

Northampton, Aug. 14, 1697."[1]

1 Judd MSS.

Northampton Declines to Appear before the Legislative Committee.

The committee named above, met on the first day of September. Hatfield was represented by three men, but the committee reported that "Northampton sent unto us, and said they would wholly decline the thing at this time. Therefore we could not hear what they had to say, and cannot give our sense therein. We make no other report."

Hatfield Files another Petition.

From the statement made by the Northampton selectmen, it appears that the controversy had been going on for some years, though they claim that the line had been repeatedly perambulated by both towns conjointly, and had been accepted as correct by Hatfield. Holding this opinion and relying upon the law of usage, they declined to meet their neighbors in the discussion of a question which they had every reason to believe had been settled for years. But Hatfield was not to be put off. On the 3^d of September, another petition was sent to the General Court, of which the following is the substance: —

They state that the committee appointed by the Court to hear the parties, view the lines, etc., went to the place "where the line should go," and some of our men with them, but "Northampton, though we gave them notice, refused to attend this motion, and so what has been done is of little effect." Reference is made to the Northampton grant of Oct. 18th, 1654, which states that the north and south line, giving them their breadth upon the river, shall be from the little meadow (above their plantation) called Capawonke, down to the head of the Falls. Their second grant, May 27th, 1685, gives them nine miles into the woods. This is all they can claim. They say further: —

"Hatfield grant, May 11, 1670, makes Northampton's northerly bounds our southerly bounds, all the land for 6 miles above them is granted to our town. If Northampton at this station at Capawonk meadow, from which place their west line is to run, do first run north 1½ miles and then a west line, which they plead was by an agreement with Hadley, but without any grant of court to Hadley or Northampton, it takes off what is properly ¼ part of our bounds, viz: 8640 acres of our land, or of land that lies directly back of our town plot." They request the General Court to appoint surveyors to run the line from Capawonk meadow west nine miles and order it to be marked out and to stand for Northampton bounds.

This document was signed by the selectmen of Hatfield.

Joseph Hawley Appointed Attorney. At a meeting held in September, the town "made choice of Mr Joseph Hawley to be their Attorney to Act in their behalfe in the management of the matter at the generall Court." No further action seems to have been taken by the Legislature in regard to the disputed boundary at this time, and it remained unsettled for twenty-two years.

Hatfield opens the case once more. Hatfield, however, continued to agitate the matter, and in February, 170⅔, accused Northampton people of cutting wood within its bounds, and voted to apply to the General Court for help. In announcing this action, in April of the same year, an elaborate appeal was made to Northampton to settle the dispute. Hatfield professed a desire to accomplish a peaceful and amicable adjustment of the difficulty, and expressed a willingness to sacrifice a portion of its rights if a satisfactory settlement could be reached. At the same time the statement was reiterated that Northampton had no right "according to the General Court's grant," to the boundary it claimed. Unless Northampton came to some speedy agreement the application to the court was to be pressed forthwith.

In answer to this communication, Medad Pomeroy, Town Clerk, addressed a letter to the citizens of Hatfield, in the month of April. In it he recites the facts about the original grant, and after an allusion to the rejection by Hatfield of a former proposition for a settlement, makes another offer which would give to Hatfield the land in dispute, owned by Mr. Parsons, in place of a somewhat larger amount (considered of less value) taken by Northampton, farther from the river. This suggestion was consented to by this town in May. Little effect, however, was produced upon either town by this correspondence, or by the petition, upon the Legislature, but the matter soon got into the local courts.

Law Suits arise in which both Towns take part. The suggestion of Hatfield, early in the controversy, that law suits were likely to grow out of the unadjusted boundary, proved true. The owners of land near the unsettled line

29

quarreled about their rights, as might naturally have been expected. Some of the Hatfield men demolished a portion of Mr. Parsons' fence on "land in Timber swamp, granted to him by the town of Northampton." Each town took the side of its own citizens. Hatfield voted that "any person may fetch away Mr. Parsons' fence set up as we account on our land; the town engages to save harmless any person who shall fetch off the fence, especially N. Dickinson, Jr." In February, 170$\frac{3}{4}$, Northampton voted to appoint a committee to investigate and act in behalf of the town, "And in case the committee shall Advise Mr Parsons to sue in An Action of trespas And the Towne of Hatfeild plead title then the Towne to vindicate Mr Parsons title respecting the land Mr Parsons had of the Towne." The committee did advise Mr. Parsons to sue, as will be seen by the following vote passed by Hatfield, February 25th, 170$\frac{3}{4}$:

"Joseph Parsons, Esq., has commenced a suit against Corp. Jona. Smith, for cutting several scores of poles on a tract of land at Dewey's swamp, which land said Parsons pretends to own. Voted that we justify said Smith and plead title to said land and order said Smith to plead title and prosecute said plea."

Northampton was then invited to choose "unconcerned men with us to view the records and see where the line is pitched." If this was refused, then Hatfield was to proceed ex-parte, and bring in evidence of boundary. "If Northampton will settle without law we will."

This case was tried before Joseph Hawley Esq., February 25th, 170$\frac{3}{4}$, and decided in favor of Parsons. Smith appealed to the Inferior Court, to try title, and the case came up at the April term in Northampton. The jury found for Parsons, awarding him 6s. damages and 28s. costs. The attorney for Hatfield, Eleazar Frary, carried the case to the Supreme Court, at Boston, but the result is not known. In April, Northampton appointed Ebenezer Pomeroy attorney with "full power to Constitute one or more Attorneys vnder him as he shall see meet."

In this connection, and in the same paragraph with the above vote, is found the following, by means of which funds were obtained for meeting the expenses of the case before the higher court : —

"At the same time the Towne voted that the three guns wch were delivered to the three Captains that did Belong to the Towne that said guns should be sold & that Ebenezar Pumry should be supplyed with money out of the effects of said guns for going to Boston And obliging Layers and Insident Charges that should be expended in said case."

No further information has been obtained in reference to these guns. Perhaps they were part of the spoils captured by Capt. Colton, three or four years before. Muskets were probably worth, at that time, about one pound each. However, Northampton seems to have trained them upon Hatfield with good effect, for they furnished the means to carry on the legal war about the boundary. The three captains to whom the weapons had been delivered, were undoubtedly Capt. Preserved Clapp, Capt. John Parsons, and Capt. Ebenezer Pomeroy. At the same meeting, the town appropriated 32s. to pay the expenses of the jury's view of the land in dispute.

Hatfield Revives the Question. No other action seems to have been taken by Hatfield for fourteen years, when the matter was once more agitated, and a vote passed again to petition the Legislature. In that document, which is dated June, 1719, Hatfield contended that the difficulty was of thirty year's standing, that Northampton refused to run the line set by the General Court, which was westerly from the Connecticut River, nine miles into the woods, but claimed from the Great River aforesaid, sixty rods, then a west line to the end of the bounds, which line came within a mile of Hatfield houses, the whole length of the town, and destroyed all their out lots, and would bring on the town scarcity of wood and stone, if fenced, and other inconveniences. They pray the Court to order the line run.

A copy of this petition was served on this town, and both parties were heard by the Court, November 20th, 1719. A committee, consisting of John Chandler, William Dudley, and Thomas How, was ordered to examine, survey and determine where the station to run nine miles west from the river, on the northerly bounds of Northampton ought to be, or what else was proper to be done.

And it is finally Settled.

The report made by this committee was accepted Nov. 20th, 1720.   It showed that the old line, first established with Hadley, when Hatfield was part of that town, was the proper one.   That boundary had been perambulated by Hatfield and Hadley, and ought to continue to be the proper division between the towns in the future.   The sum of £17.2.4, to be paid in equal proportion by both towns, was allowed by the General Court, for the expenses of the committee.   In April following, committees from both towns surveyed and established the line on the old basis.

Mr. Stoddard's Salary to be Paid in Money.

Mr. Stoddard, becoming dissatisfied with the manner in which his salary was paid, in 1697, requested the town to pay him £80 in money in semi-annual payments, instead of £100 in provisions as heretofore.   This was promptly voted, and the same year Dea. Ebenezer Strong was chosen collector to gather Mr. Stoddard's rate.

A New Bridge over Mill River Ordered.

The bridge over Mill River at South Street, had become impassable.   Twenty-five years before, after having been in agitation for ten years, a "horse bridge"[1] had been built at this point. Now the proposition was not to restore the horse bridge, but to build a new foot bridge.   This was seemingly progression backwards.   The ford at this place was excellent. It was always passable except in times of high water, which usually continued but a short time.   Whether the horse bridge had been carried away by a freshet, or worn out by constant use, is not known.   As the cost of keeping it in repair from year to year must have been slight, in all probability it had been somewhat damaged in the great flood of

1 The first bridges built in these early times were "foot bridges," in some instances consisting of a single tree felled across the stream, but generally they were more pretentious, with "one good rayle;" then followed "horse bridges" for use in times of high water, as a good ford was easily passed on horseback. These had usually a rail on one side. Afterwards, as population multiplied and transportation increased, "cart bridges" came into use. Most of these first bridges were built of logs.

$169\frac{1}{2}$,[1] and had not improved since that time. In December, 1697, the town made choice of "Mr Joseph Parsons And Enos Kingsley to Repair and make good foot Bridges ouer the Mill riuer so as to Sute the Inhabitants on that side of the riuer vpon the Towne charge in a way of proportion As we repair other high waies." At another meeting, held in the following March, the town "Allowed sd men thirty shillings out of the Towne treasury to hire workmen, and" voted "that the Surveiers manage the worke According to their order." For some reason not now patent, this work was not even commenced. Those persons most interested in it, tired of the delay, took the matter to the Court of General Sessions for the county, and the town was "presented" for not having a sufficient bridge over Mill River. At the September term of the Court in 1698, an order was passed requiring "Joseph Parsons, Esq., and Enos Kingsley to repair and make good the bridge at the town's charge, and call out men to work." If they refused they were to pay 2s. 8d. per day.

The Pauper Problem. Overseers of the Poor Appointed.
Material progress marked the years 1698 and 1699. Measures were adopted having an important bearing upon the well being of the settlement, morally and industrially. Strongly emphasizing the social and economic advancement of the community, these proceedings demand special attention. First and perhaps worthy of the highest consideration was the problem concerning the care of the town poor ; an unsolved enigma that still vexes the statute books of more modern legislation. While ready and willing to supply the wants of the truly needy, the people were opposed to harboring the idle or vicious. No drone would be tolerated. Every person able to work, was not only morally bound to earn a living, but if unwilling, was to be compelled to do so under the law. A class of paupers, requiring each year, as at the present time, a large appropriation

1 This flood, which occurred in February, $169\frac{1}{2}$, was the highest experienced in this section of the valley previous to 1801. Medad Pomeroy's account of it represents the rain as falling for five days almost continuously, during which time the "sun was not seen," and "the water rose to such a height as was scarce known in the country before." Much damage was done throughout this entire region. In "Northampton several horses were drowned and two corn mills and one saw mill much damnified." In Westfield, Springfield and Suffield, many houses were flooded and many cattle and horses drowned.

for their maintenance, was then unknown. Aged, infirm, or "distracted" persons, who became paupers, were ordinarily "boarded round" at the houses of such settlers as were willing to take charge of them.[1]

Unless other persons were specially authorized to fill the office, the selectmen were empowered to act as overseers of the poor, and up to this time they had performed all such duties. In 1699, the first separate board of officers with that title, was chosen. The vote creating the commission, gives the reasons governing the town in this matter, and is appended in full : —

"At a leagall Towne meeting, March : 7:1698, the Towne Considering of Seueral p^rsons and familes in the towne wch if they were not taken care of so that they followed some imploiment so as that they might be in Capacity to maintaine them selues or at least be more Likely to maintaine y^m selues would be a Towne Charge the Towne therefore chose Leiut. King, Isaac Shelden Senr And Enos Kingsley to be ouerseers of the poore to take care of such p^rsons by prouiding for them such things as are of nessessity And to take care that none of y^m Spend their time vnprofitably or Idly observing the direction of ye Law in Such cases : that so the Town may not be needlesly at charge to maintaine y^m."

This vote seems to have been aimed at certain families or persons who were likely to become a burden upon the town. It was an "ounce of prevention" designed to save a "pound of cure." The duties of the board were to discourage rather than administer to poverty. The modern doctrine of helping the poor to help themselves was here admirably exemplified.

Sheep Raising Encouraged. Land Sequestered for Pastures.

Foreseeing that the country must depend upon itself in a great measure for all of its supplies, the government enacted laws for the establishment and encouragement of sheep raising. Under these regulations, the industry had greatly thrived throughout the country. The price per head fell from 9s. and 8s. 6d. in 1690, to 6s. 8d. and 6s. in 1699, a pretty good indication that the number was rapidly increasing. Like all domestic animals pastured on the commons or in the woods, sheep were placed under the care

---

1 A disabled soldier of the town of Hadley, was supported by the town for a year or two. Thirty-two persons were paid for keeping him sixty-five weeks. He went from house to house like the school-master, and was kept from one to three weeks at a place. The pay was 4s. per week.—History of Hadley, p. 242.

of a keeper ; a shepherd[1] having been appointed in Northampton more than thirty years before. In this connection comes the following vote, which was passed early in
the year 1699 :—

"At a Legall Towne Meetting Janu⁷ 9 :169⅜, The Towne vpon consideration the great Advantage the Raising of A flock of Sheep might
be to them in order to their suplying of them with Clothing and other
wise And that in order there vnto it was needfull to set Apart some
Land to be cleared for the more Aduantagos raising A flock did therefore the day Aboue sd Sequester these seuerall parcels of Land following wch were to ly in Common for the free feeding of sheep the first
parcell north of the Slow bridg to Hatfeild bounds All that Land between the road wch Leads to Hatfeild and the great Riuer the second
parcell All the Common Land wch is on the west side of the road w^ch
gos out at the west end of the Towne to the pine bredge And so to the
milstone mountaine All on the north and south side of the highway
wch Leads to Brotons meadow so farr as the Brook. A third parcell is
ouer the Mill riuer on the south side of said riuer from Pancake hill to
Rockey hill and so to Sandy hill All the Common Land there."

These extensive tracts of land would seemingly be sufficient to accommodate all the sheep raisers for many years.
It is not probable, however, that all of it became immediately available, or that more than a moiety of it was
needed at that time. A portion of this land, the parcel
first mentioned, in the north-eastern section of the town,
near the great river, was still designated as "sheep pastures," on a map of Northampton, issued in 1831.

Preservation of the Forests. By-Laws concerning them. The importance of preserving the forests
and protecting the timber in them received
repeated recognition in town meeting.
Nothing destroyed their younger growth so effectually as
the frequent burnings, both by the natives and the white
men. A general sentiment prevailed throughout the valley
for many years that there was great danger of a scarcity of
timber for building purposes. In nearly all the towns, regulations were adopted, governing and restricting the transportation of lumber of various kinds, to other places.
Each town desired to preserve all that was within its own
limits for home consumption. This feeling was augmented

1 Sheep suffered greatly from the depredations of wild animals. Hurdles for
their protection, to keep them from straying, were in common use. A keeper with
hurdles was employed for many years in Hatfield. In 1683, the whole number of
sheep in that town was 291. The expense of the shepherd, hurdles, etc., which was
£18.2.3, was assessed upon the owners of the sheep.

by the constant drain upon the forests for fire wood. An indiscriminate use of them for that purpose would be likely to greatly lessen the lumber production. Consequently stringent regulations were adopted at various times to guard against the mischief. In 1699, the town adopted a by-law regulating at least one branch of the subject. The avowed reason for this enactment was, in the language of the vote,

"the great difficulty we are in to get fire wood and in future time like to be exposed to greatter difficulty by reason of a custom men haue to cut downe the young wood of stadles and the Like wch if it be not preuented is like to proue a great dammage to the Towne."

It forbade the cutting of certain sizes of young wood or staddles. Previous votes had designated the sizes of such undergrowth as it was allowable to cut, and each had become more stringent in this respect. Heretofore none that was not above "five inches over," was permitted to be used for fire-wood. Now "nine inches ouer at the stubb," was the limit. The transgressor, "if there be Aboue three stadles less than nine inches at the stub, in his Load" was to "forfeit his Load of wood or three shillings in money, one halfe to the informer the other halfe to the vse of the towne." Any one in need of small timber was to apply to the selectmen, who were empowered to grant "Liberty to him according as his need requireth." Committees were appointed in different parts of the town to see that these by-laws were properly enforced. If any member of this committee should see any "staddle wood come into the town" that did not come within these regulations, he was "to make A demand of ye wood or the three shillings aforesaid and on refusal to deliuer the wood or pay the money," the party was to be complained of to the committee appointed to prosecute such cases. If the above committees refused to act against the offenders, they were to be sued by the prosecuting committee for the fine of twenty shillings, laid against them for neglecting their duty. This last named committee—"Ebenezar Wright and Ebenezar Pumry"— were empowered to sue not only the parties who infringed the law against cutting staddles, but also to prosecute the members of the other committees who neglected their duties. This order or by-law was approved by a Justice of the Peace, and was thus made legal and binding.

Regulations about Feeding the Common Field.

During the same year, action was taken concerning the use of the common field or meadow, for universal feeding. In the early part of the year a vote was passed prohibiting free feeding therein. It was to be fenced as soon as the frost would permit and so kept throughout the year. This order was to be in force seven years. It was not satisfactory, and in September, another vote was passed providing that the common field should be free for feeding from September to December, and after that the meadow was to be kept clear of all cattle. Rates for impounding cattle were voted this year. Field drivers were to have six pence for all cattle and horses, four pence for swine, and two pence for all sheep impounded, paid them out of the town rate. All persons whose animals were impounded were to pay such prices as the county law demanded.

School Fuel.

Although the town had assumed the payment of the school-master's salary, it did not furnish fuel to keep him and his pupils warm. Parents were obliged to bring a certain quantity of wood to the school-house, for each of their children attending school. An order was adopted in March, 1699, providing "that all and euery Scholler bring one load of wood though they goe but two months that is two months from the beginning of October to yᵉ first of Aprill." Those who failed to comply were to pay a fine of four shillings. The order recites "that many that sent their Children to Schoole were negligent in bringing of wood for want whereof the Schoole oft times was omited." The day of stoves and furnaces had not then dawned, and the enormous fire-place was the only means of warming the school-room, consequently the lack of a few loads of wood was likely to make serious inroads upon school time. This vote did not remedy the defect, and the next year the selectmen were ordered to prosecute all who were delinquent in furnishing wood, according to the previous order. In a few years the selectmen were instructed to charge tuition to all children attending the town schools from other towns. The attendance from abroad could not have been very large and was probably confined to the grammar grade.

CHAPTER XXXVII.

MODERATOR—MILL RIVER—ORDINARIES—JAIL.

Town Meetings. Presiding Officers. LITTLE allusion has heretofore been made among the numerous by-laws regulating town meetings to the presiding officer. Occasionally the term "moderator" has been used on the records, but only in an incidental manner. It is not to be supposed, however, that these meetings had been carried on all this time without an organization of some kind, though the precise method of their government when first held is somewhat obscure. Town meetings, whatever may have been their first complexion, soon grew disorderly and tumultuous. The records of other towns than Northampton, notably some among those first settled in the eastern part of the state, prove this fact beyond doubt. The townsmen were the governing body of the settlement, and had charge of all secular meetings. With such a limited constituency, these gatherings must have been small. It may be inferred that the people came together and discussed questions concerning town affairs in much the same way that a committee appointed at the present day to carry out certain instructions from the town, meet and exchange views of the business in hand. Of course, as the census enlarged, the interests of the different sections or individuals began to clash, and more or less disorder was the result. It is difficult to name the precise method of procedure in such cases, but the means through which the present efficient and satisfactory way of governing and conducting deliberative assemblies of that nature, was evolved in the New England town meeting, and may be worthy of recapitulation.

By-Laws Concerning Town Meetings Summarized. In 1659, absentees from any town meeting, duly warned, were fined twelve pence, and all who failed to attend the annual meeting had to pay more than double that amount. If any one presumed to leave the meeting before adjournment without permission from the moderator, he also had a fine to pay. Fining people for non-attendance did not apparently improve their manners, and the following year considerable disorder prevailed. It was deemed necessary not only to impose fines upon unruly members, so that there should not "be more speakers than one at a time," but to provide for their collection by "distress." Within two years, trouble of a different kind appeared, and an order regarding the presentation of business was recorded. This indicates very loose practice relative to the action of the meeting, and suggests that there was no limit to the amount or character of the measures that might be presented for consideration. Consequently it was provided that all business should first be "proposed" to the townsmen, and by them submitted to the town. Here was foreshadowed the now universal method of preparing carefully beforehand and publishing by warrant, all matters upon which action can be legally taken. At the same time it was also ordered that the townsmen should appoint one of their own number to conduct the meeting. In other words, they were to appoint the moderator from among themselves. These provisions were adopted eight years after the town was settled. In a few years absenteeism again prevailed to such an extent that more effective measures against it became imperative, and a roll of "all who ought to attend town meetings" was called at every such gathering. The presiding officer, however chosen, had apparently little authority and less influence over the assembly he was expected to control. That under such conditions town meetings should be scantily attended and poorly governed, is not strange. The history of other towns in this respect seems to have repeated itself in Northampton. In several of them the same restrictions, adopted in almost the exact order named here, were found necessary, and from them very probably the by-laws in use in this town were modeled.

First Moderator
Chosen in Open
Meeting.

For forty-five years town meetings were conducted in accordance with the several enactments above enumerated. If any moderator had been appointed, no record of it is to be found. It is not known who presided at any of these meetings. Presumably a new governing officer was appointed at each of them, or which ever of the selectmen happened to be present, filled the office.[1] The inconvenience of this method at last became so obvious that in May, 1699, an order was adopted providing that at each annual meeting, when selectmen were elected, a moderator should be chosen whose duty it should be "to manage town meetings." It is presumed that the first intent of this vote was that the moderator then chosen should preside at all subsequent meetings held during that year. Such seems to have been the practice for many years. The duty of the presiding officer may have included that of preparing beforehand for, or at least becoming familiar with, whatever business was proposed for town action, as well as the actual care of the meeting while it was in progress. This provision did not go into operation till the following year. At the first meeting held in the eighteenth century, on the 4th of March, 1700, Mr. Joseph Parsons was chosen to that office. He was the first person in town elected to that position. For two years the chairman of the board of selectmen (or at least the first person named on the list), was especially designated as moderator. This method, once established, was undoubtedly continued, but for eleven years no mention is made of any such officer. Probably it was an omission of the clerk to record and not a failure of the town to elect, for when the custom was again noticed, the same practice of making the first named selectman, moderator, was resumed. From that time till the close of the first

1 Either a moderator for town meetings was not deemed essential, or a record of the appointment of such an officer was not considered of any importance in the early history of New England towns. In several instances many years elapsed after their settlement, before any allusion is made to a moderator on their records. Windsor, Ct., first settled in 1635, has no mention of any presiding officer on its records, till 1652 when seven selectmen were chosen, the first on the list being named "mod." Springfield was settled the year after, but not till 1660 was it considered of any importance that the office of moderator should be named on the records. It was then voted that the moderator should be the first officer chosen "by papers" (written votes) "before any other officer to regulate proceedings and prevent disorders." Hadley, settled in 1659, made choice of a moderator for town meetings the next year.

quarter of the century, the name of but one moderator for each year appears, except in 1721, when three are recorded. After that a presiding officer was chosen at every meeting.

Mill River. Its Course. When the first settler stood upon its banks, Mill River did not pass in its present channel through the meadows; neither were its waters discharged directly into the Connecticut. At the foot of Pleasant Street it turned sharply to the south, following closely the base of "Fort Hill," and formed the western boundary of "Munhan Meadow." It flowed through "Hulbert's Pond," and is supposed to have entered the Manhan River near its junction with the Connecticut.[1] Mill River may have entered the Connecticut through a smaller channel of its own, but it is evident that the main course of its waters was to the Manhan first.

Its Name. The name "Mill" river was applied, as was customary in those times, to the principal stream, whose waters turned the mill that ground the corn for the community.[2]   No village was long without its mill, the building of which upon its banks gave a name to the stream.   "Lickingwater"[3] was the absurd cognomen at one time applied to that portion of Mill River near the old South Street bridge.   The appellation was occasionally used upon the town records, but is now obsolete.

Manhan Meadow between Mill River and the Connecticut. Manhan meadow, or as the Indians called it "Munhan," comprised several hundred acres of rich land, lying directly east of the ridge or bluff on which South Street is situated.   It was considered extremely valuable, and in 1657, was in part divided among the inhabitants.   The vote specified that the lots were "to runn from the greate River to the Mill River."   This meadow contained, as near as can

1 Henry Woodward, who settled in Northampton about the year 1658, was granted a lot of meadow land "lying where the Mill and Manhan rivers meet." The land had Mill River for its eastern and Manhan River for its southern boundary. Manhan River has not materially changed its course since that time.

2 This was true of Northfield, Deerfield, Hatfield, Hadley, and Springfield. Each town had its Mill River, so named because of its availability for mill purposes.

3 A school house was located in the vicinity of the river on the south side, in 1784, which was for many years known as the "Lickingwater school."

now be ascertained, exclusive of sequestered land, about five hundred fifty acres, which at one time appears to have been divided into forty-four lots, varying in size from forty-six and two-thirds to four acres, owned by thirty-four individuals. Twenty-four of these lots, including three hundred sixty-five acres, "more or less," were bounded east by the "Great River" and west by Mill River, which were two hundred forty rods apart at the widest point. Some of these lots were quite narrow, the smaller ones being four rods wide by two hundred forty long.

Stopping the Mouths of the Gutters.   The former channel of the river, thus winding along the outskirts of the meadows, may yet be distinctly traced, notwithstanding the constant tillage and natural accumulations of more than two centuries. Great damage occurred in the meadows from the overflow of Mill River. Passageways or "gutters" were formed in its banks, through which its surplus waters poured into Manhan meadow, each year enlarging the outlet, increasing the flow and augmenting the damage. In 1699, the town voted

" to stop the Mouths of the gutters that carry the watter out of yᵉ mill riuer into the great Swamp And so into the meadow whereby much dammag is done Both to the highways And in the meadow: in consideration whereof they then made choice of Mʳ Joseph Hawley Esqʳ John Clark and Thomas Shelden to haue the ouersight of yᵉ work And impowred them to call out men As need required And this work to be done in the same proportion as other highway worke is done * * * all pʳsons shall worke 8 hours in a day And those wᶜʰ come with teams shall worke 6 hours."

The "Great Swamp," as it is repeatedly called in the records, extended from the lower end of Pleasant Street, just below the "meadow gate," on the westerly side of the Hockanum Ferry road, in a south-easterly direction, and covered many acres. It comprised what was known as Lyman's and Parsons' swamps, which names still attach to sections bordering on the easterly bank of Mill River. While the labor of closing these outlets must have been great, it proved of little benefit. Each year the waters reopened some of the "mouths of the gutters," and the damage was not abated. This recurring trouble led the proprietors to devise some more effectual remedy, and in a few years they adopted the heroic method of turning the channel of the river, through the great swamp, directly into Connecticut River.

A Bridge built at Enos Kingsley's Gate.

A bridge was ordered to be built across Mill River, in 1700, below Enos Kingsley's gate. Its location was probably under "Fort Hill," as the river then ran in its old channel. "Capt. Clap and Benjamin hastins" were chosen a committee to do the work. It was "to be carried on By such persons as have Land in that end of the meadow wch this highway leads too," and was to "be set off in their due in other highway work."

Tar and Turpentine.

Gathering turpentine from pine trees seems to have been a profitable business, but was not generally followed till a few years previous to the opening of the eighteenth century. Tar was produced in considerable quantities before this date, but there is no record concerning the time when the practice commenced in this section. From time to time restrictions were placed upon the "burning of candle wood to make tar," in nearly all the towns.[1] Turpentine was obtained from living pine trees. The town controled the trees on the common land, first to preserve the timber, and afterwards for purposes of revenue. In order to obtain turpentine, the trees were boxed. A hollow place was cut in the tree near the ground, and portions of the bark stripped off. Into this excavation or box the turpentine slowly flowed, and from it was dipped into barrels. Many barrels of it were gathered in Hampshire County,[2] and sent to Hart-

1 Gov. Winthrop describes the method of making tar in 1662. He states that "the most tar is made about Connecticut, about 50 miles up the river, where there be great plains of these pines on both sides of the river. Some has been made in Massachusetts and New Plymouth." The pine knots remaining from decayed trees were "gathered into heaps upon a hearth made of clay and stone, so high that the tar may run out into a vessel. The tar runs into the center of the bed or hearth and thence runs out one side in a gutter. The knots are piled up and covered with clay or loam, like a coal pit. The wood is fired and the tar runs out into a barrel or other vessel. After the tar has run out, the rest is excellent charcoal."

2 Joseph Parsons of Northampton sent down from Hampshire above five hundred barrels of turpentine from 1696 to 1700, and much was sent from Hadley by Samuel Porter and others. Many of the turpentine barrels contained about three hundred pounds. The price here for a few years after 1708, was 5s. 6d. to 6s. per one hundred twelve pounds, and in Boston about 2s. more. One hundred twelve pounds of turpentine yielded about three gallons of spirits of turpentine. It was distilled in Boston.—History of Hadley, pp. 301, 302.

ford, where it was shipped to Boston.[1] The first record of town action in this matter was made during this year, when a vote was passed forbidding the boxing of pine trees for the purpose of obtaining turpentine, within three miles of the meeting house, under penalty of "1s. for every such tree." In the succeeding year the town ordered the prosecution of every one trespassing on the commons for this purpose. All the pine trees on the north side of Manhan River were reserved for the use of the town in 1702, and "that in case any p'son or p'sons shall presume to Box Any pine tree for turpentine within the Limmits Aboue he shall forfit three shillings for euery tree so boxed: the one halfe of the fine to Be to the informer the other halfe to the vse of the Schoole."

No more "Baiting" of any "Creature" in the Meadows on Sunday. Making Sunday herdsmen of the boys, though it had been prohibited more than thirty years before, had again come into practice. Horses, cows and oxen were put into the meadows to feed on Sunday, during the close season, under the care of drovers or herdsmen. While the old folks were gathered at the meeting house, the boys were in many instances, put in charge of these animals. Under pretence of assisting in their labors, the young herders were soon surrounded by their companions, and together they turned the Sabbath into a holiday. They much preferred, puritan boys though they were, to spend that sacred day skylarking in the meadows, than attend two meetings, under the eyes and rod of the tithing-man, and reciting catechism after sermon. Intent upon their games, the beasts were allowed to wander, and much damage to crops, as well as to the morals of the youthful "cow keepers," was the result. Among the reasons given for abolishing the practice, in addition to the damage to crops, was the "profanation of the Sabbath by Bois meeting together on that occasion." Every offender was to pay a fine of 5s. besides the damages.

---

1 At the County Court, held in Northampton, December, 1708, Samuel Bartlett Jr., Preserved Bartlett and Thomas Clapp, were fined 40s. "for deceit" in some barrels of turpentine sent to Hartford and sold. The turpentine was confiscated and sold and the proceeds, including the fines, were distributed, one-half to the informer and the other half to the poor of Northampton. In addition, the parties had the costs to pay. Two other Northampton men were afterwards fined 20s. for the same offense.

Disorder in the Meeting House during Sunday Services.

Not all, and probably not the worst, of the youth were sent into the meadows to tend cattle on Sunday. Enough of them were left to create much more disturbance during services in the meeting house, than was needful in any self-respecting congregation. Notwithstanding constables, tithing-men, Sunday wardens, and deacons, disorder in the meeting house was not unknown. A side light of some significance is thrown upon this matter by an entry in the note book of the first Joseph Hawley. In his capacity as Justice of the Peace, he was called upon to hear a complaint against John Davis, "for his Disorderly Carriage at meeting upon the Sabbath; forsaking his own seat and Breaking over the Back of others seats; and for Breach of peace in kicking of Isaac Bridgman," on the 20th of July, 1701. He was found guilty and a fine of five shillings and costs imposed for breach of the peace, and ten shillings for breaking into other seats. The Justice, however, suspended "the execution of the ten shillings for the present."

Northampton and Westfield Petition for a Strip of Land.

A parcel of land three or four miles broad, lying between Northampton and Westfield, was coveted by both towns. Westfield petitioned the General Court for a grant of it in 1685, suggesting that Northampton was about to ask for the land, but to give it to that town would greatly damage Westfield. Northampton did not ask for it at that time, and no action was taken by the Court upon the request of Westfield. In 1700, both towns united in a petition requesting that the land should be equally divided between them.

Rev. Solomon Stoddard wrote to Hon. William Stoughton, Deputy-Governor, Sept. 19th, 1700, in behalf of this petition. Writing at the request of others, he says: "I have no such opinion either of worthiness in myself or partiality in you to expect you would give away the country's land for my sake, but I have some reasons to present. 1st. The necessity of the town, which was about to divide a tract adjoining this among the inhabitants, but many of the lots would be so small as to be unprofitable, unless this be added. 2d. The enlargement of the province. If this petition be granted probably many young men would plant themselves partly on this division and partly on another adjoining it, and so make a village in time. 3d. Securing the province. Lying upon the extremity of the province, the town was much exposed in case of any rising of the Indians. This grant will make the town more populous and defensible and will prevent many young men's going to the other province."

The division line was to commence at Webb's rock and run westerly to the end of the bounds. This document was signed by John Clarke, Representative from Northampton, and Isaac Phelps, Representative from Westfield. The petition, which was granted at the June session in 1701, provided that the "Springfield grant be not impinged or the right of Joseph Parsons,[1] Esq. and Samuel Cooper or any other person, reserving 400 acres to William Hulburd, when he chooses, he being wounded in his majestie's service."

More Land Sequestered for Schools. Additional land was set apart for school purposes in 1702. One lot was situated "Betwixt Samuel Pumrys home lot And the saw mill," and the other comprised "all the Low Land Below Sam[ll] Bartlets Corne Mill Downe as farr as Roberd Danks his farme." This land was all within the present limits of Easthampton. The number of acres is not named. It was leased for many years and the income applied to the maintenance of the schools.

Coombs' Fulling Mill. John Coombs had permission in 1702 to set up a Fulling Mill on Mill River. Other grants for this purpose had been previously made, and in one case at least the grantees had failed to build. This grant was made on condition that

"he preiudice not any other mill Already set vp. And also that he damnifie no man in his propriety And also that when said mill is rotten And he doth not Repair it so as to make it Servisable so as to do the worke of the Towne wch is brought to him the place to return to the Towne Againe. And prouided Also that the said Coames goe forthwith About the Setting up And finish said mill that so it may be no hindrance to Any other person that may appear to set vp a fulling mill in case Come should faile."

Coombs had been living on South Street four or five years, and had been running a fulling mill near Bartlett's

---

1 In 1661, the first Joseph Parsons bought of Thomas Cooper of Springfield, land at Warranoco (Westfield), for which Cooper paid the Indian owner upwards of £20. Parsons was to pay one-half of this sum, and if he was deprived of the land Cooper was to pay him back the £10. At this time the land was in the hands of the children of the original owners.

mill in Easthampton. He seems to have hired that mill of Samuel Bartlett. His fulling mill was probably built on Mill River in the vicinity of the old paper mill (now the cutlery works of E. E. Wood), but the exact date or location cannot be given. It was long known as Coombs' Mill, though he removed to Springfield in 1713.

Death of Col. John Pynchon.

An entry of the death of Col. John Pynchon, at the age of seventy-eight, which occurred on the 17th of January, 1703, may be found upon the records of Northampton as well as upon those of Springfield. For nearly half a century he was the foremost man in all this section. Born in England, in 1625, he came to Springfield with his father, William Pynchon, when eleven years of age, and continued a resident of that place till his death. Prominently identified with the interests of the valley, his name repeats itself in the history of Western Massachusetts more frequently than that of any other of its first settlers. Within its precincts he was a leader in civil, military, judicial, industrial and agricultural affairs. Succeeding to the business of his father in 1652, he was first of all a trader, with scattered associations throughout the colonies of Massachusetts and Connecticut. For a long time the Pynchons were the only persons licensed by the government to trade with the Indians in this portion of the colony. They paid something for this privilege, and sold rights to others. Their object, however, was not so much to gain the small pittance received from the sale of these rights, as to control the traffic in goods required for the Indian trade. Their principal profits came from the sale of beaver skins, for all goods purchased of them by other Indian traders, had to be paid in beaver, grain not being used in those transactions. The restriction on the Indian trade, however, extended only to furs. By this means they not only controlled the business with the lesser dealers, but gained a monopoly of the fur trade. They had a large warehouse in Springfield, and imported many of their goods, John Pynchon visiting England for that purpose. Among those to whom the latter sold trading rights in Northampton, were Joseph Parsons, John Webb, and David Wilton. With these men he had book accounts, extending through many years. During the first years after its settlement, the people of North-ampton were compelled to purchase their supplies else-where than in their own town, and consequently they be-came constant customers of Mr. Pynchon.

Some of his Pub-lic Duties.   Notwithstanding his large private business, he was much engaged in public affairs. In dealings with the Indians, whether for the purchase of land or the making of treaties, he was often employed by the government. Northampton, Hadley, Northfield, and other towns, were bought in part, of the natives by him, and many records of these transactions are minutely entered upon his account books.[1] Much town business fell to his lot to transact, and he was for four years deputy from Springfield. He was an assistant magistrate for a period of twenty-two years, and during that period and to the end of his life, was Chief Justice of the County Court. A member of the Council under Andros, captain of the first troop of cavalry ever formed in Hampshire County, he was also commander-in-chief of the military in the county during most of the time of King Philip's war.

Marriage.   He married Amy, daughter of Gov. George Willys of Hartford, in 1645. Mrs. Pynchon died January 9th, 1699, at the age 74. They had five chil-dren. It was owing to the ill health of his wife that Col. Pynchon resigned his commission as commander of the Hampshire forces.

His Character.   Col. Pynchon was a man of sterling integ-rity, upright, honest, and withal liberal in his dealings. Though he was a successful trader, methodi-cal and correct in all his transactions, and had the reputa-tion of exacting the full payment of all his just debts, yet he was in many cases liberal and considerate when his debtors were unfortunate. He had much land in his pos-session, portions of which he rented. Many instances of his sympathy with those in adversity, in the abatement of

1 For some of his charges to the promoters of Northampton, for the purchase of Nonotuck, see Appendix E.

agreed compensation for rent and other indebtedness, may be found upon his account books. These deductions were made because of failure in crops, because of Indian outrages, by reason of loss by floods, and other drawbacks, liable to overtake men in the ordinary course of business. He was a man of strong convictions, great will power, and one whose loss was greatly lamented wherever his influence was felt and acknowledged.

Drunkenness and Liquor Selling. Drunkenness and tippling seem to have prevailed to a considerable extent in Northampton, at the beginning of the eighteenth century. During the previous decade there had been but one licensed innholder in the town. In 1701, two were authorized, and that number was continued with but a few exceptions for the next ten years. The court record abounds in cases in which persons—women as well as men—were fined for drunkenness, and in many instances for the illegal sale of liquor. Those who plead guilty or were convicted, were fined, and some who were acquitted had the costs to pay. One-half the fines went either to the schools or the poor of the town. In addition to the innholders who were all licensed to sell, retailers of strong drink were frequently appointed. Yet notwithstanding all these legalized privileges of sale, nearly every year parties were convicted of selling contrary to law. In one case a licensed tavern keeper plead guilty to an illegal sale and was fined 40s.

The Town Decides to have but one Ordinary. An attempt was made, beginning in 1704, to abate the evil of intemperance, by restricting the sale of intoxicants. The result was not satisfactory, and after a year or two the endeavor was abandoned. In that year the "Towne voted that in their Judgment one ordinary was sufficient for this Towne A [nd] manifested their desire that there should be no more." A committee was appointed to "present their desire herein to the quarter sessions" of the County Court. In 1702, Nathaniel Dwight and John Parsons Jr., were licensed as innkeepers, and in 1704, at the September court, only Dwight's license was renewed, but at the same time Benjamin Stebbins was licensed as a "retailer." The action of the town had its effect so far as taverns were concerned, but did not greatly diminish the number of places where liquor could be obtained.

And the next year Votes to have none.

After a year's experience with but one licensed tavern, the result proved so satisfactory, that the town determined to abolish them altogether. At a meeting held in August, 1705, the following vote was passed : —

"The Towne taking into serious consideration the ill consequences that are like to acrue to y^m And to their Children by Reason of multiplying of Tauerns And tipling houses the Towne voted they desired to haue no Tauerns or tauerne But that they might haue one vitular and one retailor of strong drinke," and made choice of a committee "to communicate ye Towne's mind to the Hono^d Court."

Consequently no innholder was licensed for Northampton in 1705, and there is no record of the appointment of a victualler or retailer. In September, 1706, the Hon. Court saw fit to license Ebenezer Pomeroy and Nathaniel Dwight as innholders. No further vote in relation to this matter was passed by the town, and two tavern keepers continued to be appointed for years in succession.

One need of Taverns.

In this matter of granting innholder's licenses, the court may have considered its own convenience, as well as that of the public. The courts were held at the "ordinaries," unless upon some special occasion, till 1737, when a Court House was erected here. Strangers, gathered in attendance upon the sessions, as well as the judges and other officers of the court, needed some place of entertainment, and a trial of one year probably satisfied the authorities that taverns were a necessity.

Young Men Presented for Carousing.

Notwithstanding the attempt to limit the number of taverns, the evil influences of intoxicating liquors were visible to a considerable extent among the young people. In March, 170⅚, four young men of Northampton, belonging to its most respectable families, were "presented for being at N. Dwight's at an unseasonable time on Thursday night after Decb^r Court," and for abusive words and actions to "a couple of young men from Brookfield." The jury returned a verdict of not guilty, and the prisoners were discharged on the payment of costs. Dwight had been one of the licensed innholders, but had no license at that time, though he received one in September. Probably the young men were in the habit of carousing at these places of entertainment, especially when the sessions of the court brought boon companions from other towns, and from force of habit went to Dwight's.

Powder Sold from the Town Stock. From the town's stock of ammunition, not only the military company, but the people obtained their supply. In 1704, about the time of the outbreak of the second French and Indian war, the town voted to sell half a barrel of powder at "three shillings and foure pence per pound in present mony." The selectmen had heretofore controlled the town's supply of ammunition, but now an order was adopted placing it in the care of some "trusty man," to act for the town. Capt. Clapp, commander of the militia company, was appointed to that duty.

A New System of Fortification. The fortifications established in 1675 and renewed and enlarged in 1690, had probably fallen into decay, and when danger again threatened, a new system of defense, by means of fortified houses, was adopted. "Queen Anne's French and Indian war" commenced in 1704; in March of that year the following vote was placed upon record, and it is the only allusion to the war, though it continued nine years longer. The town

"Considering the Great desolation made by the enemy viz: french and indians in many places especialy At deerfeild did then vote And Agree to fortify Severall houses in the Towne And then chose Severall men to Joine in consultation with the committee of Militia And to consider what houses may be best to fortifie."

The expense of fortification was paid by the town. In accordance with this vote, a number of houses were strongly fortified, but it is impossible to ascertain where they were situated.

Encroachments on the Highways to be Scrutin i z e d and Remedied.

Infringements upon the highways were not confined entirely to the meadows. Throughout the town the same obliquity of vision in regard to boundary lines was observable. Special grants from them were common, and special private appropriations therefrom, in all directions, seem to have been the order of the day. Most of the roads were laid of extra width, abuttors were permitted to use them for pasturage and mowing, and in many instances portions of them were cultivated, till finally the owner found it extremely difficult to discriminate between the town land and his own home lot. The first highways were laid out before lots were granted, but in after years, when new grants were made, the town reserved the right to run highways through them whenever needed. The committees appointed at different times, and particularly in 1690, were empowered to look after encroachments upon town lands as well as upon highways. They reported the following year that they had re-established certain highways in the vicinity of what is now North street, and that the trespassers had readily agreed to rectify their bounds. But this was only one among many similar cases of encroachment, and in a short time other sections were treated in the same way.

Poor H o u s e Es-tablished.

The choice of a board of overseers of the poor was soon followed by an order for the building of a house for the poor. No very large number of persons who were unable to care for themselves could have burdened the town at that time. The severe laws against pauperism, and the number of officials —Selectmen, Constables, Tithing-men, Overseers of the Poor—whose duty it was to look after the idle, the poor, and the vicious, would seem to be sufficient to prevent all except the very unfortunate from becoming paupers. Often the courts ordered the children or other members of a family to contribute towards the support of their relatives.[1] In some cases the selectmen took charge of the

1 The children of a widow in Springfield, " who was reduced to a low and poor state for want of subsistence," were ordered by the Court of Common Pleas to contribute " 25s. yearly towards her support." There were six of them, sons and sons-in-law. " If these persons named by the court refuse, a warrant of distress shall issue."

property as well as the patient. The practice of boarding the poor in families, probably letting them out to the lowest bidder, may not have proved very satisfactory, though it seems to have been followed in after years, and this may have been deemed a more economical method of caring for them. At all events, in March, 1705, the following vote was passed :—

"The Towne considering that there was need of a house to intertaine such as were poore And not Able to prouide for themselues they therefore Agreed that a House should be Built on the Towne charge And that it should remaine for that service viz : to intertaine such as from time were poore and could not prouide for y^m selues. At the same time the Towne Agreed and voted that said house should be set up on the point of the meeting house hill where the Schole house formerly stood And they then did chose Ensigne Thomas Limon, Samuel Bartlet Sen and Thomas Shelden to be A committee to take care and manage the Building of said house with as much speed as may be."

Location of the Poor House.

This is the first mention of a "Poor House" on the town records. It was situated very nearly upon the site of the first meeting house, at the junction of Main and King Streets, as that building was used for a school house after the second meeting house was built. It was undoubtedly demolished when the new school house was erected in 1693. How long the poor house remained in use is not known. No subsequent action was taken in the matter, and it is barely possible that no almshouse was erected.

House of Correction Ordered by the Court.

No sufficient place for the detention of criminals existed in Northampton till the commencement of the last century. Though a cage had been provided in 1695, that could only have been used for their temporary confinement. In March, 170⅚, the court passed the following order :—

" Ordered that Joseph Hawley, Esq. Eben^r Pumry and Samuel Wright of Northampton be a committee to agree with some workmen to build a house of correction in Northampton and to provide materials for building said house of 24 feet long and 16 feet wide besides the chimney, and a small house at the end of said house, which said committee are hereby empowered forthwith to cause the said work to be done upon the county charge."

Its Situation.   The first house of correction ever built in Northampton was erected at the head of South Street, a short distance west of the brick building standing upon the corner, about midway between that point and the City Hall.   The lot was triangular in shape, being five or six rods on the street, and as many deep, containing about fifteen square rods.   It was an unsubstantial building, and the tradition is that it held the prisoners no longer than they were willing to stay.   In 1707, Benjamin Carpenter was appointed master of the "House of Correction at Northampton," and in 1709, John Webb was "allowed to live in and take care of the House of Correction for half a year."   In 1730, the court ordered the building repaired, and a "yard made around it."   This was the only jail in town till 1773, when a new one was built at the lower end of Pleasant Street.   The first one was undoubtedly situated upon a small lot taken from the highway and granted to William Pixley, a year or two before.   It is not probable that he ever occupied it, as he removed to Westfield, where he died in 1689.

CHAPTER XXXVIII.

QUEEN ANNE'S FRENCH AND INDIAN WAR.

Improved Condition of Affairs. DURING the few years of peace which followed the close of King William's war, the town prospered greatly. A general increase in population wrought betterments in every direction. The records which thus far have been carefully followed, show that in its moral, social, educational and industrial elements the town was improving, expanding and developing. New dwellings had been erected, better schools and school houses furnished, improved facilities for the care of the unfortunate provided, and successful efforts made to lessen the temptations that beset all classes, especially the young. Valuable additions to its territory had been secured, and altogether the town was better prepared than ever before to meet the harrassing and disturbing effects of Indian warfare.

War against France Declared in 1702. The causes that led to the rupture between England and France at this time are familiar to all, and need not be entered upon. King William, who died in March, 1702, had just previous to his death formed an alliance with certain of the continental powers against France, and Queen Anne declared war against that country in May, immediately after ascending the throne. .

The Indians still the Disturbing Element. Always an uncertain factor, the Indians had heretofore acted against the English. It was therefore of great importance for the latter either to form alliances or make treaties of neutrality with the tribes. By means of the Jesuit missionaries, who were political intriguers of the highest order, the French obtained great control over the savages and in many instances readily counteracted whatever influence the English had acquired. The French Governor of Canada made a treaty with the Iroquois, and succeeded in embroiling the eastern or Maine tribes with the English, after the ratification of a solemn treaty with the latter.

Gov. Dudley concludes a Treaty with the Abenakis Tribe.

Joseph Dudley, who ten years before had been sent out of the country a prisoner with Andros, returned in 1702, commissioned by the Queen as Governor of Massachusetts. His arrival was speedily followed by news of the proclamation of war against France, and the colony shuddered at the prospect of renewed hostilities with the French and their savage allies. One of the first acts of Gov. Dudley was to make peace with certain of the eastern tribes in Maine. This was satisfactorily accomplished at Casco, Me., in June, 1703. Determined to abrogate this compact, the Governor of Canada sent a force of French and Indians, under Lieut. Beaubassin, into Maine, who succeeded in inducing the Abenakis to join them. On the 30th of June, the treacherous red men made a binding treaty with Gov. Dudley. Less than two months after, uniting with the forces from Canada, they attacked the English, and within six weeks had ravaged every settlement on the coast.[1] Even while the treaty was in progress, they laid plans to capture the entire party of English engaged in conducting the negotiations.[2]

Two Men Captured at Deerfield.

The war thus opened in the eastern section of the colony, spread alarm and consternation throughout the province. This feeling of uncertainty and insecurity was intensified by the appearance of Indians at Deerfield. In October, 1703, Zebadiah Williams and John Nims, who went into the meadow at that place, in the evening after cattle, were captured by a straggling party of savages and carried to Canada. The need of prompt and efficient measures for defense, empha-

1 N. Y. Colonial Documents, vol 9, p. 756.
2 Penhallow's Indian Wars, p. 18.

sized by this disaster, became apparent to all, and Deerfield proceeded to renew its fortifications, having made successful application to the General Court for assistance. Connecticut decided to protect its borders, as heretofore, by defending Hampshire County.

Rev. Mr. Stoddard Suggests the use of Dogs in Indian Warfare.

Affairs in the river towns, especially in Deerfield, called out a letter from Rev. Mr. Stoddard to Gov. Dudley, dated Oct. 22^d, 1703, in which he urges the use of dogs in fighting the Indians. This letter not only presents strong arguments in favor of the proposition, but it also gives in a nutshell the then prevalent opinion concerning the Indians. He argues that dogs would strike the enemy with terror, secure our men from the danger of ambush, and prevent their coming at all. He is aware of the inhumanity of the suggestion, but says that the Indians "are to be looked upon as murderers and thieves; * * * They act like wolves and are to be dealt withall as wolves."[1]

[1] Mr. Stoddard writes: " But if dogs were trained up to hunt Inds as th do Bears; we sh. quickly be senseble of a great advantage thereby. The dogs would be an extream terrour to the Inds; they not much afraid of us, they know they can take us & leave us, if they can but get out of gun shot. * * * But these dogs would be such a terrour to them, that after a little experience it w^d prevent their comming & men would live more safely in their houses & work more safely in the fields and woods: In case the Inds sh. come near the Towne the dogs w^d readely take their track & and lead us to them. * * * Besides if we had dogs fitted for that purpose our men might follow the Inds w^h more safety, * * * they would follow their dogs with an undaunted spirit, not fearing a surprise; * * * the dogs would do a great deal of execution upon the enemy & catch many an Ind that w^d be too light of foot for us. * * * In a time of war with Inds in Virginia, they did in this way prevail over them, though all attempts before they betook themselves to this method proved vain. * * * If the Indians were as other people are, and did manage their warr fairly after the manner of other nations, it might be looked upon as inhuman to persue them in such a manner. But they are to be looked upon as theives and murderers, & they doe acts of hostility without proclaiming war, they dont appear openly in the field to bid us battle, they use those cruelly that fall into their hands, they act like wolves, & are to be dealt withall as wolves."

The suggestion of Mr. Stoddard bore fruit in 1706, when the General Court passed a bill for raising and increasing dogs for the better security of the frontiers. In 1708, a bill of £41 was paid by the Government for " Trayling dogs " on the frontier of Middlesex. In 1724, Col. John Stoddard recommended that a " number of good dogs be provided " and if they should kill an Indian " it will more effectually prevent their coming than the killing of 20 in any other way." Again in 1749, Gideon Lyman of Northampton, was paid over £250 for purchasing dogs. The same year a troop of fifty men with fifty dogs, was ordered to range the woods, and Col. Stoddard writes that he had committed the command of the men with dogs to Col. Willard and Ens. Bridgman. Hoyt speaks of the use of dogs in 1744 and 1746. They were used in New Haven colony in 1656, and " Fierce Dogs " in New Jersey, in 1758. Connecticut made use of dogs in 1708.

Apparently no notice was taken of this proposition by the government at this time, but it was acted upon quite effectively, a few years after. It will be remembered that a similar suggestion was made by Lieuts. Maudsley and Filer in 1675. [1]

Origin of the Attack upon Deerfield.   The first blow of the war in the valley fell upon Deerfield, Feb. 29th, 1704. After the raid under Beaubassin[2] the English retaliated, and a number of Indians were killed at Piggwacket, Me. The Abenakis at once sent to Canada for assistance, and in answer to this appeal, the attack on Deerfield was determined upon. This disastrous event has been so often and so thoroughly described,[3] and is so familiar to all, that only a brief statement of the principal facts relating thereto, together with a slight reference to the Northampton men engaged in it, will be given.

Early Notice of the Design.   Gov. Dudley had received information, obtained through Indian spies, from the Governor of New York, in May, 1703, that preparations were making in Canada for an attack on Deerfield, and Major Schuyler of Albany, sent a similar notification to the authorities of that town. These alarms proved premature, however, though they had the effect of causing measures for defense to be promptly taken. A garrison was stationed there through the season, and two companies were sent from Connecticut in August, but their stay was brief.

1 Lieut. Filer, in his letter to the government, written in 1675, recommending the use of dogs, makes the following barbarous proposition: " If an Indian worthy to die were baited by our fiercest dogs and fed with their flesh and so kept it would be a terrour." Capt. Mosely writes that in the same year, a squaw, captured at Springfield, was ordered to be "tourne in peeces by dogs and shee was so dealt withall."

2 " Shortly after he " (Sieur de Beaubassin) " had retired the English having killed some of these (Abenakis) Indians they sent us word of it, and at the same time demanded assistance. This obliged us My Lord, to send thither Sieur de Rouville, an officer of the line with nearly two hundred men, who attacked a fort (Deerfield) in which, according to the report of all the prisoners, there were more than 100 men under arms; they took more than one hundred and fifty prisoners, including men and women, and retreated, having lost only three men and some twenty wounded."— N. Y. Colonial Documents, vol. 9, p. 762.

3 The fullest and most accurate account of this attack may be found in Sheldon's History of Deerfield. The following sketch is mainly compiled from that source.

The Attack.   In this expedition were two hundred French and one hundred forty Indians, commanded by Major Hertel de Rouville, assisted by his two brothers. The weather was cold, the snow deep, and the march of three hundred miles or more tedious and wearisome. Moccasins and snow shoes had been provided, as well for the soldiers as for the expected captives. On the way, provisions became scarce, the French were starving and very nearly mutinied. It is asserted that they must have surrendered to the English, had the attack failed. Their Indian allies furnished a scanty supply of game, and on this they subsisted. On the evening of the 28th of February, the party reached the vicinity of Deerfield, where they spent the night making preparations for the assault. Just before dawn, ascertaining that the sentinels had been withdrawn, or according to some reports that one of them had fallen asleep, they rushed upon the village. By means of the deep snow drifts that nearly reached the top of the palisades, the enemy gained an easy entrance. Simultaneous assaults were made at different points, the surprised and bewildered inhabitants offering but little resistance. Men, women and children were dragged from their beds, bound and collected together preparatory to the march to Canada. A few escaped to the woods, but more than half the inhabitants were either killed or made prisoners.

Capture of the Williams Family.   About twenty of the enemy attacked the house of Rev. John Williams, the minister. Jumping out of bed, he presented a pistol at the breast of an Indian. It missed fire, and he was seized and bound, remaining so for an hour before he was permitted to dress. Two of his younger children and a negro woman were murdered before his eyes. Mrs. Williams, with her babe but a few weeks old, and five children, were made captives. Her husband and children were carried to Canada, herself and babe were slain on the way.

Capt. Stoddard Escapes.   John Stoddard, son of Rev. Solomon Stoddard, was one of the garrison soldiers on duty there, and was billeted at the house of Mr. Williams. Seizing his cloak he leaped from a window and made his way across Deerfield River. But half dressed and without shoes, he tore his cloak in pieces, wrapped them about his naked feet, and reached Hatfield completely exhausted. He brought the first information of the attack to the towns below, though they had already been alarmed by the light of the burning buildings.

The People make a Stout Defense. As the enemy swarmed through the village, house after house was attacked, some fell an easy prey, while others were bravely defended. In many of them, soldiers of the garrison were quartered, who gave good account of themselves. Stout resistance was made at the house of Capt. John Sheldon. Unable to effect an entrance, a hole was hacked in the front door,[1] through which Mrs. Sheldon was shot. A son of Capt. Sheldon, with his wife, jumped from a window. She sprained her ankle and was captured; he escaped and reached Hatfield in safety. An entrance was effected through the back door, and most of the family were made prisoners. A short distance from the Sheldon house stood that of Benoni Stebbins. Its inmates, seven men and a few women, made such an effective defense that all attempts to burn it were frustrated, but Hoyt says that it was accidentally burned during the fight. A palisaded house, a few rods south of the fortification, was also successfully defended. Seventeen houses and barns were burned, nine houses left standing within the fortifications, and fifteen without. The wounded and the women and children saved, were taken to Northampton, Hadley and Hatfield.

Reinforcements Arrive. Fight in the Meadows. Preparations were made for the return march to Canada, and the prisoners were collected in the house of Capt. Sheldon, one of the largest in the place. While the assailants were thus employed, about thirty men on horseback, hastily gathered from the towns below, arrived. These, together with the defenders of the block house, and such of the inhabitants as could be gathered, under the command of Capt. Wells, made a most determined attack upon the enemy. A party

---

[1] The perforated door of this house is still preserved in Pocumtuck Hall, Deerfield.

engaged in plundering houses, and wantonly slaughtering stock, was driven out of the town and pursued into a meadow. Here the enemy received reinforcements, and the English being nearly surrounded, some accounts say ambushed, were compelled to retreat, having lost nine men. This pursuit by the English, put the prisoners in great jeopardy, and Rouville, at one time anticipating defeat, issued orders to tomahawk the captives, but the messenger was killed before delivering his orders. Preparations had been made to put the captives to death, and several were bound for that purpose, but when the English retreated these barbarous orders were countermanded.[1]

Number Slain and Captured.   One hundred eleven persons were made prisoners, including three Frenchmen, residing in the village. The number slain was forty-nine.[2] The French claimed that they took more than one hundred fifty prisoners, men, women and children, lost but three Frenchmen and had twenty wounded.[3] The number of Indians killed is not known.[4]

Men in the Meadow Fight.   Deerfield was garrisoned by twenty soldiers from different towns in the county. Sergt. Wright gives the names of fifty-seven men who fought in the meadow. Thirty-eight of them were men who volunteered, when the light of the burning buildings, warned them that the attack was in progress, and who hastened to the scene of hostilities. Of these men, eight were from Northampton, thirteen belonged in Deerfield, fourteen were from Hadley, and twenty-two from Hatfield. The names of the Northampton men, as given by Sergt. Wright, were the following: Sergt. Ebenezer Wright, Joseph Clesson, Thomas Alvord, garrison soldiers, Benjamin Stebbins, Samuel Wright, Joseph

1 Hoyt's Indian wars, p. 188.

2 Sheldon's History of Deerfield, vol. 1, p. 306.

3 N. Y. Colonial Records, vol. 9, p. 762.

4 The whole number of inhabitants at Deerfield, at this time was two hundred ninety-one. Of these, twenty were garrison soldiers, two visitors from Hatfield, and two hundred sixty-eight residents. In a few hours, all but one hundred twenty-six were either killed or in captivity.—Sheldon's History of Deerfield, vol. 1, p. 310.

Wright, Preserved Strong, and John Bridgman Jr. Six of them went up on the morning of the 29th, and two belonged to the garrison. Thomas Baker was a member of the garrison, but was captured before the meadow fight.

John Bridgman Jr. Captured and Maimed. None of the Northampton men were killed. John Bridgman Jr. was captured, but escaped while the meadow fight was in progress. He suffered[1] both in person and in property, and in 1705, petitioned the General Court for remuneration. He states that he "lost considerable and was maimed, being in the service under pay. I was taken by the enemy, and while in their hands they cut off the forefinger of my right hand, by which wound I lost my time and was disabled from work four months." The court granted him £7 for his wound and the amount of his losses was made up to him from the sum voted by the Legislature for all who were engaged in the meadow fight. In the excitement of that encounter, the men threw off their outer garments, coats, jackets, waistcoats, and accoutrements.

Compensation Granted to the Soldiers. On the 9th of June, the General Court ordered that the losses of the soldiers should be repaid. The whole amounted to £34.17. Each of the widows of the four slain soldiers, were allowed £5, and as only one scalp had been obtained, the survivors of the fifty-seven men were voted £60, which was to be equally divided among them. The entire sum awarded by the Legislature to these men and their families, was £114.17, but only £108.17 was allowed. They were also given the plunder taken from the enemy, which amounted to £16.12.10. Thirty-one years after, the survivors of the fight petitioned for a grant of land. The House of Deputies voted them a township on the west side of the Connecticut River, ten miles square, adjoining Hatfield. The town was to be laid out in sixty-three equal shares, one for the first minister, one for the ministry, and one for the school.

1 His inventory of losses is as follows : 1 saddle 26s.; Leather Breeches 15s; Leather Waistcoat 20s.; Gloves 3s.; Muslin neck cloth and 1 handkerchief 6s.; Serge Waistcoat 16s.; pair of Stockings 4s.; 1 Shirt 5s.; ½ lb. of powder and 1 lb. bullets 2s. 6d.; money 14s. Total £5.11.6.

The petitioners were to settle within three years, one family on each of the sixty shares. This recommendation passed the House of Deputies, Dec. 12th, 1735, but there is no record of any action by the Council, and the petitioners failed to obtain the coveted township.

The March to Canada begun. The Captives.

After the retreat of the English, de Rouville, having collected his prisoners, began the march to Canada. This tedious, heart rending, and calamitous journey has been so frequently and so minutely described, that there is little need of its repetition here. Two men from Northampton, were captured at this time—John Bridgman Jr. and Thomas Baker. The former escaped before the march began, and the latter was carried to Canada. The cold was intense, the snow deep, and being encumbered by women and children, as well as loaded with provisions and plunder, progress was slow. Of the one hundred eleven captives, two escaped, and twenty-two were slain or perished on the way. More than half of the prisoners were under eighteen years of age; thirty-two of them less than twelve, and twelve not five years old. Rev. John Williams and family were among those carried off by the enemy. His wife and infant child were killed on the fifth day of the march. He and all his children but one, Eunice, who never came back, remained in captivity two years. On his return he published an account of the hardships he endured, under the title of the "Redeemed Captive returning to Zion."

Reinforcements quickly Forwarded.

Soldiers were promptly sent to Deerfield from the Hampshire towns and from Connecticut. On the first of March, one hundred forty-seven men came up from Hartford. The snow was so deep that it was impossible to pursue the enemy, as the troops were without snow shoes. Later in the month, Capt. Newberry, with sixty-two men arrived from Connecticut, and they remained till September. The remaining inhabitants of Deerfield had serious thoughts of again deserting the place, but after consideration they resolutely determined to maintain their plantation. About twenty-five men and from fifty to sixty women and children were all that remained, and their situation was desolate and forbidding in the extreme. In order to encourage the inhabitants to remain, Lieut. Col. Partridge of Hatfield, impressed men into the service and permanently garrisoned the town.

Attempts to Recover the Prisoners, 1704 to 1707.   All allusion to the heroic exertions made for the recovery and redemption of the captives must necessarily be brief.[1] A few months after the disaster, efforts were commenced for their return. Ens. John Sheldon, Capt. John Wells of Deerfield, and Capt. John Livingstone of Albany, set out on an expedition for this purpose in December following. They had credentials from Gov. Dudley, and letters to the Marquis de Vaudreuil. Finding the Indians unwilling to give them up without ransom, and the French government not ready for an exchange, they were able to obtain the release of but five persons, with whom they returned in the spring of 1705. Meanwhile negotiations were in progress between Gov. Dudley and the Canadian authorities for a general exchange of prisoners, and a number of French in the hands of the English were sent to Port Royal. In January, 1706, Sheldon and Wells were again commissioned as deputies and sent to Canada. After a delay of many months, they brought away with them forty-four captives, returning to Boston in August. Rev. Mr. Williams and fifty-six others, were afterwards set at liberty, and they arrived at Boston in November of the same year, under the conduct of Mr. Samuel Appleton of that city. In 1707, Mr. Sheldon was again sent to Canada, to negotiate for the release of the remaining prisoners, ninety in number. He was not well received, and as there were rumors of an English expedition against Canada, he was detained several months. He reached Albany with seven more rescued captives in August.

Story of Mary Sheldon.   Interwoven with the local history of Northampton, as well as that of Deerfield, is the story of Mary Sheldon. She was the daughter of John Sheldon, who removed from Northamp-

---

1 For a detailed account of these efforts, see Sheldon's History of Deerfield, vol. 1, pp. 324 to 351.

ton to Deerfield, in 1684. When that town was destroyed, she was among the captives, and was carried to Canada, where she remained three or four years, but was finally redeemed. Some time before her capture, when between thirteen and fourteen years of age, she engaged to marry Jonathan Strong of this town. Her first inquiry on reaching home was for her lover. Alas! he remained constant but a twelvemonth and a day, having married Mehitable Stebbins, in 1705. In 1708, she became the third wife of Samuel Clapp of Northampton. Her husband and the wife of Jonathan Strong both died in 1761, and the following year the ancient lovers were married. She was then 75 and he was 80 years of age. She died the next year, but he survived three years longer. There is a tradition that Mill River was very high at the time of the marriage, and as no boat was at hand, the bride was ferried over in an old "hopper" from the grist mill. Another story is that she helped her husband mount his horse and then got on the pillion behind him. During her captivity she was adopted by a squaw, and some of the Canada Indians became very much attached to her. In after years these Indians came to visit her at Northampton. They always came when Clapp's corn was green, and would devour it in large quantities, roasting the ears at a fire under an apple tree. On one occasion she received a visit from two squaws. Leaving their papooses in the bushes on Pancake plain, they came into the street, and found the house where Mrs. Clapp lived, by means of the step stones which had been described to them. They asked permission to bring their children, which was readily given. Mrs. Clapp received a grant of land from the General Court "between Southampton and Glascow." [1]

1 Judd MSS.

CHAPTER XXXIX.

QUEEN ANNE'S FRENCH AND INDIAN WAR.

Capt. Thomas Baker. IN this connection comes properly the romance of Capt. Baker.[1] Though the principal events occurred some years after, he first appears as an actor in the terrible tragedy at Deerfield. Capt. Thomas Baker was the son of Timothy Baker of Northampton, where he was born in 1682. He had no home but his father's house till he removed to Brookfield, in 1716. Timothy Baker was an influential citizen, often employed in town business, was chosen ensign in 1689, when the trouble occurred about the officers of the Northampton militia company, and was afterwards lieutenant. Thomas probably joined the company of which his father was lieutenant, and was one of the garrison soldiers at Deerfield, under the command of Capt. Wells, in 1703.

Taken Prisoner, he Narrowly Escapes Burning at the Stake, but Eventually gets away. While the fight in the Deerfield meadow was in progress, Thomas Baker was taken prisoner. He lost his weapons, as well as a portion of his clothing, and with the other captives endured the fearful march to Canada. In a few months he endeavored to escape from Montreal, in order to bring intelligence of the projected invasion of Chevalier Boncour [Beaucours], but was recaptured. The Indians decided to burn him alive. As they were about to bind him to the stake, by a sudden exertion of strength, he shook off his tormenters and was spared that cruel fate. Seeking refuge at the house of one Le Clair,

1 His story may be gathered from various petitions found in the Massachusetts archives; from the Journal of Capt. John Stoddard's expedition to Canada to recover prisoners in 1713; from the Otis Genealogy, in N. E. Historical and Genealogical Register, vol. 5, pp. 177 to 195; and from "True Stories of New England Captives," by Miss C. A. Baker. It is from these sources that this narrative has been compiled.

he was ransomed from the Indians by the payment ·of £5, advanced by his protector. Suspecting his design of conveying intelligence of pending military movements, the Governor of Canada put him in irons, and kept him a close prisoner four months. No sooner was he at large than he renewed his attempt to escape. In this flight he was accompanied by Joseph Petty, John Nims, and Martin Kellogg Jr., fellow prisoners taken when he himself was captured. Their march homeward was attended by much suffering and many privations. Though beset with dangers on every side, their greatest difficulty was in procuring food, but by fishing and hunting they were able to support life till they reached Deerfield, nearly dead with hunger and fatigue. In 1718, he petitioned the General Court for remuneration for his losses, and was granted £10.

Goes on a Scouting Expedition. Attacks and Disperses a Party of Indians. Rewarded by the Legislature, 1712. Restless and adventurous, Baker continued in the service, and was actively employed during the continuance of the war. In 1712, he had reached the grade of lieutenant, and with thirty-two men started on a scouting expedition. He went north-west to Coasset, on the Connecticut River, and then struck across the country to the Pemigewasset, the west branch of the Merrimac River. Here at the confluence of a small stream, since known as Baker's River, with the Merrimac, he came upon a party of Indians, which he dispersed without the loss of a man. The Indian sachem Walteonumus [Wattanummon] was killed. It is reported that Capt. Baker and the sachem leveled their guns at each other at the same time; Baker's eyebrow was grazed by the Indian bullet, but the chief was instantly killed. On the bank of the river was a wigwam filled with beaver skins. Baker's party carried away what they could, and burned the rest. A daughter of Capt. Baker, Mrs. Bean, gives a different version of this encounter, repeated undoubtedly from the statements of her father. She reports that a large party of French and Indians were discovered coming down the river in their boats; that Capt. Baker placed his men in ambush, fired upon them when they appeared, and killed so many and sunk so many canoes, that the remainder made a precipitate retreat. He obtained the accoutrements

and ornaments of a chief. In this account nothing is said
of the capture of beaver skins, nor is any account made of
them to the General Court, when compensation was voted
to the soldiers engaged in the expedition. Capt. Baker
then proceeded down the Merrimac to Dunstable, and thence
to Boston. On the 8th of May, 1712, he made application
to the General Court for payment for the services of himself and his command. But one scalp was brought by
them, yet they claimed that they had slain a number of Indians, whose scalps they could not obtain. Willing to reward the bravery and enterprise of Lieut. Baker and his
men, the court granted them £40, sufficient to pay for four
scalps. They were in active service from the 24th of March
to the 16th of May. Baker was soon after promoted to a
captaincy.

Is sent to Canada
with Col. Stod-
dard and Rev.
Mr. Williams,
1713.

The next year Col. John Stoddard and Rev.
John Williams were sent by the government to Canada to negotiate for the return
or exchange of prisoners. Capt. Baker was
an assistant, and Martin Kellogg, his companion in the
hazardous journey through the wilderness, was employed
as interpreter. These tedious negotiations, set forth minutely in the journal of Col. Stoddard, will be noted hereafter, and need not be commented on at this point. It was
during his sojourn in Canada at this time, that Capt.
Baker found the future companion of his life. Among the
prisoners was madame Le Beau. She was the daughter of
Richard Otis of Dover, N. H., and was captured while an
infant, when that place was destroyed by the Indians in
1689. The mother and infant were carried to Canada,
where the mother married a Frenchman, and the daughter
was brought up in a convent, but she resolutely refused to
take the veil.

The Priests are Un-
willing that she
should Return,
but she Sails
away with her
Lover.

At an early age she married a French gen-
tleman named Le Beau, by whom she had
three children. He died a short time before
Col. Stoddard and his party arrived. Capt.
Baker, a bachelor of thirty-two, soon fell in
love with the handsome widow, scarcely twenty-five years

old. His affection was returned, and the romance culminated in marriage a few years after. In the meantime, the French priests endeavored by every means in their power to prevent her return. It was only through her own determined will, the bravery and address of her lover, and a commendable exhibition of pluck and resolution on the part of all concerned, that her deliverance was effected. Not a penny did she receive from the estate of her husband. It was sold by the authorities and the proceeds confiscated. Christine or Christina, her Roman Catholic name, anxious to return, placed her goods upon a vessel about to sail for Boston. The authorities ordered them on shore and absolutely refused to allow her to depart. Capt. Baker, who had been sent home with dispatches, returned promptly, came to the rescue, and she decided to leave every thing and go with him. When the vessel in which the liberated prisoners were to be taken home, was ready to sail, Capt. Baker arrived at Quebec from Montreal, "bringing with him one English prisoner." The priests, baffled and enraged, renewed their endeavors to get her out of the hands of the English, but Col. Stoddard, having placed her safely on board the transport, refused to give her up, and she sailed away with her lover, leaving children, property and Catholicism behind.

And Arrives at Northampton. Capt. Baker brought her to his home, the house of his father, in Northampton. Here under the spiritual teaching of Rev. Solomon Stoddard, she renounced the Catholic religion, and was baptized into the Puritan faith. With her old religion she discarded her French name, and Margaret (the name by which it was believed she was known in infancy) was substituted for that of Christine, though she seems afterwards in one instance at least, to have used the latter name. One authority states that she joined the church at Northampton, but her name is not found upon its records. At the time of her death she was a member of the church at Dover, N. H. Capt. Baker and Madame Le Beau were married at Northampton during the year 1715. The birth of their first child, named Christian, is found upon the records in this town. Her name is there given as Margaret.

Capt. Baker Removes to Brookfield. Fruitless Journey to Canada to obtain the Children. About the year 1716, Capt. Baker removed to Brookfield,[1] where he resided many years, prominent among the leading citizens of the town. He was chosen representative to the General Court in 1719, the first elected from that town, and filled other local offices during his residence there. Mrs. Baker did not forget her children, left in Canada, and in 1721, made the journey to that country in order, if possible, to recover them. Her husband was sent by the government as bearer of dispatches, and she accompanied him. But deaf to her strongest appeal, the Romish church refused to give up the children. Both Baker and his wife received compensation from the government after their return. To him was awarded £10, while to her was given twice that amount. The next year Capt. Baker and Joseph Kellogg were sent "express" to Canada, and were paid £30 each by the government.

They Reside in various Places. Letter from the Priest, 1727-1735. Capt. Baker resided in Brookfield till 1732, when he removed to Mendon; the year following he went to Newport, R. I., and in 1735, he was at Dover, N. H., the birthplace of his wife. He died in Roxbury, the same year, while on a visit to relatives. He lost nearly all his property at Brookfield, through the trickery of a speculator, and was afterwards in straightened circumstances. He was a brave man, a good Indian fighter, somewhat rough in manners and outspoken, but evidently a man of parts, and much respected.[2] After his death, his wife obtained a license to keep a public house at Dover, and continued in the business for a number of years. Her old friends, the

---

1 The annexed extract from the Brookfield land records, gives the reason why Capt. Baker and his wife removed to that place, but nothing has been discovered concerning the occasion of the grant to his wife: "Dec. 10, 1714. Then granted to Margaret Otice, alias Le-bue, one that was a prisoner in Canada, and lately come from thence, forty acres of upland in Brookfield, and twenty acres of meadow; provided she returns not again to live in Canada, but tarries in this Province or territory, and marries to Capt. Thomas Baker."

2 The following anecdote illustrates his bluff and irreverent manner of speech, as well as the prompt rebuke administered, so characteristic of those days: Capt. Thomas Baker was tried for blasphemy on Feb 6th, 1727, "there being a discourse of God's having in his Providence put in Jos. Jennings Esq. a Justice of the Peace for the county of Hampshire. He said the following words, 'If I had been with the Almighty I would have taught him better.'" The jury returned a verdict of not guilty, and Baker was discharged on paying costs.—Judd MSS.

priests in Canada, did not forget their youthful convert. In 1727, her former confessor wrote, urging her to return to Canada and to the fold of the Holy Catholic church. Land was offered her husband, or work, if he preferred to follow a trade. This document coming to the notice of Gov. Burnett, he prepared a strong and able answer to it, refuting the claims and arguments of the priest. These letters were translated and published, and attracted considerable attention. Mrs. Baker died at Dover, in 1773.

The Village of Pascommuck Attacked by the Indians. The next and most formidable attack in the valley fell upon the hamlet of Pascommuck, then a part of Northampton. It consisted of a little cluster of houses lying at the foot of the upper peak of Mt. Tom, just where the Connecticut River swept round the northern point of the mountain, now known as Mt. Nonotuck. At that time the current of the river flowed through the great bend known as the "Ox bow," the tongue of land encircled by it being then a part of Hadley. The place had been settled but a few years, and all houses were east of the present bridge over the Manhan River. Home lots were granted there in 1698 and 1699. The entire village is now within the limits of the town of Easthampton, and is about four miles from Northampton center. But five families were living there at that time. Moses Hutchinson occupied the most northerly lot, the house being situated just beyond or west of the point where the road through Northampton meadows joined the Springfield road, then came John Searle, Samuel Janes, Benoni Jones and Benjamin Janes.

Conjectures Concerning the Attacking Party. This attack on Pascommuck was not apparently preconcerted. A party of French and Indians, under the command of Sieur de Montigny, sent from Canada in answer to an appeal from the Indians of Penaske,[1] assaulted the hamlet because they

---

[1] "The Indians of Penaske having likewise sent us word at the same time [when the Abenakis asked help after Beaubassin's raid] my Lord, that the English had killed some of their people, M. de Vaudreuil sent Sieur de Montigny thither with 4 or 5 Frenchman, as well to reassure them in the fear they entertained of the English, as to engage them to continue the war. This he effected this spring, at the head of some 50 of these Indians, having burnt an English fort and taken 23 prisoners."—N. Y. Hist. Coll., vol. 9, p. 762.

were in pressing need of provisions, and saw an opportunity of obtaining them by surprising the people. Who the Indians of Penaske[1] were is not known. No place or tribe of that name is recognized in any extant Indian vocabulary. One historian states that the party under Montigny were returning from an unsuccessful foray upon the Merrimac River, but there are no positive data corroborating the supposition. It is asserted by the same authority that the party was on the way to attack Westfield, but the water was so high that they were unable to cross that river. The position of Pascommuck was well known to some of the Indians, who were familiar with this portion of the valley, several of them having visited Northampton the year previous. On the evening before the attack, they reconnoitred the village from the mountain side, and arranged their plan of assault. Owing to the spring freshet, the Northampton meadows were overflowed, and the enemy deemed it impossible that help could come from that place. The authority[2] already quoted reports that the Indians were so nearly famished, that they had decided to surrender to the English if food could not otherwise be obtained.

The Oldest Account of the Affair. The oldest and undoubtedly the original account of this catastrophe may be found on the Recorder's Book for Hampshire County, probably entered at the time it occurred. It is short and concise, but differs in some respects from other statements:

"May 12 [13] Pascomok Fort taken by ye French & Indians, being about 72. They took and Captivated ye whole Garrison, being about 37 Persons. The English Pursueing of them caused them to nock all the captives on the head Save 5 or 6. Three they carried to Canada with them, the others escap'd and about 7 of those knocked on the head Recovered, ye rest died. Capt. John Taylor was killed in the fight, and Sam'l Bartlett wounded."

The Assault. On the 13th of May, about daybreak, the enemy delivered the assault. No watch was kept, and the inhabitants were completely surprised. The house of Benoni Jones was fortified, and the Indians were able to approach so near as to put their guns through the port holes before the sleepers were aroused. Patience,

1 Probably the Penobscot Indians are intended.
2 Rev. Solomon Williams' Historical Sermon, 1815, pp. 12, 13.

widow of Richard Webb, awakened by the alarm, looked from a window and was shot. The people made what resistance they could, firing briskly upon the savages, but the latter, gathering flax and other combustibles, soon set the house on fire, and the surviving occupants were compelled to yield themselves prisoners. Amazed, bewildered and panic stricken, the rest of the inhabitants were able to offer but a feeble opposition, and all soon surrendered.

Capt. Benj. Wright beats off the Indians.

While the main attack was in progress at Pascommuck, a detachment of ten Indians, invested the one house at Lower Farms, now Smith's Ferry, in which Capt. Benjamin Wright lived. The place was afterwards owned by Elias Lyman, and was more recently known as the Cargill homestead, or the "old Long House." Capt. Wright refused to surrender, and shot one of the Indians, breaking his arm. They then attempted to burn the house, by shooting spiked arrows dipped in brimstone upon the roof, but a young man in the house by the name of Thomas Stebbins,[1] wrapping himself in a feather bed, drew water from the well and put out the fire.[2]

The Pursuit. Death of Capt. Taylor.

Having accomplished their object, the enemy soon drew off, but fearing pursuit, sent back one of the wounded with the announcement that if the English followed them all the prisoners would be slain. The unfortunate messenger was killed by an Indian before proceeding far on his mission. According to tradition, Benjamin Janes, escaped by darting into a ravine[3] partly concealed by bushes. Taking a skiff, which he probably knew was moored there, he sailed

1 Who the young man Thomas Stebbins was is not certainly known. But two persons of that name were then living in town. One of them married Elizabeth, sister of Capt. Benjamin Wright, and was forty-two years of age. The other was his son Thomas, then fifteen years old. Probably the lad was at his uncle's house, when the attack was made, and he it was who bravely risked his life to save the property of his relative. He afterwards lived in Southampton.—See Appendix E.

2 The above account is from Rev. Solomon Williams' Historical Sermon which at this point contains the following foot note: "The season at that time was remarkably backward; for though so late in the year, being the 24th of May, according to the present style, the trees and bushes had not budded, and the year was so far advanced before the flood subsided from the meadow, that many persons doubted whether it was expedient to plant their corn; but notwithstanding, as there was no frost till late in the season, the crop of corn proved to be uncommonly good."

3 Rev. P. W. Lyman's History of Easthampton, p. 17.

through the overflowed meadows to Northampton, where he gave the first notice of the disaster.[1]   Capt. John Taylor, with a troop of horsemen, volunteers from among the citizens of Northampton, immediately started in pursuit. Passing to the westward of the present town of Easthampton, they overtook the marauders a short distance south of that village, between the highway to Westfield and Mt. Tom, near what was formerly known as "Wilton's Meadow."[2]   One of their captives having escaped, the enemy had every reason to expect that an alarm would be given, followed by an instant and vigorous pursuit.   Consequently they first killed all but one of the boys who had been captured, and placed themselves in ambush.   While the massacre was in progress, Elisha, son of John Searle, caught up a pack and ran forward with it, indicating his willingness to be useful if his life was spared.   He was not molested, and was taken to Canada.   When the pursuers came up with the enemy, Capt. Taylor, who was riding in advance of his men, was shot.   He fell at the first fire and was the only one of his party killed.[3]   Samuel Bartlett of Northampton, was severely wounded at the same time.   He was unable to labor for several months, and received a gra-

1   The most circumstantial account of this raid is found in Penhallow's "History of the French and Indian Wars" of New England, published in 1726. Rev. Solomon Williams' "Historical Sermon, delivered on the National Thanksgiving, April 13, 1815," differs in some respects from the others, giving certain details of local interest not found elsewhere. Rev. Payson W. Lyman's "History of Easthampton," published in 1866, and the Judd Manuscript, contain local allusions of importance. From these several sources the facts relative to the assault on Pascommuck, have been obtained.

2   Lyman locates this skirmish " on land now (1866) owned by Chester and the heirs of C. Edson Waite,"—see History, p. 17. "Wilton's Meadow" is two miles beyond the Easthampton Meeting House, between Southampton and Pomeroy Meadow roads. —Judd MSS.

3   Capt. Taylor, who was sixty-three years old, lived during the last years of his life on a small lot adjoining Medad Pomeroy's homestead, probably near what afterwards became the residence of Judge Joseph Lyman. The house was burned between 1705 and 1716, and much of the furniture destroyed. His widow petitioned the Legislature for help in 1705. She represents that her husband's horse and clothes were lost, and she " left a poor widow with 11 children. By his death we are drove from the improvement of a farm in the woods which we hoped to be a relief to us." The Legislature granted her £12, two of which were to pay for the horse. The " farm in the woods" was a grant of eighty acres near " Whiteloaf brook," Southampton, made in 1703.

tuity from the government.[1]   Disheartened by this unfortunate occurrence, the troops made no further demonstration, but returned in sadness, bringing the body of their slain commander.

The Slain.   Living at Pascommuck at this time, were thirty-three persons.   Of these, nineteen were killed, three escaped, eight were rescued, and three were carried to Canada.   Not anticipating an attack, the people were scattered in their own households.   The block house contained only the family of Benoni Jones, whose dwelling it was.   The slain were Samuel Janes aged forty ; his wife Sarah, and three children, viz : Obadiah aged five, Ebenezer aged three, and Sarah aged one ; four children of Benjamin Janes, viz : Hannah aged eight, Miriam aged four, Benjamin aged three, and Nehemiah aged one ; Benoni Jones[2] aged thirty-eight, and two children, viz : Ebenezer aged six, and Jonathan aged one ; John Searl and three children, viz : Abigail aged seven, John aged four, and Caleb aged two ; Moses Hutchinson aged thirty-two, and one child, Moses, aged three ; and Patience Webb aged forty-six, widow of Richard Webb. [3]

The Wounded.   Three were found who had been knocked on the head, and one of them scalped, but all were alive, and eventually recovered.   The wife of Benja-

1 In 1705, he petitioned the General Court for a gratuity.   He represented that he was wounded while on duty, May 13, 1704, and was not able to labor till August.   During the next winter he was impressed into the service, and was engaged in the " Grand Scout towards West River," under Capt. John Parsons.   While on his return his horse was drowned.   The Court granted him £3 for loss of time and for his wound, but nothing for the horse.

2 Benoni Jones was the son of Griffith Jones of Springfield.   When twelve years old, in March, 1678, he was indentured to William Clarke of Northampton, whom he was to serve till he was twenty-one years of age.   Lieut. Clarke agreed to " learn him to read and write and give him £5 at the end of his term, with sufficient clothing, such as servants usually have, and at the end of his time two suits of apparel."   His brother, Pelatiah, was indentured at the same time to William Holton Jr., of Northampton, on similar conditions, as to schooling and apparel, but he was to be taught the " art, science and trade of a weaver," and to be paid £8 at the end of his term of service.   He was then fourteen years old.

3 " Samuel Janes lived where the house of Mr. Obadiah Janes now stands; John Searls, where his son Elisha and his grandson of the same name afterwards dwelt; Benjamin Janes, where Capt. Philip Clark lives; Moses Hutchinson, near the place where Mr. Solomon Ferry's house stands."—Rev. Mr. Williams' Hist. Sermon, p. 13.

min Janes was taken to the top of Pomeroy Mountain, tomahawked, scalped, and left for dead. She was discovered by the pursuing party, carried on a litter to Northampton, and lived till she was eighty years old. For several years she was under the care of Dr. Gershom Buckley and others of Westfield. Her husband finally settled in Coventry, Ct.[1]

The Captives. Reminiscences of Elisha Searl. But three of those taken captive reached Canada, viz: Elisha Searl, son of John, aged nine years; Esther, wife of Benoni Jones (she was an Ingersoll), who died there, and her niece, Margaret Huggins, aged eighteen, who returned. Elisha Searl remained in Canada till he was twenty-eight years old. He was baptized by the French priests and named Michael.[2] While with the Indians, he accompanied them on an excursion to the Mississippi River, and in after life was fond of relating his impressions of the country. He came to Northampton in 1722, to obtain a share of his father's estate, intending to return, but was with great reluctance on his part, induced to remain. In order "to engage him to abide here and not return to Canada," the General Court granted him £10, and requested the Governor to give him a commission as Sergeant. He served in that capacity at Deerfield, in 1724, and as lieutenant at Fort Dummer the next year. Brought up under the immediate influence of the Catholic Church, like other New England children, in similar circumstances, he became strongly impressed by the Roman Catholic religion, and greatly attached to the Indian mode of life. He had so far forgotten the English language, that on his return to his former home he was unable to make himself known, and was only recognized by walking on a pair of stilts, he had been fond

---

1 Benjamin Janes, in 1707, petitioned the Governor and Council for aid, as follows: "Benjamin Janes, late of Northampton, now resident in Wethersfield, complained of his great sufferings from the French and Indian enemies, who rifled his house, killed 4 of his children and scalped his wife who long had been and still is under cure, and himself so impoverished that he is unable to satisfy the surgeons in whose hands she hath been and is like to be, for their cost and pains therein." The Governor and Council gave him a brief to beg, "craving the charity of the good people in Branford, Guilford, Killingworth and Saybrook, in Connecticut."—Judd MSS.

2 See Appendix F.

of using when a boy. He married Rebecca Danks.[1] The wife of John Searl, mother of Elisha, was one of those who were tomahawked, but she recovered.[2]

Capt. Benjamin Wright. Capt. Benjamin Wright, who so successfully beat off the Indian attack on his house at Lower Farms, was the famous Indian fighter, whose exploits fill so large a space in the history of the valley. Capt. Wright was constantly employed during the continuance of Queen Anne's war, and a brief account of his scouting expeditions, during that period, though not strictly in chronological order at this point, may not be entirely out of place, as he was then a resident of Northampton. He was the son of Samuel Wright Jr., who came to Northampton with his father in 1656. Sergt. Samuel Wright moved to Northfield when that town was first settled, and was slain by the Indians, in Sept. 1675, when Benjamin was about fifteen years old. Capt. Benjamin Wright married Thankful Taylor, March 22[d], 1681; she died in 1701, and he afterwards married Mary Baker of Springfield. He was among the inhabitants at the second settlement of Northfield, from 1685 to 1690, and returned to

1 A grandson of Elisha Searl, who had heard him relate his adventures, gave the following account to the late Sylvester Judd:—"When Pascommuck was taken by the Indians in 1704, they took a little brother of his from the bed by his feet, and dashed his brains out as if he had been a cat. They gathered the children they had taken together, and knocked them in the head, one after another. Elisha Searl ran, the Indians finding him pretty smart and active, concluded to save him. Samuel Janes attempted to run, but received a blow of a tomahawk on the side of his head above the temple, and they supposed he was dead. He always carried the mark. (He was a thriving man, and old Kentfield said he had got half of Pascommuck, and if the Indians had knocked in the other side of his head, he would have got the whole.) Elisha Searl's mother was carried to a place called ———'s Island in Broad brook, near or on Brewer's farm, when the Indians finding that she was pregnant, and thinking she would not be able to travel to Canada, tomahawked her. She recovered. Searl lived in Canada until he had imbibed all the habits and notions of the French and Indians. He came down to get the property which was left of his father's estate and not to stay. An Indian came with him for a guide. Many persons took an interest in him, and used their influence to get him to stay. They kept him away from the Indian, gave him presents, got a commission for him, etc. They finally succeeded. The Indian after remaining some months returned. He had engaged to marry a French girl in Canada. Her name was Katreen, as he pronounced it. He retained some regard for her and named one of his daughters Catherine, in remembrance of her."—Judd MSS.

2 "One of her descendants has in her possession a silver hair pin worn on the head of Mrs. Searl at the time the blow was inflicted."—Lyman's History of Easthampton, p. 17. This fact has been amplified into a silver comb of sufficient size to deaden the blow of the tomahawk, and thus save her life.

3 2

Northampton when the former place was a second time abandoned. In 1714, he returned to Northfield and became one of the permanent, as well as one of the most prominent, of its settlers. He owned a home lot on Bridge Street, Northampton, which he sold, and removed to Lower Farms, where he lived in 1704. He was a member of the Northampton military company in 1698, and was stationed with others at Deerfield. His first exploit, as commander of the expedition that rescued the boys captured in the Hatfield meadows, has been already noted. In 1708, he commanded a scouting party of English and Indians, which was sent up the Connecticut River. He ascended the river to Cowasset (now Newberry, Vt.), was absent nine weeks, but discovered no Indians.

Commands a Scouting Expedition. Encounters the Indians, and is Defeated. With a party of fifteen men[1] from Northampton, Hatfield, Deerfield and Springfield, Capt. Wright set out in April, 1709, on another scouting expedition. He followed the Connecticut to White River, and proceeded up that stream to its source. Leaving a deposit of provisions, with six men as a guard, the rest pushed on over the mountains till they reached French (or Onion) River. Here they either found or made canoes, in which they sailed down to Lake Champlain. They went out upon the lake, and coming upon a party of Indians in two canoes, fired upon them. Two were killed, two wounded, and one of the canoes captured, containing arms, ammunition and provisions. One scalp was obtained. On their return up French River, they discovered another party of Indians returning from a marauding expedition in New England, having with them William Moody, whom they had captured near Exeter. Capt. Wright fired upon the party, and killed and wounded several. Moody jumped from the canoe and swam for the shore. Lieut. Wells and John Strong went forward to help Moody, when a part of the Indian force, landing from other canoes, that had not been discovered, fired upon

1 This party consisted of Capt. Wright, John Burt, John Strong, Matthew Clesson, and Lieut. John King of Northampton; John Wells, Jonathan Hoyt, Timothy Childs, Ebenezer Severance, and Jabez Olmsted of Deerfield; Joseph Root and Joseph Wait of Hatfield; Thomas Pagan and Joseph Ephraim, two Natick Indians; and Thomas McCreeny and Henry Wright of Springfield.

them, killing Wells and wounding Strong. The English fled, leaving the prisoner Moody, who was too weak to keep up with them, to the tender mercies of the enemy. They seized and burned him on the spot. John Burt disappeared; he was lost in the woods and undoubtedly died of hunger. Strong was able to travel, and the next day coming to their canoes on White River, they retreated to Hatfield, reaching that place on the 28th of May, having been absent thirty-two days. The rear guard, left at the mouth of the river, started for home six days after the rest of the command left them. In the French account, it is stated that two Indians were killed on the lake and one on shore, and that four or five of the English were slain.

Bounty and Scalp Money Granted. Those who were engaged in this expedition, petitioned the General Court for pay and scalp bounty money. They asserted that four Indians had been killed on the lake, and presented one scalp. They also declared to Col. Partridge, who forwarded the paper, that they were sure of having killed four more on Onion River, making eight in all. The court allowed Capt. Wright £12, and £6 each to the men. It is asserted that they had a pocket compass to guide them through the forest. These instruments were not in general use here at that time, and were rarely employed in surveying till after the commencement of the eighteenth century.

"Here am I send me!" During this same year an expedition for the conquest of Canada and Nova Scotia was undertaken by the colonies. The General Court presented the matter to the home government, and the enterprise was entered upon with spirit and determination. The Queen acquiesced in the proposition and soldiers and ships were promised. This scheme was inaugurated while Capt. Wright was engaged in the scout just recounted, and on his return he endeavored to obtain employment in that army. He offered his services to the government in a short but characteristic letter, in which he used the phrase at the head of this paragraph. But the enterprise failed and nothing further is heard from him while the war was in progress. It is not to be supposed, however, that he was idle. There was plenty of work for such men as Capt. Wright, and no doubt he found ample employment. During the succeeding ten years he was actively engaged in building up the struggling town of Northfield, and in subsequent wars will again come into prominence as an Indian fighter.[1]

1 Following is the letter of Capt. Wright, offering his services to the government:

"Northampton, Sept. 19, 1709.

"May it please y^r Excellency

"With submission and under correction, I would offer my service to y^r Excellency, if that in wisdom you send forces to Canada from our parts by land, that 'Here am I, send me.' This year I have done service, and hope I may again, not that I would trouble y^r Excellency but am willing to go.

"Not else, but in duty I subscribe

y^r Excellency's most humble serv^t.

BENJAMIN WRIGHT."

CHAPTER XL

QUEEN ANNE'S FRENCH AND INDIAN WAR

Caleb Lyman Commands a Scouting Party.

IN 1704, the government having received information that the Indians had an encampment at Cowass,[1] on the Connecticut River, for the purpose of fishing and planting, determined to break it up. Orders were issued for the organization of a scouting party to reconnoitre. Only one man offered himself for that service in Hampshire County. Col. Partridge therefore requested the commander of the Connecticut forces to engage some Indians for the expedition. Major Whiting accordingly "did speedily procure five brisk Indians"[2] at Hartford, who volunteered for this service. Caleb Lyman of Northampton, was the one man who was willing to undertake the enterprise.

Mr. Lyman's Account of the Expedition.

The following report of this undertaking is copied in full from Penhallow's Indian Wars.[3] It was furnished to the author by Mr. Lyman himself, and is therefore of great interest, and thoroughly reliable : —

"Sometime in the month of May, 1704, there came intelligence from Albany, of a number of enemy Indians up Connecticut river, who had built a fort, and planted corn, at a place called Cowassuck. On the fifth of June following, we set out (by order of authority) from Northampton, and went nine days journey into the wilderness (through much difficulty, by reason of the enemy's hunting and scouting in the woods,

1 Cowassuck or Cowass, as it is generally called, was about one hundred miles above Deerfield, on the Connecticut River, near the mouth of Wells River. It was a famous rallying place for the Indians. They fished in the stream, planted the fertile meadow, and made it a general rendezvous on their way back and forth from Canada. The Pascommuck, as well as the Deerfield captives, stopped there.

2 Petition of Major Whiting, 1706, Judd MSS.

3 pp. 31 to 33.

as we perceived by their tracks and firing), and then came across some fresh tracks, which we followed till we came in sight of the abovesaid river : Supposing there might be a number of Indians at hand, we being not far from the place where the fort was said to be built. Here we made a halt to consult what methods to take ; and soon concluded to send out a spy, with green leaves for a cap and vest, to prevent his own discovery, and to find out the enemy. But before our spy was gone out of sight, we saw two Indians, at a considerable distance from us, in a canoe, and so immediately called him : And soon after we heard the firing of a gun up the river. Upon which we concluded to keep close til sun set ; and then if we could make any further discovery of the enemy, to attack them, if possible in the night. And accordingly when the evening came on, we moved towards the river, and soon perceived a smoke, at about half a mile's distance, as we thought, where we afterwards found they had taken up their lodging. But so great was the difficulty, that (though we used our utmost care and diligence in it) we were not able to make the approach till about two o'clock in the morning, when we came within twelve rods of the wigwam, where they lay. But here we met with a new difficulty, which we feared would have ruined our design. For the ground was so covered over with dry sticks and brush, for the space of five rods, that we could not pass, without making such a crackling, as we thought would alarm enemy, and give them time to escape. But while we were contriving to compass our design, God in his good providence so ordered that a very small cloud arose, which gave a smart clap of thunder, and a sudden shower of rain. And this opportunity we embraced, to run through the thicket ; and so came undiscovered within sight of the wigwam ; [1] and perceived by their noise that the enemy were awake. But however, being unwilling to lose any time, we crept on our hands and knees till we were within three or four rods of them. Then we arose, and ran to the side of the wigwam, and fired in upon them ; and flinging down our guns we surrounded them with our clubs and hatchets and knocked down several we met with. But after all our diligence, two of their number made their escape from us ; one mortally wounded, and another not hurt, as we afterwards heard.

"When we came to look over the slain, we found seven dead upon the spot ; six of whom we scalped, and left another unscalped (Our Indians saying, they would give one to the country, since we had each of us one, and so concluded we should be rich enough). When the action was thus over, we took our scalps and plunder, such as guns, skins, etc., and the enemy's canoes, in which we came down the river about twelve miles by break of day, and then thought it prudence to dismiss and break the canoes, knowing there were some of the enemy betwixt us and home.

"And now, our care being how to make a safe and comfortable return, we first looked over our provision, and found we had not more than enough for one small refreshment ; and being above one hundred

1 This wigwam, Mr. Judd says, was supposed to be twenty miles below Cowass.

miles from any English settlement, we were very thoughtful how we should subsist by the way. For having tracked about thirty of the enemy a little before us, we could not hunt for our subsistence for fear of discovery; and so we were obliged to eat buds of trees, grass and strawberry leaves for the space of four or five days, till through the goodness of God, we safely arrived at Northampton, on the 19th or 20th of the aforesaid June. And sometime after (upon our humble petition to the Great and General Court, to consider the service we had done) we received thirty-one pounds reward. And I have only this to observe, that in consequence of this action, the enemy were generally alarmed, and immediately forsook their fort and corn at Cowassuck, and never returned to this day that we could hear of, to renew their settlement at that place."

Lyman and his party Rewarded.

In November, the General Court granted Caleb Lyman[1] £21 for "his good services in killing seven Indians." The savages who composed the company, it seems could not wait the slow motions of the Court, and were paid £10 on their return, by Col. Partridge, which was refunded to him by the Legislature when the bounty was granted to Lyman. In addition, Major Whiting also paid them £8 each out of his own pocket. In 1706, he petitioned the General Court of Massachusetts for repayment. The Council at first demurred, on the ground that the Indians were in the service of Connecticut, and should be paid by that colony, but eventually granted the amount.

Fears for the Safety of Lyman and rumors of an Invading Army on the March.

This exploit completely broke up the encampment at Cowass, and the enemy fled precipitately to Canada. The expedition was extremely hazardous, and there was great solicitude for its safety. Bands of Indians were

1 Caleb Lyman, a son of John Lyman, one of the first settlers of Northampton, was born in 1678. He afterwards removed to Boston, where he was highly respected, became an elder in the church, and died at Weston, Nov. 17th, 1742. His funeral sermon was preached by Rev. Mr. Williams of Weston, in which it is said of him that "He had a pleasant temper and was useful in all relations. He had been a deacon, and then assistant to the pastor (probably an elder). He had a firm courage in his military capacity; was a man of steady loyalty. As a Justice of the Peace, he endeavored to promote order, righteousness and peace; a kind neighbor; a peace-maker, and gave £500 legacy to his minister and successors. He acquired considerable outward estate, was very kind to ministers." His wife survived him. He had a family of adopted children, but none of his own.—Judd MSS.

In October, 1704, Mr. Lyman petitioned the General Court for a reward. In that document he states that he "furnished himself with ammunition and provisions, and traveled about one hundred fifty miles with the rest, with great hazard, and was gone a full fortnight, that we slew seven of the enemy and brought six scalps to the great encouragement of these plantations. He was one of the founders of the new North Church in Boston, in 1712, and one of its first deacons.

roaming everywhere, and so small a party it was feared would be quickly dispatched. Scarcely were they out of sight before a report came that a body of French and Indians was on the way to attack Northampton and other towns in Hampshire County. This rumor became certainty when a French deserter arrived, giving full particulars of the invading army. Messengers were hurriedly dispatched to Connecticut for assistance, and all hope of the return of Lyman and his braves was abandoned. Major Whiting promptly responded, and soon arrived with a force of three hundred forty-three men, comprising representatives from every county and from nearly every town in Connecticut. Head-quarters were established at Northampton, and for many weeks the town was filled with soldiers. Three times during June and July, was this rumor of the approach of hostile forces renewed, and each time reinforcements were sent from Connecticut. No enemy appearing, the troops soon returned.

An Army sent against North-ampton, and the Causes of its Failure.

These rumors were not groundless, nor were the preparations for defense needless. The Governor of Canada still harbored the design of destroying the settlements on the Connecticut River. The report of Gov. Vaudreuil to the home government[1] of this expensive and abortive enterprise is but a tissue of explanations concerning its origin and excuses for its failure. Yielding to the importunities of his Indian allies, who after recovery from the fatigue attending the sack of Deerfield, were anxious to undertake another raid, he placed an army of about seven hundred Indians and one hundred twenty-five French soldiers, under command of Capt. Beaucours. The ultimate design of this invasion was the destruction of Northampton. It failed for several reasons, some of which are given by the French Governor, and others supplied by various English historians. Vaudreuil attributed its want of success to the desertion of a soldier, when within a day's march of the enemy, and the subsequent panic in the army. In Canada the highest expectations were entertained concerning the expedition. It started amid great rejoicings, and important re-

1 New York Colonial Documents, vol. 9, pp. 763, 764.

sults were anticipated. English historians attribute the retreat of this formidable army to internal dissensions. The rank and file, unable to decide relative to the proper distribution of the prospective spoils, mutinied, and nearly one-half deserted, marching homewards. Finding the English thoroughly prepared to receive them, the courage of the rest failed, and the enterprise collapsed.[1]

Lord Cornbury gives Information.

Vaudreuil's statement that the length of time required to gather his Indian forces, would give the enemy opportunity to obtain information of the movement, was correct. The fact that he was preparing for an attack upon New England, as well as its destination, were well known. Lord Cornbury, Governor of New York, informed the Massachusetts authorities that his scouts had ascertained that "300 French and Indians were marching with a design to attempt Northampton in New England." The very date of the commencement of their march was given in the Boston newspapers. Knowledge that their plans and movements were no secret, and that all the towns would be well prepared to make a vigorous defense, dampened their ardor, and was undoubtedly the main reason why the army "broke up."

Anxiety and Alarm Everywhere.

These constant rumors of an approaching enemy kept the country in a continued state of alarm. At no time since Philip's war, twenty-eight years previous, had there been so many soldiers in the county. They were quartered in every town, and there were marchings and counter-marchings in every direction. Indians, spies and scouts of the approaching army, filled the forests. Parties of English, many of them citizens of the river towns, incessantly ranged the woods. None of the inhabitants dared venture far beyond the fortifications without an efficient guard, and the occupations of the farming community were greatly interfered with, if not wholly suspended. The attack on Pascommuck brought the warfare to the very doors of the people of Northampton. Repeated rumors that a force of French

1 Penhallow's Indian Wars, p. 34.

and Indians was on its way to attack the town, and the
ever present dread that the blow might be delivered at any
moment, must have filled the minds of all with disquietude
ard apprehension.

Casualties in 1704.   During this year Indian murders were frequent, but no citizen of Northampton was
slain after the attack on Pascommuck. In May, John
Allen and wife were killed at Deerfield; Thomas Russell of
Hatfield, "having rambled from the party he was with,"
was slain above Deerfield, and Kidness, a friendly Indian,
was killed near Hatfield mill. Sergt. Hawks was fired
upon while riding to Hatfield, and wounded in the hand.
On the 29th of July, Thomas Battis, who had been employed in carrying dispatches to Boston, was slain on his
return, within the present town of Belchertown. His dispatches were sent to Canada. Allusion to intelligence obtained from them is made by Vaudreuil in his reports to
the home government and forms the basis of a congratula-
tory notice of the inconvenience to the English, caused by
the invading army. In August, a party of men on the
way from Northampton to Westfield, under Capt. Allen of
Connecticut, were ambushed, two of them killed and two
others made prisoners. An English scouting party fell in
with the enemy soon after, killed two of the Indians and
rescued the prisoners.

Snow Shoes.   Having become convinced by sad experience
that it was useless to undertake to pursue
the enemy in winter when the snow was deep, without
snow shoes, the General Court ordered five hundred pairs
and as many moccasins for use on the frontiers. One hundred twenty-five of them were put into the hands of the
chief military officer of Hampshire County. Only 3s. per
pair were allowed for them by the government. On petition
of Col. Partridge and other officers of Hampshire, in which
they state that a "good pair of snow shoes and magosins
and bands (the snow shoes could not be worn without moccasins) cost 10s," the price was raised in November to 5s.,
and so remained till 1712, when 7s. were allowed. Each soldier had to furnish himself with them, and the sums named
were all that the government was willing to repay the men.

The French Indisposed for further Invasion — During the year 1705, not one of the Hampshire towns was molested. There was constant apprehension of Indian raids, but none occurred. The French government in Canada, having met with heavy pecuniary losses,[1] and having also under consideration proposals for a treaty designed to bring about a cessation of hostilities, had no disposition to organize any more marauding expeditions. In anticipation of a winter attack upon some of the river towns, preparations for defence were not neglected. Northampton, Hadley, Hatfield, and Westfield, were garrisoned from January to March, by two hundred men from Connecticut, who were supplied with snow shoes, but saw no occasion to use them. Soldiers were also stationed at Deerfield and Brookfield. As usual, many rumors and reports of the approach of the enemy were rife, and the excitement and alarm did not subside.

Capt. Parsons' Scout. — Samuel Bartlett, who was wounded while pursuing the enemy after the destruction of Pascommuck, in his petition for aid, mentions the "Grand Scout towards West River," in the winter of 1705, under Capt. John Parsons, but no other allusion to the affair has been found. Capt. Parsons of Northampton, certifies that Bartlett was impressed for the service.

Several Persons Killed in 1706 and 1707. — No Indian attack occurred in Hampshire in 1706 and 1707, though several persons lost their lives within its limits. At Springfield, Samuel Chapin was wounded; at Brookfield, widow Mary McIntosh was killed; and at Sheffield, Judah Trumbull was slain. These casualties which took place in 1706, were undoubtedly the work of straggling parties of Indians. Edward Bancroft of Westfield, was the only person killed by the Indians in this County in 1707.

Memorable Expedition of Capt. John Stoddard. — One of the most important scouting expeditions of the year was that of Capt. John Stoddard of Northampton. He started from Deerfield, on the 28th of April, 1707, with twelve men. For

---

1 The annual store ship with supplies, covering "two millions of wealth" was captured by the English. The vessel had also ecclesiastical as well as material supplies on board, and the Bishop of Quebec and twenty priests were made prisoners.

a fortnight they tracked the Indians, crossing the State of Vermont, and coming out upon Lake Champlain, without overtaking the enemy. They followed the trail to French River, and down that stream to the last carrying place, when, concluding that the Indians were too far in advance for further pursuit, they retraced their steps, arriving at home on the 30th of May. This was the first party of soldiers that went from Connecticut River to the Lake.[1]

Several Northampton Men Slain. In 1708, the depredations by detached and roving bands of Indians were continued, and a number of persons killed. Two sons of Capt. John Parsons of Northampton, Samuel aged twenty-three, and Joseph aged fourteen, were killed on the 9th of July, while in the woods, searching for cattle. On the 26th, Aaron Parsons, a soldier, son of Samuel Parsons of Northampton, and Benajah Hulburt of Enfield, another soldier, were slain by a party of Indians who suddenly assaulted the house of Lieut. Abel Wright, at Skipmuck, Springfield. At the same time they scalped the wife of Lieut. Wright, who afterwards died, and killed Hannah, wife of Lieut. Wright's son Henry.[2] The infant son of Henry Wright, and his daughter Hannah, were in the same cradle; the former was killed and the latter was knocked on the head, but she survived the blow.

Other Casualties. In October, Abijah Bartlett was killed at Brookfield, John Wolcott captured and three others wounded. A few days after, Ebenezer, son of John Field of Hatfield, was slain at Bloody Brook, in Deerfield. Soldiers from Connecticut were present at different times during the year, but no enemy appeared in force.

De Rouville Raids Haverhill. Though no attack was made in this section during this year, the French were not idle. An expedition of several hundred French and Indians, commanded by Hertel de Rouville, was sent out. The intention was to attack the settlements on the Maine coast, and lay waste that territory. Before proceed-

1 Judd's History of Hadley, p. 276.
2 **Henry Wright** was then serving with Capt. Benjamin Wright in the scouting expedition to Lake Champlain.

ing far, however, a large portion of the Indians deserted, and the principal object of the raid had to be abandoned. Having received orders to proceed with the remainder of his force and surprise if possible some outlying settlement, Rouville pressed forward, and on the 29th of August, surprised the town of Haverhill. About forty persons were killed and many taken prisoners. The citizens rallied as quickly as possible, pursued and attacked the retreating enemy. De Rouville's brother and a number of other Frenchmen were killed, and many of the captives rescued. Fearing that the enemy would next attack the river towns, preparations for defense were hastily made in all of them, and reinforcements sent up from Connecticut. That party, however, did not come in this direction, but made the best of its way back to Canada.

Captivity of Mehuman Hinsdale   While on his way homeward from Northampton, Mehuman Hinsdale of Deerfield, was captured by two Indians, about half a mile from Pine Bridge, in this town. The forest trees had not yet put forth their leaves, and he anticipated no danger. He was taken to Canada, where he was compelled to run the gauntlet. This was his second captivity, and the Governor, who knew him, attempted to obtain information concerning the designs and movements of the English. Refusing to give the desired intelligence, he was ordered into close confinement. Soon after the Indians asked the Governor to surrender Hinsdale to them, as they desired to burn an Englishman before starting out on the war path, and he was delivered into their custody. The Indians, however, were plotting to desert to the English, and desired the good offices of Hinsdale to ensure a favorable reception. Their design was discovered, and he was again remanded to prison. The next year, in company with Joseph Clesson, who had been captured in the meantime, he was sent to France. Here the prisoners were well received, hospitably treated, and were at length sent to England. Great kindness was shown them by the English, and they were eventually shipped to New England, and landed in Rhode Island. Hinsdale was absent from home about three and one-half years.[1]

1 Sheldon's History of Deerfield, vol. 1, pp. 367, 368.

Another Raid under Rouville.

The scouting expedition of Capt. Benjamin Wright, which took place this year, and in which he encountered the enemy· on Lake Champlain, and on French River, has already been described. The Indians surprised by him, on their return home, chagrined and crestfallen, were anxious for revenge, and asked of Vaudreuil permission to make another raid. He assented to their request, and a party of about one hundred eighty French and Indians, commanded by De Rouville, started on the 22^d of June. They were discovered in the vicinity of Deerfield, and driven off, having succeeded in capturing Joseph Clesson and John Arms. In the skirmish, Jonathan Williams was killed, and Matthew Clesson mortally wounded.

Killed at Brookfield in 1709 and 1710.

On the 9th of August, 1709, John Clary and Robert Granger, were slain at Brookfield. July 22^d of the following year, six men who were making hay at that place, were surprised and killed. They were the only persons slain in the county during that year.

Samuel Strong Wounded and Captured. His son Killed.

Samuel Strong of Northampton, and his son Samuel, started on the morning of the 10th of August, 1711, to get a load of grain from the meadows. They went through Kingsley's gate, very near where the present High Street enters the meadows. When they reached the bottom of the hill, three shots were fired at them by Indians in ambush. The people living on South Street heard the guns and ran to the spot. They found the young man dead and the team standing quiet. The father was wounded, captured, and on his way to Canada. According to a tradition handed down in the family, Mr. Strong, in recounting his adventures, stated that when the party reached a hill, whence Northampton could be seen, he took, as he supposed, his last look upon his beloved home and town, with feelings that cannot be described. It is not known how long he remained in Canada, nor how he obtained his liberty. He returned on a Lecture Day, and entered the meeting house to the surprise and joy of the entire congregation, who received him as one risen from the dead. He was the sixth son of Elder John Strong and lived on South Street. His son Samuel was twenty-four years of age.

Expeditions into the Enemy's Country, 1707 to 1711.

While the French were constantly fitting out and sending expeditions across our frontiers to plunder and destroy, the colonies were also active in carrying war into the country of the enemy. In 1707, an expedition was prepared by Massachusetts, Rhode Island and New Hampshire, for a descent upon Nova Scotia. An army, a thousand strong, under command of Col. March, convoyed by an English frigate, besieged Port Royal. The place was so well defended, that after an investment of two weeks, the invading army ingloriously embarked and sailed away. An aggressive but fruitless attempt against Canada was made by the English in 1709. An address to the Queen, seeking aid to an enterprise for the invasion of that country was well received, and preparations on a large scale undertaken. A sufficient naval force and five regiments of the regular army were detailed for the undertaking. The colonies of Massachusetts and Rhode Island were to raise and equip a force of twelve hundred men. This army was destined for the capture of Quebec, while fifteen hundred soldiers from the colonies farther west, were to march by land against Montreal. These forces were promptly mustered, the first named at Boston, and the latter at Wood Creek, near the south end of Lake Champlain. For several months these troops remained in camp, waiting the arrival of their allies. The English contingent failed to appear, and the expedition came to naught.[1] Reverses to the English arms in Portugal, caused the diversion of the troops intended for it, to the seat of hostilities in that country. These menacing preparations caused great excitement and alarm in Canada. All the available troops were gathered, fortifications repaired, and the inhabitants ordered to concentrate within the walls of Montreal and Quebec, on the south shore, and on the north the women and children, and the cattle were sent into the woods.[2] So

1 Palfrey's History of New England, vol. 4, pp. 271-277.

2 New York Colonial Documents, vol. 9, pp. 828, 832.

thoroughly and promptly were these orders carried out that a considerable portion of the crops were left unharvested from lack of laborers to do the work.   An expedition was fitted out in Canada against the army at Wood Creek, which had become weakened by an epidemic.   Gen. Nicholson, Lieut.-Governor of New York, the commander, had obtained intelligence of the approach of the enemy, and after a slight skirmish hastily retreated.

During the next year another expedition was launched against Port Royal.   A naval force of thirty-six vessels, from the royal navy and from the colonies, with four regiments from New England, and a regiment of royal marines, proceeded against that place capturing it after a siege of about a week.   In 1711, another formidable demonstration against Canada was organized.   It consisted of fifteen men-of-war and forty transports, conveying more than five thousand troops.   Massachusetts ordered a levy of nine hundred men.   The squadron set sail on the 30th of July, Gen. Hill commanding.   Misfortune and failure attended the enterprise.   After reaching the St. Lawrence River, eleven ships were driven on shore by tempestuous weather, and more than one thousand persons lost.   Defeated by the elements, the commander had no resource but retreat, and with the remnant of the disabled fleet, sailed for home. This was the last adventure during the war against Canada. No soldiers had been enlisted in Hampshire County for these undertakings till the last.   Among the eighteen companies furnished by Massachusetts, was one enlisted in this county.   It was commanded by Capt. Ebenezer Pomeroy of Northampton, and was under pay from June 2d to Oct. 26th, 1711.   The pay roll amounted to £367.2.10, but the muster roll of the company has not been preserved.   These several expeditions cost Massachusetts in the aggregate about £80,000.

Scouting Expedition and Exchange of Prisoners.   In 1712, two companies of snow shoe men from the Bay, were in service in this county during the month of January.   In March, Lieut. William Crocker had orders to raise a company and scout in the vicinity of Coasset, but there remains no record of any such duty performed by him.

The expedition of Capt. Thomas Baker, previously sketched, occurred in April. In accordance with a suggestion of Vaudreuil concerning an exchange of prisoners, a party of French captives was collected at Deerfield, and under command of Lieut. Williams, protected by a flag of truce, marched to Canada in July. He returned September 24th, with nine English prisoners.

One more Indian Raid.

In July, occurred the last Indian raid during Queen Anne's war. Two parties of savages, numbering twenty in all, one of them commanded by the afterwards famous chief, Gray Lock, left Canada to lay waste English territory, on the 13th of that month. On the 30th, Benjamin Wright, was taken by this latter party at Skipmuck, and soon after killed; Samuel Andrews of Hartford, was slain in the vicinity of Deerfield, and Benjamin Barrett of Deerfield, and William Sandford, a soldier from Connecticut, were captured. Fortunately the party for the purpose of exchanging prisoners, was then in Canada, and these two men were brought back. This was the closing act in the war.

Peace Proclaimed.

A proclamation by the Queen, announcing a cessation of hostilities, was made public at Boston in October, 1712, and in the following March peace was once more established by the treaty of Utrecht.

Number Killed, Wounded and Captured in Hampshire Co.

During the ten year's duration of this war, one hundred nineteen persons were killed in Hampshire County, twenty-five were wounded, and one hundred twenty-five captured. Twenty-five of the number killed, nine or ten of the wounded, and five of the captives, were citizens of Northampton.[1] All the prisoners returned with the exception of Esther, wife of Benoni Jones. She died in Canada, "retaining her faith and hope in the midst of the Jesuits."

War Expenses and War Taxes.

The expenses of this war were grievous and irksome. To Massachusetts the burden was oppressive, amounting to nearly a million of dollars. Taxes were heavy and there was little to pay

1 For list of soldiers in Queen Anne's War, see Appendix G.

3 3

them with. An average of about £227,000 per year, in taxes, were levied upon the people. Every year province bills were issued, and when the war closed, not far from £127,000 were still unredeemed. The debt was large, probably somewhat in excess of that sum. It need hardly be said that the re-establishment of peace was received by all with joy and thanksgiving. In 1702, the province tax of Northampton was £72; in 1703 it was £125.5; in 1704 it had risen to £200; and during the remainder of the war, did not vary greatly from £220.10 each year. For a number of years the Province Tax of Hampshire County was £1046.10.

CHAPTER XLI.

TURNING MILL RIVER—JOSEPH HAWLEY.

Unsettled State of Affairs. WHILE these stirring events were in progress, town affairs were conducted as usual. Military matters were left to the proper authorities, and little or no mention is made of them upon the records. During these years, as has already been made manifest, there were reiterated rumors of armies on the march, having for their object an attack upon Northampton. Though scouting parties were continually patroling the forests, and strict watch and ward were kept in every hamlet, events had more than once proved that there was no real security from sudden surprise or unexpected attack. Northampton was the head-quarters of the army in this section of the valley, and many of its citizens, either enlisted as soldiers or acting as volunteers, were constantly on duty, some in scouting expeditions and others in garrisoning the more exposed towns. After the experience at Pascommuck, more than usual courage was needed to attend the common duties of the farm. It was dangerous to venture unattended far into the meadows.

By-Law concerning Wood for the School. Yet the business of the town was by no means neglected. Town meetings were held and routine matters of the municipality were carefully considered. The records of those eventful years do not vary greatly from those that preceded them. One difficulty, that of keeping the school room warm in cold weather, had not been surmounted, and a more efficient remedy was adopted. In November, 1706, a stringent by-law was enacted, ordering every person who had children at school from the 26th of October to the 26th of April, to bring a sufficient load of wood for each pupil, during the first week after entering the school, or forfeit 6s. The selectmen were to name the day when the wood should be delivered, and the fine was to be paid within six days of that time, or the selectmen were to bring suit against the delinquent. That this new law did not work altogether in a satisfactory manner may be inferred from the fact that not long after its passage the selectmen were ordered by special vote to prosecute all who had not complied with its requirements. How much effect these threats and orders to bring suit may have had is not apparent, but it is not difficult to imagine the quality of some of the fuel that was palmed off upon the schools. Probably the school rooms, with nothing but the open fire-place, were very insufficiently warmed till the town assumed the responsibility and bought and paid for the heating material.

Seating the Meeting House. Upon a committee, chosen annually for that purpose, devolved the duty of seating the meeting house. The seat in the meeting house gave to each person a certain dignity on Sunday, however much he might swerve from it on week days. It graded to every one his rank as he appeared to deserve it according to the formula adopted by the town. Social distinction in the sanctuary was one of the disquieting influences in every locality. In many places bitterness of feeling and neighborhood feuds grew out of the practice. It was found necessary, in some instances, to pass ordinances with penalties attached, to prevent people from disregarding the action of the seating committee and forcing themselves into seats awarded to others. In order to reconcile somewhat the dissatisfaction arising from this source, it became customary to "dignify the meeting," that is to give to those seats in one portion of the house equal rank with others in different locations.[1] To award to their own

1 Only a single record remains of any such action having been taken in Northampton, and that was when the new meeting house, built in 1735, was first occupied. In 1701, the town of Hatfield voted that they "esteem the fore side seat below equal with the 4th in the body: the hind seat equal with the 8th in the body; the fore seat in the front gallery equal with the 3d seat below in the body; the side foreseat in the gallery equal with the 5th seat below." The seating committee of Hatfield were instructed to consider "age, estates and places of trust," in awarding seats; in South Hadley, "age, estate and qualifications;" in Rowly "age, office and amount paid towards the house;" in Watertown they were "to have regard to age, honor, usefulness, and to real and personal estate."

neighbors and friends a "position according to age, estate, qualifications, only respecting commissioned officers and impartiality," was not a task that many would voluntarily undertake. Probably those appointed were always ready to resign the honor, but very seldom were any excused. That much dissatisfaction resulted from the action of the seating committee is noticeable in other places, but there is nothing to show that discord resulted therefrom in this town. Human nature is much the same everywhere, and in the absence of evidence that people were less strenuous for their rights or less ready to show resentment for fancied slights here than elsewhere, it may be surmised that more or less trouble resulted from this universal cause of jealousy. One intimation that there was little complaint here is found in the fact that a permanent seating committee was chosen. The vote reads:—

"At the time aboue said (March 3, 170$\frac{8}{9}$) the Towne made choice of Mr Hawley, Elder Clap, and Elder Strong to be A standing committee who from time to time w^r impowered to Seat p^{r}sons in the metting house as there should be occation And their power to Remaine And continue till the Towne sees reason to call it in;" it was also voted "that they should desire Mr Stodard to assist y^m in said work."

In 1712, two other persons were chosen to fill vacancies on the committee, caused by death. No special instructions were given at this time for the government of the committee. The regulations previously adopted and still in force, were undoubtedly deemed sufficient.

Exemption from the Payment of Pol^l Taxes.   Some young men who had served during the war, claimed exemption from the payment of Poll Taxes, on that account, and the County Court had interfered to protect them. In June, 1708, Preserved Clapp, one of the selectmen for that year, petitioned the General Court, in behalf of the town, concerning the matter. He represented that they had difficulties about taxing polls of young men who had been "improved in her Majestie's service; we have taxed them knowing no law to the contrary, but our Justices have freed them from poll money." He asks for an explanatory act that the assessors may know their duty. The Court in response held that no persons were exempt from country tax but those by law exempted. The assessors were to be the Judges about the polls and not the Quarter Sessions.

The order prohibiting the cutting of "staddles" above a certain size, passed in 170⅜,
seems to have become a dead letter or was
only partially enforced, for it was again adopted in 1709,
with added requirements to secure its enforcement. It was
voted "that the said Act and euery claus and parragraph
therein mentioned shall be vigurously put in execution."
The penalty was increased to five shillings for every transgression, the committee for enforcing the act was enlarged,
and a determination manifested to put in full force all
votes relating to the matter.

Notwithstanding the unsettled state of affairs during the years of strife, bloodshed
and uncertainty, attending the French and Indian war, an
undertaking of great importance to the welfare of the
town, involving no inconsiderable outlay of money, was
inaugurated in 1710. The damage in the common field,
arising from the annual overflow of Mill River, still continued, in spite of the efforts made eleven years before to
remedy the evil. It was believed that the most effectual
way of "stopping the mouths of the gutters" would be to
change the course of the river, from its circuitous route on
the border to one more direct through the meadows. By
this means the river bed would be straightened and shortened, the water carried by a swifter current, the damage
by flooding be reduced to a minimum, and the entire meadows much benefitted by an extensive system of drainage.
The most disastrous results undoubtedly occurred from sudden freshets in Mill River, when the Connecticut was not
high enough to overflow its banks. Reference to the map,
surveyed especially for this work, showing the location of
the home lots of the earliest settlers, exhibits the original
course of Mill River. Remains of the old bed, still distinctly visible close under "Fort Hill," afford a very nearly
accurate guide to its re-location. Its crooked course, turning in places almost back upon itself, indicates a nearly
level passage-way, whose banks would be speedily overflowed and broken in times of freshet.

Changing the Course
of the Stream.

To change completely the course of so large a stream, would to-day be considered an engineering feat of considerable magnitude. Nothing accurate is known concerning the topography of the meadows at that time. It is evident, however, that there was much swampy land in them, and that the new channel of the river was carried where their drainage would be most effectual. The town having paid the expense of the method already attempted, an effort was made to bring the burden of this proposed scheme upon it also. Accordingly when the question came before a meeting held on the 6th of March, 1710, the following vote was passed : —

"The Towne taking into Consideration A motion made concerning Turning the Mill Riuer through the common feild in which motion was set forth the great inconuenience and damage done both to the publick and private by reason of the Riuers ouerflowing and so wronging men's Land.

"The towne'rejected the motion of turning sd Riuer on the Townes charge : But voted Liberty for those that had their Land damnified to Turne the Riuer throug the common feild as Aboue said, prouided the proprietors of the damnified Land wil be at the whole charge of it."

A Sewer Commission Appointed.

Having received permission to turn the river through the common field, a petition, signed by Joseph Parsons and others, was forwarded to the Governor and Council

"Praying for a Commission of Sewers to be grantd to some discreet persons as the Law directs for the cutting out a passage, for the conveying the Water of a small River running through the said Meadow (and often overflowing a considerable part thereof), into the great River of Connecticut agreeable to a vote of the Town approving there of and to apportion the charge there of according to each persons benefit thereby."

On the 8th of June, the following named persons were appointed for that service : —

"Samuel Partridge [Hatfield], Aaron Cook & Samuel Porter Esqrs [Hadley], Ebenezar Pomrey [Northampton], John White [Hatfield], Peter Montague [Hadley], & Ebenezar Wright [Northampton], Gentn."
"Any four of the sd Commissrs to make a valid act whereof Partridge or Porter to be one."

Undoubtedly they entered immediately upon the work, but no minutes are at hand showing when or at what point they began.

Present Course of
the River.

When the first building lots were laid off at the lower end of Pleasant Street, Mill River was divided into two branches, at that point, and Maple and Fruit Streets were swamps. It is possible that the excavation may have been commenced near the bridge (one document indicating that such was the case), in order to relieve the swamps immediately adjoining, and it is also probable that the two branches were united at the same time. At whatever point the work began, the river was carried through the meadows in a course very nearly straight, forming afterwards the eastern instead of the western boundary of Manhan meadow. It was entered into the Connecticut near the north-easterly turn of the "ox bow," a little west of the present line of the Connecticut River railroad, making an abrupt turn in that direction, just before reaching the Great River. When the railroad was built, the channel of the river near its mouth, was again changed to its present position.

The Work Proceeds,
and the old Com-
mission asks a re-
appointment.

Acting under the powers conferred upon them by the law, the commission proceeded with the work. Several years were undoubtedly required in which to accomplish the undertaking, but how long a time elapsed before the current of the river flowed in the new channel, has not been ascertained. Very possibly the work was in progress for eight or ten years, as it was not till 1720, that land in the old bed of the river was disposed of by the town. During that year the surviving commissioners, two of them, Aaron Cook and Samuel Porter, "being now dead," petitioned the authorities for a renewal of the old commission or the appointment of a new one. In it they say:—

"Wee the Commissioners within mentioned have Proceeded to turn a considerable River, which has made considerable Land by Dreyning the same, and been very Profitable to the Towne, In some Respects, and Grately advantagous to Particular Persons. And there being still considerable Labour to be accounted for, and Damages to be answered for, and this Commission being of such an Ancient Date. Wee fearing that s^d Power may not be suffishent to Proceed, and there being absolute nesesaty that something further should be done, In order to equal justice. Wee Pray that this Commission may be Revived again, or a new one, to us, or others to finish the s^d work."

The Powers of the old Commission are Renewed.

Long previous to this time the main portion of the labor had been performed, and the entire practicability of the scheme made manifest. In order to make sure that their authority had not lapsed through limitation, and the decease of two members, the commissioners sought to be reinstated in their position or have others put in their places. It was necessary that the matter should be closed up forthwith, hence the petition. Some delay occurred, however, for no action was taken by the Governor and Council for two years. In November, 1722, authority was granted to the surviving parties named in the first document, and they proceeded to close up their accounts.

An Assessment made which certain Persons refuse to Pay.

In March of the following year, an assessment of £94.3.6 was made by the commissioners, and placed in the hands of the proper persons for collection. This action was opposed by certain men, and they appealed to the Governor and Council for redress. The controversy entered into the politics of the day, and the choice of representative in 1723, hinged upon it in part, Joseph Parsons being chosen in opposition to Col. John Stoddard. In regard to this matter, Col. Stoddard writes in a letter to Gov. Dummer, in May, 1723, as follows:—

"I hear that Mr Parsons has promised * * * to obtain the dismission of the Commission of Sewers and review some of their acts. He and some others have served their own purposes and made considerable estates out of that which was of no value, to the hurt of many, and the ruin of some mean land, and pretty much at the charge of other men, and now to pretend to avoid the paying of their rate and to have the committee dismissed is such a piece of injustice that one would wonder that a christian should make any offer at it."

Petition of the Remonstrants.

In November, 1723, Joseph Parsons and twenty-three others remonstrated against the legality of this assessment. The commissioners allege that the rate is made to "Defrey and make paym't of some more charges & Damages that has accrewed by the Great Drain & by some small Drains made in ye meadows." To this the objectors answer in substance:

"That it is unjust to put the charge of any small Drains upon yᵉ subscribers, who have Liberty by the Law and by the Town, to do what they have done. That it is illegal for these Five Gentlemen to make a Rate to pay Pretended Damages done up the river, half a mile above the places dug to Drain s'd Land, for if any damage has been done by s'd Drain, the Law is open for them. That if any pʳsons have Recd any Damage by yᵉ River Running where it now does, It is the Town of Northampton's Right to pay it who were the occasion of the Rivers Running there by Diging a Trench for a mill above Fifty years ago. They also claim that the Commission granted, in 1722, was unjustly taken out, inasmuch as the petition requesting it was not signed by a majority of the proprietors, and ought to be recalled."

Was the River Turned into the Mill Trench? From this statement it may be inferred that the work was commenced at some distance up the river—probably above South Street bridge—and that as a result the course of the stream had been diverted into the old Mill Trench. This may have been done, but in 1770, the town took action to prevent Mill River from "shifting its course again into the old Mill Trench, northward of the Island where Amos Hull dwelt." If the commissioners carried the river into the trench, it had evidently been put back into its old channel, and the people were determined that it should stay there.

A Petition against the Remonstrants. This action of Parsons and others was followed by a petition from Thomas Alvord and twenty others, in favor of sustaining the acts of the commissioners. Their land evidently lay at some distance from the great drain, towards which they had already paid considerable taxes, "in the expectation of small outlets being made to answer their ends."

Action of the Governor and Council. The hearing on these petitions was ordered to be held in December, but was postponed from time to time, for various reasons, and did not take place till the 14th of November, 1724. Ebenezer Pomeroy was appointed attorney for the commissioners, and his reply in substance is as follows:—

He argues that the Commissioners have power to order an assessment for small drains as well as for the large one. In order to make the drain they must purchase the land on which to dig it, and the cost must be assessed upon the proprietors benefitted. In regard to the Mill trench, he states that there was not 20s. assessed in that section, and that the town voted that the drain was to be at the charge of the proprietors. In relation to the claim that the remonstrants had not requested a commission, and had no occasion for one, the answer was: In the Commission first made it was at the request of the proprietors, and this new commission, as they call it, was only a reviving of the first one. These proprietors had their end answered by the first commission: that land that was not worth twelve pence an acre (except because it was possible to drain it) was now worth £30 and more an acre, and by their advantage other men are damnified, and many have labored and received no recompence. Many men had paid considerable "whose land lieth at some small distance, and them we assessed before informing them that small drains should be made from and through their land into the great drain. We know no other way but to tax those who have received so great benefit as some of the proprietors have done."

The Council dismissed the petition of Parsons, ordered the commissioners to finish their work with all convenient speed, and present their account to the board for allowance.

Parsons and his Party still keep up the Contest. But Joseph Parsons and his supporters were by no means inclined to abandon the fight. Two weeks afterwards they again appeared before the Council with another petition, containing forty names. In this document, on which a hearing was held on the 28th of November, they claimed that the commissioners had not rated all the land by the great drain in due proportion according to law; because they rate them "to pay men that have done no work at all to the Removing the stoppages in the River which drown our Land;" and also because they are rated "to pay Damage to some men that are greatly Benefitted by the Drain and to others that we have done no Damage to." They also pray for the appointment of "some suitable and indifferent persons" to view the land, and to hear "our exceptions," who were to report to the Council.

The Council thereupon issued an order appointing "Major John Pynchon, Samuel Barnard Esq. & Dr. Thomas Hastings" a committee to "inquire into the matters of complaint and report to this Board, as soon as may be;" the collection of rates was to be stayed in the meantime, and the petitioners to bear the charges of the investigation.

The Rates ordered to be Collected. In February, 1727, no report having been made by the special committee, the Council ordered "that the Commissioners of Sewers, or those of them that survive do proceed, and that the rates be collected." This ended the controversy, and the river still runs in the channel provided by the commission, greatly to the benefit of the entire south meadow.

The Commissioners ask Pay for their Services. In accordance with the order of the authorities, the commissioners reported the amount of labor they had performed, and their accounts were allowed. Samuel Partridge, John White and Peter Montague, sought compensation for six days' work each, and Ebenezer Pomeroy and Ebenezer Wright for eight days each ; they also desired payment for time and expense in making their defense. This claim probably covered only the time occupied in closing up the accounts and making the assessment.

Land in the old Bed of the River sold by the Town. Though the town refused to pay any portion of the expense of this undertaking, it was quite ready to take advantage of certain benefits accruing from changing the river channel. The fact that the town voted in 1720 to "Sell the Land where the Mill River formerly Run," proves conclusively that the course of the river had been permanently changed previous to that date. Some of the land was sold, some granted to abuttors, certain portions were given as compensation for making meadow fences, and for other duties for which the town paid in land.[1]

Joseph Hawley Joseph Hawley, the first of the name who came to Northampton, and grandfather of Hon. Joseph Hawley, the renowned patriot and statesman, died in 1711. He was in his fifty-

---

1 During the Revolutionary war, a detachment of Hessian soldiers, prisoners captured from Bourgoyne's army, was quartered here, and there is a tradition that one of the officers, an engineer, suggested the feasibility of turning the course of the river, and that under his direction, and by the troops under his command, that labor was performed. Hessian prisoners were billeted here after the Battle of Bennington, and they may have been employed in cleaning, straightening and enlarging the channel, but the work of turning the stream had been accomplished between fifty and sixty years before that date.

seventh year, in the full vigor and maturity of his powers, when his popularity was well established, and his influence universally acknowledged. For many years he was one of the most able and efficient men in Northampton. Brief as had been his residence in the town of his adoption—he lived here but thirty-seven years—he stood in the front rank as a man of education, energy and practical business talent.

Birth and Education.   The son of Thomas Hawley, he was born in Roxbury, January 28, 165$\frac{4}{5}$, and removed to this town, when nineteen years of age. Graduating from Harvard College, in 1674, with the design of entering upon the ministerial profession, he followed the usual practice of his time, and commenced teaching school. In the fall of that year, he came here, and was at once employed as school-master; indeed it is possible that his engagement as teacher antedated his graduation, as it was the custom to "improve" young collegians in "that capacity." Licensed to preach before or soon after reaching town, he supplied in person the pulpits in various churches about the county, as opportunity offered, in a very acceptable manner. However, he soon became so engrossed in secular affairs that he renounced the ministry, though it seemed that he had certain adverse influences to contend against that hindered and possibly prevented his success in that profession.[1] From that time onward he was more and more employed in municipal business to the end of his life. His career as a school-master has already been outlined in these pages. Major Cook asserts that it was the underhand influence of John King and others that decided Mr. Hawley to give up preaching; that may have been one of the causes, but it is more than probable, that finding insufficient time to pursue his theological studies, he settled the matter on other grounds. Such good success attended his pedagogic labors, that they were continued for nearly ten years.

1 Capt. Aaron Cook, in a letter heretofore quoted (see p. 406), speaks as follows of Mr. Hawley:—"Mr. Joseph Hawley is my Lieut. who came a schoolmaster to us and was improved in teaching school, and preached on occasion at the neighboring towns, who gave a good testimony of him, so likewise his schooling gave good content, but this King and others, by secret plots and acts weakened his hand to his ministerial work, and being employed in town business, he joined in fining King for bad fences."

School Teacher, Farmer, Merchant, Lawyer.
He seems to have combined with school-teaching, farming, the mercantile business, and the practice of law; at least he commenced with the first, and afterwards carried on the other branches. During the latter part of his life he was the principal lawyer in Northampton. Although the records show that litigation was constant, the people had little use for lawyers. While the most trivial matters were brought before the legal tribunals, there seems to have been little occasion for a professional interpreter of the statutes. There is no evidence that Mr. Hawley ever studied law, still he was appointed by the town to conduct nearly every suit in which Northampton was a party, during the latter half of his life.

His Judicial Services.
Mr. Hawley received his first judicial appointment from Gov. Andros. In 1687, he was commissioned as one of the five justices for Hampshire County, and assisted in holding the County Courts during his administration.[1] The old order of things prevailed for the next three years, and in July, 1692, after the new charter went into effect, Mr. Hawley was again appointed a Justice of the Peace, in which capacity he served as one of the Associate Justices in the Court of "General Sessions of the Peace," during his lifetime.

Extant Account Books show him to have been Accurate and Methodical in all Business Matters.
That he was methodical in all his transactions, careful, accurate and pains-taking in all his dealings, the several account books, which have been preserved, abundantly prove. These books, commenced in 1674, and carried on till his death, show the varied business affairs of his daily life. Not only were his school accounts, his farm and mercantile transactions, entered upon these volumes, but very many of the law cases in which he acted as justice, are also recorded. This latter

1 It is highly probable that no Commissioners to End Small Causes were appointed here under Andros, as Mr. Hawley's books contain notes of cases tried before him in 1687 and 1688, and his record was not resumed till 1693, after his second appointment as Justice. The last vote relative to commissioners, was in 1685, when "The Towne voted to have commissioners And Left it to the Court to Appoint the Persons."

book, four by six inches in size, bound in leather, now black and warped with age, seems to have served originally as a college note book, or may possibly have been used in preparatory studies. It contains many pages of English sentences translated into Latin, some Latin rendered into English, and many others written entirely in "Latine." Apparently it had been in use before it came into the possession of Mr. Hawley, as most of the school-boy notes differ orthographically from those made by him. The law entries commence in 1687, when he received his first appointment as magistrate, and end in 1710, one year before his death. They consist mainly of minutes of cases tried before him, though there are a few marriages recorded and a number of deaths.

Mr. Hawley as a Merchant. It is not probable that his mercantile business was ever very extensive. The first of these account books was commenced about the year 1679. His wife's grandfather, David Wilton, died in 1678, leaving his property to his widow and grandchildren. He was an Indian trader, and carried a general stock of goods, usually found at that day. The retail traffic of Mr. Hawley seems to have been confined principally to the sale of what remained of Wilton's stock in trade, though he probably continued to deal in some articles after that had been closed out. He sold goods for produce, of which he also bought much for the Boston market. From 1681 to 1693 he shipped pork, flour, winter wheat and peas to Boston, and sent home from that city in the former year a lot of kitchen utensils, a barrel of rum, and a bale of miscellaneous goods. It was a barter trade almost exclusively. Hawley sold his goods for such kinds of produce as the farmers had to buy with, and exchanged it for other articles with which to refill his shelves. Indian corn was much used in this kind of trade, but little or none of it was ever sent to Boston. It is evident that Mr. Hawley sold considerable rum. He dealt to some extent in school and other books, among which were catechisms, primers, psalters and Bibles; he also sold writing paper, and disposed of a few of Mrs. Rowlandson's little book, narrating her captivity among the Indians. Mr. Hawley transacted considerable business at Windsor, Ct., renting lands, and selling goods. He owned an orchard and pasture there, which brought him in a yearly revenue of £3, in wheat, peas and cider in equal proportion. There are many accounts for boating on the river, and for fire and candle wood sold.

As a Military Offi-
cer.   Like all prominent men of his day, he had some military experience. He served in the militia, but never rose above the rank of Lieutenant, and was probably never in actual warfare. During "King William's War," he was not a member of the company, having resigned when the local militia troubles occurred, just before it broke out. The title of Captain is given him in some records, but there is no positive evidence that he ever attained that rank. The original commission as Lieutenant, in the Northampton company, signed by Edward Randolph, Sec'y, in 1686, and another containing the signature of Andros in 168⅚, are preserved among the papers comprising the Judd MSS. There is also among them still another document, dated in 1691, investing him with the authority of excise collector for this county, and signed by Samuel Gookin. Under this latter commission, he was required to collect the duty or revenue from innholders and dealers in liquors.

Employed in "Queen
Anne's War."   In 1704, he was actively employed in public business, though he did not then hold a military commission. The same year he was at Hartford, engaged in settling the colony boundary line, and in Deerfield soon after the attack upon that town. He went several times to the latter place in connection with Col. Partridge and Major Pynchon, and assisted in "forting" the town. When "Northampton was beset" in May, and Pascommuck was destroyed, he was among the men who turned out to fight the enemy. When the soldiers from Connecticut and the Bay filled the town, he had much to do about billeting and subsisting them. All the inhabitants at that and in similar crises, seem to have kept open houses, or rather their dwellings were turned into hotels by the authorities. His account books, like those of Wilton, contain the names of many of the officers then in service in the county.

Some of his Official Duties. In 1680, he was first chosen upon the board of selectmen, and was eight times re-elected to that office, the last date being that of 1702. Chosen Deputy to the General Court in 1683, he served in that capacity six times, extending over a period of sixteen years. When the new law under Andros, establishing the office of tax commissioner, went into effect, Mr. Hawley was chosen to the post. During the time when the law requiring that certain probate and other legal business should be transacted in Boston, was in existence, he was much employed in duties of that nature, and of necessity made frequent visits to that city. In 1682, he was appointed by the General Court, one of the surveyors for this county, his duty being to survey all lands granted by the Legislature in the County of Hampshire.

Whenever the town had a case either in the local courts or before the Legislature, Mr. Hawley was almost always chosen to manage the affair. In the boundary controversy with Hatfield, and in the unpleasantness with Sergt. King, he served the town with good results. He was a loyal supporter of the existing government, and though he accepted various offices under Andros, yet he was in sympathy with the patriots who effected the revolution in Massachusetts, in 1689.

Boston Orders from Everybody. Nothing illustrates more fully the generous spirit of neighborhood comity then prevailing, than the universal practice of errand serving expected of and rendered by all whom business or pleasure called to the larger centres of trade or population. The nature of very many of these requests gives an insight into the minor needs of the community, and serves as well to show the scarcity of the smaller items of household convenience on the shelves of the traders. Whoever went to Boston, had usually as many demands to meet, as he had time or generosity to execute. Mr. Hawley, in consequence of his frequent visits to that city, had much business of this kind to transact. For instance, in one of his note books, containing a list of such orders, may be found for one man "a whisk and 1000 pins," for another "2 psalters, a bason, and quart pot," for a third, one

34

shilling's worth of "plumb & spice," still another sent for a "hat band," another for "a box of Lockier's pills," one man wanted "an inkhorn," some one else, whether man or woman is not stated, sent for "small laces," and last, though not least, a person, probably just elected to the office, sent for a "tithingman's order." Another catalogue of similar demands shows that he was to "get a place for Mary Holton;" for "son Joseph speckled red ribbon, whistle, buckles and fish hooks;" for Capt. Partridge, "a dial and dish kettle;" for his wife "half a yard such stuff as my wife's, as her cloak." Some persons sent for knitting-needles; Mr. Stoddard ordered sealing wax; others wanted goose and duck shot, and a person owing money in Boston, sent the cash to pay the debt. These minutes are usually without dates, but in many cases the cost of the articles is given.

An Honorable, Patriotic and Able Man.   Joseph Hawley was a man of profound patriotism and stern integrity. Not readily carried away by excitement, he never allowed personal prejudice to warp his judgment. Like all his contemporaries, he was much identified with the local contests of the time, and took a decided stand in whatever cause he espoused.

Mr. Hawley's Home Lot.   The original Hawley homestead was situated on "Pudding Lane," now Hawley Street. A home lot was granted him in 1682, on the easterly side of Round Hill, and previous to this in the time of King Philip's War, a small plot of land was given him near Meeting House Hill, but there is no evidence that he ever resided on either of them. In fact, he was released from the obligation of building upon the last named lot by a special vote of the town. In 1682, he bought of Godfrey Nims a parcel of land with a dwelling house on it, which house he occupied at the time of his death. This lot was situated on the west side of Hawley Street, covering in part the present location of Belding's Silk Mill. He willed the property to his sons Joseph and Ebenezer. Joseph bought a homestead on the opposite side of Hawley Street, in 1723, to which he removed.

Ebenezer's portion came eventually into the possession of his nephew, Major Joseph, who gave it to the town of Northampton.

Death of Lieut. Joseph Hawley. His death occurred May 19th, 1711, and was caused by a wound inflicted by the horn of an ox. He left a will dated May 7th, 1711, but it was not signed. When it came before the Probate Court, Medad Pomeroy testified that it was the will of the deceased, and that it was his intention thus to dispose of his property. The widow and children consented to it, and the Court confirmed the document. In 1677, he married Lydia, daughter of the famous Capt. Samuel Marshall, of Windsor, who was killed in the Narragansett fight, and whose wife was the daughter of David Wilton. They had seven children, three daughters and four sons. His real estate was given two-thirds to his eldest son Joseph, and one-third to Ebenezer, the youngest.

Grammar School to be Continued Twenty Years Longer. In 1688, the town established a Grammar School, and five years afterwards voted that the scholars should "goe free." The following year, in spite of considerable opposition, this enactment was ordered to continue "for the space of twenty years;" near the close of that period the following action was taken : —

"At a Leegall Towne Meetting, July 16:1712, it was then voted that the Towne would maintaine a grammer Schoole in the Towne for twenty years next comming And to be paid by the Towne in the same kind And portion other taxes are paid And that the Selectmen for the time being annually take care to hire A Schoole master the best way And manner they can And this Act to continue till the Towne shall for cause reecied from it."

The Meadow Fence. The importance of a proper regulation of the Meadow Fence, is everywhere manifest, and frequent action by the town has been noted. In 1662, the first vote was passed, establishing the several divisions. Again the question came before the town in 1679, when a new measurement carried with it a new apportionment. Numerous contracts and agreements with parties owning land in and adjoining the meadows, were entered

into at the time of every change.   In 1702, the matter being once more under discussion, other arrangements were
adopted, and in 1710 it was again made prominent by
further readjustment.   Three years after there was a general overhauling of the entire system.

New Regulations   In 1713, the proprietors determined upon a
Suggested and   general and comprehensive reapportion-
Adopted.   ment of the meadow fence.   A committee
was appointed to measure all the meadow land, "or by
some other method to come to the knowledge of all the
land in the meadow;" they were also ordered to measure
"all the fence About the meadow," and the following provisions in reference to the matter were adopted : —

   "1ly That the Committee should consider & determine what Ponds,
Creeks and Wast Land In the medow should be exempted from making
fence.

   "2ly That the Committee should have full Power & authority to Sell
off all the fence from Munhan River unto the Land belonging unto the
heirs of Decon John Clark Deces^d. as also over Munhan River &
through Nashawannack To Jeremiah Weed [Webb] and Robert Danks,
or any other Persons, or either of them and for a Reccompence for the
making & maintaining s'd fence to Pay them In Land upon Richard
Weebbs Fort and to take Good Security for the maintenance of the s'd
fence.

   "3ly That whereas there is about 27 Rods of Fence downe the River
below Pascommock Bridge 'tis Proposed to be maintained By the Proprietors till an oppertunity Presents to Put it off with a Peise of Land.

   "4ly That the sd Committee shall examine the Records and see there
what Contracts there is made between the Towne and Particular Persons for making Either of more fence, or Less than their Proportion.

   "5ly That the s'd Committee shall have full Power to Bargain with
some Persons to make and maintaine fence across all the Water
Courses that the fence Croseth Also to make & maintaine all the Gates
Belonging to the medow, for such a Sertain number of Rods of fence
as they can Agree.

   "6ly Then what Land is not fenced for as aforesaid, and what fence
then doth Remain, shall be alloted or distrubuted to each man according to each man's number of acres of Land In the medow.

   "7ly Tis Proposed that Every mans fence shall be together, or In one
Peise, unless In some Exempt Cases which shall be Left to the discression of the s'd Committee.

   "8ly That the s'd Committee shall have full Power to allott or Set out
to any Particular Person his Part of fence In any Particular Place
where it will sute his Intreast, and more Especially where his Intreast
and the Public is Congruous together.

"9ˡʸ Then those persons as have not Got there Fence from the afore-said methods, what then remains Shall bee drawn by Lott, which if any Person is abcent att the time appointed by the Committee for the drawing of Lotts having had due warning, or Present refuses to draw, the Commitee shall one draw a Lott for him.

"10ˡʸ That those Persons as by assignment of the Commitee, or by Lott shall come Into the Place of another man's fence. The origenall owner upon due warning Given shall have Liberty to fetch of his fence if he cant agree & sell it to his neighbore."

These propositions were "all ten of them sepparatively voted upon the affirmative," on the 2ᵈ of November. On the 26ᵗʰ of the same month, the committee reported the name of, as well as the number of acres belonging to, each owner, stating that "The totall of the Land In the medow that is to make fence is 2469 acres & three Quarters." One hundred thirty-four names are recorded as the owners of this land. The committee also reported as follows concerning the length of fence and the limits of the several divisions :—

"And the fence begining In the Great River beyond Capᵗ John Parsones house to 27 rods below Pascommock Bridge is : 1817 Rods 16 foot and 5 Inches : Whareof By the Law & Contracts with Particular Persons there is 536 Rods 15 foot & one Inch made : which substracted out of the totall then there Remains 1309 Rods 11 foot & 04 Inches to be made In Proportion upon the aforesaid 2469 acres & three quarters of Land In the medow, which is to Each acre Eight foot & nine Inches : which fence is divided Into four divitions and here followeth a List of Each divition successively : The first divition begins in the Great River as aforesaid and Ends att the Gate formerly called Bartlett's Gate, * * * which Is 507 Rods 2 foot and 10 Inches."

"Then at Bartletts Gat begins The 2ᵈ divition and Goes to Kingsleys Gatt," and "the sum totall of the fence In this 2ᵈ divition is 468 Rod 12 foot and 9 Inches."

The third division "begins att Nashawannuck, at the beginning of that Farm and so to take in Kingsleys Gate."

"The 4ᵗʰ divition begins att Nashawannuck and Ends Twenty-seven Rods below Pascommock bridge."

A Possible Reason for the new Fence Regula-tions.
It may be that this careful and complete investigation of the matter was occasioned by the change in the channel of Mill River, then in progress, but not completed. The next readjustment of the fence was made in 1744, when another list of meadow land owners was obtained, and a new apportionment made and recorded.

CHAPTER XLII.

COL. STODDARD'S MISSION TO CANADA.

Northampton Men Distinguished in the Service. MANY citizens of Northampton were in active service throughout the war, closed by the treaty of Utrecht. They fought in the ranks or commanded in action, and everywhere exhibited courage and ability. Of those who carried the heavy and cumbersome flint lock musket, risked their lives in pursuing the savages through the mazes of the forest, or fought them in the bloody skirmish, little is known; many of the muster rolls have disappeared, and in some of those yet in existence, no town is given, so that it is difficult to place them with accuracy. Some of the prominent leaders in the many scouting expeditions, or commanders in the more hazardous enterprises, have already been named. Capt. Benjamin Wright, Capt. Thomas Baker, Caleb Lyman, Capt. John Taylor, Capt. Ebenezer Pomeroy, Capt. John Parsons, and Capt. John King, all citizens of Northampton, were men whose deeds have found a place upon the pages of the historian. In addition to all these and more prominent than any of them, was Col. John Stoddard. Some of his exploits have already been chronicled, and others are yet to be noted as this narrative progresses. Though scarcely twenty-two years of age, his abilities were at once recognized and his services were in constant requisition during the war. He was second in command in Hampshire County, under Col. Samuel Partridge, who succeeded to the control of affairs in this section of the valley on the death of Col. Pynchon. During the war, Col. Stoddard disbursed for the government in payment of the soldiers in his division, nearly £5,000. This was in addition to the sum which passed through the hands of Col. Par-

534

tridge.   In 1706, he was promoted to the rank of major, and at the close of the war held that of colonel.   Soon after the declaration of peace, he was appointed by Gov. Dudley, one of the commissioners to conduct negotiations with the Canadian government for the return of the English prisoners then held in that country.   He entered upon this enterprise with his usual energy and sagacity, though not able entirely to circumvent the duplicity of the French Governor, or the machinations of the Jesuits.   The Frenchmen determined that none of the English captives should be returned if they could prevent it, and the result, meagre as it was, all things considered, reflects great credit upon the men to whom the work was entrusted.

The Exchange of Prisoners Unsatisfactory.   Gov. Dudley had reason to be dissatisfied with the results of the attempts at exchanging prisoners with the authorities of Canada.   It was altogether too one-sided an affair.   All the Canadian prisoners held in this section, who were willing to go back, were forwarded, but only a scattering few of the English were returned from time to time, numbers sadly out of proportion to the aggregate held in bondage. Lieut. Williams, who escorted the French captives from Deerfield, was able to rescue but a small number, by no means what was to have been expected, when it was understood that upwards of an hundred English were at that time held by the French and their Indian allies.   Efforts had been directed towards the rescue of Eunice, daughter of Rev. John Williams, but without avail.   She never returned.   The several attempts to obtain her release have been fully given to the public and need not be rehearsed. The King of France having given an order for the release of divers prisoners in Canada, Gov. Dudley sent, in accordance with a vote of the General Court, two commissioners to Canada to negotiate for the redemption of the captives remaining in that country.

Personnel of the Party.   For this duty he appointed Col. John Stoddard of Northampton, and Rev. John Williams, minister at Deerfield, the latter having been captured at the sack of Deerfield, and carried to

Canada. From the journal of Col. Stoddard,[1] detailing
the events of his journey and the course of the negotiations, the following narrative has been condensed. The
party consisted of six persons, viz. : the two commissioners, Capt. Thomas Baker of Northampton, and Martin Kellogg of Deerfield, both of whom had been prisoners in
Canada, and had escaped, together with two attendants,
Eleazar Warner and Jonathan Smith.

The Journey to Canada.

Starting from Boston, on the 5th of November, the party reached Northampton on the
9th. After remaining here four days, they
set out on their journey, on horseback. The route lay
through Westfield and Kinderhook, and on the 16th they
reached Albany. For more than two months they were
detained at the latter place by stress of weather. A thaw
had set in, the river was filled with floating ice, and the
forests were impassable. It was not till the 22d of January
that they began the march to Canada. On the 24th, Sara-
toga was passed, and on the 31st they reached Crown Point.
Finding open water on the Lake, they were compelled to
make a detour by land, and did not arrive at Chamblee till
the 8th of February. From that point they were forwarded
in carryalls (carriole, a French sleigh), to Quebec, reaching
that city on the 16th of the month.

After a Favorable Reception, they meet with Ob-stacles.

An audience was held with the French Governor the next day, when credentials were
presented and the object of the mission explained. Vaudreuil received them with
professions of great friendliness. He assured them that
all the prisoners should have full liberty to return, that the
commissioners might visit them or send for them to their
lodgings, and have free speech with the religious. Elated
by this auspicious reception, the commissioners anticipated
speedy and gratifying results. But they were soon unde-
ceived. Within five days they discovered that there was
strong opposition to their purpose, and that obstacles were
being placed in their way. On the 21st a note was addressed to the Governor, in which they complained that the

---

1 Historical and Genealogical Register, 1851, vol. 5, p. 21.

laity and priests were endeavoring to prevent the return of the prisoners. They averred that persons went from house to house soliciting the English to remain ; some the priests endeavored to terrify by suggesting their danger of perdition ; from others they threatened to take away their property, wives and children. The commissioners entreated the Governor to prevent such interference. Vaudreuil replied "that he could as easily alter the course of the waters as prevent the priests endeavors." In a few days he sent for the commissioners and informed them "that there was a considerable number of English people that the King (after divers objections) had naturalized; therefore they could not have liberty to return." The commissioners afterwards ascertained that eighty-four persons had thus been imposed upon. To the demand that all the captives under age should be compelled to return, the Governor promptly agreed. Astounded by the naturalization pretence, the commissioners demanded a copy of the papers and time to answer. Their reply was a clear and cogent argument showing naturalization to be a mere pretext, contrary to the order of the King, and in conflict with the articles of peace. Some of those named among the naturalized were ordered to be set at liberty by the King. They refreshed the Governor's memory by quoting his oft repeated statement that he cared not "how few staid in this country, the fewer the better."

Still further Opposition from the French.

On the 27th the commissioners went to Montreal, the better probably to confer with the prisoners. At another interview with Vaudreuil, they boldly taxed him with insincerity, relating how he at first agreed to release all, but now objected to the return of a great number, and desired to know what they might expect. If none were allowed to go, there was no need for them to tarry longer. He replied that he was "afraid to release those that were naturalized, but would write to the King." This they contended would only delay matters and was disobeying the King's orders, but if he was resolute in the matter one of the commission would carry the letter to the King. Again they offer to show that naturalization was a fraud and a deceit. He admitted that it might be so, and gave them liberty to smuggle these men on board their ship and he would never send after them. They next demanded that men and women might not be entangled with their marriages, and parents with their children. He conceded that French women might have liberty to go with their English husbands, and that English women should not be compelled to stay with French husbands, but demurred to the claim that children might go with their parents. He also "sent word that he did not approve of those persons coming to divine service who had embraced the Romish Religion." The next day they demanded "that all the English Prisoners should be gathered to Quebec, there to give their answer whether they would return or not (presuming that when they were gotten from the priests, their acquaintance, and should see others ready to embark, they would easily be persuaded to go with them.)" To this Vaudreuil readily assented. The commissioners then requested an answer concerning the status of children born during the sojourn of their parents in Canada. The Governor declined to give an opinion, alleging that "he knew not what to determine," but proposed to refer the matter to Gov. Dudley, requesting his "reasons why they should not be held as subjects of the King of France." The commissioners, having no instructions on this point, gave their "opinion, and reasons for it, and left the matter for the present." At the same time they requested a list of all the English persons in the country, which the Governor agreed to furnish. He then sent word that "he would not allow any English to visit" the embassy on the Sabbath. Against this order they "wrangled long" with the Governor, but "at last found his fixed resolution more forcible than our arguments."

Further Unsuc-   On the 26th, a written opinion concerning
cessful Diplo-   the question about children returning with
macy.   their parents, was forwarded to the French
Governor. Afterwards there was further discourse on this point, but they "could not obtain a full answer." Having informed the Governor that it was their design to send some prisoners home by land, he stated that any who would say before him that they would go home, should have permission. John Carter (a Deerfield youth) was sent for, he having told the commissioners that he wanted to return,

but when he was brought before the Governor, overawed by his presence, declared that he would stay. Permission for the commissioners to talk with Carter in private, was reluctantly granted, and he agreed to go before the authorities, and avow his desire to go home. This he did, the Governor became very angry, and declared that he should not go by land, but should wait for the ship, to see whether he would persevere in his resolution. Influences were afterwards brought to bear upon him, and he remained in Canada. In another case a boy, who wanted to return home had permission from the Governor, and Capt. Baker supplied him with clothing. In a short time, the priest with whom the boy had lived, in the absence of Capt. Baker, took away the clothes that had been given him, and prevailed upon him to stay. Vaudreuil sent for the boy and kept him some time in Quebec, but as Stoddard says, it was "too late, the same priest had made too thorough work with his proselyte."

A Wrangle with the Lord Intendant. The commissioners waited upon the Lord Intendant and solicited his aid. Like Vaudreuil, he was at first full of fair promises, but at a subsequent interview with them strongly condemned the practice of preaching religion to the prisoners, threatening to confine the commissioners to their chambers unless it was discontinued. Col. Stoddard intimated to him that the Governor had control of such matters and had given permission for such discourse, diplomatically suggesting to him that it was none of his business. The Intendant further told them "that the priests had informed him that we, in a moment, undid all they had done in seven years' endeavors to establish our people in their religion." A very thorough compliment to the persuasive powers of the Deerfield minister. It was the priests who were placing the greatest obstacles in the way of releasing the prisoners.

More Evasion and Subterfuge on the part of the French. After that the commissioners let the Intendant alone severely for many days, but they recapitulated to Gov. Vaudreuil the "chief particulars which he formerly promised" them. He again assented to them, with exceptions only to the return of those who had been naturalized, and to children born in Canada. Their quarrel with the Intendant seemed to please the Governor, who encouraged them with the intimation that their affairs should in no wise be determined by him. Rev. Mr. Williams made earnest endeavors to obtain the release of his daughter Eunice, but without avail. An interview with her was denied him. The conversion to the Catholic faith of the daughter of a Puritan clergyman, was something for the priests to boast of among their ignorant followers, and they held her with a grip of iron. Definite answers were demanded to the questions already discussed, but evasion and subterfuge, the constant postponing of direct promises, were all that could be obtained from the French authorities. Several other prisoners having signified their desire to return home, were influenced by the priests or overawed by the officials, and dared not make the attempt. Vaudreuil refused the list of prisoners he had promised, and required the commissioners to give him the names of those they desired to take, and he would assemble them when their ship arrived. They sent him the list, with the information that when the commissioners were absent the priests would prevail upon any of the prisoners to remain in Canada. An interview was had with some of the Cagnawaga Indian chiefs, at which were present Jesuits and others. The Governor spoke to them, urging them to restore the prisoners. But the chiefs, apparently tutored by the priests, replied that the captives, especially the children, had been adopted into their families, and were not held as prisoners, but as children, members of their households, that they would not compel any to return, but "leave them their own liberty." A private conference with these Indians failed to convince them, and nothing could be accomplished.

Case of Ebenezer Nims and his Wife. The circumstances relative to the position of Madame Le Beau, already introduced in the notice of Capt. Baker, are treated at some length. Ebenezer Nims, one of the Deerfield captives, his wife and child, were obtained with great difficulty. Nims was seventeen years old when captured, and was adopted by a squaw. Sarah Hoyt was made prisoner at the same time. In the course of a few years efforts were made to force her to marry a Frenchman. She objected strongly, but offered to marry any one of the captives. Ebenezer Nims joyfully responded, and they were married. Both were anxious to return homeward, but were afraid to make known their desire. The commissioners demanded that Nims and his wife should be brought from Lorette, which after much delay, and persistent and reiterated solicitation by Stoddard and Williams, was finally accomplished. Nims was brought first, and it was intimated that his wife was sick and unable to travel. Stoddard sent his own physician to see her, who pronounced her in good health, and eventually she walked to Quebec. On signifying their desire to go home, they were permitted to embark. A number of Indians accompanied them from Lorette, and after they had been placed on ship board, endeavored to entice them on shore again.

The Negotiations come to Naught, At last after dallying months with the commissioners, making promises one day only to break them the next, Vaudreuil had the cheek to suggest that they had better go home. He said "that our Governor pretended to send a vessel to Quebec early in the spring, but although the summer was now far advanced, yet was not arrived, and therefore he thought it best for us to return." They had been long in the country, had put the King to great expense, and he refused to subsist them longer. When they represented to him that the ship had probably been delayed by contrary winds and would arrive within eight or ten days, he promised to maintain them that length of time.

And the Commissioners Sail for Home. Capt. Baker, who had been sent to Boston with dispatches, returned on the 23d of July, and on the 4th of August, the long expected ship appeared. Consequently the commissioners once more reiterated their demands, at which Vaudreuil "manifested some discontent at our insisting on those things we had so often discussed." It all came to naught. Though repeatedly promised, the prisoners were never convened, and only those who could not on any pretext be prevented, were allowed to return.

Satisfied that nothing further could be accomplished, in fact dismissed by the French Governor, the commissioners sailed for Boston on the 24th of August. Mr. Stoddard sums up the results as follows : —

"In the morning we sailed from Quebec with twenty-six prisoners, having lost three men who had declared to the Governor that they would go home, and five others, who pretended to embark just before we sailed,— not having received the list that the Governor had promised us; without having our people assembled at Quebec; without having one half of our people asked, before us, whether they would return or not, and several that were at Quebec while we were there,—or one minor compelled; having never seen many of our prisoners while we were in the country."

They Arrive at Boston in September. After an absence of ten months, the commissioners reached Boston early in September. Col. Stoddard must have become well acquainted with the French method of "how not to do it." The commissioners had danced attendance on Vaudreuil, month after month, urging, demanding, arguing, beseeching, only fair play. They desired simply that the prisoners should be allowed to decide for themselves whether to go or stay, uninfluenced by either side. The Jesuits determined to keep as many as possible, by fair means or foul, and none of the children were allowed to be taken, they were food for the church. The Governor was a mere tool in their hands, which he had the frankness to acknowledge. All sorts of objections were urged against the removal of those who expressed a desire to return. They were intimidated by the priests, overawed by official authority, and were not permitted to decide for themselves. The few who were rescued were obtained only through the persistent labor of the commissioners.

CHAPTER XLIII.

SAW MILL—MINISTER'S SALARY—COMMON LANDS.

Prosperity Returns. RELIEVED of military pressure, things soon resumed their normal condition in the Connecticut valley. During the next ten years the quiet avocations of peace absorbed the energies of the people, and prosperity once more showered its blessings upon the land. Everywhere the inhabitants were industriously solving the life problem of the hour:—endeavoring to pay taxes, to "make both ends meet," and to recover the losses attendant upon the recent disastrous times. In an agricultural community like that of Northampton, little of exciting interest or of more than ordinary note can be anticipated. Grave and sober citizens with little beyond the daily struggle for existence to enter into their lives, do not make history rapidly, or prominently mark its eras with stirring events. Within this period only the usual affairs of the community, such as have already formed the staple of this narrative, come into prominence, and the monotony of the records is but slightly varied.

Ordinary Topics Engross Attention. Topics of momentous interest to the inhabitants of that day have but slight attraction for modern readers. Yet they are links in the chain of events that connect the present with the past, and are neither valueless nor uninstructive. As noted year by year, they serve to portray the character of the times and indicate the general growth and tendency of the public mind. Everywhere will be noticed the necessity for economy, as well in the conduct of municipal affairs as in the more minute details of private life. The country had not yet recovered from the financial embarrassments occasioned by the war, scarcely a twelve month ended. Taxes were heavy, with little margin after meeting household expenses, for paying them.

The common place round of events incident upon the home life of an inland settlement once more absorbed the interest of the community. Building bridges, making new regulations concerning the boxing of pine trees upon the commons, granting saw mill privileges, providing means for religious and educational purposes, were among the most conspicuous subjects under consideration during this year.

Protecting Pine Trees.   When the subject of protecting pine trees from general and indiscriminate piracy, through boxing, bleeding and scraping, was considered, an order found its way upon the records prohibiting people from molesting such trees, on any of the commons, divided or undivided, under penalty of 5s., "for the vse of the poore of the Towne: And any Prson may take out Any turpentine out of Any such trees And haue it himselfe for his pinns," meaning that he might confiscate to his own use whatever he found gathered in an illegal manner, in such places. A couple of years afterwards the pine trees on the commons were made a source of revenue, being leased to individuals.

A Sexton Employed.   To care for the meeting house and to ring the bell had been duties devolving upon the selectmen. But this year "The Towne voted that the selectmen Annually for the time Being should have power to hire a Sexton to Look After the Meting house." This is the first time the word is used on the records. It was a new name for an old office, and while it involved no new duties, added a certain amount of dignity to the incumbent.

A Saw Mill Site Granted to Benjamin Stebbins.   On the petition of Benjamin Stebbins for the grant of a saw mill privilege, he was given "a Liberty of the Stream at the foot of the mountain in the old Cart Road for A Saw mill (that is the Towne Right)." This location was at Pascommuck,

on the brook at the base of Mt. Tom, west of that mountain. The significance of this grant lies in the conditions
attached to it, viz. : —

··(1) that he shall take no partners out of this Towne. 2 that he
shall not damnifie the Road or highway, that some times is Oca-
tionaly vsed. 3 that he shall sell bords to Any of the Inhabitants of
this Towne for their own vse shall bee at twenty Shilling per Thousand
for the time of four years from the time the mill was first set vp."

Stebbins accepted the grant and the conditions, and in
1714, sold one-half the right to Joseph Parsons, they agreeing to build the mill that spring. The mill was erected on
Broad Brook, a short distance from the main road, and was
in use for many years. Eventually it passed into the
hands of Abijah Wait, and he sold one-half of it in 1783,
to Elias Lyman. Evidently it was not the intention to
allow the mill privilege to be used for speculative purposes
by outside parties. The mill was for the benefit of the
town, it must be managed by townsmen, and the work
done at reasonable rates. Unwilling to risk the possibilities of what in modern days might develop into a saw mill
trust, or leave the matter of prices to the tender mercies of
saw mill combination, special terms were made with the
prospective owners.

**Fencing the Bury-
ing Yard.** Encroaching upon town lands, more especially upon highways, has been frequently
noted in these pages, but this year it was
found necessary to check the depredations that were being
made upon the sequestered land on what is now Bridge
Street. A committee was accordingly appointed to

"examine the Records And to see who it is that hath encroached
vpon the sequestered land on the pine plaine, And Also to contriue
About fenceing in the buriing place with stone and to make Report to
the Town About the same."

The burying ground occupied the north-east corner of
the present Bridge Street cemetery. As has already been
stated, six years subsequent to the arrival of the first settlers, ten acres were set apart on the pine plain, "sequestered as a standing lot for the ministry." Two years afterwards, a portion of it, apparently without definite bounds,
was selected for a burying place. Adjoining owners had
undoubtedly taken unwarranted liberties with the "seques-

35

tered minister's lot," as it was called, and it became necessary to define carefully its limits.   A favorable report was
made, and the work of fencing the burying place was put
into the hands of a committee.   The dimensions of the cemetery were fixed at "tenn rods square," which gave an enclosure of a little more than half an acre.   The fencing
was to be done by the same rule as highway work.   This
wall was very probably composed of the loose stones gathered upon the commons, and piled into the usual symmetry
of an ordinary agricultural fence.   At this time a highway
extended along the north line of the sequestered land, connecting Bridge and Market Streets.   In the course of years
this little enclosure became too small, and it was gradually
enlarged from the surrounding plain, till eventually the
burying place embraced about one-half the land originally
sequestered in that vicinity. [1]   Thirty-five years afterwards
the fence was rebuilt in a much more substantial manner,
and within it undoubtedly much additional land was then
enclosed.   The cost of that work was £175.9.6, divided substantially as follows :—285 loads of stone at 8s., £114; 78
days work laying stone at 12s., £46.16; 18 days work by
masters at 16s., £14.8.6; moving stone, etc., £0.10.

Increasing the Min-   For more than forty years, Rev. Mr. Stod-
ister's Salary   dard had officiated as pastor of the church.
The town had greatly increased in popula-
tion and wealth, and his labors had been abundantly
blessed.   That the people appreciated his services is made
evident by the fact that in 1715 his salary was increased,
apparently without solicitation on his part.   When first
settled he received £100 in the currency of the time, produce and provisions; afterwards this was changed at his
request, to £80 in money.   It was now voted

"to giue to the Rev[d] M[r] Stodderd Sixty pounds for the time past in
like mony as we paid him in the year past.   And to giue him one hundreed pounds a year So long as he continues In the work of the ministry
in like money as we haue paid him in time past in such mony for the
time to come as shall be currant with the marchants."

1 Sylvester Judd states that the old burying yard was only eight rods wide at the
north or north-easterly end, and about twenty-five rods wide at the opposite side and
not far from forty rods long on the north line.   Its probable average width was from
eighteen to twenty rods, and it contained from four and one-half to five acres.   In
1833, the cemetery was enlarged by the purchase of about five acres more, on the
north-westerly side.

Mr. Stoddard acknowledged his acceptance of the proposition over his own signature, upon the town books. Whether the £60 was a gift, or was intended to even up his back pay, to make up for deficiencies in previous years, is not apparent. Be that as it may, the addition of twenty pounds per year to his salary was a generous act, duly appreciated by the hard working pastor, for the depreciation in the currency and the hard times that followed the expensive and exhaustive wars, must have rendered difficult the payment of the minister's rate, even at the previous figures.

Common Lands. A new deal ordered. This year commenced the wrangle over the Common Lands, which was not permanently adjusted for more than half a century. It originated in dissatisfaction with the distribution of the commons, made in 1700. Afterwards disagreement arose concerning privileges allowed the community at large in the divided property. That, however, occurred many years subsequent, and was the occasion of another heated controversy. The real causes that led up to this contention are not easy to ascertain. Action was first taken in the matter in March, $17\frac{13}{14}$. At that meeting a vote was passed :—

" Att the same time it was voted to Throw up Three Mille of the West End of the Westardly division of Commons, and to Lay sd three Mille Into two Ranges, and each Proprietor shall draw again for the sd three Mille, and to draw by the same Rule as before : Except some Persons that was Left out who are then to haue a draught." Att the same time it was voted that " a notification to be posted upon the meeting house, seven days before such meeting, Signifying the time and occasion of such meeting, shall always be accounted a Sufficient warning for a Proprietors meeting."

The Old Division Unsatisfactory. A Protest against it. Apparently much feeling existed throughout the town concerning the untrustworthiness of the division of the common lands made in 1684, on which that of sixteen years later, was founded, the legality of that distribution being strongly questioned. A document is in existence, drawn up in $17\frac{14}{15}$, in which is set forth with considerable minuteness the reasons for that opinion. It was main-

tained that persons were admitted to participate in it who
had no right; that some were excluded who were entitled
to the privileges of that division; that others had received
more than their just proportion, while many others had
less. Again it was urged that the rule adopted in 1684 was
not adhered to; that ownership of the lands thus divided
descended to successors and not to heirs and assigns, and
consequently it was for the present proprietors to make the
rule of division. Another point was that the list of names
according to which the division was made, was the work of
a committee who had no authority from the proprietors or
selectmen, and that it was therefore void; that the committee was instructed to report to the town in order that its
doings might be reviewed; that this had not been done,
and the committee had proceeded without such authority.
And finally it was contended that there was no recorded
vote authorizing them to carry out the distribution.

A Legal Opinion   Because of this adverse sentiment, the pro-
Solicited.   prietors voted to take legal advice upon the
                        matter. They sought the opinion of lead-
ing lawyers in Connecticut, and sent a committee to lay the
case before them. In February, the following vote was
passed: —

"Att a Legall Proprietors meeting, Feb. 11:17$\frac{14}{15}$, The Proprietors
then voted to send to William Pitpin [Pitkin] of Hartford, John Eliot
and Roger Wilcot Both of Windsor Esqr for their advise Respecting
the former divisions of the Commons In Northampton for their opinion
whether it be Legal or nott, the Proprietors did then make choise of
Maj. John Stoddard & Joseph Parsons Esqr to represent the case to the
aforesaid Gentlemen."

No report from this committee, nor of the decision rendered by the referees, was ever entered upon the records.
It is believed, however, that the legality of the former division was sustained. The committee who acted in 1699,
recorded the results of their labors, giving the amount of
each man's estate, as well as the width of each lot. In
1754, a survey of the "Inner Commons" and "Long Division" in part, was made by Nathaniel Dwight, and the figures on the map made by him are identical with this record.

Origin of the Trouble Possibly the dissatisfaction arose in part from the fact that some persons had been omitted in this deal, and partly because some of the property had already been twice divided. In explanation of the above mentioned action, it will be needful to go back a few years and recall the proceedings by which the division in 1699 and 1700 had been determined. No allusion to this transaction was made upon the town record books, but the whole may be found on the Proprietors' Land Book, or Registry of Deeds.

The Previous Division in 1700. The last distribution of common land previous to this date had been made in 1684, and was apparently satisfactory. For fifteen years it remained unchallenged. At that time, in 1699, considerable dissatisfaction seems to have been manifested among those individuals to whom small lots, scattered throughout the town, had been assigned. This apportionment of land into so many small parcels in different sections of the town, widely dispersed ownership, and rendered any effectual use of the land troublesome and laborious. Consequently in 169$\frac{8}{9}$, a committee was appointed by the proprietors to devise some method for remedying the difficulty. They were directed "to propound to the Towne some way more advantageous for men to have their land together that men might be in better capacity to improve their land." Previous assignment of common land had designated no less than four divisions in which each inhabitant had a share, and there was a large section still undivided. To put this latter into possession of individuals was part of the design of the proposed movement. In order, therefore, to obviate the prevailing difficulty, and yet give every man his proper proportion in all sections, the committee proposed that the existing divisions, four in number, should be made into two, and that every proprietor should have his part in each division, in accordance with the rule hereafter agreed upon, and that each one should "draw lots to determine the place where his lot should fall." This committee was composed of Joseph Hawley, Joseph Parsons, Preserved Clapp, John King, Medad Pumry, Ebenezer Strong, James Wright Jr., Judah Wright, Enos Kingsley, Thomas Lyman, John Clark.

The Divisions Proposed by the Committee, and Accepted. In the month of February, 169⅜, the proposition of the committee was adopted. The four divisions named by them were as follows :—The first one commenced at Hatfield bounds and extended to Pine Bridge, known in later years as Burt's Bridge, and included Broughton's Meadow. The second "begins at Brotton's Meadow Plaine and ends at Munhan Saw Mil Plaine." The third division was newly laid out and began at the "bounds between Hatfield and the Towne, the north end whereof was to front east of the Broad Brook Swamp and so to turne something westward toward the south end of bare [Bear] hill and from thence on a southerly line to Munhan Saw Mill." This was known as "Long Division." The fourth was laid "betweene the county road and the common fence" from Sandy Hill near "Pancake Plain" to Munhan River, and embraced the two small divisions known as "Hatefield" and "Lovefield." The last named division, as well as the first, lying east of the Long Division line, was known as the "Inner Commons."

Order about Running the Lines. A meeting was held January 15, 1699-1700, at which the matter seems to have been further debated, and the question of finding the starting point and running the lines was decided in the following manner :—

"The proprietors considering that they had laid out several devisions of land in the commons wch were to ly east and west : and in order to determine the east and west line it was then agreed that observation should be taken by the North Starr and from that an exact square should be set east and west : and accordingly the lines between the divisions of men's lots should be settled, and the proprietors then chose John Clark, Sam'l Wright and Judah Hutchinson, a committee to run the liens."

The Committee then proceeded to make a readjustment of the old divisions and a proper distribution of the new tract of land in the western part of the town. Their proceedings, the rule of division as well as the share alloted to each individual, are carefully carried out upon the proprietors' book of records. The new adjustment was not made upon the basis of the previous one, adopted in 1684, which was the appropriation of a certain number of acres to every pound of valuation, rating every head of a family at

£100; every young man twenty-one or more years of age at £30; and all other males under that age at £15. A somewhat different and more simple method was substituted. It was based solely on the amount of real estate owned by each individual. Every one was directed to bring in to the selectmen or the committee, a true list of his rateable estate. The total amount of real estate in town divided by the distance in length of the land to be disposed of, gave the proportion in width to every pound of valuation represented in real estate. The aggregate valuation of the real estate in town returned to the authorities, is figured at £30,496. From Hatfield line to Manhan River, the distance on the east line of "Long Division" is called 6½ miles; this is equivalent to 34,320 feet, or 411,840 inches. This would allow to each pound of estate, 13½ inches in width of land; but the estimate or calculation of the committee seems to have been a trifle less than that, about 13⅓ inches. An estate valued at £100 drew, according to the record, 107 feet, equal to 6½ rods in width, or 6 rods and 8 feet, as recorded. A rod seems to have been called 16 feet. To estates of £50, the same amount of land was allowed as to others of twice that value. These lots extended to the western boundary of the town, and were 250 rods in length. The smallest lot was but four rods wide, and the largest seventy. It was most appropriately named "Long Division." These lots were all numbered, ranging from one to ninety, in two divisions, but in the smallest, called "Little Division," there were ninety-two owners.

No change made in the matter of Division. Such was the method pursued and the results obtained in the division of 1699-1700, which was now called in question. Apparently the work had been carefully done, and in an acceptable manner. No dissatisfaction had heretofore been manifested. The reason for any objection to this deal, brought up thirteen years afterwards, nowhere appears. Certainly the protest heretofore quoted, has no weight against its validity. In reality there seems to have been little gained by this readjustment of holdings, as people still owned land in four different sections of the town. There was an omission, however, in regard to certain privileges heretofore allowed to the community at large in the divided lands, and this was many years afterwards the occasion of another serious controversy, which will be treated in its proper sequence.

No further Action taken by the Town.   This controversy over the commons quietly died out, and there seems to have been no redivision of the common land at this time. Probably the referees reported in favor of the legality of the old division, and no other tenable ground seems to have existed for its molestation.   At all events no further action by the town in reference to the vote to throw up three miles of the westwardly division of the commons, was taken at that time.

Reasons offered for the Proposed Re-division of the Commons.   In connection with the above, there comes pertinently to notice a paper prepared at this time, apparently for presentation at a meeting of the Proprietors, but without signature, and lacking endorsement of any kind, indicating that it was ever acted upon.   It is dated January 27, 17$\frac{14}{15}$, and is of importance principally because it gives certain reasons for making any division at this time.   The opening paragraphs of the preamble read as follows :—

"The Proprietors taking into consideration, 1^{ly} their ability to Improve the commons, by Reason of the Increase of the Inhabitants, and termenating the warr: and 2^{ly} Their necessity for the same, by the much failling of the meadows Especially for Winter Grain, and the multiplication of the Inhabitants that want Sustenance or must be under a necessity to Remove."

"Therefore the Proprietors upon the day abousaid concluded and agreed to divide all the Commons belonging to the towne of Northampton or att Least so much of it as is fitt for Plowing, Mowing or Pasturing, which fitness shall be determined by a committee after mentioned which divition shall be according to the manner & Rules heretofore Prescribed."

Following these are seven articles providing for the manner of division, the method of adjustment with those who had already acquired possession of any of these lands, and other essentials to the carrying out of the vote.

Apparently some of those persons who had large holdings of meadow lands, which were beginning to depreciate in fertility, wanted to grab a part of the commons to compensate for their loss.   There is no reason to believe that they succeeded.

CHAPTER XLIV.

MEDAD POMEROY—FINANCES—PUBLIC BANK.

In December, 1716, the town was bereft of one of its most prominent and influential citizens, by the death of Medad Pomeroy, or Pumry, as the name was pronounced and usually written. Full of years, honored and respected, he had been identified more than any other citizen then living, with the earlier history of the place. The son of Eltweed Pomeroy, he was descended from a long line of English ancestry, dating back in unbroken succession to the time of William the Conqueror. His father emigrated to this country about 1630, settled first in Dorchester, and removed with Rev. Mr. Warham's company to Windsor, Ct., where Medad was born in 1638. When old and infirm, he removed to Northampton, and lived with Medad. Eldad, Caleb and Joshua, brothers of Medad, also settled in this town.

A Blacksmith by Trade, he follows his calling here.

When twenty-one years of age, Medad Pomeroy came to Northampton. Of his father, who was a gunsmith, he learned the trade of blacksmith, which he followed through life. It is presumed, though nothing remains to prove the supposition, that he also was a maker of guns. At all events, that trade was afterwards continued in the family through seven generations. He was not, however, the first blacksmith who settled here. John Webb preceded him, and had carried on the trade some years before his arrival. It may be reasonably conjectured that Pomeroy at first found employment in the shop of Webb, where his ability was soon recognized by the public. Webb was a speculator in land, a hunter, an agitator, and apparently did not apply himself closely to business. Within a year af-

553

ter the coming of Pomeroy, Webb relinquished blacksmithing.   His tools were purchased by the town, offered "on
terms" to Pomeroy, and afterwards given to him outright.

Pomeroy's Home   His home lot, granted by the town, was sit-
Lot.   uated in the vicinity of the Bridge Street
              cemetery.   It is somewhat doubtful whether
he ever occupied these premises.   The lot was afterwards
enclosed within the limits of the cemetery.   He sold this
property, or rather exchanged with Richard Weller, for
a lot on South Street, within three years, and it was not
till 1665, that he occupied the homestead in the center of
the town, which descended to his heirs.   In that year he
bought one acre on the westerly side of Thomas Salmon's
home lot, on Meeting House Hill, where he resided till his
death.   Probably he occupied the shop formerly used by
Webb, which stood in the highway in front of his home
lot.   Webb then lived at the corner of Main and South
Streets.   In 1661, the town gave Pomeroy "the land his
shop stands on," which undoubtedly formed part of the
highway.   This shop, whether built by Pomeroy or Webb,
stood, as is believed, nearly in front of Memorial Hall.
Six years afterwards, he had a grant of one and one-half
acres of land adjoining the lot "whereon Medad Pumrys
dwelling house and shop stands."   In a few years he
bought the rest of Salmon's home lot of his brother Caleb,
to whom it had been sold by the original owner.   The
south line of this property extended from Elm Street on
the west, to the homestead of the late Judge Lyman, which
was included within its limits, on the east.   His house, as
nearly as can be ascertained, stood near what is now Ma-
sonic Street, in the vicinity, if not on the site of, what was
once "Colonade Row," known also as "Curtis' Tavern."

He is granted   Medad Pomeroy was not only a skilled me-
Privileges for a   chanic and a thorough business man, but he
Saw and Fulling
Mill.   was also a person of great public spirit,
                  ready to undertake any enterprise that
would develop and build up the town.   In connection with
John King, he had the first grant of a saw mill privilege
ever made by the town.   For some reason they were unable
to carry out the condition of the grant, and at the end of

the time specified, it was transferred to other parties. Again in 1682, he was granted a place for a "fulling mill," but there is no evidence that he ever prosecuted that enterprise. Though he failed, whether through lack of capital or some other good and sufficient reason, to carry out these particular measures, yet his movements in that direction stimulated others, and the business establishments he projected, soon found parties willing to perfect them.

Official Life.   His record as a public officer is both honorable and varied. In 1678, he was appointed "Clerk of the Writs," a position he held till near the close of his life. It has been claimed that he was a lawyer, but the holding of the above office was as near as he ever came to being enrolled as a member of that profession. For many years he was Recorder of Lands (Register of Deeds); was chosen Town Clerk in 1692, and was annually re-elected for twenty-one consecutive years. In 1695, when towns were first authorized by legislative enactment to choose treasurers, he was elected to fill the place, and was continued in it till 1716. Chosen one of the Commissioners to end Small Causes, in 1684, he was a few years afterwards appointed one of the Associate Justices of the County Court. From 1669 to 1704, he was twenty-seven times elected a member of the board of selectmen. First chosen Deputy in 1677, he was six times re-elected to that important post, the last service being in 1692. He was chosen County Treasurer in 1698, and was a number of times re-elected to that office. In 1675, he was made a Deacon of the church. It appears that in some years, he held not less than six important town offices at the same time. In the expressive language of to-day, he seems to have been the "champion" office holder of his time. He not only held various judicial offices, but was much employed in the settlement of estates.

Licensed to Sell Wine.   He was never an innholder, but as selling wine for the stomach's sake was considered by the magistrates as an act of charity, he was given a license to perform such benevolent duties. In the record of a court held in 1684, the following entry may be found:—

"Dea. Medad Pumry of Northampton, showing this court that the inhabitants of this town are many times in streights in times of sickness and weakness for want of wine for their relief; there is no meet person allowed to sell drinks and he showing that he meets with much trouble respecting that matter and desiring libertie to sell as aforesaid, this court allows him such charitable work."

His Family.   Dea. Pomeroy was three times married, and was the father of twelve children. His first wife, to whom he was married in 1661, was Experience, daughter of Henry Woodward, one of the early settlers of Northampton. She died in 1686, and the same year he married Abigail, daughter of Elder John Strong, and widow of Rev. Nathaniel Chauncey. Her death occurred in 1704, and the following year, he married Hannah, widow of Thomas Noble of Westfield. Of his twelve children, seven survived him, three sons and four daughters.

His Character. A Contemporary with Joseph Hawley.   Medad Pomeroy was a man of strong natural common sense, rough and rugged in manners and expression, as were the majority of his contemporaries, but just in all his dealings, and conscientious in the discharge of every duty. A strong will, and withal a domineering manner, made him a leader in a community where tenacity of purpose, physical endurance, and acuteness of intellect, rather than mental culture, were the chief characteristics. He was prominent in the military controversy, already dwelt upon, and seems to have carried his point, though he never attained to any military rank. A man of the people, he belonged to the town party, and labored for the good of the whole. One of his strongest co-laborers was Joseph Hawley, the school-master and lawyer. Both were men of more than ordinary ability, both were leaders, and both were conspicuous in establishing, promoting and building up the settlement. Pomeroy came here a few years earlier and lived a few years longer than Hawley, but for thirty-seven years they were contemporaries. Often on the board of selectmen together, Associate Justices about the same time, though seldom acting at the same court, they transacted much town and county business together. For legislative honors they seem to have been rivals, each for several years alternating with the other. In the local contentions of that day, they were sometimes in opposition and sometimes labored in unison. In the quarrel about militia officers, they were in hostile ranks. Both of these men left descendants who took high position during "the times that tried men's souls." The grandsons of each were eminent men, and their names will live in the history of the nation. Gen. Seth Pomeroy, the Revolutionary Patriot, and Major Joseph Hawley, the renowned statesman, rendered valuable service in the early days of the republic.

Deeds his Home Lot to Ebenezer.

Dea. Pomeroy died Dec. 30, 1716, in the seventy-ninth year of his age, and his monument may still be seen in the Bridge Street cemetery. In 1709, he deeded the home lot, and the adjoining land in his possession, about nine acres in all, to his son Ebenezer. The deed conveys the homestead "with housing, barns, shops, water courses and all appurtenances." The water courses refer to an aqueduct supplying the place with water, the pipes or logs extending to a reservoir on a lot on Elm Street, afterwards the property of Elijah Clark.

Grant of Land to Ebenezer Pomeroy.

"Hon. Ebenezer Pomeroy Esq.," as he is designated on the records, was one of the leading citizens of Northampton. He was a son of Medad, a gunsmith, and a man of energy and ability. In 1711, he led a company of soldiers in the expedition to Canada, and was for many years afterwards High Sheriff of the county. Whether in recognition for his services, or for some other good and sufficient reason not named, he was granted in 1716, a large quantity of land between Northampton and Springfield. The grant comprised "all the Remaining part of the Half mile Square: Between us and Springfield, Saueing what was Before Granted to Capt. John Taylor and his two sons, viz: Thomas And Sam[ll]." The grant to Capt. Taylor was made in 1703, and consisted of eighty acres near Whiteloaf brook, in what was afterwards the town of Southampton. This property descended to Capt. Lemuel Pomeroy, son of Col. Seth, and grandson of Ebenezer, who settled in Southampton, in 1776. The present boundary line between Southampton and Holyoke, at the south-east corner of the former town, shows an indentation, as though a corner had been cut out of Holyoke (which was a part of Springfield at that time). This was without doubt a part of the half mile square granted to Capts. Taylor and Pomeroy, and it was in this vicinity that Capt. Lemuel lived.

Ebenezer Sheldon Allowed to set his House partly in the Highway.
In 1718, Ebenezer Sheldon was granted permission to "sett His House in the Highway, nott exceeding fiue foote beyond Where His House now is." With all the land available in those days, it seems as though no man could get enough. What they failed to obtain by encroachment they managed to get by grant. An encroachment upon the highway of but five feet would appear to have been entirely unnecessary, a fact which the town virtually acknowledges, when it was expressly voted that the privilege was granted as a "full compensation for two Peices of Land: His father Had In the Town: att or neer the Meetting House Hill." This home lot was on Bridge Street, on the east side of the highway, where the bluff descends abruptly into the meadow. It was very probably because so little space remained between the street and the bluff, that the house was built partly in the highway. This was part of the homestead occupied in more recent years by Isaac and Theodore Sheldon.

Town Stock of Ammunition.
It was voted in 1719 that the "Selecttmen" should "examine and take care of the Powder that was delivered to the Respective Garrisons, and take the town stock out of Elder Claps Hand (He being desirous to Part with it)." According to the inventory it consisted of "one Barrell and Half of Powder: one Hundred and fiuteen Pouns of Bulletts: and three Hundred and Eighty-six flints, being the whole of the Town Stock now to be obtained." This was placed in the care of Thomas Sheldon.

Ear Marks for Cattle.
The method of marking cattle, or other domestic animals, so as to substantiate ownership, then in use, was that of mutilating their ears. Branding, now so common everywhere, was then used as a punishment for criminals, and the early set-

tlers had too much respect for their "creatures" or "critters," as they were usually called, to humiliate them by such a criminal process. It was necessary when almost every man had more or less stock feeding upon the commons, that all such marks should be registered. No action, however, seems to have been taken in this direction till 1719. In March of that year the town voted

"that Every man Should Haue a Distinct Ear Mark For His Creatures to be apointed Him by the Selectt men ; and entered in the Town book, Pursuant whereto we the Select men Haue this 30ᵗʰ of March : 1719 ordered the following marks to be vsed Each mark Respectiuely by Him to whose name such mark is affixed."

Then follow several pages of such marks, on which may be found one hundred fifty-five of them, some paring the ears of the poor animals out of all natural shape. A part of the clippings were upon both ears, and not a few were to be on "yᵉ neer Ear" or "yᵉ off Ear."

Bounty on Sheep.   Another attempt to encourage and protect the business of sheep raising, was made in 1718 and 1719. Frequent allusion has already been made to this subject. Its manifest benefit to the colony, collectively and individually, was duly recognized by the General Court, and brought to the attention of the towns. A bounty on sheep had been offered and many persons profited thereby. Entries upon the account books of the second Joseph Hawley, indicate that he received "sheep money" or "bounty money for sheep," for many persons, giving them credit for the amount collected. It varied from five to twenty-five shillings.

A Meeting called to Stimulate the Industry.   In January, 17$\frac{18}{19}$, the selectmen warned the inhabitants of Northampton living "in the East Military Division" to meet for the purpose of considering the report of a committee about the "encouragement of a flock of sheep in said town." Who created this committee, or empowered it to act, is unknown. The town records fail to disclose any action ever taken for such a purpose. Though no record of its proceedings is extant, the outcome of this meeting seems to have been the adoption of by-laws concerning the pasturage and protection of these animals.

Clearing the Sheep
Pastures.

The year previous the town passed a vote providing for the special preparation of the pastures expressly set apart for the feeding of sheep.   The vote was as follows : —

"that Every man from sixteen years old to Sixty : Work one or Two Days (In Each year as the Selectt men for the time being shall Directt) att clearing the commons for Sheep : the men to work in Small companys, att Such Time and In such Place, and under the Inspection of such men as the Selectt men shall a Point, None To fail of any of the above Injuncttions under the Penalty of fiue Shillings forefitture."

By-Law against
Dogs.

A stringent vote against dogs running at large was adopted the following year.   In this vote is recited a bit of history not unlike that which has since been many times repeated.   In May, 1719

"The town taking into Consideration the Dearness[1] of Sheeps Wooll and cloathing ; and so Consequently the Growing nessity of keeping and Encreasing a Flock of Sheep In the town, and also considering the Prosperous Success We Have Had In our Small beginning In that affair and also our Experience Has taught us How Pernicious and Destructive Doggs : as well as Woulues Haue been to Sheep : and altho there Has been many Endeavours for the Destroying of Doggs out of the town : with very considerable Success yett some few Parsons Either out of Hope of Private Gain or Disregard to the Publick Enterest Doe keep and maintain Large Doggs Going at Large and are In Great Danger of putting a Check unto our Growing Endeavours unto such a Designe that is Like to Proue such a Benefitt and advantage to the Town."

"The town therefore upon the Day aboue sd voted that if any Dogg more than twelue Inches High Sall goe at Large without being with His Master or Keeper : the Respectiue owner master or keeper of such Dogg shall Pay a fine of twenty Shillings : for Every time He is found or seen at large as aforesd : for the vse of the Poor of the Town of Northamp', to be Recouerd as the Law Directts."

A New Seating Com-
mittee Chosen

Seating the meeting house was a matter that was by no means neglected, though for a number of years, there is only an occasional allusion to the subject.   The method adopted in 1707, of entrusting that duty to a permanent committee, seems to have been quite satisfactory, and only when it became

1   From 1670 to 1681, wool was sold at 1s., 1s. 3d. and 1s. 6d. per lb., from 1683 to 1697, it varied from 9d., 1s., 1s. 4d. to 1s. 6d. per lb., in pay or barter ; from 1701 to 1709, the price in money was 1s., 1s. 2d., 1s. 3d. and 1s. 4d ; in 1718, the price had nearly doubled, being sold at 2s.

necessary to fill vacancies on the committee, was there any further record concerning the matter till 1721. At that time an entirely new committee was chosen, composed of Joseph Parsons, Ebenezer Wright, Jonathan Hunt, Timothy Baker and Benjamin Edwards Jr. It was also decided at that time to renew the instructions to the seating committee. They were as follows :—"1ˢᵗ : to Haue Regard to persons Age. 2 : to Estate. 3 : to Haue Some Regard to mens vsefullness." These directions were substantially the same as those adopted in 1663, and were similar to the rules adopted for that purpose in other places.

Finances of the Province. Colony Bills of Credit, 1690. While the financial condition of the province does not directly concern this narrative, except so far as it affects the interests of Northampton, yet an allusion to the more important financial measures of that time is necessary in order to a clear comprehension of town action in such matters. When the heavy expenses of the several wars, more especially of the futile attempt upon Canada, under Sir William Phips, in 1690, had rendered the government nearly bankrupt, the General Court commenced the manufacture of paper money. These promises to pay were called "Bills of Credit," and they were issued in denominations varying from 2s. to £5. They answered a temporary purpose only, and soon fell in value; but subsequently when a considerable portion of the amount in circulation had been retired, they rose nearly to par. Never very plentiful in the valley towns, this emission of paper money did not take the place to any great extent of the long established circulating medium, wheat, corn, and other articles of produce.

Province Bills of Credit substituted for them. The Province of Massachusetts Bay continued the issue of Colony Bills of Credit till 1702, although the new charter had been in force for ten years. In that year they were superceded by a new kind of paper currency, not essentially different from the old issue except in name. They were denominated "Province Bills," and their emission was continued for nearly half a century. Taxes were laid sufficient to cover the amount represented by the annual issue of these bills, and the Treasurer of the Province paid the expenses of government with them. Although they were received in payment of rates and duties, and although all of them thus received were annually destroyed, the amount of paper money in circulation was constantly increasing. The usual result followed : the value of Province Bills decreased in proportion to the ratio of their augmentation.

A Public Banking System Devised. Trustees to Loan to Individuals. Province bills to the amount of £10,000 were issued in 1702. During the succeeding five years other issues were made, each one of which was to be redeemed in two years. Then the time of redemption for other emissions was lengthened three, four and five years, till 1711, when the limit was placed at six years. Financial matters grew worse and worse till 1714, when a public banking system was devised, by which a specified amount of paper money, issued by the government, was brought within the reach of individuals. In November of that year, bills of credit to the amount of £50,000 were issued, and placed in the hands of five Trustees. They were authorized to loan this money directly to the people, for periods not exceeding five years, with interest annually at five per cent. A yearly payment of one-fifth of the amount loaned was exacted, and the loan was secured by a first mortgage on the real estate of the borrower. Not more than £500 nor less than £50 could be awarded to any one person. This arrangement proved satisfactory, and the system was known as the "Public Bank."

Capital Increased. Loans by Counties, 1716-1717. Two years afterwards the capital of the Public Bank was considerably increased and facilities adopted for placing the loans in all sections of the Province. The sum of £100,000 was apportioned to the several counties, in proportion to the amount of Province tax assessed in each. Five trustees were appointed in each county to distribute the money among the inhabitants. This issue was to run ten years, at five per cent. per annum, and the loans ranged in amount from £25 to £500. The trustees for Hampshire County were "John Pinchon, Springfield; Mr Henry Dwight, Hatfield; Mr Luke Hitchcock, Springfield; John Ashley, Westfield and Mr John Partridge, Hatfield." To Hampshire County the sum of £4947 was apportioned, and this was loaned to the citizens of the several towns, in amounts varying from £25 to £250. Being a first lien on unincumbered real estate, the whole may be found recorded in the Registry of Deeds at Springfield. Twelve men in Northampton availed themselves of this opportunity, and borrowed money of the Province upon their farms. The entire amount loaned to citizens of this town was £975. The largest sum borrowed by any individual was £125, and the smallest £40. Borrowers absorbed the principal alloted to Hampshire County within nine months of the year 1717. Other loans of a similar character were made in this vicinity during the next three years, but very little more was taken in this town. The loans placed in Northampton were all repaid, and undoubtedly this system was the means of building up business in all sections of the Province.

Money Loaned Directly to the Town. In 1721, additional capital was added to the bank, and its facilities for accommodating the people greatly enlarged. This loan, amounting to £50,000, was issued to the several towns, and made payable in nine years. Of this sum, £486.15 were appropriated to Northampton. The amount was to be repaid in yearly instalments, of one-fifth of the principal, commencing in 1726; the whole to be liquidated in 1730. Towns were required to appoint trustees to loan the money to individuals, and to have the general oversight of the transaction. In September, 1721, the following named trustees were elected: Capt. Ebenezer Pomeroy, Lieut. Joseph Hawley, and Ens. Benjamin Lyman. A proposition was made in October, by Ebenezer Parsons, Jonathan Sheldon and John Clark, to take the entire amount,

"and duly pay to the trustees the severall paymentts of the Princaple Sum so that the Paymentts may be Seasonablely made to the Province Treasurer and Wholly Endemnyfy the town from any trouble: and that they Will Pay all the cost and charge ariseing from the Letting out and Recieuing and paying In sd Bills and all other charge there aboute from this time and forward. Together With three pounds ten shillings p' annum for each Hundred Pounds and so pro rato During the Whole term: and that they Will Give Sufficientt Security for the performance of these proposalls."

The above scheme was accepted with the provision that the parties gave satisfactory security. This money was to be distributed in December, but the syndicate not having perfected its arrangements, the town voted early in that month, that if the proper security was not forthcoming, then the trustees were to let out the money, and "take Such Security either Reall' or parsonall as they think most for the Enterestt of The Town."

The Loan Received, and its Manage-ment. On the 14th of December, 1721, the money was received, and within five months was loaned by the trustees to twenty persons at six per cent. per annum. Henry Dwight received 15s. for bringing the money from Boston, and 10s. was paid to each of the trustees for services during the first year. From the income obtained from the borrowers, the town paid all necessary expenses and the salary of the trustees. They received 83s. in 1723, to pay for their "trouble in letting out the money, writing bonds, keeping accounts and collecting interest." Ens. Benjamin Lyman died in 1724, and Ebenezer Strong was chosen to fill the vacancy. One hundred pounds of accrued interest was used in 1727 "towards settling Mr. Edwards." Payments of one-fifth of the principal to the Province Treasurer were commenced in 1726, and during that and the succeeding four years annual instalments of £97.7 were made till the entire amount was refunded. When the account was closed in 1732, there remained £82.3.6 in the town treasury, the avails of the interest on the loans. By this transaction, the town, after paying all expenses, realized during eight years £182.3.6.

Another Loan to the Town. The capital of the Public Bank was still further replenished in 172⅞, when £60,000 in Bills of Credit were loaned to the towns, at six per cent. per annum, for ten years. This time a little different arrangement was entered upon. The towns were no longer allowed to appropriate the interest, but were required to pay four per cent. to the Province, retaining two per cent. Northampton received £488.10. It was put into the hands of the same trustees. Eleazar Porter brought the funds in May, 1728, for which service he was paid 8s. This money was loaned to twelve persons. For five years the interest at four per cent.—£19.10.10—was paid annually to the Province Treasurer. At that time the first instalment on the principal, amounting to £97.14, was paid. Each year thereafter the same amount became due, but for some reason, possibly on account of the expenditures attending the erection of the new meeting house, the payment for the year 1736 was omitted. It was made up the next year, and the loan was cancelled in 1739. After 1732, the balance of the £50,000 loan was added to this one and but one account was kept.

Net Results of the two Loans. When the account was balanced and settled, the town had a net credit of £157 accruing from the two loans, after paying all expenses. About £75 were obtained from the last one. During the eighteen years over which these loans extended, the town received £257. When the two loans were joined in the same account, the balance of £82.3.6, from the first one, was added to the principal, and the accumulations from it helped to swell the aggregate. This system of Province loaning was termed the "Town Bank," and the account seems to have been kept under that heading by the Town Treasurer. The only drawback noted in the Public Banking scheme was the reception of one counterfeit bill of the value of £5, which was promptly charged over to profit and loss.

Counterfeiting Bills of Credit. The enormous quantity of paper money in circulation was a great temptation to counterfeiters, and many cases in court are reported, in which parties were tried and punished for this crime. In the year 1721, Ebenezer Bridgman of Northampton, was tried for altering and passing a bill of the value of 5s. raised to that of £5. He was found guilty of passing the bill, but not of altering it, and was fined £5 and costs, amounting in all to £10. Ovid Rushbrook was the terror of the settlements on the Connecticut River, in the matter of counterfeiting.   He was a weaver, probably an Englishman, and lived in Springfield, but did not follow his trade very industriously.   He was arrested for counterfeiting, and tried in Northampton, in 1718, but nothing was proved against him.   He was again on trial the following · year in Hartford, and was before the court here again in September, 1721, when he was convicted of engraving plates and with them printing spurious bills of credit.   The court sentenced him to be set in the pillory at Springfield, to have one ear cut off, to be imprisoned one year, to be branded F on the right cheek with a hot iron, and to pay double damages to those whom he had defrauded.   This punishment did not reform him, as he was several years afterwards again under suspicion.

Highway Rates   Up to this date the practice had been to lay
Changed.   a special rate for highway expenses.   In
                1722, a change was made in this respect. Payments for work done upon the highways were ordered to be made from the town rate, and surveyors were instructed "to take good and effectuall care that people be warned to work att highways for some proportion according as they bear of the town charge."   The price was fixed at 5s. for teams in the summer, 2s. 6d. for "hands," and 4s. in the fall for teams, and 2s. for "hands" per diem.   For that year highway work amounted to £20.15.10, made out in one bill, which also included plank for bridges. About one hundred sixty-five day's work were reported as having been performed.

Increased Bounty   When the town entered upon the work of
  for Killing   encouraging sheep raising, it not only made
Wolves.   war on all dogs over a foot high, but it also endeavored to stimulate the onslaught on wolves, by increasing the bounty offered for their ears to £4 'per pair. This was higher than had ever before been given, but it was none too large, as the destruction by wild animals was much greater than by tame ones.   This increase of bounty depleted the treasury to the amount of £16.   During the

year the ears of four full grown wolves were brought to the selectmen, and the premiums on them paid.

Ringing the Meeting House Bell.
The customary price paid for "ringing the bell" was £4 annually, and with it was coupled the work of sweeping the meeting house. When the amount of bell ringing required in those days is considered, the price does not seem exorbitant. Indeed, if the labor was as wearing upon the ringer as upon the rope, he was but poorly paid. Almost every year the rope had to be renewed or repaired, and frequent accounts for mending the ringing machinery are to be found. During the latter half of the eighteenth century, and for more than half of the present one, the meeting house bell was heard at least twice a day, and at times much oftener. For many years it was rung at twelve o'clock, to warn people working in the meadows and elsewhere (for few farmers owned or carried watches then) that the dinner hour had arrived, and again at nine o'clock at night to signify that bed time was at hand. The first notice of a nine o'clock bell in the Connecticut valley was at Hartford in 1665, when it was rung for the purpose of preventing disorderly Meetings.[1] The practice soon spread throughout the valley, though it is not to be supposed for the same purpose as in Hartford, and became general before the opening of the present century. In some towns in Hampshire County, votes were passed controlling the matter, but nothing of the kind is recorded here. Over a large section of the country the practice prevailed of ringing the bell at marriages and funerals, and many persons are familiar with the now obsolete custom of ringing the bell for every death, tolling at the end the age of the deceased.

Grant to Col. Stoddard.
Thirty acres of land were granted to Col. John Stoddard, in 1722, for his services in obtaining a settlement of the division line between this town and Hatfield. The land was to be taken near the north-west corner of the town, adjoining the Hatfield line.

1 Judd's History of Hadley, p. 52.

Cow Keeper or
Herdsman, 1663
to 1722.
At the second meeting of the proprietors in 1655, the necessity of a "cow keeper or calf keeper," was recognized. Though there is no record of the appointment of any officer at that time, it is altogether probable that the election of a herdsman was scarcely ever omitted. The owners of the stock comprising the herd were responsible to the keeper for his pay, though the town sometimes designated the amount. A refusal to pay the cow herd brought out the following vote in 1663: "Wheare as some of our Nighbors refused to pay to the cow keeper because there cows went not in the hard as they Sayd it was voted by the Towne that they should all pay theare full pay with thear Nighbors." The next year an agreement was made with "Matthew Clesson to keepe the cowes upon the same termes Samuel Allin did the last yere except he is to have pay in wheate at 3^s 3^d p^r bush." Then follows a vote "that all the cowes y^t goe on the commons shalbee payable to the cow keeper, except those over the river, but dry cattle and yearlings shall bee halfe price." The above are among the very few times in which the herdsmen were designated by name. In 1665, the town voted "that they were willing to haue a dry heard, and therefore to further that work they also agreed thatt all dry cattell aboue one yere old except oxen should pay toward the keeping of a herd." Possibly for a few years, cows had not been under the care of a herdsman, as at the same time the above was adopted another vote was passed "that they would haue a heard of cows kept as formerly." A few years later the term "constant herdsmen" is used, and all who had cattle upon the commons except working oxen were to pay to him. Soon after a dry herd in the remote parts of the town was provided.

How long the appointment of the herdsman remained in the control of the town, is uncertain, but it seems eventually to have fallen under the supervision of the owners of the stock, who provided for their care while pasturing on the commons. In 1722, a number of persons made a contract with Abram Miller to keep their cows. They agreed to pay him "six pence a week for each cow sent out to him to be kept, or so much as to make him three shillings per day for his service." He was to be paid at the end of each week, in money, corn or otherwise to his satisfaction. They also agreed to bring their "cows to the meeting house hill every morning by sun half an hour high." Probably they were brought back to the same place in the afternoon, "sun half an hour high," that being the practice in other towns. Thirteen persons joined in this contract, furnishing thirty-six cows, which at six pence each, gave the cow herd the stipulated three shillings per day. Some of the parties had four cows, others three, and several but one.

APPENDIX.

A.

CONTRIBUTIONS FROM NORTHAMPTON TO HARVARD COLLEGE.

Page 225. Among the original papers in the Judd MSS. is the following list of contributions to Harvard College, made in Northampton in 167⅔. The first entries of the material in which the gifts were made were written by David Wilton, and afterwards each name is again given and the value of the donation carried out in £ s. d., by Rev. Solomon Stoddard. The list copied by Mr. Stoddard contains eighty-five subscribers, but the following has a few additional names.

	£ s. d.
Mr Stoddard 13b a peck & more wheate	02.00.00
Decon Holton 7 bushels wheate	01.01.00
Tho. Mason toe bushels wheate	00.06.00
Thomas Stronge toe bushels wheate,	00.06.00
George Lankton toe bushels wheate	00.06.00
Decon Hanchet toe bushels wheate and 4℔ flaxe	00.10.00
Samuell Mason toe ℔ flaxe	00.02.00
John Marsh payd in wheate ten shillings	00.10.00
Samuell Dauis payd toe ℔ flaxe	00.02.00
Gorge Allexander 5℔ flaxe	00.05.00
Christover Smith half bushell wheat	00.01.06
Samuell Curtis half bushell wheate	00.01.06
Ensigene Limon 4 bushels wheate	00.12.00
Robert Bartlet payd 4 bushels wheate	00.12.00
Nathaniell Weller half bushel w	00.01.06
John Hanchet toe ℔ flaxe	00.02.00
Richard Weller toe bushels wheate	
Nathaniell Curtis half bushell wheate	00.01.06
John Kinge 5℔ flaxe	00.05.00
John Stebbinge toe bushel halfe of wheate & toe ℔ halfe of flaxe	00.10.00
Nathaniell Phelps fiue ℔ flaxe	00.05.00
Mathew Clesson toe ℔ halfe of flaxe	00.02.06
Alexander Alford 4 ℔ flaxe	00.04.00
Enos Kingsley 3℔ flax	00.03.00
Jededia Stronge bushell wheat 3℔ flax	00.06.00

	£ s. d.
Cornelius Merri 3℔ flaxe	00.03.00
Leift Clarke ten bushels wheat . . .	01.02.00
Tho Liman toe ℔ flax	00.02.00
Jonathan Hunt 6℔ flaxe	00.06.00
Richard Liman 4℔ flaxe	00.04.00
Isacke Shilden 9 flaxe	00.09.00
Israell Rust toe bushels wheat	00.06.00
Jams Bredgeman 6℔ flaxe	00.06.00
Joseph Leeds on bushell wheate 7℔ flax . .	00.10.00
Tho Bascomb Senʳ 4℔ flaxe	00.04.00
John Bridgeman 3℔ flax	00.03.00
Joseph Baker toe bushels wheate and one half .	00.07.06
Samuell Wright on bushell & halfe wheate . .	00.04.06
Tho Salmon on pound flax	00.01.00
Mʳ Williams 5℔ flax and for Elder Stronge 6℔ ½ .	00.05.00
William Hannum 2℔ flaxe	00.02.00
Samuell Smith 3℔ flax	00.03.00
frome that line aboue and now all set down vnder	
& 3℔ & halfe more is pck into the greate barrell	
John Hannum 3℔ flaxe ` . . .	00.03.00
Henry Coudliue [Cunliffe] on pound flaxe 20℔ bacon	00.10.00
John Searle toe pound flaxe . . .	00.02.00
Robert Liman toe pound thre quarters flaxe . .	00.02.09
Elder Stronge 13℔ ½ flaxe	00.15.00
Calib Pumary 3℔ flaxe	00.03.00
William Hulburd pay in wompom seauen shillings	00.07.00
Richard ingraham payd 2ˢ	00.02.00
Tho Bascomb Junʳ 2℔ ½ of flaxe . . .	00.02.06
Joshua Pumary 4℔ flaxe	00.04.00
Hinery Woodward 8℔ flaxe . . .	00.08.00
Nehemia Allen 6℔ flaxe	00.06.00
John Woodward 6℔ flaxe	00.06.00
free Nims 5℔ flaxe	00.05.00
Samuell Edwards on ℔ flaxe . . .	00.01.00
John Allen on ℔ flaxe	00.01.00
Judeth Wright 4 ℔ ¾ flaxe	00.04.09
hepziba Marsh 4℔ flaxe	00.04.00
Allexander Edwards 8℔ fla	00.08.00
Praysever Turner 14℔ flaxe . . .	00.14.00
Samuell Allen 5℔ flaxe	00.05.00
Joseph Edwards on pound flaxe . . .	00.01.00
John Hulburd 3℔ flaxe	00.03.00
Elisabeth Liman 2℔ flaxe	00.02.00
David Wilton payd by Caredge . . .	01.10.00
and by a barrell	00.02.06
Joseph Parsons Sen pay 520℔ of flower at 12 per ℔	02.14.06
John Tayler payd in Cartinge	00.03.00

	£ s. d.
Mr Jeans payd for him selfe and toe Sowns in Carttinge	00.10.00
Nathaniell Allexander on pound flaxe .— .	00.01.00
David Burt 3℔ flaxe	00.03.00
Joseph Root 4℔ flaxe	00.04.00
John Webb in worke	00.05.00
Jonathan Marsh on bushell	00.03.00
Medad Pumary thre bushels & ½ wheat . .	00.10.06
Thomas Roote Senr bushell ½ & ½ peck wheate .	00.05.00
William Smeade payd by a barrell . .	00.02.06
Ebenezer Stronge on bushell wheate . . .	00.06.00
Mary Stronge	00.01.00
Goodman Willard	00.06.00
Samuell Marshall	00.02.00
Sarah Clarke	00.05.00
John Clarke	00.03.00
John Strong	00.15.00
John Weller	00.03.00
John Parsons	00.03.00
John Earle	00.05.00
Samuell Strong	00.01.00
Abigail Strong	00.01.00
Sam: Strong	00.02.00
Joseph Parsons jun^r	00.02.06
William Hulburd S^1	00.05.00
Received in Cash	00.12.04
	———
Totall Some is	29.17.10

thus reseaued in acount for the Colledge

	£ s. d.
payd out on the Colledge acount	
It. sent toe Windsor 60 b w	09.00.00
by toe barrels flower 520 weight from Joseph Parsons	
Senr	03.02.00
by toe barrels flaxe 224½	11.04.06
by the fwer barrels	00.10.00
by a peece bacon sent toe Windsor that I tooke of	
brother Coundliue	00.09.00
by Carttinge the 60 b w	03.00.00
by Carttinge the 2 barrels flaxe toe Windsor . .	00.06.00
by selver deliuared Mr Stodderd . . .	00.12.04
by dept vnpayd on the acount	01.01.00
by shrinkinge in the wheat toe bushels a peck & half	00.07.00
by bootinge the goods to Hartford houseing at Winsor	
and measuringe & cartinge toe waters side all	00.13.00
	———
	30.14.10

                                              £   s.   d.
rest dew toe David Wilton toe ballance I
    say dew 00.17.00   .   .   .   30.14.10
                                              29.17.10
                                              _____
                                              00.17.00

The twelve shillings & four pence in silver delivered to me I payed to
Left. Wilton for seventeen Shillings which was due to him.

                    per me   SOL STODDARD.

B.

RECORD OF HOUSES IN HAMPSHIRE TOWNS.

Page 278.   The following statistics relating to certain towns on the
Connecticut River, giving the number of houses in each, in 1675, are
from a paper in the Manuscript Department of the British Museum,
communicated through the courtesy of Lieut. C. D. Parkhurst of Fort
Monroe.   It purports to be "an account of all the trading Townes and
Ports lying upon the sea, and navigable rivers, with number of houses
in each Towne."   Those of special interest to this work are given
below : —

Weathersfield,	150	Hadley,	100
Hartford,	500	Northampton,	100
Winsor,	400	Hatfield,	50
Harmington [Farmington],	100	Northfield,	30
Springfield Burnt	50	Deerfield,	30

C.

NORTHAMPTON SOLDIERS IN THE FALLS FIGHT.

Page 332.   List of Northampton men who were engaged in the fight
at Turner's Falls, May 19, 1676 : —

                          CITIZENS.

Nathaniel Alexander,	John Lyman,
Thomas Alvord,	Cornelius Merry,
Timothy Baker,	Godfrey Nims,
James Bennet,[1]	Caleb Pomeroy,
Peter Bushrod,	Medad Pomeroy,
Preserved Clapp,	Robert Price,
William Clark,	William Smead,
Benjamin Edwards,	Benoni Stebbins,
Abel Janes,	John Webb,
Francis Keet,	Richard Webb.
John King,	James Wright.

1 Killed.

The names only of the garrison soldiers from Northampton who were killed, have been preserved.

Peter Guerin,
Thomas Roberts,
Joshua Langsbury,
Samuel Ransford,
William Howard, Salem,
John Miller,
John Walker,

John Foster,
John Whitterage, Salem,
Jacob Burton, Topsfield,
Joseph Fowler, Ipswich,
George Buckley,
Thomas Lyon.

D.

NORTHAMPTON SOLDIERS IN KING WILLIAM'S WAR.

Page 441.   Below are the names of the Northampton men who served from 1688 to 1698 : —

Timothy Baker,
John Bridgman,
John Burt,[1]
Preserved Clapp,
Joseph Clesson,[1]
John Field,[1]
John King,[1]
William King,[1]
Ebenezer Kingsley,
John Lyman,[1]
Thomas Lyman,[1]
Samuel Marshall,
John Parsons,[1]

Ebenezer Pomeroy,[1]
Joseph Pomeroy,[1]
Nathaniel Rust,[1]
Joseph Sheldon,[1]
Benjamin Stebbins,
Jeremiah Strong,[1]
John Taylor,
Jonathan Taylor,
Ebenezer Wells,[1]
Benjamin Wright,
Ebenezer Wright,[1]
Joseph Wright.[1]

E.

PURCHASE OF NONOTUCK.

Page 468.   When Nonotuck was purchased of the Indians, the price agreed upon was "100 fathoms of Wampum by tale and for Tenn coates (besides some small gifts) in hand to the said Sachems and owners."   This amount was paid to the natives by Mr. Pynchon, and he charged the same to the settlers.   The town records contain but a single allusion to the cost of the plantation, that of 1659 (p. 85), when a vote was passed debarring non-residents, whether or not they had paid anything for the purchase, from obtaining a title to any land in

1 At Deerfield, September 16th, 1696, named in Joseph Parsons' account book.

the township. The cost of the land was probably between £25 and
£40. One hundred fathoms of wampum at 5s. per fathom, which seems
to have been the average price at that time, would have been worth
just £25. The cost of the ten coats, it is now impossible to ascertain,
and the small gifts could not have been very valuable, the whole being
possibly between £5 and £10.

Mr. Pynchon's account books contain the only information on this
point, but they do not apparently cover the entire expenditure. He
makes charges for only £19 of the purchase money. Other portions
may have been carried to the accounts of other settlers, who traded
with him, without having been itemized. The following statement,
copied from Mr. Pynchon's day book, shows the amount definitely
charged to persons who were interested in the new settlement. Apparently he received payment from but six persons, who did not by any
means pay a uniform rate. Only three of them settled here, and no
land was awarded to any of the others. Dea. Holton paid more than
any one else and that may possibly account in some measure for his
prominence in the first business transactions of the town. The following items are transcribed from Mr. Pynchon's books:—

"Purchase of Nonotuck & Nootuck.

"1653, Oct. William Clark of Hartford, for the purchase of Nanotuck	00.30.00
"1653, Nov. Edward Elmer of Hartford, for the purchase of Naotuck	00.40.00
"1653. John Coale of Hartford, for the purchase of Naotuck	00.30.00
"Brother Wyllis" is charged "for Nalwotog" .	00.20.00
Rowland Thomas "Due on Nalwotog purchase"	00.20.00
William Holton of Hartford is charged "for the purchase of Nanotuck," (he paid in Pork)	03.00.00
	10.00.00

"Nalwotog Towne as Dr.

"Imp. To what is resting due to me for the purchase of yᵉ place £7 being behind, for which expect they should allow me 50 shillings unless they will let my land there goe rate free till it be paid me." To the £7 he adds £2.10 and calls the whole	09.00.00
	19.00.00

THOMAS STEBBINS.

Page 493. Thomas Stebbins was the son of Thomas Stebbins and
Elizabeth, daughter of Samuel Wright Jr., who was killed at Northfield, in 1675. He married Sarah Searl in 1750. He was deranged at intervals and several times attempted suicide. In 1735, he cut his throat
and again in 1752, tried to make way with himself. He was living in

Southampton, and the good people had a meeting to pray for him. He was sent to Northampton, June 15th, and not being sufficiently guarded, threw himself into a well and perished. His sister called for help and immediately descended into the well and held his head above the water till assistance arrived. His skull was fractured.

F.

ELISHA SEARL.

Page 496. Baptism of Elisha Searl, from the Montreal Parish Records, copied and translated by Miss C. Alice Baker:—

"On Tuesday the 29th day of September, in the year 1705, the ceremonies of baptism have been by me, the undersigned priest, given to an English child, named in his own country, Elisha, son of the deceased John Searls and of his wife Abigail Pumry, who was born at Northampton, in New England, the ———— having been captured the 11th of March of the year 1704, and brought to Canada, lives with Mr. John Baptist Beloron, Esq., Seignior de Blainville and Captain of a company of the detachment of the marine. He had for his godfather the said Seignoir de Blainville, who gave him the name of Michael, and for his godmother Madame Mary Anne Le Moyne, wife of Mr. John Baptist, Seignior de la Chassaque Captain of a company of the same regiment who haue signed with me."

The signatures of Father Meriel and of the godparents follow.

G.

NORTHAMPTON SOLDIERS IN QUEEN ANNE'S WAR

Page 513. Who served from 1704 to 1713:—

Joseph Alexander,	Benjamin Lyman,
Thomas Alvord,	Aaron Parsons,[1]
Thomas Baker,	Ebenezer Pomeroy, Capt.,
Samuel Bartlett,	Benjamin Stebbins,
John Bridgman Jr.,	John Strong,
John Burt,[1]	Preserved Strong,
Joseph Clesson,	John Stoddard, Capt.,
Joseph Hawley Jr.,	John Taylor, Capt.,[1]
John Hunt,	Benjamin Wright,
Joseph Ingersoll,[1]	Ebenezer Wright, Sergt.,
David King,	Joseph Wright,
John King, Lieut.,	Samuel Wright.
Caleb Lyman,	

[1] Killed.

3 7

INDEX.

41

CPSIA information can be obtained
at www.ICGtesting.com
Printed in the USA
LVHW051010221218
600913LV00006B/61/P